STIFFNESS AND FUNDAMENTAL VIBRATION FREQUENCY

springs of series $\frac{1}{k} = \frac{1}{k_1} + \frac{1}{k_2} + \frac{1}{k_3} + \cdots$

springs in parallel $k = k_1 + k_2 + k_3 + \cdots$

Longitudinal 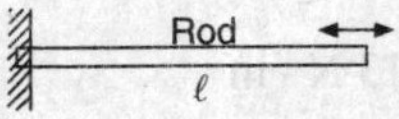

$k = \frac{AE}{l}$ lb/in. $\quad \omega_n = (2n-1)\frac{\pi}{2l}\sqrt{\frac{E}{\rho}}$ $\quad \rho$ = mass density $\quad n = 1, 2, 3 \ldots$

Torsion 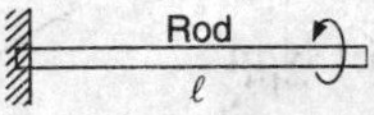

$K = \frac{I_p G}{l}$ lb · in./rad $\quad \omega_n = (2n-1)\frac{\pi}{2l}\sqrt{\frac{G}{\rho}}$ $\quad n = 1, 2, 3 \ldots$

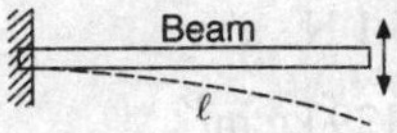

$k = \frac{3EI}{l^3}$ lb/in. $\quad \omega_1 = 3.52\sqrt{\frac{EI}{ml^4}}$ $\quad m$ = mass/length

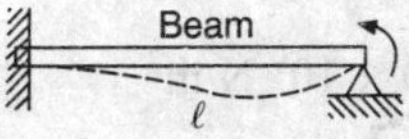

$K = \frac{4EI}{l}$ lb · in./rad $\quad \omega_1 = 15.42\sqrt{\frac{EI}{ml^4}}$

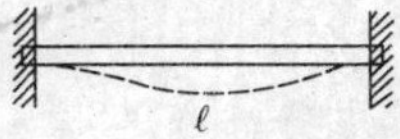

$\omega_1 = 22.37\sqrt{\frac{EI}{ml^4}}$

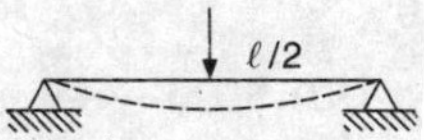

$k = \frac{48EI}{l^3}$ lb/in. $\quad \omega_1 = \pi^2\sqrt{\frac{EI}{ml^4}}$

QUANTITY	ENGLISH SYSTEM	S.I. SYSTEM
force	1 lb	4.448 Newtons (N)
mass	$1\ lb \cdot sec^2/ft$ (slug)	14.59 kg (kilogram)
length	1ft	0.3048 meters (m)
mass density	$1\ lb/ft^3$	$16.02\ kg/m^3$
torque or moment	$1\ lb \cdot in.$	$0.113\ N \cdot m$
acceleration	$1\ ft/sec^2$	$0.3048\ m/s^2$
accel. of gravity	$32.2\ ft/s^2 = 386\ in./sec^2$	$9.81\ m/s^2$
spring constant k	1 lb/in.	175.1 N/m
spring constant K	$1\ lb \cdot in./rad$	$0.113\ N \cdot m/rad$
damping constant c	$1\ lb \cdot sec/in.$	$175.1\ N \cdot s/m$
mass moment of inertia	$1\ lb.\ in.\ sec^2$	$0.1129\ kg\ m^2$
modulus of elasticity	$10^6\ lb/in.^2$	$6.895 \times 10^9\ N/m^2$
modulus of elastidty of steel	$29 \times 10^6\ lb/in.^2$	$200 \times 10^9\ N/m^2$
angle	1 degree	1/57.3 radian

CONTENTS

PREFACE

This book is the fifth edition of the *Theory of Vibration with Application*. For a classical subject like Vibration, an explanation for another revision is in order.

Although the subject of Vibration does not greatly change, the development of new and sophisticated digital techniques keep advancing and increasing the wide variety of problems to be solved and discussed in class.

MATLAB® is a versatile computer software program that is commercially available and adopted by many engineering schools. It is compatible with the previous computational methods of the 4th edition and we have decided to augment and broaden the computer capabilities of the 4th edition with its use in the 5th edition.To undertake this revision, our editor and I have engaged a competent co-author. Dr. Marie D. Dahleh, of our Engineering Department, to work with me on this task.

The authors recognize that problem solving is a vital part of the learning process, and the use of a versatile new computer, technique will enhance the student's capabilities not only in the field of Vibration, but to other fields as well. To use MATLAB, or any other new computer method, it is not necessary to completely understand the detailed mathematics on which the software program is based. On this point, I am reminded of a timely quotation by Oliver Heavyside, a famous British mathematician and engineer of the early 20th century, who was being criticized for his innovative mathematics. His response to them was; "Should I refuse my dinner because I do not understand the process of my digestion?"

As in earlier editions, the first four chapters, which deal with single-degree-of-freedom systems, need very few changes. However, wherever appropriate MATLAB has been introduced to familiarize the reader with the MATLAB commands that will be necessary to make use of this facility. At the end of Chapter 4, where the first extensive calculations with finite difference and Runge–Kutta were made, the MATLAB method is demonstrated with parallel computations for comparison.

Systems with two or more degrees of freedom, introduced in Chapter 5, offers a logical opportunity to present the matrix notation. The Mass and the Stiffness Matrices are defined here and the digital computation in Fortran has been completely replaced by MATLAB.The importance of normal mode vibration is emphasized in this chapter and free vibrations are demonstrated to be composed of normal modes with specified initial conditions. Forced vibrations are again presented in terms of frequency ratio of forced to normal modes, and the important application of vibration absorbers and dampers is retained unchanged. Orthogonality of eigenvectors, the modal matrix and its orthonormal form enable concise presentation of basic equations for the diagonal eigenvalue matrix that forms the basis for the computation of the eigenvalue-eigenvector problem. They also provide a background for the normal mode summation method. The chapter concludes with the modal damping and examples of equal roots and degenerate systems.

Chapter 6 presents the energy method using physical coordinates followed by the classic method of Lagrange, which is associated with virtual work and generalized coordinates. Included in this chapter is the method of assumed modes, which enables the determination of eigenvalues and eigenvectors of continuous systems in terms of smaller equations of discrete system equations. The

Lagrangian method offers an all-encompassing view of the entire field of dynamics, a knowledge of which should be acquired by all readers interested in a serious study of dynamics.

Chapter 7, "Computational Methods," examines the basic methods of computation that are utilized by the digital computer. Most engineering and science students today acquire knowledge of computers and programming in their freshman year and, given the basic background for vibration calculation, they can generally follow computer programs for eigenvalues and eigenvectors. Covered in this chapter are the following subjects; Polynomial method, Gauss elimination, Matrix iteration, the Dynamic matrix, Standard computer form, Cholesky Decomposition, Jacobi Diogonalization, and the QR Decomposition. As stated earlier, for those who feel intimidated by the somewhat difficult mathematics may ignore these sections or even skip the entire Chapter 7 and still acquire the skills of using these newer computer programs. The former computations made by Fortran are now replaced and plotted by MATLAB.

Chapter 8, "Vibration of Continuous Systems," Rods and beams of uniformly distributed mass and stiffness represent continuous systems of infinite degrees of freedom. To analyse the vibration of such system requires the use of partial differential equation, presented in the first part of this chapter. As example of how these solutions can be adopted to more complex structures, an example of the vibration of the Tacoma Narrows suspension bridge is presented. When the continuous structure is discretized into repeated identical sections, simple analytic expressions are available for the natural frequencies and mode shapes by the use of difference equations. Here the method demonstrates the technique of matching boundary conditions.

Chapters 9 and 10: These two chapters, "Mode Summation Procedures for Continuous Systems," and "Classical Methods" have been retained as in the previous edition. Being essentially computing methods, MATLAB has been advantageously used. Holzer and Myklestad methods have been placed into MATLAB files for available use.

Chapter 11, "Introduction to the Finite Element Method," remains unchanged except that the computing is done entirely by MATLAB and the stiffness of framed structures is presented first to bring out the introductory basics of the finite element method presented later in this chapter. A few helpful hints have been injected in some places, and the section on generalized force proportional to displacement has been substantially expanded by detailed computation of rotating helicopter blades. Brought out by this example is the advantage of forming equal element sections of length l = 1 (all l's can be arbitrarily equated to unity inside of the mass and stiffness matrices when the elements are of equal lengths) for the compiling of the mass and stiffness matrices and converting the final results to those of the original system only after the computation is completed.

Chapter 12. "Random Vibrations": Random vibration became of interest to the engineer with the development of jet engines for airplanes. It is a nondeterministic phenomena which require a probabilistic solution. The presentation of the subject here is mainly from the mathematical treatment to familiarize the students with the new terminology. Progress in this field is largely through instruments developed to make measurements useful to engineering design.

Chapter 13, "Nonlinear Vibrations", can be described as a behavior which cannot be solved mathematically by superposition. The understanding of its behavior is best studied by means of the phase-plane. Presented in this chapter are some terminology for nonlinear systems, its stability and limit cycle and the computer programs of Runge–Kutta used for its digital solution. A number of problems suitable for the computer are listed in the problem section and marked with a capital M.

Finally I wish to acknowledge my appreciation to my coauthor and to Dr. Igor Mezic of our Mechanical Engineering Department, who corrected and assembled the Solutions Manual for the fifth edition and added several new problems throughout the text.

William T. Thomson
Marie Dillon Dahleh

The contents of the fifth edition have been reorganized and additional examples have been included where necessary, to make this edition beneficial to the students of Indian Universities.

Chandramouli Padmanabhan

Note: To find the M files referenced in the text and the Solution Manual log on to the Pearson Education's World Wide Web site at: http://www.pearsoned.com/williamtthomson and access the files.

The SI System of Units

THE SI SYSTEM OF UNITS

The English system of units that has dominated the United States from historical times is now being replaced by the SI system of units. Major industries throughout the United States either have already made, or are in the process of making, the transition, and engineering students and teachers must deal with the new SI units as well as the present English system. We present here a short discussion of the SI units as they apply to the vibration field and outline a simple procedure to convert from one set of units to the other.

The basic units of the SI system are

Units	Name	Symbol
Length	Meter	m
Mass	Kilogram	kg
Time	Second	s

The following quantities pertinent to the vibration field are derived from these basic units:

Force	Newton	N (= $kg \cdot m/s^2$)
Stress	Pascal	Pa (= N/m^2)
Work	Joule	J (= $N \cdot m$)
Power	Watt	W (= J/s)
Frequency	Hertz	Hz (= 1/s)

Moment of a force	$N \cdot m$ (= $kg \cdot m^2/s^2$)
Acceleration	m/s^2
Velocity	m/s
Angular velocity	1/s
Moment of inertia (area)	m^4 ($mm^4 \times 10^{-12}$)
Moment of inertia (mass)	$kg \cdot m^2$ ($kg \cdot cm^2 \times 10^{-4}$)

Because the meter is a large unit of length, it will be more convenient to express it as the number of millimeters multiplied by 10^{-3}. Vibration instruments, such as accelerometers, are in general calibrated in terms of $g = 9.81\ m/s^2$, and hence expressed in nondimensional units. It is advisable to use nondimensional representation whenever possible.

In the English system, the weight of an object is generally specified. In the SI system, it is more common to specify the mass, a quantity of matter that remains unchanged with location.

In working with the SI system, it is advisable to think directly in SI units. This will require some time, but the following rounded numbers will help to develop a feeling of confidence in the use of SI units.

The newton is a smaller unit of force than the pound. One pound of force is equal to 4.4482 newtons, or approximately four and a half times the value for the pound. (An apple weighs approximately $\frac{1}{4}$ lb, or approximately 1 newton.)

One inch is 2.54 cm, or 0.0254 meter. Thus, the acceleration of gravity, which is 386 in./s^2 in the English system, becomes $386 \times 0.0254 = 9.81$ m/s^2, or approximately 10 m/s^2.

Table of Approximate Equivalents

1 lb	$\cong$	4.5 N
Acceleration of gravity g	$\cong$	10 m/s^2
Mass of 1 slug	$\cong$	15 kg
1 ft	$\cong$	$\frac{1}{3}$ m

SI conversion. A simple procedure to convert from one set of units to another follows: Write the desired SI units equal to the English units, and put in canceling unit factors. For example, if we wish to convert torque in English units into SI units, we proceed as follows:

Example 1

$$[\text{Torque SI}] = [\text{Torque English}] \times [\text{multiplying factors}]$$

$$[\text{N} \cdot \text{M}] = [\cancel{\text{lb}} \cdot \cancel{\text{in}}]\left(\frac{\text{N}}{\cancel{\text{lb}}}\right)\left(\frac{\text{m}}{\cancel{\text{in.}}}\right)$$

$$= [\text{lb} \cdot \text{in.}](4.448)(0.0254)$$

$$= [\text{lb} \cdot \text{in.}](0.1129)$$

■

Example 2

$$[\text{Moment of inertia SI}] = [\text{Moment of inertia English}] \times [\text{multiplying factors}]$$

$$[\text{kg} \cdot \text{m}^2 = \text{n} \cdot \text{m} \cdot \text{s}^2] = [\cancel{\text{lb}} \cdot \cancel{\text{in.}} \cdot \text{s}^2]\left(\frac{\text{N}}{\cancel{\text{lb}}} \cdot \frac{\text{m}}{\cancel{\text{in.}}}\right)$$

$$= [\text{lb} \cdot \text{in.} \cdot \text{s}^2](4.448 \times 0.0254)$$

$$= [\text{lb} \cdot \text{in.} \cdot \text{s}^2](0.1129)$$

■

Example 3

Modulus of Elasticity, E:

$$\left[\mathrm{N/m^2}\right] = \left[\frac{\not{\mathrm{lb}}}{\not{\mathrm{in}}.^2}\right]\left(\frac{\mathrm{N}}{\not{\mathrm{lb}}}\right)\left(\frac{\not{\mathrm{in}}.}{\mathrm{m}}\right)^2$$

$$= \left[\frac{\mathrm{lb}}{\mathrm{in.}^2}\right](4.448)\left(\frac{1}{0.0254}\right)^2$$

$$= \left[\frac{\mathrm{lb}}{\mathrm{in.}^2}\right](6{,}894.7)$$

■

E of steel $\mathrm{N/m^2} = (29 \times 10^6 \mathrm{lb/in.}^2)\,(6894.7) = 200 \times 10^9 \mathrm{N/m^2}$

Example 4

Spring Stiffness, K:

$$[\mathrm{N/m}] = [\mathrm{lb/in.}] \times (175.13)$$

Mass, M:

$$[\mathrm{kg}] = [\mathrm{lb.s^2/in.}] \times (175.13)$$

■

Conversion Factors* U.S.–British Units to SI Units

To Convert From	To	Multiply By
Acceleration:		
foot/second^2 (ft/s^2)	meter/second^2 (m/s^2)	$3.048 \times 10^{-1*}$
inch/second^2 (in./s^2)	meter/second^2 (m/s^2)	$2.54 \times 10^{-2*}$
Area:		
foot^2 (ft^2)	meter^2 (m^2)	9.2903×10^{-2}
inch^2 (in.^{2})	meter^2 (m^2)	$6.4516 \times 10^{-4*}$
yard^2 (yd^2)	meter^2 (m^2)	8.3613×10^{-1}
Density:		
pound mass/inch^3 (lbm/in.^{3})	kilogram/meter^3 (kg/m^3)	2.7680×10^4
pound mass/foot^3 (lbm/ft^3)	kilogram/meter^3 (kg/m^3)	1.6018×10
Energy, Work:		
British thermal unit (Btu)	joule (J)	1.0551×10^3
foot-pound force (ft · Ibf)	joule (J)	1.3558
kilowatt-hour (kw · h)	joule (J)	$3.60 \times 10^{6*}$
Force:		
kip (1000 Ibf)	newton(N)	4.4482×10^3
pound force (Ibf)	newton (N)	4.4482
ounce force	newton (N)	2.7801×10^{-1}

Conversion Factors* U.S.–British Units to SI Units

To Convert From	To	Multiply By
Length:		
foot (ft)	meter (m)	$3.048 \times 10^{-1*}$
inch (in.)	meter (m)	$2.54 \times 10^{-2*}$
mile (mi) (U.S. statute)	meter (m)	1.6093×10^{3}
mile (mi) (international nautical)	meter (m)	$1.852 \times 10^{3*}$
yard (yd)	meter (m)	$9.144 \times 10^{-1*}$
Mass:		
pound · mass (lbm)	kilogram (kg)	4.5359×10^{-1}
slug (lbf · s^2/ft)	kilogram (kg)	1.4594×10
ton (2000 lbm)	kilogram (kg)	9.0718×10^{2}
Power:		
foot-pound/minute (ft · lbf/min)	watt (W)	2.2597×10^{-2}
horsepower (550 ft · /s)	watt (W)	7.4570×10^{2}
Pressure, stress:		
atmosphere (std) (14.7 lbf/in.^{2})	newton/meter^2 (N/m^2 or Pa)	1.0133×10^{5}
pound/foot^2 (lbf/ft^2)	newton/meter^2 (N/m^2 or Pa)	4.7880×10
pound/inch^2 (lbf/in.^{2}, or psi)	newton/meter^2 (N/m^2 or Pa)	6.8948×10^{3}
Velocity:		
foot/minute (ft/min)	meter/second (m/s)	$5.08 \times 10^{-3*}$
foot/second (ft/s)	meter/second (m/s)	$3.048 \times 10^{-1*}$
knot (nautical mi/h)	meter/second (m/s)	5.1444×10^{-1}
mile/hour (mi/h)	meter/second (m/s)	$4.4704 \times 10^{-1*}$
mile/hour (mi/h)	kilometer/hour (km/h)	1.6093
mile/second (mi/s)	kilometer/second (km/s)	1.6093
Volume:		
foot^3 (ft^3)	meter^3 (m^3)	2.8317×10^{-2}
inch^3 (in.^{3})	meter^3 (m^3)	1.6387×10^{-5}

*Exact value.

Source: J. L. Meriam, *Dynamics*, 2nd Ed. (SI Version) (New York: John Wiley, 1975). *The International System of Units (SI)*, July 1974, National Bureau of Standards, Special Publication 330.

CHAPTER 1

Oscillatory Motion

The study of vibration is concerned with the oscillatory motions of bodies and the forces associated with them. All bodies possessing mass and elasticity are capable of vibration. Thus, most engineering machines and structures experience vibration to some degree, and their design generally requires consideration of their oscillatory behavior.

Oscillatory systems can be broadly characterized as *linear* or *nonlinear*. For linear systems, the principle of superposition holds, and the mathematical techniques available for their treatment are well developed. In contrast, techniques for the analysis of nonlinear systems are less well known, and difficult to apply. However, some knowledge of nonlinear systems is desirable, because all systems tend to become nonlinear with increasing amplitude of oscillation.

There are two general classes of vibrations—free and forced. *Free vibration* takes place when a system oscillates under the action of forces inherent in the system itself, and when external impressed forces are absent. The system under free vibration will vibrate at one or more of its *natural frequencies*, which are properties of the dynamical system established by its mass and stiffness distribution.

Vibration that takes place under the excitation of external forces is called *forced vibration*. When the excitation is oscillatory, the system is forced to vibrate at the excitation frequency. If the frequency of excitation coincides with one of the natural frequencies of the system, a condition of *resonance* is encountered, and dangerously large oscillations may result. The failure of major structures such as bridges, buildings, or airplane wings is an awesome possibility under resonance. Thus, the calculation of the natural frequencies is of major importance in the study of vibrations.

Vibrating systems are all subject to *damping* to some degree because energy is dissipated by friction and other resistances. If the damping is small, it has very little influence on the natural frequencies of the system, and hence the calculations for the natural frequencies are generally made on the basis of no damping. On the other hand, damping is of great importance in limiting the amplitude of oscillation at resonance.

The number of independent coordinates required to describe the motion of a system is called *degrees of freedom* of the system. Thus, a free particle undergoing general motion in space will have three degrees of freedom, and a rigid body will have six degrees of freedom, i.e., three components of position and three angles defining its orientation. Furthermore, a continuous elastic body will require an infinite number of coordinates (three for each point on the body) to describe its motion; hence, its degrees of freedom must be infinite. However, in many cases, parts of such bodies may be assumed to be rigid, and the system may be considered to be dynamically equivalent to one having finite degrees of freedom. In fact, a surprisingly large number of vibration problems can be treated with sufficient accuracy by reducing the system to one having a few degrees of freedom.

1.1 HARMONIC MOTION

Oscillatory motion may repeat itself regularly, as in the balance wheel of a watch, or display considerable irregularity, as in earthquakes. When the motion is repeated in equal intervals of time τ, it is called *periodic motion*. The repetition time τ is called the *period* of the oscillation, and its reciprocal, $f = 1/\tau$, is called the *frequency*. If the motion is designated by the time function $x(t)$, then any periodic motion must satisfy the relationship $x(t) = x(t + \tau)$.

The simplest form of periodic motion is *harmonic motion*. It can be demonstrated by a mass suspended from a light spring, as shown in Fig. 1.1.1. If the mass is displaced from its rest position and released, it will oscillate up and down. By placing a light source on the oscillating mass, its motion can be recorded on a light-sensitive filmstrip, which is made to move past it at a constant speed.

The motion recorded on the filmstrip can be expressed by the equation

$$x = A \sin 2\pi \frac{t}{\tau} \tag{1.1.1}$$

where A is the amplitude of oscillation, measured from the equilibrium position of the mass, and τ is the period. The motion is repeated when $t = \tau$.

Harmonic motion is often represented as the projection on a straight line of a point that is moving on a circle at constant speed, as shown in Fig. 1.1.2. With the angular speed of the line $0 - p$ designated by ω, the displacement x can be written as

$$x = A \sin \omega t \tag{1.1.2}$$

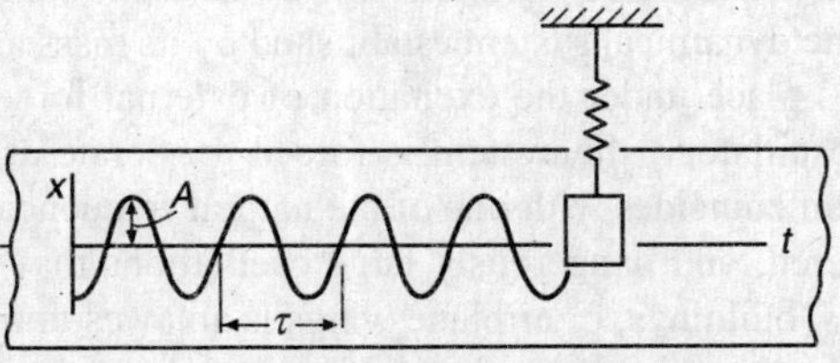

FIGURE 1.1.1. Recording harmonic motion.

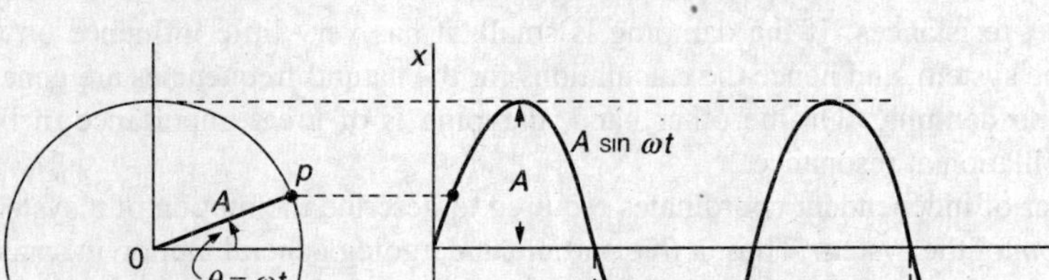

FIGURE 1.1.2. Harmonic motion as a projection of a point moving on a circle.

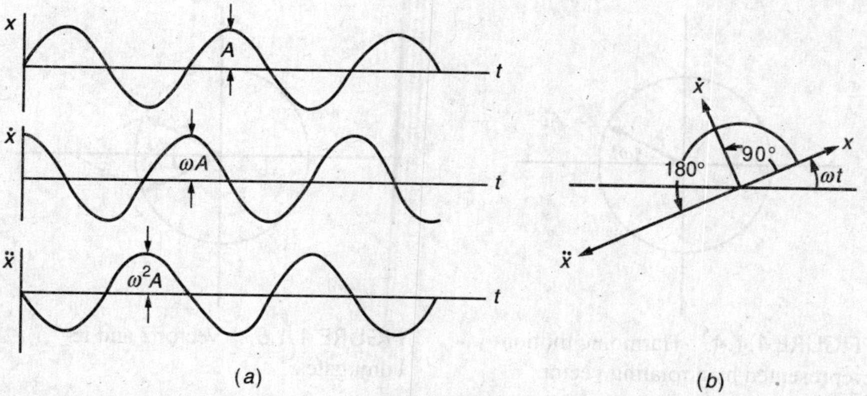

FIGURE 1.1.3. In harmonic motion, the velocity and acceleration lead the displacement by $\pi/2$ and π.

The quantity ω is generally measured in radians per second, and is referred to as the *circular frequency.** Because the motion repeats itself in 2π radians, we have the relationship

$$\omega = \frac{2\pi}{\tau} = 2\pi f \tag{1.1.3}$$

where τ and f are the period and frequency of the harmonic motion, usually measured in seconds and cycles per second, respectively.

The velocity and acceleration of harmonic motion can be simply determined by differentiation of Eq. (1.1.2). Using the dot notation for the derivative, we obtain

$$\dot{x} = \omega A \cos \omega t = \omega A \sin(\omega t + \pi/2) \tag{1.1.4}$$

$$\ddot{x} = -\omega^2 A \sin \omega t = \omega^2 A \sin(\omega t + \pi) \tag{1.1.5}$$

Thus, the velocity and acceleration are also harmonic with the same frequency of oscillation, but lead the displacement by $\pi/2$ and π radians, respectively. Figure 1.1.3 shows both time variation and the vector phase relationship between the displacement, velocity, and acceleration in harmonic motion.

Examination of Eqs. (1.1.2) and (1.1.5) reveals that

$$\ddot{x} = -\omega^2 x \tag{1.1.6}$$

so that in harmonic motion, the acceleration is proportional to the displacement and is directed toward the origin. Because Newton's second law of motion states that the acceleration is proportional to the force, harmonic motion can be expected for systems with linear springs with force varying as kx.

Exponential form. The trigonometric functions of sine and cosine are related to the exponential function by Euler's equation

$$e^{i\theta} = \cos\theta + i \sin\theta \tag{1.1.7}$$

*The word *circular* is generally deleted, and ω and f are used without distinction for frequency.

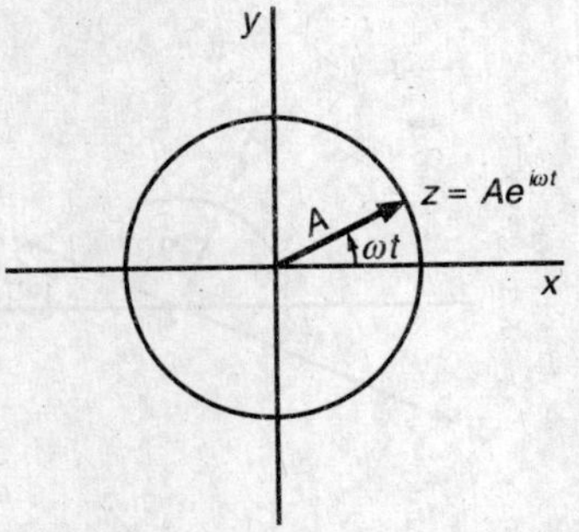

FIGURE 1.1.4. Harmonic motion represented by a rotating vector.

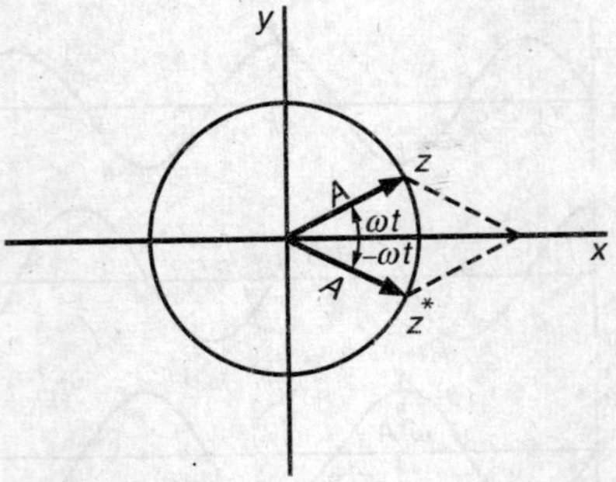

FIGURE 1.1.5. Vector z and its conjugate z^*.

A vector of amplitude A rotating at constant angular speed ω can be represented as a complex quantity z in the Argand diagram, as shown in Fig. 1.1.4.

$$\begin{aligned} z &= Ae^{i\omega t} \\ &= A\cos\omega t + iA\sin\omega t \\ &= x + iy \end{aligned} \tag{1.1.8}$$

The quantity z is referred to as the *complex sinusoid*, with x and y as the real and imaginary components, respectively. The quantity $z = Ae^{i\omega t}$ also satisfies the differential equation (1.1.6) for harmonic motion.

Figure 1.1.5 shows z and its conjugate $z^* = Ae^{-i\omega t}$, which is rotating in the negative direction with angular speed $-\omega$. It is evident from this diagram that the real component x is expressible in terms of z and z^* by the equation

$$x = \tfrac{1}{2}(z + z^*) = A\cos\omega t = \operatorname{Re} Ae^{i\omega t} \tag{1.1.9}$$

where Re stands for the real part of the quantity z. We will find that the exponential form of the harmonic motion often offers mathematical advantages over the trigonometric form.

Some of the rules of exponential operations between $z_1 = A_1 e^{i\theta_1}$ and $z_2 = A_2 e^{i\theta_2}$ are as follows:

$$\begin{aligned} &\text{Multiplication} \quad & z_1 z_2 &= A_1 A_2 e^{i(\theta_1+\theta_2)} \\ &\text{Division} & \frac{z_1}{z_2} &= \left(\frac{A_1}{A_2}\right) e^{i(\theta_1-\theta_2)} \\ &\text{Powers} & z^n &= A^n e^{in\theta} \\ & & z^{1/n} &= A^{1/n} e^{i\theta/n} \end{aligned} \tag{1.1.10}$$

1.2 PERIODIC MOTION

It is quite common for vibrations of several different frequencies to exist simultaneously. For example, the vibration of a violin string is composed of the fundamental frequency f and all its harmonics, $2f$, $3f$, and so forth. Another example is the free vibration of a multidegree-of-freedom system, to which

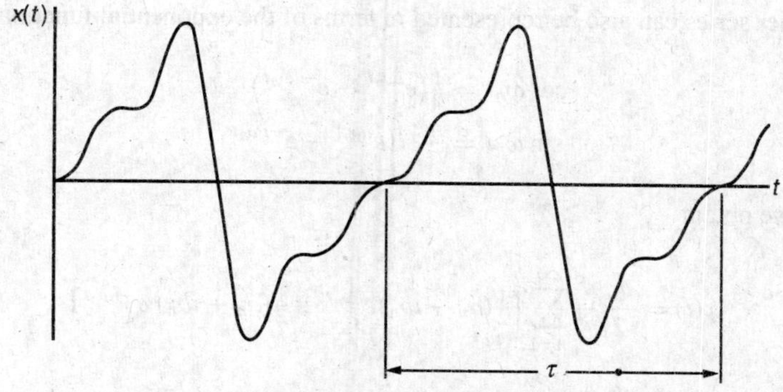

FIGURE 1.2.1. Periodic motion of period τ.

the vibrations at each natural frequency contribute. Such vibrations result in a complex waveform, which is repeated periodically as shown in Fig. 1.2.1.

The French mathematician J. Fourier (1768–1830) showed that any periodic motion can be represented by a series of sines and cosines that are harmonically related. If $x(t)$ is a periodic function of the period τ, it is represented by the Fourier series

$$\begin{aligned} x(t) = \frac{a_0}{2} &+ a_1 \cos \omega_1 t + a_2 \cos \omega_2 t + \cdots \\ &+ b_1 \sin \omega_1 t + b_2 \sin \omega_2 t + \cdots \end{aligned} \tag{1.2.1}$$

where

$$\omega_1 = \frac{2\pi}{\tau}$$
$$\omega_n = n\omega_1$$

To determine the coefficients a_n and b_n, we multiply both sides of Eq. (1.2.1) by $\cos \omega_n t$ or $\sin \omega_n t$ and integrate each term over the period τ. By recognizing the following relations,

$$\begin{aligned} \int_{-\tau/2}^{\tau/2} \cos \omega_n t \cos \omega_m t \, dt &= \begin{cases} 0 & \text{if } m \neq n \\ \tau/2 & \text{if } m = n \end{cases} \\ \int_{-\tau/2}^{\tau/2} \sin \omega_n t \sin \omega_m t \, dt &= \begin{cases} 0 & \text{if } m \neq n \\ \tau/2 & \text{if } m = n \end{cases} \\ \int_{-\tau/2}^{\tau/2} \cos \omega_n t \sin \omega_m t \, dt &= \begin{cases} 0 & \text{if } m \neq n \\ 0 & \text{if } m = n \end{cases} \end{aligned} \tag{1.2.2}$$

all terms except one on the right side of the equation will be zero, and we obtain the result

$$\begin{aligned} a_n &= \frac{2}{\tau} \int_{-\tau/2}^{\tau/2} x(t) \cos \omega_n t \, dt \\ b_n &= \frac{2}{\tau} \int_{-\tau/2}^{\tau/2} x(t) \sin \omega_n t \, dt \end{aligned} \tag{1.2.3}$$

The Fourier series can also be represented in terms of the exponential function. Substituting

$$\cos \omega_n t = \tfrac{1}{2}\left(e^{i\omega_n t} + e^{-i\omega_n t}\right)$$
$$\sin \omega_n t = -\tfrac{1}{2} i\left(e^{i\omega_n t} - e^{-i\omega_n t}\right)$$

in Eq. (1.2.1), we obtain

$$\begin{aligned} x(t) &= \frac{a_0}{2} + \sum_{n=1}^{\infty}\left[\tfrac{1}{2}(a_n - ib_n)e^{i\omega_n t} + \tfrac{1}{2}(a_n + ib_n)\,e^{-i\omega_n t}\right] \\ &= \frac{a_0}{2} + \sum_{n=1}^{\infty}\left[c_n e^{i\omega_n t} + c_n^* e^{-i\omega_n t}\right] \qquad (1.2.4) \\ &= \sum_{n=-\infty}^{\infty} c_n e^{i\omega_n t} \end{aligned}$$

where

$$\begin{aligned} c_0 &= \tfrac{1}{2} a_0 \\ c_n &= \tfrac{1}{2}(a_n - ib_n) \end{aligned} \qquad (1.2.5)$$

Substituting for a_n and b_n from Eq. (1.2.3), we find c_n to be

$$\begin{aligned} c_n &= \frac{1}{\tau}\int_{-\tau/2}^{\tau/2} x(t)(\cos \omega_n t - i \sin \omega_n t)\, dt \\ &= \frac{1}{\tau}\int_{-\tau/2}^{\tau/2} x(t)e^{-i\omega_n t}\, dt \end{aligned} \qquad (1.2.6)$$

Some computational effort can be minimized when the function $x(t)$ is recognizable in terms of the even and odd functions:

$$x(t) = E(t) + O(t) \qquad (1.2.7)$$

An even function $E(t)$ is symmetric about the origin, so that $E(t) = E(-t)$, i.e., $\cos \omega t = \cos(-\omega t)$. An odd function satisfies the relationship $O(t) = -O(-t)$, i.e., $\sin \omega t = -\sin(-\omega t)$. The following integrals are then helpful:

$$\int_{-\tau/2}^{\tau/2} E(t) \sin \omega_n t\, dt = 0 \qquad (1.2.8)$$

$$\int_{-\tau/2}^{\tau/2} O(t) \cos \omega_n t\, dt = 0$$

When the coefficients of the Fourier series are plotted against frequency ω_n, the result is a series of discrete lines called the *Fourier spectrum*. Generally plotted are the absolute values $|2c_n| = \sqrt{a_n^2 + b_n^2}$ and the phase $\phi_n = \tan^{-1}(b_n/a_n)$, an example of which is shown in Fig. 1.2.2. Fourier analysis including the Fourier transform are discussed in more detail in Chapter 12.

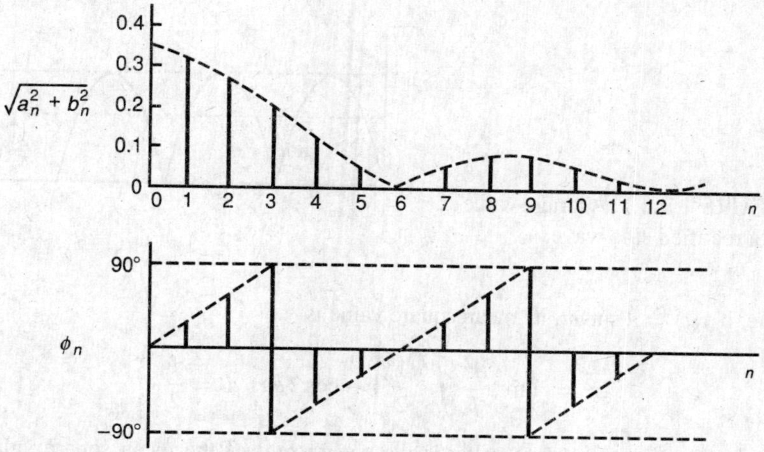

FIGURE 1.2.2. Fourier spectrum for pulses shown in Prob. 1.16, $k = \frac{1}{3}$.

With the aid of the digital computer, harmonic analysis today is efficiently carried out. A computer algorithm known as the *fast Fourier transform*[1] (FFT) is commonly used to minimize the computation time.

1.3 VIBRATION TERMINOLOGY

Certain terminologies used in vibration analysis need to be represented here. The simplest of these are the *peak value* and the *average value.*

The peak value generally indicates the maximum stress that the vibrating part is undergoing. It also places a limitation on the "rattle space" requirement.

The average value indicates a steady or static value, somewhat like the dc level of an electrical current. It can be found by the time integral

$$\bar{x} = \lim_{T\to\infty} \frac{1}{T} \int_0^T x(t)\,dt \tag{1.3.1}$$

For example, the average value for a complete cycle of a sine wave, $A \sin t$, is zero; whereas its average value for a half-cycle is

$$\bar{x} = \frac{A}{\pi} \int_0^{\pi} \sin t\,dt = \frac{2A}{\pi} = 0.637A$$

It is evident that this is also the average value of the rectified sine wave shown in Fig. 1.3.1.

The square of the displacement generally is associated with the energy of the vibration for which the mean square value is a measure. The *mean square value* of a time function $x(t)$ is found from the average of the squared values, integrated over some time interval T:

$$\overline{x^2} = \lim_{T\to\infty} \frac{1}{T} \int_0^T x^2(t)\,dt \tag{1.3.2}$$

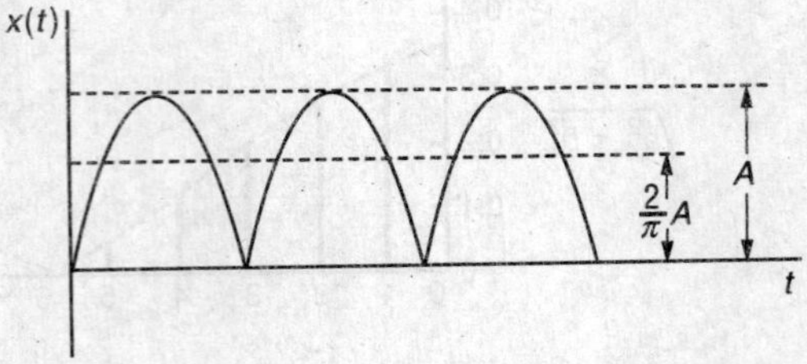

FIGURE 1.3.1. Average value of a rectified sine wave.

For example, if $x(t) = A \sin \omega t$, its mean square value is

$$\overline{x^2} = \lim_{T\to\infty} \frac{A^2}{T} \int_0^T \frac{1}{2}(1 - \cos 2\,\omega t)\; dt = \frac{1}{2} A^2$$

The *root mean square* (rms) value is the square root of the mean square value. From the previous example, the rms of the sine wave of amplitude A is $A/\sqrt{2} = 0.707A$. Vibrations are commonly measured by rms meters.

The *decibel* is a unit of measurement that is frequently used in vibration measurements. It is defined in terms of a power ratio.

$$\begin{aligned} \text{dB} &= 10 \log_{10}\left(\frac{p_1}{p_2}\right) \\ &= 10 \log_{10}\left(\frac{x_1}{x_2}\right)^2 \end{aligned} \tag{1.3.3}$$

The second equation results from the fact that power is proportional to the square of the amplitude or voltage. The decibel is often expressed in terms of the first power of amplitude or voltage as

$$\text{dB} = 20 \log_{10}\left(\frac{x_1}{x_2}\right) \tag{1.3.4}$$

Thus an amplifier with a voltage gain of 5 has a decibel gain of

$$20 \log_{10}(5) = +14$$

Because the decibel is a logarithmic unit, it compresses or expands the scale.

When the upper limit of a frequency range is twice its lower limit, the frequency span is said to be an *octave*. For example, each of the frequency bands in the following table represents an octave band.

Band	Frequency Range (Hz)	Frequency Bandwidth
1	10–20	10
2	20–40	20
3	40–80	40
4	200–400	200

REFERENCE

[1] J. S. BENDAT and A. G. PIERSOL, *Random Data* (New York: John Wiley, 1971), pp. 305–306.

PROBLEMS

1.1. A harmonic motion has a frequency of 15 cps and its maximum velocity is 6 m/s. Determine its amplitude, its period, and its maximum acceleration.

1.2. A harmonic motion has an amplitude of 0.20 cm and a period of 0.25 s. Determine the maximum velocity and acceleration.

1.3. An accelerometer indicates that a structure is vibrating harmonically at 95.5 cps with a maximum acceleration of 50 g. Determine the amplitude of vibration.

1.4. Find the sum of two harmonic motions of equal amplitude but of slightly different frequencies. Discuss the beating phenomena that result from this sum.

1.5. Add two complex vectors $(8 + 5i)$ and $(3 - 2i)$, expressing the result as $A\angle\theta$.

1.6. Express the complex vector $8 + 6i$ in the exponential form $Ae^{i\theta}$.

1.7. Determine the sum of two vectors $4e^{i\pi/4}$ and $5e^{i\pi/6}$ and find the angle between the resultant and the first vector.

1.8. Show that the multiplication of a vector $z = Ae^{+i\omega t}$ by $+i$ rotates it by $+90°$.

1.9. Determine the Fourier series for the triangular wave shown in Fig. P1.9.

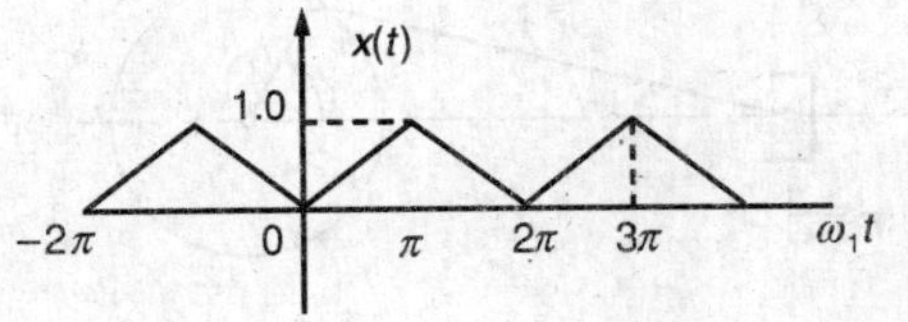

FIGURE P1.9.

1.10. Determine the Fourier series for the sawtooth curve shown in Fig. P1.10. Express the result of Prob. 1.10 in the exponential form of Eq. (1.2.4).

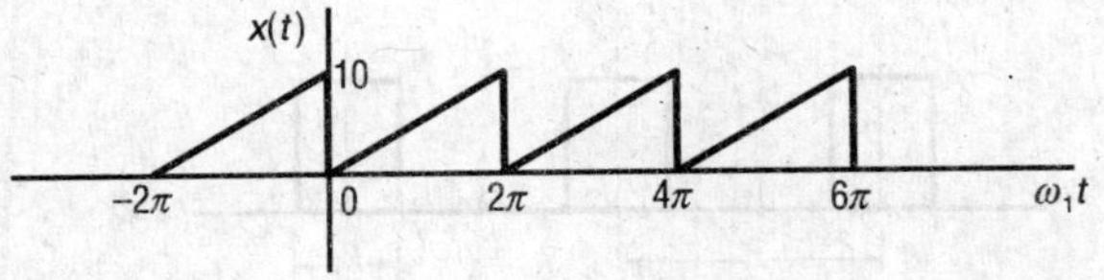

FIGURE P1.10.

1.11. Determine the Fourier series for the rectangular wave shown in Fig. P1.11.

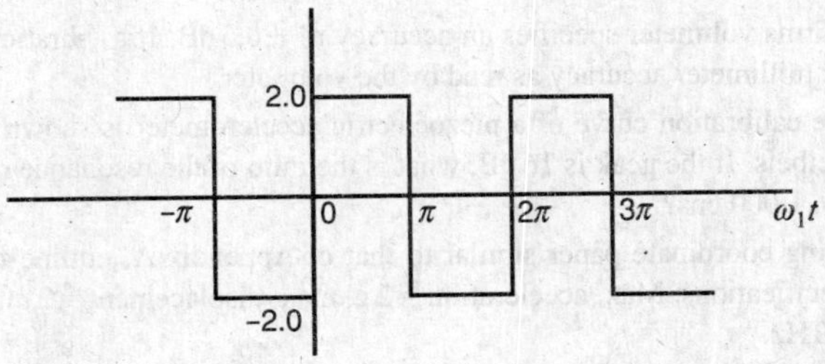

FIGURE P1.11.

1.12. If the square wave of Prob. 1.11 is shifted to the right by $\pi/2$, determine the Fourier series.

1.13. Determine the mean square value of the sawtooth wave of Prob. 1.10. using the squared curve and from the Fourier series representation.

1.14. Determine the rms value of a wave consisting of the negative portions of a sine wave.

1.15. Plot the frequency spectrum for the triangular wave of Prob. 1.9.

1.16. Determine the Fourier series of a series of rectangular pulses shown in Fig. P1.16. Plot c_n and ϕ_n versus n when $k = \frac{1}{3}$.

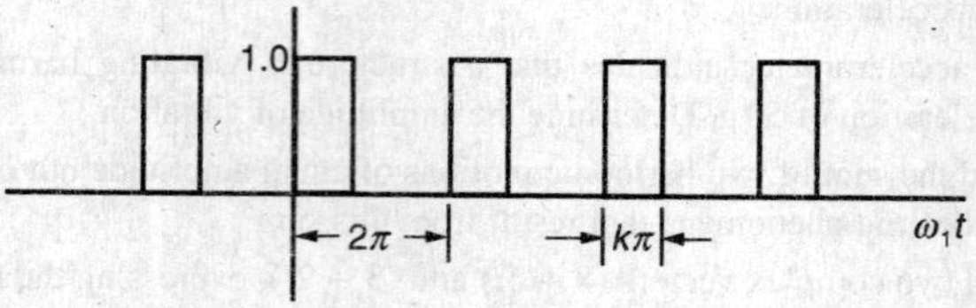

FIGURE P1.16.

1.17. Write the equation for the displacement s of the piston in the crank-piston mechanism shown in Fig. P1.17, and determine the harmonic components and their relative magnitudes. If $r/l = 1/4$, what is the ratio of the second harmonic compared to the first?

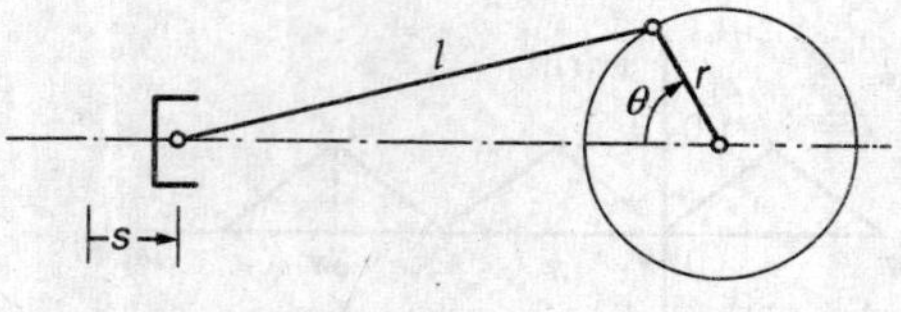

FIGURE P1.17.

1.18. Determine the mean square value of the triangular wave of Fig. P1.9.

1.19. Determine the mean square of the rectangular pulse shown in Fig. P1.19 for $k = 0.20$. If the amplitude is A, what would an rms voltmeter read?

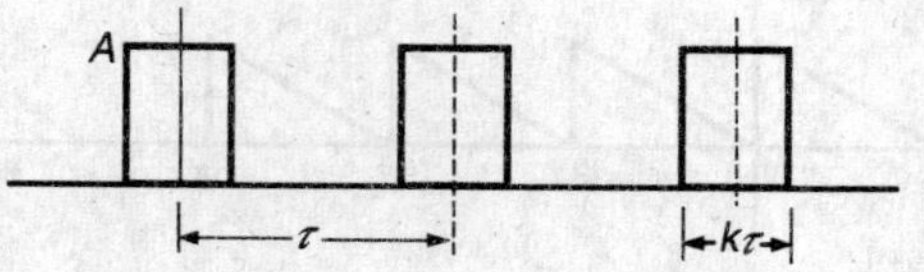

FIGURE P1.19.

1.20. Amplification factors on a voltmeter used to measure the vibration output from an accelerometer are given as 5, 10, and 50. What are the decibel steps?

1.21. An rms voltmeter specifies an accuracy of ± 0.5 dB. If a vibration of 3 mm rms is measured, determine the millimeter accuracy as read by the voltmeter.

1.22. The calibration curve of a piezoelectric accelerometer is shown in Fig. P1.22 where the ordinate is in decibels. If the peak is 16 dB, what is the ratio of the resonance response to that at some low frequency, say, 1,000 cps?

1.23. Using coordinate paper similar to that of Appendix A, outline the bounds for the following vibration specifications. Max. acceleration = 2 g, max. displacement = 2 mm min. and max. frequencies: 1 Hz and 200 Hz.

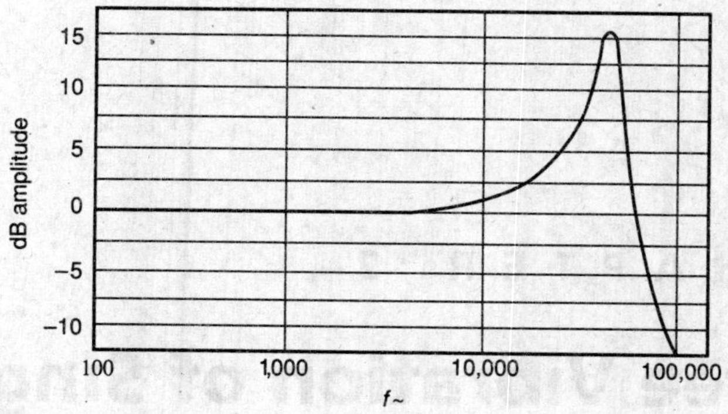

FIGURE P1.22.

1.24. Show that every function $f(t)$ can be represented as a sum of an odd function $O(t)$ and an even function $E(t)$.

1.25. Assume a pulse occurs at integer times and lasts for 1 s. It has a random amplitude with the probability of having the amplitude equal 1 or -1 being $p(1) = p(-1) = 1/2$. What is the mean value and the mean square value of the amplitude?

CHAPTER 2

Free Vibration of Single Degree-of-Freedom Systems

All systems possessing mass and elasticity are capable of free vibration, or vibration that takes place in the absence of external excitation. Of primary interest for such a system is its natural frequency of vibration. Our objectives here are to learn to write its equation of motion and evaluate its natural frequency, which is mainly a function of the mass and stiffness of the system.

Damping in moderate amounts has little influence on the natural frequency and may be neglected in its calculation. The system can then be considered to be conservative, and the principle of conservation of energy offers another approach to the calculation of the natural frequency. The effect of damping is mainly evident in the diminishing of the vibration amplitude with time. Although there are many models of damping, only those that lead to simple analytic procedures are considered in this chapter.

2.1 VIBRATION MODEL

The basic vibration model of a simple oscillatory system consists of a mass, a massless spring, and a damper. The mass is considered to be lumped and measured in the SI system as kilograms. In the English system, the mass is $m = w/g$ lb $\cdot$ s^2/in.

The spring supporting the mass is assumed to be of negligible mass. Its force-deflection relationship is considered to be linear, following Hooke's law, $F = kx$, where the stiffness k is measured in newtons/meter or pounds/inch.

The viscous damping, generally represented by a dashpot, is described by a force proportional to the velocity, or $f = c\dot{x}$. The damping coefficient c is measured in newtons/meter/second or pounds/inch/second.

2.2 EQUATIONS OF MOTION: NATURAL FREQUENCY

Figure 2.2.1 shows a simple undamped spring-mass system, which is assumed to move only along the vertical direction. It has 1 degree of freedom (DOF), because its motion is described by a single coordinate x.

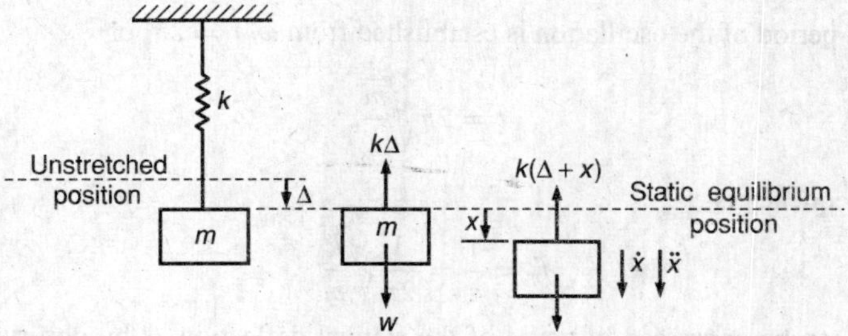

FIGURE 2.2.1. Spring-mass system and free-body diagram.

When placed into motion, oscillation will take place at the natural frequency f_n, which is a property of the system. We now examine some of the basic concepts associated with the free vibration of systems with 1 DOF.

Newton's second law is the first basis for examining the motion of the system. As shown in Fig. 2.2.1 the deformation of the spring in the static equilibrium position is Δ, and the spring force $k\Delta$ is equal to the gravitational force w acting on mass m:

$$k\Delta = w = mg \tag{2.2.1}$$

By measuring the displacement x from the static equilibrium position, the forces acting on m are $k(\Delta + x)$ and w. With x chosen to be positive in the downward direction, all quantities—force, velocity, and acceleration—are also positive in the downward direction.

We now apply Newton's second law of motion to the mass m:

$$m\ddot{x} = \sum F = w - k(\Delta + x)$$

and because $k\Delta = w$, we obtain

$$m\ddot{x} = -kx \tag{2.2.2}$$

It is evident that the choice of the static equilibrium position as reference for x has eliminated w, the force due to gravity, and the static spring force $k\Delta$ from the equation of motion, and the resultant force on m is simply the spring force due to the displacement x.

By defining the circular frequency ω_n by the equation

$$\omega_n^2 = \frac{k}{m} \tag{2.2.3}$$

Eq. (2.2.2) can be written as

$$\ddot{x} + \omega_n^2 x = 0 \tag{2.2.4}$$

and we conclude by comparison with Eq. (1.1.6) that the motion is harmonic. Equation (2.2.4), a homogeneous second-order linear differential equation, has the following general solution:

$$x = A \sin \omega_n t + B \cos \omega_n t \tag{2.2.5}$$

where A and B are the two necessary constants. These constants are evaluated from initial conditions $x(0)$ and $\dot{x}(0)$, and Eq. (2.2.5) can be shown to reduce to

$$x = \frac{\dot{x}(0)}{\omega_n} \sin \omega_n t + x(0) \cos \omega_n t \tag{2.2.6}$$

The natural period of the oscillation is established from $\omega_n \tau = 2\pi$, or

$$\tau = 2\pi\sqrt{\frac{m}{k}} \tag{2.2.7}$$

and the natural frequency is

$$f_n = \frac{1}{\tau} = \frac{1}{2\pi}\sqrt{\frac{k}{m}} \tag{2.2.8}$$

These quantities can be expressed in terms of the statical deflection Δ by observing Eq. (2.2.1), $k\Delta = mg$. Thus, Eq. (2.2.8) can be expressed in terms of the statical deflection Δ as

$$f_n = \frac{1}{2\pi}\sqrt{\frac{g}{\Delta}} \tag{2.2.9}$$

Note that τ, f_n, and ω_n depend only on the mass and stiffness of the system, which are properties of the system.

Although our discussion was in terms of the spring-mass system of Fig. 2.2.1, the results are applicable to all single-DOF systems, including rotation. The spring can be a beam or torsional member and the mass can be replaced by a mass moment of inertia. A table of values for the stiffness k for various types of springs is presented at the end of the chapter.

Example 2.2.1

A $\frac{1}{4}$-kg mass is suspended by a spring having a stiffness of 0.1533 N/mm. Determine its natural frequency in cycles per second. Determine its statical deflection.

Solution The stiffness is

$$k = 153.3\,\text{N/m}$$

By substituting into Eq. (2.2.8), the natural frequency is

$$f = \frac{1}{2\pi}\sqrt{\frac{k}{m}} = \frac{1}{2\pi}\sqrt{\frac{153.3}{0.25}} = 3.941\ \text{Hz}$$

The statical deflection of the spring suspending the $\frac{1}{4}$-kg mass is obtained from the relationship $mg = k\Delta$

$$\Delta = \frac{mg}{k_{\text{N/mm}}} = \frac{0.25 \times 9.81}{0.1533} = 16.0\ \text{mm}$$

■

Example 2.2.2

Determine the natural frequency of the mass M on the end of a cantilever beam of negligible mass shown in Fig. 2.2.2.

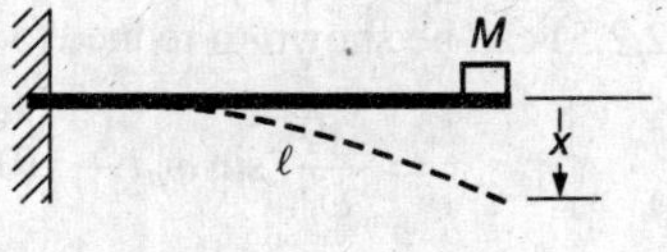

FIGURE 2.2.2.

Solution The deflection of the cantilever beam under a concentrated end force P is

$$x = \frac{Pl^3}{3EI} = \frac{P}{k}$$

where EI is the flexural rigidity. Thus, the stiffness of the beam is $k = 3EI/l^3$, and the natural frequency of the system becomes

$$f_n = \frac{1}{2\pi}\sqrt{\frac{3EI}{Ml^3}}$$

■

Example 2.2.3

An automobile wheel and tire are suspended by a steel rod 0.50 cm in diameter and 2 m long, as shown in Fig. 2.2.3. When the wheel is given an angular displacement and released, it makes 10 oscillations in 30.2 s. Determine the polar moment of inertia of the wheel and tire.

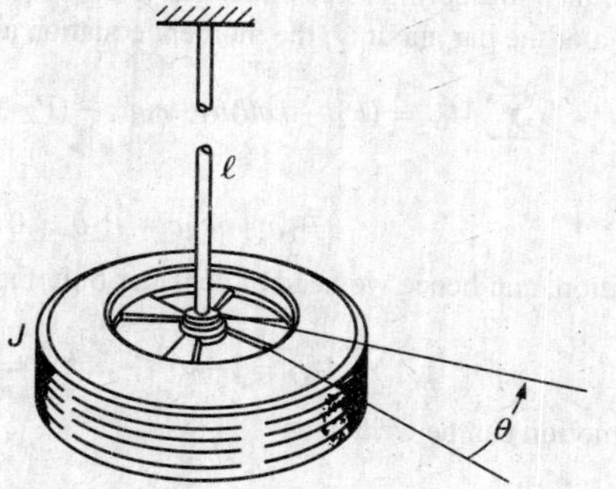

FIGURE 2.2.3.

Solution The rotational equation of motion corresponding to Newton's equation is

$$J\ddot{\theta} = -K\theta$$

where J is the rotational mass moment of inertia, K is the rotational stiffness, and θ is the angle of rotation in radians. Thus, the natural frequency of oscillation is equal to

$$\omega_n = 2\pi\frac{10}{30.2} = 2.081 \text{ rad/s}$$

The torsional stiffness of the rod is given by the equation $K = GI_p/l$, where $I_p = \pi d^4/32$ = polar moment of inertia of the circular cross-sectional area of the rod, l = length, and $G = 80 \times 10^9 \text{ N/m}^2$ = shear modulus of steel.

$$I_p = \frac{\pi}{32}\left(0.5 \times 10^{-2}\right)^4 = 0.006136 \times 10^{-8} \text{ m}^4$$

$$K = \frac{80 \times 10^9 \times 0.006136 \times 10^{-8}}{2} = 2.455 \text{ N} \cdot \text{m/rad}$$

By substituting into the natural frequency equation, the polar moment of inertia of the wheel and tire is

$$J = \frac{K}{\omega_n^2} = \frac{2.455}{(2.081)^2} = 0.567 \text{ kg} \cdot \text{m}^2$$

■

Example 2.2.4

Figure 2.2.4 shows a uniform bar pivoted about point O with springs of equal stiffness k at each end. The bar is horizontal in the equilibrium position with spring forces P_1 and P_2. Determine the equation of motion and its natural frequency.

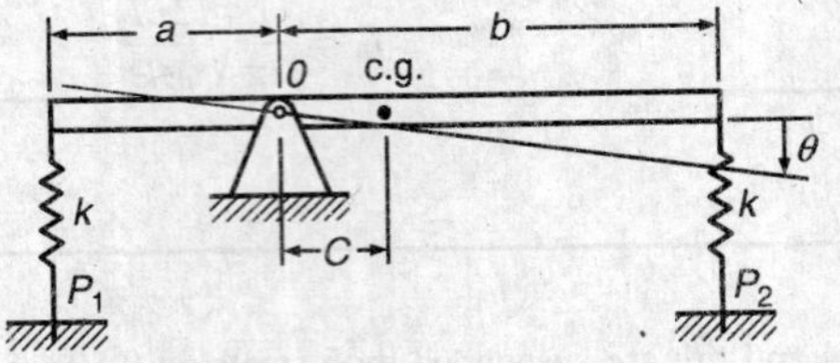

FIGURE 2.2.4.

Solution Under rotation θ, the spring force on the left is decreased and that on the right is increased. With J_O as the moment of inertia of the bar about O, the moment equation about O is

$$\sum M_O = (P_1 - ka\theta)a + mgc - (P_2 + kb\theta)b = J_O\ddot{\theta}$$

However,

$$P_1 a + mgc - P_2 b = 0$$

in the equilibrium position, and hence we need to consider only the moment of the forces due to displacement θ, which is

$$\sum M_O = (-ka^2 - kb^2)\theta = J_O\ddot{\theta}$$

Thus, the equation of motion can be written as

$$\ddot{\theta} + \frac{k(a^2 + b^2)}{J_O}\theta = 0$$

and, by inspection, the natural frequency of oscillation is

$$\omega_n = \sqrt{\frac{k(a^2 + b^2)}{J_O}}$$

2.3 VISCOUSLY DAMPED FREE VIBRATION

Viscous damping force is expressed by the equation

$$F_d = c\dot{x} \tag{2.3.1}$$

where c is a constant of proportionality. Symbolically, it is designated by a dashpot, as shown in Fig. 2.3.1. From the free-body diagram, the equation of motion is seen to be

$$m\ddot{x} + c\dot{x} + kx = F(t) \tag{2.3.2}$$

The solution of this equation has two parts. If $F(t) = 0$, we have the homogeneous differential equation whose solution corresponds physically to that of *free-damped vibration*. With $F(t) \neq 0$, we obtain the particular solution that is due to the excitation irrespective of the homogeneous solution.

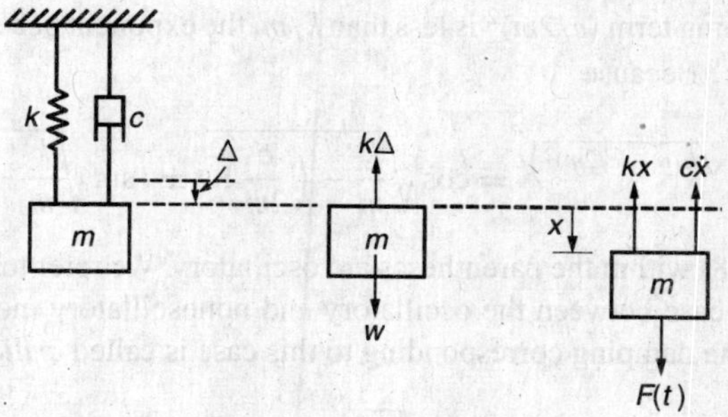

FIGURE 2.3.1.

We will first examine the homogeneous equation that will give us some understanding of the role of damping.

With the homogeneous equation

$$m\ddot{x} + c\dot{x} + kx = 0 \tag{2.3.3}$$

the traditional approach is to assume a solution of the form

$$x = e^{st} \tag{2.3.4}$$

where s is a constant. Upon substitution into the differential equation, we obtain

$$(ms^2 + cs + k)e^{st} = 0$$

which is satisfied for all values of t when

$$s^2 + \frac{c}{m}s + \frac{k}{m} = 0 \tag{2.3.5}$$

Equation (2.3.5), which is known as the *characteristic equation*, has two roots:

$$s_{1,2} = -\frac{c}{2m} \pm \sqrt{\left(\frac{c}{2m}\right)^2 - \frac{k}{m}} \tag{2.3.6}$$

Hence, the general solution is given by the equation

$$x = Ae^{s_1 t} + Be^{s_2 t} \tag{2.3.7}$$

where A and B are constants to be evaluated from the initial conditions $x(0)$ and $\dot{x}(0)$.

Equation (2.3.6) substituted into (2.3.7) gives

$$x = e^{-(c/2m)t}\left(Ae^{\left(\sqrt{(c/2m)^2-k/m}\right)t} + Be^{-\left(\sqrt{(c/2m)^2-k/m}\right)t}\right) \tag{2.3.8}$$

The first term, $e^{-(c/2m)t}$, is simply an exponentially decaying function of time. The behavior of the terms in the parentheses, however, depends on whether the numerical value within the radical is positive, zero, or negative.

When the damping term $(c/2m)^2$ is larger than k/m, the exponents in the previous equation are real numbers and no oscillations are possible. We refer to this case as *overdamped*.

When the damping term $(c/2m)^2$ is less than k/m, the exponent becomes an imaginary number, $\pm i\sqrt{k/m-(c/2m)^2}t$. Because

$$e^{\pm i\left(\sqrt{k/m-(c/2m)^2}\right)t} = \cos\sqrt{\frac{k}{m}-\left(\frac{c}{2m}\right)^2}\,t \pm i\sin\sqrt{\frac{k}{m}-\left(\frac{c}{2m}\right)^2}\,t$$

the terms of Eq. (2.3.8) within the parentheses are oscillatory. We refer to this case as *underdamped*.

In the limiting case between the oscillatory and nonoscillatory motion, $(c/2m)^2 = k/m$ and the radical is zero. The damping corresponding to this case is called *critical damping*, c_c.

$$c_c = 2m\sqrt{\frac{k}{m}} = 2m\omega_n = 2\sqrt{km} \tag{2.3.9}$$

Any damping can then be expressed in terms of the critical damping by a nondimensional number ζ, called the *damping ratio*:

$$\zeta = \frac{c}{c_c} \tag{2.3.10}$$

and we can also express $s_{1,2}$ in terms of ζ as follows:

$$\frac{c}{2m} = \zeta\left(\frac{c_c}{2m}\right) = \zeta\omega_n$$

Equation (2.3.6) then becomes

$$s_{1,2} = \left(-\zeta \pm \sqrt{\zeta^2-1}\right)\omega_n \tag{2.3.11}$$

The three cases of damping discussed here now depend on whether ζ is greater than, less than, or equal to unity. Furthermore, the differential equation of motion can now be expressed in terms of ζ and ω_n as

$$\ddot{x} + 2\zeta\omega_n\dot{x} + \omega_n^2 x = \frac{1}{m}F(t) \tag{2.3.12}$$

This form of the equation for single-DOF systems will be found to be helpful in identifying the natural frequency and the damping of the system. We will frequently encounter this equation in the modal summation for multi-DOF systems.

Figure 2.3.2 shows Eq. (2.3.11) plotted in a complex plane with ζ along the horizontal axis. If $\zeta = 0$, Eq. (2.3.11) reduces to $s_{1,2}/\omega_n = \pm i$ so that the roots on the imaginary axis correspond to the undamped case. For $0 \le \zeta \le 1$, Eq. (2.3.11) can be rewritten as

$$\frac{s_{1,2}}{\omega_n} = -\zeta \pm i\sqrt{1-\zeta^2} \quad \text{for } \zeta < 1 \tag{2.3.13}$$

The roots s_1 and s_2 are then conjugate complex points on a circular arc converging at the point $s_{1,2}/\omega_n = -1.0$. As ζ increases beyond unity, the roots separate along the horizontal axis and remain real numbers. With this diagram in mind, we are now ready to examine the solution given by Eq. (2.3.8).

Oscillatory motion. [$\zeta < 1.0$ (Underdamped Case).] By substituting Eq. (2.3.11) into (2.3.7), the general solution becomes

$$x = e^{-\zeta\omega_n t}\left(Ae^{i\sqrt{1-\zeta^2}\omega_n t} + Be^{-i\sqrt{1-\zeta^2}\omega_n t}\right) \tag{2.3.14}$$

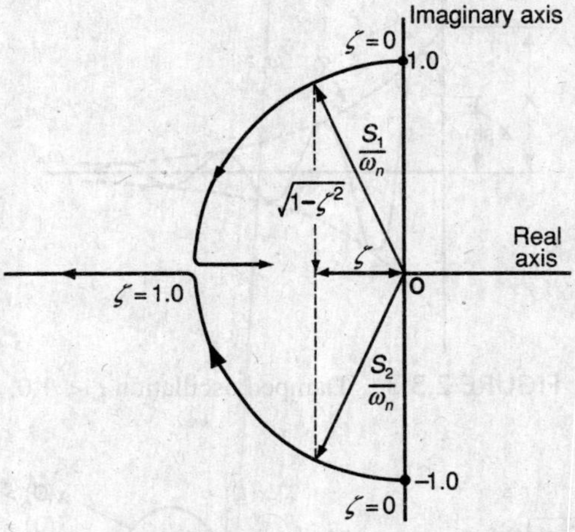

FIGURE 2.3.2.

This equation can also be written in either of the following two forms:

$$x = Xe^{-\zeta\omega_n t}\sin\left(\sqrt{1-\zeta^2}\,\omega_n t + \phi\right) \tag{2.3.15}$$

$$= e^{-\zeta\omega_n t}\left(C_1 \sin\sqrt{1-\zeta^2}\,\omega_n t + C_2\cos\sqrt{1-\zeta^2}\,\omega_n t\right) \tag{2.3.16}$$

where the arbitrary constants X, ϕ, or C_1, C_2 are determined from initial conditions. With initial conditions $x(0)$ and $\dot{x}(0)$, Eq. (2.3.16) can be shown to reduce to

$$x = e^{-\zeta\omega_n t}\left(\frac{\dot{x}(0)+\zeta\omega_n x(0)}{\omega_n\sqrt{1-\zeta^2}}\sin\sqrt{1-\zeta^2}\,\omega_n t + x(0)\cos\sqrt{1-\zeta^2}\,\omega_n t\right) \tag{2.3.17}$$

The equation indicates that the *frequency of damped oscillation* is equal to

$$\omega_d = \frac{2\pi}{\tau_d} = \omega_n\sqrt{1-\zeta^2} \tag{2.3.18}$$

Figure 2.3.3 shows the general nature of the oscillatory motion.

Nonoscillatory motion. [$\zeta > 1.0$ (Overdamped Case).] As ζ exceeds unity, the two roots remain on the real axis of Fig. 2.3.2 and separate, one increasing and the other decreasing. The general solution then becomes

$$x = Ae^{\left(-\zeta+\sqrt{\zeta^2-1}\right)\omega_n t} + Be^{\left(-\zeta-\sqrt{\zeta^2-1}\right)\omega_n t} \tag{2.3.19}$$

where

$$A = \frac{\dot{x}(0) + \left(\zeta+\sqrt{\zeta^2-1}\right)\omega_n x(0)}{2\omega_n\sqrt{\zeta^2-1}} \tag{2.3.20}$$

and

$$B = \frac{-\dot{x}(0) - \left(\zeta-\sqrt{\zeta^2-1}\right)\omega_n x(0)}{2\,\omega_n\sqrt{\zeta^2-1}} \tag{2.3.21}$$

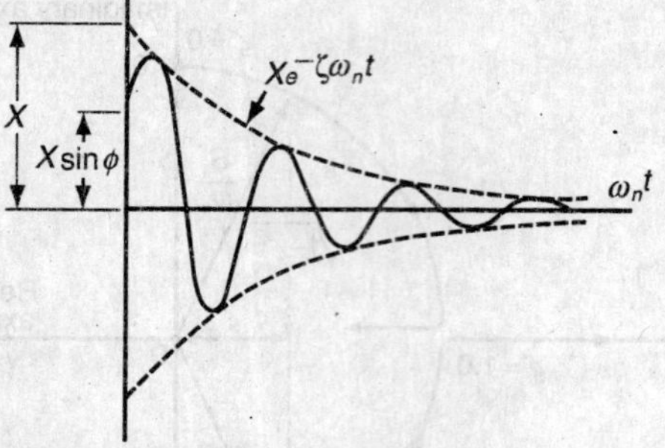

FIGURE 2.3.3. Damped oscillation $\zeta < 1.0$.

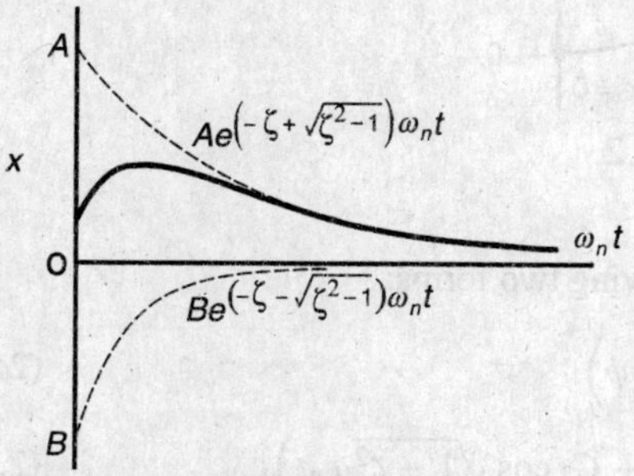

FIGURE 2.3.4. Aperiodic motion $\zeta > 1.0$.

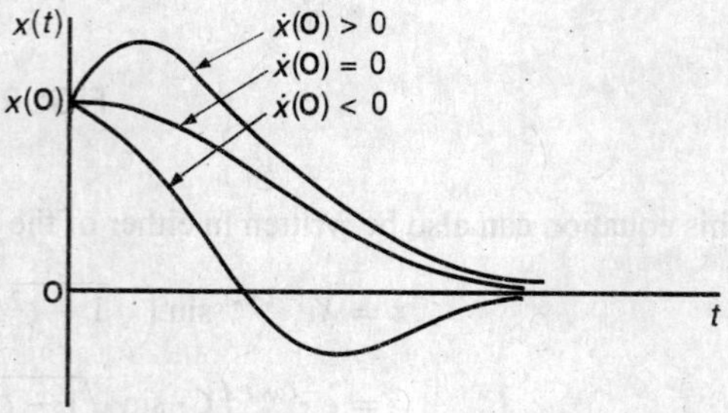

FIGURE 2.3.5. Critically damped motion $\zeta = 1.0$.

The motion is an exponentially decreasing function of time, as shown in Fig. 2.3.4, and is referred to as *aperiodic*.

Critically damped motion. [$\zeta = 1.0$.] For $\zeta = 1$, we obtain a double root, $s_1 = s_2 = -\omega_n$, and the two terms of Eq. (2.3.7) combine to form a single term, which is lacking in the number of constants required to satisfy the two initial conditions.

The correct general solution is

$$x = (A + Bt)e^{-\omega_n t} \tag{2.3.22}$$

which for the initial conditions $x(0)$ and $\dot{x}(0)$ becomes

$$x = \{x(0) + [\dot{x}(0) + \omega_n x(0)]t\}e^{-\omega_n t} \tag{2.3.23}$$

This can also be found from Eq. (2.3.17) by letting $\zeta \rightarrow 1$. Figure 2.3.5 shows three types of response with initial displacement $x(0)$.

2.4 LOGARITHMIC DECREMENT

A convenient way to determine the amount of damping present in a system is to measure the rate of decay of free oscillations. The larger the damping, the greater will be the rate of decay.

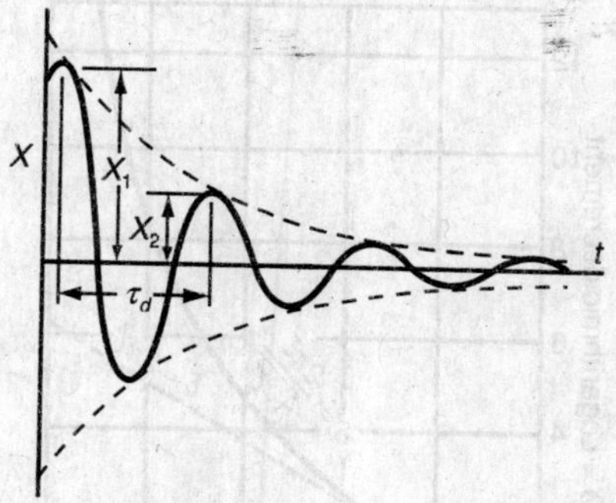

FIGURE 2.4.1. Rate of decay of oscillation measured by the logarithmic decrement.

Consider a damped vibration expressed by the general equation (2.3.15)

$$x = Xe^{-\zeta\omega_n t}\sin\left(\sqrt{1-\zeta^2}\,\omega_n t + \phi\right)$$

which is shown graphically in Fig. 2.4.1. We introduce here a term called the *logarithmic decrement*, which is defined as the natural logarithm of the ratio of any two successive amplitudes. The expression for the logarithmic decrement then becomes

$$\delta = \ln\frac{x_1}{x_2} = \ln\frac{e^{-\zeta\omega_n t_1}\sin\left(\sqrt{1-\zeta^2}\,\omega_n t_1 + \phi\right)}{e^{-\zeta\omega_n(t_1+\tau_d)}\sin\left[\sqrt{1-\zeta^2}\,\omega_n(t_1+\tau_d) + \phi\right]} \tag{2.4.1}$$

and because the values of the sines are equal when the time is increased by the damped period τ_d, the preceding relation reduces to

$$\delta = \ln\frac{e^{-\zeta\omega_n t_1}}{e^{-\zeta\omega_n(t_1+\tau_d)}} = \ln e^{\zeta\omega_n\tau_d} = \zeta\omega_n\tau_d \tag{2.4.2}$$

By substituting for the damped period, $\tau_d = 2\pi/\omega_n\sqrt{1-\zeta^2}$, the expression for the logarithmic decrement becomes

$$\delta = \frac{2\pi\zeta}{\sqrt{1-\zeta^2}} \tag{2.4.3}$$

which is an exact equation.

When ζ is small, $\sqrt{1-\zeta^2} \cong 1$, and an approximate equation

$$\delta \cong 2\pi\zeta \tag{2.4.4}$$

is obtained. Figure 2.4.2 shows a plot of the exact and approximate values of δ as a function of ζ.

Example 2.4.1

The following data are given for a vibrating system with viscous damping: $m = 4.5\,\text{kg}$, $k = 5250\,\text{N/m}$, and $c = 21\,\text{Ns/m}$. Determine the logarithmic decrement and the ratio of any two successive amplitudes.

Solution The undamped natural frequency of the system in radians per second is

$$\omega_n = \sqrt{\frac{k}{m}} = \sqrt{\frac{5250}{4.5}} = 34.2\ \text{rad/s}$$

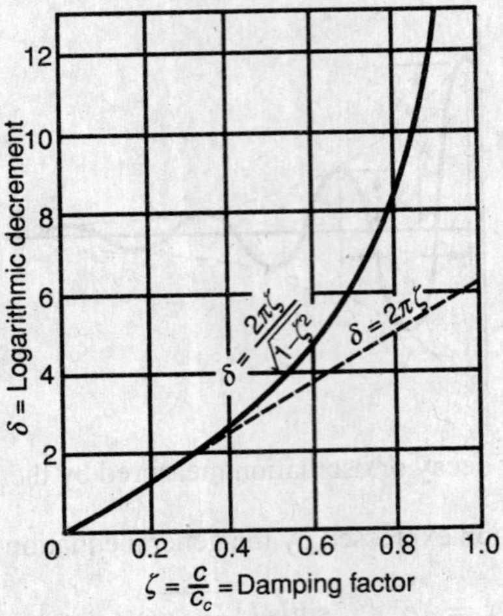

FIGURE 2.4.2. Logarithmic decrement as function of ζ.

The critical damping coefficient c_c and damping factor ζ are

$$c_c = 2m\omega_n = 307.4\,\text{Ns/m}$$

$$\zeta = \frac{c}{c_c} = \frac{21}{307.4} = 0.0683$$

The logarithmic decrement, from Eq. (2.4.3), is

$$\delta = \frac{2\pi\zeta}{\sqrt{1-\zeta^2}} = \frac{2\pi \times 0.0683}{\sqrt{1-(0.0683)^2}} = 0.430$$

The amplitude ratio for any two consecutive cycles is

$$\frac{x_1}{x_2} = e^{\delta} = e^{0.430} = 1.54$$

■

Example 2.4.2

Show that the logarithmic decrement is also given by the equation

$$\delta = \frac{1}{n}\ln\frac{x_0}{x_n}$$

where x_n represents the amplitude after n cycles have elapsed. Plot a curve giving the number of cycles elapsed against ζ for the amplitude to diminish by 50 percent.

Solution The amplitude ratio for any two consecutive amplitudes is

$$\frac{x_0}{x_1} = \frac{x_1}{x_2} = \frac{x_2}{x_3} = \cdots = \frac{x_{n-1}}{x_n}e^{\delta}$$

The ratio x_0/x_n can be written as

$$\frac{x_0}{x_n} = \left(\frac{x_0}{x_1}\right)\left(\frac{x_1}{x_2}\right)\left(\frac{x_2}{x_3}\right)\cdots\left(\frac{x_{n-1}}{x_n}\right) = (e^{\delta})^n = e^{n\delta}$$

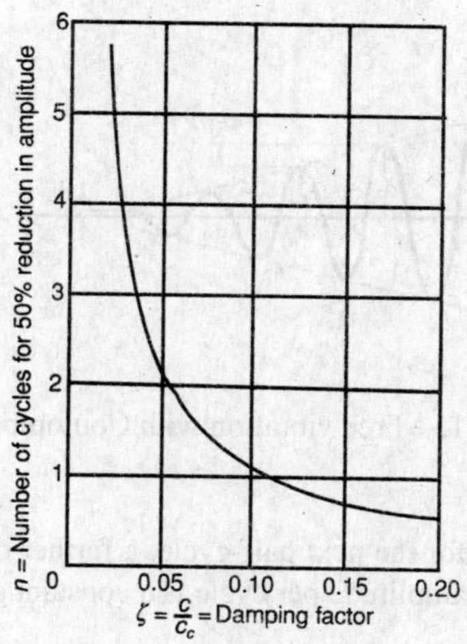

FIGURE 2.4.3.

from which the required equation is obtained as

$$\delta = \frac{1}{n} \ln \frac{x_0}{x_n}$$

To determine the number of cycles elapsed for a 50-percent reduction in amplitude, we obtain the following relation from the preceding equation:

$$\delta \cong 2\pi\zeta = \frac{1}{n} \ln 2 = \frac{0.693}{n}$$

$$n\zeta = \frac{0.693}{2\pi} = 0.110$$

The last equation is that of a rectangular hyperbola and is plotted in Fig. 2.4.3.

■

2.5 COULOMB DAMPING

Coulomb damping results from the sliding of two dry surfaces. The damping force is equal to the product of the normal force and the coefficient of friction μ and is assumed to be independent of the velocity, once the motion is initiated. Because the sign of the damping force is always opposite to that of the velocity, the differential equation of motion for each sign is valid only for half-cycle intervals.

To determine the decay of amplitude, we resort to the work-energy principle of equating the work done to the change in kinetic energy. By choosing a half-cycle starting at the extreme position with velocity equal to zero and the amplitude equal to X_1, the change in the kinetic energy is zero and the work done on m is also zero.

$$\tfrac{1}{2}k(X_1^2 - X_{-1}^2) - F_d(X_1 + X_{-1}) = 0$$

or

$$\tfrac{1}{2}k(X_1 - X_{-1}) = F_d$$

where X_{-1} is the amplitude after the half-cycle, as shown in Fig. 2.5.1.

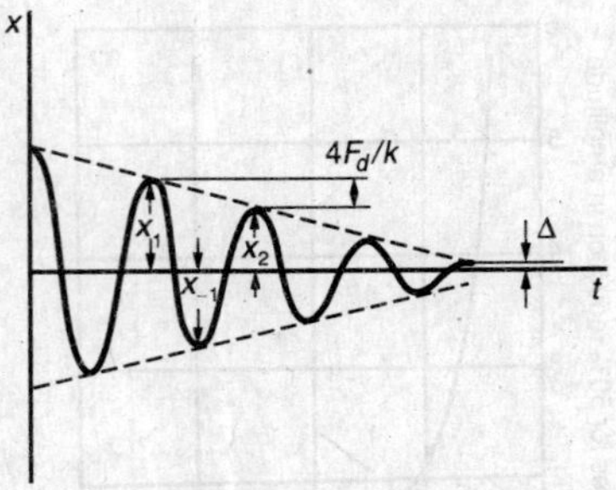

FIGURE 2.5.1. Free vibration with Coulomb damping.

By repeating this procedure for the next half-cycle, a further decrease in amplitude of $2F_d/k$ will be found, so that the decay in amplitude per cycle is a constant and equal to

$$X_1 - X_2 = \frac{4F_d}{k} \tag{2.5.1}$$

The motion will cease, however, when the amplitude becomes less than Δ, at which position the spring force is insufficient to overcome the static friction force, which is generally greater than the kinetic friction force. It can also be shown that the frequency of oscillation is $\omega_\mu = \sqrt{k/m}$, which is the same as that of the undamped system.

Figure 2.5.1 shows the free vibration of a system with Coulomb damping. It should be noted that the amplitudes decay linearly with time.

Numerical methods. Throughout the course of this book numerical techniques are introduced when appropriate. The finite difference method is discussed in Secs. 4.7 and 5.12. The Runge-Kutta method appears in Secs. 4.8 and 13.8. Chapter 7 is devoted to computational methods. It includes techniques for finding the roots of a polynomial, Sec. 7.1; eigenvalues and eigenvectors, Secs. 7.2, 7.3, 7.9, and 7.10; and the Cholesky decomposition, Sec. 7.8. The finite element method is the subject of Chapter 11. The equations for a bar are contained in Sec. 11.6 and those for a beam are in 11.10. The Holzer method is found in Secs. 10.4 and 10.5. Section 10.6 is devoted to the Myklestad's method. A brief discussion of these programs is found in Appendix F. All of these programs are written in MATLAB®. An introduction to MATLAB® is provided in Appendix E.

PROBLEMS

2.1. A spring-mass system, k_1 and m, has a natural frequency of f_1. If a second spring k_2 is added in series with the first spring, the natural frequency is lowered to $\frac{1}{4}f_1$. Determine k_2 in terms of k_1.

2.2. A 0.5-kg mass attached to a light spring elongates it by 0.98 mm. Determine the natural frequency of the system. Find the stiffness of the spring.

2.3. An unknown mass of m kg attached to the end of an unknown spring k has a natural frequency of 100 cpm. When a $\frac{1}{2}$-kg mass is added to m, the natural frequency is lowered to 75 cpm. Determine the unknown mass m and the spring constant k N/m.

2.4. A 5-kg mass attached to the lower end of a spring whose upper end is fixed vibrates with a natural period of 0.5 s. Determine the natural period when a 2.5-kg mass is attached to the midpoint of the same spring with the upper and lower ends fixed.

2.5. A flywheel weighing 30 kg was allowed to swing as a pendulum about a knife-edge at the inner side of the rim, as shown in Fig. P2.5. If the measured period of oscillation was 1 s, determine the moment of inertia of the flywheel about its geometric axis.

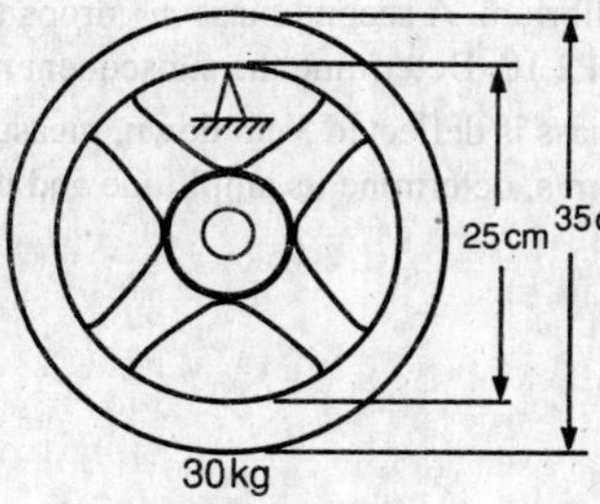

FIGURE P2.5.

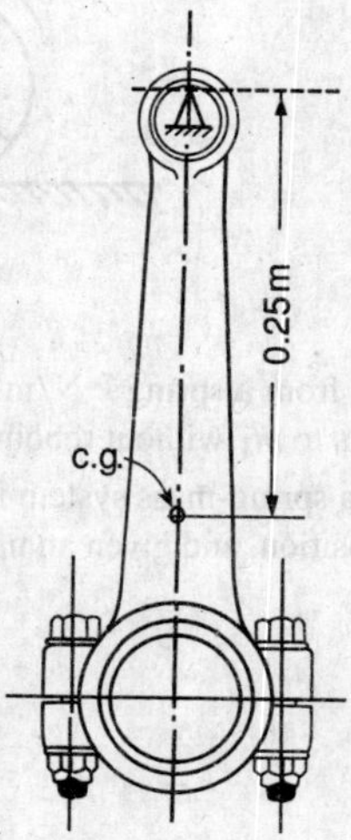

FIGURE P2.6.

2.6. A connecting rod weighing 19.6 N oscillates 45 times in 1 min when suspended as shown in Fig. P2.6. Determine its moment of inertia about its center of gravity, which is located 0.25 m from the point of support.

2.7. A flywheel of mass M is suspended in the horizontal plane by three wires of 1.829-m length equally spaced around a circle of 0.254-m radius. If the period of oscillation about a vertical axis through the center of the wheel is 2.17 s, determine its radius of gyration.

2.8. A wheel and axle assembly of moment of inertia J is inclined from the vertical by an angle α, as shown in Fig. P2.8. Determine the frequency of oscillation due to a small unbalance weight w N at a distance a in. from the axle.

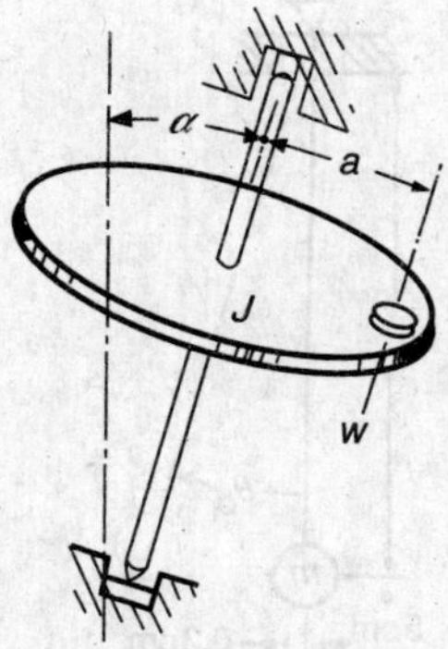

FIGURE P2.8.

2.9. A cylinder of mass m and mass moment of inertia J_0 is free to roll without slipping, but is restrained by the spring k, as shown in Fig. P2.9. Determine the natural frequency of oscillation.

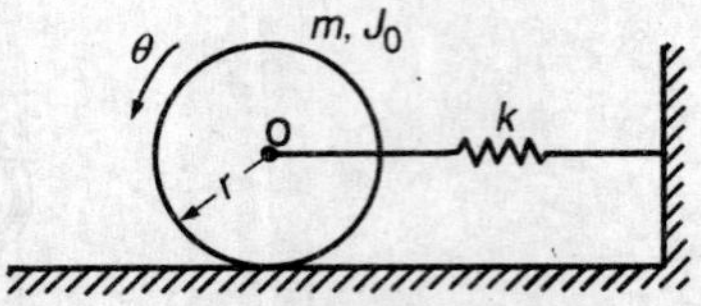

FIGURE P2.9.

2.10. A mass m_1 hangs from a spring k N/m and is in static equilibrium. A second mass m_2 drops through a height h and sticks to m_1 without rebound, as shown in Fig. P2.10. Determine the subsequent motion.

2.11. The ratio k/m of a spring-mass system is given as 9. If the mass is deflected 3 cm down, measured from its equilibrium position, and given an upward velocity of 6 cm/s, determine its amplitude and maximum acceleration.

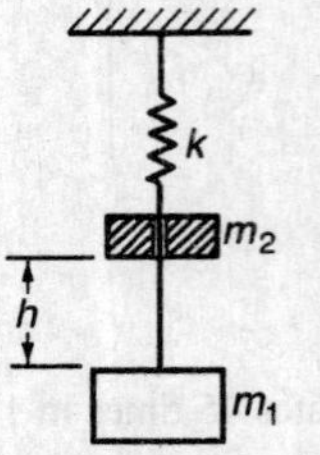

FIGURE P2.11.

2.12. A chronograph is to be operated by a 2-s pendulum of length L shown in Fig. P2.12. A platinum wire attached to the bob completes the electric timing circuit through a drop of mercury as it swings through the lowest point. (a) What should be the length L of the pendulum? (b) If the platinum wire is in contact with the mercury for 0.3 cm of the swing, what must be the amplitude θ to limit the duration of contact 0.01 s? (Assume that the velocity during contact is constant and that the amplitude of oscillation is small.)

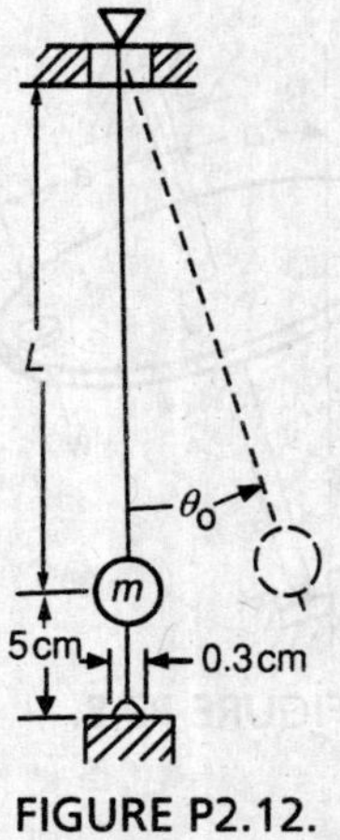

FIGURE P2.12.

2.13. A hydrometer float, shown in Fig. P2.13, is used to measure the specific gravity of liquids. The mass of the float is 0.0372 kg, and the diameter of the cylindrical section protruding above the surface is 0.0064 m. Determine the period of vibration when the float is allowed to bob up and down in a fluid of specific gravity 1.20.

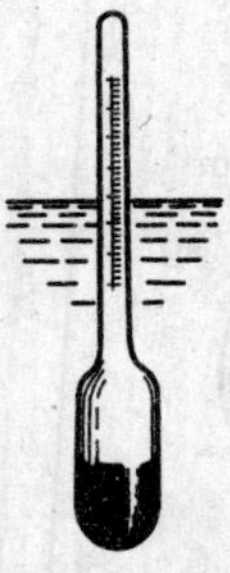

FIGURE P2.13.

2.14. A spherical buoy 1 m in diameter is weighted to float half out of water, as shown in Fig. P2.14. The center of gravity of the buoy is 20 cm below its geometric center, and the period of oscillation in rolling motion is 1.3 s. Determine the moment of inertia of the buoy about its rotational axis.

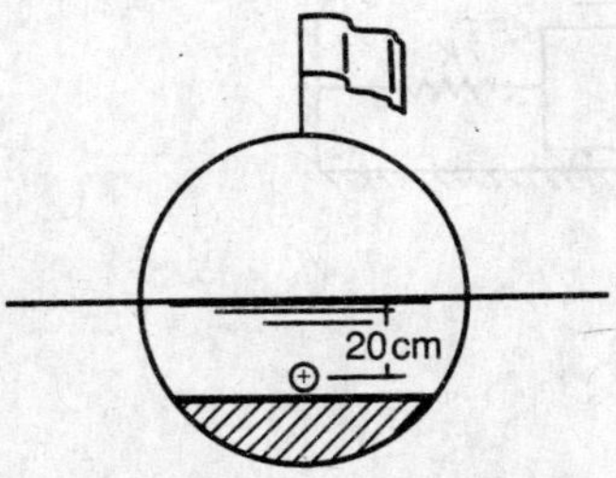

FIGURE P2.14.

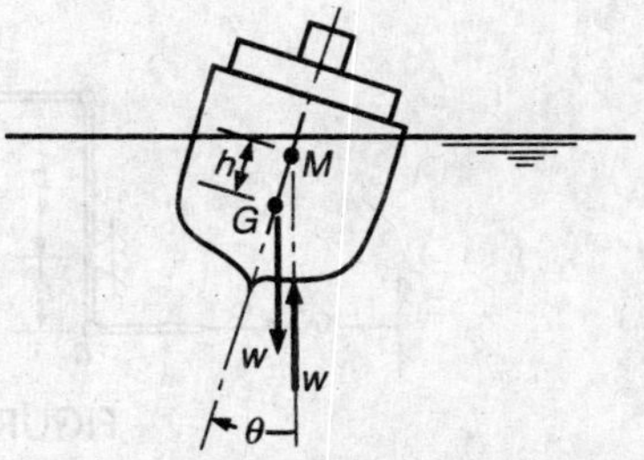

FIGURE P2.15.

2.15. The oscillatory characteristics of ships in rolling motion depend on the position of the metacenter M with respect to the center of gravity G. The metacenter M represents the point of intersection of the line of action of the buoyant force and the center line of the ship, and its distance h measured from G is the metacentric height, as shown in Fig. P2.15. The position of M depends on the shape of the hull and is independent of the angular inclination θ of the ship for small values of θ. Show that the period of the rolling motion is given by

$$\tau = 2\pi\sqrt{\frac{J}{Wh}}$$

where J is the mass moment of inertia of the ship about its roll axis, and W is the weight of the ship. In general, the position of the roll axis is unknown and J is obtained from the period of oscillation determined from a model test.

2.16. A uniform bar of radius of gyration k about its center of gravity is suspended horizontally by two vertical strings of length h, at distances a and b from the mass center. Prove that the bar will oscillate about the vertical line through the mass center, and determine the frequency of oscillation.

2.17. A steel shaft 110-cm long and 37.5 mm in diameter is used as a torsion spring for the wheels of a light automobile, as shown in Fig. P2.17. Determine the natural frequency of the system if the weight of the wheel and tire assembly is 17 kg and its radius of gyration about its axle is 225 mm. Discuss the difference in the natural frequency with the wheel locked and unlocked to the arm.

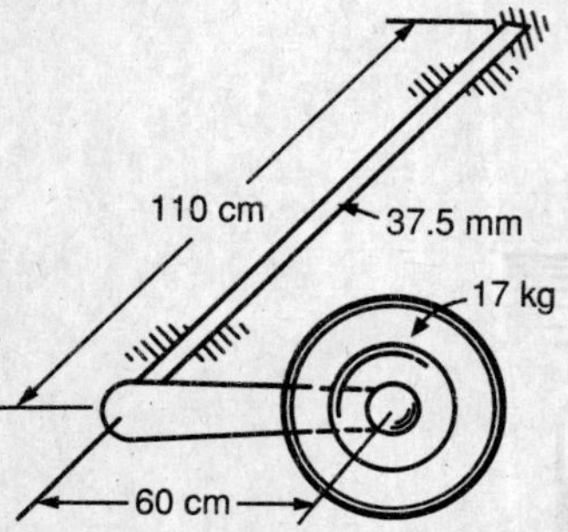

FIGURE P2.17.

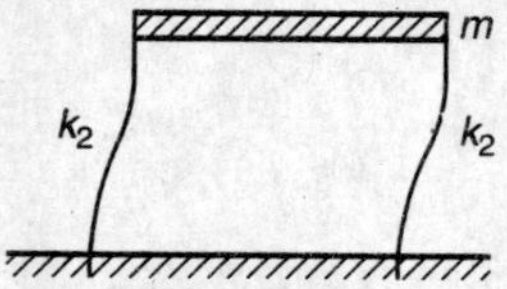

FIGURE P2.18.

2.18. Figure P2.18 shows a simplified model of a single-story building. The columns are assumed to be rigidly embedded at the ends. Determine its natural period τ. Refer to the table of stiffness on page 29.

2.19. Determine the natural frequency for the system shown in Fig. P2.19.

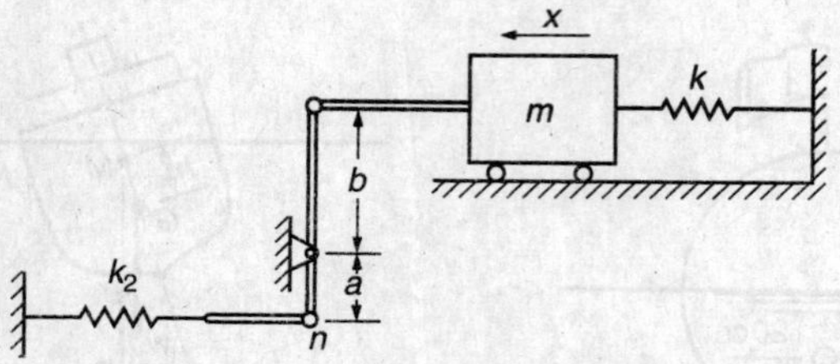

FIGURE P2.19.

2.20. Determine the stiffness at m_0, and write the expression for the natural frequency, for the system shown in Fig. P2.20.

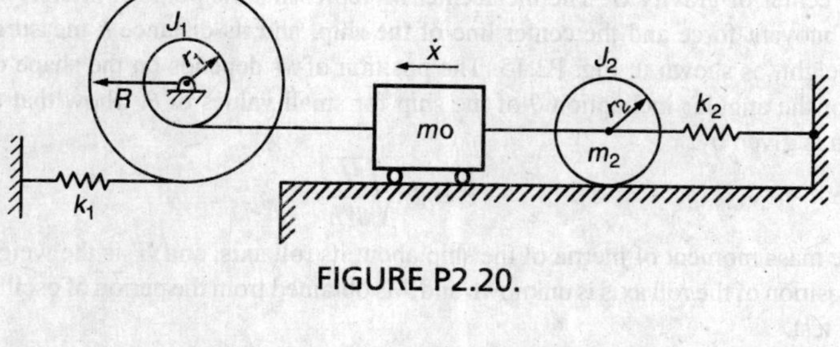

FIGURE P2.20.

2.21. Tachometers are a reed-type frequency-measuring instrument consisting of small cantilever beams with weights attached at the ends. When the frequency of vibration corresponds to the natural frequency of one of the reeds, it will vibrate, thereby indicating the frequency. How large a weight must be placed on the end of a reed made of spring steel 0.1016-cm thick, 0.635-cm wide, and 8.890-cm long for a natural frequency of 20 cps?

Table of Spring Stiffness

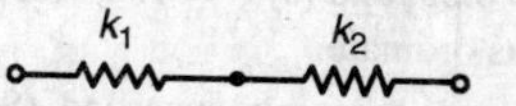

$$k = \frac{1}{1/k_1 + 1/k_2}$$

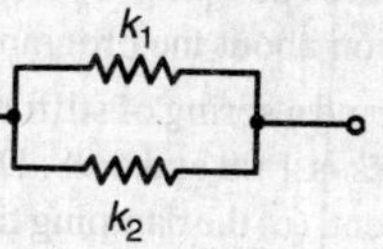

$$k = k_1 + k_2$$

$$k = \frac{EI}{l}$$ I = moment of inertia of cross-sectional area

l = total length

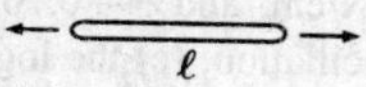

$$k = \frac{EA}{l}$$ A = cross-sectional area

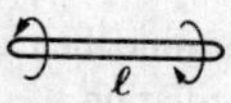

$$k = \frac{GJ}{l}$$ J = torsion constant of cross section

$$k = \frac{Gd^4}{64nR^3}$$ n = number of turns

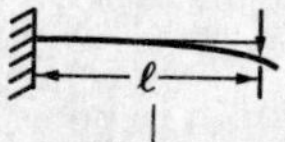

$$k = \frac{3EI}{l^3}$$ k at position of load

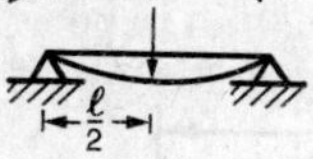

$$k = \frac{48EI}{l^3}$$

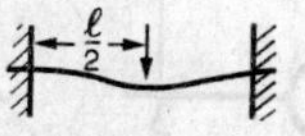

$$k = \frac{192EI}{l^3}$$

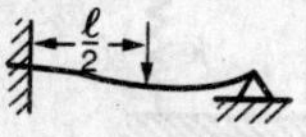

$$k = \frac{768EI}{7l^3}$$

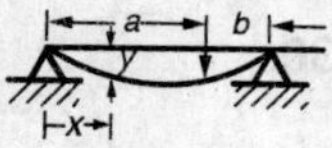

$$k = \frac{3EIl}{a^2b^2} \qquad y_x = \frac{Pbx}{6EIl}(l^2 - x^2 - b^2)$$

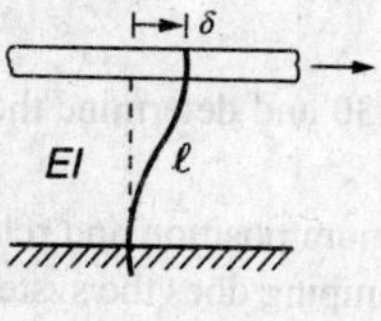

$$k = \frac{12EI}{l^3}$$

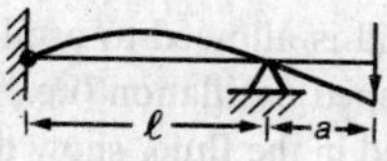

$$k = \frac{3EI}{(1+a)a^2}$$

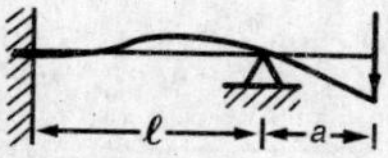

$$k = \frac{24EI}{a^2(3l + 8a)}$$

2.22. A mass of 1 kg is attached to the end of a spring with a stiffness of 20 N/cm. Determine the critical damping coefficient.

2.23. To calibrate a dashpot, the velocity of the plunger was measured when a given force was applied to it. If a 0.25-kg weight produced a constant velocity of 5 cm/s, determine the damping factor ζ when used with the system of Prob. 2.22.

M **2.24.** A vibrating system is started under the following initial conditions: $x = 0$ and $\dot{x} = v_0$. Determine the equation of motion when (a) $\zeta = 1.5$, (b) $\zeta = 0.25$, and (c) $\zeta = 1.0$. Plot nondimensional curves for the three cases with $\omega_n t$ as abscissa and $x\omega_n/v_0$ as ordinate.

M **2.25.** In Prob. 2.24, compare the peak values for the three dampings specified. (See Appendix E for information about MATLAB® and Appendix F for information about the programs.)

2.26. A vibrating system consisting of a mass of 2 kg and a spring of stiffness 20 N/cm is viscously damped such that the ratio of any two consecutive amplitudes is 1.00 and 0.98. Determine (a) the natural frequency of the damped system, (b) the logarithmic decrement, (c) the damping factor, and (d) the damping coefficient.

2.27. A vibrating system consists of a mass of 4.534 kg, a spring of stiffness 35.0 N/cm, and a dashpot with a damping coefficient of 0.1243 N/cm/s. Find (a) the damping factor, (b) the logarithmic decrement, and (c) the ratio of any two consecutive amplitudes.

2.28. A vibrating system has the following constants: $m = 17.5$ kg, $k = 70.0$ N/cm, and $c = 0.70$ N/cm/s. Determine (a) the damping factor, (b) the natural frequency of damped oscillation, (c) the logarithmic decrement, and (d) the ratio of any two consecutive amplitudes.

2.29. Set up the differential equation of motion for the system shown in Fig. P2.29. Determine the expression for (a) the critical damping coefficient, and (b) the natural frequency of damped oscillation.

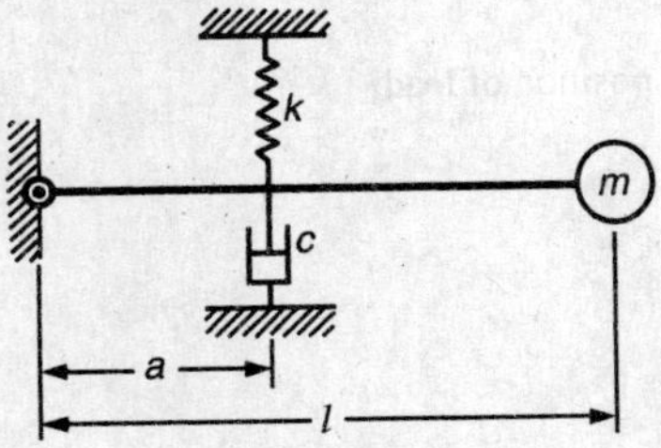

FIGURE P2.29.

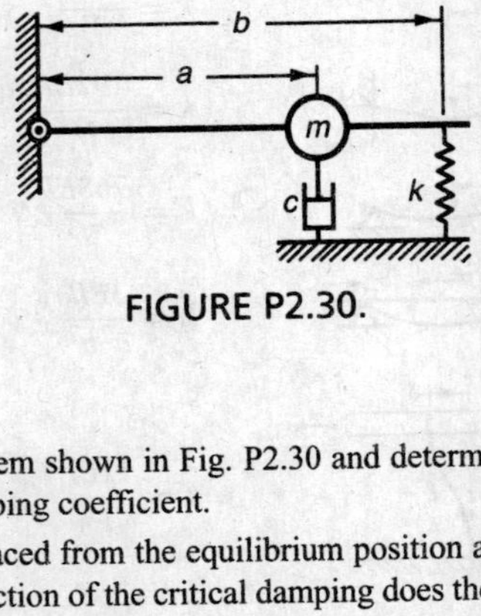

FIGURE P2.30.

2.30. Write the differential equation of motion for the system shown in Fig. P2.30 and determine the natural frequency of damped oscillation and the critical damping coefficient.

2.31. A spring-mass system with viscous damping is displaced from the equilibrium position and released. If the amplitude diminished by 5% each cycle, what fraction of the critical damping does the system have?

2.32. A thin plate of area A and weight W is attached to the end of a spring and is allowed to oscillate in a viscous fluid, as shown in Fig. P2.32. If τ_1 is the natural period of undamped oscillation (i.e., with the system oscillating in air) and τ_2 the damped period with the plate immersed in the fluid, show that

$$\mu = \frac{2\pi W}{gA\tau_1\tau_2}\sqrt{\tau_2^2 - \tau_1^2}$$

where the damping force on the plate is $F_d = \mu 2Av$, $2A$ is the total surface area of the plate, and v is its velocity.

2.33. A gun barrel weighing 544 kg has a recoil spring of stiffness 29,864 N/m. If the barrel recoils 1.22 m on firing, determine (a) the initial recoil velocity of the barrel, (b) the critical damping coefficient of a dashpot that is engaged at the end of the recoil stroke, and (c) the time required for the barrel to return to a position 51 mm. from its initial position.

FIGURE P2.32.

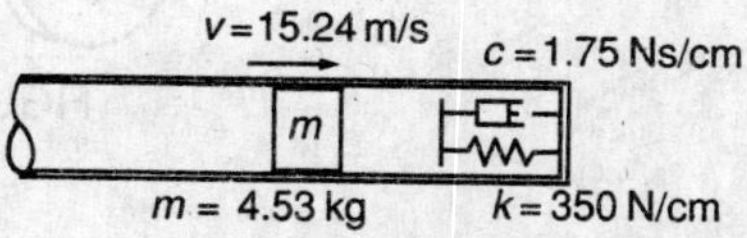

FIGURE P2.34.

2.34. A piston of mass 4.53 kg is traveling in a tube with a velocity of 15.24 m/s and engages a spring and damper, as shown in Fig. P2.34. Determine the maximum displacement of the piston after engaging the spring-damper. How many seconds does it take?

2.35. A shock absorber is to be designed so that its overshoot is 10% of the initial displacement when released. Determine ζ_1. If ζ is made equal to $\frac{1}{2}\zeta_1$, what will be the overshoot?

2.36. Determine the effective stiffness of the springs shown in Fig. P2.36.

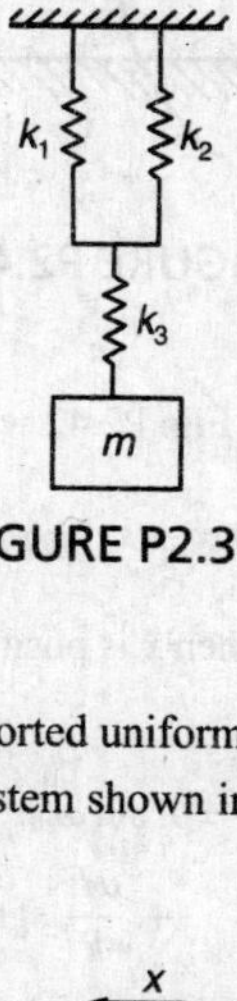

FIGURE P2.36.

2.37. Determine the flexibility of a simply supported uniform beam of length L at a point $\frac{1}{3}L$ from the end.

2.38. Determine the effective stiffness of the system shown in Fig. P2.38, in terms of the displacement x.

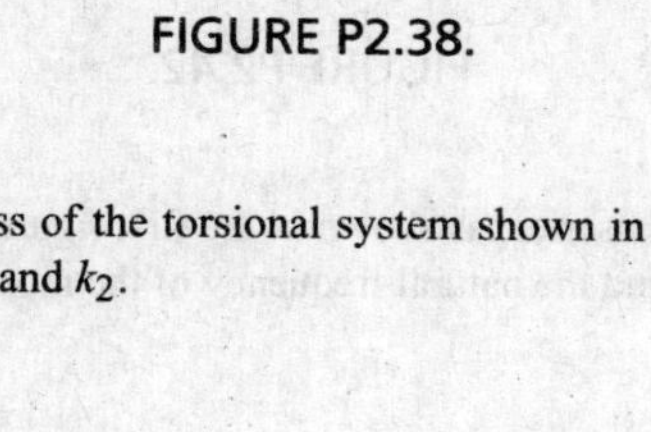

FIGURE P2.38.

2.39. Determine the effective stiffness of the torsional system shown in Fig. P2.39. The two shafts in series have torsional stiffnesses of k_1 and k_2.

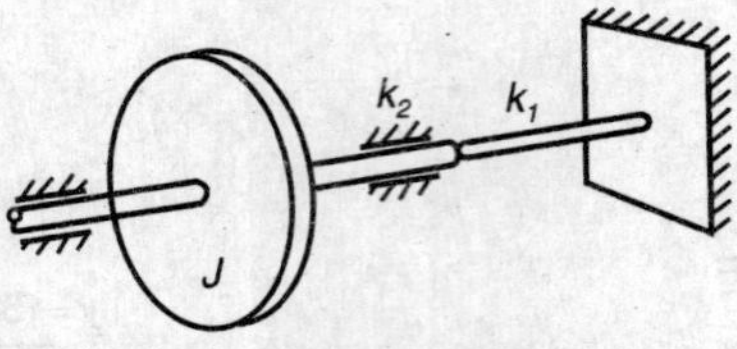

FIGURE P2.39.

M **2.40.** A spring-mass system, m and k, is started with an initial displacement of unity and an initial velocity of zero. Plot $\ln X$ versus n, where X is the amplitude at cycle n for (a) viscous damping with $\zeta = 0.05$, and (b) Coulomb damping with damping force $F_d = 0.05k$. When will the two amplitudes be equal?

2.41. Determine the differential equation of motion and establish the critical damping for the system shown in Fig. P2.41.

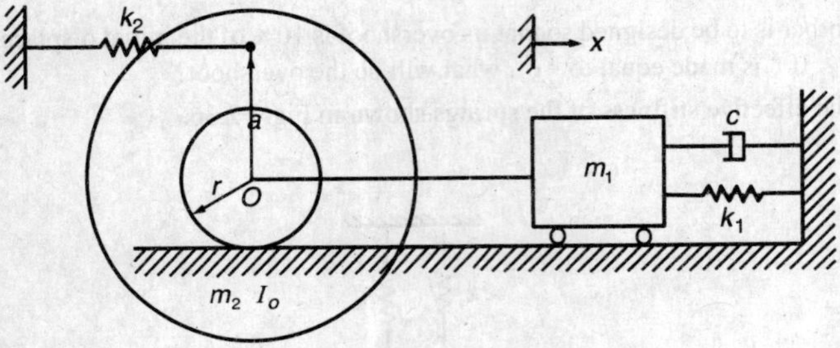

FIGURE P2.41.

2.42. The equation of motion for the system of Fig. P2.42 with Coulomb damping can be written as

$$m\ddot{x} + kx = \mu F \operatorname{sgn}(\dot{x})$$

where $\operatorname{sgn}(\dot{x}) = \pm 1$ (i.e., $\operatorname{sgn}(\dot{x}) = +1$ when $\dot{x}$ is positive and -1 when $\dot{x}$ is negative). The general solution to this equation is

$$x(t) = A \sin \omega_m t + B \cos \omega_m t + \frac{\mu F}{k} \operatorname{sgn}(\dot{x})$$

Evaluate the constants A and B if the motion is started with the initial conditions $x(0) = x_0$ and $\dot{x}(0) = 0$.

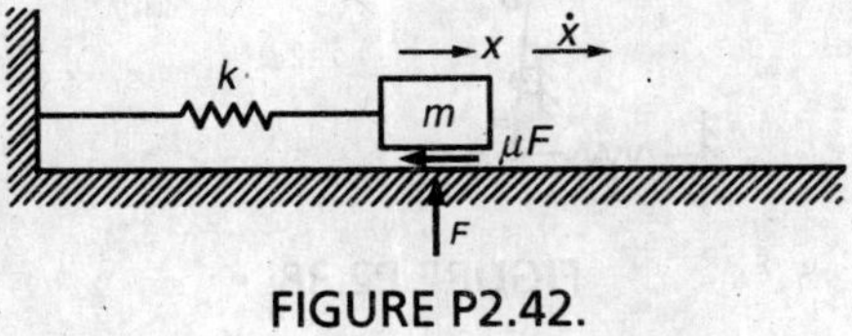

FIGURE P2.42.

2.43. If two springs are connected in series, as shown in the first figure in the table of spring stiffness, derive the resulting spring stiffness and the natural frequency of the motion.

2.44. If two springs are connected in parallel, as shown in the second figure in the table of spring stiffness, derive the resulting spring stiffness and the natural frequency of the motion.

2.45. Write down the equations of motion and find the effective spring constant for the system shown in Fig. P2.45.

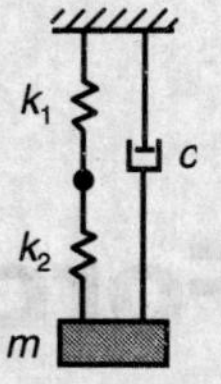

FIGURE P2.45.

CHAPTER 3

Harmonically Forced Vibration of Single Degree-of-Freedom Systems

When a system is subjected to harmonic excitation, it is forced to vibrate at the same frequency as that of the excitation. Common sources of harmonic excitation are unbalance in rotating machines, forces produced by reciprocating machines, and the motion of the machine itself. These excitations may be undesirable for equipment whose operation may be disturbed or for the safety of the structure if large vibration amplitudes develop. Resonance is to be avoided in most cases, and to prevent large amplitudes from developing, dampers and absorbers are often used. Discussion of their behavior is of importance for their intelligent use. Finally, the theory of vibration-measuring instruments is presented as a tool for vibration analysis.

3.1 FORCED HARMONIC VIBRATION

Harmonic excitation is often encountered in engineering systems. It is commonly produced by the unbalance in rotation machinery. Although pure harmonic excitation is less likely to occur than periodic or other types of excitation, understanding the behavior of a system undergoing harmonic excitation is essential in order to comprehend how the system will respond to more general types of excitation. Harmonic excitation may be in the form of a force or displacement of some point in the system.

We will first consider a single-DOF system with viscous damping, excited by a harmonic force $F_0 \sin \omega t$, as shown in Fig. 3.1.1. Its differential equation of motion is found from the free-body diagram to be

$$m\ddot{x} + c\dot{x} + kx = F_0 \sin \omega t \tag{3.1.1}$$

The solution to this equation consists of two parts, the *complementary function*, which is the solution of the homogeneous equation, and the *particular integral*. The complementary function, in this case, is a damped free vibration that was discussed in Chapter 2.

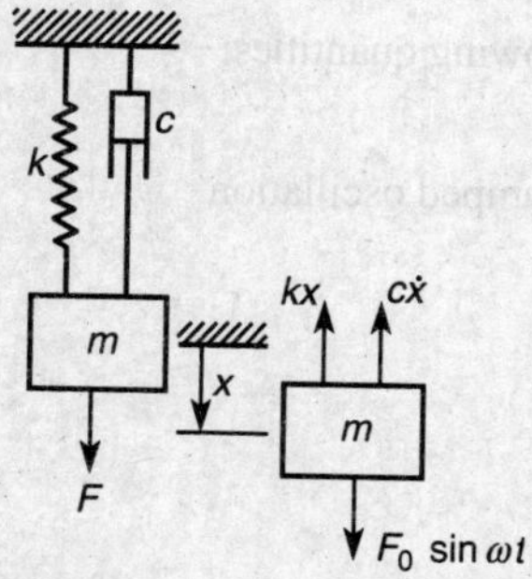

FIGURE 3.1.1. Viscously damped system with harmonic excitation.

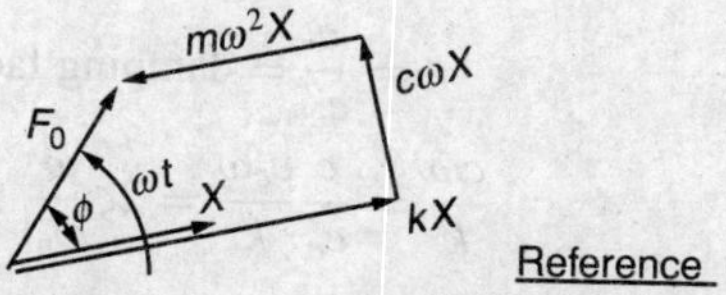

FIGURE 3.1.2. Vector relationship for forced vibration with damping.

The particular solution to the preceding equation is a steady-state oscillation of the same frequency ω as that of the excitation. We can assume the particular solution to be of the form

$$x = X\sin(\omega t - \phi) \tag{3.1.2}$$

where X is the amplitude of oscillation and ϕ is the phase of the displacement with respect to the exciting force.

The amplitude and phase in the previous equation are found by substituting Eq. (3.1.2) into the differential equation (3.1.1). Remembering that in harmonic motion the phases of the velocity and acceleration are ahead of the displacement by 90° and 180°, respectively, the terms of the differential equation can also be displayed graphically, as in Fig. 3.1.2. It is easily seen from this diagram that

$$X = \frac{F_0}{\sqrt{(k - m\omega^2)^2 + (c\omega)^2}} \tag{3.1.3}$$

and

$$\phi = \tan^{-1}\frac{c\omega}{k - m\omega^2} \tag{3.1.4}$$

We now express Eqs. (3.1.3) and (3.1.4) in nondimensional form that enables a concise graphical presentation of these results. Dividing the numerator and denominator of Eqs. (3.1.3) and (3.1.4) by k, we obtain

$$X = \frac{\dfrac{F_0}{k}}{\sqrt{\left(1 - \dfrac{m\omega^2}{k}\right)^2 + \left(\dfrac{c\omega}{k}\right)^2}} \tag{3.1.5}$$

and

$$\tan\phi = \frac{\dfrac{c\omega}{k}}{1 - \dfrac{m\omega^2}{k}} \tag{3.1.6}$$

These equations can be further expressed in terms of the following quantities:

$$\omega_n = \sqrt{\frac{k}{m}} = \text{natural frequency of undamped oscillation}$$

$$c_c = 2m\omega_n = \text{critical damping}$$

$$\zeta = \frac{c}{c_c} = \text{damping factor}$$

$$\frac{c\omega}{k} = \frac{c}{c_c}\frac{c_c\omega}{k} = 2\zeta\frac{\omega}{\omega_n}$$

The nondimensional expressions for the amplitude and phase then become

$$\frac{Xk}{F_0} = \frac{1}{\sqrt{\left[1-\left(\frac{\omega}{\omega_n}\right)^2\right]^2 + \left[2\zeta\left(\frac{\omega}{\omega_n}\right)\right]^2}} \tag{3.1.7}$$

and

$$\tan\phi = \frac{2\zeta\left(\frac{\omega}{\omega_n}\right)}{1-\left(\frac{\omega}{\omega_n}\right)^2} \tag{3.1.8}$$

These equations indicate that the nondimensional amplitude Xk/F_0 and the phase ϕ are functions only of the frequency ratio ω/ω_n and the damping factor ζ and can be plotted as shown in Fig. 3.1.3. These curves show that the damping has a large influence on the amplitude and phase angle in the frequency region near resonance. Further understanding of the behavior of the system can be obtained

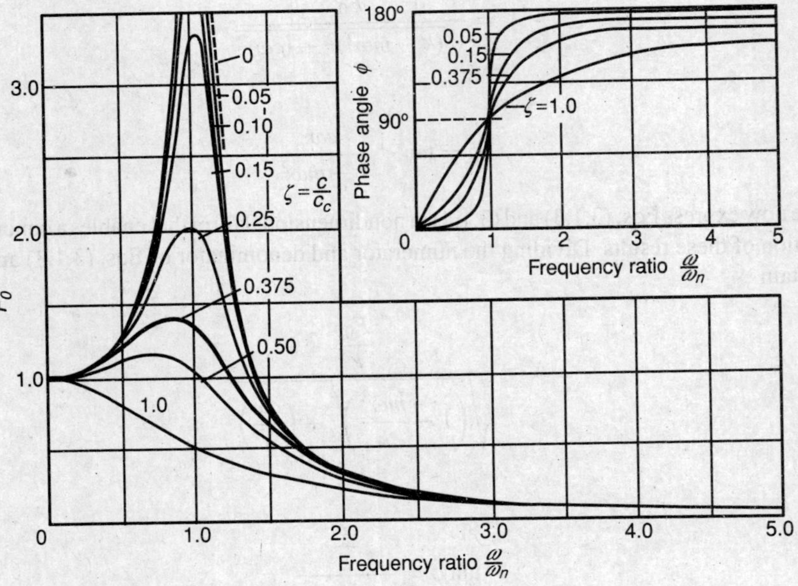

FIGURE 3.1.3. Plot of Eqs. (3.1.7) and (3.1.8).

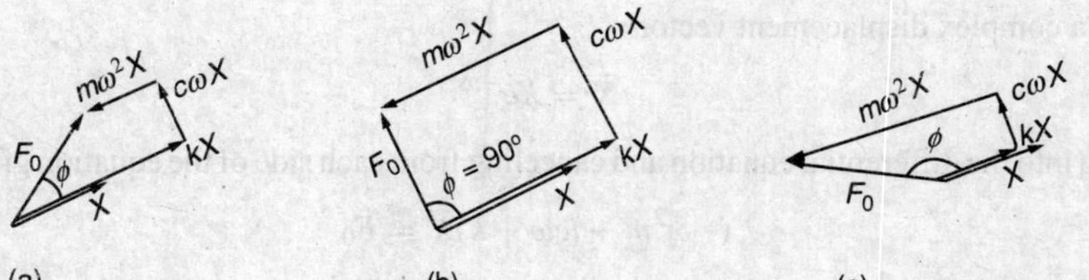

FIGURE 3.1.4. Vector relationship in forced vibration. (a) $\omega/\omega_n \ll 1$; (b) $\omega/\omega_n = 1$; (c) $\omega/\omega_n \gg 1$.

by studying the force diagram corresponding to Fig. 3.1.2 in the regions ω/ω_n small, $\omega/\omega_n = 1$, and ω/ω_n large.

For small values of $\omega/\omega_n \ll 1$, both the inertia and damping forces are small, which results in a small phase angle ϕ. The magnitude of the impressed force is then nearly equal to the spring force, as shown in Fig. 3.1.4(a).

For $\omega/\omega_n = 1.0$, the phase angle is 90° and the force diagram appears as in Fig. 3.1.4(b). The inertia force, which is now larger, is balanced by the spring force, whereas the impressed force overcomes the damping force. The amplitude at resonance can be found, either from Eqs. (3.1.5) or (3.1.7) or from Fig. 3.1.4(b), to be

$$X = \frac{F_0}{c\omega_n} = \frac{F_0}{2\zeta k} \tag{3.1.9}$$

At large values of $\omega/\omega_n \gg 1, \phi$ approaches 180°, and the impressed force is expended almost entirely in overcoming the large inertia force as shown in Fig. 3.1.4(c).

In summary, we can write the differential equation and its complete solution, including the transient term as

$$\ddot{x} + 2\zeta\omega_n\dot{x} + \omega_n^2 x = \frac{F_0}{m}\sin\omega t \tag{3.1.10}$$

$$x(t) = \frac{F_0}{k}\frac{\sin(\omega t - \phi)}{\sqrt{\left[1 - \left(\frac{\omega}{\omega_n}\right)^2\right]^2 + \left[2\zeta\frac{\omega}{\omega_n}\right]^2}} + X_1 e^{-\zeta\omega_n t}\sin\left(\sqrt{1-\zeta^2}\,\omega_n t + \phi_1\right) \tag{3.1.11}$$

Complex frequency response. From the vector force polygon of Fig. 3.1.2, it is easily seen that the terms of Eq. (3.1.1) are projections of the vectors on the vertical axis. If the force had been $F_0 \cos\omega t$ instead of $F_0 \sin\omega t$, the vector force polygon would be unchanged and the terms of the equation then would have been the projections of the vectors on the horizontal axis. Taking note of this, we could let the harmonic force be represented by

$$F_0(\cos\omega t + i\sin\omega t) = F_0 e^{i\omega t} \tag{3.1.12}$$

This would be equivalent to multiplying the quantities along the vertical axis by $i = \sqrt{-1}$ and using complex vectors. The displacement can then be written as

$$x = Xe^{i(\omega t - \phi)} = (Xe^{-i\phi})e^{i\omega t} = \overline{X}e^{i\omega t} \tag{3.1.13}$$

where $\overline{X}$ is a complex displacement vector:

$$\overline{X} = Xe^{-i\phi} \tag{3.1.14}$$

Substituting into the differential equation and canceling from each side of the equation give the results

$$(-\omega^2 m + ic\omega + k)\overline{X} = F_0$$

and

$$\overline{X} = \frac{F_0}{(k - \omega^2 m) + i(c\omega)} = \frac{F_0/k}{1 - (\omega/\omega_n)^2 + i(2\zeta\omega/\omega_n)} \tag{3.1.15}$$

It is now convenient to introduce the complex frequency response $H(\omega)$ defined as the output divided by the input:

$$H(\omega) = \frac{\overline{X}}{F_0} = \frac{1/k}{1 - (\omega/\omega_n)^2 + i2\zeta\omega/\omega_n} \tag{3.1.16}$$

(Often the factor $1/k$ is considered together with the force, leaving the frequency response a nondimensional quantity.) Thus, $H(\omega)$ depends only on the frequency ratio and the damping factor.

The real and imaginary parts of $H(\omega)$ can be identified by multiplying and dividing Eq. (3.1.16) by the complex conjugate of the denominator. The result is

$$H(\omega) = \frac{1 - (\omega/\omega_n)^2}{[1 - (\omega/\omega_n)^2]^2 + [2\zeta\omega/\omega_n]^2} - i\frac{2\zeta\omega/\omega_n}{[1 - (\omega/\omega_n)^2]^2 + [2\zeta\omega/\omega_n]^2} \tag{3.1.17}$$

This equation shows that at resonance, the real part is zero and the response is given by the imaginary part, which is

$$H(\omega) = -i\frac{1}{2\zeta} \tag{3.1.18}$$

It is easily seen that the phase angle is

$$\tan\phi = \frac{2\zeta\omega/\omega_n}{1 - (\omega/\omega_n)^2}$$

3.2 VIBRATION ISOLATION

Vibratory forces generated by machines and other causes are often unavoidable; however, their effects on a dynamical system can be minimized by proper isolator design. An isolation system attempts either to protect a delicate object from excessive vibration transmitted to it from its supporting structure or to prevent vibratory forces generated by machines from being transmitted to its surroundings. The basic problem is the same for these two objectives, that of reducing the transmitted force.

Figure 3.6.2 for $|X/Y|$ shows that the motion transmitted from the supporting structure to the mass m is less than 1 when the ratio ω/ω_n is greater than $\sqrt{2}$. This indicates that the natural frequency ω_n of the supported system must be small compared to that of the disturbing frequency ω. This requirement can be met by using a soft spring.

The other problem of reducing the force transmitted by the machine to the supporting structure has the same requirement. The force to be isolated is transmitted through the spring and damper, as shown in Fig. 3.2.1. Its equation is

$$F_T = \sqrt{(kX)^2 + (c\omega X)^2} = kX\sqrt{1 + \left(\frac{2\zeta\omega}{\omega_n}\right)^2} \tag{3.2.1}$$

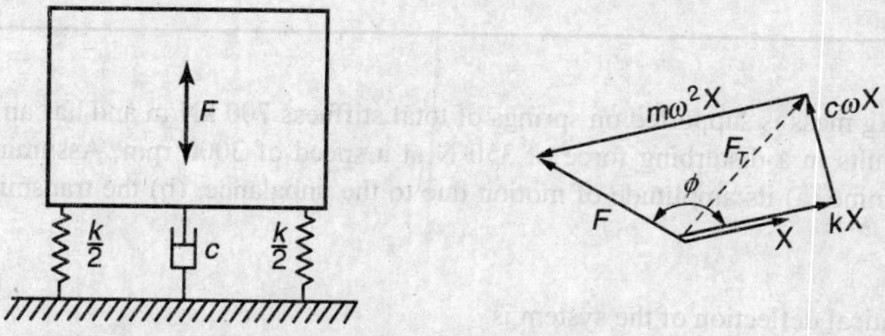

FIGURE 3.2.1. Disturbing force transmitted through springs and damper.

With the disturbing force equal to $F_0 \sin \omega t$, the value of X in the preceding equation is

$$X = \frac{F_0/k}{\sqrt{[1-(\omega/\omega_n)^2]^2 + [2\zeta\omega/\omega_n]^2}} \tag{3.2.1a}$$

The transmissibility TR, defined as the ratio of the transmitted force to that of the disturbing force, is then

$$TR = \left|\frac{F_T}{F_0}\right| = \sqrt{\frac{1+(2\zeta\omega/\omega_n)^2}{[1-(\omega/\omega_n)^2]^2 + [2\zeta\omega/\omega_n]^2}} \tag{3.2.2}$$

Comparison of the preceding equation with Eq. (3.6.8) shows that

$$TR = \left|\frac{F_T}{F_0}\right| = \left|\frac{X}{Y}\right|$$

When the damping is negligible, the transmissibility equation reduces to

$$TR = \frac{1}{(\omega/\omega_n)^2 - 1} \tag{3.2.3}$$

where it is understood that the value of ω/ω_n to be used is always greater than $\sqrt{2}$. On further replacing ω_n by Δ/g, where g is the acceleration of gravity and Δ is the statical deflection, Eq. (3.2.3) can be expressed as

$$TR = \frac{1}{(2\pi f)^2 \Delta/g - 1}$$

To reduce the amplitude X of the isolated mass m without changing TR, m is often mounted on a large mass M, as shown in Fig. 3.2.2. The stiffness k must then be increased to keep the ratio $k/(m+M)$ constant. The amplitude X is, however, reduced because k appears in the denominator of Eq. (3.2.1a).

Because in the general problem the mass to be isolated may have 6 DOF (three translation and three rotation), the designer of the isolation system must use his or her intuition and ingenuity. The results of the single-DOF analysis should, however, serve as a useful guide. Shock isolation for pulse excitation is discussed in Secs. 4.5 and 4.6 in Chapter 4.

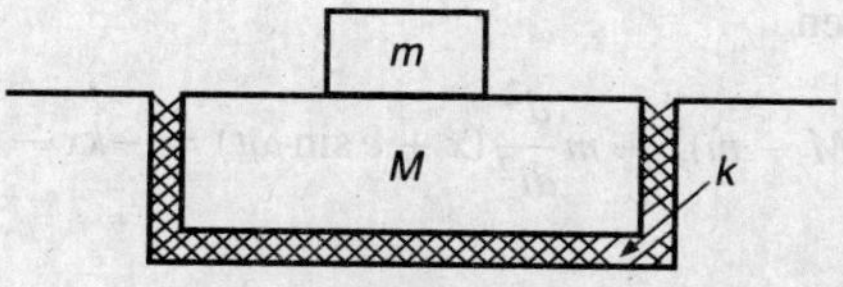

FIGURE 3.2.2.

Example 3.2.1

A machine of 100-kg mass is supported on springs of total stiffness 700 kN/m and has an unbalanced rotating element, which results in a disturbing force of 350 N at a speed of 3000 rpm. Assuming a damping factor of $\zeta = 0.20$, determine (a) its amplitude of motion due to the unbalance, (b) the transmissibility, and (c) the transmitted force.

Solution The statical deflection of the system is

$$\frac{100 \times 9.81}{700 \times 10^3} = 1.401 \times 10^{-3}\ \text{m} = 1.401\ \text{mm}$$

and its natural frequency is

$$f_n = \frac{1}{2\pi}\sqrt{\frac{9.81}{1.401 \times 10^{-3}}} = 13.32\ \text{Hz}$$

(a) By substituting into Eq. (3.1.5), the amplitude of vibration is

$$X = \frac{\frac{350}{700\times 10^3}}{\sqrt{\left[1-\left(\frac{50}{13.32}\right)^2\right]^2 + \left[2 \times 0.20 \times \frac{50}{13.32}\right]^2}}$$

$$= 3.79 \times 10^{-5}\ \text{m}$$

$$= 0.0379\ \text{mm}$$

(b) The transmissibility from Eq. (3.2.2) is

$$TR = \frac{\sqrt{1+\left(2 \times 0.20 \times \frac{50}{13.32}\right)^2}}{\sqrt{\left[1-\left(\frac{50}{13.32}\right)^2\right]^2 + \left(2 \times 0.20 \times \frac{50}{13.32}\right)^2}} = 0.137$$

(c) The transmitted force is the disturbing force multiplied by the transmissibility.

$$F_{TR} = 350 \times 0.137 = 47.89\ \text{N}$$

■

3.3 ROTATING UNBALANCE

Unbalance in rotating machines is a common source of vibration excitation. We consider here a spring-mass system constrained to move in the vertical direction and excited by a rotating machine that is unbalanced, as shown in Fig. 3.3.1. The unbalance is represented by an eccentric mass m with eccentricity e that is rotating with angular velocity ω. By letting x be the displacement of the nonrotating mass $(M - m)$ from the static equilibrium position, the displacement of m is

$$x + e \sin \omega t$$

The equation of motion is then

$$(M - m)\ddot{x} + m\frac{d^2}{dt^2}(x + e \sin \omega t) = -kx - c\dot{x}$$

which can be rearranged to

$$M\ddot{x} + c\dot{x} + kx = (me\omega^2) \sin \omega t \tag{3.3.1}$$

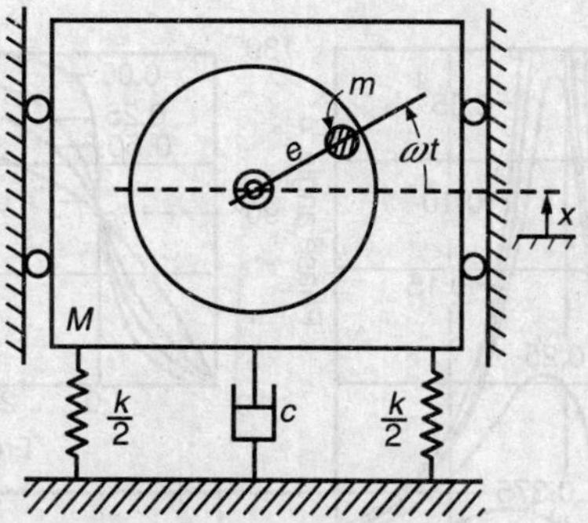

FIGURE 3.3.1. Harmonic disturbing force resulting from rotating unbalance.

It is evident, then, that this equation is identical to Eq. (3.1.1) where F_0 is replaced by $me\omega^2$, and hence the steady-state solution of the previous section can be replaced by

$$X = \frac{me\omega^2}{\sqrt{(k - M\omega^2)^2 + (c\omega)^2}} \tag{3.3.2}$$

and

$$\tan\phi = \frac{c\omega}{k - M\omega^2} \tag{3.3.3}$$

These can be further reduced to nondimensional form:

$$\frac{M}{m}\frac{X}{e} = \frac{\left(\frac{\omega}{\omega_n}\right)^2}{\sqrt{\left[1 - \left(\frac{\omega}{\omega_n}\right)^2\right]^2 + \left[2\zeta\frac{\omega}{\omega_n}\right]^2}} \tag{3.3.4}$$

and

$$\tan\phi = \frac{2\zeta\left(\frac{\omega}{\omega_n}\right)}{1 - \left(\frac{\omega}{\omega_n}\right)^2} \tag{3.3.5}$$

and presented graphically as in Fig. 3.3.2. The complete solution is given by

$$x(t) = X_1 e^{-\zeta\omega_n t}\sin\left(\sqrt{1-\zeta^2}\,\omega_n t + \phi_1\right)$$
$$+ \frac{me\omega^2}{\sqrt{\left(k - M\omega^2\right)^2 + (c\omega)^2}}\sin(\omega t - \phi) \tag{3.3.6}$$

Example 3.3.1

A counterrotating eccentric weight exciter is used to produce the forced oscillation of a spring-supported mass, as shown in Fig. 3.3.3. By varying the speed of rotation, a resonant amplitude of 0.60 cm was recorded. When

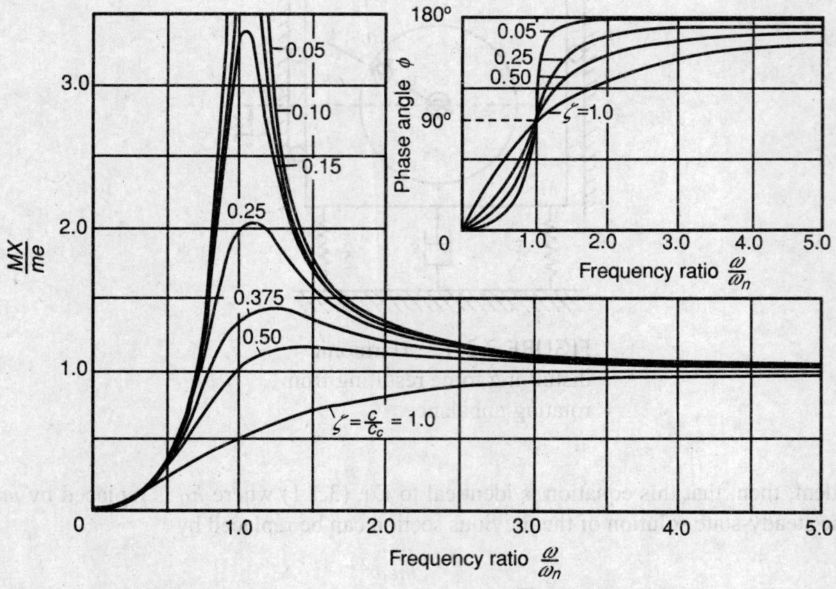

FIGURE 3.3.2. Plot of Eqs. (3.3.4) and (3.3.5) for forced vibration with rotating unbalance.

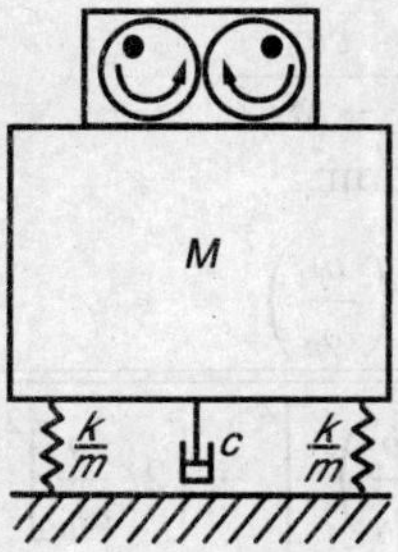

FIGURE 3.3.3.

the speed of rotation was increased considerably beyond the resonant frequency, the amplitude appeared to approach a fixed value of 0.08 cm. Determine the damping factor of the system.

Solution From Eq. (3.3.4), the resonant amplitude is

$$X = \frac{\frac{me}{M}}{2\zeta} = 0.60\,\text{cm}$$

When ω is very much greater than ω_n, the same equation becomes

$$X = \frac{me}{M} = 0.08\,\text{cm}$$

By solving the two equations simultaneously, the damping factor of the system is

$$\zeta = \frac{0.08}{2 \times 0.60} = 0.0666$$

■

3.4 ROTOR UNBALANCE

In Sec. 3.3 the system was idealized to a spring-mass-damper unit with a rotating unbalance acting in a single plane. It is more likely that the unbalance in a rotating wheel or rotor is distributed in several planes. We wish now to distinguish between two types of rotating unbalance.

Static unbalance. When the unbalanced masses all lie in a single plane, as in the case of a thin rotor disk, the resultant unbalance is a single radial force. As shown in Fig. 3.4.1, such unbalance can be detected by a static test in which the wheel-axle assembly is placed on a pair of horizontal rails. The wheel will roll to a position where the heavy point is directly below the axle. Because such unbalance can be detected without spinning the wheel, it is called *static unbalance*.

Dynamic unbalance. When the unbalance appears in more than one plane, the resultant is a force and a rocking moment, which is referred to as *dynamic unbalance*. As previously described, a static test may detect the resultant force, but the rocking moment cannot be detected without spinning the rotor. For example, consider a shaft with two disks, as shown in Fig. 3.4.2. If the two unbalanced masses are equal and 180° apart, the rotor will be statically balanced about the axis of the shaft. However, when the rotor is spinning, each unbalanced disk would set up a rotating centrifugal force, tending to rock the shaft on its bearings.

In general, a long rotor, such as a motor armature or an automobile engine crankshaft, can be considered to be a series of thin disks, each with some unbalance. Such rotors must be spun in order to detect the unbalance. Machines to detect and correct the rotor unbalance are called *balancing machines*. Essentially, the balancing machine consists of supporting bearings that are spring-mounted so as to detect the unbalanced forces by their motion, as shown in Fig. 3.4.3. By knowing the amplitude of each bearing and their relative phase, it is possible to determine the unbalance of the rotor and correct for them. The problem is that of 2 DOF, because both translation and angular motion of the shaft take place simultaneously.

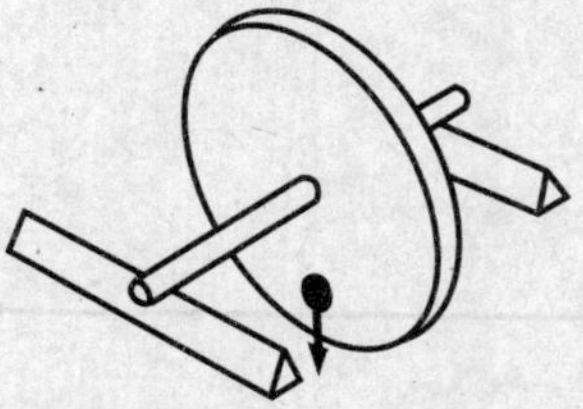

FIGURE 3.4.1. System with static unbalance.

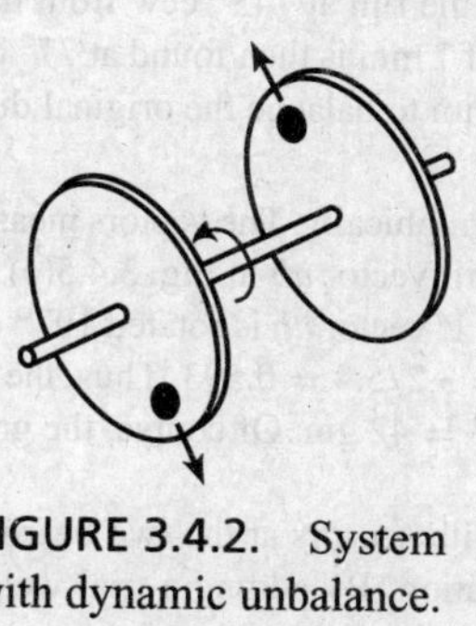

FIGURE 3.4.2. System with dynamic unbalance.

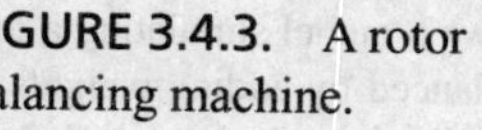

FIGURE 3.4.3. A rotor balancing machine.

Example 3.4.1

Although a thin disk can be balanced statically, it can also be balanced dynamically. We describe one such test that can be simply performed.

The disk is supported on spring-restrained bearings that can move horizontally, as shown in Fig. 3.4.4. With the disk running at any predetermined speed, the amplitude X_0 and the wheel position a at maximum excursion are noted. An accelerometer on the bearing and a stroboscope can be used for this observation. The amplitude X_0, due to the original unbalance m_0, is drawn to scale on the wheel in the direction from o to a.

FIGURE 3.4.4. Experimental balancing of a thin disk.

Next, a trial mass m_1 is added at any point on the wheel and the procedure is repeated at the same speed. The new amplitude X_1 and wheel position b, which are due to the original unbalance m_0 and the trial mass m_1, are represented by the vector ob. The difference vector ab is then the effect of the trial mass m_1 alone. If the position of m_1 is now advanced by the angle ϕ shown in the vector diagram, and the magnitude of m_1 is increased to $m_1\ (oa/ab)$, the vector ab will become equal and opposite to the vector oa. The wheel is now balanced because X_1 is zero.

■

Example 3.4.2

A thin disk is supported on spring-mounted bearings, as shown in Fig. 3.4.5. When run at 300 rpm counterclockwise (ccw), the original disk indicates a maximum amplitude of 3.2 mm at 30° ccw from a reference mark on the disk. Next, a trial weight of 71 gm is added to the rim at 143° ccw from the reference mark, and the wheel is again run at 300 rpm ccw. The new amplitude of 7 mm is then found at 77° ccw from the reference mark. Determine the correction weight to be placed on the rim to balance the original disk.

Solution The diagrams of Fig. 3.4.5 display the solution graphically. The vectors measured by the instrument and the position of the trial weight are shown in Fig. 3.4.5(b). Vector ab in Fig. 3.4.5(c) is found graphically to be equal to 5.4 mm, and the angle ϕ is measured to be 107°. If vector ab is rotated 107° ccw, it will be opposite the vector oa. To cancel oa it must be shortened by $oa/ab = 3.2/5.4 = 0.593$. Thus, the trial mass $m_t = 71$ gm must be rotated 107° ccw and reduced in size to $71 \times 0.593 = 42$ gm. Of course, the graphical solution for ab and ϕ can be found mathematically by the law of cosines.

Figure 3.4.6 shows a model simulating a long rotor with sensors at the two bearings. The two end disks may be initially unbalanced by adding weights at any location. By adding a trial weight at one of the disks and recording the amplitude and phase and then removing the first trial weight and placing a second trial

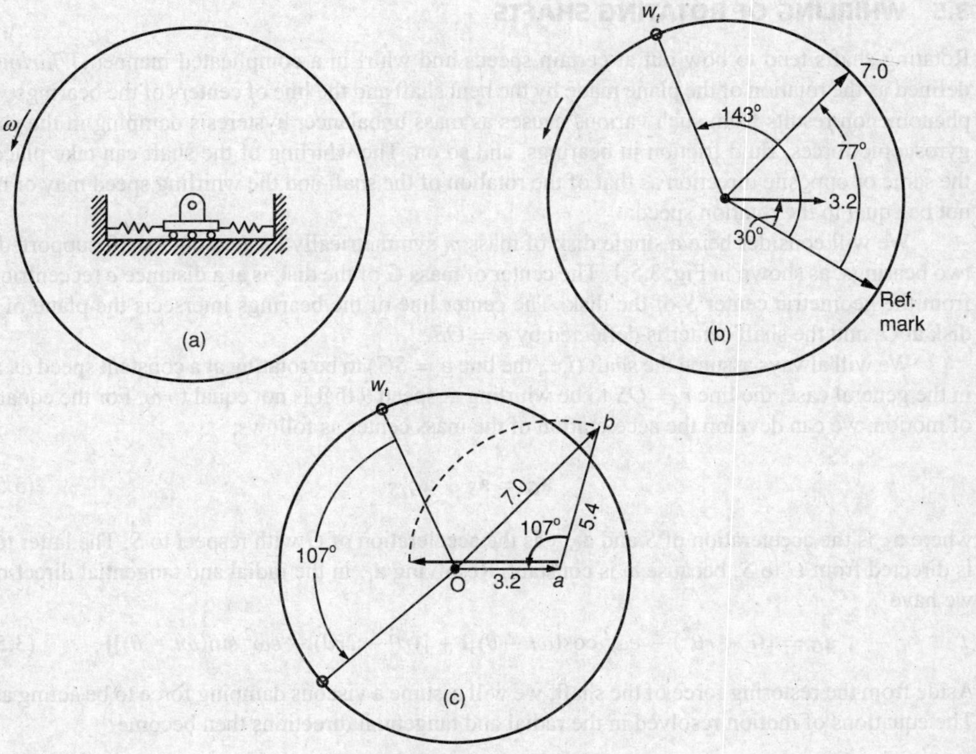

FIGURE 3.4.5.

FIGURE 3.4.6. The plane-balancing experiment. (*Courtesy of UCSB Mechanical Engineering Undergraduate Laboratory.*)

weight to the other disk and making similar measurements, the initial unbalance of the simulated rotor can be determined.

■

3.5 WHIRLING OF ROTATING SHAFTS

Rotating shafts tend to bow out at certain speeds and whirl in a complicated manner. *Whirling* is defined as the rotation of the plane made by the bent shaft and the line of centers of the bearings. The phenomenon results from such various causes as mass unbalance, hysteresis damping in the shaft, gyroscopic forces, fluid friction in bearings, and so on. The whirling of the shaft can take place in the same or opposite direction as that of the rotation of the shaft and the whirling speed may or may not be equal to the rotation speed.

We will consider here a single disk of mass m symmetrically located on a shaft supported by two bearings, as shown in Fig. 3.5.1. The center of mass G of the disk is at a distance e (eccentricity) from the geometric center S of the disk. The center line of the bearings intersects the plane of the disk at O, and the shaft center is deflected by $r = OS$.

We will always assume the shaft (i.e., the line $e = SG$) to be rotating at a constant speed ω, and in the general case, the line $r = OS$ to be whirling at speed $\dot{\theta}$ that is not equal to ω. For the equation of motion, we can develop the acceleration of the mass center as follows:

$$\mathbf{a}_G = \mathbf{a}_S + \mathbf{a}_{G/S} \tag{3.5.1}$$

where $\mathbf{a}_S$ is the acceleration of S and $\mathbf{a}_{G/S}$ is the acceleration of G with respect to S. The latter term is directed from G to S, because ω is constant. Resolving $\mathbf{a}_G$ in the radial and tangential directions, we have

$$\mathbf{a}_G = [(\ddot{r} - r\dot{\theta}^2) - e\omega^2 \cos(\omega t - \theta)]\mathbf{i} + [(r\ddot{\theta} - 2\dot{r}\dot{\theta}) - e\omega^2 \sin(\omega t - \theta)]\mathbf{j} \tag{3.5.2}$$

Aside from the restoring force of the shaft, we will assume a viscous damping force to be acting at S. The equations of motion resolved in the radial and tangential directions then become

$$-kr - c\dot{r} = m\left[\ddot{r} - r\dot{\theta}^2 - e\omega^2 \cos(\omega t - \theta)\right]$$
$$-cr\dot{\theta} = m\left[r\ddot{\theta} + 2\dot{r}\dot{\theta} - e\omega^2 \sin(\omega t - \theta)\right]$$

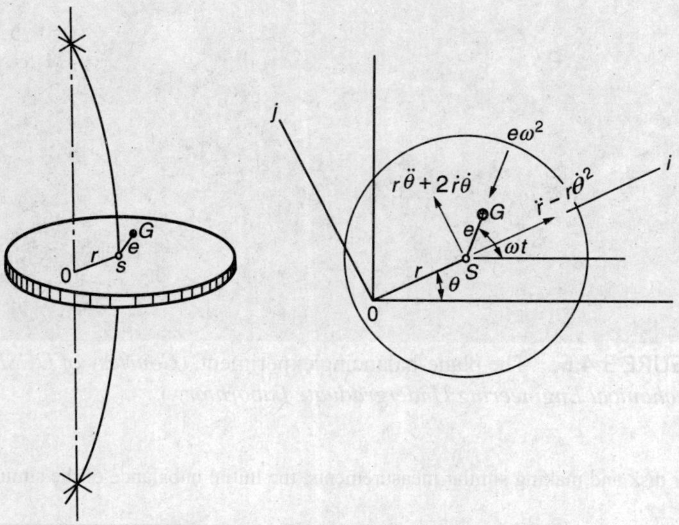

FIGURE 3.5.1. Whirling of shaft.

which can be rearranged to

$$\ddot{r} + \frac{c}{m}\dot{r} + \left(\frac{k}{m} - \dot{\theta}^2\right)r = e\omega^2 \cos(\omega t - \theta) \tag{3.5.3}$$

$$r\ddot{\theta} + \left(\frac{c}{m}r + 2\dot{r}\right)\dot{\theta} = e\omega^2 \sin(\omega t - \theta) \tag{3.5.4}$$

The general case of whirl as described by the foregoing equations comes under the classification of self-excited motion, where the exciting forces inducing the motion are controlled by the motion itself. Because the variables in these equations are r and θ, the problem is that of 2 DOF. However, in the steady-state synchronous whirl, where $\dot{\theta} = \omega$ and $\ddot{\theta} = \ddot{r} = \dot{r} = 0$, the problem reduces to that of 1 DOF.

Synchronous whirl. For the synchronous whirl, the whirling speed $\dot{\theta}$ is equal to the rotation speed ω, which we have assumed to be constant. Thus, we have

$$\dot{\theta} = \omega$$

and on integrating we obtain

$$\theta = \omega t - \phi$$

where ϕ is the phase angle between e and r, which is now a constant, as shown in Fig. 3.5.1. With $\ddot{\theta} = \ddot{r} = \dot{r} = 0$, Eqs. (3.5.3) and (3.5.4) reduce to

$$\left(\frac{k}{m} - \omega^2\right)r = e\omega^2 \cos\phi$$

$$\frac{c}{m}\omega r = e\omega^2 \sin\phi \tag{3.5.5}$$

Dividing, we obtain the following equation for the phase angle:

$$\tan\phi = \frac{\dfrac{c}{m}\omega}{\dfrac{k}{m} - \omega^2} = \frac{2\zeta\dfrac{\omega}{\omega_n}}{1 - \left(\dfrac{\omega}{\omega_n}\right)^2} \tag{3.5.6}$$

where $\omega_n = \sqrt{k/m}$ is the critical speed, and $\zeta = c/c_c$. Noting from the vector triangle of Fig. 3.5.2 that

$$\cos\phi = \frac{\dfrac{k}{m} - \omega^2}{\sqrt{\left(\dfrac{k}{m} - \omega^2\right)^2 + \left(\dfrac{c}{m}\omega\right)^2}}$$

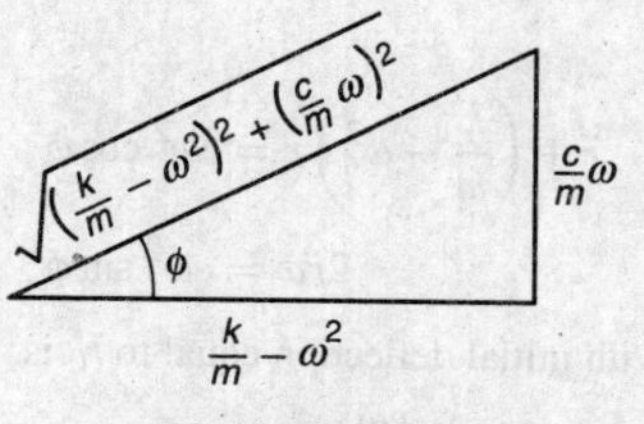

FIGURE 3.5.2.

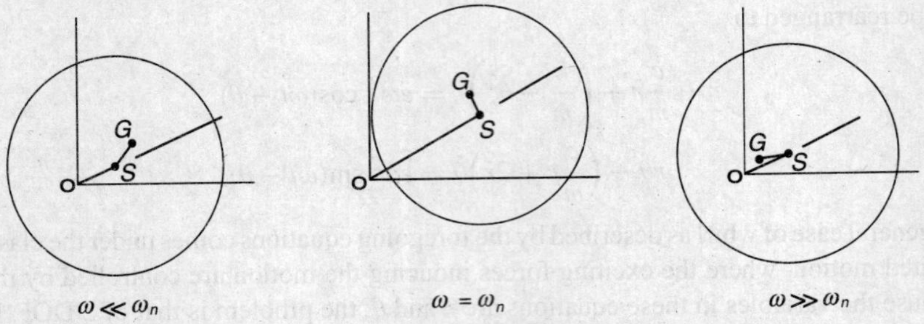

FIGURE 3.5.3. Phase of different rotation speeds.

and substituting into the first of Eq. (3.5.5) gives the amplitude equation

$$r = \frac{me\omega^2}{\sqrt{(k - m\omega^2)^2 + (c\omega)^2}} = \frac{e\left(\dfrac{\omega}{\omega_n}\right)^2}{\sqrt{\left[1 - \left(\dfrac{\omega}{\omega_n}\right)^2\right]^2 + \left[2\zeta\left(\dfrac{\omega}{\omega_n}\right)\right]^2}} \tag{3.5.7}$$

These equations indicate that the eccentricity line $e = SG$ leads the displacement line $r = OS$ by the phase angle ϕ, which depends on the amount of damping and the rotation speed ratio ω/ω_n. When the rotation speed coincides with the critical speed $\omega_n = \sqrt{k/m}$, or the natural frequency of the shaft in lateral vibration, a condition of resonance is encountered in which the amplitude is restrained only by the damping. Figure 3.5.3 shows the disk-shaft system under three different speed conditions. At very high speeds, $\omega \gg \omega_n$, the center of mass G tends to approach the fixed point O, and the shaft center S rotates about it in a circle of radius e.

It should be noted that the equations for synchronous whirl appear to be the same as those of Sec. 3.3. This is not surprising, because in both cases the exciting force is rotating and equal to $me\omega^2$. However, in Sec. 3.3 the unbalance was in terms of the small unbalanced mass m, whereas in this section, the unbalance is defined in terms of the total mass m with eccentricity e. Thus, Fig. 3.3.2 is applicable to this problem with the ordinate equal to r/e instead of MX/me.

Example 3.5.1

Turbines operating above the critical speed must run through dangerous speed at resonance each time they are started or stopped. Assuming the critical speed ω_n to be reached with amplitude r_0, determine the equation for the amplitude buildup with time. Assume zero damping.

Solution We will assume synchronous whirl as before, which makes $\dot{\theta} = \omega =$ constant and $\ddot{\theta} = 0$. However, $\ddot{r}$ and $\dot{r}$ terms must be retained unless shown to be zero. With $c = 0$ for the undamped case, the general equations of motion reduce to

$$\ddot{r} + \left(\frac{k}{m} - \omega^2\right) r = e\omega^2 \cos\phi$$

$$2\dot{r}\omega = e\omega^2 \sin\phi \tag{a}$$

The solution of the second equation with initial deflection equal to r_0 is

$$r = \frac{e\omega}{2} t \sin\phi + r_0 \tag{b}$$

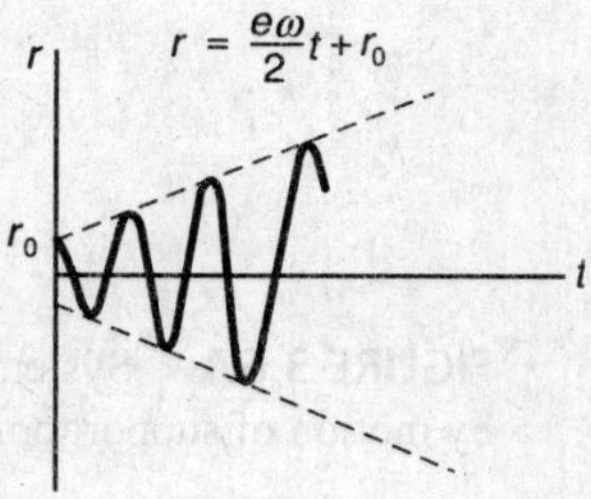

FIGURE 3.5.4. Amplitude and phase relationship of synchronous whirl with viscous damping.

Differentiating this equation twice, we find that $\ddot{r} = 0$; so the first equation with the aforementioned solution for r becomes

$$\left(\frac{k}{m} - \omega^2\right)\left(\frac{e\omega}{2} t \sin\phi + r_0\right) = e\omega^2 \cos\phi \tag{c}$$

Because the right side of this equation is constant, it is satisfied only if the coefficient of t is zero:

$$\left(\frac{k}{m} - \omega^2\right) \sin\phi = 0 \tag{d}$$

which leaves the remaining terms:

$$\left(\frac{k}{m} - \omega^2\right) r_0 = e\omega^2 \cos\phi \tag{e}$$

With $\omega = \sqrt{k/m}$, the first equation is satisfied, but the second equation is satisfied only if $\cos\phi = 0$ or $\phi = \pi/2$. Thus, we have shown that at $\omega = \sqrt{k/m}$, or at resonance, the phase angle is $\pi/2$ as before for the damped case, and the amplitude builds up linearly according to the equation shown in Fig. 3.5.4.

3.6 SUPPORT MOTION

In many cases, the dynamical system is excited by the motion of the support point, as shown in Fig. 3.6.1. We let y be the harmonic displacement of the support point and measure the displacement x of the mass m from an inertial reference.

In the displaced position, the unbalanced forces are due to the damper and the springs, and the differential equation of motion becomes

$$m\ddot{x} = -k(x - y) - c(\dot{x} - \dot{y}) \tag{3.6.1}$$

By making the substitution

$$z = x - y \tag{3.6.2}$$

Eq. (3.6.1) becomes

$$\begin{aligned} m\ddot{z} + c\dot{z} + kz &= -m\ddot{y} \\ &= m\omega^2 Y \sin\omega t \end{aligned} \tag{3.6.3}$$

where $y = Y \sin\omega t$ has been assumed for the motion of the base. The form of this equation is identical to that of Eq. (3.3.1), where z replaces x and $m\omega^2 Y$ replaces $me\omega^2$. Thus, the solution can

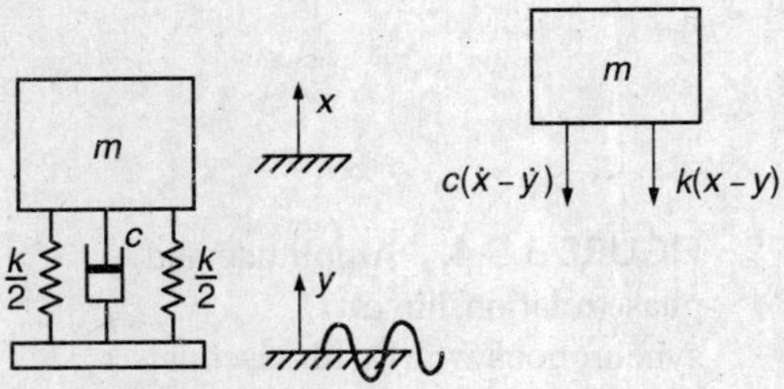

FIGURE 3.6.1. System excited by motion of support point.

be immediately written as

$$z = Z\sin(\omega t - \phi)$$

$$Z = \frac{m\omega^2 Y}{\sqrt{(k - m\omega^2)^2 + (c\omega)^2}} \tag{3.6.4}$$

$$\tan\phi = \frac{c\omega}{k - m\omega^2} \tag{3.6.5}$$

and the curves of Fig. 3.3.2 are applicable with the appropriate change in the ordinate.

If the absolute motion x of the mass is desired, we can solve for $x = z + y$. Using the exponential form of harmonic motion gives

$$\begin{aligned} y &= Ye^{i\omega t} \\ Z &= Ze^{i(\omega t - \phi)} = (Ze^{-i\phi})e^{i\omega t} \\ x &= Xe^{i(\omega t - \psi)} = (Xe^{-i\psi})e^{i\omega t} \end{aligned} \tag{3.6.6}$$

Substituting into Eq. (3.6.3), we obtain

$$Ze^{-i\phi} = \frac{m\omega^2 Y}{k - m\omega^2 + i\omega c}$$

and

$$\begin{aligned} x &= (Ze^{-i\phi} + Y)e^{i\omega t} \\ &= \left(\frac{k + i\omega c}{k - m\omega^2 + i\omega c}\right) Ye^{i\omega t} \end{aligned} \tag{3.6.7}$$

The steady-state amplitude and phase from this equation are

$$\left|\frac{X}{Y}\right| = \sqrt{\frac{k^2 + (\omega c)^2}{(k - m\omega^2)^2 + (c\omega)^2}} \tag{3.6.8}$$

and

$$\tan\psi = \frac{mc\omega^3}{k(k - m\omega^2) + (\omega c)^2} \tag{3.6.9}$$

which are plotted in Fig. 3.6.2. It should be observed that the amplitude curves for different damping have the same value of $|X/Y| = 1.0$ at the frequency $\omega/\omega_n = \sqrt{2}$.

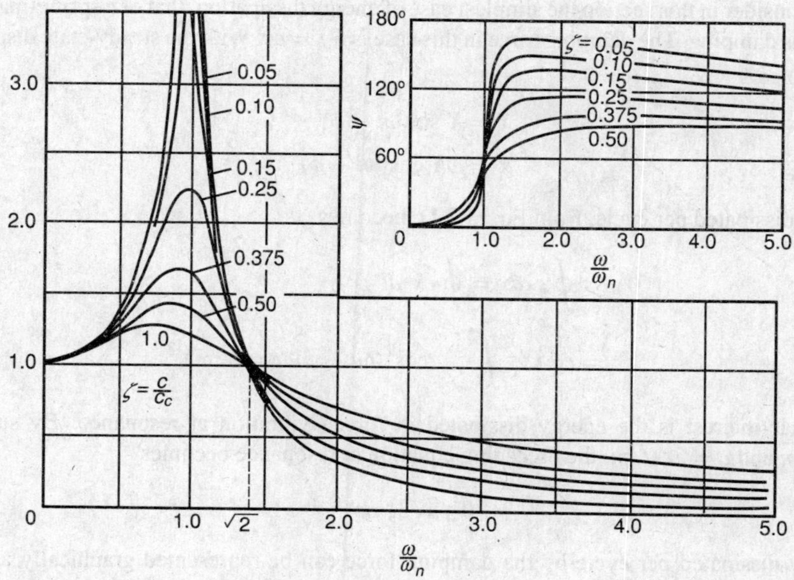

FIGURE 3.6.2. Plot of Eqs. (3.6.8) and (3.6.9).

3.7 ENERGY DISSIPATED BY DAMPING

Damping is present in all oscillatory systems. Its effect is to remove energy from the system. Energy in a vibrating system is either dissipated into heat or radiated away. Dissipation of energy into heat can be experienced simply by bending a piece of metal back and forth a number of times. We are all aware of the sound that is radiated from an object given a sharp blow. When a buoy is made to bob up and down in the water, waves radiate out and away from it, thereby resulting in its loss of energy.

In vibration analysis, we are generally concerned with damping in terms of system response. The loss of energy from the oscillatory system results in the decay of amplitude of free vibration. In steady-state forced vibration, the loss of energy is balanced by the energy that is supplied by the excitation.

A vibrating system can encounter many different types of damping forces, from internal molecular friction to sliding friction and fluid resistance. Generally, their mathematical description is quite complicated and not suitable for vibration analysis. Thus, simplified damping models have been developed that in many cases are found to be adequate in evaluating the system response. For example, we have already used the viscous damping model, designated by the dashpot, which leads to manageable mathematical solutions.

Energy dissipation is usually determined under conditions of cyclic oscillations. Depending on the type of damping present, the force–displacement relationship when plotted can differ greatly. In all cases, however, the force–displacement curve will enclose an area, referred to as the *hysteresis loop*, that is proportional to the energy lost per cycle. The energy lost per cycle due to a damping force F_d is computed from the general equation

$$W_d = \oint F_d dx \tag{3.7.1}$$

In general, W_d depends on many factors, such as temperature, frequency, or amplitude.

We consider in this section the simplest case of energy dissipation, that of a spring-mass system with viscous damping. The damping force in this case is $F_d = c\dot{x}$. With the steady-state displacement and velocity

$$x = X \sin(\omega t - \phi)$$
$$\dot{x} = \omega X \cos(\omega t - \phi)$$

the energy dissipated per cycle, from Eq. (3.7.1), becomes

$$\begin{aligned} W_d &= \oint c\dot{x}dx = \oint c\dot{x}^2 dt \\ &= c\omega^2 X^2 \int_0^{2\pi/\omega} \cos^2(\omega t - \phi)dt = \pi c \omega X^2 \end{aligned} \tag{3.7.2}$$

Of particular interest is the energy dissipated in forced vibration at resonance. By substituting $\omega_n = \sqrt{k/m}$ and $c = 2\zeta\sqrt{km}$, the preceding equation at resonance becomes

$$W_d = 2\zeta\pi k X^2 \tag{3.7.3}$$

The energy dissipated per cycle by the damping force can be represented graphically as follows. Writing the velocity in the form

$$\begin{aligned} \dot{x} &= \omega X \cos(\omega t - \phi) = \pm\omega X \sqrt{1 - \sin^2(\omega t - \phi)} \\ &= \pm\omega\sqrt{X^2 - x^2} \end{aligned}$$

the damping force becomes

$$F_d = c\dot{x} = \pm c\omega\sqrt{X^2 - x^2} \tag{3.7.4}$$

By rearranging the foregoing equation to

$$\left(\frac{F_d}{c\omega X}\right)^2 + \left(\frac{x}{X}\right)^2 = 1 \tag{3.7.5}$$

we recognize it as that of an ellipse with F_d and x plotted along the vertical and horizontal axes, respectively, as shown in Fig. 3.7.1(a). The energy dissipated per cycle is then given by the area enclosed by the ellipse. If we add to F_d the force kx of the lossless spring, the hysteresis loop is rotated as shown in Fig. 3.7.1(b). This representation then conforms to the *Voigt model*, which consists of a dashpot in parallel with a spring.

Damping properties of materials are listed in many different ways, depending on the technical areas to which they are applied. Of these, we list two relative energy units that have wide usage. First of these is *specific damping capacity*, defined as the energy loss per cycle W_d divided by the peak potential energy U:

$$\frac{W_d}{U} \tag{3.7.6}$$

The second quantity is the *loss coefficient*, defined as the ratio of damping energy loss per radian $W_d/2\pi$ divided by the peak potential or strain energy U:

$$\eta = \frac{W_d}{2\pi U} \tag{3.7.7}$$

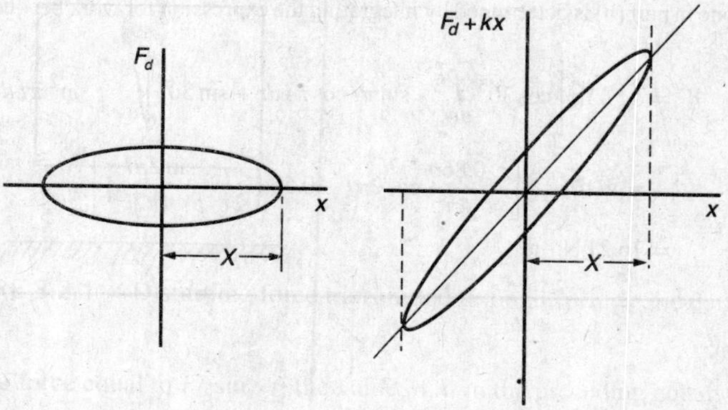

FIGURE 3.7.1. Energy dissipated by viscous damping.

For the case of linear damping, where the energy loss is proportional to the square of the strain or amplitude, the hysteresis curve is an ellipse. When the damping loss is not a quadratic function of the strain or amplitude, the hysteresis curve is no longer an ellipse.

Example 3.7.1

Determine the expression for the power developed by a force $F = F_0 \sin(\omega t + \phi)$ acting on a displacement $x = X_0 \sin \omega t$.

Solution Power is the rate of doing work, which is the product of the force and velocity.

$$
\begin{aligned}
P = F\frac{dx}{dt} &= (\omega X_0 F_0)\sin(\omega t + \phi)\cos\omega t \\
&= (\omega X_0 F_0)[\cos\phi \cdot \sin\omega t \cos\omega t + \sin\phi \cdot \cos^2\omega t] \\
&= \frac{1}{2}\omega X_0 F_0[\sin\phi + \sin(2\omega t + \phi)]
\end{aligned}
$$

The first term is a constant, representing the steady flow of work per unit time. The second term is a sine wave of twice the frequency, which represents the fluctuating component of power, the average value of which is zero over any interval of time that is a multiple of the period.

■

Example 3.7.2

A force $F = 10 \sin \pi t$ N acts on a displacement of $x = 2\sin(\pi t - \pi/6)$ m. Determine (a) the work done during the first 6 s; (b) the work done during the first $\frac{1}{2}$ s.

Solution Rewriting Eq. (3.7.1) as $W = \int F\dot{x}dt$ and substituting $F = F_0 \sin\omega t$ and $x = X\sin(\omega t - \phi)$ gives the work done per cycle of

$$W = \pi F_0 X \sin\phi$$

For the force and displacement given in this problem, $F_0 = 10\,\text{N}$, $X = 2\,\text{m}$, $\phi = \pi/6$, and the period $\tau = 2\,\text{s}$. Thus, in the 6 s specified in (a), three complete cycles take place, and the work done is

$$W = 3(\pi F_0 X \sin\phi) = 3\pi \times 10 \times 2 \times \sin 30^\circ = 94.2\,\text{N}\cdot\text{m}$$

The work done in part (b) is determined by integrating the expression for work between the limits 0 and $\frac{1}{2}$ s.

$$W = \omega F_0 X_0 \left[\cos 30^\circ \int_0^{1/2} \sin \pi t \cos \pi t \, dt + \sin 30^\circ \int_0^{1/2} \sin^2 \pi t \, dt \right]$$

$$= \pi \times 10 \times 2 \left[-\frac{0.866}{4\pi} \cos 2\pi t + 0.50 \left(\frac{t}{2} - \frac{\sin 2\pi t}{4\pi} \right) \right]_0^{1/2}$$

$$= 16.21 \text{ N} \cdot \text{m}$$

3.8 EQUIVALENT VISCOUS DAMPING

The primary influence of damping on oscillatory systems is that of limiting the amplitude of response at resonance. As seen from the response curves of Fig. 3.1.3, damping has little influence on the response in the frequency regions away from resonance.

In the case of viscous damping, the amplitude at resonance, Eq. (3.1.9), was found to be

$$X = \frac{F_0}{c\omega_n} \tag{3.8.1}$$

For other types of damping, no such simple expression exists. It is possible, however, to approximate the resonant amplitude by substituting an equivalent damping c_{eq} in the foregoing equation.

The equivalent damping c_{eq} is found by equating the energy dissipated by the viscous damping to that of the nonviscous damping force with assumed harmonic motion. From Eq. (3.7.2),

$$\pi c_{eq} \omega X^2 = W_d \tag{3.8.2}$$

where W_d must be evaluated from the particular type of damping force.

Example 3.8.1

Bodies moving with moderate speed (3 to 20 m/s) in fluids, such as water or air are resisted by a damping force that is proportional to the square of the speed. Determine the equivalent damping for such forces acting on an oscillatory system, and find its resonant amplitude.

Solution Let the damping force be expressed by the equation

$$F_d = \pm a\dot{x}^2$$

where the negative sign must be used when $\dot{x}$ is positive, and vice versa. Assuming harmonic motion with the time measured from the position of extreme negative displacement,

$$x = -X \cos \omega t$$

the energy dissipated per cycle is

$$W_d = 2 \int_{-X}^{X} a\dot{x}^2 dx = 2a\omega^2 X^3 \int_0^{\pi} \sin^3 \omega t \, d(\omega t)$$

$$= \frac{8}{3} a\omega^2 X^3$$

The equivalent viscous damping from Eq. (3.8.2) is then

$$c_{eq} = \frac{8}{3\pi} a\omega X$$

The amplitude at resonance is found by substituting $c = c_{eq}$ in Eq. (3.8.1) with $\omega = \omega_n$:

$$X = \sqrt{\frac{3\pi F_0}{8a\omega_n^2}}$$

Example 3.8.2

Find the equivalent viscous damping for Coulomb damping.

Solution We assume that under forced sinusoidal excitation, the displacement of the system with Coulomb damping is sinusoidal and equal to $x = X \sin \omega t$. The equivalent viscous damping can then be found from Eq. (3.8.2) by noting that the work done per cycle by the Coulomb force F_d is equal to $W_d = F_d \times 4X$. Its substitution into Eq. (3.8.2) gives

$$\pi c_{eq} \omega X^2 = 4F_d X$$

$$c_{eq} = \frac{4F_d}{\pi \omega X}$$

The amplitude of forced vibration can be found by substituting c_{eq} into Eq. (3.1.3):

$$X = \frac{F_0}{\sqrt{(k - m\omega^2)^2 + \left(\frac{4F_d\omega}{\pi\omega X}\right)^2}}$$

Solving for X, we obtain

$$|X| = \frac{\sqrt{F_0^2 - \left(\frac{4F_d}{\pi}\right)^2}}{k - m\omega^2} = \frac{F_0}{k} \frac{\sqrt{1 - \left(\frac{4F_d}{\pi F_0}\right)^2}}{1 - \left(\frac{\omega}{\omega_n}\right)^2}$$

We note here that unlike the system with viscous damping, X/δ_{st} goes to ∞ when $\omega = \omega_n$. For the numerator to remain real, the term $4F_d/\pi F_0$ must be less than 1.0.

3.9 STRUCTURAL DAMPING

When materials are cyclically stressed, energy is dissipated internally within the material itself. Experiments by several investigators[1,2] indicate that for most structural metals, such as steel or aluminum, the energy dissipated per cycle is independent of the frequency over a wide frequency range and proportional to the square of the amplitude of vibration. Internal damping fitting this classification is called *solid damping* or *structural damping*. With the energy dissipation per cycle proportional to the square of the vibration amplitude, the loss coefficient is a constant and the shape of the hysteresis curve remains unchanged with amplitude and independent of the strain rate.

Energy dissipated by structural damping can be written as

$$W_d = \alpha X^2 \tag{3.9.1}$$

where α is a constant with units of force/displacement. By using the concept of equivalent viscous damping, Eq. (3.8.2) gives

$$\pi c_{eq}\omega X^2 = \alpha X^2$$

or

$$c_{eq} = \frac{\alpha}{\pi\omega} \tag{3.9.2}$$

By substituting c_{eq} for c, the differential equation of motion for a system with structural damping can be written as

$$m\ddot{x} + \left(\frac{\alpha}{\pi\omega}\right)\dot{x} + kx = F_0 \sin \omega t \tag{3.9.3}$$

Complex stiffness. In the calculation of the flutter speeds of airplane wings and tail surfaces, the concept of *complex stiffness* is used. It is arrived at by assuming the oscillations to be harmonic, which enables Eq. (3.9.3) to be written as

$$m\ddot{x} + \left(k + i\frac{\alpha}{\pi}\right)x = F_0 e^{i\omega t}$$

By factoring out the stiffness k and letting $\gamma = \alpha/\pi k$, the preceding equation becomes

$$m\ddot{x} + k(1 + i\gamma)x = F_0 e^{i\omega t} \tag{3.9.4}$$

The quantity $k(1 + i\gamma)$ is called the *complex stiffness* and γ is the *structural damping factor*.

Using the concept of complex stiffness for problems in structural vibrations is advantageous in that one needs only to multiply the stiffness terms in the system by $(1 + i\gamma)$. The method is justified, however, only for harmonic oscillations. With the solution $x \equiv \overline{X}e^{i\omega t}$, the steady-state amplitude from Eq. (3.9.4) becomes

$$\overline{X} = \frac{F_0}{(k - m\omega^2) + i\gamma k} \tag{3.9.5}$$

The amplitude at resonance is then

$$|X| = \frac{F_0}{\gamma k} \tag{3.9.6}$$

Comparing this with the resonant response of system with viscous damping

$$|X| = \frac{F_0}{2\zeta k}$$

we conclude that with equal amplitudes at resonance, the structural damping factor is equal to twice the viscous damping factor.

Frequency response with structural damping. By starting with Eq. (3.9.5), the complex frequency response for structural damping can be shown to be a circle. Letting $\omega/\omega_n = r$ and multiplying and dividing by its complex conjugate give a complex frequency response of

$$H(r) = \frac{1}{(1 - r^2) + i\gamma} = \frac{1 - r^2}{(1 - r^2)^2 + \gamma^2} + i\frac{-\gamma}{(1 - r^2) + \gamma^2} = x + iy$$

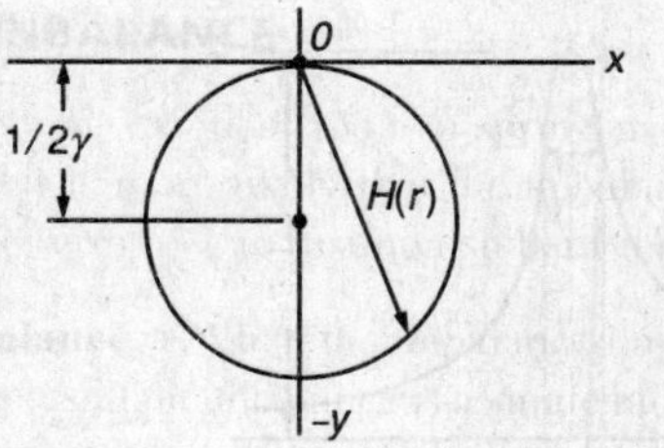

FIGURE 3.9.1. Frequency response with structural damping.

where

$$x = \frac{1-r^2}{(1-r^2)^2+\gamma^2} \quad \text{and} \quad y = \frac{-\gamma}{(1-r^2)^2+\gamma^2}$$

The following algebra leads to

$$y + \frac{1}{2\gamma} = \frac{(1-r^2)^2-\gamma^2}{2\gamma[(1-r^2)^2+\gamma^2]}$$

$$x^2 + \left(y+\frac{1}{2\gamma}\right)^2 = \frac{4\gamma^2(1-r^2)^2+(1-r^2)^4-2\gamma^2(1-r^2)^2+\gamma^4}{4\gamma^2[(1-r^2)^2+\gamma^2]^2}$$

$$= \left(\frac{1}{2\gamma}\right)^2$$

$$x^2 + \left(y+\frac{1}{2\gamma}\right)^2 = \left(\frac{1}{2\gamma}\right)^2$$

This is a circle of radius $1/2\gamma$ with center $-1/2\gamma$, as shown in Fig. 3.9.1.

Every point on the circle represents a different frequency ratio r. At resonance, $r = 1, x = 0$, $y = -1/\gamma$, and $H(r) = -i/\gamma$.

3.10 SHARPNESS OR RESONANCE

In forced vibration, there is a quantity Q related to damping that is a measure of the sharpness of resonance. To determine this quantity, we assume viscous damping and start with Eq. (3.1.7).

When $\omega/\omega_n = 1$, the resonant amplitude is $x_{res} = (F_0/k)/2\zeta$. We now seek the two frequencies on either side of resonance (often referred to as *sidebands*), where X is $0.707X_{res}$. These points are also referred to as the *half-power points* and are shown in Fig. 3.10.1.

Letting $X = 0.707X_{res}$ and squaring Eq. (3.1.7), we obtain

$$\frac{1}{2}\left(\frac{1}{2\zeta}\right)^2 = \frac{1}{\left[1-\left(\frac{\omega}{\omega_n}\right)^2\right]^2+\left[2\zeta\left(\frac{\omega}{\omega_n}\right)\right]^2}$$

or

$$\left(\frac{\omega}{\omega_n}\right)^4 - 2(1-2\zeta^2)\left(\frac{\omega}{\omega_n}\right)^2 + (1-8\zeta^2) = 0 \tag{3.10.1}$$

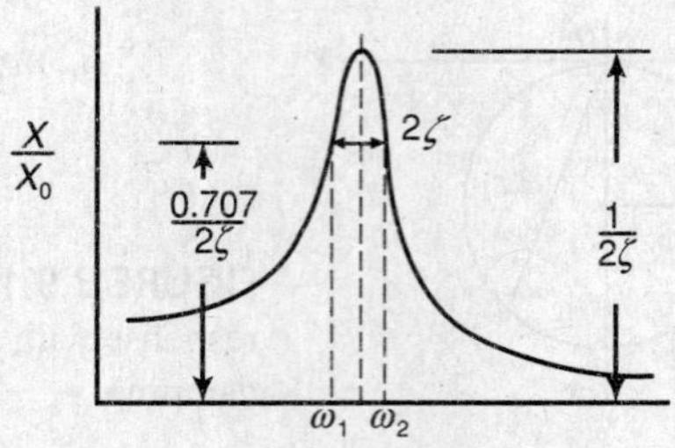

FIGURE 3.10.1.

Solving for $(\omega/\omega_n)^2$, we have

$$\left(\frac{\omega}{\omega_n}\right)^2 = (1 - 2\zeta^2) \pm 2\zeta\sqrt{1 - \zeta^2} \tag{3.10.2}$$

Assuming $\zeta \ll 1$ and neglecting higher-order terms of ζ, we arrive at the result

$$\left(\frac{\omega}{\omega_n}\right)^2 = 1 \pm 2\zeta \tag{3.10.3}$$

Letting the two frequencies corresponding to the roots of Eq. (3.10.3) be ω_1 and ω_2, we obtain

$$4\zeta = \frac{\omega_2^2 - \omega_1^2}{\omega_n^2} \cong 2\left(\frac{\omega_2 - \omega_1}{\omega_n}\right)$$

The quantity Q is then defined as

$$Q = \frac{\omega_n}{\omega_2 - \omega_1} = \frac{f_n}{f_2 - f_1} = \frac{1}{2\zeta} \tag{3.10.4}$$

Here, again, equivalent damping can be used to define Q for systems with other forms of damping. Thus, for structural damping, Q is equal to

$$Q = \frac{1}{\gamma} \tag{3.10.5}$$

3.11 VIBRATION-MEASURING INSTRUMENTS

The basic element of many vibration-measuring instruments is the seismic unit of Fig. 3.11.1. Depending on the frequency range utilized, displacement, velocity, or acceleration is indicated by the relative motion of the suspended mass with respect to the case.

To determine the behavior of such instruments, we consider the equation of motion of m, which is

$$m\ddot{x} = -c(\dot{x} - \dot{y}) - k(x - y) \tag{3.11.1}$$

where x and y are the displacement of the seismic mass and the vibrating body, respectively, both measured with respect to an inertial reference. Letting the relative displacement of the mass m and the case attached to the vibrating body be

$$z = x - y \tag{3.11.2}$$

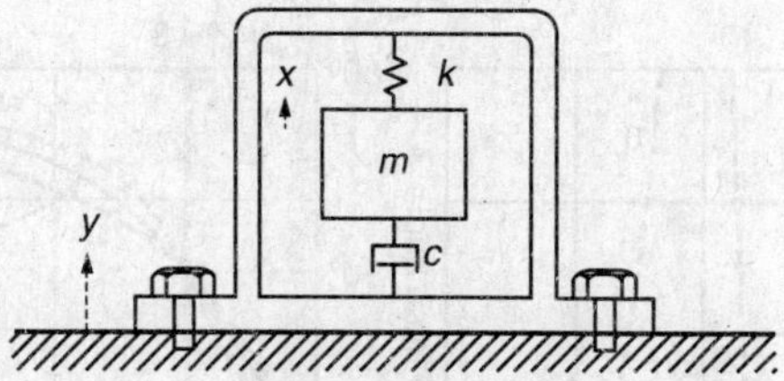

FIGURE 3.11.1.

and assuming sinusoidal motion $y = Y \sin \omega t$ of the vibrating body, we obtain the equation

$$m\ddot{z} + c\dot{z} + kz = m\omega^2 Y \sin \omega t \tag{3.11.3}$$

This equation is identical in form to Eq. (3.3.1) with z and $m\omega^2 Y$ replacing x and $me\omega^2$, respectively. The steady-state solution $z = Z \sin(\omega t - \phi)$ is then available from inspection to be

$$Z = \frac{m\omega^2 Y}{\sqrt{(k - m\omega^2)^2 + (c\omega)^2}} = \frac{Y\left(\dfrac{\omega}{\omega_n}\right)^2}{\sqrt{\left[1 - \left(\dfrac{\omega}{\omega_n}\right)^2\right]^2 + \left[2\zeta\dfrac{\omega}{\omega_n}\right]^2}} \tag{3.11.4}$$

and

$$\tan \phi = \frac{\omega c}{k - m\omega^2} = \frac{2\zeta\dfrac{\omega}{\omega_n}}{1 - \left(\dfrac{\omega}{\omega_n}\right)^2} \tag{3.11.5}$$

It is evident then that the parameters involved are the frequency ratio ω/ω_n and the damping factor ζ. Figure 3.11.2 shows a plot of these equations and is identical to Fig. 3.4.2 except that Z/Y replaces MX/me. The type of instrument is determined by the useful range of frequencies with respect to the natural frequency ω_n of the instrument.

Seismometer: instrument with low natural frequency. When the natural frequency ω_n of the instrument is low in comparison to the vibration frequency ω to be measured, the ratio ω/ω_n approaches a large number, and the relative displacement Z approaches Y regardless of the value of the damping ζ, as indicated in Fig. 3.11.2. The mass m then remains stationary while the supporting case moves with the vibrating body. Such instruments are called *seismometers*.

One of the disadvantages of the seismometer is its large size. Because $Z = Y$, the relative motion of the seismic mass must be of the same order of magnitude as that of the vibration to be measured.

The relative motion z is usually converted to an electric voltage by making the seismic mass a magnet moving relative to coils fixed in the case, as shown in Fig. 3.11.3. Because the voltage generated is proportional to the rate of cutting of the magnetic field, the output of the instrument will be proportional to the velocity of the vibrating body. Such instruments are called *velometers*. A typical instrument of this kind can have a natural frequency from 1 to 5 Hz and a useful frequency range of 10 to 2000 Hz. The sensitivity of such instruments can be in the range of 20 to 350 mV/cm/s, with the maximum displacement limited to about 0.5 cm peak to peak.

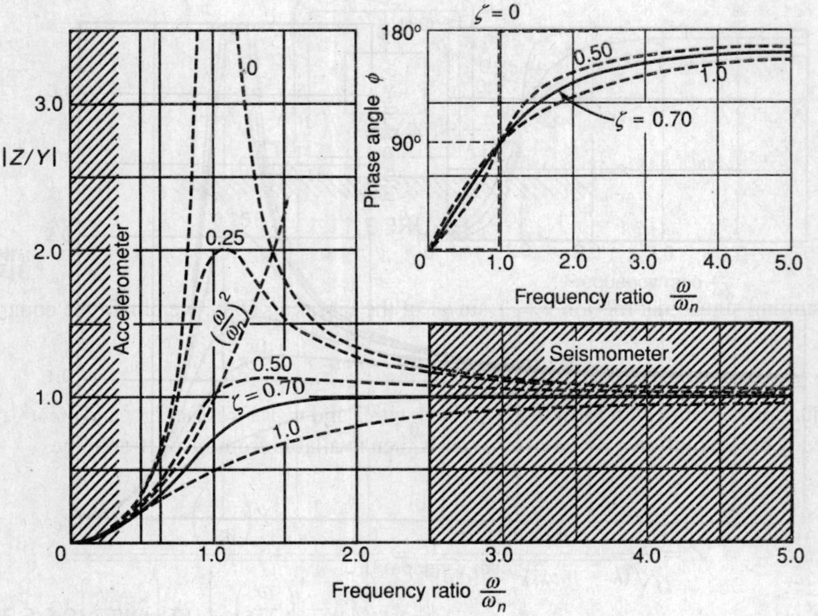

FIGURE 3.11.2. Response of a vibration-measuring instrument.

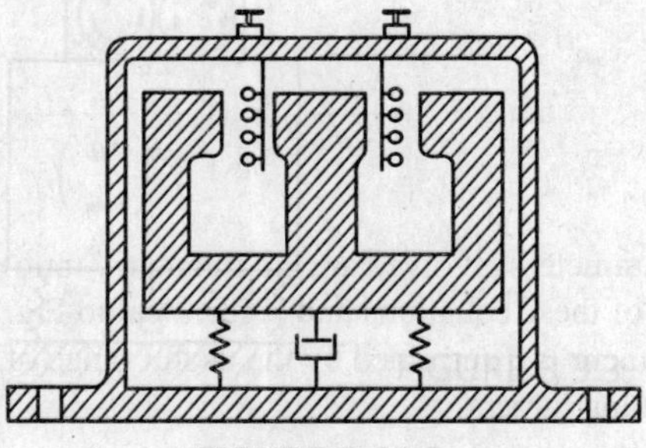

FIGURE 3.11.3.

Both the displacement and acceleration are available from the velocity-type transducer by means of the integrator or the differentiator provided in most signal conditioner units.

Figure 3.11.4 shows the Ranger seismometer, which because of its high sensitivity was used in the U.S. lunar space program. The Ranger seismometer incorporates a velocity-type transducer with the permanent magnet as the seismic mass. Its natural frequency is nominally 1 Hz with a mass travel of ±1 mm. Its size is 15 cm in diameter and it weighs 5 kg.

Accelerometer: instrument with high natural frequency. When the natural frequency of the instrument is high compared to that of the vibration to be measured, the instrument indicates acceleration. Examination of Eq. (3.11.4) shows that the factor

$$\sqrt{\left[1-\left(\frac{\omega}{\omega_n}\right)^2\right]^2+\left(2\zeta\frac{\omega}{\omega_n}\right)^2}$$

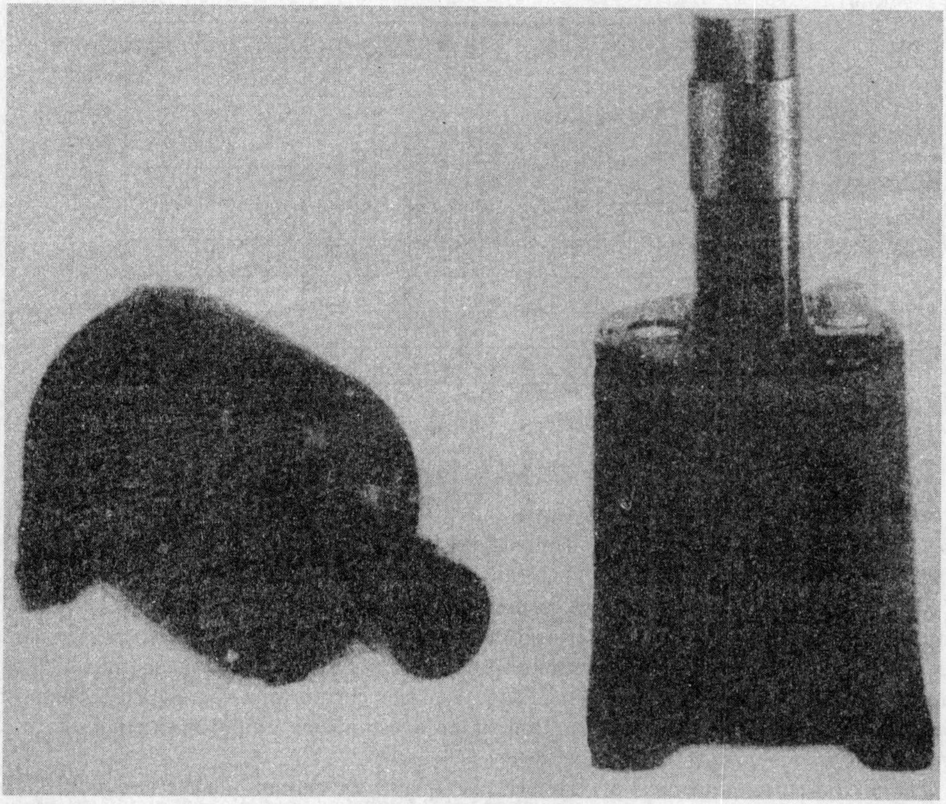

FIGURE 3.11.4. Ranger seismometer. (*Courtesy of Kinemetrics, Inc., Pasadena, California.*)

approaches unity for $\omega/\omega_n \to 0$, so that

$$Z = \frac{\omega^2 Y}{\omega_n^2} = \frac{\text{acceleration}}{\omega_n^2} \tag{3.11.6}$$

Thus, Z becomes proportional to the acceleration of the motion to be measured with a factor $1/\omega_n^2$. The useful range of the accelerometer can be seen from Fig. 3.11.5, which is a magnified plot of

$$\frac{1}{\sqrt{\left[1-\left(\frac{\omega}{\omega_n}\right)^2\right]^2 + \left(2\zeta\frac{\omega}{\omega_n}\right)^2}}$$

for various values of damping ζ. The diagram shows that the useful frequency range of the undamped accelerometer is somewhat limited. However, with $\zeta = 0.7$, the useful frequency range is $0 \le \omega/\omega_n \le 0.20$ with a maximum error less than 0.01 percent. Thus, an instrument with a natural frequency of 100 Hz has a useful frequency range from 0 to 20 Hz with negligible error. Electromagnetic-type accelerometers generally utilize damping around $\zeta = 0.7$, which not only extends the useful frequency range, but also prevents phase distortion for complex waves, as will be shown later. On the other hand, very high natural-frequency instruments, such as the piezoelectric

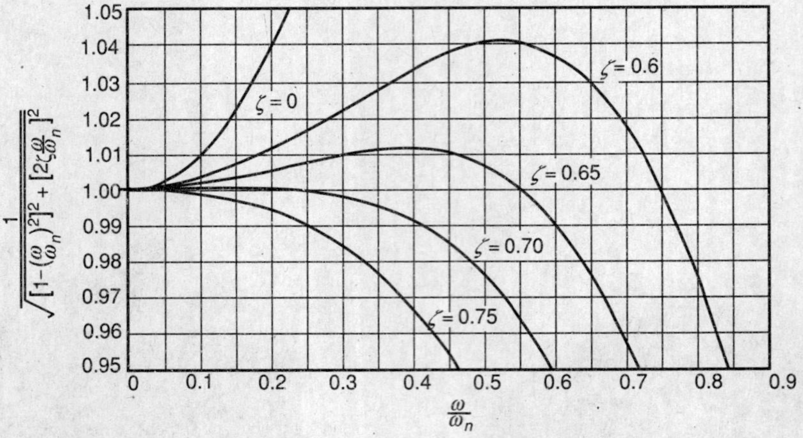

FIGURE 3.11.5. Acceleration error vs. frequency with ζ as a parameter.

crystal accelerometers, have almost zero damping and operate without distortion up to frequencies of $0.06f_n$.

Several different accelerometers are in use today. The seismic mass accelerometer is often used for low-frequency vibration, and the supporting springs may be four electric strain gage wires connected in a bridge circuit. A more accurate variation of this accelerometer is one in which the seismic mass is servo-controlled to have zero relative displacement; the force necessary to accomplish this becomes a measure of the acceleration. Both of these instruments require an external source of electric power.

The piezoelectric properties of crystals like quartz or barium titanate are utilized in accelerometers for higher-frequency measurements. The crystals are mounted so that under acceleration, they are either compressed or bent to generate an electric charge. Figure 3.11.6 shows one such arrangement. The natural frequency of such accelerometers can be made very high, in the 50,000-Hz range, which enables acceleration measurements to be made up to 3000 Hz. The size of the crystal accelerometer is very small, approximately 1 cm in diameter and height, and it is remarkably rugged and can stand shocks as high as 10,000 g's.

The sensitivity of the crystal accelerometer is given either in terms of charge (picocoulombs = pC = 10^{-12} Coulombs) per g, or in terms of voltage (millivolts = mV = 10^{-3} V) per g. Because the voltage is related to the charge by the equation $E = Q/C$, the capacitance of the crystal, including the shunt capacitance of the connecting cable, must be specified. Typical sensitivity for a crystal accelerometer is 25 pC/g with crystal capacitance of 500 pF (picofarads). The equation $E = Q/C$ then gives 25/500 = 0.050 mV/g = 50 mV/g for the sensitivity in terms of voltage. If the accelerometer is connected to a vacuum-tube voltmeter through a 3-m length of cable of capacitance 300 pF, the open-circuit output voltage of the accelerometer will be reduced to

$$50 \times \frac{500}{500 + 300} = 31.3 \text{ mV/g}$$

This severe loss of signal can be avoided by using a charge amplifier, in which case, the capacitance of the cable has no effect.

Phase distortion. To reproduce a complex wave such as the one shown in Fig. 3.11.7 without changing its shape, the phase of all harmonic components must remain unchanged with respect to

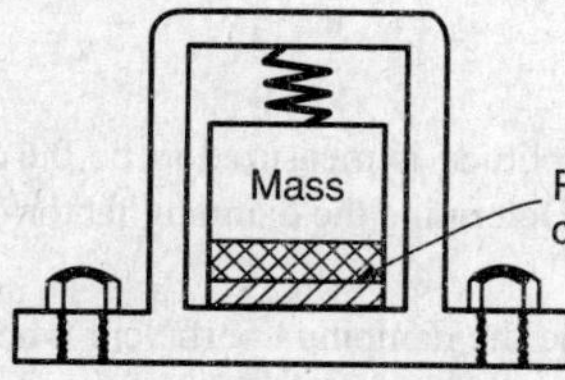

FIGURE 3.11.6.

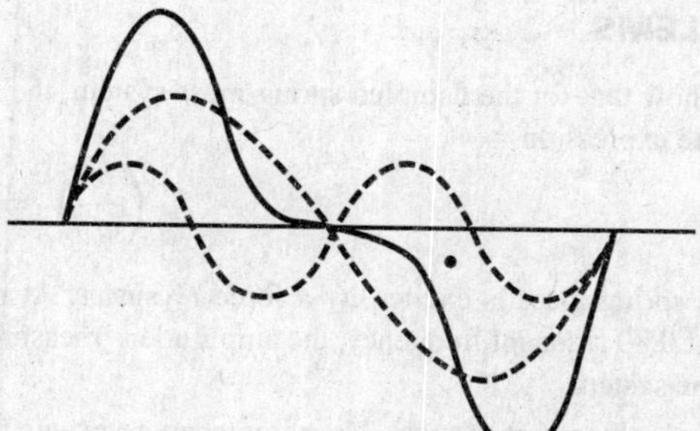

FIGURE 3.11.7.

the fundamental. This requires that the phase angle be zero or that all the harmonic components must be shifted equally. The first case of zero phase shift corresponds to $\zeta = 0$ for $\omega/\omega_n < 1$. The second case of an equal time-wise shift of all harmonics is nearly satisfied for $\zeta = 0.70$ for $\omega/\omega_n < 1$. As shown in Fig. 3.11.2, when $\zeta = 0.70$, the phase for $\omega/\omega_n < 1$ can be expressed by the equation

$$\phi \cong \frac{\pi}{2}\frac{\omega}{\omega_n}$$

Thus, for $\zeta = 0$, or 0.70, the phase distortion is practically eliminated.

Example 3.11

Investigate the output of an accelerometer with damping $\zeta = 0.70$ when used to measure a periodic motion with the displacement given by the equation

$$y = Y_1 \sin \omega_1 t + Y_2 \sin \omega_2 t$$

Solution For $\zeta = 0.70$, $\phi \cong \pi/2 \times \omega/\omega_n$, so that $\phi_1 = \pi/2 \times \omega_1/\omega_n$ and $\phi_2 = \pi/2 \times \omega_2/\omega_n$. The output of the accelerometer is then

$$z = Z_1 \sin(\omega_1 t - \phi_1) + Z_2 \sin(\omega_2 t - \phi_2)$$

By substituting for Z_1 and Z_2 from Eq. (3.11.6), the output of the instrument is

$$z = \frac{1}{\omega_n^2}\left[\omega_1^2 Y_1 \sin \omega_1\left(t - \frac{\pi}{2\omega_n}\right) + \omega_2^2 Y_2 \sin \omega_2\left(t - \frac{\pi}{2\omega_n}\right)\right]$$

Because the time functions in both terms are equal $(t - \pi/2\omega_n)$, the shift of both components along the time axis is equal. Thus, the instrument faithfully reproduces the acceleration $\ddot{y}$ without distortion. It is obvious that if ϕ_1 and ϕ_2 are both zero, we again obtain zero phase distortion.

■

REFERENCES

[1] A. L. KIMBALL, "Vibration Damping, Including the Case of Solid Damping," *Trans. ASME*, APM 51–52 (1929).

[2] B. J. LAZAN, *Damping of Materials and Members in Structural Mechanics* (Elmsford, NY: Pergamon Press, 1968).

PROBLEMS

3.1. Show that for the damped spring-mass system, the peak amplitude occurs at a frequency ratio given by the expression

$$\left(\frac{\omega}{\omega_n}\right)_p = \sqrt{1-2\zeta^2}$$

3.2. A spring-mass is excited by a force $F_0 \sin \omega t$. At resonance, the amplitude is measured to be 0.6 cm. At 0.80 resonant frequency, the amplitude is measured to be 0.45 cm. Determine the damping factor ζ of the system.

3.3. A machine part of mass 2 kg vibrates in a viscous medium. Determine the damping coefficient when a harmonic exciting force of 25 N results in a resonant amplitude of 2 cm with a period of 0.20 s.

3.4. If the system of Prob. 3.3 is excited by a harmonic force of frequency 4 cps, what will be the percentage increase in the amplitude of forced vibration when the dashpot is removed?

3.5. A weight attached to a spring of stiffness 600 N/m has a viscous damping device. When the weight is displaced and released, the period of vibration is 2 s, and the ratio of consecutive amplitudes is 4 to 1.0. Determine the amplitude and phase when a force $F = 2\cos 3t$ acts on the system.

3.6. For the system shown in Fig. P3.6, set up the equation of motion and solve for the steady-state amplitude and phase angle by using complex algebra.

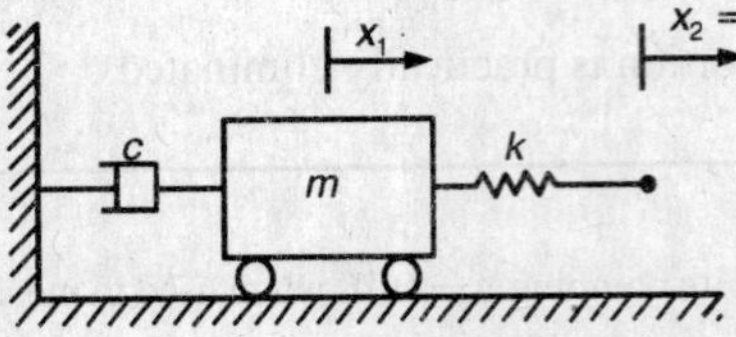

FIGURE P3.6.

3.7. Shown in Fig. P3.7 is a cylinder of mass m connected to a spring of stiffness k excited through viscous friction c to a piston with motion $y = A \sin \omega t$. Determine the amplitude of the cylinder motion and its phase with respect to the piston.

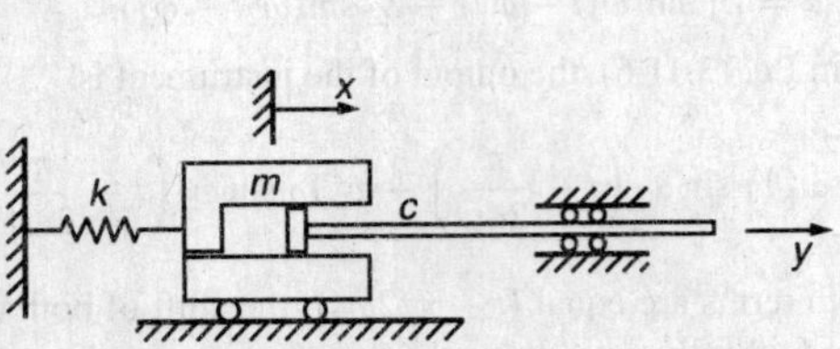

FIGURE P3.7.

M **3.8.** Plot the real and imaginary parts of Eq. (3.1.17) for $\zeta = 0.02$ and 0.10. (See Appendix E for information about MATLAB®.)

3.9. An industrial machine of mass 500 kg is supported on springs with a static deflection of 0.5 cm. If the machine has a rotating unbalance of 0.25 kg·m, determine (a) the force transmitted to the floor at 1200 rpm and (b) the dynamic amplitude at this speed. (Assume damping to be negligible.)

3.10. If the machine of Prob. 3.9 is mounted on a large concrete block of mass 1200 kg and the stiffness of the springs or pads under the block is increased so that the statical deflection is still 0.5 cm, what will be the dynamic amplitude?

3.11. An aircraft radio weighing 98.1 N is to be isolated from engine vibrations ranging in frequencies from 1500 to 2400 cpm. What statical deflection must the isolators have for 85% isolation?

3.12. A refrigerator unit weighing 30 kg is to be supported by three springs of stiffness k N/mm each. If the unit operates at 580 rpm, what should be the value of the spring constant k if only 10% of the shaking force of the unit is to be transmitted to the supporting structure?

3.13. An electric motor of mass 70 kg is mounted on an isolator block of mass 1200 kg and the natural frequency of the total assembly is 150 cpm with a damping factor of $\zeta = 0.10$ (see Fig. P3.13). If there is an unbalance in the motor that results in a harmonic force of $F = 120 \sin 31.4t$, determine the amplitude of vibration of the block and the force transmitted to the floor.

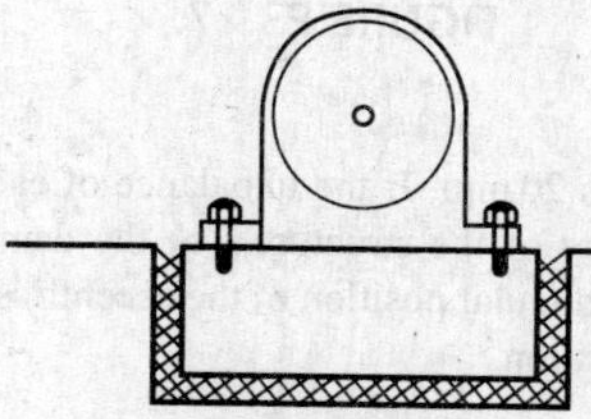

FIGURE P3.13.

3.14. A sensitive instrument with mass 110 kg is to be installed at a location where the acceleration is 20 cm/s^2 at a frequency of 18 Hz. It is proposed to mount the instrument on a rubber pad with the following properties: $k = 3000$ N/cm and $\zeta = 0.12$. What acceleration is transmitted to the instrument?

3.15. If the instrument of Prob. 3.14 can tolerate an acceleration of only 2 cm/s^2, suggest a solution assuming that the same rubber pad is the only isolator available. Give numerical values to substantiate your solution.

M **3.16.** For the system shown in Fig. P3.16, verify that the transmissibility $TR = |x/y|$ is the same as that for force. Plot the transmissibility in decibels, $20 \log |TR|$ versus ω/ω_n between $\omega/\omega_n = 1$ to 15 with $\zeta = 0.01, 0.02, \ldots, 0.15$.

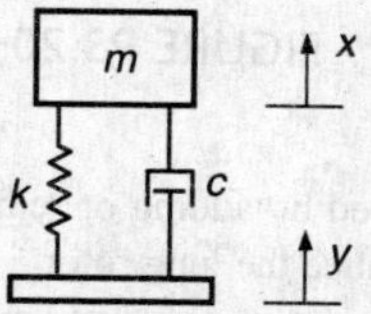

FIGURE P3.16.

3.17. A thin disk is supported on spring-mounted bearings with vibration pickup and strobotac, as shown in Fig. P3.17. Running at 500 rpm ccw, the original disk indicates a maximum amplitude of 3 mm at 45° cw from a reference mark on the disk. Next a trial weight of 65 g is added at the rim in a position 91.5° cw from the reference mark and run at the same speed. If now the new unbalance is 6.0 mm at 80° cw from the reference mark, determine the position and weight necessary to balance the original disk.

3.18. If for the same disk of Prob. 3.17, the trial weight of 65 g is placed at 135° cw from the reference mark, the new unbalance is found to be 4.3 mm at 111° cw. Show that the correct balance weight is unchanged.

3.19. If the wheel of Prob. 3.17 shows resonance at 800 rpm with damping of $\zeta = 0.10$, determine the phase lag of the original unbalance and check the vector diagrams of Probs. 3.17 and 3.18.

3.20. A counterrotating eccentric mass exciter shown in Fig. P3.20 is used to determine the vibrational characteristics of a structure of mass 180 kg. At a speed of 1000 rpm, a stroboscope shows the eccentric masses to be at the top at the instant the structure is moving upward through its static equilibrium position,

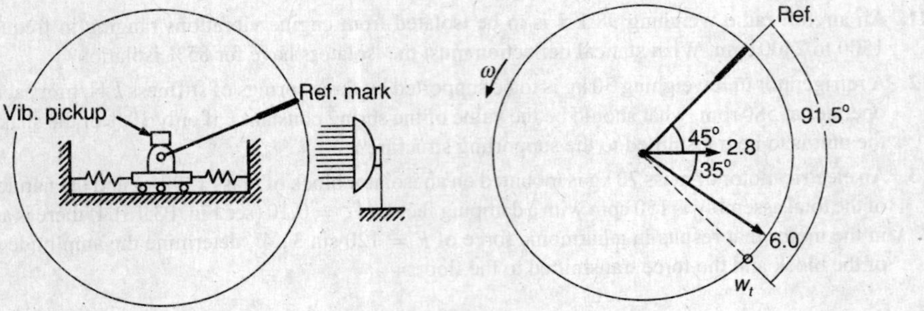

FIGURE P3.17.

and the corresponding amplitude is 20 mm. If the unbalance of each wheel of the exciter is 0.1 kg · m, determine (a) the natural frequency of the structure, (b) the damping factor of the structure, (c) the amplitude at 1200 rpm, and (d) the angular position of the eccentrics at the instant the structure is moving upward through its equilibrium position.

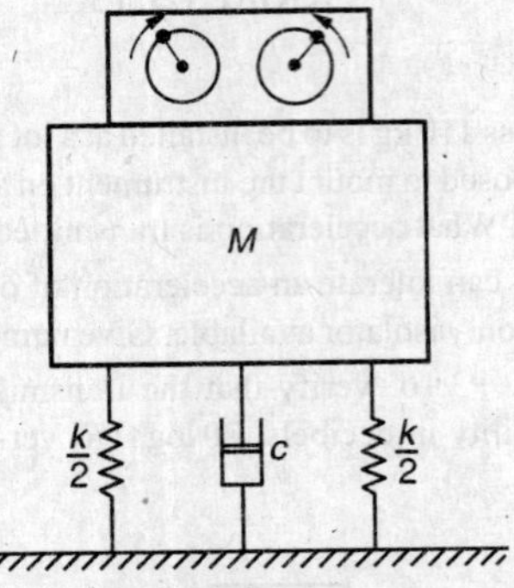

FIGURE P3.20.

3.21. Prove that a long rotor can be balanced by adding or removing weights in any two parallel planes, and modify the single disk method to balance the long rotor.

3.22. A balanced wheel supported on springs, as shown in Fig. P3.22, is rotating at 1200 rpm. If a bolt weighing 15 g and located 4 cm from center suddenly comes loose and flies off, determine the buildup of vibration if the natural frequency of the system is 20 cps with damping of $\zeta = 0.15$.

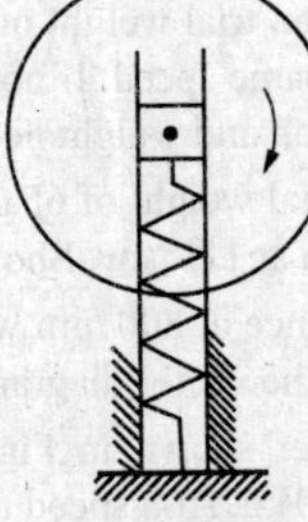

FIGURE P3.22.

3.23. Solve Eq. (3.3.1) for the complex amplitude, i.e., let $(me\omega^2)\sin\omega t = \overline{F}e^{i\omega t}$ and $x = X_e^{i(\omega t-\phi)} = (Xe^{-i\phi})e^{i\omega t} = \overline{X}e^{i\omega t}$.

3.24. A solid disk weighing 4.5 kg is keyed to the center of a 12-mm steel shaft 60 cm between bearings. Determine the lowest critical speed. (Assume the shaft to be simply supported at the bearings.)

3.25. The rotor of a turbine 14-kg in mass is supported at the midspan of a shaft with bearings 0.5-m apart, as shown in Fig. P3.25. The rotor is known to have an unbalance of 0.25 kg · cm. Determine the forces exerted on the bearings at a speed of 5500 rpm if the diameter of the steel shaft is 2.50 cm. Compare this result with that of the same rotor mounted on a steel shaft of diameter 2 cm. (Assume the shaft to be simply supported at the bearings.)

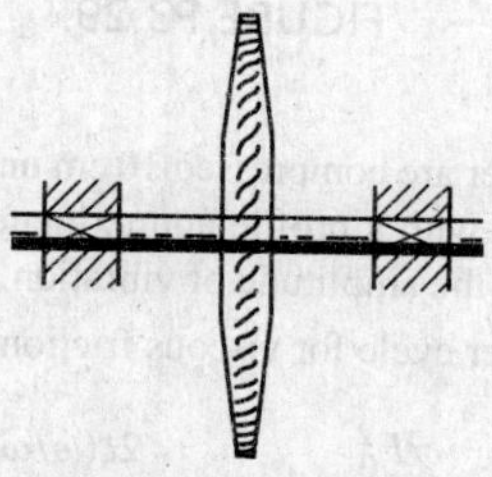

FIGURE P3.25.

3.26. For turbines operating above the critical speed, stops are provided to limit the amplitude as they run through the critical speed. In the turbine of Prob. 3.25, if the clearance between the 2.50-cm shaft and the stops is 0.05 cm, and if the eccentricity is 0.02 cm, determine the time required for the shaft to hit the stops. Assume that the critical speed is reached with zero amplitude.

3.27. The point of suspension of a simple pendulum is given by a harmonic motion $x_0 = X_0 \sin\omega t$ along a horizontal line, as shown in Fig. P3.27. Write the differential equation of motion for a small amplitude of oscillation using the coordinates shown. Determine the solution for x/x_0, and show that when $\omega = \sqrt{2}\omega_n$, the node is found at the midpoint of l. Show that in general the distance h from the mass to the node is given by the relation $h = l(\omega_n/\omega)^2$, where $\omega_n = \sqrt{g/l}$.

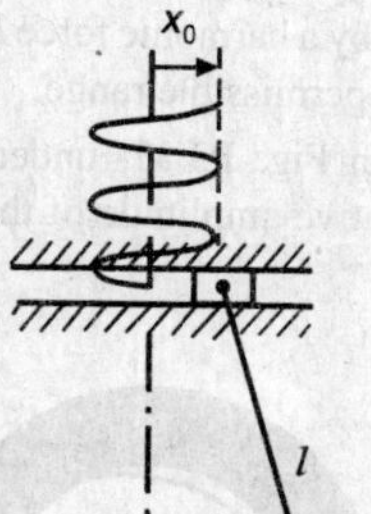

FIGURE P3.27.

3.28. Derive Eqs. (3.6.8) and (3.6.9) for the amplitude and phase by letting $y = Y\sin\omega t$ and $x = X\sin(\omega t - \phi)$ in the differential equation (3.6.1).

3.29. Figure P3.29 represents a simplified diagram of a spring-supported vehicle traveling over a rough road. Determine the equation for the amplitude of W as a function of the speed, and determine the most unfavorable speed.

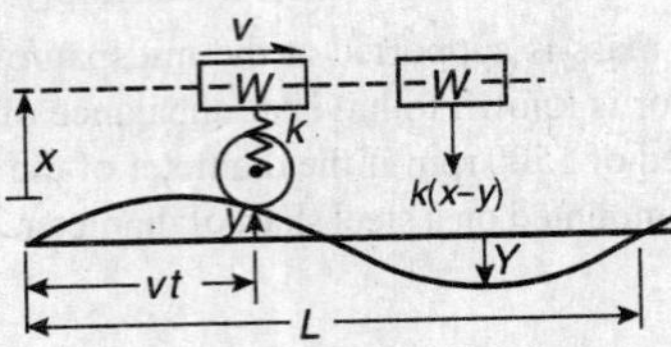

FIGURE P3.29.

3.30. The springs of an automobile trailer are compressed 10 cm under its weight. Find the critical speed when the trailer is traveling over a road with a profile approximated by a sine wave of amplitude 7.5 cm and wavelength of 15 m. What will be the amplitude of vibration at 60 km/h? (Neglect damping.)

3.31. Show that the energy dissipated per cycle for viscous friction can be expressed by

$$W_d = \frac{\pi F_0^2}{k} \frac{2\zeta(\omega/\omega_n)}{[1-(\omega/\omega_n)^2]^2 + [2\zeta(\omega/\omega_n)]^2}$$

3.32. Show that for viscous damping, the loss factor η is independent of the amplitude and proportional to the frequency.

3.33. Express the equation for the free vibration of a single-DOF system in terms of the loss factor η at resonance.

3.34. Show that τ_n/τ_d plotted against ζ is a quarter circle where τ_d is the damped natural period, and τ_n is the undamped natural period.

3.35. For small damping, the energy dissipated per cycle divided by the peak potential energy is equal to 2δ and also to $1/Q$. [See Eq. (3.7.6).] For viscous damping, show that

$$\delta = \frac{\pi c \omega_n}{k}$$

3.36. Coulomb damping between dry surfaces is a constant D always opposed to the motion. Determine the equivalent viscous damping. Using the result determine the amplitude of motion of a spring-mass system with Coulomb damping when excited by a harmonic force $F_0 \sin \omega t$. Under what condition can this motion be maintained? Plot the results in the permissible range.

3.37. The shaft of a torsiograph, shown in Fig. P3.37, undergoes harmonic torsional oscillation $\theta_0 \sin \omega t$. Determine the expression for the relative amplitude of the outer wheel with respect to (a) the shaft and (b) a fixed reference.

FIGURE P3.37.

3.38. A commercial-type vibration pickup has a natural frequency of 5 cps and a damping factor $\zeta = 0.65$. What is the lowest frequency that can be measured with (a) 1% error and (b) 2% error?

3.39. An undamped vibration pickup having a natural frequency of 0.8 cps is used to measure a harmonic vibration of 4 cps. If the amplitude indicated by the pickup (relative amplitude between pickup mass and frame) is 0.05 cm, what is the correct amplitude?

3.40. A manufacturer of vibration-measuring instruments gives the following specifications for one of its vibration pickups:

Frequency range: Velocity response flat from 20 to 1000 cps.
Sensitivity: 8.1 V/cm/s, both volts and velocity in rms values.
Amplitude range: Almost no lower limit to maximum stroke between stops of 0.5 cm.

(a) This instrument was used to measure the vibration of a machine with a known frequency of 30 cps. If a reading of 0.025 V is indicated, determine the rms amplitude.

(b) Could this instrument be used to measure the vibration of a machine with known frequency of 24 cps and double amplitude of 0.80 cm? Give reasons.

3.41. A vibration pickup has a sensitivity of 35 mV/cm/s from $f = 20$ to 1500 Hz. If 1-g acceleration is maintained over this frequency range, what will be the output voltage at (a) 20 Hz and (b) 1500 Hz?

3.42. Using the equations of harmonic motion, obtain the relationship for the velocity versus frequency applicable to the velocity pickup.

3.43. A vibration pickup has a sensitivity of 20 mV/cm/s. Assuming that 2 mV (rms) is the accuracy limit of the instrument, determine the upper frequency limit of the instrument for 1-g excitation. What voltage would be generated at 200 Hz?

3.44. The sensitivity of a certain crystal accelerometer is given as 20 pC/g, with its capacitance equal to 500 pF. It is used with a vacuum-tube voltmeter with connecting cable 5-m long with a capacitance of 50 pF/m. Determine its voltage output per g.

3.45. Specific damping capacity W_d/U is defined as the energy loss per cycle W_d divided by the peak potential energy $U = \frac{1}{2}kX^2$. Show that this quantity is equal to

$$\frac{W_d}{U} = 4\pi\zeta\left(\frac{\omega}{\omega_n}\right)$$

where $\zeta = c/c_{cr}$.

3.46. Logarithmic decrement δ for small damping is equal to $\delta \cong 2\pi\zeta$. Show that δ is related to the specific damping capacity by the equation

$$\frac{W_d}{U} = 2\delta\left(\frac{\omega}{\omega_n}\right)$$

3.47. For a system with hysteresis damping, show that the structural damping factor γ is equal to the loss factor at resonance.

3.48. For viscous damping, the complex frequency response can be written as

$$H(r) = \frac{1}{(1 - r^2) + i(2\zeta r)}$$

where $r = \omega/\omega_n$, and $\zeta = c/c_{cr}$. Show that the plot of $H = x + iy$ leads to the equation

$$x^2 + \left(y + \frac{1}{4\zeta r}\right)^2 = \left(\frac{1}{4\zeta r}\right)^2$$

which cannot be a circle because the center and the radius depend on the frequency ratio.

M **3.49.** The following problem uses the programs **runga.m** and **f.m** where **f.m** contains the forcing function, [force] $= \sin(t)$. You should use the following parameters for all of the problem: spring constant, $k = 1$; initial position $x(0) = 0$; time step, $\delta t = 0.2$; and initial time, $t_0 = 0$. Produce a plot for each of the cases considered.

(a) For the next two cases $m = 1, c = 1$, and t final = 20.

i. initial velocity $x'(0) = 1$

ii. initial velocity $x'(0) = 10$

iii. How does the initial velocity affect the response of the system?

(b) For the next three cases, the initial velocity is fixed $x'(0) = 10$.

i. $c = 10, m = 1$, and t final = 40.

ii. $c = 1, m = 10$, and t final = 40.

iii. $c = 1, m = 10$, and t final = 100.

iv. Discuss why it takes the two systems different amounts of time to reach the steady state solution.

M **3.50.** Consider the system forced with two frequencies given by

$$m\ddot{x} + c\dot{x} + kx = F_1 \sin(\omega_1 t) + F_2 \sin(\omega_2 t).$$

Solve the equations of motion. Find the relationship between the amplitudes of the motion and the ratios of frequencies $\omega_1/\omega, \omega_2/\omega$. Plot the results in MATLAB®.

M **3.51.** Consider the system shown in Fig. P3.51, with the viscous damping coefficient c and spring stiffness k. Derive the equation of motion when the system is forced by a sinusoidal force $F_0 \sin(\omega t)$. What is the effective damping for this system? What is the energy dissipated over one cycle? Compare this system with the system in which the spring and the damper are connected in parallel.

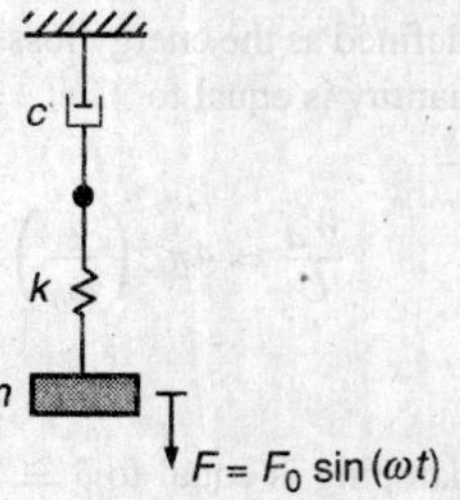

FIGURE P3.51.

M **3.52.** Consider the problem of Example 3.8.1. Solve the equations of motion numerically in MATLAB® and plot the average amplitude of oscillation versus the frequency ratio. Compare with the result obtained in Example 3.8.1 where the equivalent viscous damping approach is used.

M **3.53.** A table-tennis ball is jumping on the table that is oscillating periodically in time. The position of the table is given by $y(t) = A \sin(\omega t)$. It is assumed that the coefficient of restitution is 1, so when the ball leaves the table it does so with the velocity V given by

$$V = 2W - U$$

where W is the velocity of the table at that moment in time and U is the velocity of the ball at the impact. Simulate the motion in MATLAB® and plot the results in the following form: Record the velocity of the ball v_j and time t_j at every impact with the table. Do this for different initial conditions and for different forcing frequencies ω. Plot the average of the amplitude of the ball over time versus the forcing frequency.

CHAPTER 4

Transient Vibration of Single Degree-of-Freedom Systems

When a dynamical system is excited by a suddenly applied nonperiodic excitation $F(t)$, the response to such excitation is called *transient response*, since steady-state oscillations are generally not produced. Such oscillations take place at the natural frequencies of the system with the amplitude varying in a manner dependent on the type of excitation.

We first study the response of a spring-mass system to an impulse excitation because this case is important in the understanding of the more general problem of transients.

4.1 IMPULSE EXCITATION

Impulse is the time integral of the force, and we designate it by the notation $\hat{F}$:

$$\hat{F} = \int F(t)\,dt \tag{4.1.1}$$

We frequently encounter a force of very large magnitude that acts for a very short time but with a time integral that is finite. Such forces are called *impulsive*.

Figure 4.1.1 shows an impulsive force of magnitude $\hat{F}/\epsilon$ with a time duration of ϵ. As ϵ approaches zero, such forces tend to become infinite; however, the impulse defined by its time

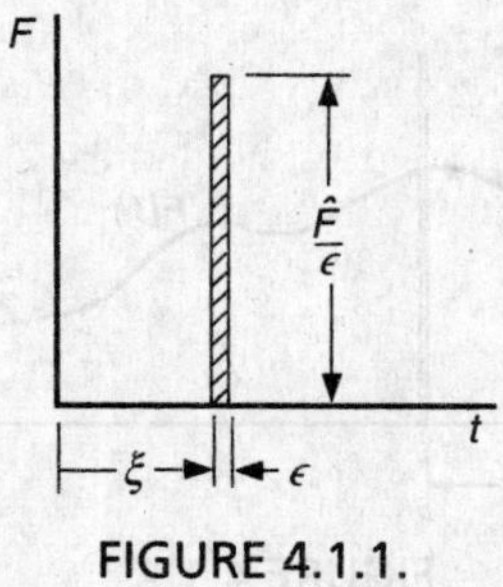

FIGURE 4.1.1.

integral is $\hat{F}$, which is considered to be finite. When $\hat{F}$ is equal to unity, such a force in the limiting case $\epsilon \to 0$ is called the *unit impulse*, or the *delta function*. A delta function at $t = \xi$ is identified by the symbol $\delta(t - \xi)$ and has the following properties:

$$\delta(t-\xi) = 0 \qquad \text{for all } t \neq \xi$$

$$= \text{greater than any assumed value for } t = \xi$$

$$\int_0^\infty \delta(t-\xi)dt = 1.0 \qquad 0 < \xi < \infty \tag{4.1.2}$$

If $\delta(t - \xi)$ is multiplied by any time function $f(t)$, as shown in Fig. 4.1.2, the product will be zero everywhere except at $t = \xi$, and its time integral will be

$$\int_0^\infty f(t)\,\delta(t-\xi)\,dt = f(\xi) \qquad 0 < \xi < \infty \tag{4.1.3}$$

Because $F\,dt = m\,dv$, the impulse $\hat{F}$ acting on the mass will result in a sudden change in its velocity equal to $\hat{F}/m$ without an appreciable change in its displacement. Under free vibration, we found that the undamped spring-mass system with initial conditions $x(0)$ and $\dot{x}(0)$ behaved according to the equation

$$x = \frac{\dot{x}(0)}{\omega_n}\sin\omega_n t + x(0)\cos\omega_n t$$

Hence, the response of a spring-mass system initially at rest and excited by an impulse $\hat{F}$ is

$$x = \frac{\hat{F}}{m\omega_n}\sin\omega_n t = \hat{F}h(t) \tag{4.1.4}$$

where

$$h(t) = \frac{1}{m\omega_n}\sin\omega_n t \tag{4.1.5}$$

is the response to a unit impulse.

When damping is present, we can start with the free-vibration equation, Eq. (2.3.17), with $x(0) = 0$:

$$x = \frac{\dot{x}(0)e^{-\zeta\omega_n t}}{\omega_n\sqrt{1-\zeta^2}}\sin\sqrt{1-\zeta^2}\,\omega_n t$$

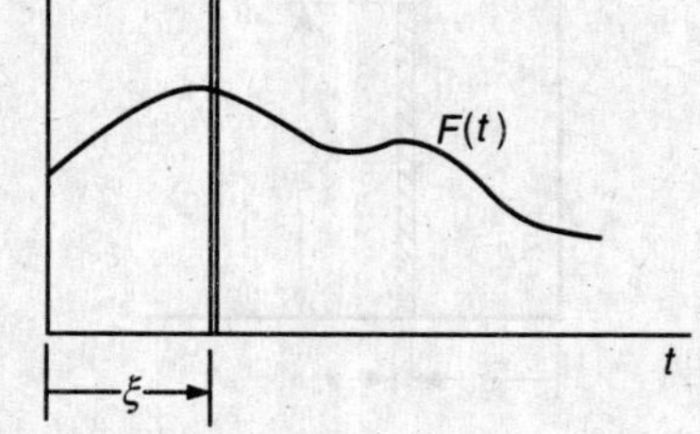

FIGURE 4.1.2.

Substituting for the initial condition $\dot{x}(0) = \hat{F}/m$, we arrive at the equation

$$x = \frac{\hat{F}}{m\omega_n\sqrt{1-\zeta^2}} e^{-\zeta\omega_n t} \sin \sqrt{1-\zeta^2}\omega_n t \tag{4.1.6}$$

The response to the unit impulse is of importance to the problems of transients and is identified by the special designation $h(t)$. Thus, in either the damped or undamped case, the equation for the impulsive response can be expressed in the form

$$x = \hat{F}h(t) \tag{4.1.7}$$

where the right side of the equation is given by either Eq. (4.1.4) or (4.1.6).

4.2 ARBITRARY EXCITATION

By having the response $h(t)$ to a unit impulse excitation, it is possible to establish the equation for the response of the system excited by an arbitrary force $f(t)$. For this development, we consider the arbitrary force to be a series of impulses, as shown in Fig. 4.2.1. If we examine one of the impulses (shown crosshatched) at time $t = \xi$, its strength is

$$\hat{F} = f(\xi)\,\Delta\xi$$

and its contribution to the response at time t is dependent upon the elapsed time $(t - \xi)$, or

$$f(\xi)\,\Delta\xi h(t-\xi)$$

where $h(t-\xi)$ is the response to a unit impulse started at $t = \xi$. Because the system we are considering is linear, the principle of superposition holds. Thus, by combining all such contributions, the response to the arbitrary excitation $f(t)$ is represented by the integral

$$x(t) = \int_0^t f(\xi)h(t-\xi)\,d\xi \tag{4.2.1}$$

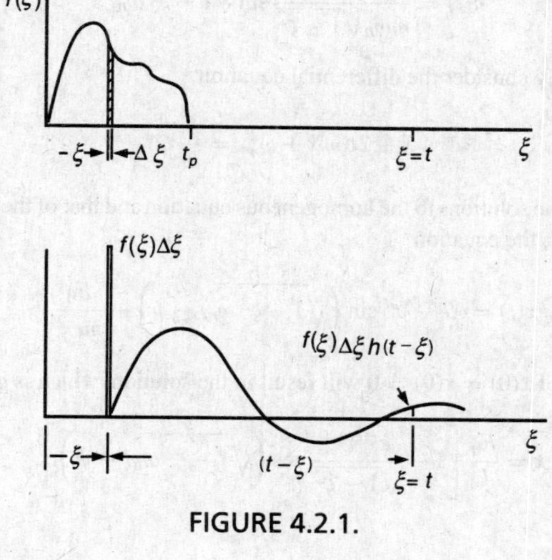

FIGURE 4.2.1.

This integral is called the *convolution integral* and is sometimes referred to as the *superposition integral.*

Example 4.2.1

Determine the response of a single-DOF system to the step excitation shown in Fig. 4.2.2.

FIGURE 4.2.2. Step function excitation.

Solution Considering the undamped system, we have

$$h(t) = \frac{1}{m\omega_n} \sin \omega_n t$$

By substituting into Eq. (4.2.1), the response of the undamped system is

$$\begin{aligned} x(t) &= \frac{F_0}{m\omega_n} \int_0^t \sin \omega_n (t - \xi)\, d\xi \\ &= \frac{F_0}{k}(1 - \cos \omega_n t) \end{aligned} \tag{4.2.2}$$

This result indicates that the peak response to the step excitation of magnitude F_0 is equal to twice the statical deflection.

For a damped system, the procedure can be repeated with

$$h(t) = \frac{e^{-\zeta\omega_n t}}{m\omega_n\sqrt{1-\zeta^2}} \sin \sqrt{1 - \zeta_2}\, \omega_n t$$

or, alternatively, we can simply consider the differential equation

$$\ddot{x} + 2\zeta\omega_n \dot{x} + \omega_n^2 x = \frac{F}{m}$$

whose solution is the sum of the solutions to the homogeneous equation and that of the particular solution, which for this case is $F_0/m\omega_n^2$. Thus, the equation

$$x(t) = Xe^{-\zeta\omega_n t} \sin\left(\sqrt{1-\zeta^2}\, \omega_n t - \phi\right) + \frac{F_0}{m\omega_n^2}$$

fitted to the initial condition of $x(0) = \dot{x}(0) = 0$ will result in the solution, which is given as

$$x = \frac{F_0}{k}\left[1 - \frac{e^{-\zeta\omega_n t}}{\sqrt{1-\zeta^2}} \cos\left(\sqrt{1-\zeta^2}\, \omega_n t - \psi\right)\right] \tag{4.2.3}$$

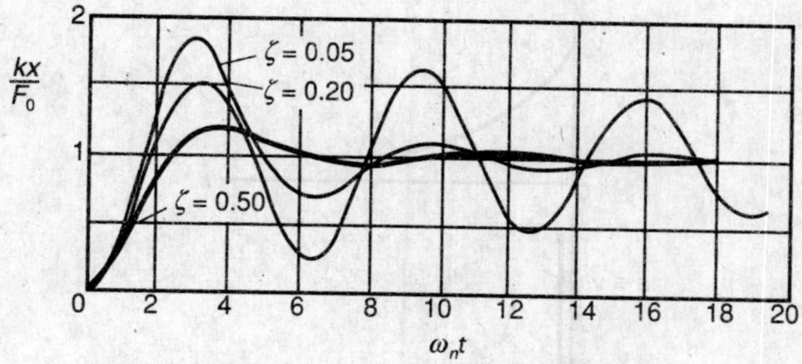

FIGURE 4.2.3. Response to a unit step function.

where

$$\tan\psi = \frac{\zeta}{\sqrt{1-\zeta^2}}$$

Figure 4.2.3 shows a plot of xk/F_0 versus $\omega_n t$ with ζ as a parameter, and it is evident that the peak response is less than $2F_0/k$ when damping is present.

■

Base excitation. Often, the support of the dynamical system is subjected to a sudden movement specified by its displacement, velocity, or acceleration. The equation of motion can then be expressed in terms of the relative displacement $z = x - y$ as follows:

$$\ddot{z} + 2\zeta\omega_n\dot{z} + \omega_n^2 z = -\ddot{y} \tag{4.2.4}$$

and, hence, all of the results for the force-excited system apply to the base-excited system for z when the term F/m is replaced by $-\ddot{y}$ or the negative of the base acceleration.

For an undamped system initially at rest, the solution for the relative displacement becomes

$$z = -\frac{1}{\omega_n}\int_0^t \ddot{y}(\xi)\sin\omega_n(t-\xi)\,d\xi \tag{4.2.5}$$

Example 4.2.2

Consider an undamped spring-mass system where the motion of the base is specified by a velocity pulse of the form

$$\dot{y}(t) = v_0 e^{-t/t_0}u(t)$$

where $u(t)$ is a unit step function. The velocity together with its time rate of change is shown in Fig. 4.2.4.

Solution The velocity pulse at $t = 0$ has a sudden jump from zero to v_0, and its rate of change (or acceleration) is infinite. Differentiating $\dot{y}(t)$ and recognizing that $(d/dt)u(t) = \delta(t)$, a delta function at the origin, we obtain

$$\ddot{y} = v_0 e^{-t/t_0}\delta(t) - \frac{v_0}{t_0}e^{-t/t_0}u(t)$$

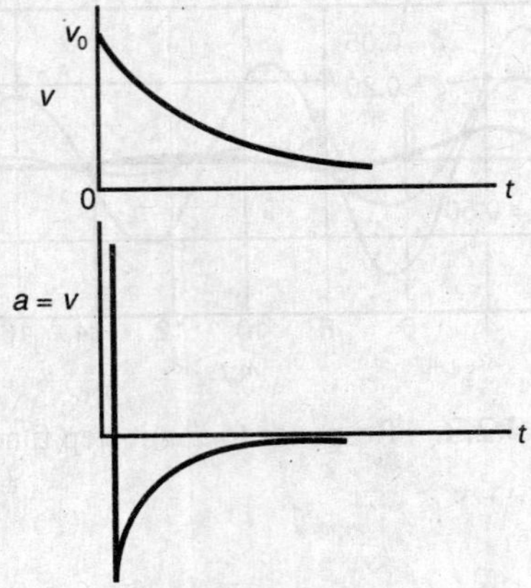

FIGURE 4.2.4.

By substituting $\ddot{y}$ into Eq. (4.2.5), the result is

$$\begin{aligned}
z(t) &= -\frac{v_0}{\omega_n}\int_0^t \left[e^{-\xi/t_0}\delta(\xi) - \frac{1}{t_0}e^{-\xi/t_0}u(\xi) \right] \sin\omega_n(t-\xi)\,d\xi \\
&= -\frac{v_0}{\omega_n}\int_0^t \delta(\xi)e^{-\xi/t_0}\sin\omega_n(t-\xi)\,d\xi + \frac{v_0}{\omega_n t_0}\int_0^t e^{-\xi/t_0}\sin\omega_n(t-\xi)\,d\xi \\
&= \frac{v_0 t_0}{1+(\omega_n t_0)^2}\left(e^{-t/t_0} - \omega_n t_0 \sin\omega_n t - \cos\omega_n t\right) \qquad (4.2.6)
\end{aligned}$$

■

4.3 LAPLACE TRANSFORM FORMULATION

Tie Laplace transform method of solving the differential equation provides a complete solution, yielding both transient and forced vibrations. For those unfamiliar with this method, a brief presentation of the Laplace transform theory is given in Appendix B. In this section, we illustrate its use by some simple examples.

Example 4.3.1

Formulate the Laplace transform solution of a viscously damped spring-mass system with initial conditions $x(0)$ and $\dot{x}(0)$.

Solution The equation of motion of the system excited by an arbitrary force $F(t)$ is

$$m\ddot{x} + c\dot{x} + kx = F(t)$$

Taking its Laplace transform, we find

$$m[s^2\bar{x}(s) - x(0)s - \dot{x}(0)] + c[s\bar{x}(s) - x(0)] + k\bar{x}(s) = \bar{F}(s)$$

Solving for $\bar{x}(s)$, we obtain the *subsidiary equation*:

$$\bar{x}(s) = \frac{\bar{F}(s)}{ms^2+cs+k} + \frac{(ms+c)x(0) + m\dot{x}(0)}{ms^2+cs+k} \qquad (4.3.1a)$$

FIGURE 4.3.1. Block diagram.

The response $x(t)$ is found from the inverse of Eq. (4.3.1); the first term represents the forced vibration and the second term represents the transient solution due to the initial conditions.

For the more general case, the subsidiary equation can be written in the form

$$\overline{x}(s) = \frac{A(s)}{B(s)} \tag{4.3.1b}$$

where $A(s)$ and $B(s)$ are polynomials and $B(s)$, in general, is of higher order than $A(s)$.

If only the forced solution is considered, we can define the *impedance transform* as

$$\frac{\overline{F}(s)}{\overline{x}(s)} = z(s) = ms^2 + cs + k \tag{4.3.1c}$$

Its reciprocal is the admittance transform

$$H(s) = \frac{1}{z(s)} \tag{4.3.1d}$$

Frequently, a block diagram is used to denote input and output, as shown in Fig. 4.3.1. The admittance transform $H(s)$ then can also be considered as the *system transfer function*, defined as the ratio in the subsidiary plane of the output over the input with all initial conditions equal to zero.

■

Example 4.3.2 (Drop Test)

The question of how far a body can be dropped without incurring damage is of frequent interest. Such considerations are of paramount importance in the landing of airplanes or the cushioning of packaged articles. In this example, we discuss some of the elementary aspects of this problem by idealizing the mechanical system in terms of linear spring-mass components.

Consider the spring-mass system of Fig. 4.3.2 dropped through a height h. If x is measured from the position of m at the instant $t = 0$ when the spring first contacts the floor, the differential equation of motion for m applicable as long as the spring remains in contact with the floor is

$$m\ddot{x} + kx = mg \tag{4.3.2a}$$

Taking the Laplace transform of this equation with the initial conditions $x(0) = 0$ and $\dot{x}(0) = \sqrt{2gh}$, we can write the subsidiary equation as

$$\overline{x}(s) = \frac{\sqrt{2gh}}{s^2 + \omega_n^2} + \frac{g}{s(s^2 + \omega_n^2)} \tag{4.3.2b}$$

where $\omega_n = \sqrt{k/m}$ is the natural frequency of the system. From the inverse transformation of $\overline{x}(s)$, the displacement equation becomes

$$\begin{aligned} x(t) &= \frac{2gh}{\omega_n} \sin \omega_n t + \frac{g}{\omega_n^2}(1 - \cos \omega_n t) \\ &= \sqrt{\frac{2gh}{\omega_n^2} + \left(\frac{g}{\omega_n^2}\right)^2} \sin(\omega_n t - \phi) + \frac{g}{\omega_n^2} \quad x(t) > 0 \end{aligned} \tag{4.3.2c}$$

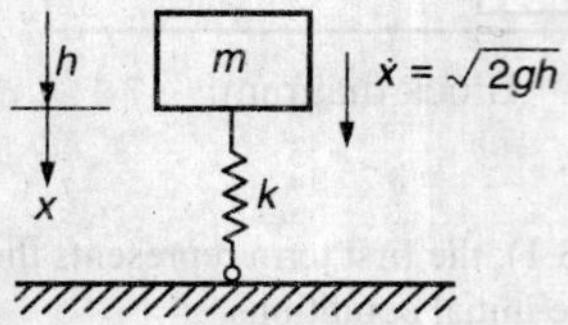

FIGURE 4.3.2.

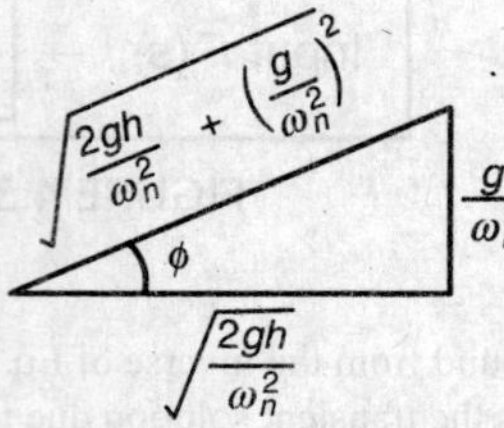

FIGURE 4.3.3.

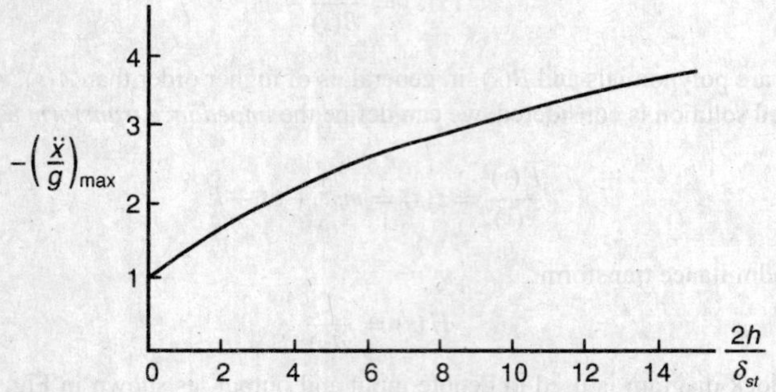

FIGURE 4.3.4.

where the relationship is shown in Fig. 4.3.3. By differentiation, the velocity and acceleration are

$$\dot{x}(t) = \omega_n \sqrt{\frac{2gh}{\omega_n^2} + \left(\frac{g}{\omega_n^2}\right)^2} \cos(\omega_n t - \phi)$$

$$\ddot{x}(t) = -\omega_n^2 \sqrt{\frac{2gh}{\omega_n^2} + \left(\frac{g}{\omega_n^2}\right)^2} \sin(\omega_n t - \phi)$$

We recognize here that $g/\omega^2 = \delta_{st}$ and that the maximum displacement and acceleration occur at $\sin(\omega_n t - \phi) = 1.0$. Thus, the maximum acceleration in terms of gravity is found to depend only on the ratio of the distance dropped to the statical deflection as given by the equation

$$\frac{\ddot{x}}{g} = -\sqrt{\frac{2h}{\delta_{st}} + 1} \tag{4.3.2d}$$

A plot of this equation is shown in Fig. 4.3.4.

Example 4.3.3

For a man in a seated position, as when driving an automobile, the single-DOF model of Fig. 4.3.5 is often assumed for forensic studies. From extensive biomechanical tests, the spinal stiffness of 81,000 N/m = 458 lb/in.* is assumed for the spring k supporting the body mass W/g. By assuming $m = 73$ kg, this results in a static

*See Ref. [1].

deflection of $\delta_{st} = (73 \times 9.81)/81000 = 8.9$ mm. Let us assume that in hitting an obstacle, the driver not restrained by a seat belt is thrown upward and drops 75 mm in free fall onto an unpadded stationary seat. Determine the g acceleration transmitted by his spinal cord.

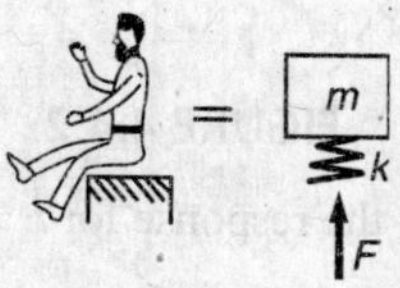

FIGURE 4.3.5.

Solution The result for this problem is simply obtained from Eq. (4.3.2) as

$$\frac{\ddot{x}}{g} = -\sqrt{\frac{2h}{\delta_{st}} + 1} = -\sqrt{\frac{2 \times 75}{8.9} + 1} = -4.23$$

■

4.4 PULSE EXCITATION AND RISE TIME

In this section, we consider the time response of the undamped spring-mass system to three different excitations shown in Fig. 4.4.1. For each of these force excitations, the time response must be considered in two parts, $t < t_1$ and $t > t_1$.

Rise time. The input can be considered to be the sum of two ramp functions, as shown in Fig. 4.4.2. For the first ramp function, the terms of the convolution integral are

$$f(t) = F_0\left(\frac{t}{t_1}\right)$$
$$h(t) = \frac{1}{m\omega_n}\sin\omega_n t = \frac{\omega_n}{k}\sin\omega_n t \tag{4.4.1}$$

and the response becomes

$$\begin{aligned} x(t) &= \frac{\omega_n}{k}\int_0^1 F_0\frac{\xi}{t_1}\sin\omega_n(t-\xi)d\xi \\ &= \frac{F_0}{k}\left(\frac{t}{t_1} - \frac{\sin\omega_n t}{\omega_n t_1}\right) \qquad t < t_1 \end{aligned} \tag{4.4.2}$$

For the second ramp function starting at t_1, the solution can be written by inspection of the foregoing equation as

$$x(t) = -\frac{F_0}{k}\left[\frac{t-t_1}{t_1} - \frac{\sin\omega_n(t-t_1)}{\omega_n t_1}\right]$$

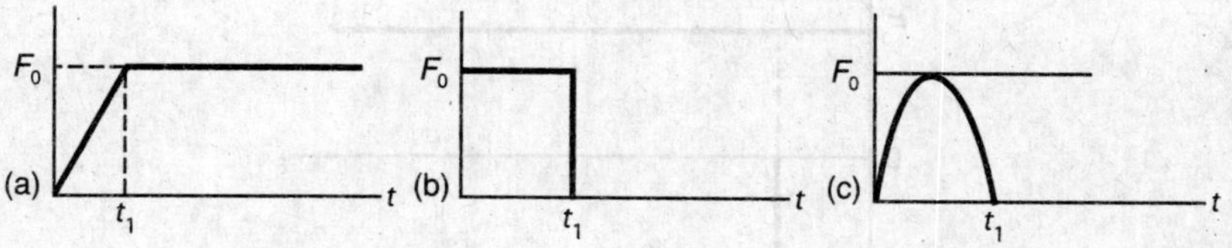

FIGURE 4.4.1. (a) Constant with rise time; (b) rectangular pulse; (c) half-sine pulse.

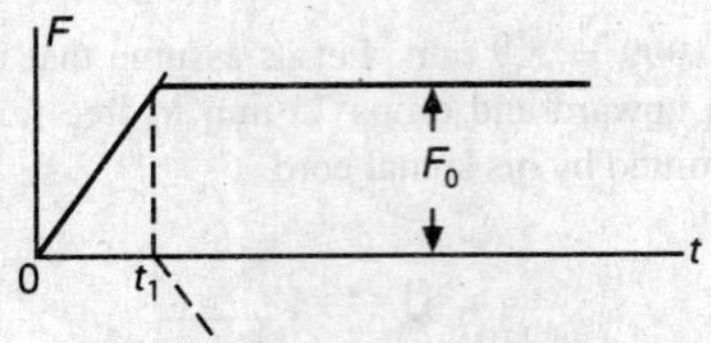

FIGURE 4.4.2.

By superimposing these two equations, the response for $t > t_1$ becomes

$$x(t) = \frac{F_0}{k}\left[1 - \frac{\sin \omega_n t}{\omega_n t_1} + \frac{1}{\omega_n t_1} \sin \omega_n (t - t_1)\right] \quad t > t_1 \tag{4.4.3}$$

Rectangular pulse. The input pulse here can be considered as the sum of two step functions, as shown in Fig. 4.4.3.

We already have the response to the step function as

$$\frac{kx}{F_0} = [1 - \cos \omega_n t] \quad t < t_1 \tag{4.4.4}$$

The peak response here is obviously equal to 2.0 at $t = \frac{1}{2}\tau$.

The response to the second step function started at $t = t_1$ is

$$\frac{kx}{F_0} = -[1 - \cos \omega_n (t - t_1)] \tag{4.4.5}$$

and by adding, the response in the second interval $t > t_1$ becomes

$$\begin{aligned} \frac{kx}{F_0} &= \{[1 - \cos \omega_n t] - [1 - \cos \omega_n (t - t_1)]\} \\ &= -\cos \omega_n t + \cos \omega_n (t - t_1) \quad t > t_1 \end{aligned} \tag{4.4.6}$$

Half-sine pulse. For a pulse of time duration t_1, the excitation is

$$\begin{aligned} F(t) &= F_0 \sin \frac{\pi t}{t_1} && \text{for } t < t_1 \\ &= 0 && \text{for } t > t_1 \end{aligned} \tag{4.4.7}$$

and the differential equation of motion is

$$\ddot{x} + \omega_n^2 x = \frac{F_0}{m} \sin \frac{\pi t}{t_1} \quad t < t_1 \tag{4.4.8}$$

The general solution is the sum of the free vibration and the particular solution

$$x(t) = A \sin \omega_n t + B \cos \omega_n t + \frac{F_0}{m} \frac{\sin pt}{\omega_n^2 - p^2} \tag{4.4.9}$$

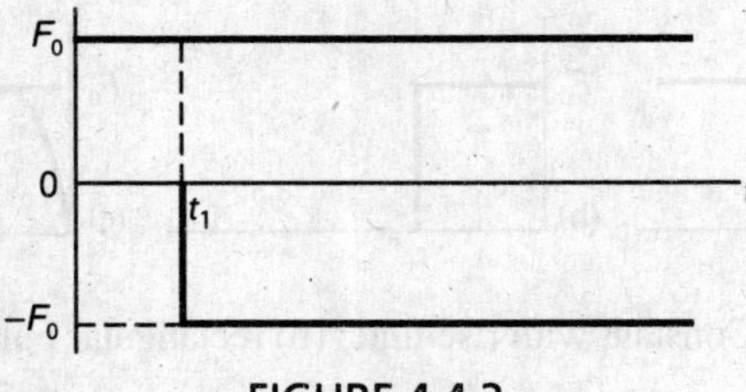

FIGURE 4.4.3.

where $p = \pi/t_1$. To satisfy the initial conditions $x(0) = \dot{x}(0) = 0$, we find

$$B = 0 \quad \text{and} \quad A = -\frac{F_0}{k}\frac{\frac{p}{\omega_n}}{1-\left(\frac{p}{\omega_n}\right)^2}$$

and the previous solution reduces to

$$\left(\frac{xk}{F_0}\right) = \frac{-\frac{p}{\omega_n}}{1-\left(\frac{p}{\omega_n}\right)^2}\sin\omega_n t + \frac{1}{1-\left(\frac{p}{\omega_n}\right)^2}\sin pt$$

$$= \frac{1}{\frac{\tau}{2t_1}-\frac{2t_1}{\tau}}\left[\sin\frac{2\pi t}{\tau} - \left(\frac{2t_1}{\tau}\right)\sin\frac{\pi t}{t_1}\right] \qquad t < t_1 \tag{4.4.10}$$

To determine the solution for $t > t_1$, we use Eq. (4.4.10) but with t replaced by $(t - t_1)$. However, we choose a different procedure, noting that for $t > t_1$, the excitation force is zero and we can obtain the solution as a free vibration [see Eq. (2.3.17)] with $t' = (t - t_1)$.

$$x(t) = \frac{\dot{x}(t_1)}{\omega_n}\sin\omega_n t + x(t_1)\cos\omega_n t \tag{4.4.11}$$

The initial values $x(t_1)$ and $\dot{x}(t_1)$ can be obtained from Eq. (4.4.10), noting that $pt_1 = \pi$.

$$\frac{kx(t_1)}{F_0} = \frac{1}{1-\left(\frac{p}{\omega_n}\right)^2}\left[\sin pt_1 - \left(\frac{p}{\omega_n}\right)\sin\omega_n t_1\right] = \frac{1}{1-\left(\frac{p}{\omega_n}\right)^2}\left[-\frac{p}{\omega_n}\sin\omega_n t_1\right]$$

$$\frac{k\dot{x}(t_1)}{F_0} = \frac{1}{1-\left(\frac{p}{\omega_n}\right)^2}[p\cos pt_1 - p\cos\omega_n t_1] = \frac{-p}{1-\left(\frac{p}{\omega_n}\right)^2}[1+\cos\omega_n t_1]$$

Substituting these results into Eq. (4.4.11), we obtain

$$\frac{xk}{F_0} = \frac{-\frac{p}{\omega_n}}{1-\left(\frac{p}{\omega_n}\right)^2}[(1+\cos\omega_n t_1)\sin\omega_n t' + \sin\omega_n t_1\cos\omega_n t']$$

$$= \frac{-\frac{p}{\omega_n}}{1-\left(\frac{p}{\omega_n}\right)^2}[\sin\omega_n t' + \sin\omega_n(t'+t_1)] \tag{4.4.12}$$

$$= \frac{1}{\frac{\tau}{2t_1}-\frac{2t_1}{\tau}}\left[\sin\frac{2\pi t}{\tau} + \sin 2\pi\left(\frac{t}{\tau}-\frac{t_1}{\tau}\right)\right] \qquad t > t_1$$

4.5 SHOCK RESPONSE SPECTRUM

In the previous section, we solved for the time response of an undamped spring-mass system to pulse excitation of time duration t_1. When the time duration t_1 is small compared to the natural period τ

of the spring-mass oscillator, the excitation is called a *shock*. Such excitation is often encountered by engineering equipment that must undergo shock-vibration tests for certification of satisfactory design. Of particular interest is the maximum peak response, which is a measure of the severity of the shock. In order to categorize all types of shock excitation, the single-DOF undamped oscillator (spring-mass system) is chosen as a standard.

Engineers have found the concept of the shock response spectrum to be useful in design. The *shock response spectrum* (SRS) is a plot of the maximum peak response of the single-DOF oscillator as a function of the natural period of the oscillator. The maximum of the peaks, often labeled *maximax*, represents only a single point on the time response curve. It does not uniquely define the shock input because it is possible for two different shock pulses to have the same maximum peak response. In spite of this limitation, the SRS is a useful concept that is extensively used, especially for preliminary design.

In Eq. (4.2.1), the response of a system to arbitrary excitation $f(t)$ was expressed in terms of the impulse response $h(t)$. For the undamped single-DOF oscillator, we have

$$h(t) = \frac{1}{m\omega_n} \sin \omega_n t$$

so that the peak response to be used in the response spectrum plot is given by the equation

$$x(t)_{\max} = \left| \frac{1}{m\omega_n} \int_0^t f(\xi) \sin \omega_n (t - \xi)\, d\xi \right|_{\max} \tag{4.5.1}$$

In the case where the shock is due to the sudden motion of the support point, $f(t)$ is replaced by $-\ddot{y}(t)$, the acceleration of the support point, as in Eq. (4.2.5).

$$z(t)_{\max} = \left| \frac{-1}{\omega_n} \int_0^t \ddot{y}(\xi) \sin \omega_n (t - \xi)\, d\xi \right|_{\max} \tag{4.5.2}$$

With τ as the natural period of the oscillator, the maximum value of $x(t)$ or $z(t)$ is plotted as a function of t_1/τ, where τ is the natural period of the oscillator and t_1 is the pulse duration time.

To graphically describe the concept of the SRS, we choose the time response to the rectangular pulse previously given in Sec. 4.4. For $t > t_1$, the response is given by Eq. (4.4.6), which clearly represents two step functions started at times $t = 0$ and $t = t_1$. These are plotted in Fig. 4.5.1 for

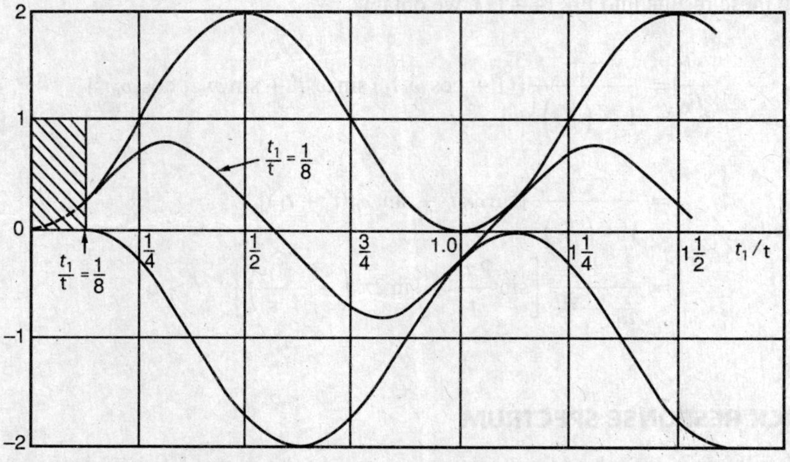

FIGURE 4.5.1. Response for $t_1/\tau = \frac{1}{8}$, which gives $(xk/F_0)_{\max} = 0.80$ at $t_m = 0.32\tau$.

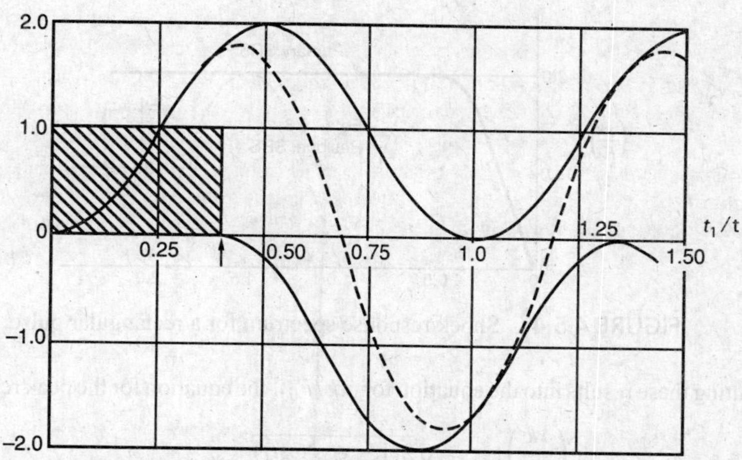

FIGURE 4.5.2. Response for $t_1/\tau = 0.40$, which gives $(xk/F_0)_{\max} = 1.82$ at $t_m = 0.45\tau$.

$t_1/\tau = \frac{1}{8}$. Their difference, which is the response of the oscillator for $t > t_1$, is shown by the dark line and the peak response is $(xk/F_0)_{\max} = 0.80$ at time $t_m = 0.32\tau$. Thus, we have one point, 0.80, on the SRS plot of $|xk/F_0|_{\max}$ vs. t_1/τ.

If we change the pulse duration time to $t_1/\tau = 0.40$, a similar plot shown in Fig. 4.5.2 indicates that the peak response is now equal to $|xk/F_0|_{\max} = 1.82$ at time $t_m = 0.45\tau$. This then gives us a second point on the SRS plot, etc.

To avoid the laborious procedure described previously, we can start with Eq. (4.4.6) and differentiate with respect to time to obtain the peak response as follows:

$$\left(\frac{xk}{F_0}\right) = \{[1 - \cos \omega_n t] - [1 - \cos \omega_n (t - t_1)]\}$$

$$\frac{d}{dt}\left(\frac{xk}{F_0}\right) = \omega_n\left[\sin \omega_n t_p - \sin \omega_n (t_p - t_1)\right] = 0$$

where t_p is the time corresponding to the peak response. It follows then that

$$\tan \omega_n t_p \doteq \frac{\sin \omega_n t_1}{-(1 - \cos \omega_n t_1)}$$

which is shown in Fig. 4.5.3. From this figure, two other relations are found:

$$\sin \omega_n t_p = \frac{\sin \omega_n t_1}{\sqrt{2(1 - \cos \omega_n t_1)}}$$

$$\cos \omega_n t_p = \frac{-(1 - \cos \omega_n t_1)}{\sqrt{2(1 - \cos \omega_n t_1)}} = \frac{1}{\sqrt{2}}\sqrt{(1 - \cos \omega_n t_1)}$$

FIGURE 4.5.3.

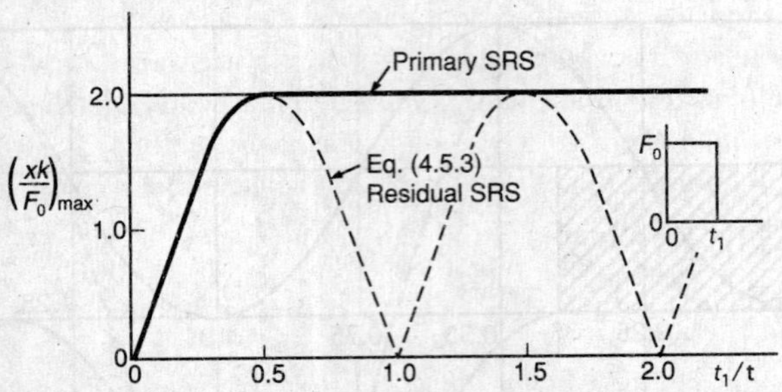

FIGURE 4.5.4. Shock response spectrum for a rectangular pulse.

By substituting these results into the equation for (xk/F_0), the equation for the peak response becomes

$$\left(\frac{xk}{F_0}\right)_{\max} = \sqrt{2(1 - \cos\omega_n t_1)}$$

$$= 2\sin\tfrac{1}{2}\omega_n t_1 = 2\sin\frac{\pi t_1}{\tau} \qquad t > t_1 \tag{4.5.3}$$

The SRS for the rectangular pulse given by this equation can now be displayed by the plot of Fig. 4.5.4. Note the two points x found from the time response plots. The dashed-line curves are called the *residual spectrum*, and the upper curve, which is equal to 2.0 for $t_1/\tau > 0.50$, represents the envelope of all peaks, including the peaks of the time response curve for $t < t_1$, which is easily seen from Eq. (4.2.2).

Figures 4.5.5 and 4.5.6 show the SRS for the half-sine pulse and the triangular pulse, which are often good approximations to the actual pulse shapes.

For the half-sine pulse, the equation for the primary shock spectrum $(t < t_1)$ is obtained from the maximum of Eq. (4.4.6):

$$\left(\frac{xk}{F_0}\right)_{\max} = \frac{1}{1 - \dfrac{\tau}{2t_1}} \sin \frac{2\pi n\left(\dfrac{\tau}{2t_1}\right)}{1 + \dfrac{\tau}{2t_1}} \tag{4.5.4}$$

whereas for the residual shock spectrum $(t > t_1)$, the maximum values of Eq. (4.4.6) are

$$\left(\frac{xk}{F_0}\right)_{\max} = \left(\frac{2}{\dfrac{\tau}{2t_1} - \dfrac{2t_1}{\tau}}\right)\cos\frac{\pi t_1}{\tau} \tag{4.5.5}$$

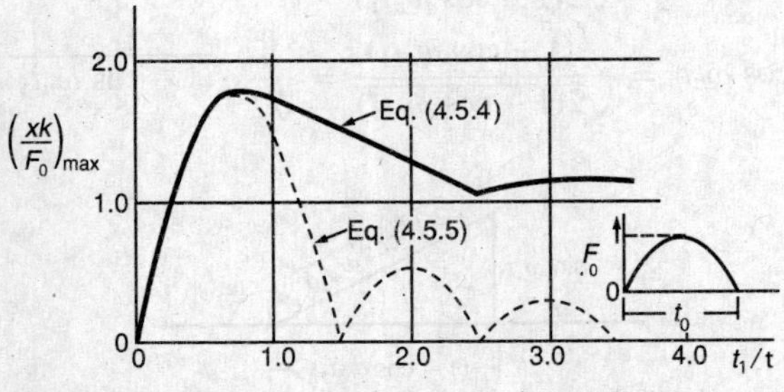

FIGURE 4.5.5. Shock response spectrum for half-sine wave.

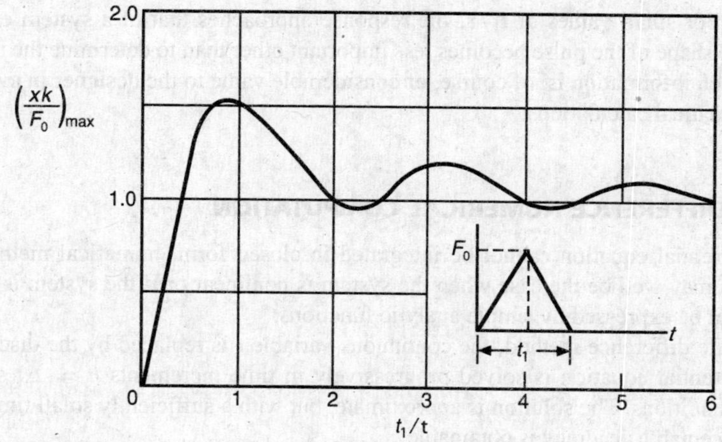

FIGURE 4.5.6. Shock response spectrum for triangular pulse.

4.6 SHOCK ISOLATION

For shock isolation, the maximum peak response or the transmissibility must be less than unity. Thus, for the rectangular pulse, this requires [see Eq. (4.5.3)]

$$2 \sin \frac{\pi t_1}{\tau} < 1.0$$

$$\frac{\pi t_1}{\tau} < 30° = \frac{\pi}{6}$$

Vibration isolation is then possible for

$$\frac{t_1}{\tau} < \frac{1}{6}$$

$$\omega_n < \frac{\pi}{3t_1}$$

and the natural period of the isolated system must be greater than six times the pulse time.

Next, consider a more general pulse bounded by a rectangular pulse, such as those shown in Fig. 4.6.1. The impulse of these force pulses is clearly less than that of the rectangular pulse. By remembering that the impulse is equal to the change in momentum, it is reasonable to assume that the maximum peak response of the rectangular pulse must be the upper bound to that of the enclosed pulse of general shape. We also find that for small t_1/τ, the peak response occurs in the

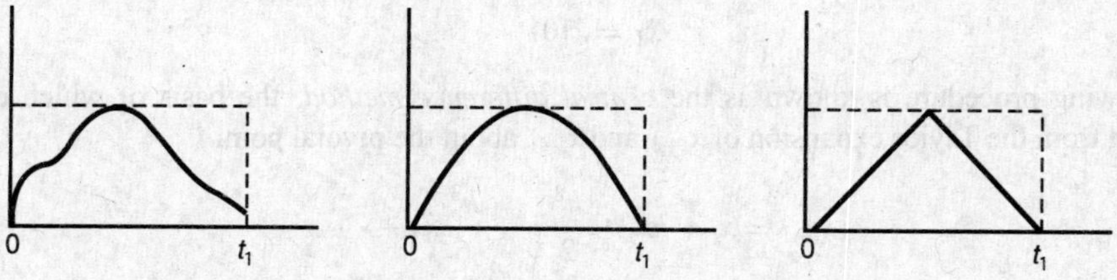

FIGURE 4.6.1. Shock pulses bounded by a rectangular pulse.

region $t > t_1$. For small values of t_1/τ, the response approaches that of a system excited by an impulse and the shape of the pulse becomes less important other than to determine the magnitude of the impulse. Such information is, of course, of considerable value to the designer in avoiding some difficult mathematical calculations.

4.7 FINITE DIFFERENCE NUMERICAL COMPUTATION

When the differential equation cannot be integrated in closed form, numerical methods must be employed. This may well be the case when the system is nonlinear or if the system is excited by a force that cannot be expressed by simple analytic functions.

In the finite difference method, the continuous variable t is replaced by the discrete variable t_i and the differential equation is solved progressively in time increments $h = \Delta t$ starting from known initial conditions. The solution is approximate, but with a sufficiently small time increment, a solution of acceptable accuracy is obtainable.

Although there are a number of different finite difference procedures available, in this chapter, we consider only two methods chosen for their simplicity. Merits of the various methods are associated with the accuracy, stability, and length of computation, which are discussed in a number of texts on numerical analysis listed at the end of the chapter.

The differential equation of motion for a dynamical system, which may be linear or nonlinear, can be expressed in the following general form:

$$\begin{aligned} \ddot{x} &= f(x, \dot{x}, t) \\ x_1 &= x(0) \\ \dot{x}_1 &= \dot{x}(0) \end{aligned} \tag{4.7.1}$$

where the initial conditions x_1 and $\dot{x}_1$ are presumed to be known. (The subscript 1 is chosen to correspond to $t = 0$ because most computer languages do not allow subzero.)

In the first method, the second-order equation is integrated without change in form; in the second method, the second-order equation is reduced to two first-order equations before integration. The equation then takes the form

$$\begin{aligned} \dot{x} &= y \\ \dot{y} &= f(x, y, t) \end{aligned} \tag{4.7.2}$$

We first discuss the method of solving the second-order equation directly. We also limit, at first, the discussion to the undamped system, whose equations are

$$\begin{aligned} \ddot{x} &= f(x, t) \\ x_1 &= x(0) \\ \dot{x}_1 &= \dot{x}(0) \end{aligned} \tag{4.7.3}$$

The following procedure is known as the *central difference method*, the basis of which can be developed from the Taylor expansion of x_{i+1} and x_{i-1} about the pivotal point i.

$$\begin{aligned} x_{i+1} &= x_i + h\dot{x}_i + \frac{h^2}{2}\ddot{x}_i + \frac{h^3}{6}\dddot{x}_i + \cdots \\ x_{i-1} &= x_i - h\dot{x}_i + \frac{h^2}{2}\ddot{x}_i - \frac{h^3}{6}\dddot{x}_i + \cdots \end{aligned} \tag{4.7.4}$$

where the time interval is $h = \Delta t$. Subtracting and ignoring higher-order terms, we obtain

$$\dot{x}_i = \frac{1}{2h}(x_{i+1} - x_{i-1}) \tag{4.7.5}$$

Adding, we find

$$\ddot{x}_i = \frac{1}{h^2}(x_{i-1} - 2x_i + x_{i+1}) \tag{4.7.6}$$

In both Eqs. (4.7.5) and (4.7.6), the ignored terms are of order h^2. By substituting from the differential equation, Eq. (4.7.3), Eq. (4.7.6) can be rearranged to

$$x_{i+1} = 2x_i - x_{i-1} + h^2 f(x_i, t_i) \quad i \geq 2 \tag{4.7.7}$$

which is known as the *recurrence formula.*

(Starting the computation.) If we let $i = 2$ in the recurrent equation, we note that it is not self-starting, i.e., x_1 is known, but we need x_2 to find x_3. Thus, to start the computation, we need another equation for x_2. This is supplied by the first of Taylor's series, Eq. (4.7.4), ignoring higher-order terms, which gives

$$x_2 = x_1 + h\dot{x}_1 + \frac{h^2}{2}\ddot{x}_1 = x_1 + h\dot{x}_1 + \frac{h^2}{2}f(x_1, t) \tag{4.7.8}$$

Thus, Eq. (4.7.8) enables one to find x_2 in terms of the initial conditions, after which $x_3, x_4, \ldots$ are available from Eq. (4.7.7).

In this development we have ignored higher-order terms that introduce what is known as *truncation errors*. Other errors, such as round-off errors, are introduced due to loss of significant figures. These are all related to the time increment $h = \Delta t$ in a rather complicated way, which is beyond the scope of this text. In general, better accuracy is obtained by choosing a smaller Δt, but the number of computations will then increase together with errors generated in the computation. A safe rule to use with this method is to choose $h \leq \tau/10$, where τ is the natural period of the system.

A flow diagram for the digital calculation is shown in Fig. 4.7.1. From the given data in block Ⓐ, we proceed to block Ⓑ, which is the differential equation. Going to © for the first time, I is not greater than 1, and hence we proceed to the left, where x_2 is calculated. Increasing I by 1, we complete the left loop Ⓑ and ©, where I is now equal to 2, so we proceed to the right to calculate x_3. Assuming N intervals of Δt, the path is to the No direction and the right loop is repeated N times until $I = N + 1$, at which time the results are printed out.

Example 4.7.1

Solve numerically the differential equation

$$4\ddot{x} + 2000x = F(t)$$

with initial conditions

$$x_1 = \dot{x}_1 = 0$$

and the forcing function shown in Fig. 4.7.2.

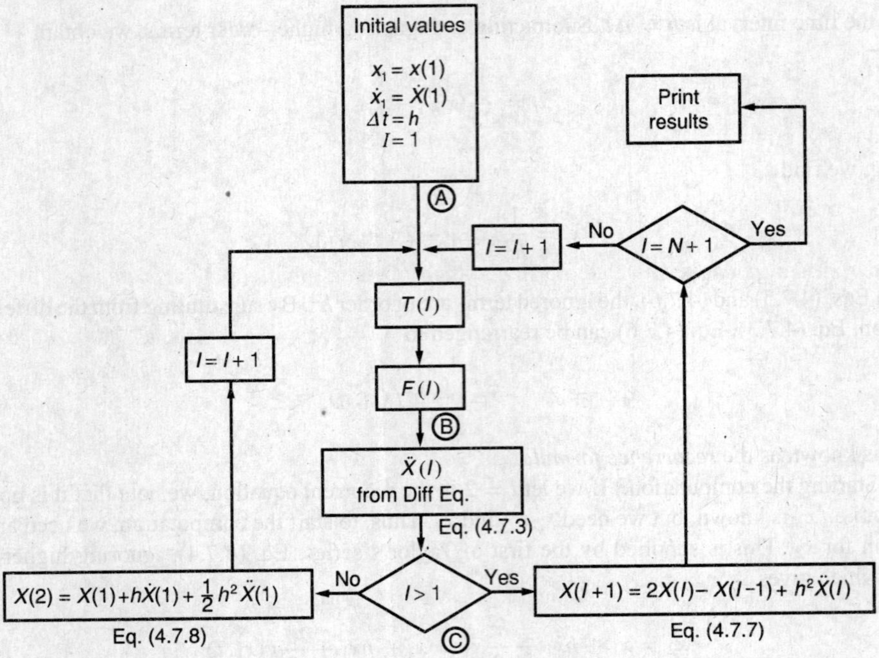

FIGURE 4.7.1. Flow diagram (undamped system).

Solution The natural period of the system is first found as

$$\omega = \frac{2\pi}{\tau} = \sqrt{\frac{2000}{4}} = 22.36 \text{ rad/s}$$

$$\tau = \frac{2\pi}{22.36} = 0.281 \text{ s}$$

According to the rule $h \leq \tau/10$ and for convenience for representing $F(t)$, we choose $h = 0.020$ s.

From the differential equation, we have

$$\ddot{x} = f(x, t) = \frac{1}{4}F(t) - 500x$$

Equation (4.7.8) gives $x_2 = \frac{1}{2}(25)(0.02)^2 = 0.005$. x_3 is then found from Eq. (4.7.7).

$$x_3 = 0.005 - 0 + (0.02)^2(25 - 500 \times 0.005) = 0.0190$$

The following values of x_4, x_5, etc. are now available from Eq. (4.7.7).

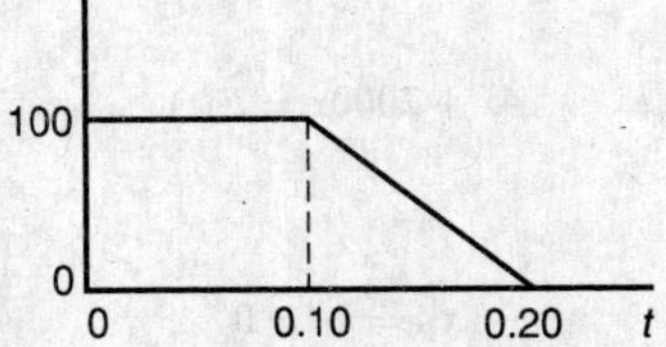

FIGURE 4.7.2.

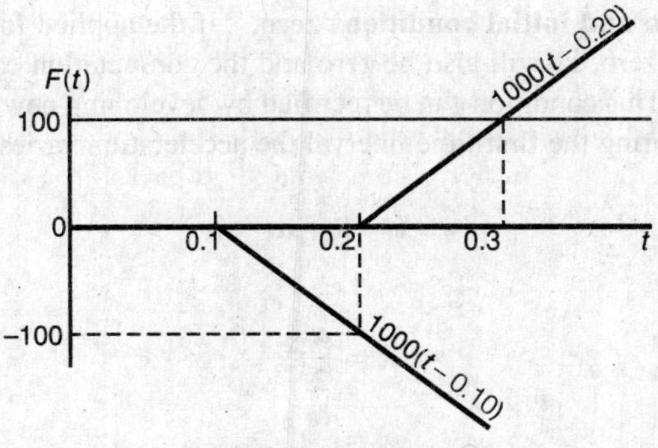

FIGURE 4.7.3.

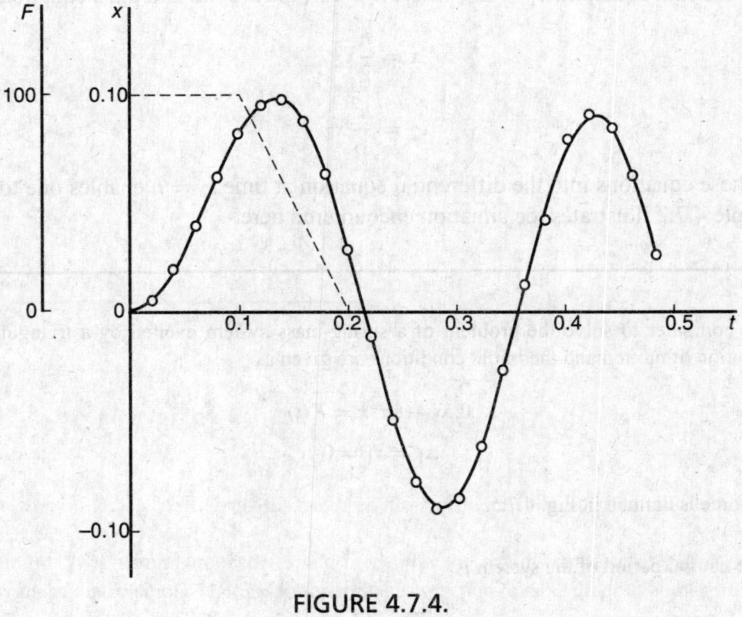

FIGURE 4.7.4.

The exact solution was obtained by the superposition of the solutions for the step function and the ramp function in the following manner. Figure 4.7.3 shows the superposition of forces. The equations to be superimposed for the exact solution are

$$x_1 = 0.05(1 - \cos 22.36t) \quad 0 \le t \le 0.1 \tag{4.7.9}$$

$$x_2 = -\left[\frac{1}{2}(t - 0.1) - 0.02236 \sin 22.36(t - 0.10)\right] \quad \text{add at } t = 0.1 \tag{4.7.10}$$

$$x_3 = +\left[\frac{1}{2}(t - 0.2) - 0.02236 \sin 22.36(t - 0.2)\right] \quad \text{add at } t = 0.2 \tag{4.7.11}$$

Both computations were carried out with MATLAB® and Fig. 4.7.4 shows the computed values compared with the exact solution.

Initial acceleration and initial conditions zero. If the applied force is zero at $t = 0$ and the initial conditions are zero, $\ddot{x}_1$ will also be zero and the computation cannot be started because Eq. (4.7.8) gives $x_2 = 0$. This condition can be rectified by developing new starting equations based on the assumption that during the first-time interval the acceleration varies linearly from $\ddot{x}_1 = 0$ to $\ddot{x}_2$ as follows:

$$\ddot{x} = 0 + \alpha t$$

Integrating, we obtain

$$\dot{x} = \frac{\alpha}{2}t^2$$

$$x = \frac{\alpha}{6}t^3$$

Because from the first equation, $\ddot{x}_2 = \alpha h$, where $h = \Delta t$, the second and third equations become

$$\dot{x} = \frac{h}{2}\ddot{x}_2 \tag{4.7.12}$$

$$x_2 = \frac{h^2}{6}\ddot{x}_2 \tag{4.7.13}$$

Substituting these equations into the differential equation at time $t_2 = h$ enables one to solve for $\ddot{x}_2$ and x_2. Example 4.7.2 illustrates the situation encountered here.

Example 4.7.2

Use the digital computer to solve the problem of a spring-mass system excited by a triangular pulse. The differential equation of motion and the initial conditions are given as

$$0.5\ddot{x} + 8\pi^2 x = F(t)$$

$$x_1 = \dot{x}_1 = 0$$

The triangular force is defined in Fig. 4.7.5.

Solution The natural period of the system is

$$\tau = \frac{2\pi}{\omega} = \frac{2\pi}{4\pi} = 0.50$$

The time increment is chosen as $h = 0.05$, and the differential equation is reorganized as

$$\ddot{x} = f(x, t) = 2F(t) - 16\pi^2 x$$

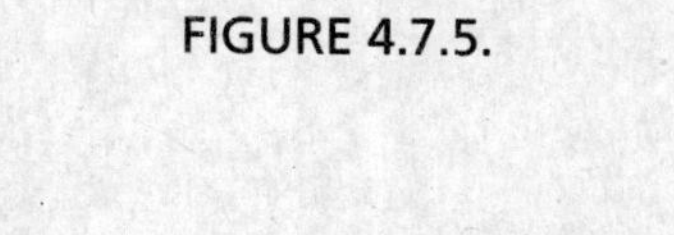

FIGURE 4.7.5.

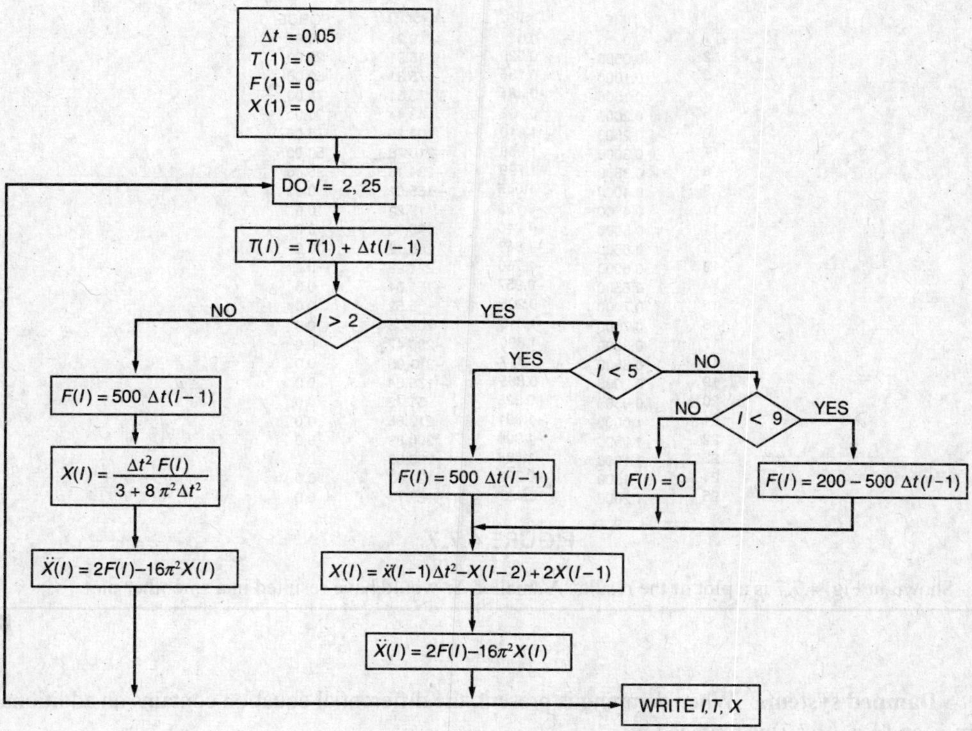

FIGURE 4.7.6.

This equation is to be solved together with the recurrence equation, Eq. (4.7.7),

$$x_{i+1} = 2x_i - x_{i-1} + h^2 f(x, t)$$

Because the force and the acceleration are zero at $t = 0$, it is necessary to start the computational process with Eqs. (4.7.12) and (4.7.13) and the differential equation:

$$x_2 = \frac{1}{6}\ddot{x}_2(0.05)^2 = 0.000417\ddot{x}_2$$

$$\ddot{x}_2 = 2F(0.05) - 16\pi^2 x_2 = 50 - 158x_2$$

Their simultaneous solution leads to

$$x_2 = \frac{(0.05)^2 F(0.05)}{3 + 8\pi^2(0.05)^2} = 0.0195$$

$$\ddot{x}_2 = 46.91$$

The flow diagram for the computation is shown in Fig. 4.7.6. With $h = 0.05$, the time duration for the force must be divided into regions $I = 1$ to 5, $I = 6$ to 9, and $I > 9$. The index I controls the computation path on the diagram.

J	TIME	DISPL	ACCLRTN	FORCE
1	0.0	0.0	0.0	0.0
2	0.0500	0.020	46.91	25.00
3	0.1000	0.156	75.31	50.00
4	0.1500	0.481	73.31	75.00
5	0.2000	0.992	43.44	100.00
6	0.2500	1.610	−104.25	75.00
7	0.3000	1.968	−210.78	50.00
8	0.3500	1.799	−234.10	25.00
9	0.4000	1.045	−165.01	0.00
10	0.4500	−0.122	19.22	0.0
11	0.5000	−1.240	195.86	0.0
12	0.5500	−1.869	295.19	0.0
13	0.6000	−1.760	277.98	0.0
14	0.6500	−0.957	151.04	0.0
15	0.7000	0.225	−35.52	0.0
16	0.7500	1.318	−208.06	0.0
17	0.8000	1.890	−298.47	0.0
18	0.8500	1.717	−271.05	0.0
19	0.9000	0.865	−136.64	0.0
20	0.9500	−0.328	51.72	0.0
21	1.0000	−1.391	219.66	0.0
22	1.0500	−1.906	300.89	0.0
23	1.1000	−1.668	263.33	0.0
24	1.1500	−0.772	121.83	0.0
25	1.2000	0.429	−67.77	0.0

FIGURE 4.7.7.

Shown in Fig. 4.7.7 is a plot of the results. A smaller Δt would have resulted in a smoother plot. ■

Damped system. When damping is present, the differential equation contains an additional term $\dot{x}_i$ and Eq. (4.7.7) is replaced by

$$x_{i+1} = 2x_i - x_{i-1} + h^2 f(x_i, \dot{x}_i, t_i) \qquad i \geq 2 \tag{4.7.7'}$$

We now need to calculate the velocity at each step as well as the displacement.

Considering again the first three terms of the Taylor series, Eq. (4.7.4), we see that x_2 is available from the expansion of x_{i+1} with $i = 1$:

$$x_2 = x_1 + \dot{x}_1 h + \frac{h^2}{2} f(x_1, \dot{x}_1, t_1)$$

The quantity $\dot{x}_2$ is found from the second equation for x_{i-1} with $i = 2$:

$$x_1 = x_2 - \dot{x}_2 h + \frac{h^2}{2} f(x_1, \dot{x}_2, t_2)$$

With these results, x_3 can be calculated from Eq. (4.7.7′). The procedure is thus repeated for other values of x_i and $\dot{x}_i$ using the Taylor series.

4.8 RUNGE–KUTTA METHOD

The Runge–Kutta computation procedure is popular because it is self-starting and results in good accuracy. A brief discussion of its basis is presented here.

In the Runge–Kutta method, the second-order differential equation is first reduced to two first-order equations. As an example, consider the differential equation for the single-DOF system, which can be written as

$$\ddot{x} = \frac{1}{m}[f(t) - kx - c\dot{x}] = F(x, \dot{x}, t) \tag{4.8.1}$$

By letting $\dot{x} = y$, this equation is reduced to the following two first-order equations:

$$\begin{aligned} \dot{x} &= y \\ \dot{y} &= F(x, y, t) \end{aligned} \tag{4.8.2}$$

Both x and y in the neighborhood of x_i and y_i can be expressed in terms of the Taylor series. Letting the time increment be $h = \Delta t$, we have

$$\begin{aligned} x &= x_i + \left(\frac{dx}{dt}\right)_i h + \left(\frac{d^2x}{dt^2}\right)_i \frac{h^2}{2} + \cdots \\ y &= y_i + \left(\frac{dy}{dt}\right)_i h + \left(\frac{d^2y}{dt^2}\right)_i \frac{h^2}{2} + \cdots \end{aligned} \tag{4.8.3}$$

Instead of using these expressions, it is possible to replace the first derivative by an average slope and ignore higher-order derivatives:

$$\begin{aligned} x &= x_i + \left(\frac{dx}{dt}\right)_{iav} h \\ y &= y_i + \left(\frac{dy}{dt}\right)_{iav} h \end{aligned} \tag{4.8.4}$$

If we used Simpson's rule, the average slope in the interval h becomes

$$\left(\frac{dy}{dt}\right)_{iav} = \frac{1}{6}\left[\left(\frac{dy}{dt}\right)_{t_i} + 4\left(\frac{dy}{dt}\right)_{t_i+h/2} + \left(\frac{dy}{dt}\right)_{t_i+h}\right]$$

The fourth-order Runge–Kutta method is very similar to the preceding computations, except that the center term of the given equation is split into two terms and four values of $t, x, y,$ and f are computed for each point i as follows:

t	x	$y = \dot{x}$	$f = \dot{y} = \ddot{x}$
$T_1 = t_i$	$X_1 = x_i$	$Y_1 = y_i$	$F_1 = f(T_1, X_1, Y_1)$
$T_2 = t_i + \frac{h}{2}$	$X_2 = x_i + Y_1\frac{h}{2}$	$Y_2 = y_i + F_1\frac{h}{2}$	$F_2 = f(T_2, X_2, Y_2)$
$T_3 = t_i + \frac{h}{2}$	$X_3 = x_i + Y_2\frac{h}{2}$	$Y_3 = y_i + F_2\frac{h}{2}$	$F_3 = f(T_3, X_3, Y_3)$
$T_4 = t_i + h$	$X_4 = x_i + Y_3 h$	$Y_4 = y_i + F_3 h$	$F_4 = f(T_4, X_4, Y_4)$

These quantities are then used in the following recurrence formula:

$$x_{i+1} = x_i + \frac{h}{6}(Y_1 + 2Y_2 + 2Y_3 + Y_4) \tag{4.8.5}$$

$$y_{i+1} = y_i + \frac{h}{6}(F_1 + 2F_2 + 2F_3 + F_4) \tag{4.8.6}$$

where it is recognized that the four values of Y divided by 6 represent an average slope dx/dt and the four values of F divided by 6 result in an average of dy/dt as defined by Eqs. (4.8.4).

Example 4.8.1

Solve Example 4.7.1 by the Runge–Kutta method.

Solution The differential equation of motion is

$$\ddot{x} = \frac{1}{4}f(t) - 500x$$

Let $y = \dot{x}$; then

$$\dot{y} = F(x, t) = \frac{1}{4}f(t) - 500x$$

With $h = 0.02$, the following table is calculated:

	t	x	$y = \dot{x}$	f
$t_1 =$	0	0	0	25
	0.01	0	0.25	25
	0.01	0.0025	0.25	23.75
$t_2 =$	0.02	0.0050	0.475	22.50

The calculation for x_2 and y_2 follows:

$$x_2 = 0 + \frac{0.02}{6}(0 + 0.50 + 0.50 + 0.475) = 0.00491667$$

$$y_2 = 0 + \frac{0.02}{6}(25 + 50 + 47.50 + 22.50) = 0.4833333$$

To continue to point 3, we repeat the foregoing table:

	t	x	$y = \dot{x}$	f
$t_2 =$	0.02	0.00491667	0.4833333	22.541665
	0.03	0.0097500	0.70874997	20.12500
	0.03	0.01200417	0.6845833	18.997915
$t_3 =$	0.04	0.01860834	0.8632913	15.695830

We then calculate x_3 and y_3:

$$\begin{aligned} x_3 &= 0.00491667 \\ &+ \frac{0.02}{6}(0.483333 + 1.4174999 + 1.3691666 + 0.8632913) \\ &= 0.00491667 + 0.01377764 = 0.01869431 \end{aligned}$$

$$y_3 = 0.483333 + 0.38827775 = 0.87161075$$

To complete the calculation, the example was performed in MATLAB® and the results showed excellent accuracy. Table 4.8.1 gives the numerical values for the central difference method, which is discussed in Example 4.7.1, and the Runge–Kutta method compared with the analytical solution [see Eqs. (4.7.9)–(4.7.11)].

TABLE 4.8.1 Comparison of Methods for Example 4.8.1

Time t	Exact Solution	Central Difference	Runge–Kutta
0	0	0	0
0.02	0.00492	0.00500	0.00492
0.04	0.01870	0.01900	0.01869
0.06	0.03864	0.03920	0.03862
0.08	0.06082	0.06159	0.06076
0.10	0.08086	0.08167	0.08083
0.12	0.09451	0.09541	0.09447
0.14	0.09743	0.09807	0.09741
0.16	0.08710	0.08712	0.08709
0.18	0.06356	0.06274	0.06359
0.20	0.02949	0.02782	0.02956
0.22	−0.01005	−0.01267	−0.00955
0.24	−0.04761	−0.05063	−0.04750
0.26	−0.07581	−0.07846	−0.07571
0.28	−0.08910	−0.09059	−0.08903
0.30	−0.08486	−0.08461	−0.08485
0.32	−0.06393	−0.06171	−0.06400
0.34	−0.03043	−0.02646	−0.03056
0.36	0.00906	0.01407	0.00887
0.38	0.04677	0.05180	0.04656
0.40	0.07528	0.07916	0.07509
0.42	0.08898	0.09069	0.08886
0.44	0.08518	0.08409	0.08516
0.46	0.06436	0.06066	0.06473
0.48	0.03136	0.02511	0.03157

■

Although the Runge–Kutta method does not require the evaluation of derivatives beyond the first, its higher accuracy is achieved by four evaluations of the first derivatives to obtain agreement with the Taylor series solution through terms of order h^4.

Moreover, the versatility of the Runge–Kutta method is evident in that it can be used for a single variable or several variables.

For two variables, x and y, as in this example, we can let $z = \begin{Bmatrix} x \\ y \end{Bmatrix}$ and write the two first-order equations as

$$z = \begin{Bmatrix} \dot{x} \\ \dot{y} \end{Bmatrix} = \begin{Bmatrix} y \\ f(x, y, t) \end{Bmatrix} = F(x, y, t)$$

or

$$\dot{z} = F(x, y, t)$$

Thus, the vector equation is identical in form to the equation in one variable and can be treated in the same manner.

Example 4.8.2

Solve the equation $2\ddot{x} + 8\dot{x} + 100x = f(t)$ using RUNGA, with $f(t)$ vs. t, as shown in Fig. 4.8.1.

Solution The computer program RUNGA is essentially the same as the one presented in Sec. 4.8. It includes damping.

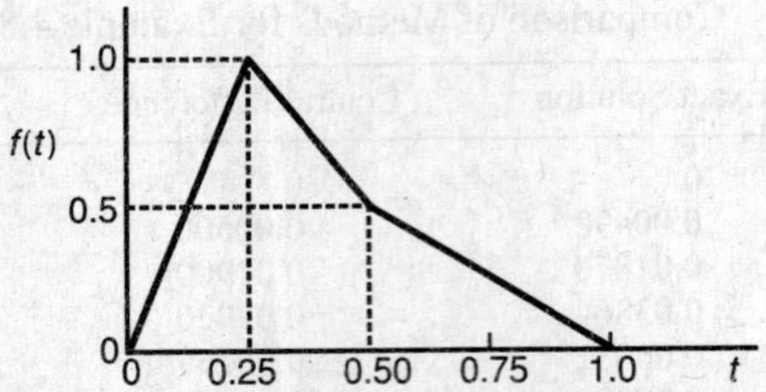

FIGURE 4.8.1.

The use of the program RUNGA is illustrated here for Example 4.8.2. The program solves the differential equation

$$m\frac{d^2x}{dt^2} + c\frac{dx}{dt} + kx = f(t)$$

The program RUNGA requires a function file called **f.m** which contains the expression for the forcing function. The following is a listing for the function in Fig. 4.8.1.

```
function [force] = f(t)
if t < 0.25
force = 4 * t;
elseif t < 0.5
force = -2 * (t - 0.25) + 1.0;
elseif t < 1
force = -1 * (t - 0.5) + 0.5;
else
force = 0;
end
```

The computer program asks for the numerical values of m, c, and k and the initial position and velocity which for this problem are $m = 2$, $c = 8$, $k = 100$, and $x(0) = \dot{x}(0) = 0$. With this input the program calculates the natural period, $\tau = 2\pi\sqrt{\frac{m}{k}}$. It then asks the user to input the time interval h. The method generally performs well for a time interval $\tau/10$. The program then proceeds with the computation of the solution. The results presented are the displacement $x(t)$ and the velocity $\dot{x}(t)$ and a plot for the displacement.

Time	Displ.	Vel.
0	0	0
0.0700	0.0001	0.0044
0.1400	0.0008	0.0151
0.2100	0.0023	0.0285
0.2800	0.0047	0.0399
0.3500	0.0075	0.0377
0.4200	0.0097	0.0239
0.4900	0.0107	0.0043
0.5600	0.0104	−0.0147
0.6300	0.0088	−0.0282
0.7000	0.0066	−0.0346
0.7700	0.0041	−0.0343
0.8400	0.0001	−0.0289

0.9100	0.0001	−0.0210
0.9800	−0.0010	−0.0126
1.0500	−0.0017	−0.0052
1.1200	−0.0018	0.0014
1.1900	−0.0015	0.0061
1.2600	−0.0010	0.0084
1.3300	−0.0004	0.0084
1.4000	0.0002	0.0066
1.4700	0.0005	0.0039
1.5400	0.0007	0.0010
1.6100	0.0007	−0.0014
1.6800	0.0005	−0.0029
1.7500	0.0003	−0.0034
1.8200	0.0001	−0.0031
1.8900	−0.0001	−0.0022
1.9600	−0.0002	−0.0011
2.0300	−0.0003	−0.0000
2.1000	−0.0003	0.0008
2.1700	−0.0002	0.0013
2.2400	−0.0001	0.0013
2.3100	0.0000	0.0011
2.3800	0.0001	0.0007
2.4500	0.0001	0.0003
2.5200	0.0001	−0.0001
2.5900	0.0001	−0.0004
2.6600	0.0001	−0.0005
2.7300	0.0000	−0.0005
2.8000	−0.0000	−0.0004
2.8700	−0.0000	−0.0002
2.9400	−0.0000	−0.0000
3.0100	−0.0000	0.0001

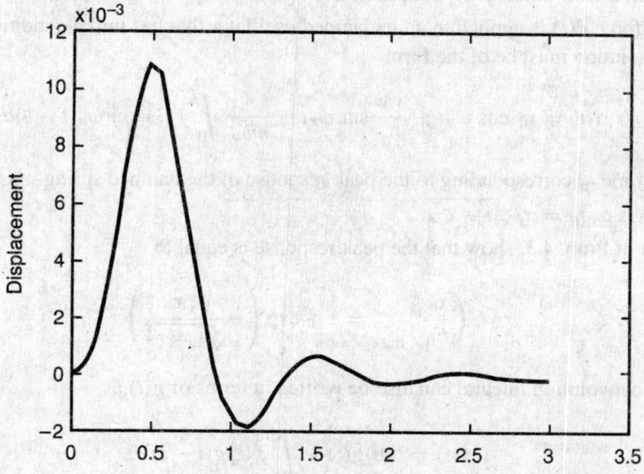

FIGURE 4.8.2.

FURTHER READING

[1] CREDE, C. E. *Vibration & Shock Isolation*. New York: John Wiley & Sons, 1951.

[2] HARRIS, C. M. and CREDE, C. E. *Shock & Vibration Handbook*, Vol. 1. New York: McGraw-Hill, 1961, Chapter 8.

[3] JACOBSEN, L. S. and AYRE, R. S. *Engineering Vibrations*. New York: McGraw-Hill, 1958.

[4] NELSON, F. C. *Shock & Vibration Isolation: Breaking the Academic Paradigm. Proceedings of the 61st Shock & Vibration Symposium*, Vol. 1, October 1990.

REFERENCE

[1] SACZALSKI, K. J. *Vibration Analysis Methods Applied to Forensic Engineering Problems, ASME Conference Proceedings on Structural Vibrations and Acoustics, Design Engineering Division*, Vol. 34, pp. 197–206.

PROBLEMS

4.1. Determine the peak displacement for the impulsively excited spring-mass system, and show that it can be expressed in the form

$$\frac{x_{\text{peak}}\sqrt{km}}{\hat{F}} = \exp\left(-\frac{\zeta}{\sqrt{1-\zeta^2}}\tan^{-1}\frac{\sqrt{1-\zeta^2}}{\zeta}\right)$$

4.2. Show that the time t_p corresponding to the peak response for the impulsively excited spring-mass system is given by the equation

$$\tan\sqrt{1-\zeta^2}\,\omega_n t_p = \sqrt{1-\zeta^2}/\zeta$$

Plot this result as a function of ζ.

4.3. For the rectangular pulse of time duration t_1, derive the response equation for $t > t_1$ using the free-vibration equation with initial conditions $x(t_1)$ and $\dot{x}(t_1)$. Compare with Eq. (4.4.6).

4.4. If an arbitrary force $f(t)$ is applied to an undamped oscillator that has initial conditions other than zero, show that the solution must be of the form

$$x(t) = x_0 \cos\omega_n t + \frac{v_0}{\omega_n}\sin\omega_n t + \frac{1}{m\omega_n}\int_0^t f(\xi)\sin\omega_n(t-\xi)d\xi$$

4.5. Show that the time t_p corresponding to the peak response of the damped spring-mass system excited by a step force F_0 is $\omega_n t_p = \pi/\sqrt{1-\zeta^2}$.

4.6. For the system of Prob. 4.3, show that the peak response is equal to

$$\left(\frac{xk}{F_0}\right)_{\max} = 1 + \exp\left(-\frac{\zeta\pi}{\sqrt{1-\zeta^2}}\right)$$

4.7. Show that the convolution integral can also be written in terms of $g(t)$ as

$$x(t) = f(0)g(t) + \int_0^t \dot{f}(\xi)g(t-\xi)\,d\xi$$

where $g(t)$ is the response to a unit step function.

4.8. Show that the response to a unit step function, designated by $g(t)$, is related to the impulsive response $h(t)$ by the equation $h(t) = \dot{g}(t)$.

4.9. In Sec. 4.3, the subsidiary equation for the viscously damped spring-mass system was given by Eq. (4.3.la). Evaluate the second term due to initial conditions by the inverse transforms.

4.10. An undamped spring-mass system is given a base excitation of $\dot{y}(t) = 10(1-2t)$. If the natural frequency for the system is $\omega_n = 5\,\mathrm{s}^{-1}$, determine the maximum relative displacement.

4.11. For the triangular pulse shown in Fig. P4.11, show that the response is

$$x = \frac{2F_0}{k}\left(\frac{t}{t_1} - \frac{\tau}{2\pi t_1}\sin 2\pi\frac{t}{\tau}\right), \quad 0 < t < \frac{1}{2}t_1$$

$$x = \frac{2F_0}{k}\left\{1 - \frac{t}{t_1} + \frac{\tau}{2\pi t_1}\left[2\sin\frac{2\pi}{\tau}\left(t - \frac{1}{2}t_1\right) - \sin 2\pi\frac{t}{\tau}\right]\right\}, \quad \frac{1}{2}t_1 < t < t_1$$

$$x = \frac{2F_0}{k}\left\{\frac{\tau}{2\pi t_1}\left[2\sin\frac{2\pi}{\tau}\left(t - \frac{1}{2}t_1\right) - \sin\frac{2\pi}{\tau}(t - t_1) - \sin 2\pi\frac{t}{\tau}\right]\right\}, \quad t > t_1$$

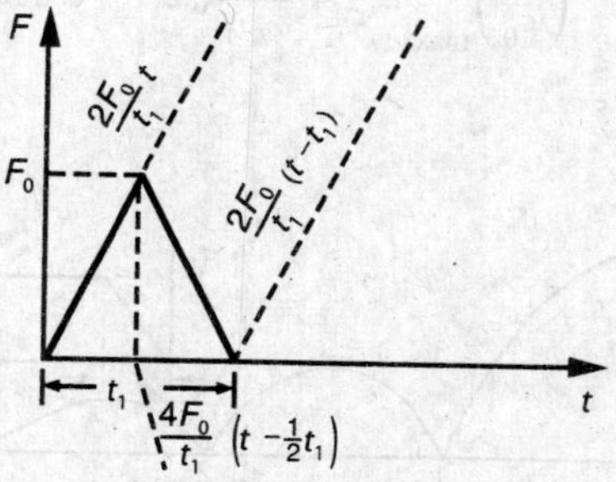

FIGURE P4.11.

4.12. A half-sine pulse is the result of two sine waves shown in Fig. P4.12. Derive Eq. (4.4.12) for $t > t_1$ from Eq. (4.4.10) and its shifted equation.

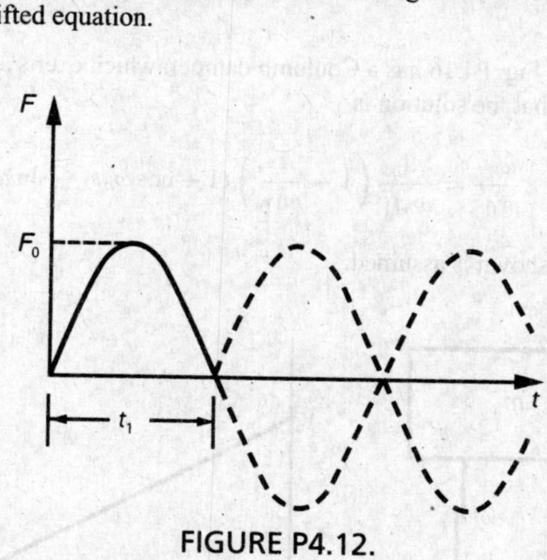

FIGURE P4.12.

4.13. A 175 N weight is supported on several springs whose combined stiffness is 1132 N/m. If the system is lifted so that the bottoms of the springs are just free and released, determine the maximum displacement of m, and the time for maximum compression.

4.14. A spring-mass system slides down a smooth 30° inclined plane, as shown in Fig. P4.14. Determine the time elapsed from first contact of the spring until it breaks contact again.

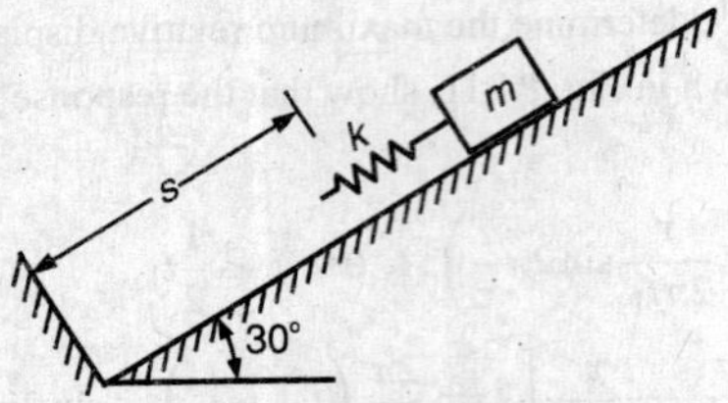

FIGURE P4.14.

4.15. For $t > t_1$, show that the maximum response of the ramp function of Fig. 4.4.2 is equal to

$$\left(\frac{xk}{F_0}\right)_{\max} = 1 + \frac{1}{\omega_n t_1}\sqrt{2(1 - \cos \omega_n t_1)}$$

which is plotted as Fig. P4.15.

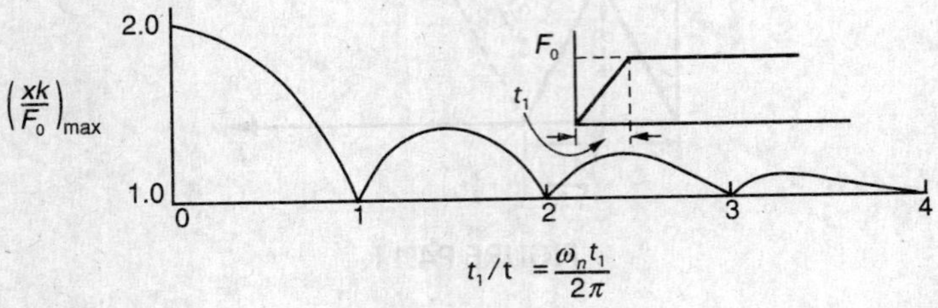

FIGURE P4.15.

4.16. A spring-mass system of Fig. P4.16 has a Coulomb damper, which exerts a constant friction force f. For a base excitation, show that the solution is

$$\frac{\omega_n z}{v_0} = \frac{1}{\omega_n t_1}\left(1 - \frac{f t_1}{m v_0}\right)(1 - \cos \omega_n t) - \sin \omega_n t$$

where the base velocity shown is assumed.

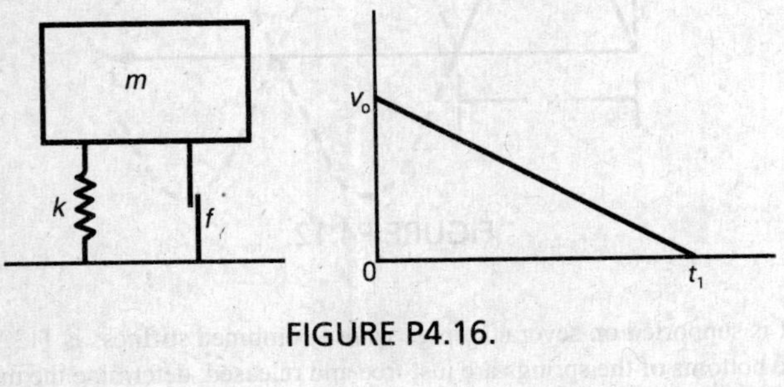

FIGURE P4.16.

4.17. Show that the peak response for Prob. 4.15 is

$$\frac{\omega_n z_{\max}}{v_0} = \frac{1}{\omega_n t_1}\left(1 - \frac{ft_1}{mv_0}\right)\left\{1 - \frac{\frac{1}{\omega_n t_1}\left(1 - \frac{ft_1}{mv_0}\right)}{\sqrt{1 + \left[\frac{1}{\omega_n t_1}\left(1 - \frac{ft_1}{mv_0}\right)\right]^2}}\right\} - \frac{1}{\sqrt{1 + \left[\frac{1}{\omega_n t_1}\left(1 - \frac{ft_1}{mv_0}\right)\right]^2}}$$

By dividing by $\omega_n t_1$, the quantity $z_{\max}/v_0 t_1$ can be plotted as a function of $\omega_n t_1$, with ft_1/mv_0 as a parameter.

4.18. In Prob. 4.16, the maximum force transmitted to m is

$$F_{\max} = f + |kz_{\max}|$$

To plot this quantity in nondimensional form, multiply by t_1/mv_0 to obtain

$$\frac{F_{\max} t_1}{mv_0} = \frac{ft_1}{mv_0} + (\omega_n t_1)^2\left(\frac{z_{\max}}{v_0 t_1}\right)$$

which again can be plotted as a function of ωt_1 with parameter ft_1/mv_0. Plot $|\omega_n z_{\max}/v_0|$ and $|z_{\max}/v_0 t_1|$ as a function of $\omega_n t_1$ for ft_1/mv_0 equal to 0, 0.20, and 1.0.

4.19. For a triangular pulse of duration t_1, show that when $t_1/\tau = \frac{1}{2}$, the peak response occurs at $t = t_1$, which can be established from the equation

$$2\cos\frac{2\pi t_1}{\tau}\left(\frac{t_p}{t_1} - 0.5\right) - \cos 2\pi\frac{t_1}{\tau}\left(\frac{t_p}{t_1} - 1\right) - \cos\frac{2\pi t_1}{\tau}\frac{t_p}{t_1} = 0$$

found by differentiating the equation for the displacement for $t > t_1$. The response spectrum for the triangular pulse is shown in Fig. P4.19.

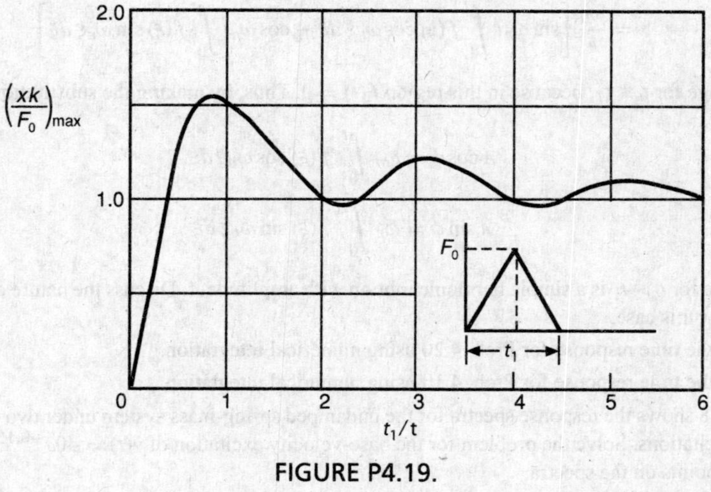

FIGURE P4.19.

4.20. An undamped spring-mass system with $w = 72$ N has a natural period of 0.5 s. It is subjected to an impulse of 9 N · s, which has a triangular shape with time duration of 0.40 s. Determine the maximum displacement of the mass.

4.21. Shown in Fig. 4.5.5 is the response spectrum for the sine pulse. Show that for small values of $t_1\tau$, the peak response occurs in the region $t > t_1$. Determine t_p/t_1 when $t_1/\tau = \frac{1}{2}$.

4.22. Derive Eqs. (4.5.4) and (4.5.5) for the half-sine pulse, and verify the primary and the residual SRS curves of Fig. 4.5.5. (Note that $n = 2$ for $t_1/\tau > 1.5$ in the primary SRS equation.)

4.23. The base of an undamped spring-mass system, m and k, is given a velocity pulse, as shown in Fig. P4.23. Show that if the peak occurs at $t < t_1$, the response spectrum is given by the equation

$$\frac{\omega_n z_{\max}}{v_0} = \frac{1}{\omega_n t_1} - \frac{1}{\omega_n t_1\sqrt{1+(\omega_n t_1)^2}} - \frac{\omega_n t_1}{\sqrt{1+(\omega_n t_1)^2}}$$

Plot this result.

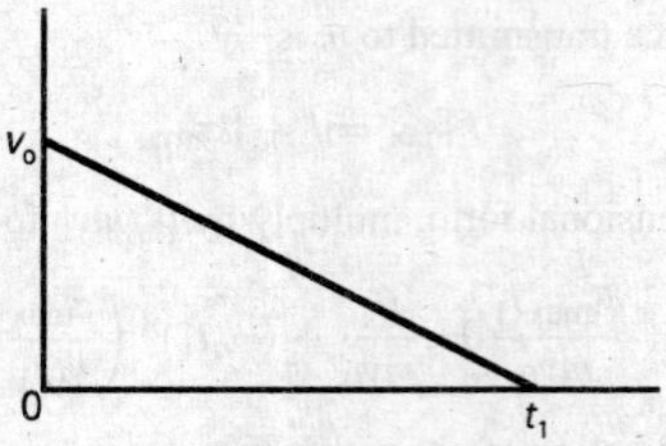

FIGURE P4.23.

4.24. In Prob. 4.23, if $t > t_1$, show that the solution is

$$\frac{\omega_n z}{v_0} = -\sin\omega_n t + \frac{1}{\omega_n t_1}[\cos\omega_n(t-t_1) - \cos\omega_n t]$$

4.25. If the natural period τ of the oscillator is large compared to that of pulse duration t_1, the maximum peak response will occur in the region $t > t_1$. For the undamped oscillator, the integrals written as

$$x = \frac{\omega_n}{k}\left[\sin\omega_n t\int_0^t f(\xi)\cos\omega_n\xi\,d\xi - \cos\omega_n t\int_0^t f(\xi)\sin\omega_n\xi\,d\xi\right]$$

do not change for $t > t_1$, because in this region $f(t) = 0$. Thus, by making the substitution

$$A\cos\phi = \omega_n\int_0^{t_1} f(\xi)\cos\omega_n\xi\,d\xi$$

$$A\sin\phi = \omega_n\int_0^{t_1} f(\xi)\sin\omega_n\xi\,d\xi$$

the response for $t > t_1$ is a simple harmonic motion with amplitude A. Discuss the nature of the response spectrum for this case.

M **4.26.** Determine the time response for Prob. 4.20 using numerical integration.

M **4.27.** Determine the time response for Prob. 4.10 using numerical integration.

4.28. Figure P4.28 shows the response spectra for the undamped spring-mass system under two different base-velocity excitations. Solve the problem for the base-velocity excitation of $\dot{y}(t) = 40e^{-0.15t}$, and verify a few of the points on the spectra.

4.29. If the driver of Example 4.3.3 is sitting on a cushion of stiffness $k = 9000$ N/m, what acceleration would be experienced assuming the same drop distance?

4.30. During ejection from a military airplane, the pilot's acceleration must not exceed 16 g if injury is to be avoided (see Ref. [1]). Assuming the ejection pulse to be triangular, what is the maximum peak

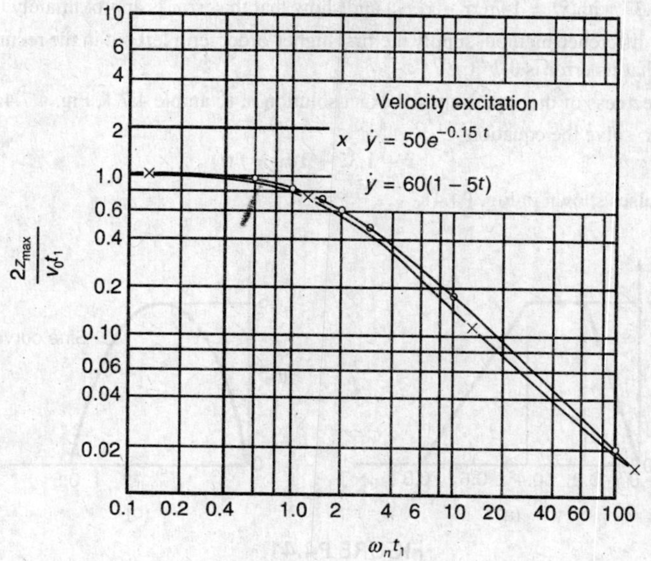

FIGURE P4.28.

acceleration of the ejection pulse applied to the pilot? Assume as in Example 4.3.3 that the seated pilot of 73 kg can be modeled with a spinal spring stiffness of $k = 80{,}000$ N/m.

4.31. Assume that a lightly damped system is driven by a force $F_0 \sin \omega_n t$, where ω_n is the natural frequency of the system. Determine the equation if the force is suddenly removed. Show that the amplitude decays to a value e^{-1} times the initial value in the time $t = 1/f_n\delta$.

4.32. A spring-mass system with viscous damping is initially at rest with zero displacement. If the system is activated by a harmonic force of frequency $\omega = \omega_n = \sqrt{k/m}$, determine the equation for its motion.

4.33. In Prob. 4.32, show that with small damping, the amplitude will build up to a value $(1 - e^{-1})$ times the steady-state value in time $t = 1/f_1, \delta$ (δ = logarithmic decrement).

4.34. Determine the response of an undamped spring-mass system to the alternating square wave of force shown in Fig. P4.34 by superimposing the solution to the step function and matching the displacement and velocity at each transition time. Plot the result and show that the peaks of the response will increase as straight lines from the origin.

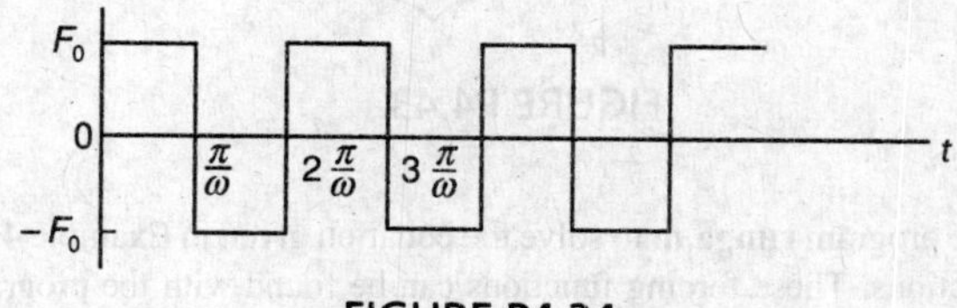

FIGURE P4.34.

M **4.35.** Write a MATLAB® program for the damped system excited by base motion $y(t)$ with initial conditions $x(0) = X_1$ and $\dot{x}(0) = V_1$. The base motion is a half-sine wave.

M **4.36.** Set up a computer program for Example 4.7.1.

4.37. Consider a curve of $x = 2t^3$ and determine x_i at $t = 0.8, 0.9, 1.0, 1.1$, and 1.2. Calculate $\dot{x}_{1.0}$ by using $\dot{x}_i = \frac{1}{2h}(x_{i+1} - x_{i-1})$, with $h = 0.20$ and $h = 0.10$, and show that the error is approximately $0(h^2)$.

4.38. Repeat Prob. 4.37 with $\dot{x}_i = 1/h(x_i - x_{i-1})$ and show that the error is approximately $0(h)$.

4.39. For the central difference method, supply the first higher-order term left out in the recurrence formula for $\ddot{x}_i$, and verify that its error is $0(h^2)$.

4.40. Verify the correctness of the superimposed exact solution in Example 4.7.1, Fig. 4.7.4.

M **4.41.** Using RUNGA, solve the equation

$$\ddot{x} + 1.3\dot{x} + 10x = f(t)$$

for the force pulses shown in Fig. P4.41.

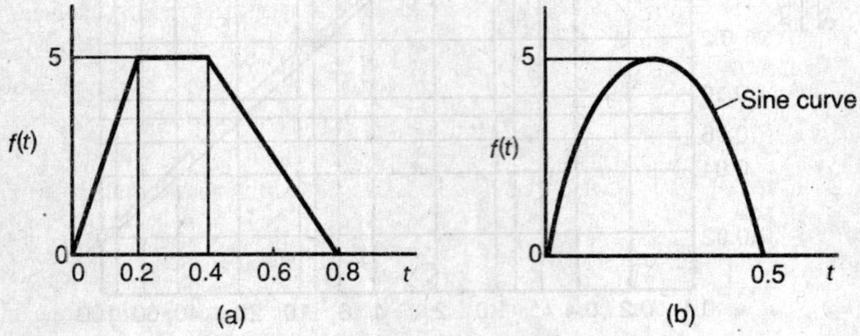

FIGURE P4.41.

M **4.42.** Calculate the problem in Example 4.7.2 by using the Runge–Kutta computer program RUNGA (see Appendix F).

4.43. A large box of weight W resting on a barge is to be hoisted by a crane, as shown in Fig. P4.43. Assuming the stiffness of the crane boom to be k_c, determine the equation of motion of the extended point if the boom is given a displacement $x = Vt$. Use the method of Laplace transformation.

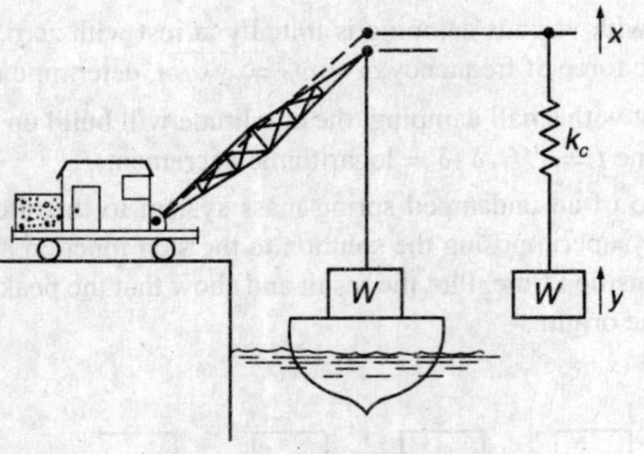

FIGURE P4.43.

M **4.44.** This problem uses the program **runga.m** to solve the equation given in Example 4.7.1, the text with three different forcing functions. These forcing functions can be found with the programs. To see how these forcing functions differ from the example, plot each one of them. Produce a plot of the response and discuss how the response differs as the forcing function is changed.

(a) The MATLAB® code is **force1.m.**

(b) The MATLAB® code is **force2.m.**

(c) The MATLAB® code is **force3.m.**

M **4.45.** In Example 4.8.1 add damping of $c = 0.2c_c$ and solve using computer program RUNGA. Compare response with Example 4.8.1.

M **4.46.** The forced Van der Pol oscillator is described by the following equation:

$$\ddot{x} - \mu\dot{x}(1 - x^2) + x = F(t)$$

(cf. Example 13.4.2). Determine the equivalent damping. Solve this equation numerically in MATLAB® with $F(t)$ given by the step function excitation and ramp excitation, for $\mu = 0.01, 0.1, 1$.

M **4.47.** Consider the problem of Example 3.8.1. Solve numerically for the transient response of the system under impulse excitation and ramp excitation (see Fig. 4.4.4). Determine numerically the response spectra.

M **4.48.** Consider the equation for the forced oscillation of a damped system with hardening spring given by

$$m\ddot{x} + c\dot{x} + kx + \mu x^3 = F(t)$$

(cf. Prob. 13.25). Solve this equation numerically in MATLAB® with $F(t)$ given by the step function excitation and ramp excitation, $m = 1, c = 0.5, k = 1$, and $\mu = 0.01, 0.1, 1$. Compare with the results obtained when $\mu = 0$.

CHAPTER 5

Multi-Degree-of-Freedom System Vibrations

When a system requires more than one coordinate to describe its motion, it is called a multi-DOF system, or an N-DOF system, where N is the number of coordinates required. Thus, a 2-DOF system requires two independent coordinates to describe its motion, and it is the simplest of the N-DOF systems.

The N-DOF system differs from that of the single-DOF system in that it has N natural frequencies, and for each of the natural frequencies, there corresponds a natural state of vibration with a displacement configuration known as the *normal mode*. Mathematical terms related to these quantities are known as *eigenvalues* and *eigenvectors*. They are established from the N simultaneous equations of motion of the system and possess certain dynamic properties associated with the system.

Normal mode vibrations are free undamped vibrations that depend only on the mass and stiffness of the system and how they are distributed. When vibrating at one of these normal modes, all points in the system undergo simple harmonic motion that passes through their equilibrium positions simultaneously. To initiate a normal mode vibration, the system must be given specific initial conditions corresponding to its normal mode. For the more general initial conditions, such as an impulsive blow, the resulting free vibration may contain all the normal modes simultaneously.

As in the single-DOF system, forced harmonic vibration of the N-DOF system takes place at the frequency of the excitation. When the excitation frequency coincides with one of the natural frequencies of the system, a condition of resonance is encountered, with large amplitudes limited only by the damping. Again, damping is generally omitted except when its concern is of importance in limiting the amplitude of vibration or in examining the rate of decay of the free oscillation.

In this chapter, we begin with the determination of the natural frequencies and normal modes of the 2-DOF system. All of the fundamental concepts of the multi-DOF system can be described in terms of the 2-DOF system without becoming burdened with the algebraic difficulties of the multi-DOF system. Numerical results are easily obtained for the 2-DOF system and they provide a simple introduction to the behavior of systems of higher DOF.

For systems of higher DOF, matrix methods are essential, and although they are not necessary for the 2-DOF system, we introduce them here as a preliminary to the material in the chapters to follow. They provide a compact notation and an organized procedure for their analysis and solution.

For systems of DOF higher than 2, computers are necessary. A few examples of systems of higher DOF are introduced near the end of the chapter to illustrate some of the computational difficulties.

5.1 THE NORMAL MODE ANALYSIS

We now describe the basic method of determining the normal modes of vibration for any system by means of specific examples. The method is applicable to all multi-DOF systems, although for systems of higher DOF, there are more efficient methods, which we will describe in later chapters.

Example 5.1.1 Translational System

Figure 5.1.1 shows an undamped 2-DOF system with specific parameters. With coordinates x_1 and x_2 measured from the initial reference, the free-body diagrams of the two masses lead to the differential equations of motion where all forces to the right are considered positive:

$$\begin{aligned} m\ddot{x}_1 &= -kx_1 + k(x_2 - x_1) \\ 2m\ddot{x}_2 &= -k(x_2 - x_1) - kx_2 \end{aligned} \tag{5.1.1}$$

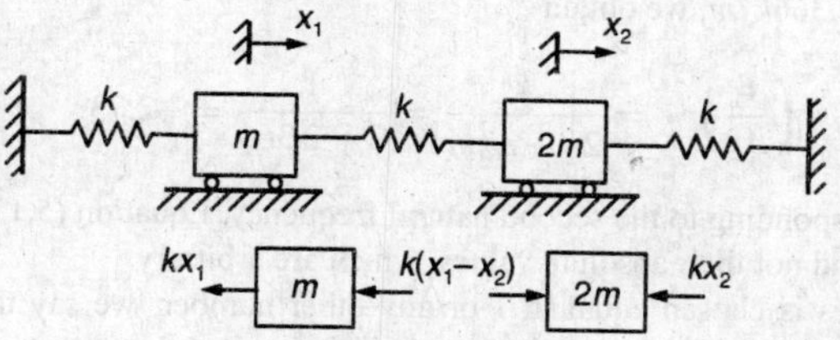

FIGURE 5.1.1.

For the normal mode of oscillation, each mass undergoes harmonic motion of the same frequency, passing through the equilibrium position simultaneously. For such motion, we can let

$$\begin{aligned} x_1 &= A_1 \sin \omega t \quad \text{or} \quad A_1 e^{i\omega t} \\ x_2 &= A_2 \sin \omega t \quad \text{or} \quad A_2 e^{i\omega t} \end{aligned} \tag{5.1.2}$$

Substituting these into the differential equations, we have

$$\begin{aligned} (2k - \omega^2 m)A_1 - kA_2 &= 0 \\ -kA_1 + (2k - 2\omega^2 m)A_2 &= 0 \end{aligned} \tag{5.1.3}$$

$$\begin{bmatrix} (2k - \omega^2 m) & -k \\ -k & (2k - 2\omega^2 m) \end{bmatrix} \begin{bmatrix} A_1 \\ A_2 \end{bmatrix} = \begin{bmatrix} 0 \\ 0 \end{bmatrix} \tag{5.1.4}$$

This equation is satisfied for any A_1 and A_2 if the determinant of the above equations is zero.

$$\begin{vmatrix} (2k - \omega^2 m) & -k \\ -k & (2k - 2\omega^2 m) \end{vmatrix} = 0 \tag{5.1.5}$$

Letting $\omega^2 = \lambda$ and multiplying out, the foregoing determinant results in a second-degree algebraic equation that is called the *characteristic equation.*

$$\lambda^2 - \left(3\frac{k}{m}\right)\lambda + \frac{3}{2}\left(\frac{k}{m}\right)^2 = 0 \tag{5.1.6}$$

The two roots λ_1 and λ_2 of this equation are the *eigenvalues* of the system:

$$\begin{aligned} \lambda_1 &= \left(\frac{3}{2} - \frac{1}{2}\sqrt{3}\right)\frac{k}{m} = 0.634\frac{k}{m} \\ \lambda_2 &= \left(\frac{3}{2} + \frac{1}{2}\sqrt{3}\right)\frac{k}{m} = 2.366\frac{k}{m} \end{aligned} \tag{5.1.7}$$

and the *natural frequencies* of the system are

$$\omega_1 = \lambda_1^{1/2} = \sqrt{0.634\frac{k}{m}}$$

$$\omega_2 = \lambda_2^{1/2} = \sqrt{2.366\frac{k}{m}}$$

From Eq. (5.1.3), two expressions for the ratio of the amplitudes are found:

$$\frac{A_1}{A_2} = \frac{k}{2k - \omega^2 m} = \frac{2k - 2\omega^2 m}{k} \tag{5.1.8}$$

Substitution of the natural frequencies in either of these equations leads to the ratio of the amplitudes. For $\omega_1^2 = 0.634k/m$, we obtain

$$\left(\frac{A_1}{A_2}\right)^{(1)} = \frac{k}{2k - \omega_1^2 m} = \frac{1}{2 - 0.634} = 0.731$$

which is the amplitude ratio corresponding to the first natural frequency.

Similarly, using $\omega_2^2 = 2.366k/m$, we obtain

$$\left(\frac{A_1}{A_2}\right)^{(2)} = \frac{k}{2k - \omega_2^2 m} = \frac{1}{2 - 2.366} = -2.73$$

for the amplitude ratio corresponding to the second natural frequency. Equation (5.1.8) enables us to find only the ratio of the amplitudes and not their absolute values, which are arbitrary.

If one of the amplitudes is chosen equal to 1 or any other number, we say that the amplitude ratio is *normalized* to that number. The normalized amplitude ratio is then called the *normal mode* and is designated by $\phi_i(x)$.

The two normal modes of this example, which we can now call *eigenvectors*, are

$$\phi_1(x) = \begin{Bmatrix} 0.731 \\ 1.00 \end{Bmatrix} \qquad \phi_2(x) = \begin{Bmatrix} -2.73 \\ 1.00 \end{Bmatrix}$$

Each normal mode oscillation can then be written as

$$\begin{Bmatrix} x_1 \\ x_2 \end{Bmatrix}^{(1)} = A_1 \begin{Bmatrix} 0.731 \\ 1.00 \end{Bmatrix} \sin(\omega_1 t + \psi_1)$$

$$\begin{Bmatrix} x_1 \\ x_2 \end{Bmatrix}^{(2)} = A_2 \begin{Bmatrix} -2.73 \\ 1.00 \end{Bmatrix} \sin(\omega_2 t + \psi_2)$$

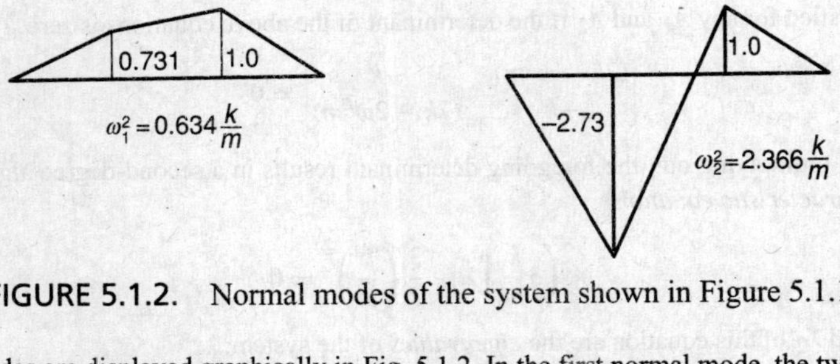

FIGURE 5.1.2. Normal modes of the system shown in Figure 5.1.1.

These normal modes are displayed graphically in Fig. 5.1.2. In the first normal mode, the two masses move in phase; in the second mode, the two masses move in opposition, or out of phase with each other. ■

Example 5.1.2 Rotational System

We now describe the rotational system shown in Fig. 5.1.3 with coordinates θ_1 and θ_2 measured from the inertial reference. From the free-body diagram of two disks, the torque equations are

$$\begin{aligned} J_1\ddot{\theta}_1 &= -K_1\theta_1 + K_2(\theta_2 - \theta_1) \\ J_2\ddot{\theta}_2 &= -K_2(\theta_2 - \theta_1) - K_3\theta_2 \end{aligned} \tag{5.1.9}$$

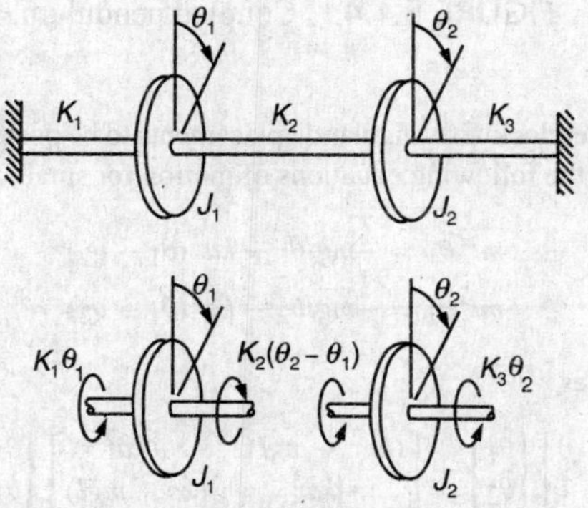

FIGURE 5.1.3.

It should be noted that Eqs. (5.1.9) are similar in form to those of Eqs. (5.1.1) and only the symbols are different. The rotational moment of inertia J now replaces the mass m, and instead of the translational stiffness k, we have the rotational stiffness K.

At this point, we introduce the matrix notation, writing Eqs. (5.1.9) in the concise form:

$$\begin{bmatrix} J_1 & 0 \\ 0 & J_2 \end{bmatrix} \begin{Bmatrix} \ddot{\theta}_1 \\ \ddot{\theta}_2 \end{Bmatrix} + \begin{bmatrix} (K_1 + K_2) & -K_2 \\ -K_2 & (K_2 + K_3) \end{bmatrix} \begin{Bmatrix} \theta_1 \\ \theta_2 \end{Bmatrix} = \begin{Bmatrix} 0 \\ 0 \end{Bmatrix} \tag{5.1.10}$$

By following the rules for matrix operations in Appendix C, the equivalence of the two equations can be easily shown.

The matrix

$$\begin{bmatrix} J_1 & 0 \\ 0 & J_2 \end{bmatrix}$$

is known as the mass matrix and the matrix

$$\begin{bmatrix} (K_1 + K_2) & -K_2 \\ -K_2 & (K_2 + K_3) \end{bmatrix}$$

is known as the stiffness matrix. Both of these matrices will be discussed in detail in Chapter 11.

A few points of interest should be noted. The stiffness matrix is symmetric about the diagonal and the mass matrix is diagonal. Thus, the square matrices are equal to their transpose, i.e., $[k]^T = [k]$, and $[m]^T = [m]$. In addition, for the discrete mass system with coordinates chosen at each mass, the mass matrix is diagonal and its inverse is simply the inverse of each diagonal element, i.e., $[m]^{-1} = [1/m]$.

■

Example 5.1.3 Coupled Pendulum

In Fig. 5.1.4 the two pendulums are coupled by means of a weak spring k, which is unstrained when the two pendulum rods are in the vertical position. Determine the normal mode vibrations.

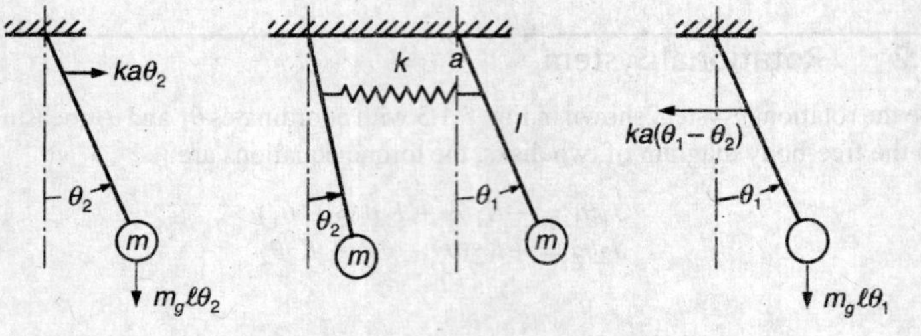

FIGURE 5.1.4. Coupled pendulum.

Solution Assuming the counterclockwise angular displacements to be positive and taking moments about the points of suspension, we obtain the following equations of motion for small oscillations

$$ml^2\ddot{\theta}_1 = -mgl\theta_1 - ka^2(\theta_1 - \theta_2)$$
$$ml^2\ddot{\theta}_2 = -mgl\theta_2 - ka^2(\theta_1 - \theta_2)$$

which in matrix notation becomes

$$ml^2\begin{bmatrix}1 & 0\\ 0 & 1\end{bmatrix}\begin{Bmatrix}\ddot{\theta}_1\\ \ddot{\theta}_2\end{Bmatrix} + \begin{bmatrix}(ka^2+mgl) & -ka^2\\ -ka^2 & (ka+mgl)\end{bmatrix}\begin{Bmatrix}\theta_1\\ \theta_2\end{Bmatrix} = \begin{Bmatrix}0\\ 0\end{Bmatrix} \tag{5.1.11}$$

Assuming the normal mode solutions as

$$\theta_1 = A_1\cos\omega t \quad \text{or} \quad A_1e^{i\omega t}$$
$$\theta_2 = A_2\cos\omega t \quad \text{or} \quad A_2e^{i\omega t}$$

the natural frequencies and mode shapes are

$$\omega_1 = \sqrt{\frac{g}{l}} \qquad \omega_2 = \sqrt{\frac{g}{l} + 2\frac{k}{m}\frac{a^2}{l^2}}$$

$$\left(\frac{A_1}{A_2}\right)^{(1)} = 1.0 \quad \left(\frac{A_1}{A_2}\right)^{(2)} = -1.0$$

Thus, in the first mode, the two pendulums move in phase and the spring remains unstretched. In the second mode, the two pendulums move in opposition and the coupling spring is actively involved with a node at its midpoint. Consequently, the natural frequency is higher.

■

5.2 INITIAL CONDITIONS

When the normal mode frequencies and mode shapes are known, it is possible to determine the free vibration of the system for any initial conditions by the proper summation of the normal modes. For example, we have found the normal modes of the system of Fig. (5.1.1) to be

$$\omega_1 = \sqrt{0.654k/m} \quad \phi_1 = \begin{Bmatrix}0.732\\ 1.000\end{Bmatrix}$$

$$\omega_2 = \sqrt{2.366k/m} \quad \phi_2 = \begin{Bmatrix}-2.732\\ 1.000\end{Bmatrix}$$

For free vibration to take place in one of the normal modes for any initial conditions, the equation of motion for mode i must be of the form

$$\begin{Bmatrix} x_1 \\ x_2 \end{Bmatrix}^{(i)} = c_i \phi_i \sin(\omega_i t + \psi_i) \quad i = 1, 2 \tag{5.2.1}$$

The constants c_i and ψ_i are necessary to satisfy the initial conditions, and ϕ_i ensures that the amplitude ratio for the free vibration is proportional to that of mode i.

For initial conditions in general, the free vibration contains both modes simultaneously and the equations of motion are of the form

$$\begin{Bmatrix} x_1 \\ x_2 \end{Bmatrix} = c_1 \begin{Bmatrix} 0.732 \\ 1.000 \end{Bmatrix} \sin(\omega_1 t + \psi_1) + c_2 \begin{Bmatrix} -2.732 \\ 1.000 \end{Bmatrix} \sin(\omega_2 t + \psi_2) \tag{5.2.2}$$

where c_1, c_2, ψ_1 and ψ_2 are the four necessary constants for the two differential equations of second order. Constants c_1 and c_2 establish the amount of each mode, and phases ψ_1 and ψ_2 allow the freedom of time origin for each mode. To solve for the four arbitrary constants, we need two more equations, which are available by differentiating Eq. (5.2.2) for the velocity:

$$\begin{Bmatrix} \dot{x}_1 \\ \dot{x}_2 \end{Bmatrix} = \omega_1 c_1 \begin{Bmatrix} 0.732 \\ 1.000 \end{Bmatrix} \cos(\omega_1 t + \psi_1) + \omega_2 c_2 \begin{Bmatrix} -2.732 \\ 1.000 \end{Bmatrix} \cos(\omega_2 t + \psi_2) \tag{5.2.3}$$

By letting $t = 0$ and specifying the initial conditions, the four constants can be found.

Example 5.2.1

Determine the free vibration for the system of Fig. 5.1.1 for the initial conditions

$$\begin{Bmatrix} x_1(0) \\ x_2(0) \end{Bmatrix} = \begin{Bmatrix} 2.0 \\ 4.0 \end{Bmatrix} \quad \text{and} \quad \begin{Bmatrix} \dot{x}_1(0) \\ \dot{x}_2(0) \end{Bmatrix} = \begin{Bmatrix} 0 \\ 0 \end{Bmatrix}$$

Substituting these initial conditions into Eqs. (5.2.2) and (5.2.3), we have

$$\begin{Bmatrix} 2.0 \\ 4.0 \end{Bmatrix} = c_1 \begin{Bmatrix} 0.732 \\ 1.000 \end{Bmatrix} \sin\psi_1 + c_2 \begin{Bmatrix} -2.732 \\ 1.000 \end{Bmatrix} \sin\psi_2 \tag{5.2.2a}$$

$$\begin{Bmatrix} 0 \\ 0 \end{Bmatrix} = \omega_1 c_1 \begin{Bmatrix} 0.732 \\ 1.000 \end{Bmatrix} \cos\psi_1 + \omega_2 c_2 \begin{Bmatrix} -2.732 \\ 1.000 \end{Bmatrix} \cos\psi_2 \tag{5.2.3a}$$

To determine $c_1 \sin\psi_1$, we can multiply the second equation of Eq. (5.2.2a) by 2.732 and add the results to the first equation. To determine $c_2 \sin\psi_2$ multiply the second equation of Eq. (5.2.2a) by -0.732 and add the results to the first equation. In similar manner we can solve for $\omega_1 c_1 \cos\psi_1$ and $\omega_2 c_2 \cos\psi_2$ to arrive at the following four results:

$$12.928 = 3.464 c_1 \sin\psi_1$$

$$-0.928 = -3.464 c_2 \sin\psi_2$$

$$0 = 3.464 \omega_1 c_1 \cos\psi_1$$

$$0 = -3.464 \omega_2 c_2 \cos\psi_2$$

From the last two of the foregoing equations, it is seen that $\cos\psi_1 = \cos\psi_2 = 0$, or $\psi_1 = \psi_2 = 90°$. Constants c_1 and c_2 are then found from the first two of the foregoing equations:

$$c_1 = 3.732$$

$$c_2 = 0.268$$

and the equations for the free vibration of the system for the initial conditions stated for the example become

$$\begin{Bmatrix} x_1 \\ x_2 \end{Bmatrix} = 3.732 \begin{Bmatrix} 0.732 \\ 1.000 \end{Bmatrix} \cos\omega_1 t + 0.268 \begin{Bmatrix} -2.732 \\ 1.000 \end{Bmatrix} \cos\omega_2 t$$

$$= \begin{Bmatrix} 2.732 \\ 3.732 \end{Bmatrix} \cos\omega_1 t + \begin{Bmatrix} -0.732 \\ 0.268 \end{Bmatrix} \cos\omega_2 t$$

which clearly shows that the free vibration under the initial condition is the sum of the normal modes of the system.

These equations show that for the given initial conditions, most of the response is due to the first mode ϕ_1. This is to be expected because the ratio of the initial displacements

$$\begin{Bmatrix} 2 \\ 4 \end{Bmatrix} = \begin{Bmatrix} 0.50 \\ 1.00 \end{Bmatrix}$$

is somewhat close to that of the first normal mode and quite different from that of the second normal mode.

Example 5.2.2 Beating

If the coupled pendulum of Example 5.1.3 is set into motion with initial conditions differing from those of the normal modes, the oscillations will contain both normal modes simultaneously. For example, if the initial conditions are $\theta_1(0) = A, \theta_2(0) = 0$, and $\dot\theta_1(0) = \dot\theta_2(0) = 0$, the equations of motion will be

$$\theta_1(t) = \frac{1}{2}A\cos\omega_1 t + \frac{1}{2}A\cos\omega_2 t$$

$$\theta_2(t) = \frac{1}{2}A\cos\omega_1 t + \frac{1}{2}A\cos\omega_2 t$$

Consider the case in which the coupling spring is very weak, and show that a beating phenomenon takes place between the two pendulums.

Solution The preceding equations can be rewritten as follows:

$$\theta_1(t) = A\cos\left(\frac{\omega_1 - \omega_2}{2}\right)t\cos\left(\frac{\omega_1 + \omega_2}{2}\right)t$$

$$\theta_2(t) = -A\sin\left(\frac{\omega_1 - \omega_2}{2}\right)t\sin\left(\frac{\omega_1 + \omega_2}{2}\right)t$$

Because $(\omega_1 - \omega_2)$ is very small, $\theta_1(t)$ and $\theta_2(t)$ will behave like $\cos(\omega_1 + \omega_2)t/2$ and $\sin(\omega_1 + \omega_2)t/2$ with slowly varying amplitudes, as shown in Fig. 5.2.1. Since the system is conservative, energy is transferred from one pendulum to the other.

The beating sound, which is often audible, is that of the peak amplitudes, which repeat in π radians. Thus,

$$\left(\frac{\omega_1 - \omega_2}{2}\right)\tau_b = \pi \quad \text{or} \quad \tau_b = \frac{2\pi}{\omega_1 - \omega_2}$$

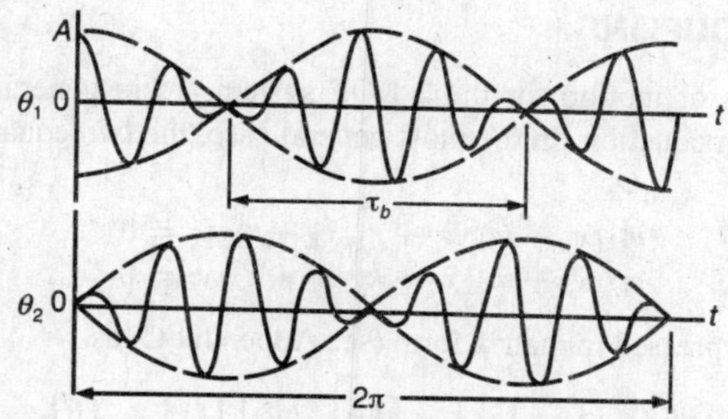

FIGURE 5.2.1. Exchange of energy between pendulums.

The beat frequency is then given by the equation

$$\omega_b = \frac{2\pi}{\tau_b} = \omega_1 - \omega_2$$

A simple demonstration model is shown in Fig. 5.2.2.

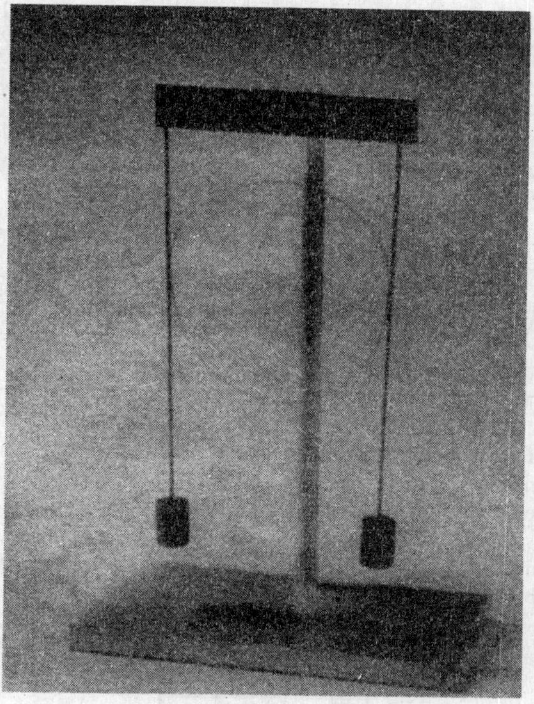

FIGURE 5.2.2. Demonstration model for exchange of energy by beating. (*Courtesy of UCSB Mechanical Engineering Undergraduate Laboratory.*)

■

5.3 COORDINATE COUPLING

The differential equations of motion for the 2-DOF system are in general *coupled*, in that both coordinates appear in each equation. In the most general case, the two equations for the undamped system have the form

$$\begin{aligned} m_{11}\ddot{x}_1 + m_{12}\ddot{x}_2 + k_{11}x_1 + k_{12}x_2 &= 0 \\ m_{21}\ddot{x}_1 + m_{22}\ddot{x}_2 + k_{21}x_1 + k_{22}x_2 &= 0 \end{aligned} \tag{5.3.1}$$

These equations can be expressed in matrix form (see Appendix C) as

$$\begin{bmatrix} m_{11} & m_{12} \\ m_{21} & m_{22} \end{bmatrix} \begin{Bmatrix} \ddot{x}_1 \\ \ddot{x}_2 \end{Bmatrix} + \begin{bmatrix} k_{11} & k_{12} \\ k_{21} & k_{22} \end{bmatrix} \begin{Bmatrix} x_1 \\ x_2 \end{Bmatrix} = \begin{Bmatrix} 0 \\ 0 \end{Bmatrix} \tag{5.3.2}$$

which immediately reveals the type of coupling present. Mass or *dynamical coupling* exists if the mass matrix is nondiagonal, whereas stiffness or *static coupling* exists if the stiffness matrix is nondiagonal.

It is also possible to establish the type of coupling from the expressions for the kinetic and potential energies. Cross products of coordinates in either expression denote coupling, dynamic or static, depending on whether they are found in T or U. The choice of coordinates establishes the type of coupling, and both dynamic and static coupling may be present.

It is possible to find a coordinate system that has neither form of coupling. The two equations are then decoupled and each equation can be solved independently of the other. Such coordinates are called *principal coordinates* (also called *normal coordinates*).

Although it is always possible to decouple the equations of motion for the undamped system, this is not always the case for a damped system. The following matrix equations show a system that has zero dynamic and static coupling, but the coordinates are coupled by the damping matrix.

$$\begin{bmatrix} m_{11} & 0 \\ 0 & m_{22} \end{bmatrix} \begin{Bmatrix} \ddot{x}_1 \\ \ddot{x}_2 \end{Bmatrix} + \begin{bmatrix} c_{11} & c_{12} \\ c_{21} & c_{22} \end{bmatrix} \begin{Bmatrix} \dot{x}_1 \\ \dot{x}_2 \end{Bmatrix} + \begin{bmatrix} k_{11} & 0 \\ 0 & k_{22} \end{bmatrix} \begin{Bmatrix} x_1 \\ x_2 \end{Bmatrix} = \begin{Bmatrix} 0 \\ 0 \end{Bmatrix} \tag{5.3.3}$$

If in the foregoing equation, $c_{12} = c_{21} = 0$, then the damping is said to be *proportional* (to the stiffness or mass matrix), and the system equations become uncoupled.

Example 5.3.1

Figure 5.3.1 shows a rigid bar with its center of mass not coinciding with its geometric center, i.e., $l_1 \neq l_2$, and supported by two springs, k_1 and k_2. It represents a 2-DOF system, because two coordinates are necessary to describe its motion. The choice of the coordinates will define the type of coupling that can be immediately determined from the mass and stiffness matrices. Mass or *dynamical coupling* exists if the mass matrix is nondiagonal, whereas stiffness or *static coupling* exists if the stiffness matrix is nondiagonal. It is also possible to have both forms of coupling.

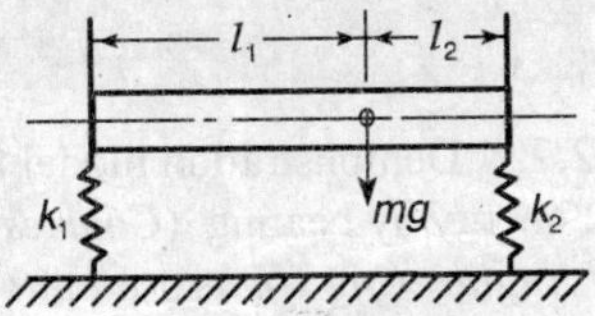

FIGURE 5.3.1.

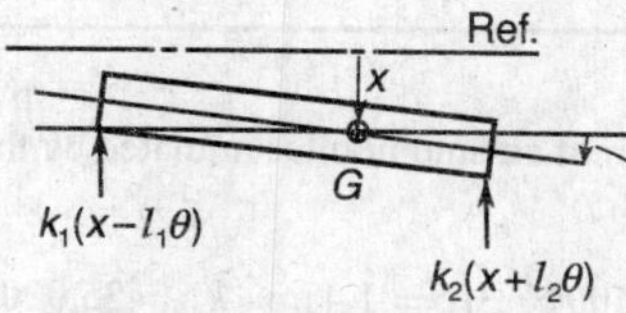

FIGURE 5.3.2. Coordinates leading to static coupling.

Static coupling. Choosing coordinates x and θ, shown in Fig. 5.3.2, where x is the linear displacement of the center of mass, the system will have static coupling, as shown by the matrix equation

$$\begin{bmatrix} m & 0 \\ 0 & J \end{bmatrix} \begin{Bmatrix} \ddot{x} \\ \ddot{\theta} \end{Bmatrix} + \begin{bmatrix} (k_1+k_2) & (k_2l_2-k_1l_1) \\ (k_2l_2-k_1l_1) & (k_1l_1^2+k_2l_2^2) \end{bmatrix} \begin{Bmatrix} x \\ \theta \end{Bmatrix} = \begin{Bmatrix} 0 \\ 0 \end{Bmatrix}$$

If $k_1l_1 = k_2l_2$, the coupling disappears, and we obtain uncoupled x and θ vibrations.

Dynamic coupling. There is some point C along the bar where a force applied normal to the bar produces pure translation; i.e., $k_1l_3 = k_2l_4$ (see Fig. 5.3.3). The equations of motion in terms of x_c and θ can be shown to be

$$\begin{bmatrix} m & me \\ me & J_c \end{bmatrix} \begin{Bmatrix} \ddot{x}_c \\ \ddot{\theta} \end{Bmatrix} + \begin{bmatrix} (k_1+k_2) & 0 \\ 0 & (k_1l_3^2+k_2l_4^2) \end{bmatrix} \begin{Bmatrix} x_c \\ \theta \end{Bmatrix} = \begin{Bmatrix} 0 \\ 0 \end{Bmatrix}$$

which shows that the coordinates chosen eliminated the static coupling and introduced dynamic coupling.

Static and dynamic coupling. If we choose $x = x_1$ at the end of the bar, as shown in Fig. 5.3.4, the equations of motion become

$$\begin{bmatrix} m & ml_1 \\ ml_1 & J_1 \end{bmatrix} \begin{Bmatrix} \ddot{x}_1 \\ \ddot{\theta} \end{Bmatrix} + \begin{bmatrix} (k_1+k_2) & k_2l \\ k_2l & k_2l^2 \end{bmatrix} \begin{Bmatrix} x_1 \\ \theta \end{Bmatrix} = \begin{Bmatrix} 0 \\ 0 \end{Bmatrix}$$

and both static and dynamic coupling are now present.

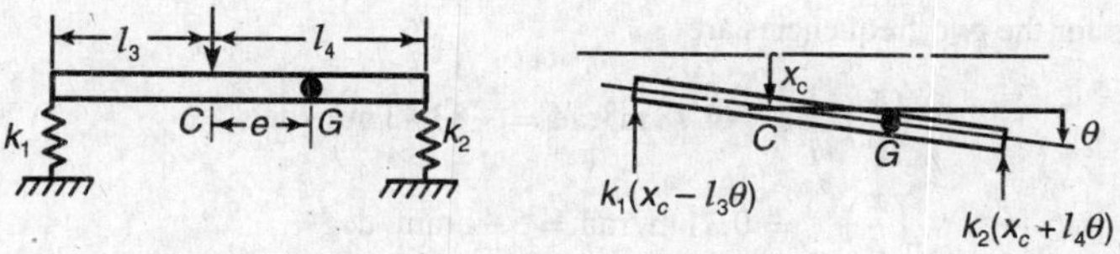

FIGURE 5.3.3. Coordinates leading to dynamic coupling.

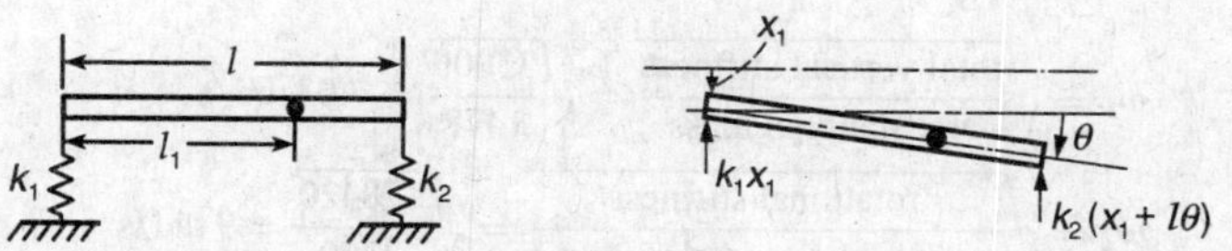

FIGURE 5.3.4. Coordinates leading to static and dynamic coupling.

Example 5.3.2

Determine the normal modes of vibration of an automobile simulated by the simplified 2-DOF system with the following numerical values (see Fig. 5.3.5):

$$W = 14{,}500\,\text{N} \quad l_1 = 1.4\,\text{m} \quad k_1 = 35{,}000\,\text{N/m}$$
$$J_c = \frac{W}{g} r^2 \quad l_2 = 1.7\,\text{m} \quad k_2 = 38{,}000\,\text{N/m}$$
$$r = 1.22\,\text{m} \quad l = 3.1\,\text{m}$$

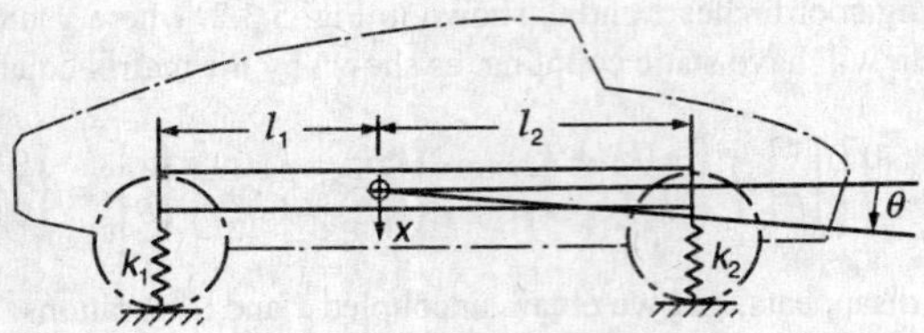

FIGURE 5.3.5.

The equations of motion indicate static coupling.

$$m\ddot{x} + k_1(x - l_1\theta) + k_2(x + l_2\theta) = 0$$

$$J_c\ddot{\theta} - k_1(x - l_1\theta)l_1 + k_2(x + l_2\theta)l_2 = 0$$

Assuming harmonic motion, we have

$$\begin{bmatrix} (k_1 + k_2 - \omega^2 m) & -(k_1 l_1 - k_2 l_2) \\ -(k_1 l_1 - k_2 l_2) & (k_1 l_1^2 + k_2 l_2^2 - \omega^2 J_c) \end{bmatrix} \begin{Bmatrix} x \\ \theta \end{Bmatrix} = \begin{Bmatrix} 0 \\ 0 \end{Bmatrix}$$

From the determinant of the matrix equation, the two natural frequencies are

$$\omega_1 = 6.87\,\text{rad/s} = 1.09\,\text{cps}$$

$$\omega_2 = 9.13\,\text{rad/s} = 1.45\,\text{cps}$$

The amplitude ratios for the two frequencies are

$$\left(\frac{x}{\theta}\right)_{\omega_1} = -4.78\,\text{m/rad} = -83.43\,\text{mm/deg}$$

$$\left(\frac{x}{\theta}\right)_{\omega_2} = 0.31\,\text{m/rad} = 5.41\,\text{mm/deg}$$

The mode shapes are illustrated by the diagrams of Fig. 5.3.6.

In interpreting these results, the first mode, $\omega_1 = 6.87$ rad/s is largely vertical translation with very small rotation, whereas the second mode, $\omega_2 = 9.13$ rad/s is mostly rotation. This suggests that we could have made a rough approximation for these modes as two 1-DOF systems.

$$\omega_1 \cong \sqrt{\frac{\text{total vertical stiffness}}{\text{translational mass}}} = \sqrt{\frac{73000}{1478}} = 7.03\,\text{rad/s}$$

$$\omega_2 \cong \sqrt{\frac{\text{rotational stiffness}}{\text{rotational moment of inertia}}} = \sqrt{\frac{178420}{2200}} = 9\,\text{rad/s}$$

Note that these uncoupled values are inside of the coupled natural frequencies by small amounts, as shown in Fig. 5.3.7.

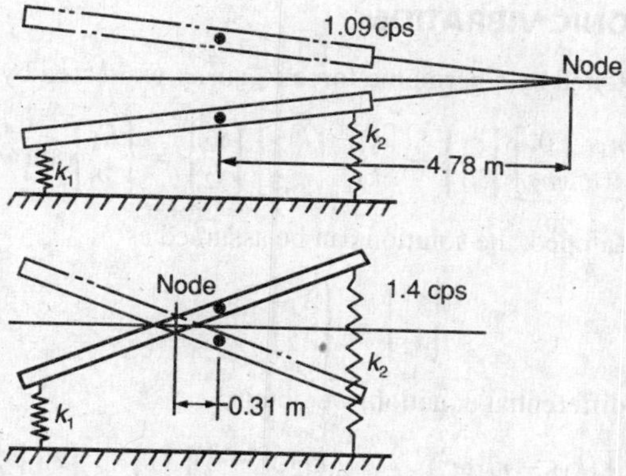

FIGURE 5.3.6. Normal modes of the system shown in Fig. 5.3.5.

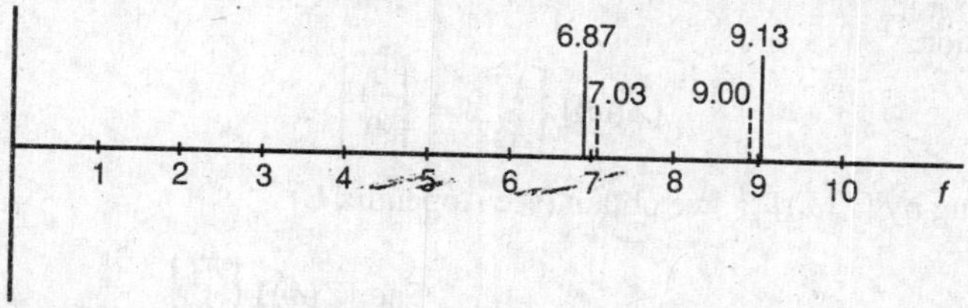

FIGURE 5.3.7. Uncoupled frequencies relative to coupled frequencies.

FIGURE 5.3.8. Two-DOF model of an automobile. The auto body is represented by the meter stick with adjustable weights. The model is inverted with the springs and ground above the body. Shakers can be excited individually to simulate the ground. (*Courtesy of UCSB Mechanical Engineering Undergraduate Laboratory.*)

One other observation is worth mentioning. For the simplified model used, the wheels and tires had been omitted. This justification is assigned in Prob. 5.27 with data as to weights of wheels and stiffness of tires.

Figure 5.3.8 shows an inverted laboratory model of the automobile.

■

5.4 FORCED HARMONIC VIBRATION

Consider here a system excited by a harmonic force $F_1 \sin \omega t$ expressed by the matrix equation

$$\begin{bmatrix} m_1 & 0 \\ 0 & m_2 \end{bmatrix} \begin{Bmatrix} \ddot{x}_1 \\ \ddot{x}_2 \end{Bmatrix} + \begin{bmatrix} k_{11} & k_{12} \\ k_{21} & k_{22} \end{bmatrix} \begin{Bmatrix} x_2 \\ x_2 \end{Bmatrix} = \begin{Bmatrix} F_1 \\ 0 \end{Bmatrix} \sin \omega t \tag{5.4.1}$$

Because the system is undamped, the solution can be assumed as

$$\begin{Bmatrix} x_1 \\ x_2 \end{Bmatrix} = \begin{Bmatrix} X_1 \\ X_2 \end{Bmatrix} \sin \omega t$$

Substituting this into the differential equation, we obtain

$$\begin{bmatrix} (k_{11} - m_1\omega^2) & k_{12} \\ k_{21} & (k_{22} - m_2\omega^2) \end{bmatrix} \begin{Bmatrix} X_1 \\ X_2 \end{Bmatrix} = \begin{Bmatrix} F_1 \\ 0 \end{Bmatrix} \tag{5.4.2}$$

or, in simpler notation,

$$[Z(\omega)] \begin{Bmatrix} X_1 \\ X_2 \end{Bmatrix} = \begin{Bmatrix} F_1 \\ 0 \end{Bmatrix}$$

Premultiplying by $[Z(\omega)]^{-1}$, we obtain (see Appendix C)

$$\begin{Bmatrix} X_1 \\ X_2 \end{Bmatrix} = [Z(\omega)]^{-1} \begin{Bmatrix} F_1 \\ 0 \end{Bmatrix} = \frac{\operatorname{adj}[Z(\omega)] \begin{Bmatrix} F_1 \\ 0 \end{Bmatrix}}{|Z(\omega)|} \tag{5.4.3}$$

By referring to Eq. (5.4.2), the determinant $|Z(\omega)|$ can be expressed as

$$|Z(\omega)| = m_1 m_2 (\omega_1^2 - \omega^2)(\omega_2^2 - \omega^2) \tag{5.4.4}$$

where ω_1 and ω_2 are the normal mode frequencies. Thus, Eq. (5.4.3) becomes

$$\begin{Bmatrix} X_1 \\ X_2 \end{Bmatrix} = \frac{1}{|Z(\omega)|} \begin{bmatrix} (k_{22} - m_2\omega^2) & -k_{12} \\ -k_{21} & (k_{11} - m_1\omega^2) \end{bmatrix} \begin{Bmatrix} F_1 \\ 0 \end{Bmatrix} \tag{5.4.5}$$

and the amplitudes of the force vibration are

$$X_1 = \frac{(k_{22} - m_2\omega^2)F_1}{m_1 m_2 (\omega_1^2 - \omega^2)(\omega_2^2 - \omega^2)}$$
$$X_2 = \frac{-k_{21}F_1}{m_1 m_2 (\omega_1^2 - \omega^2)(\omega_2^2 - \omega^2)} \tag{5.4.6}$$

Example 5.4.1

Apply Eqs. (5.4.6) to the system shown in Fig. 5.4.1 when m_1 is excited by the force $F_1 \sin \omega t$. Plot its frequency response curve.

Solution The equation of motion for the system is

$$\begin{bmatrix} m & 0 \\ 0 & m \end{bmatrix} \begin{Bmatrix} \ddot{x}_1 \\ \ddot{x}_2 \end{Bmatrix} + \begin{bmatrix} 2k & -k \\ -k & 2k \end{bmatrix} \begin{Bmatrix} x_1 \\ x_2 \end{Bmatrix} = \begin{Bmatrix} F_1 \\ 0 \end{Bmatrix} \sin \omega t$$

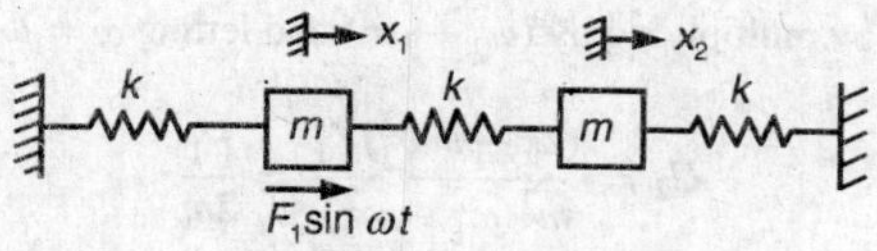

FIGURE 5.4.1. Forced vibration of a 2-DOF system.

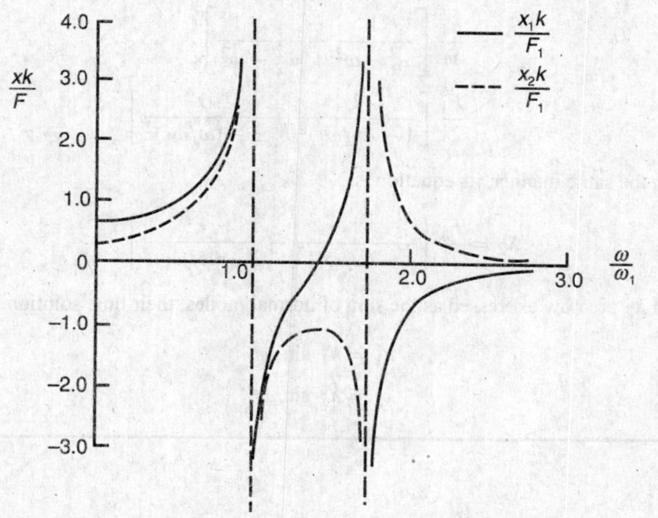

FIGURE 5.4.2. Forced response of a 2-DOF system.

Thus, we have $k_{11} = k_{22} = 2k$ and $k_{12} = k_{21} = -k$. Equations (5.4.6) then become

$$X_1 = \frac{(2k - m\omega^2)F_1}{m^2(\omega_1^2 - \omega^2)(\omega_2^2 - \omega^2)}$$

$$X_2 = \frac{kF_1}{m^2(\omega_1^2 - \omega^2)(\omega_2^2 - \omega^2)}$$

where $\omega_1^2 = k/m$ and $\omega_2^2 = 3k/m$ are obtained from the determinant of the matrix equation. When plotted, these results appear as in Fig. 5.4.2.

■

Example 5.4.2 Forced Vibration in Terms of Normal Mode Summation

Express the equations for X_1 and X_2 in Example 5.4.1 as the sum of the normal modes.

Solution Consider X_1 and expand the equation in terms of partial fractions.

$$\frac{(2k - m\omega^2)F_1}{m^2(\omega_1^2 - \omega^2)(\omega_2^2 - \omega^2)} = \frac{C_1}{\omega_1^2 - \omega^2} + \frac{C_2}{\omega_2^2 - \omega^2}$$

To solve for C_1, multiply by $(\omega_1^2 - \omega^2)$ and let $\omega = \omega_1$:

$$C_1 = \frac{(2k - m\omega_1^2)F_1}{m^2(\omega_2^2 - \omega_1^2)} = \frac{F_1}{2m}$$

Similarly, C_2 is evaluated by multiplying by $(\omega_2^2 - \omega^2)$ and letting $\omega = \omega_2$:

$$C_2 = \frac{(2k - m\omega_2^2)F_1}{m^2(\omega_1^2 - \omega_2^2)} = \frac{F_1}{2m}$$

An alternative form of X_1 is then

$$X_1 = \frac{F_1}{m}\left[\frac{1}{\omega_1^2 - \omega^2} + \frac{1}{\omega_2^2 - \omega^2}\right]$$

$$= \frac{F_1}{2k}\left[\frac{1}{1 - (\omega/\omega_1)^2} + \frac{1}{3 - (\omega/\omega_1)^2}\right]$$

Treating X_2 in the same manner, its equation is

$$X_2 = \frac{F_1}{2k}\left[\frac{1}{1 - (\omega/\omega_1)^2} - \frac{1}{3 - (\omega/\omega_1)^2}\right]$$

Amplitudes X_1 and X_2 are now expressed as the sum of normal modes, their time solution being

$$x_1 = X_1 \sin \omega t$$

$$x_2 = X_2 \sin \omega t$$

■

5.5 ORTHOGONALITY OF EIGENVECTORS

The normal modes, or the eigenvectors of the system, can be shown to be orthogonal with respect to the mass and stiffness matrices. By using the notation ϕ_i for the ith eigenvector, the normal mode equation for the ith mode is

$$K\phi_i = \lambda_i M\phi_i \tag{5.5.1}$$

Premultiplying the ith equation by the transpose ϕ_j^T, of mode j, we obtain

$$\phi_j^T K\phi_i = \lambda_i \phi_j^T M\phi_i \tag{5.5.2}$$

If next we start with the equation for the jth mode and premultiplying by ϕ_i^T, we obtain a similar equation with i and j interchanged:

$$\phi_i^T K\phi_j = \lambda_j \phi_i^T M\phi_j \tag{5.5.3}$$

Because K and M are symmetric matrices, the following relationships hold.

$$\phi_j^T \begin{bmatrix} K \\ \text{or} \\ M \end{bmatrix} \phi_i = \phi_i^T \begin{bmatrix} K \\ \text{or} \\ M \end{bmatrix} \phi_j \tag{5.5.4}$$

Thus, subtracting Eq. (5.5.3) from Eq. (5.5.2), we obtain

$$(\lambda_i - \lambda_j)\phi_i^T M\phi_j = 0 \tag{5.5.5}$$

If $\lambda_i \neq \lambda_j$ the foregoing equation requires that

$$\phi_i^T M\phi_j = 0 \quad i \neq j \tag{5.5.6}$$

It is also evident from Eq. (5.5.2) or Eq. (5.5.3) that as a consequence of Eq. (5.5.6),

$$\phi_i^T K \phi_j = 0 \quad i \neq j \tag{5.5.7}$$

Equations (5.5.6) and (5.5.7) define the orthogonal character of the normal modes.

Finally, if $i = j$, $(\lambda_i - \lambda_j) = 0$ and Eq. (5.5.5) is satisfied for any finite value of the products given by Eq. (5.5.5) or (5.5.6). We therefore have

$$\begin{aligned} \phi_i^T M \phi_i &= M_{ii} \\ \phi_i^T K \phi_i &= K_{ii} \end{aligned} \tag{5.5.8}$$

The quantities M_{ii} and K_{ii} are called the *generalized mass* and the *generalized stiffness*, respectively. We will have many occasions to refer to the generalized mass and generalized stiffness later.

Expansion Theorem. Consider the problem of initiating the free vibration of a system with a specified arbitrary displacement. As previously stated, free vibrations are the superposition of normal modes, which is referred to as the Expansion Theorem. We now wish to determine how much of each mode will be present in the free vibration.

We will express first the arbitrary displacement at time zero by the equation:

$$X(0) = c_1\phi_1 + c_2\phi_2 + c_3\phi_3 + \cdots + c_i\phi_i + \cdots$$

where ϕ_i are the normal modes and c_i are the coefficients indicating how much of each mode is present. Premultiplying the above equation by $\phi_i^T M$ and taking note of the orthogonal property of ϕ_i, we obtain

$$\phi_i^T MX(0) = 0 + 0 + 0 + \cdots + c_i\phi_i^T M\phi_i + 0 + \cdots$$

The coefficient c_i of any mode is then found as

$$c_i = \frac{\phi_i^T MX(0)}{\phi_i^T M\phi_i}$$

Orthonormal modes. If each of the normal modes ϕ_i is divided by the square root of the generalized mass M_{ii}, it is evident from the first equation of Eq. (5.5.8) that the right side of the foregoing equation will be unity. The new normal mode is then called the *weighted normal mode* or the *orthonormal mode* and designated as $\tilde{\phi}_i$. It is also evident from Eq. (5.5.1) that the right side of the second equation of Eq. (5.5.8) becomes equal to the eigenvalue λ_i. Thus, in place of Eq. (5.5.8), the orthogonality in terms of the orthonormal modes becomes

$$\begin{aligned} \tilde{\phi}_i^T M \tilde{\phi}_i &= 1 \\ \tilde{\phi}_i^T K \tilde{\phi}_i &= \lambda_i \end{aligned} \tag{5.5.9}$$

5.6 MODAL MATRIX *P*

When the N normal modes (or eigenvectors) are assembled into a square matrix with each normal mode represented by a column, we call it the *modal matrix P*. Thus, the modal matrix for a 3-DOF system can appear as

$$P = \left[\begin{Bmatrix} x_1 \\ x_2 \\ x_3 \end{Bmatrix}^{(1)} \begin{Bmatrix} x_1 \\ x_2 \\ x_3 \end{Bmatrix}^{(2)} \begin{Bmatrix} x_1 \\ x_2 \\ x_3 \end{Bmatrix}^{(3)} \right] = [\phi_1\ \phi_2\ \phi_3] \tag{5.6.1}$$

The modal matrix makes it possible to include all of the orthogonality relations of Sec. 5.5 into one equation. For this operation, we need also the transpose of P, which is

$$P^T = \begin{bmatrix} (x_1 x_2 x_3)^{(1)} \\ (x_1 x_2 x_3)^{(2)} \\ (x_1 x_2 x_3)^{(3)} \end{bmatrix} = [\phi_1 \; \phi_2 \; \phi_3]^T \tag{5.6.2}$$

with each new row corresponding to a mode. If we now form the product $P^T MP$ or $P^T KP$, the result will be a diagonal matrix, because the off-diagonal terms simply express the orthogonality relations, which are zero.

For example, consider a 3-DOF system. Performing the indicated operation with the modal matrix, we have

$$\begin{aligned} P^T MP &= [\phi_1 \; \phi_2 \; \phi_3]^T [M][\phi_1 \; \phi_2 \; \phi_3] \\ &= \begin{bmatrix} \phi_1^T M\phi_1 & \phi_1^T M\phi_2 & \phi_1^T M\phi_3 \\ \phi_2^T M\phi_1 & \phi_2^T M\phi_2 & \phi_2^T M\phi_3 \\ \phi_3^T M\phi_1 & \phi_3^T M\phi_2 & \phi_3^T M\phi_3 \end{bmatrix} = \begin{bmatrix} M_{11} & 0 & 0 \\ 0 & M_{22} & 0 \\ 0 & 0 & M_{33} \end{bmatrix} \end{aligned} \tag{5.6.3}$$

In this equation, the off-diagonal terms are zero because of orthogonality, and the diagonal terms are the generalized mass M_{ii}.

It is evident that a similar formation applies also to the stiffness matrix that results in the following equation:

$$P^T KP = \begin{bmatrix} K_{11} & 0 & 0 \\ 0 & K_{22} & 0 \\ 0 & 0 & K_{33} \end{bmatrix} \tag{5.6.4}$$

The diagonal terms here are the generalized stiffness K_{ii}.

When the normal modes ϕ_i in the P matrix are replaced by the *orthonormal modes* $\tilde{\phi}_i$, the modal matrix is designated as $\tilde{P}$. It is easily seen then that the orthogonality relationships are

$$\tilde{P}^T M\tilde{P} = I \tag{5.6.5}$$

$$\tilde{P}^T K\tilde{P} = \Lambda \tag{5.6.6}$$

where Λ is the diagonal matrix of the eigenvalues.

$$\Lambda = \begin{bmatrix} \lambda_1 & 0 & 0 \\ 0 & \lambda_2 & 0 \\ 0 & 0 & \lambda_3 \end{bmatrix} \tag{5.6.7}$$

Equations (5.6.5) and (5.6.6) show that if the eigenvectors are known then one can easily calculate the eigenvalues. These relationships will be used in the discussion of numerical methods for eigenvalues and eigenvectors (see Sec. 7.9).

Example 5.6.1

Verify the results of the system considered in Example 5.1.1 (see Fig. 5.6.1) by substituting them into the equations of Sec. 5.6.

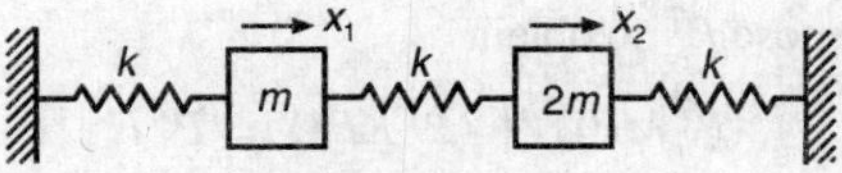

FIGURE 5.6.1.

Solution The mass and stiffness matrices are

$$M = m\begin{bmatrix} 1 & 0 \\ 0 & 2 \end{bmatrix} \quad K = k\begin{bmatrix} 2 & -1 \\ -1 & 2 \end{bmatrix}$$

The eigenvalues and eigenvectors for Example 5.1.1 are

$$\lambda_1 = \frac{\omega_1^2 m}{k} = 0.634 \quad \phi_1 = \begin{Bmatrix} 0.731 \\ 1.000 \end{Bmatrix}$$

$$\lambda_2 = \frac{\omega_2^2 m}{k} = 2.366 \quad \phi_2 = \begin{Bmatrix} -2.73 \\ 1.00 \end{Bmatrix}$$

Forming the modal matrix P, we have

$$P = \begin{bmatrix} 0.731 & -2.73 \\ 1.00 & 1.00 \end{bmatrix}$$

$$P^T MP = \begin{bmatrix} 0.731 & 1.0 \\ -2.73 & 1.0 \end{bmatrix}\begin{bmatrix} 1 & 0 \\ 0 & 2 \end{bmatrix}\begin{bmatrix} 0.731 & -2.73 \\ 1 & 1 \end{bmatrix}$$

$$= \begin{bmatrix} 2.53 & 0 \\ 0 & 9.45 \end{bmatrix} = \begin{bmatrix} M_{11} & 0 \\ 0 & M_{22} \end{bmatrix}$$

Thus, the generalized mass are 2.53 and 9.45.

If instead of P we use the orthonormal modes, we obtain

$$\tilde{P} = \left[\frac{1}{\sqrt{2.53}}\begin{Bmatrix} 0.731 \\ 1.00 \end{Bmatrix} \frac{1}{\sqrt{9.45}}\begin{Bmatrix} -2.73 \\ 1.00 \end{Bmatrix}\right] = \begin{bmatrix} 0.459 & -0.888 \\ 0.628 & 0.3252 \end{bmatrix}$$

$$\tilde{P}^T M\tilde{P} = \begin{bmatrix} 0.459 & 0.628 \\ -0.888 & 0.325 \end{bmatrix}\begin{bmatrix} 1 & 0 \\ 0 & 2 \end{bmatrix}\begin{bmatrix} 0.459 & -0.888 \\ 0.628 & 0.325 \end{bmatrix}\begin{bmatrix} 1.00 & 0 \\ 0 & 1.00 \end{bmatrix}$$

$$\tilde{P}^T K\tilde{P} = \begin{bmatrix} 0.459 & 0.628 \\ -0.888 & 0.325 \end{bmatrix}\begin{bmatrix} 2 & -1 \\ -1 & 2 \end{bmatrix}\begin{bmatrix} 0.459 & -0.888 \\ 0.628 & 0.325 \end{bmatrix}$$

$$= \begin{bmatrix} 0.635 & 0 \\ 0 & 2.365 \end{bmatrix} = \begin{bmatrix} \lambda_1 & 0 \\ 0 & \lambda_2 \end{bmatrix}$$

Thus, the diagonal terms agree with the eigenvalues of Example 5.1.1.

5.7 DECOUPLING FORCED VIBRATION EQUATIONS

When the normal modes of the system are known, the modal matrix P or $\widetilde{P}$ can be used to decouple the equations of motion. Consider the following general equation of the forced undamped system:

$$M\ddot{X} + KX = F \tag{5.7.1}$$

By making the coordinate transformation $X = PY$, the foregoing equation becomes

$$MP\ddot{Y} + KPY = F$$

Next, premultiply by the transpose P^T to obtain

$$(P^T MP)\ddot{Y} + (P^T KP)Y = P^T F \tag{5.7.2}$$

Because the products $P^T MP$ and $P^T KP$ are diagonal matrices due to orthogonality, the new equations in terms of Y are uncoupled and can be solved as a system of 1 DOF. The original coordinates X can then be found from the transformation equation

$$X = PY \tag{5.7.3}$$

Example 5.7.1

Consider the two-story building of Fig. 5.7.1 excited by a force $F(t)$ at the top. Its equation of motion is

$$m\begin{bmatrix} 2 & 0 \\ 0 & 1 \end{bmatrix}\begin{Bmatrix} \ddot{x}_1 \\ \ddot{x}_2 \end{Bmatrix} + k\begin{bmatrix} 3 & -1 \\ -1 & 1 \end{bmatrix}\begin{Bmatrix} x_1 \\ x_2 \end{Bmatrix} = \begin{Bmatrix} 0 \\ F \end{Bmatrix}$$

The normal modes of the homogeneous equation are

$$\phi_1 = \begin{Bmatrix} 0.5 \\ 1 \end{Bmatrix} \qquad \phi_2 = \begin{Bmatrix} -1 \\ 1 \end{Bmatrix}$$

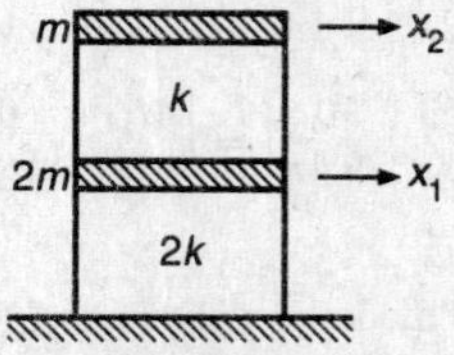

FIGURE 5.7.1.

from which the P matrix is assembled as

$$P = \begin{bmatrix} 0.5 & -1 \\ 1 & 1 \end{bmatrix}$$

Writing out the terms of Eq. (5.7.2), we have

$$m\begin{bmatrix} 0.5 & 1 \\ -1 & 1 \end{bmatrix}\begin{bmatrix} 2 & 0 \\ 1 & 1 \end{bmatrix}\begin{bmatrix} 0.5 & -1 \\ 1 & 1 \end{bmatrix}\begin{Bmatrix} \ddot{y}_1 \\ \ddot{y}_2 \end{Bmatrix}$$

$$+ k\begin{bmatrix} 0.5 & 1 \\ -1 & 1 \end{bmatrix}\begin{bmatrix} 3 & -1 \\ -1 & 1 \end{bmatrix}\begin{bmatrix} 0.5 & -1 \\ 1 & 1 \end{bmatrix}\begin{Bmatrix} y_1 \\ y_2 \end{Bmatrix} = \begin{bmatrix} 0.5 & 1 \\ -1 & 1 \end{bmatrix}\begin{Bmatrix} 0 \\ F_2 \end{Bmatrix}$$

or

$$m\begin{bmatrix} 1.5 & 0 \\ 0 & 3 \end{bmatrix}\begin{Bmatrix} \ddot{y}_1 \\ \ddot{y}_2 \end{Bmatrix} + k\begin{bmatrix} 0.75 & 0 \\ 0 & 6 \end{bmatrix}\begin{Bmatrix} y_1 \\ y_2 \end{Bmatrix} = \begin{Bmatrix} F_2 \\ F_2 \end{Bmatrix}$$

which are uncoupled.

The solutions for y_1 and y_2 are in the form

$$y_i = y_i(0)\cos\omega_i t + \frac{\dot{y}_i(0)}{\omega_i}\sin\omega_i t + \frac{F_2}{k_i}\frac{\sin\omega t}{1-(\omega/\omega_i)^2}$$

which can be expressed in terms of the original coordinates by the P matrix as

$$\begin{Bmatrix} x_1 \\ x_2 \end{Bmatrix} = \begin{bmatrix} 0.5 & -1 \\ 1 & 1 \end{bmatrix}\begin{Bmatrix} y_1 \\ y_2 \end{Bmatrix}$$

■

Example 5.7.2

For Example 5.7.1, determine the generalized mass and the $\widetilde{P}$ matrix. Numerically, verify Eqs. (5.6.5) and (5.6.6).

Solution The calculations for the generalized mass are

$$M_1 = (0.5 \quad 1)\begin{bmatrix} 2 & 0 \\ 0 & 1 \end{bmatrix}\begin{Bmatrix} 0.5 \\ 1 \end{Bmatrix} = 1.5$$

$$M_2 = (-1 \quad 1)\begin{bmatrix} 2 & 0 \\ 0 & 1 \end{bmatrix}\begin{Bmatrix} -1 \\ 1 \end{Bmatrix} = 3.0$$

By dividing the first column of P by $\sqrt{M_1}$ and the second column by $\sqrt{M_2}$, the $\widetilde{P}$ matrix becomes

$$\widetilde{P} = \begin{bmatrix} 0.4083 & -0.5773 \\ 0.8165 & 0.5773 \end{bmatrix}$$

Equations (5.6.5) and (5.6.6) are simply verified by substitution.

■

5.8 MODAL DAMPING IN FORCED VIBRATION

The equation of motion of an N-DOF system with viscous damping and arbitrary excitation $F(t)$ can be presented in matrix form:

$$M\ddot{X} + C\dot{X} + KX = F \tag{5.8.1}$$

It is generally a set of N coupled equations.

We have found that the solution of the homogeneous undamped equation

$$M\ddot{X} + KX = 0 \tag{5.8.2}$$

leads to eigenvalues and eigenvectors that describe the normal modes of the system and the modal matrix P or $\widetilde{P}$. If we let $X = \widetilde{P}Y$ and premultiply Eq. (5.8.1) by $\widetilde{P}^T$ as in Sec. 5.7, we obtain

$$\widetilde{P}^T M\widetilde{P}\ddot{Y} + \widetilde{P}^T C\widetilde{P}\dot{Y} + \widetilde{P}^T K\widetilde{P}Y = \widetilde{P}^T F \tag{5.8.3}$$

We have already shown that $\widetilde{P}^T M\widetilde{P}$ and $\widetilde{P}^T K\widetilde{P}$ are diagonal matrices. In general, $\widetilde{P}^T C\widetilde{P}$ is not diagonal and the preceding equation is coupled by the damping matrix.

If C is proportional to M or K, it is evident that $\widetilde{P}^T C\widetilde{P}$ becomes diagonal, in which case we can say that the system has *proportional damping*. Equation (5.8.3) is then completely uncoupled and its ith equation will have the form

$$\ddot{y}_i + 2\zeta_i\omega_i\dot{y}_i + \omega_i^2 y_i = \widetilde{f}_i(t) \tag{5.8.4}$$

Thus, instead of N coupled equations, we would have N uncoupled equations similar to that of a single-DOF system.

Rayleigh damping. Rayleigh introduced proportional damping in the form

$$C = \alpha M + \beta K \tag{5.8.5}$$

where α and β are constants. The application of the weighted modal matrix $\widetilde{P}$ here results in

$$\begin{aligned}\widetilde{P}^T C \widetilde{P} &= \alpha \widetilde{P}^T M \widetilde{P} + \beta \widetilde{P}^T K \widetilde{P} \\ &= \alpha I + \beta \Lambda\end{aligned} \tag{5.8.6}$$*

where I is a unit matrix, and Λ is a diagonal matrix of the eigenvalues [see Eq. 5.6.6)].

$$\Lambda = \begin{bmatrix} \omega_1^2 & & & \\ & \omega_2^2 & & \\ & & \ddots & \\ & & & \omega_n^2 \end{bmatrix} \tag{5.8.7}$$

Thus, instead of Eq. (5.8.4), we obtain for the ith equation

$$\ddot{y}_i + (\alpha + \beta\omega_i^2)\dot{y}_i + \omega_i^2 y_i = \widetilde{f}_i(t) \tag{5.8.8}$$

and the modal damping can be defined by the equation

$$2\zeta_i \omega_i = \alpha + \beta \omega_i^2 \tag{5.8.9}$$

5.9 NORMAL MODE SUMMATION

The forced vibration equation for the N-DOF system

$$M\ddot{X} + C\dot{X} + KX = F \tag{5.9.1}$$

can be routinely solved by the digital computer. However, for systems of large numbers of degrees of freedom, the computation can be costly. It is possible, however, to cut down the size of the computation (or reduce the degrees of freedom of the system) by a procedure known as the *mode summation method.* Essentially, the displacement of the structure under forced excitation is approximated by the sum of a limited number of normal modes of the system multiplied by generalized coordinates.

For example, consider a 50-story building with 50 DOF. The solution of its undamped homogeneous equation will lead to 50 eigenvalues and 50 eigenvectors that describe the normal modes of the structure. If we know that the excitation of the building centers around the lower frequencies, the higher modes will not be excited and we would be justified in assuming the forced response to be the superposition of only a few of the lower-frequency modes; perhaps $\phi_1(x), \phi_2(x)$ and $\phi_3(x)$ may be sufficient. Then the deflection under forced excitation can be written as

$$x_i = \phi_1(x_i)q_1(t) + \phi_2(x_i)q_2(t) + \phi_3(x_i)q_3(t) \tag{5.9.2}$$

or in matrix notation the position of all n floors can be expressed in terms of the modal matrix P composed of only the three modes. (See Fig. 5.9.1.)

$$\begin{Bmatrix} x_1 \\ x_2 \\ \vdots \\ x_n \end{Bmatrix} = \begin{bmatrix} \phi_1(x_1) & \phi_2(x_1) & \phi_3(x_1) \\ \cdot & \cdot & \cdot \\ \vdots & \vdots & \vdots \\ \phi_1(x_n) & \phi_2(x_n) & \phi_3(x_n) \end{bmatrix} \begin{Bmatrix} q_1 \\ q_2 \\ \vdots \\ q_n \end{Bmatrix} \tag{5.9.3}$$

*It can be shown that $C = \alpha M^n + \beta K^n$ can also be diagonalized (see Probs. 5.48 and 5.49).

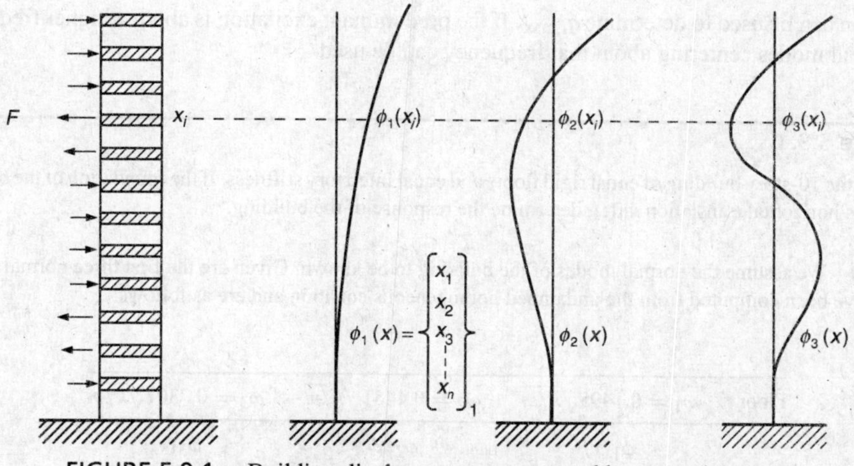

FIGURE 5.9.1. Building displacement represented by normal modes.

The use of the limited modal matrix then reduces the system to that equal to the number of modes used. For example, for the 50-story building, each of the matrices such as K is a 50×50 matrix; using three normal modes, P is a 50×3 matrix and the product $P^T KP$ becomes

$$P^T KP = (3 \times 50)(50 \times 50)(50 \times 3) = (3 \times 3) \text{ matrix}$$

Thus, instead of solving the 50 coupled equations represented by Eq. (5.9.1), we need only solve the three by three equations represented by

$$P^T MKP\ddot{q} + P^T CP\dot{q} + P^T KPq = P^T F \tag{5.9.4}$$

If the damping matrix is assumed to be proportional, the preceding equations become uncoupled, and if the force $F(x, t)$ is separable to $p(x)f(t)$, the three equations take the form

$$\ddot{q}_i + 2\zeta_i\omega_i\dot{q}_i + \omega_i^2 q_i = \Gamma_i f(t) \tag{5.9.5}$$

where the term

$$\Gamma_i = \frac{\sum_j \phi_i(x_j)P(x_j)}{\sum_j m_j\phi_i^2(x_j)} \tag{5.9.6}$$

is called the *mode participation factor*.

In many cases, we are interested only in the maximum peak value of x_i, in which case, the following procedure has been found to give acceptable results. We first find the maximum value of each $q_j(t)$ and combine them in the form

$$|x_i|_{\max} = |\phi_1(x_i)q_{1,\max}| + \sqrt{|\phi_2(x_i)q_{2,\max}|^2 + |\phi_3(x_i)q_{3,\max}|^2} \tag{5.9.7}$$ *

Thus, the first mode response is supplemented by the square root of the sum of the squares of the peaks for the higher modes. For the previous computations, a shock spectrum for the particular

*The method is used by the shock and vibration groups in various industries and the military.

excitation can be used to determine $q_{i,\max}$. If the predominant excitation is about a higher frequency, the normal modes centering about that frequency can be used.

Example 5.9.1

Consider the 10-story building of equal rigid floors and equal interstory stiffness. If the foundation of the building undergoes horizontal translation $u_0(t)$, determine the response of the building.

Solution We assume the normal modes of the building to be known. Given are the first three normal modes, which have been computed from the undamped homogeneous equation and are as follows:

Floor	$\omega_1 = 0.1495\sqrt{k/m}$	$\omega_2 = 0.4451\sqrt{k/m}$	$\omega_3 = 0.7307\sqrt{k/m}$
	$\phi_1(x)$	$\phi_2(x)$	$\phi_3(x)$
10	1.0000	1.0000	1.0000
9	0.9777	0.8019	0.4662
8	0.9336	0.4451	−0.3165
7	0.8686	0.0000	−0.9303
6	0.7840	−0.4451	−1.0473
5	0.6822	−0.8019	−0.6052
4	0.5650	−1.0000	1.6010
3	0.4352	−1.0000	0.8398
2	0.2954	−0.8019	1.0711
1	0.1495	−0.4451	0.7307
0	0.0000	0.0000	0.0000

The equation of motion of the building due to ground motion $u_0(t)$ is

$$M\ddot{X} + C\dot{X} + KX = -M1\ddot{u}_0(t)$$

where 1 is a unit vector and X is a 10×1 vector. Using the three given modes, we make the transformation

$$X = Pq$$

where P is a 10×3 matrix and q is a 3×1 vector, i.e.,

$$P = \begin{bmatrix} \phi_1(x_1) & \phi_2(x_1) & \phi_3(x_1) \\ \phi_1(x_2) & \phi_2(x_2) & \phi_3(x_3) \\ \vdots & \vdots & \vdots \\ \phi_1(x_{10}) & \phi_2(x_{10}) & \phi_3(x_{10}) \end{bmatrix} \qquad q = \begin{Bmatrix} q_1 \\ q_2 \\ q_3 \end{Bmatrix}$$

Premultiplying by P^T, we obtain

$$P^T MP\ddot{q} + P^T CP\dot{q} + P^T KPq = -P^T M1u_0(t)$$

and by assuming C to be a proportional damping matrix, the foregoing equation results in three uncoupled equations:

$$m_{11}\ddot{q}_1 + c_{11}\dot{q}_1 + k_{11}q_1 = -\ddot{u}_0(t)\sum_{i=1}^{10} m_i\phi_1(x_i)$$

$$m_{22}\ddot{q}_2 + c_{22}\dot{q}_2 + k_{22}q_2 = -\ddot{u}_0(t)\sum_{i=1}^{10} m_i\phi_2(x_i)$$

$$m_{33}\ddot{q}_3 + c_{33}\dot{q}_3 + k_{33}q_3 = -\ddot{u}_0(t)\sum_{i=1}^{10} m_i\phi_3(x_i)$$

where m_{ii}, c_{ii}, and k_{ii} are generalized mass, generalized damping, and generalized stiffness. The $q_j(t)$ are then independently solved from each of the foregoing equations. The displacement x_i of any floor must be found from the equation $X = Pq$ to be

$$x_i = \phi_1(x_i)q_1(t) + \phi_2(x_i)q_2(t) + \phi_3(x_i)q_3(t)$$

Thus, the time solution for any floor is composed of the normal modes used.

From the numerical information supplied on the normal modes, we now determine the numerical values for the first equation, which can be rewritten as

$$\ddot{q}_1 + 2\zeta_1\omega_1 q_1 = -\frac{\sum m\phi_1}{\sum m\phi_1^2}\ddot{u}(t)$$

We have, for the first mode,

$$m_{11} = \sum m\phi_1^2 = 5.2803m$$

$$\frac{c_{11}}{m_{11}} = 2\zeta_1\omega_1 = 0.299\sqrt{\frac{k}{m}}\,\zeta_1$$

$$\frac{k_{11}}{m_{11}} = \omega_1^2 = 0.02235\frac{k}{m}$$

$$\sum m\phi_1 = 6.6912m$$

The equation for the first mode then becomes

$$\ddot{q}_1 + 0.299\sqrt{\frac{k}{m}}\zeta_1\dot{q}_1 + 0.02235\frac{k}{m}q_1 = -1.2672\ddot{u}_0(t)$$

Thus, given the values for k/m and ζ_1, the above equation can be solved for any $\ddot{u}_0(t)$.

■

5.10 EQUAL ROOTS

When equal roots are found in the characteristic equation, the corresponding eigenvectors are not unique and a linear combination of such eigenvectors may also satisfy the equation of motion. To illustrate this point, let ϕ_1 and ϕ_2 be eigenvectors belonging to a common eigenvalue λ_0, and ϕ_3 be a third eigenvector belonging to λ_3 that is different from λ_0. We can then write

$$A\phi_1 = \lambda_0\phi_1$$
$$A\phi_2 = \lambda_0\phi_2$$
$$A\phi_3 = \lambda_3\phi_3$$

By multiplying the second equation by a constant b and adding it to the first, we obtain another equation:

$$A(\phi_1 + b\phi_2) = \lambda_0(\phi_1 + b\phi_2)$$

Thus, a new eigenvector $\phi_{12} = (\phi_1 + b\phi_2)$, which is a linear combination of the first two, also satisfies the basic equation:

$$A\phi_{12} = \lambda_0\phi_{12}$$

and hence no unique mode exists for λ_0.

Any of the modes corresponding to λ_0 must be orthogonal to ϕ_3 if it is to be a normal mode. If all three modes are orthogonal, they are linearly independent and can be combined to describe the free vibration resulting from any initial condition.

The eigenvectors associated with the equal eigenvalues are orthogonal to the remaining eigenvectors, but they may not be orthogonal to each other.

Example 5.10.1

Consider the system of Fig. 5.10.1 of a flexible beam with three lumped masses. Of the three possible modes shown, the first two represent rigid body motion of translation and rotation corresponding to zero frequency, and the third mode is that of symmetric vibration of the flexible beam. With the mass matrix equal to

$$M = \begin{bmatrix} 1 & 0 & 0 \\ 0 & 2 & 0 \\ 0 & 0 & 1 \end{bmatrix}$$

the modes are easily shown to be orthogonal to each other, i.e.,

$$\phi_1^T M\phi_2 = \phi_1^T M\phi_3 = \phi_2^T M\phi_3 = 0$$

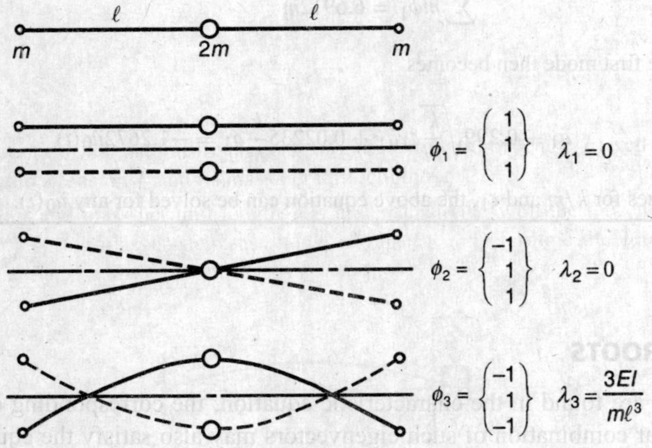

FIGURE 5.10.1.

Next, multiply ϕ_2 by a constant b and add it to ϕ_1 to form a new modal vector ϕ_{12}:

$$\phi_{12} = \phi_1 + b\phi_2 = \begin{Bmatrix} 1 \\ 1 \\ 1 \end{Bmatrix} + b \begin{Bmatrix} -1 \\ 0 \\ 1 \end{Bmatrix} = \begin{Bmatrix} 1-b \\ 1 \\ 1+b \end{Bmatrix}$$

It is seen that ϕ_{12} is orthogonal to ϕ_3, i.e.,

$$\phi_3^T M \phi_{12} = (-1 \quad 1 \quad -1) \begin{bmatrix} 1 & 0 & 0 \\ 0 & 2 & 0 \\ 0 & 0 & 1 \end{bmatrix} \begin{Bmatrix} 1-b \\ 1 \\ 1+b \end{Bmatrix} = 0$$

Thus, the new eigenvector formed by a linear combination of ϕ_1 and ϕ_2 is orthogonal to ϕ_3. However, we find that ϕ_1 and ϕ_2 are not orthogonal to ϕ_{12}.

$$\phi_1^T M \phi_{12} = (1 \quad 1 \quad 1) \begin{bmatrix} 1 & 0 & 0 \\ 0 & 2 & 0 \\ 0 & 0 & 1 \end{bmatrix} \begin{Bmatrix} 1-b \\ 1 \\ 1+b \end{Bmatrix} = 4 \neq 0$$

$$\phi_2^T M \phi_{12} = (-1 \quad 0 \quad 1) \begin{bmatrix} 1 & 0 & 0 \\ 0 & 2 & 0 \\ 0 & 0 & 1 \end{bmatrix} \begin{Bmatrix} 1-b \\ 1 \\ 1+b \end{Bmatrix} = 2b \neq 0$$

■

5.11 UNRESTRAINED (DEGENERATE) SYSTEMS

A vibrational system that is unrestrained is free to move as a rigid body as well as vibrate. An airplane in flight or a moving train is such an unrestrained system. The equation of motion for such a system will generally include rigid-body modes as well as vibrational modes, and its characteristic equation will contain zero frequencies corresponding to the rigid-body modes.

Example 5.11.1

Figure 5.11.1 shows a three-mass torsional system that is unrestrained to rotate freely in bearings. Its equation of motion is

$$\begin{bmatrix} J_1 & 0 & 0 \\ 0 & J_2 & 0 \\ 0 & 0 & J_3 \end{bmatrix} \begin{Bmatrix} \ddot{\theta}_1 \\ \ddot{\theta}_2 \\ \ddot{\theta}_3 \end{Bmatrix} + \begin{bmatrix} K_1 & -K_1 & 0 \\ -K_1 & (K_1 + K_2) & -K_2 \\ 0 & -K_2 & K_2 \end{bmatrix} \begin{Bmatrix} \theta_1 \\ \theta_2 \\ \theta_3 \end{Bmatrix} = \begin{Bmatrix} 0 \\ 0 \\ 0 \end{Bmatrix}$$

We will here assume that $J_1 = J_2 = J_3 = J$ and $K_1 = K_2 = K$, and let $\lambda = \omega^2 J/K$, in which case, the preceding equation reduces to

$$\left[-\lambda \begin{bmatrix} 1 & 0 & 0 \\ 0 & 1 & 0 \\ 0 & 0 & 1 \end{bmatrix} + \begin{bmatrix} 1 & -1 & 0 \\ -1 & 2 & -1 \\ 0 & -1 & 1 \end{bmatrix} \right] \begin{Bmatrix} \theta_1 \\ \theta_2 \\ \theta_3 \end{Bmatrix} = \begin{Bmatrix} 0 \\ 0 \\ 0 \end{Bmatrix}$$

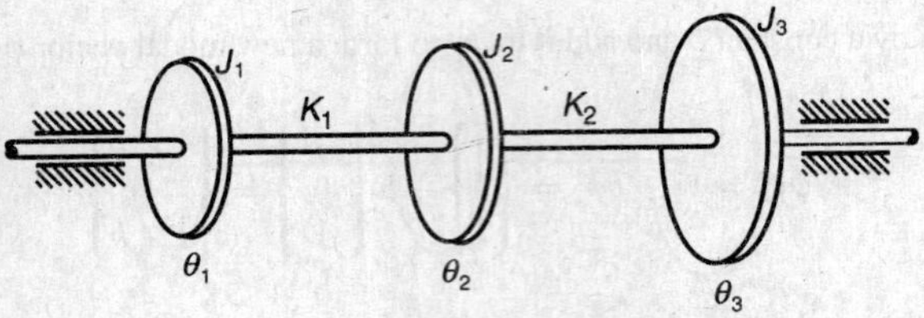

FIGURE 5.11.1.

The characteristic determinant for the system is

$$\begin{vmatrix} (1-\lambda) & -1 & 0 \\ -1 & (2-\lambda) & -1 \\ 0 & -1 & (1-\lambda) \end{vmatrix} = 0$$

which when multiplied out becomes

$$\lambda(1-\lambda)(\lambda-3) = 0$$

Thus, the roots of the eigenvalues for the system are

$$\lambda_1 = 0$$
$$\lambda_2 = 1$$
$$\lambda_3 = 3$$

To identify the corresponding eigenvectors, each of the λ's is substituted into the equation of motion:

$$\begin{bmatrix} (1-\lambda) & -1 & 0 \\ 0 & (2-\lambda) & -1 \\ 0 & -1 & (1-\lambda) \end{bmatrix} \begin{Bmatrix} \theta_1 \\ \theta_2 \\ \theta_3 \end{Bmatrix} = \begin{Bmatrix} 0 \\ 0 \\ 0 \end{Bmatrix}$$

When $\lambda_1 = 0$ is substituted, the result is $\theta_1 = \theta_2 = \theta_3$ and its normal mode, or eigenvector, is

$$\phi_1 = \begin{Bmatrix} 1 \\ 1 \\ 1 \end{Bmatrix}$$

which describes the rigid body motion [see Fig. 5.11.2(a)].

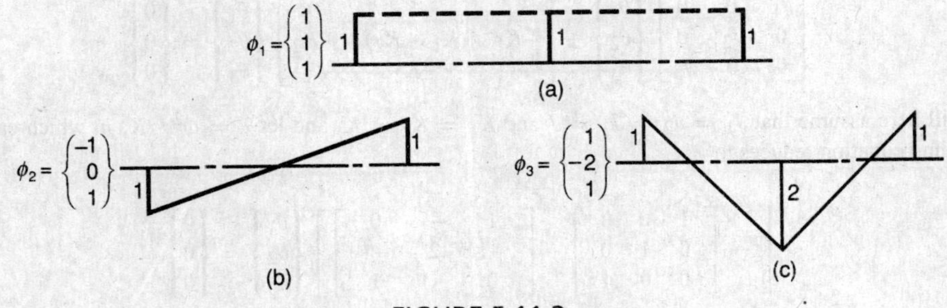

FIGURE 5.11.2.

Similarly, the second and third modes [see Figs. 5.11.2(b) and (c), respectively] are found and displayed as

$$\phi_2 = \begin{Bmatrix} -1 \\ 0 \\ 1 \end{Bmatrix} \quad \phi_3 = \begin{Bmatrix} 1 \\ -2 \\ 1 \end{Bmatrix}$$

5.12 FINITE DIFFERENCE METHOD FOR SYSTEMS OF EQUATIONS

The finite difference method of Sec. 4.7 can easily be extended to the solution of systems with two DOF. The procedure is illustrated by the following problem, which is programmed and solved by the digital computer.

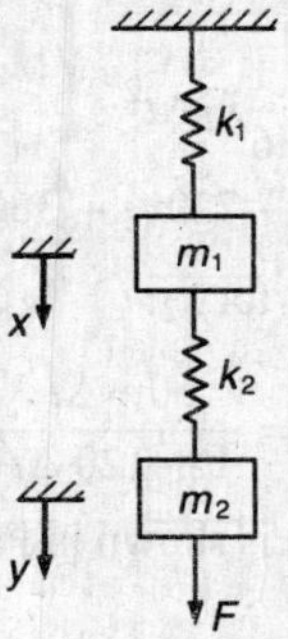

FIGURE 5.12.1.

The system to be solved is shown in Fig. 5.12.1. To avoid confusion with subscripts, we let the displacements be x and y.

$$k_1 = 36\,\text{kN/m}$$
$$k_2 = 36\,\text{kN/m}$$
$$m_1 = 100\,\text{kg}$$
$$m_2 = 25\,\text{kg}$$
$$F = \begin{cases} 4000\,\text{N}, & t > 0 \\ 0, & t < 0 \end{cases}$$

Initial conditions:

$$x = \dot{x} = y = \dot{y} = 0$$

The equations of motions are

$$100\ddot{x} = -36{,}000x + 36{,}000(y - x)$$
$$25\ddot{y} = -36{,}000(y - x) + F$$

which can be rearranged to

$$\ddot{x} = -720x + 360y$$
$$\ddot{y} = 1440(x - y) + 160$$

These equations are to be solved together with the recurrence equations of Sec. 4.7.

$$x_{i+1} = \ddot{x}_i \Delta t^2 + 2x_i - x_{i-1}$$
$$y_{i+1} = \ddot{y}_i \Delta t^2 + 2y_i - y_{i-1}$$

Calculations for the natural periods of the system reveal that they do not differ substantially. They are $\tau_1 = 0.3803$ and $\tau_2 = 0.1462$ s. We therefore arbitrarily choose a value of $\Delta t = 0.01$ s which is smaller than $\tau_2/10$.

To start the computation, note that the initial accelerations are $\ddot{x}_1 = 0$ and $\ddot{y}_1 = 160$, so that the starting equation, Eq. (4.7.8), can be used only for y.

$$y_2 = \frac{1}{2}\ddot{y}_1 \Delta t^2$$

For the calculation of x_2, the special starting equation (Eq. 4.7.13), must be used together with the differential equations

$$x_2 = \frac{1}{6}\ddot{x}_2 \Delta t^2$$
$$\ddot{x}_2 = -720x_2 + 360y_2$$

Eliminating $\ddot{x}_2$ gives the following equation for x_2:

$$x_2 = \frac{60y_2 \Delta t^2}{1 + 120\,\Delta t^2}$$

The flow diagram for the computation is shown in Fig. 5.12.2. A plot of the computed result is presented in Fig 5.12.3.

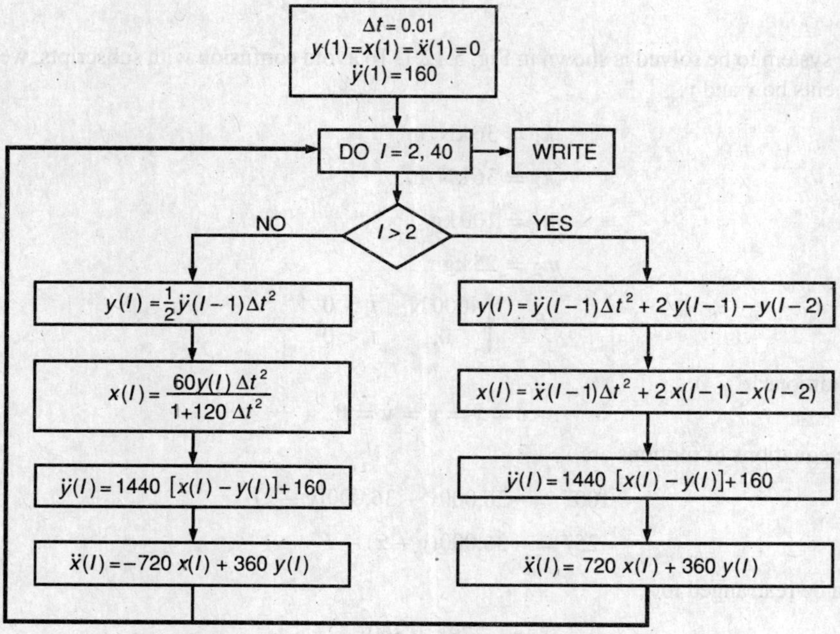

FIGURE 5.12.2. Flow diagram for computation.

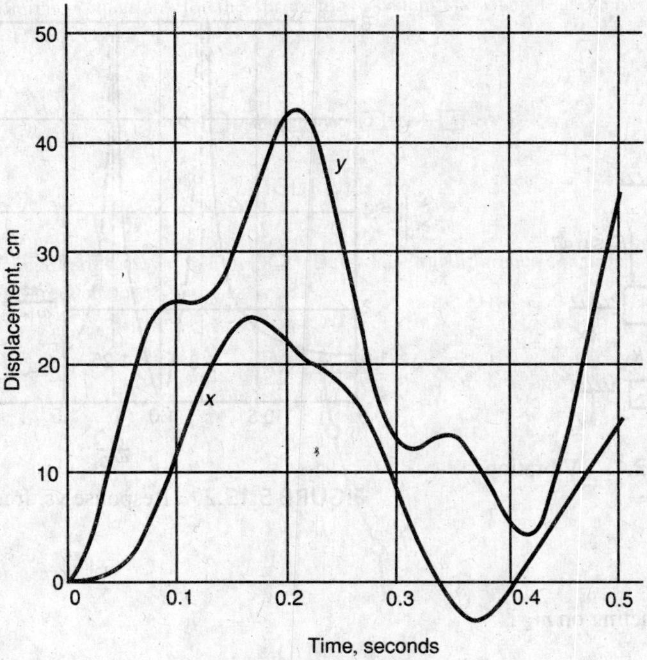

FIGURE 5.12.3.

5.13 VIBRATION ABSORBER

As a practical application of the 2-DOF system, we can consider here the spring-mass system of Fig. 5.13.1. By tuning the system to the frequency of the exciting force such that $\omega^2 = k_2/m_2$, the system acts as a vibration absorber and reduces the motion of the main mass m_1 to zero. Making the substitution

$$\omega_{11}^2 = \frac{k_1}{m_1} \qquad \omega_{22}^2 = \frac{k_2}{m_2}$$

and assuming the motion to be harmonic, the equation for the amplitude X_1 can be shown to be equal to

$$\frac{X_1 k_1}{F_0} = \frac{\left[1 - \left(\frac{\omega}{\omega_{22}}\right)^2\right]}{\left[1 + \frac{k_2}{k_1} - \left(\frac{\omega}{\omega_{11}}\right)^2\right]\left[1 - \left(\frac{\omega}{\omega_{22}}\right)^2\right] - \frac{k_2}{k_1}} \tag{5.13.1}$$

Figure 5.13.2 shows a plot of this equation with $\mu = m_2/m_1$ as a parameter. Note that $k_2/k_1 = \mu(\omega_{22}/\omega_{11})^2$. Because the system is one of 2 DOF, two natural frequencies exist. These are shown against μ in Fig. 5.13.3.

So far nothing has been said about the size of the absorber mass. At $\omega = \omega_{22}$, amplitude $X_1 = 0$, but the absorber mass has an amplitude equal to

$$X_2 = -\frac{F_0}{k_2} \tag{5.13.2}$$

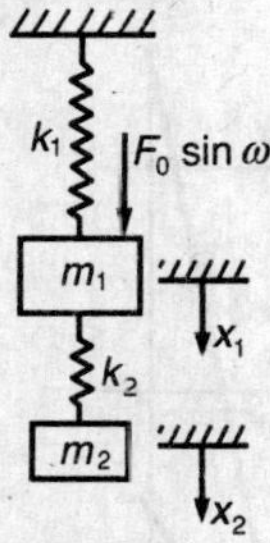

FIGURE 5.13.1. Vibration absorber.

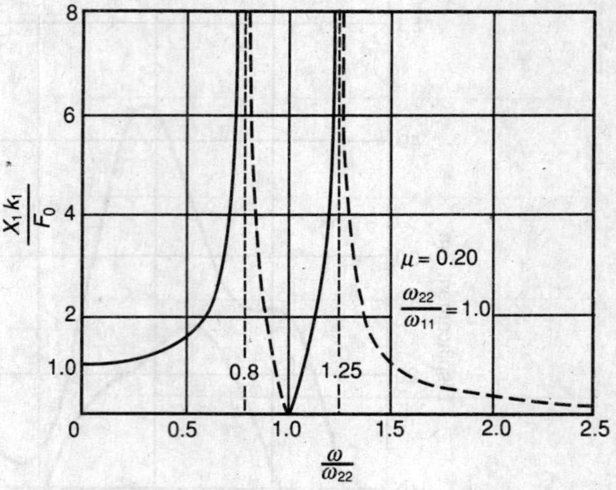

FIGURE 5.13.2. Response vs. frequency.

Because the force acting on m_2 is

$$k_2 X_2 = \omega^2 m_2 X_2 = -F_0$$

the absorber system k_2, m_2 exerts a force equal and opposite to the disturbing force. Thus, the size of k_2 and m_2 depends on the allowable value of X_2.

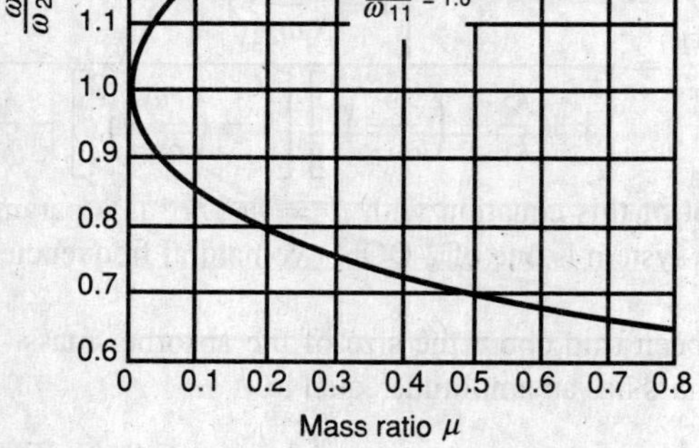

FIGURE 5.13.3. Natural frequencies vs. μ vs. m_2/m_1.

5.14 CENTRIFUGAL PENDULUM VIBRATION ABSORBER

The vibration absorber of Sec. 5.13 is only effective at one frequency, $\omega = \omega_{22}$. Also, with resonant frequencies on each side of ω_{22}, the usefulness of the spring-mass absorber is limited to a narrow frequency range.

For a rotating system such as an automobile engine, the exciting torques are proportional to the rotational speed n, which can vary over a wide range. Thus, for the absorber to be effective, its natural frequency must also be proportional to the speed. The characteristics of the centrifugal pendulum are ideally suited for this purpose.

Figure 5.14.1 shows the essentials of the centrifugal pendulum. It is a 2-DOF nonlinear system; however, we limit the oscillations to small angles, thereby reducing its complexity.

By placing the coordinates through point O' parallel and normal to r, line r rotates with angular velocity $(\dot{\theta} + \dot{\phi})$. The acceleration of m is equal to the vector sum of the acceleration of O' and the acceleration of m relative to O'.

$$\begin{aligned} a_m &= \left[R\ddot{\theta} \sin \phi - R\dot{\theta}^2 \cos \phi - r(\dot{\theta} + \dot{\phi})^2\right] i \\ &\quad + \left[R\ddot{\theta} \cos \phi - R\dot{\theta}^2 \sin \phi + r(\ddot{\theta} + \ddot{\phi})\right] j \end{aligned} \tag{5.14.1}$$

Because for the pendulum the moment about O' is zero, we have, from the j-component of a_m,

$$M_{O'} = m[R\ddot{\theta} \cos \phi + R\dot{\theta}^2 \sin \phi + r(\ddot{\theta} + \ddot{\phi})]r = 0 \tag{5.14.2}$$

Assuming ϕ to be small, we let $\cos \phi = 1$ and $\sin \phi = \phi$ in Eq. (5.14.2) and arrive at the differential equation for the pendulum:

$$\ddot{\phi} + \left(\frac{R}{r}\dot{\theta}^2\right)\phi = -\left(\frac{R+r}{r}\right)\ddot{\theta} \tag{5.14.3}$$

If we assume the motion of the wheel to be a steady rotation n plus a small sinusoidal oscillation of frequency ω, we can write

$$\begin{aligned} \theta &= nt + \theta_0 \sin \omega t \\ \dot{\theta} &= n + \omega\theta_0 \cos \omega t \cong n \\ \ddot{\theta} &= -\omega^2\theta_0 \sin \omega t \end{aligned} \tag{5.14.4}$$

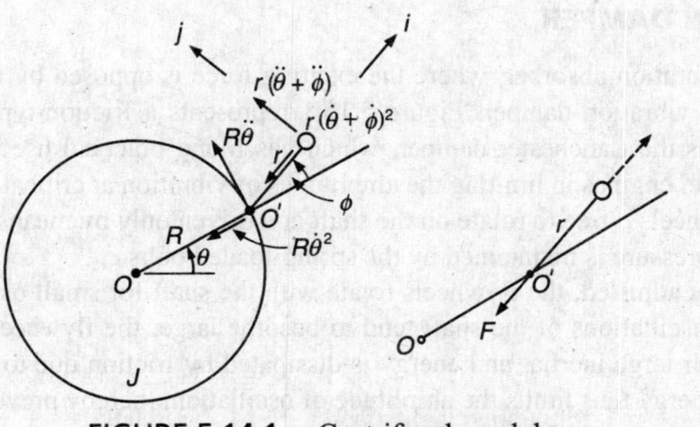

FIGURE 5.14.1. Centrifugal pendulum.

Then Eq. (5.14.3) becomes

$$\ddot{\phi} + \left(\frac{R}{r}n^2\right)\phi = \left(\frac{R+r}{r}\right)\omega^2\theta_0 \sin \omega t \tag{5.14.3'}$$

and we recognize the natural frequency of the pendulum to be

$$\omega_n = n\sqrt{\frac{R}{r}} \tag{5.14.5}$$

and its steady-state solution to be

$$\phi = \frac{(R+r)/r}{-\omega^2 + Rn^2/r}\omega^2\theta_0 \sin \omega t \tag{5.14.6}$$

The same pendulum in a gravity field would have a natural frequency of $\sqrt{g/r}$, so it can be concluded that for the centrifugal pendulum, the gravity field is replaced by the centrifugal field Rn^2.

We next consider the torque exerted by the pendulum on the wheel. With the j-component of a_m equal to zero, the pendulum force is a tension along r, given by m times the i-component of a_m. By recognizing that the major term of ma_m is $-(R+r)n^2$, the torque exerted by the pendulum on the wheel is

$$T = -m(R+r)n^2R\phi \tag{5.14.7}$$

Substituting for ϕ from Eq. (5.14.6) into the last equation, we obtain

$$T = -\frac{m(R+r)^2Rn^2/r}{Rn^2/r - \omega^2}\omega^2\theta_0 \sin \omega t = -\left[\frac{m(R+r)^2}{1 - r\omega^2/Rn^2}\right]\ddot{\theta}$$

Because we can write the torque equation as $T = J_{\text{eff}}\ddot{\theta}$, the pendulum behaves like a wheel of rotational inertia:

$$J_{\text{eff}} = -\frac{m(R+r)^2}{1 - r\omega^2/Rn^2} \tag{5.14.8}$$

which can become infinite at its natural frequency.

This poses some difficulties in the design of the pendulum. For example, to suppress a disturbing torque of frequency equal to four times the rotational speed n, the pendulum must meet the requirement $\omega^2 = (4n)^2 = n^2R/r$, or $r/R = \frac{1}{16}$. Such a short effective pendulum has been made possible by the Chilton bifilar design (see Prob. 5.67).

5.15 VIBRATION DAMPER

In contrast to the vibration absorber, where the exciting force is opposed by the absorber, energy is dissipated by the vibration damper. Figure 5.15.1 represents a friction-type vibration damper, commonly known as the Lanchester damper, which has found practical use in torsional systems such as gas and diesel engines in limiting the amplitudes of vibration at critical speeds. The damper consists of two flywheels a free to rotate on the shaft and driven only by means of the friction rings b when the normal pressure is maintained by the spring-loaded bolts c.

When properly adjusted, the flywheels rotate with the shaft for small oscillations. However, when the torsional oscillations of the shaft tend to become large, the flywheels do not follow the shaft because of their large inertia, and energy is dissipated by friction due to the relative motion. The dissipation of energy thus limits the amplitude of oscillation, thereby preventing high torsional stresses in the shaft.

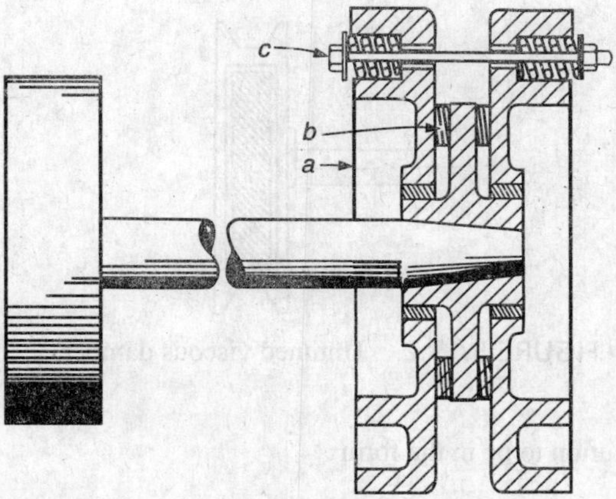

FIGURE 5.15.1. Torsional vibration damper.

In spite of the simplicity of the torsional damper, the mathematical analysis for its behavior is rather complicated. For instance, the flywheels can slip continuously, for part of the cycle, or not at all, depending on the pressure exerted by the spring bolts. If the pressure on the friction ring is either too great for slipping or zero, no energy is dissipated, and the damper becomes ineffective. Maximum energy dissipation takes place at some intermediate pressure, resulting in optimum damper effectiveness.

Obviously, the damper should be placed in a position where the amplitude of oscillation is the greatest. This position generally is found on the side of the shaft away from the main flywheel, because the node is usually near the largest mass.

Untuned viscous vibration damper. In this section, we discuss another interesting application of a vibration damper, which has found practical use in suppressing the torsional vibrations of automobile engines. In a rotating system such as an automobile engine, the disturbing frequencies for torsional oscillations are proportional to the rotational speed. However, there is generally more than one such frequency, and the centrifugal pendulum has the disadvantage that several pendulums tuned to the order number of the disturbance must be used. In contrast to the centrifugal pendulum, the untuned viscous torsional damper is effective over a wide operating range. It consists of a free rotational mass within a cylindrical cavity filled with viscous fluid, as shown in Fig. 5.15.2. Such a system is generally incorporated into the end pulley of a crankshaft that drives the fan belt, and is often referred to as the Houdaille damper.

We can examine the untuned viscous damper as a 2-DOF system by considering the crankshaft, to which it is attached, as being fixed at one end with the damper at the other end. With the torsional stiffness of the shaft equal to K in. · lb/rad, the damper can be considered to be excited by a harmonic torque $M_0e^{i\omega t}$. The damper torque results from the viscosity of the fluid within the pulley cavity, and we will assume it to be proportional to the relative rotational speed between the pulley and the free mass. Thus, the two equations of motion for the pulley and the free mass are

$$
\begin{aligned}
J\ddot{\theta} + K\theta + c(\dot{\theta} - \dot{\phi}) &= M_0e^{i\omega t} \\
J_d\ddot{\phi} - c(\dot{\theta} - \dot{\phi}) &= 0
\end{aligned}
\qquad (5.15.1)
$$

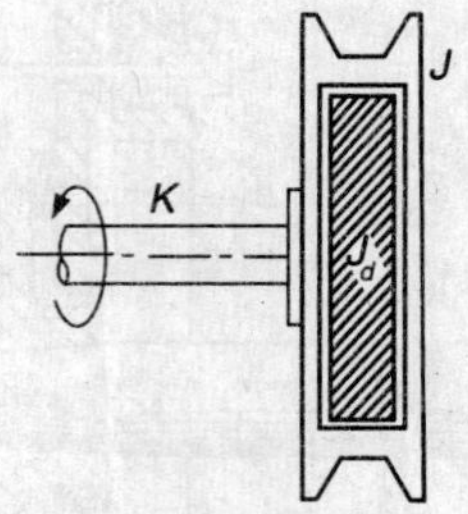

FIGURE 5.15.2. Untuned viscous damper.

By assuming the solution to be in the form

$$\begin{aligned}\theta &= \theta_0 e^{i\omega t}\\ \phi &= \phi_0 e^{i\omega t}\end{aligned} \tag{5.15.2}$$

where θ_0 and ϕ_0 are complex amplitudes, their substitution into the differential equations results in

$$\left[\left(\frac{K}{J} - \omega^2\right) + i\frac{c\omega}{J}\right]\theta_0 - \frac{ic\omega}{J}\phi_0 = \frac{M_0}{J}$$

and

$$\left(-\omega^2 + i\frac{c\omega}{J_d}\right)\phi_0 = \frac{ic\omega}{J_d}\theta_0 \tag{5.15.3}$$

By eliminating ϕ_0 between the two equations, the expression for the amplitude θ_0 of the pulley becomes

$$\frac{\theta_0}{M_0} = \frac{\omega^2 J_d - ic\omega}{[\omega^2 J_d(K - J\omega^2)] + ic\omega[\omega^2 J_d - (K - J\omega^2)]} \tag{5.15.4}$$

Letting $\omega_n^2 = K/J$ and $\mu = J_d/J$, the critical damping is

$$c_c = 2J\omega_n, \quad c = \frac{c}{c_c}2J\omega_n = 2\zeta J\omega_n$$

The amplitude equation then becomes

$$\left|\frac{K\theta_0}{M_0}\right| = \sqrt{\frac{\mu^2(\omega/\omega_n)^2 + 4\zeta^2}{\mu^2(\omega/\omega_n)^2(1 - \omega^2/\omega_n^2)^2 + 4\zeta^2[\mu(\omega/\omega_n)^2 - (1 - \omega^2/\omega_n^2)]^2}} \tag{5.15.5}$$

which indicates that $|K\theta_0/M_0|$ is a function of three parameters, ζ, μ, and (ω/ω_n).

This rather complicated equation lends itself to the following simple interpretation. It $\zeta = 0$ (zero damping), we have an undamped single-DOF system with resonant frequency of $\omega_1 = \sqrt{K/J}$. A plot of $|K\theta_0/M_0|$ vs. the frequency ratio will approach ∞ at this frequency. If $\zeta = \infty$, the damper mass and the wheel will move together as a single mass, and again we have an undamped single-DOF system, but with a lower natural frequency of $\sqrt{K/(J + J_d)}$.

Thus, like the Lanchester damper of the previous section, there is an optimum damping ζ_0 for which the peak amplitude is a minimum, as shown in Fig. 5.15.3. The result can be presented as a plot of the peak values as a function of ζ for any given μ, as shown in Fig. 5.15.4.

$$\zeta_0 = \frac{\mu}{\sqrt{2(1 + \mu)(2 + \mu)}} \tag{5.15.6}$$

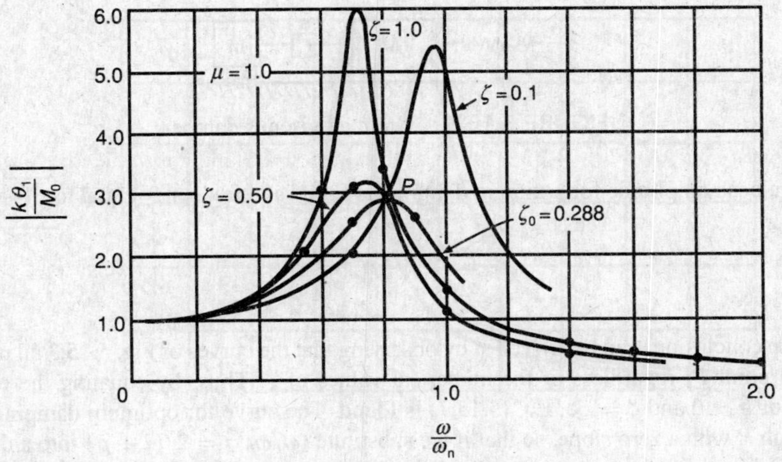

FIGURE 5.15.3. Response of an untuned viscous damper (all curves pass through P).

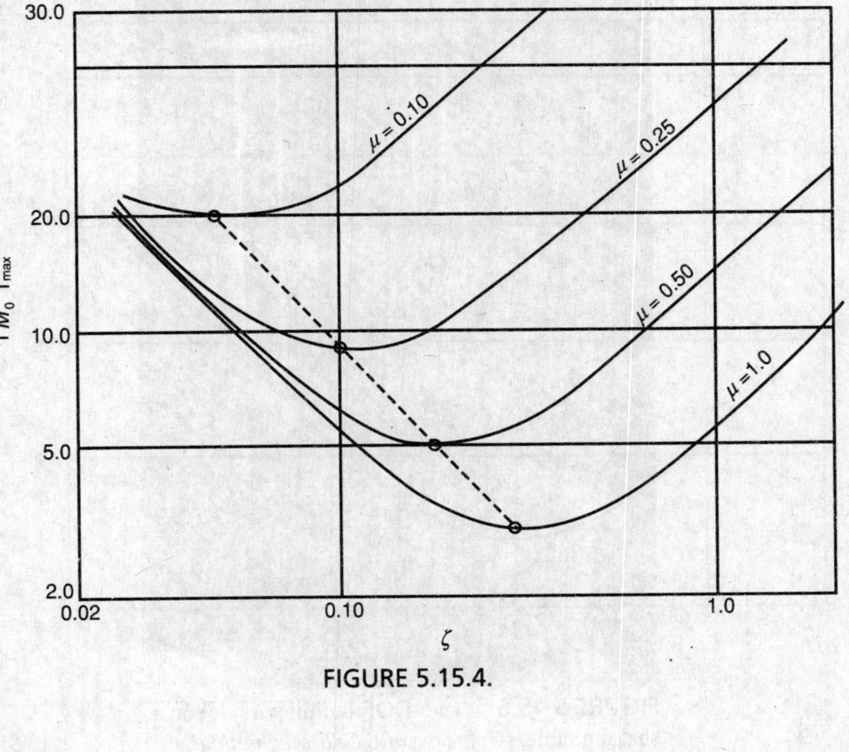

FIGURE 5.15.4.

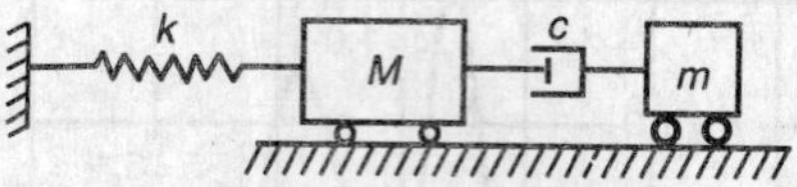

FIGURE 5.15.5. Untuned viscous damper.

and that the peak amplitude for optimum damping is found at a frequency equal to

$$\frac{\omega}{\omega_n} = \sqrt{2/(2+\mu)} \tag{5.15.7}$$

These conclusions can be arrived at by observing that the curves of Fig. 5.15.3 all pass through a common point P, regardless of the numerical values of ζ. Thus, by equating the equation for $|K\theta_0/M|$ for $\zeta = 0$ and $\zeta = \infty$, Eq. (5.15.7) is found. The curve for optimum damping then must pass through P with a zero slope, so that if we substitute $(\omega/\omega_n)^2 = 2/(2+\mu)$ into a derivative of Eq. (5.15.5) equated to zero, the expression for ζ_0 is found. It is evident that these conclusions apply also to the linear spring-mass system of Fig. 5.15.5, which is a special case of the damped vibration absorber with the damper spring equal to zero.

Fig. 5.15.6 shows a laboratory model of a 2-DOF building excited by the ground motion.

FIGURE 5.15.6. Two-DOF building model on a shaking table. (*Courtesy of UCSB Mechanical Engineering Undergraduate Laboratory.*)

PROBLEMS

5.1. Determine the natural frequencies and mode shapes of the system shown in Fig. P5.1.

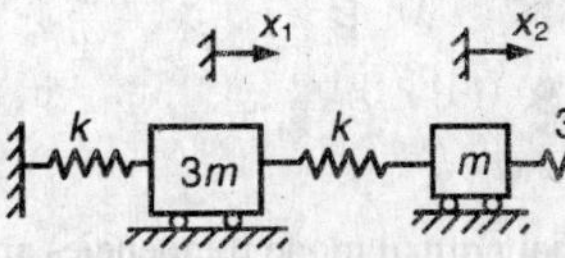

FIGURE P5.1.

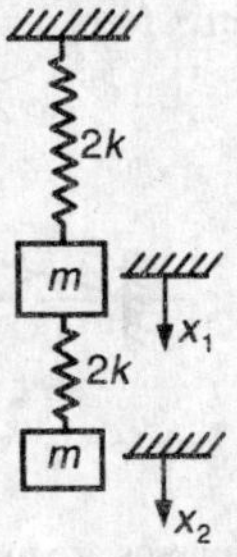

FIGURE P5.2.

5.2. Write the equations of motion for the system shown in Fig. P5.2, and determine its natural frequencies and mode shapes.

5.3. Determine the normal modes and frequencies of the system shown in Fig. P5.3 when $n = 1$.

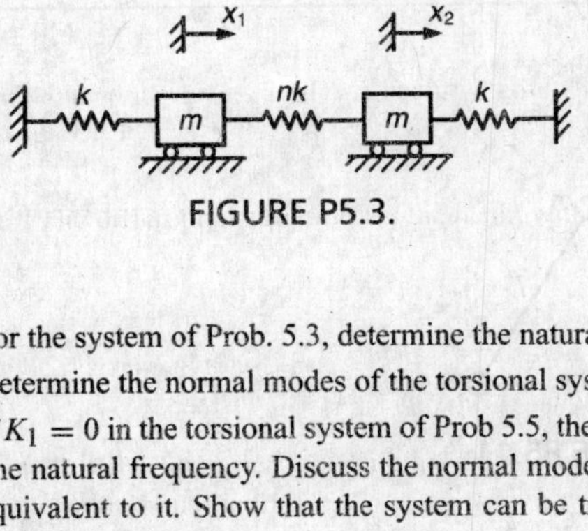

FIGURE P5.3.

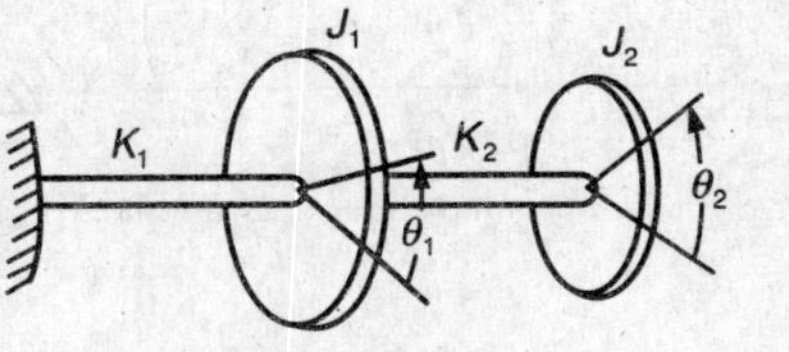

FIGURE P5.5.

5.4. For the system of Prob. 5.3, determine the natural frequencies as a function of *n*.

5.5. Determine the normal modes of the torsional system shown in Fig. P5.5 for $K_1 = K_2$ and $J_1 = J_2$.

5.6. If $K_1 = 0$ in the torsional system of Prob 5.5, the system becomes a degenerate 2-DOF system with only one natural frequency. Discuss the normal modes of this system as well as a linear spring-mass system equivalent to it. Show that the system can be treated as one of a single DOF by using the coordinate $\phi = (\theta_1 - \theta_2)$.

5.7. An electric train made up of two cars, each weighing 20,000 kg, is connected by couplings of stiffness equal to 2.8×10^6 N/m, as shown in Fig. P5.7. Determine the natural frequency of the system.

FIGURE P5.7.

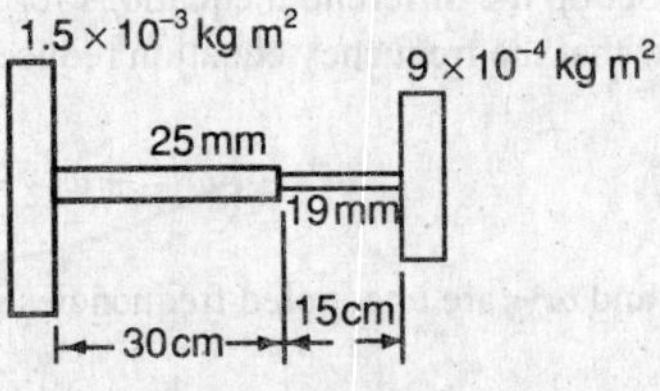

FIGURE P5.8.

5.8. Determine the natural frequency of the torsional system shown in Fig. P5.8, and draw the normal mode curve. $G = 8 \times 10^{10}\ \text{N/m}^2$.

5.9. Two masses, m_1 and m_2, are attached to a light string with tension T, as shown in Fig. P5.9. Assuming that T remains unchanged when the masses are displaced normal to the string, write the equations of motion expressed in matrix form.

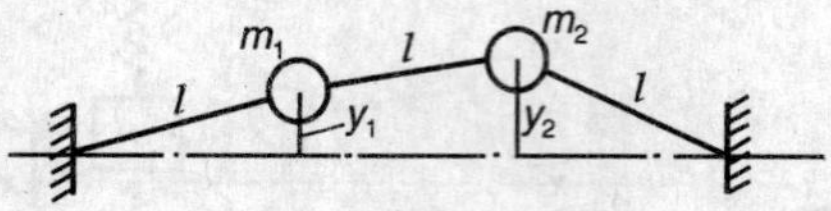

FIGURE P5.9.

5.10. In Prob. 5.9, if the two masses are made equal, show that normal mode frequencies are $\omega = \sqrt{T/ml}$ and $\omega_2 = \sqrt{3T/ml}$. Establish the configuration for these normal modes.

5.11. Assuming small amplitudes, set up the differential equations of motion for the double pendulum using the coordinates shown in Fig. P5.11. Show that the natural frequencies of the system are given by the equation

$$\omega = \sqrt{\frac{g}{l}(2 \pm \sqrt{2})}$$

Determine the ratio of amplitudes x_1/x_2 and locate the nodes for the two modes of vibration.

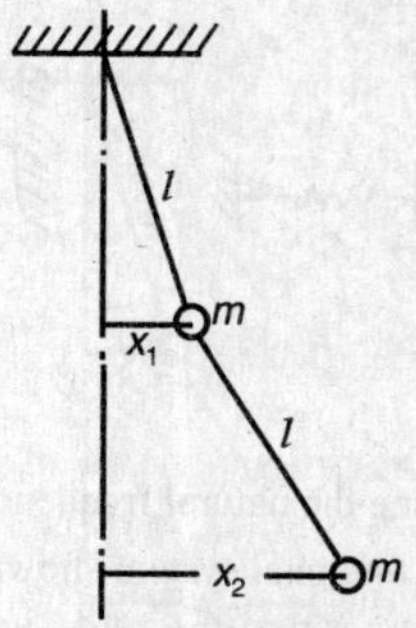

FIGURE P5.11.

5.12. Set up the equations of motion of the double pendulum in terms of angles θ_1 and θ_2 measured from the vertical.

5.13. A torsional system shown in Fig. P5.13 is composed of a shaft of stiffness K_1, a hub of radius r and moment of inertia J_1, four leaf springs of stiffness k_2, and an outer wheel of radius R and moment of inertia J_2. Set up the differential equations for torsional oscillation, assuming one end of the shaft to be fixed. Show that the frequency equation reduces to

$$\omega^4 - \left(\omega_{11}^2 + \omega_{22}^2 + \frac{J_2}{J_1}\omega_{22}^2\right)\omega^2 + \omega_{11}^2\omega_{22}^2 = 0$$

where ω_{11} and ω_{22} are uncoupled frequencies given by the expressions

$$\omega_{11}^2 = \frac{K_1}{J_1} \quad \text{and} \quad \omega_{22}^2 = \frac{4k_2R^2}{J_2}$$

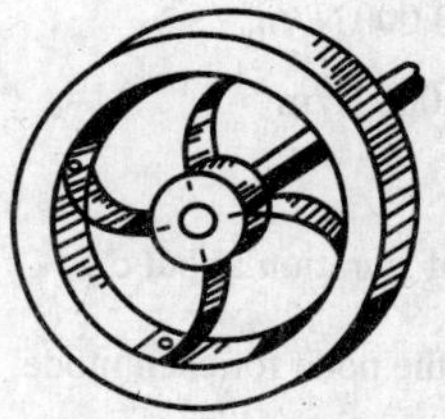

FIGURE P5.13.

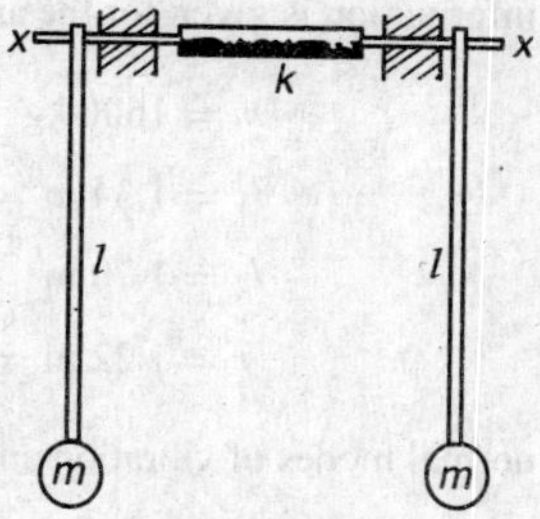

FIGURE P5.14.

5.14. Two equal pendulums free to rotate about the x–x axis are coupled together by a rubber hose of torsional stiffness k Nm/rad, as shown in Fig. P5.14. Determine the natural frequencies for the normal modes of vibration, and describe how these motions may be started.

If $l = 500$ mm, $mg = 0.01$ kg, and $k = 2.3$ Nm/rad, determine the beat period for a motion started with $\theta_1 = 0$ and $\theta_2 = \theta_0$. Examine carefully the phase of the motion as the amplitude approaches zero.

5.15. Determine the equations of motion for the system of Prob. 5.1 when the initial conditions are $x_1(0) = A$, $\dot{x}_1(0) = \dot{x}_2(0) = 0$.

5.16. The lower mass of Prob. 5.2 is given a sharp blow, imparting to it an initial velocity $\dot{x}_2(0) = V$. Determine the equation of motion.

5.17. If the system of Prob. 5.2 is started with initial conditions $x_1(0) = 0, x_2(0) = 1.0$, and $\dot{x}_1(0) = \dot{x}_2(0) = 0$, show that the equations of motion are

$$x_1(t) = 0.447 \cos \omega_1 t - 0.447 \cos \omega_2 t$$

$$x_2(t) = 0.722 \cos \omega_1 t + 0.278 \cos \omega_2 t$$

$$\omega_1 = \sqrt{2}\sqrt{0.382k/m} \quad \omega_2 = \sqrt{2}\sqrt{2.618k/m}$$

5.18. The double pendulum of Prob. 5.11 is started with the following initial conditions: $x_1(0) = x_2(0) = X$, $\dot{x}_1(0) = \dot{x}_2(0) = 0$. Determine the equations of motion.

5.19. Set up the matrix equation of motion for the system shown in Fig. P5.19 using coordinates x_1 and x_2 at m and $2m$. Determine the equation for the normal mode frequencies and describe the mode shapes.

5.20. In Prob. 5.19, if the coordinates x at m and θ are used, what form of coupling will result?

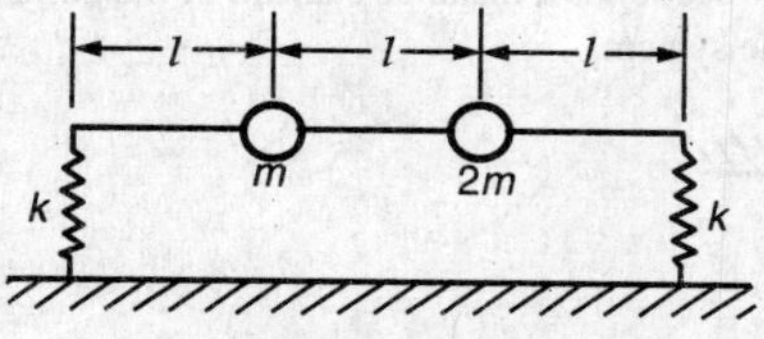

FIGURE P5.19.

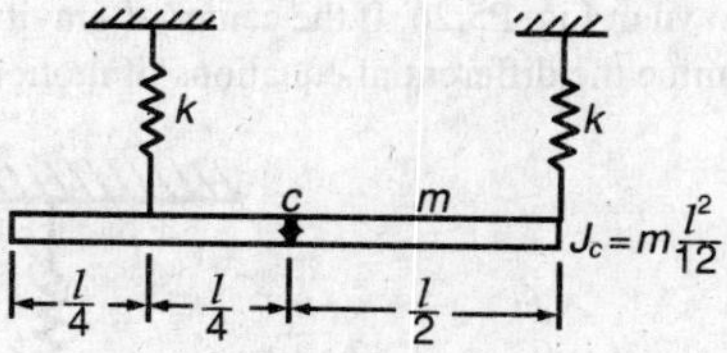

FIGURE P5.21.

5.21. Choose coordinates x for the displacement of c and θ clockwise for the rotation of the uniform bar shown in Fig. P5.21, and determine the natural frequencies and mode shapes.

5.22. Compare Probs. 5.11 and 5.12 in matrix form and indicate the type of coupling present in each coordinate system.

5.23. The following information is given for the automobile shown in Fig. P5.23.

$$m = 1600\text{ kg} \quad k_1 = 30{,}000\text{ N/m}$$
$$l_1 = 1.34\text{ m} \quad k_2 = 36{,}000\text{ N/m}$$
$$l_2 = 1.70\text{ m}$$
$$r = 1.22\text{ m} = \text{radius of gyration about c.g.}$$

Determine the normal modes of vibration and locate the node for each mode.

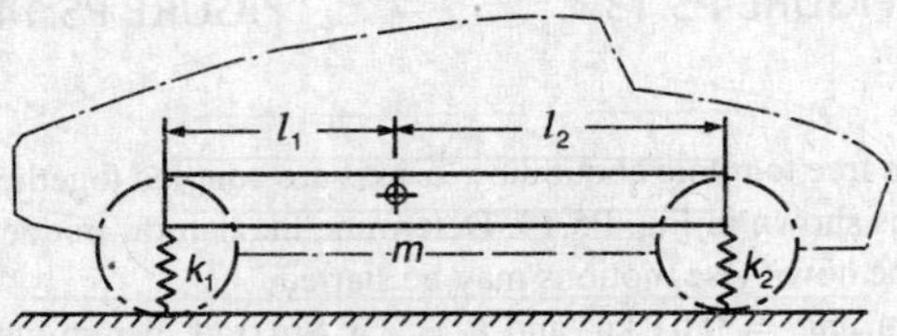

FIGURE P5.23.

5.24. Referring to Prob. 5.23 prove in general that the uncoupled natural frequencies are always between the coupled natural frequencies.

5.25. For Prob. 5.23, if we include the mass of the wheels and the stiffness of the tires, the problem becomes that of 4 DOF. Draw the spring-mass model and show that its equation of motion is

$$\begin{bmatrix} m & & & \\ & J & & \\ & & m_0 & \\ & & & m_0 \end{bmatrix}\begin{Bmatrix} \ddot{x} \\ \ddot{\theta} \\ \ddot{x}_1 \\ \ddot{x}_2 \end{Bmatrix} + \begin{bmatrix} (k_1 + k_2) & (k_2 l_2 - k_1 l_1) & -k_1 & -k_2 \\ (k_2 l_2 - k_1 l_1) & (k_1 l_1^2 - k_2 l_2^2) & k_1 l_1 & -k_2 l_2 \\ -k_1 & k_1 l_1 & (k_0 + k_1) & 0 \\ -k_2 & -k_2 l_2 & 0 & (k_0 + k_2) \end{bmatrix}\begin{Bmatrix} x \\ \theta \\ x_1 \\ x_2 \end{Bmatrix} = \begin{Bmatrix} 0 \\ 0 \\ 0 \\ 0 \end{Bmatrix}$$

5.26. An airfoil section to be tested in a wind tunnel is supported by a linear spring k and a torsional spring K, as shown in Fig. P5.26. If the center of gravity of the section is a distance e ahead of the point of support, determine the differential equations of motion of the system.

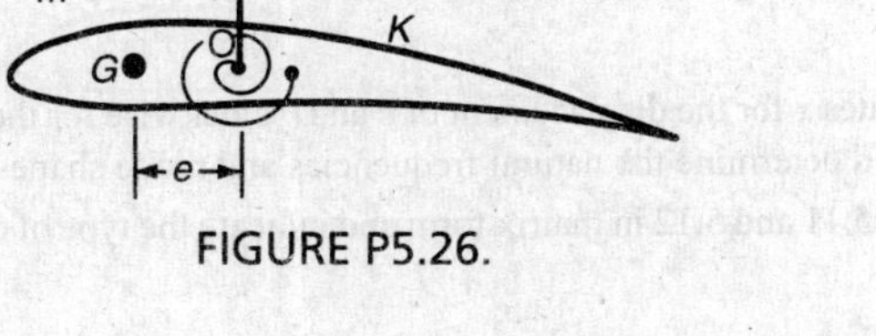

FIGURE P5.26.

5.27. To justify the 2-DOF simplified model of the automobile in Example 5.3.2, assume the mass of each wheel, hub, and tire to be approximately 35 kg, and the tire stiffness per wheel to be 330,000 N/m. Determine the natural frequency of its wheel–tire system, and explain why the simplified model is adequate.

5.28. Determine the natural frequencies and normal modes of the system shown in Fig. P5.28 when

$$m_1 = 1.5\,\text{kg} \qquad k_1 = 3500\,\text{N/m}$$
$$m_2 = 0.75\,\text{kg} \qquad k_2 = 1750\,\text{N/m}$$

When forced by $F_1 = F_0 \sin \omega t$, determine the equations for the amplitudes and plot them against ω/ω_{11}.

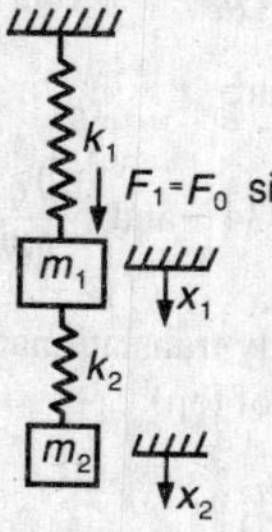

FIGURE P5.28.

5.29. A rotor is mounted in bearings that are free to move in a single plane, as shown in Fig. P5.29. The rotor is symmetrical about 0 with total mass M and moment of intertia J_0 about an axis perpendicular to the shaft. If a small unbalance mr acts at an axial distance b from its center O, determine the equations of motion for a rotational speed ω.

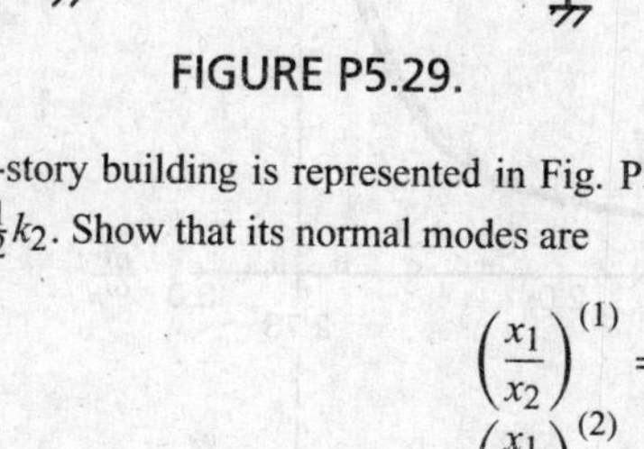

FIGURE P5.29.

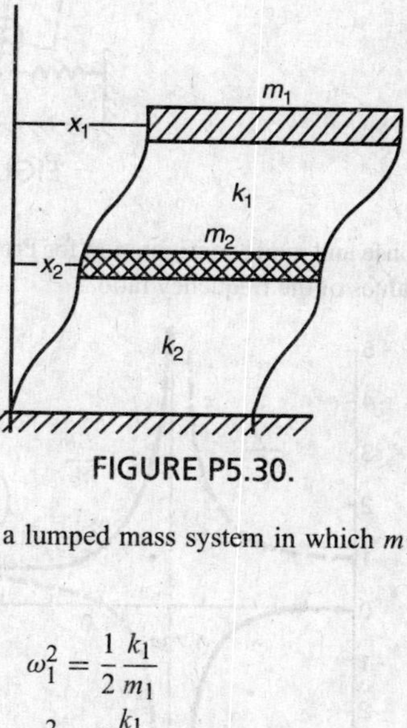

FIGURE P5.30.

5.30. A two-story building is represented in Fig. P5.30 by a lumped mass system in which $m_1 = \frac{1}{2}m_2$ and $k_1 = \frac{1}{2}k_2$. Show that its normal modes are

$$\left(\frac{x_1}{x_2}\right)^{(1)} = 2 \qquad \omega_1^2 = \frac{1}{2}\frac{k_1}{m_1}$$
$$\left(\frac{x_1}{x_2}\right)^{(2)} = -1 \qquad \omega_2^2 = 2\frac{k_1}{m_1}$$

If a force is applied to m_1 to deflect it by unity and the system is released from this position, determine the equation of motion of each mass by the normal mode summation method.

5.31. Repeat Prob. 5.30 if the load is applied to m_2, displacing it by unity.

5.32. Assume in Prob. 5.30 that an earthquake causes the ground to oscillate in the horizontal direction according to the equation $x_g = X_g \sin \omega t$. Determine the response of the building and plot it against ω/ω_1.

5.33. To simulate the effect of an earthquake on a rigid building, the base is assumed to be connected to the ground through two springs: K_h for the translational stiffness, and K_r for the rotational stiffness. If the ground is now given a harmonic motion, $Y_g = Y_G \sin \omega t$, set up the equations of motion in terms of the coordinates shown in Fig. P5.33. Solve the equations by letting

$$\omega_h^2 = \frac{K_h}{M} \qquad \left(\frac{\rho_c}{l_0}\right)^2 = \frac{1}{3}$$

$$\omega_r^2 = \frac{K_r}{M\rho_c^2} \qquad \left(\frac{\omega_r}{\omega_h}\right)^2 = 4$$

The first natural frequency and mode shape are

$$\frac{\omega_1}{\omega_h} = 0.734 \quad \text{and} \quad \frac{Y_0}{l_0\theta} = -1.14$$

which indicate a motion that is predominantly translational. Establish the second natural frequency and its mode ($Y_1 = Y_0 - 2l_0\theta_0 =$ displacement of top).

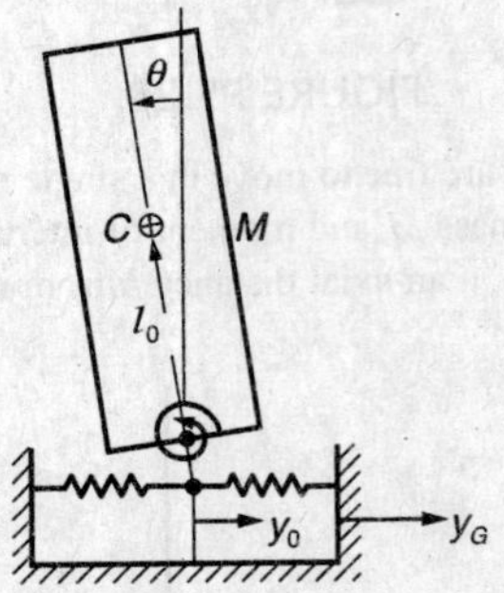

FIGURE P5.33.

5.34. The response and mode configuration for Prob. 5.33 are shown in Fig. P5.34. Verify the mode shapes for several values of the frequency ratio.

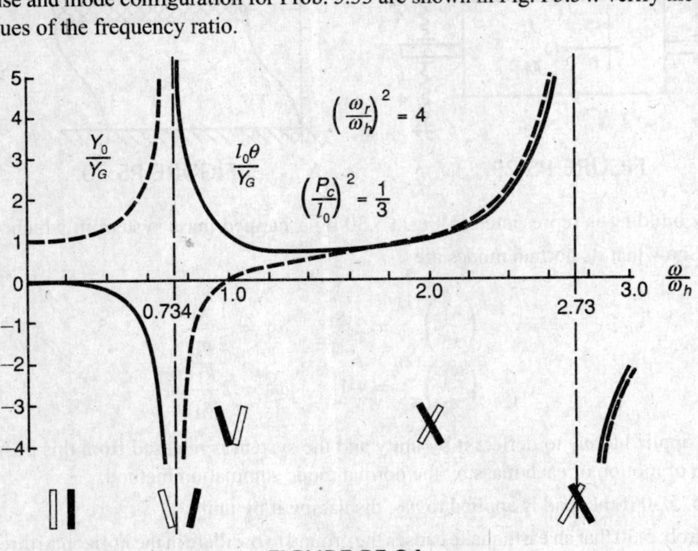

FIGURE P5.34.

5.35. The expansion joints of a concrete highway are 14 m apart. These joints cause a series of impulses at equal intervals to affect cars traveling at a constant speed. Determine the speeds at which pitching motion and up-and-down motion are most apt to arise for the automobile of Prob. 5.23.

5.36. For the system shown in Fig. P5.36, write the equation of motion in matrix form and determine the normal modes from the adjoint matrix.

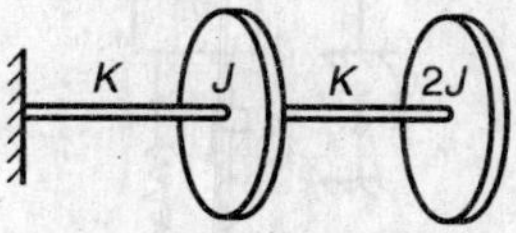

FIGURE P5.36.

5.37. Using the adjoint matrix, determine the normal modes of the spring-mass system shown in Fig. P5.37.

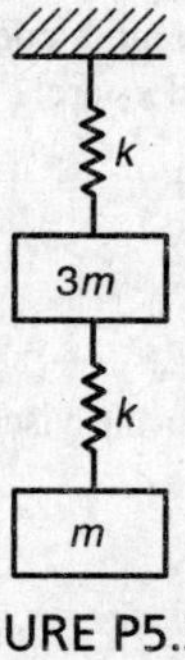

FIGURE P5.37.

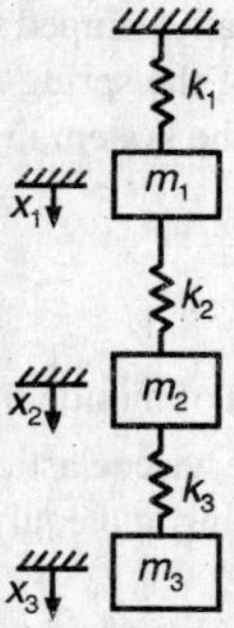

FIGURE P5.38.

5.38. Determine the flexibility matrix for the spring-mass system of three DOF shown in Fig. P5.38 and write its equation of motion in matrix form.

5.39. Determine the modal matrix P and the weighted modal matrix $\widetilde{P}$ for the system shown in Fig. P5.39 and diagonalize the stiffness matrix, thereby decoupling the equations.

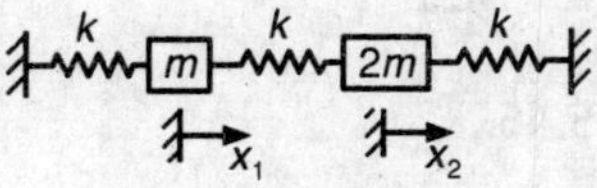

FIGURE P5.39.

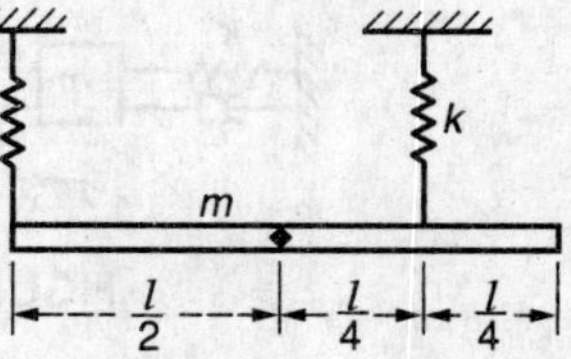

FIGURE P5.41.

5.40. Determine $\widetilde{P}$ for a double pendulum with coordinates θ_1 and θ_2. Show that $\widetilde{P}$ decouples the equations of motion.

5.41. Determine the modal matrix P and the weighted modal matrix $\widetilde{P}$ for the system shown in Fig. P5.41. Show that P or $\widetilde{P}$ will diagonalize the stiffness matrix.

5.42. If the lower end of the frame of Prob. 11.11 is rigidly fixed to the ground, the rotation of the corners will differ. Determine its stiffness matrix and determine its matrix equation of motion for m_i, J_i at the corners.

5.43. If in Prob. 11.10 masses and mass moment of inertia, m_1, J_1 and m_2, J_2, are attached to the corners so that they rotate as well as translate, determine the equations of motion and find the natural frequencies and mode shapes. Repeat the Problem 5.43 with the frame of Fig. 11.11.

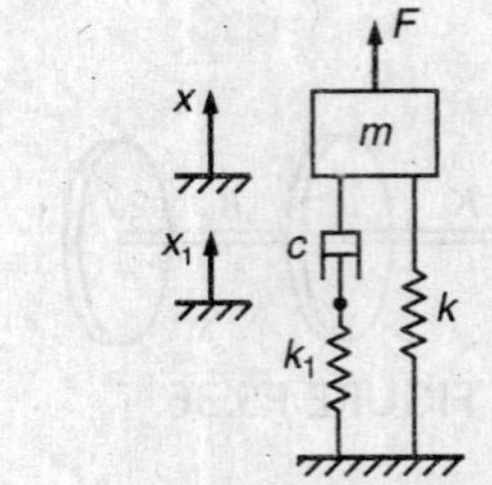

FIGURE P5.44.

5.44. Consider the viscoelastically damped system of Fig. P5.44. The system differs from the viscously damped system by the addition of the spring k_1, which introduces one more coordinate, x_1, to the system. The equations of motion for the system in inertial coordinates x and x_1 are

$$m\ddot{x} = -kx - c(\dot{x} - \dot{x}_1) + F$$

$$0 = c(\dot{x} - \dot{x}_1) - k_1 x_1$$

Write the equation of motion in matrix form.

5.45. Show, by comparing the viscoelastic system of Fig. P5.44 to the viscously damped system, that the equivalent viscous damping and equivalent stiffness are

$$c_{eq} = \frac{c}{1 + \left(\frac{\omega c}{k_1}\right)^2}$$

$$k_{eq} = \frac{k + (k_1 + k)\left(\frac{\omega c}{k_1}\right)^2}{1 + \left(\frac{\omega c}{k_1}\right)^2}$$

5.46. Determine the damping matrix for the system presented in Fig. P5.46 and show that it is not proportional.

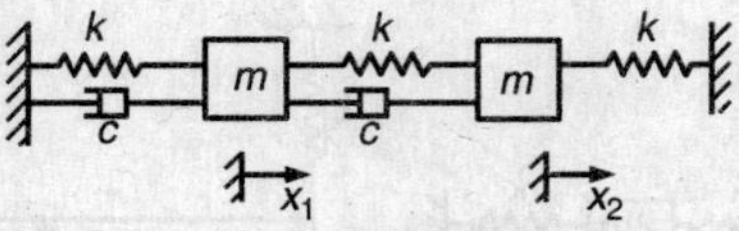

FIGURE P5.46.

5.47. Using the modal matrix $\widetilde{P}$, reduce the system of Prob. 5.46 to one that is coupled only by damping and solve by the Laplace transform method.

5.48. Verify the relationship of Eq. (5.5.7)

$$\phi_i^T K \phi_j = 0 \qquad i \neq j$$

by applying it to Prob. 5.36.

5.49. Starting with the matrix equation

$$K\phi_s = \omega_s^2 M \phi_s$$

premultiply first by KM^{-1} and, using the orthogonality relation $\phi_r^T M\phi_s = 0$, show that

$$\phi_r^T KM^{-1}K\phi_s = 0$$

Repeat to show that

$$\phi_r^T [KM^{-1}]^h K\phi_s = 0$$

for $h = 1, 2, \ldots, n$, where n is the number of degrees of freedom of the system.

5.50. In a manner similar to Prob. 5.49, show that

$$\phi_r^T [MK^{-1}]^h M\phi_s = 0, \quad h = 1, 2, \ldots$$

5.51. Evaluate the numerical coefficients for the equations of motion for the second and third modes of Example 5.9.1.

5.52. If the acceleration $\ddot{u}(t)$ of the ground in Example 5.9.1 is a single sine pulse of amplitude a_0 and duration t_1, as shown in Fig. P5.52, determine the maximum q for each mode and the value of x_{max} as given in Sec. 5.9.

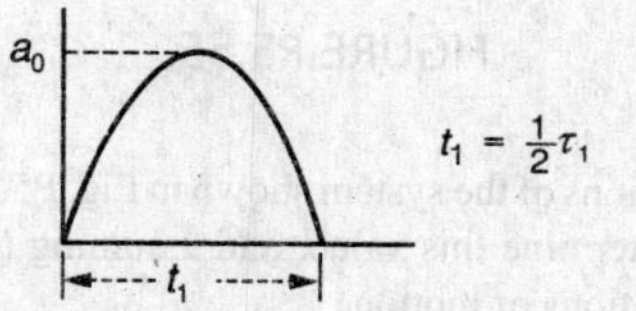

FIGURE P5.52.

5.53. The normal modes of the double pendulum of Prob. 5.11 are given as

$$\omega_1 = 0.764\sqrt{\frac{g}{l}} \qquad \omega_2 = 1.850\sqrt{\frac{g}{l}}$$

$$\phi_1 = \begin{Bmatrix}\theta_1\\ \theta_2\end{Bmatrix}_{(1)} = \begin{Bmatrix}0.707\\ 1.00\end{Bmatrix},$$

$$\phi_2 = \begin{Bmatrix}\theta_1\\ \theta_2\end{Bmatrix}_{(2)} = \begin{Bmatrix}-0.707\\ 1.00\end{Bmatrix}$$

If the lower mass is given an impulse $F_0\delta(t)$, determine the response in terms of the normal modes.

5.54. The normal modes of the three-mass torsional system of Fig. P11.7 are given for $J_1 = J_2 = J_3$ and $K_1 = K_2 = K_3$.

$$\phi_1 = \begin{Bmatrix}0.328\\ 0.591\\ 0.737\end{Bmatrix} \qquad \lambda_1 = \frac{J\omega_1^2}{k} = 0.198,$$

$$\phi_2 = \begin{Bmatrix}0.737\\ 0.328\\ -0.591\end{Bmatrix} \qquad \lambda_2 = 1.555,$$

$$\phi_3 = \begin{Bmatrix}0.591\\ -0.737\\ 0.328\end{Bmatrix} \qquad \lambda_3 = 3.247$$

Determine the equations of motion if a torque $M(t)$ is applied to the free end. If $M(t) = M_0 u(t)$, where $u(t)$ is a unit step function, determine the time solution and the maximum response of the end mass from the shock spectrum.

5.55. Using two normal modes, set up the equations of motion for the five-storey building whose foundation stiffness in translation and rotation is k_t and $K_r = \infty$, respectively (see Fig. P5.55).

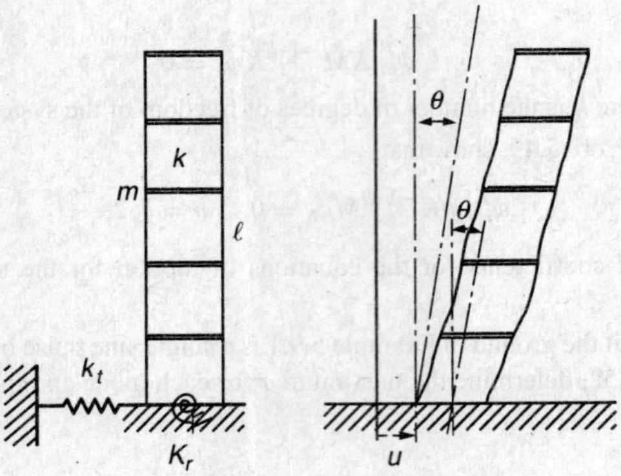

FIGURE P5.55.

5.56. The lateral and torsional oscillations of the system shown in Fig. P5.56 will have equal natural frequencies for a specific value of a/L. Determine this value, and assuming that there is an eccentricity e of mass equal to me, determine the equations of motion.

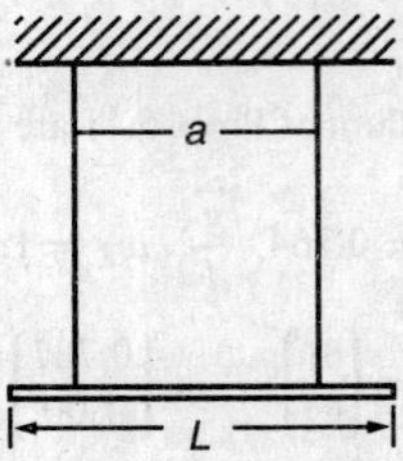

FIGURE P5.56.

5.57. Assume that a three-storey building with rigid floor girders has Rayleigh damping. If the modal dampings for the first and second modes are 0.05% and 0.13%, respectively, determine the modal damping for the third mode.

5.58. The normal modes of a 3-DOF system with $m_1 = m_2 = m_3$ and $k_1 = k_2 = k_3$, are given as

$$\phi_1 = \begin{Bmatrix} 0.737 \\ 0.591 \\ 0.328 \end{Bmatrix}, \quad \phi_2 = \begin{Bmatrix} -0.591 \\ 0.328 \\ 0.737 \end{Bmatrix}, \quad \phi_3 = \begin{Bmatrix} 0.328 \\ -0.737 \\ 0.591 \end{Bmatrix}$$

Verify the orthogonal properties of these modes. The system is given an initial displacement of

$$X = \begin{Bmatrix} 0.520 \\ -0.100 \\ 0.205 \end{Bmatrix}$$

and released. Determine how much of each mode will be present in the free vibration.

5.59. In general, the free vibration of an undamped system can be represented by the modal sum

$$X(t) = \sum_i A_i\phi_i \sin \omega_i t + \sum_i B_i\phi_i \cos \omega_i t$$

If the system is started from zero displacement and an arbitrary distribution of velocity $\dot{X}(0)$, determine the coefficients A_i and B_i.

5.60. Figure P5.60 shows a shaft supported by a bearing that has translational and rotational flexibility. Show that the left side of the shaft flexibility Eq. (11.1.1) or (11.1.2) of Example 11.1.4 should now be replaced by

$$\begin{Bmatrix} \eta \\ \theta - \beta \end{Bmatrix}$$

From the relationship between η, β, y, θ, and loads P and M, determine the new flexibility equation

$$\begin{Bmatrix} y \\ \theta \end{Bmatrix} = \begin{bmatrix} \bar{a}_{11} & \bar{a}_{12} \\ \bar{a}_{21} & \bar{a}_{22} \end{bmatrix} \begin{Bmatrix} P \\ M \end{Bmatrix}$$

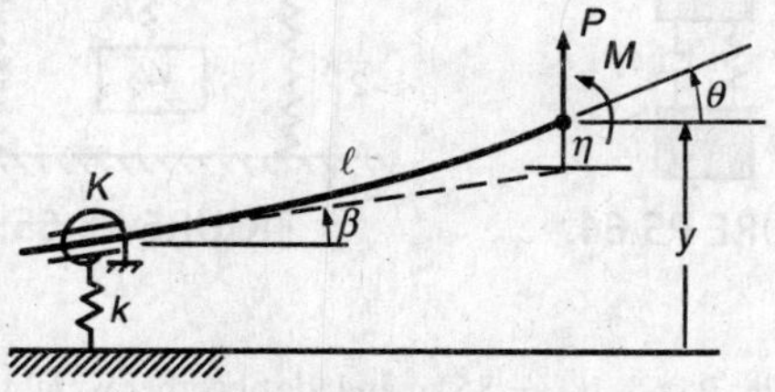

FIGURE P5.60.

5.61. Set up the matrix equation of motion for the 3-DOF system of Fig. P5.38 in terms of stiffness. Transform it to the standard eigen-problem form, where A is symmetric.

[M] **5.62.** In Example 5.9.1 for the forced vibration of a 10-storey building, the equation of motion for the first mode was given as

$$\ddot{q}_1 + 0.299\sqrt{\frac{k}{m}}\zeta_1\dot{q}_1 + 0.02235\frac{k}{m}q_1 = -1.2672\ddot{u}_0(t)$$

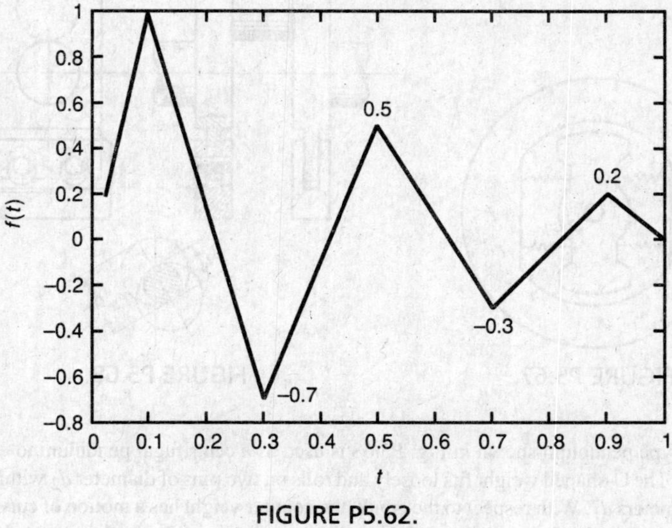

FIGURE P5.62.

Assume the values $\sqrt{k/m} = 3.0$ and $\zeta_1 = 0.10$, and solve for the time response using RUNGA when the ground acceleration is given by Fig. P5.62. You will have to write a function **file f.m** that contains an expression for the function given in Fig. P5.62.

5.63. Determine the stiffness matrix for the system of two pendula coupled by a rubber hose in Fig. P5.14.

5.64. Consider the system given in Fig. P5.64, with the damping force proportional to the square of the velocity. Is it possible to develop an equivalent damping approach for this problem (cf. Sec. 3.8)?

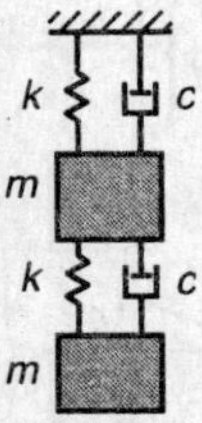

FIGURE P5.64.

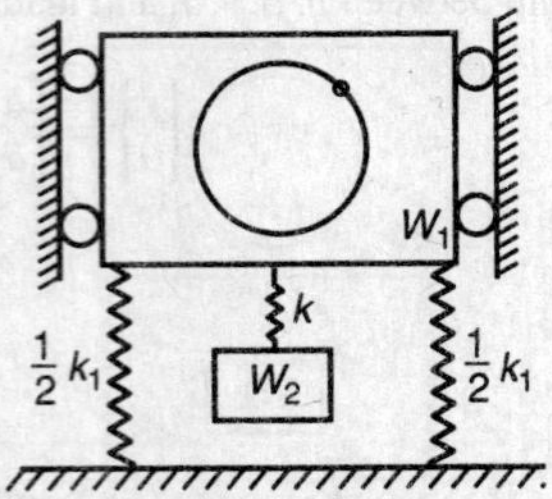

FIGURE P5.65.

5.65. For the system shown in Fig. P5.65, $W_1 = 85$ kg and the absorber weight $W_2 = 21.5$ kg. If W_1 is excited by a 23 g m, unbalance rotating at 1800 rpm, determine the proper value of the absorber spring k_2. What will be the amplitude of W_2?

5.66. In Prob. 5.65, if a dashpot c is introduced between W_1 and W_2, determine the amplitude equations by the complex algebra method.

5.67. A flywheel with moment of inertia I has a torsional absorber with moment of inertia I_d free to rotate on the shaft and connected to the flywheel by four springs of stiffness k N/m, as shown in Fig. P5.67. Set up the differential equations of motion for the system, and discuss the response of the system to an oscillatory torque.

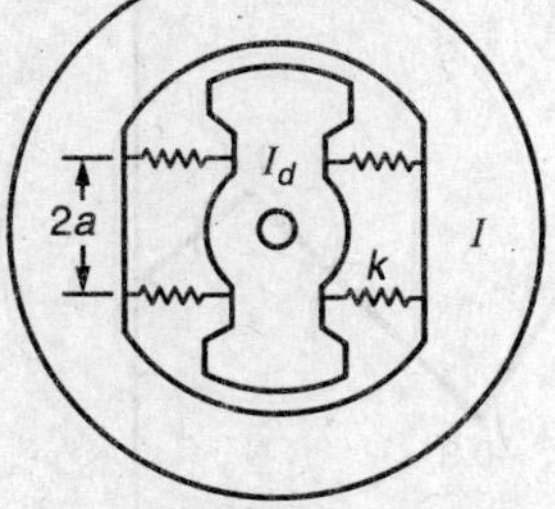

FIGURE P5.67.

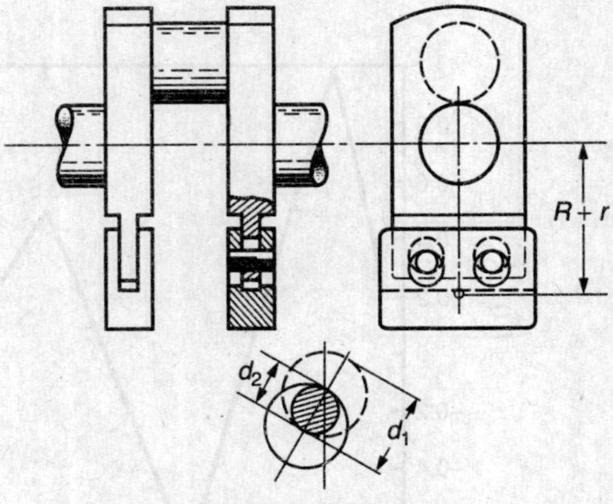

FIGURE P5.68.

5.68. The bifilar-type pendulum shown in Fig. P5.68 is used as a centrifugal pendulum to eliminate torsional oscillations. The U-shaped weight fits loosely and rolls on two pins of diameter d_2 within two larger holes of equal diameters d_1. With respect to the crank, the counterweight has a motion of curvilinear translation with each point moving in a circular path or radius $r = d_1 - d_2$. Prove that the U-shaped weight does indeed move in a circular path of $r = d_1 - d_2$.

5.69. A bifilar-type centrifugal pendulum is proposed to eliminate a torsional disturbance of frequency equal to four times the rotational speed. If the distance R to the center of gravity of the pendulum mass is 100 mm and $d_1 = 19$ mm, what must be the diameter d_2 of the pins?

5.70. A jig used to size coal contains a screen that reciprocates with a frequency of 600 cpm. The jig weighs 228 kg and has a fundamental frequency of 400 cpm. If an absorber weighing 57 kg is to be installed to eliminate the vibration of the jig frame, determine the absorber spring stiffness. What will be the resulting two natural frequencies of the system?

5.71. In a certain refrigeration plant, a section of pipe carrying the refrigerant vibrated violently at a compressor speed of 232 rpm. To eliminate this difficulty, it was proposed to clamp a spring-mass system to the pipe to act as an absorber. For a trial test, a 1 kg absorber tuned to 232 cpm resulted in two natural frequencies of 198 and 272 cpm. If the absorber system is to be designed so that the natural frequencies lie outside the region 160 to 320 cpm, what must be the weight and spring stiffness?

5.72. A type of damper frequently used on automobile crankshafts is shown in Fig. P5.72. J represents a solid disk free to spin on the shaft, and the space between the disk and case is filled with a silicone oil of coefficient of viscosity μ. The damping action results from any relative motion between the two. Derive an equation for the damping torque exerted by the disk on the case due to a relative velocity of ω.

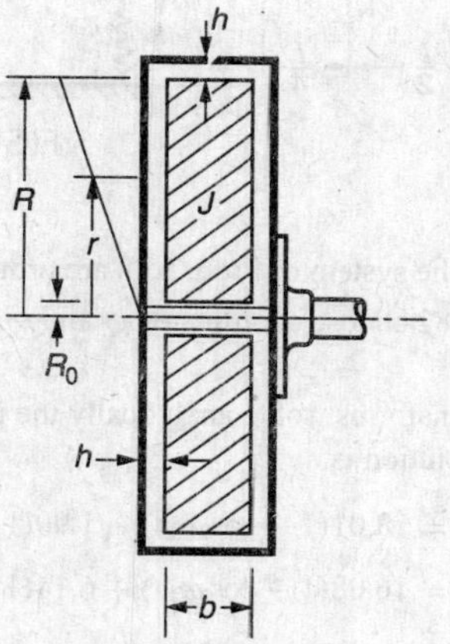

FIGURE P5.72.

5.73. For the Houdaille viscous damper with mass ratio $\mu = 0.25$, determine the optimum damping ζ_0 and the frequency at which the damper is most effective.

5.74. If the damping for the viscous damper of Prob. 5.73 is equal to $\zeta = 0.10$, determine the peak amplitude as compared to the optimum.

5.75. Establish the relationships given by Eqs. (5.15.6) and (5.15.7).

5.76. Derive the equations of motion for the two masses in Fig. 5.15.5 and follow the parallel development of the untuned torsional vibration-damper problem.

M **5.77.** Develop the MATLAB® program for the computation of the response of the system shown in Prob. 5.1 when the mass $3m$ is excited by a rectangular pulse of magnitude 50 N and duration $6\pi\sqrt{m/ks}$.

M **5.78.** In Prob. 5.30 assume the following data: $k_1 = 7 \times 10^5$ N/m, $k_2 = 10.5 \times 10^5$ N/m, and $m_1 = m_2 = 1000$ kg. Develop the MATLAB® program for the case in which the ground is given a displacement $y = 0.25 \sin \pi t$ for 4 s.

5.79. Figure P5.79 shows a degenerate 3 DOF. Its characteristic equation yields one zero root and two elastic vibration frequencies. Discuss the physical significance that three coordinates are required but only two natural frequencies are obtained.

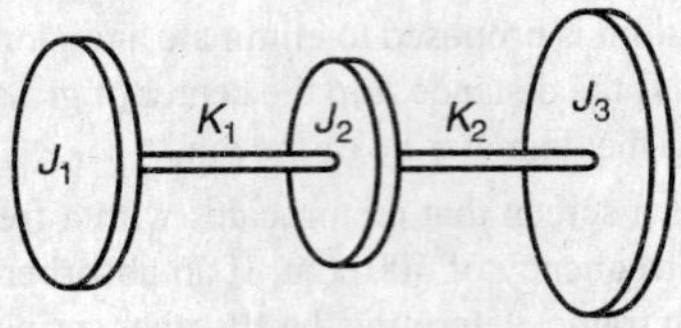

FIGURE P5.79.

5.80. The two uniform rigid bars shown in Fig. P5.80 are of equal length but of different masses. Determine the equations of motion and the natural frequencies and mode shapes using matrix methods.

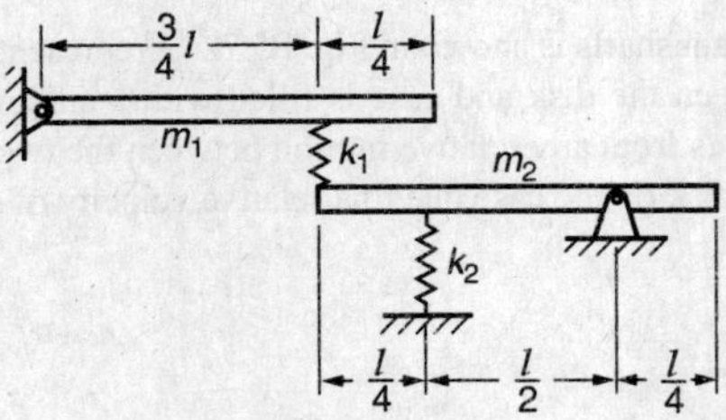

FIGURE P5.80.

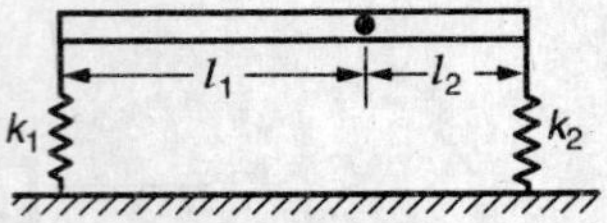

FIGURE P5.82.

5.81. Show that the normal modes of the system of Prob. 5.78 are orthogonal.

5.82. For the system shown in Fig. P5.82 choose coordinates x_2 and x_2 at the ends of the bar and determine the type of coupling this introduces.

5.83. Using the method of Laplace transforms, solve analytically the problem solved by the digital computer in Sec. 5.12 and show that the solution is

$$x_{cm} = 13.01(1 - \cos\omega_1 t) - 1.90(1 - \cos\omega_2 t)$$

$$y_{cm} = 16.08(1 - \cos\omega_1 t) + 6.14(1 - \cos\omega_2 t)$$

5.84. Consider the free vibration of any two degrees-of-freedom system with arbitrary initial conditions, and show by examination of the subsidiary equations of Laplace transforms that the solution is the sum of normal modes.

5.85. Determine by the method of Laplace transformation the solution to the forced-vibration problem shown in Fig. P5.85. Initial conditions are $x_1(0)$, $\dot{x}_1(0)$, $x_2(0)$, and $\dot{x}_2(0)$.

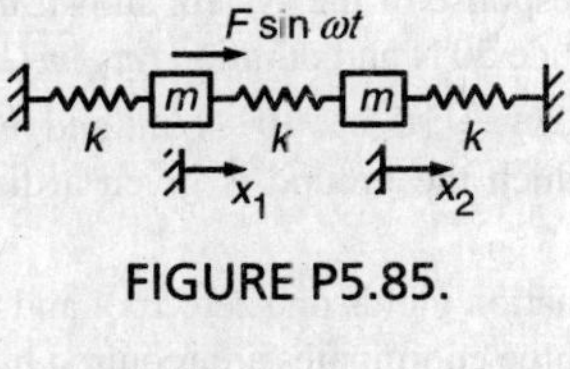

FIGURE P5.85.

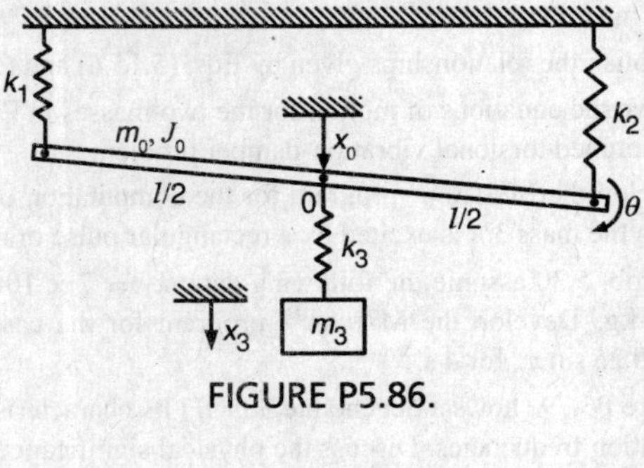

FIGURE P5.86.

5.86. Determine the matrix equation of motion for the system shown in Fig. P5.86.

5.87. Determine the matrix equation of motion for the system shown in Fig. P5.87.

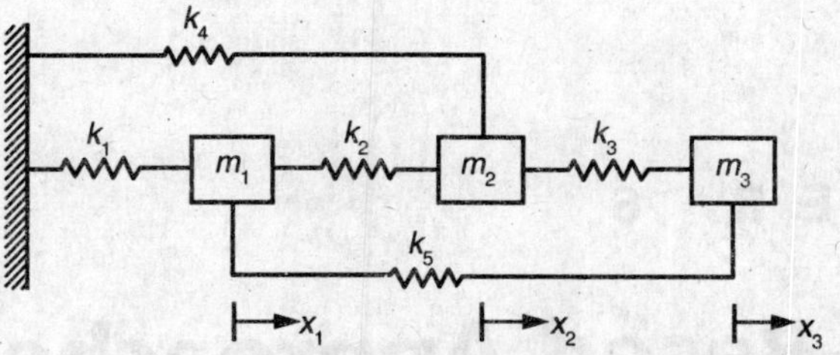

FIGURE P5.87.

M **5.88.** Consider the system with two coupled pendula of Example 5.1.3, and do not assume small displacement from the vertical position. It is assumed that the pendula are coupled via a force varying linearly with the difference in angles of the pendula $F = -ka\sin(\theta_1 - \theta_2)$ being the force on pendulum 1. Derive the equations of motion. Simulate the system in MATLAB® with different initial conditions. Plot the angles θ_1 and θ_2 versus time. What can you conclude about the exchange of energy between the pendula (cf. Example 5.2.2)?

5.89. Consider the following coupled system for the rectilinear motion of two particles:

$$\ddot{x}_1 = f_1(x_1, x_2)$$

$$\ddot{x}_2 = f_2(x_1, x_2)$$

Show that if the form of the equations stays the same when $x_1 + c$, $x_2 + c$ is inserted instead of x_1, x_2 (i.e., the system is invariant with respect to translations), then the system reduces to one equation for the variable $y = x_2 - x_1$,

$$\ddot{y} = f(y).$$

This is an example of using symmetries to reduce the dimensionality of the system. In this case, we have reduced the number of degrees of freedom by 1.

5.90. Consider the system shown in Figure P5.90 that models the motion of seats of a ski-lift. Determine the equations of motion. Determine the natural frequencies. Should the stiffness of the spring (which models the cable on which the seats are mounted) be high or low in order for the skiers *not* to experience very fast oscillations of the seat?

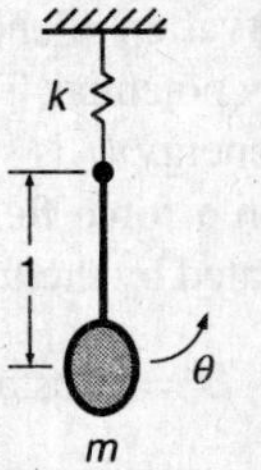

FIGURE P5.90.

CHAPTER 6

Energy-Based Approaches

In our previous discussions, the Newton's vector method offered a simple approach for systems of a few degrees of freedom. The necessity for the consideration of forces of constraints and free-body diagrams in this method leads to algebraic difficulties for systems of higher degrees of freedom.

An energy method can overcome the difficulties of the vector method. But the energy principle in terms of physical coordinates provides only one equation, which limits its use to single DOF systems.

The limitations of both the Newton's method and energy approach can be overcome using the principle of virtual work. However, it is not entirely a scalar procedure in that vector considerations of forces are necessary to determine the scalar virtual work quantity.

Joseph L.C. Lagrange (1736–1813) developed a general treatment of dynamical systems formulated from the scalar quantities of kinetic energy T, potential energy U, and work W. Lagrange's equations are in terms of generalized coordinates. This chapter begins with a look at the energy method using physical coordinates, followed by a look at virtual work and Lagrange's equations.

6.1 ENERGY METHOD

In a conservative system, the total energy is constant, and the differential equation of motion can also be established by the principle of conservation of energy. For the free vibration of an undamped system, the energy is partly kinetic and partly potential. The kinetic energy T is stored in the mass by virtue of its velocity, whereas the potential energy U is stored in the form of strain energy in elastic deformation or by a spring or work done in a force field such as gravity. The total energy being constant, its rate of change is zero, as illustrated by the following equations:

$$T + U = \text{constant} \tag{6.1.1}$$

$$\frac{d}{dt}(T + U) = 0 \tag{6.1.2}$$

If our interest is only in the natural frequency of the system, it can be determined by the following considerations. From the principle of conservation of energy, we can write

$$T_1 + U_1 = T_2 + U_2 \tag{6.1.3}$$

where 1 and 2 represent two instances of time. Let 1 be the time when the mass is passing through its static equilibrium position and choose $U_1 = 0$ as reference for the potential energy. Let 2 be the time corresponding to the maximum displacement of the mass. At this position, the velocity of the mass is zero, and hence $T_2 = 0$. We then have

$$T_1 + 0 = 0 + U_2 \tag{6.1.4}$$

However, if the system is undergoing harmonic motion, then T_1 and U_2 are maximum values, and hence

$$T_{max} = U_{max} \tag{6.1.5}$$

The preceding equation leads directly to the natural frequency.

Example 6.1.1

Determine the natural frequency of the system shown in Fig. 6.1.1.

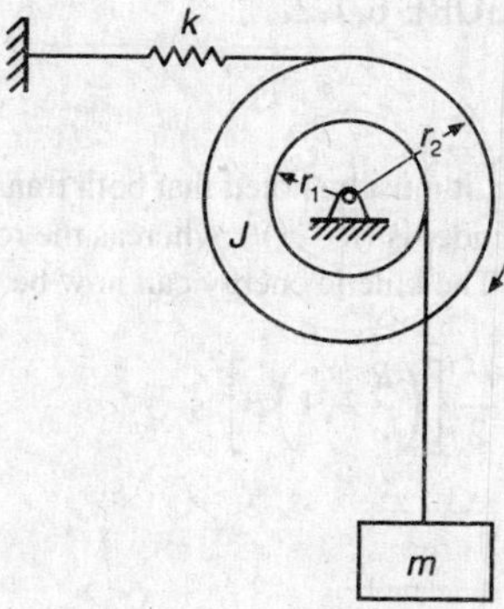

FIGURE 6.1.1.

Solution Assume that the system is vibrating harmonically with amplitude θ from its static equilibrium position. The maximum kinetic energy is

$$T_{max} = \left[\frac{1}{2}J\dot{\theta}^2 + \frac{1}{2}m(r_1\dot{\theta})^2\right]_{max}$$

The maximum potential energy is the energy stored in the spring, which is

$$U_{max} = \frac{1}{2}k(r_2\theta)^2_{max}$$

Equating the two, the natural frequency is

$$\omega_n = \sqrt{\frac{kr_2^2}{J + mr_1^2}}$$

The student should verify that the loss of potential energy of m due to position $r_1\theta$ is canceled by the work done by the equilibrium force of the spring in the position $\theta = 0$.

■

Example 6.1.2

A cylinder of weight w and radius r rolls without slipping on a cylindrical surface of radius R, as shown in Fig. 6.1.2. Determine its differential equation of motion for small oscillations about the lowest point. For no slipping, we have $r\phi = Rv$.

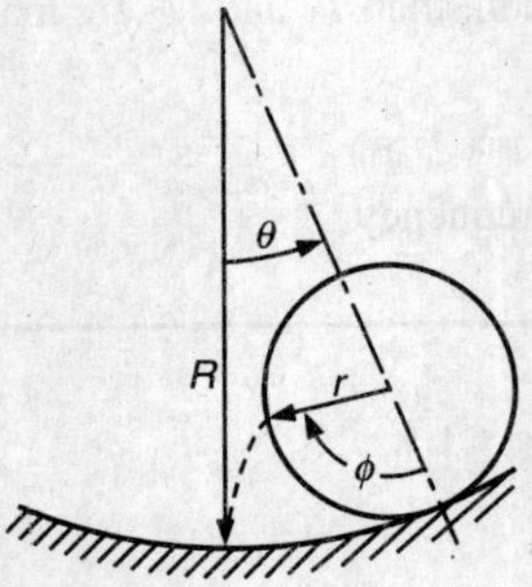

FIGURE 6.1.2.

Solution In determining the kinetic energy of the cylinder, it must be noted that both translation and rotation take place. The translational velocity of the center of the cylinder is $(R - r)\dot{\theta}$, whereas the rotational velocity is $(\dot{\phi} - \dot{\theta}) = (R/r - 1)\dot{\theta}$, because $\dot{\phi} = (R/r)\dot{\theta}$ for no slipping. The kinetic energy can now be written as

$$T = \frac{1}{2}\frac{w}{g}[(R-r)\dot{\theta}]^2 + \frac{1}{2}\frac{w}{g}\frac{r^2}{2}\left[\left(\frac{R}{r} - 1\right)\dot{\theta}\right]^2$$
$$= \frac{3}{4}\frac{w}{g}(R-r)^2\dot{\theta}^2$$

where $(w/g)(r^2/2)$ is the moment of inertia of the cylinder about its mass center.

The potential energy referred to its lowest position is

$$U = w(R-r)(1 - \cos\theta)$$

which is equal to the negative of the work done by the gravity force in lifting the cylinder through the vertical height $(R - r)(1 - \cos\theta)$.

Substituting into Eq. (6.1.2)

$$\left[\frac{3}{2}\frac{w}{g}(R-r)^2\ddot{\theta} + w(R-r)\sin\theta\right]\dot{\theta} = 0$$

and letting $\sin\theta = \theta$ for small angles, we obtain the familiar equation for harmonic motion

$$\ddot{\theta} + \frac{2g}{3(R-r)}\theta = 0$$

By inspection, the circular frequency of oscillation is

$$\omega_n = \sqrt{\frac{2g}{3(R-r)}}$$

■

6.2 RAYLEIGH METHOD: EFFECTIVE MASS

The energy method can be used for multimass systems or for distributed mass systems, provided the motion of every point in the system is known. In systems in which masses are joined by rigid links, levers, or gears, the motion of the various masses can be expressed in terms of the motion $\dot{x}$ of some specific point and the system is simply one of a single DOF, because only one coordinate is necessary. The kinetic energy can then be written as

$$T = \frac{1}{2} m_{\text{eff}} \dot{x}^2 \tag{6.2.1}$$

where m_{eff} is the *effective mass* or *an equivalent lumped mass* at the specified point. If the stiffness at that point is also known, the natural frequency can be calculated from the simple equation

$$\omega_n = \sqrt{\frac{k}{m_{\text{eff}}}} \tag{6.2.2}$$

In distributed mass systems such as springs and beams, a knowledge of the distribution of the vibration amplitude becomes necessary before the kinetic energy can be calculated. Rayleigh[1] showed that with a reasonable assumption for the shape of the vibration amplitude, it is possible to take into account previously ignored masses and arrive at a better estimate for the fundamental frequency. The following examples illustrate the use of both of these methods.

Example 6.2.1

Determine the effect of the mass of the spring on the natural frequency of the system shown in Fig. 6.2.1.

Solution With $\dot{x}$ equal to the velocity of the lumped mass m, we will assume the velocity of a spring element located at distance y from the fixed end to vary linearly with y as follows:

$$\dot{x}\frac{y}{l}.$$

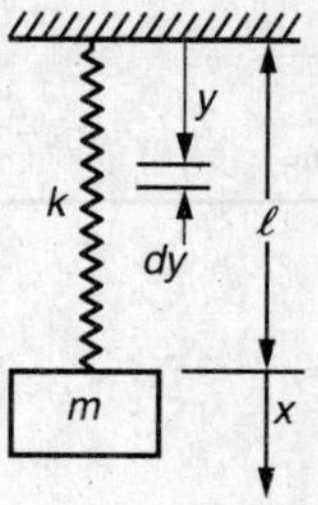

FIGURE 6.2.1. Effective mass of spring.

The kinetic energy of the spring can then be integrated to

$$T_{\text{add}} = \frac{1}{2}\int_0^l \left(\dot{x}\frac{y}{l}\right)^2 \frac{m_s}{l}\,dy = \frac{1}{2}\frac{m_s}{3}\dot{x}^2$$

and the effective mass is found to be one-third the mass of the spring. Adding this to the lumped mass, the revised natural frequency is

$$\omega_n = \sqrt{\frac{k}{m + \frac{1}{3}m_s}}$$

Example 6.2.2

A simply supported beam of total mass m_b has a concentrated mass M at midspan. Determine the effective mass of the system at midspan and find its fundamental frequency. The deflection under the load due to a concentrated force P applied at midspan is $Pl^3/48EI$. (See Fig. 6.2.2 and table of stiffness at the end of the chapter.)

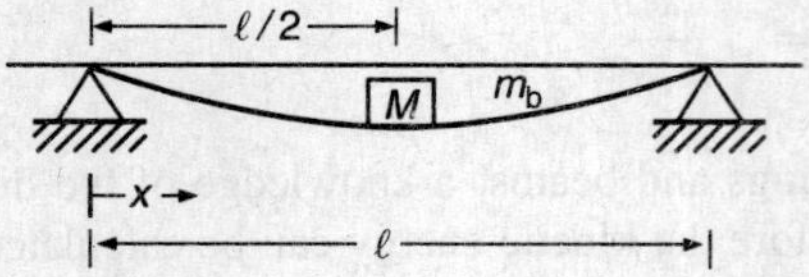

FIGURE 6.2.2. Effective mass of beam.

Solution We will assume the deflection of the beam to be that due to a concentrated load at midspan or

$$y = y_{\max}\left[\frac{3x}{l} - 4\left(\frac{x}{l}\right)^3\right] \quad \left(\frac{x}{l} \leqslant \frac{1}{2}\right)$$

The maximum kinetic energy of the beam itself is then

$$T_{\max} = \frac{1}{2}\int_0^{l/2} \frac{2m_b}{l}\left\{\dot{y}_{\max}\left[\frac{3x}{l} - 4\left(\frac{x}{l}\right)^3\right]\right\}^2 dx = \frac{1}{2}(0.4857m_b)\dot{y}^2_{\max}$$

The effective mass at midspan is then equal to

$$m_{\text{eff}} = M + 0.4857m_b$$

and its natural frequency becomes

$$\omega_n = \sqrt{\frac{48EI}{l^3(M + 0.4857m_b)}}$$

6.3 GENERALIZED COORDINATES

Generalized coordinates are any set of independent coordinates equal in number to the degrees of freedom of the system. Thus, the equations of motion of the previous chapter were formulated in terms of generalized coordinates.

In more complex systems, it is often convenient to describe the system in terms of coordinates, some of which may not be independent. Such coordinates may be related to each other by *constraint equations*.

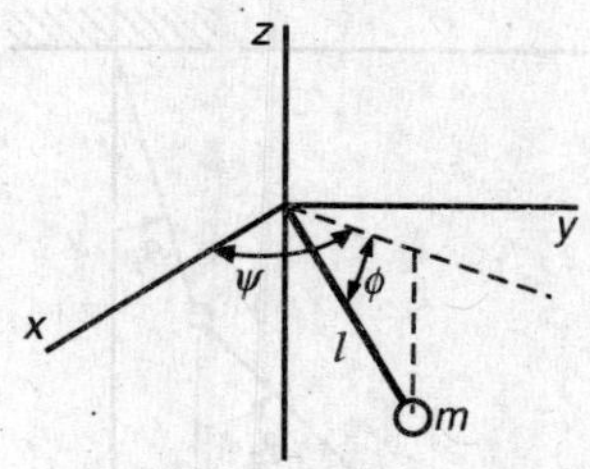

FIGURE 6.3.1.

Constraints. Motions of bodies are not always free, and are often constrained to move in a predetermined manner. As a simple, the position of the spherical pendulum of Fig. 6.3.1 can be completely defined by the two independent coordinates ψ and ϕ. Hence, ψ and ϕ are generalized coordinates, and the spherical pendulum represents a system of two degrees of freedom.

The position of the spherical pendulum can also be described by the three rectangular coordinates, x, y, z, which exceed the degrees of freedom of the system by 1. Coordinates x, y, z are, however, not independent, because they are related by the *constraint equation*:

$$x^2 + y^2 + z^2 - l^2 = 0 \tag{6.3.1}$$

One of the coordinates can be eliminated by the preceding equation, thereby reducing the number of necessary coordinates to 2.

The excess coordinates exceeding the number of degrees of freedom of the system are called *superfluous coordinates*, and constraint equations equal in number to the superfluous coordinates are necessary for their elimination. Constraints are called *holonomic* if the excess coordinates can be eliminated through equations of constraint. We will deal only with holonomic systems in this text.

Examine now the problem of defining the position of the double pendulum of Fig. 6.3.2. The double pendulum has only 2 DOF and the angles θ_1 and θ_2 completely define the position of m_1 and m_2. Thus, θ_1 and θ_2 are generalized coordinates, i.e., $\theta_1 = q_1$ and $\theta_2 = q_2$.

The position of m_1 and m_2 can also be expressed in rectangular coordinates x, y. However, they are related by the constraint equations

$$l_1^2 = x_1^2 + y_1^2$$
$$l_2^2 = (x_2 - x_1)^2 + (y_2 - y_1)^2$$

and hence are not independent. We can express the rectangular coordinates x_i, y_i in terms of the generalized coordinates θ_1 and θ_2

$$x_1 = l_1 \sin\theta_1, \quad x_2 = l_1 \sin\theta_1 + l_2 \sin\theta_2$$
$$y_1 = l_1 \cos\theta_1, \quad y_2 = l_1 \cos\theta_1 + l_2 \cos\theta_2$$

and these can also be considered as constraint equations.

To determine the kinetic energy, the squares of the velocity can be written in terms of the generalized coordinates:

$$v_1^2 = \dot{x}_1^2 + \dot{y}_1^2 = (l_1\dot{\theta}_1)^2$$
$$v_2^2 = \dot{x}_2^2 + \dot{y}_2^2 = [l_1\dot{\theta}_1 + l_2\dot{\theta}_2 \cos(\theta_2 - \theta_1)]^2 + [l_2\dot{\theta}_2 \sin(\theta_2 - \theta_1)]^2$$

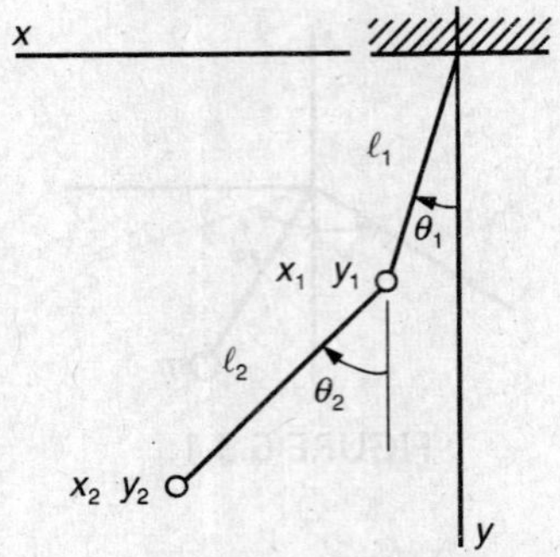

FIGURE 6.3.2.

The kinetic energy

$$T = \frac{1}{2}m_1 v_1^2 + \frac{1}{2}m_2 v_2^2$$

is then a function of both $q = \theta$ and $\dot{q} = \dot{\theta}$:

$$T = T(q_1, q_2, \ldots, \dot{q}_1, \dot{q}_2, \ldots) \tag{6.3.2}$$

For the potential energy, the reference can be chosen at the level of the support point:

$$U = -m_1(l_1 \cos\theta_1) - m_2(l_1 \cos\theta_1 + l_2 \cos\theta_2)$$

The potential energy is then seen to be a function only of the generalized coordinates:

$$U = U(q_1, q_2, \ldots) \tag{6.3.3}$$

Example 6.3.1

Consider the plane mechanism shown in Fig. 6.3.3, where the members are assumed to be rigid. Describe all possible motions in terms of generalized coordinates.

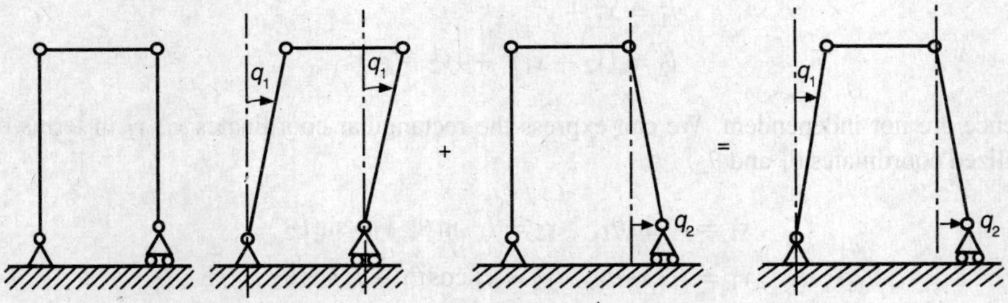

FIGURE 6.3.3.

Solution As shown in Fig. 6.3.3, the displacements can be obtained by the superposition of two displacements q_1 and q_2. Because q_1 and q_2 are independent, they are generalized coordinates, and the system has 2 DOF. ■

Example 6.3.2

The plane frame shown in Fig. 6.3.4 has flexible members. Determine a set of generalized coordinates of the system. Assume that the corners remain at 90°.

Solution There are two translational modes, q_1 and q_2, and each of the four corners can rotate independently, making a total of six generalized coordinates, $q_1, q_2, \ldots, q_6$. By allowing each of these displacements to take place with all others equal to zero, the displacement of the frame can be seen to be the superposition of the six generalized coordinates.

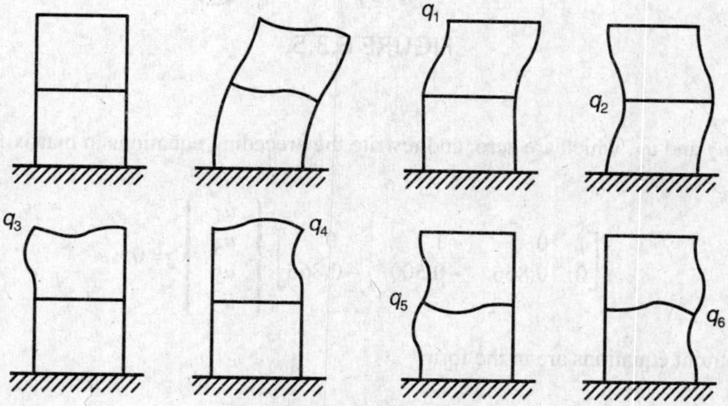

FIGURE 6.3.4.

■

Example 6.3.3

In defining the motion of a framed structure, the number of coordinates chosen often exceeds the number of degrees of freedom of the system so that constraint equations are involved. It is then desirable to express all of the coordinates u in terms of the fewer generalized coordinates q by a matrix equation of the form

$$u = Cq$$

The generalized coordinates q can be chosen arbitrarily from the coordinates u.

As an illustration of this equation, we consider the framed structure of Fig. 6.3.5 consisting of four beam elements. We will be concerned only with the displacement of the joints and not the stresses in the members, which would require an added consideration of the distribution of the masses.

In Fig. 6.3.5, we have four element members with three joints that can undergo displacement. Two linear displacements and one rotation are possible for each joint. We can label them u_1 to u_9. For compatibility of displacement, the following constraints are observed:

$$u_2 = u_8 = 0 \quad \text{(no axial extension)}$$

$$u_1 = u_5 \quad \text{(axial length remains unchanged)}$$

$$(u_4 \cos 30° - u_5 \cos 60°) - (u_7 \cos 30° - u_8 \cos 60°) = 0$$

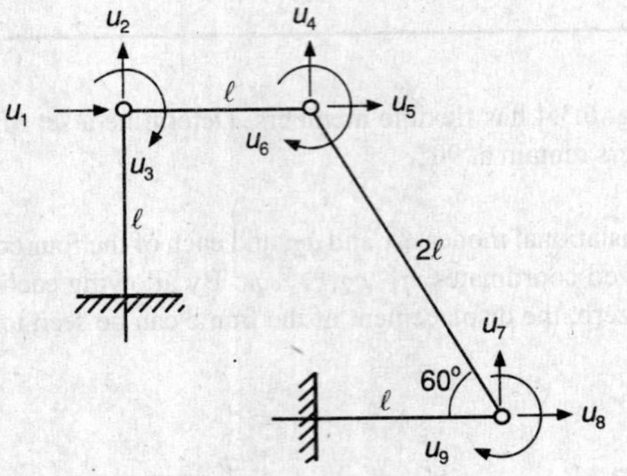

FIGURE 6.3.5.

We now disregard u_2 and u_8, which are zero, and rewrite the preceding equations in matrix form:

$$\begin{bmatrix} 1 & 0 & -1 & 0 \\ 0 & 0.866 & -0.500 & -0.866 \end{bmatrix} \begin{Bmatrix} u_1 \\ u_4 \\ u_5 \\ u_7 \end{Bmatrix} = 0 \tag{a}$$

Thus, the two constraint equations are in the form

$$[A]\{u\} = 0 \tag{b}$$

We actually have seven coordinates $(u_1, u_3, u_4, u_5, u_6, u_7, u_9)$ and two constraint equations. Thus, the degrees of freedom of the system are $7 - 2 = 5$, indicating that of the seven coordinates, five can be chosen as generalized coordinates q.

Of the four coordinates in the constraint equation, we choose u_5 and u_7 as two of the generalized coordinates and partition Eq. (a) as

$$[a|b]\begin{Bmatrix} u \\ - \\ q \end{Bmatrix} = [a]\{u\} + [b]\{q\} = 0 \tag{c}$$

Thus, the superfluous coordinates u can be expressed in terms of q as

$$\{u\} = -[a]^{-1}[b]\{q\} \tag{d}$$

Applying the preceding procedure to Eq. (a), we have

$$\begin{bmatrix} 1 & 0 \\ 0 & 0.866 \end{bmatrix}\begin{Bmatrix} u_1 \\ u_4 \end{Bmatrix} + \begin{bmatrix} -1 & 0 \\ -0.5 & -0.866 \end{bmatrix}\begin{Bmatrix} u_5 \\ u_7 \end{Bmatrix} = \begin{Bmatrix} 0 \\ 0 \end{Bmatrix}$$

$$\begin{Bmatrix} u_1 \\ u_4 \end{Bmatrix} = \begin{bmatrix} 1 & 0 \\ 0 & \frac{1}{0.866} \end{bmatrix}\begin{bmatrix} 1 & 0 \\ 0.5 & 0.866 \end{bmatrix}\begin{Bmatrix} u_5 \\ u_7 \end{Bmatrix} = \begin{bmatrix} 1 & 0 \\ 0.578 & 1 \end{bmatrix}\begin{Bmatrix} u_5 \\ u_7 \end{Bmatrix}$$

By supplying the remaining q_i as identities, all the u's can be expressed in terms of the q's as

$$\{u\} = [C]\{q\} \tag{e}$$

where the left side includes all the u's and the right column contains only the generalized coordinates. Thus, in our case, the seven u's expressed in terms of the five q's become

$$\begin{Bmatrix} u_1 \\ u_3 \\ u_4 \\ u_5 \\ u_6 \\ u_7 \\ u_9 \end{Bmatrix} = \begin{bmatrix} 0 & 1 & 0 & 0 & 0 \\ 1 & 0 & 0 & 0 & 0 \\ 0 & 0.578 & 0 & 1 & 0 \\ 0 & 1 & 0 & 0 & 0 \\ 0 & 0 & 1 & 0 & 0 \\ 0 & 0 & 0 & 1 & 0 \\ 0 & 0 & 0 & 0 & 1 \end{bmatrix} \begin{Bmatrix} u_3 \\ u_5 \\ u_6 \\ u_7 \\ u_9 \end{Bmatrix} \tag{f}$$

In Eq. (e) or (f), matrix C is the constraint matrix relating u to q.

■

Example 6.3.4

In the lumped-mass models we treated earlier, n coordinates were assigned to the n masses of the n-DOF system, and each coordinate was independent and qualified as a generalized coordinate. For the flexible continuous body of infinite degrees of freedom, an infinite number of coordinates is required. Such a body can be treated as a system of a finite number of degrees of freedom by considering its deflection to be the sum of its normal modes multiplied by generalized coordinates:

$$y(x,t) = \phi_1(x)q_1(t) + \phi_2(x)q_2(t) + \phi_3(x)q_3(t) + \cdots$$

In many problems, only a finite number of normal modes are sufficient, and the series can be terminated at n terms, thereby reducing the problem to that of a system of n DOF. For example, the motion of a slender free-free beam struck by a force P at point (a) can be described in terms of two rigid-body motions of translation and rotation plus its normal modes of elastic vibration, as shown in Fig. 6.3.6.

$$y(x,t) = \phi_T q_T + \phi_R q_R + \phi_1(x)q_1 + \phi_2(x)q_2 + \cdots$$

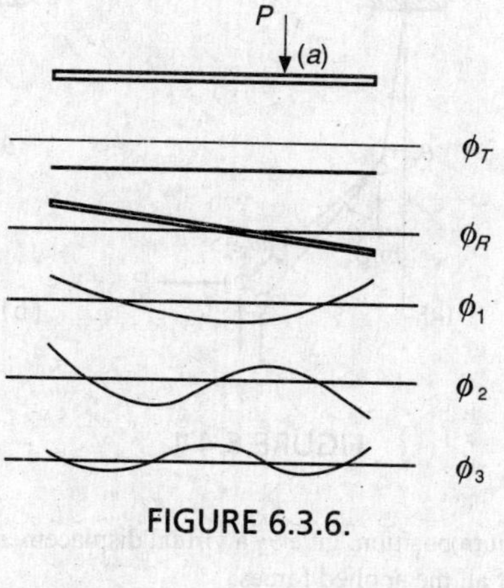

FIGURE 6.3.6.

■

6.4 VIRTUAL WORK

The advantage of the virtual work method over the vector method is considerably greater for multi-DOF systems. For interconnected bodies of many degrees of freedom, Newton's vector method is burdened with the necessity of accounting for all joint and constraint forces in the free-body diagrams, whereas these forces are excluded in the virtual work method.

In reviewing the method of virtual work, we summarize the virtual work equation as

$$\delta W = \sum_i \overline{F}_i \cdot \delta \overline{r}_i = 0 \tag{6.4.1}$$

where $\overline{F}_i$ are the applied forces excluding all constraint forces and internal forces of frictionless joints and $\delta\overline{r}_i$ are the virtual displacements. By including D'Alembert's inertia forces, $-m_i\ddot{\overline{r}}_i$, the procedure is extended to dynamical problems by the equation

$$\delta W = \sum_i (\overline{F}_i - m\ddot{\overline{r}}_i) \cdot \delta \overline{r}_i = 0 \tag{6.4.2}$$

This later equation leads to Lagrange's equation when the displacement $\overline{r}_i$ is expressed in terms of generalized coordinates.

The virtual displacements $\delta\overline{r}_i$ in these equations are arbitrary variations of the coordinates irrespective of time but compatible with the constraints of the system. Being an infinitesimal quantity, $\delta\overline{r}_i$ obeys all the rules of differential calculus. The difference between $\delta\overline{r}_i$ and $d\overline{r}_i$ is that $d\overline{r}_i$ takes place in the time dt, whereas $\delta\overline{r}_i$ is an arbitrary number that may be equal to $d\overline{r}_i$ but is assigned instantaneously irrespective of time. Although the virtual displacement $\delta\overline{r}$ is distinguished from $d\overline{r}$, the latter is often substituted for $\delta\overline{r}$ to ensure compatibility of displacement.

Example 6.4.1

We first illustrate the virtual work method for a problem of static equilibrium. Figure 6.4.1 shows a double pendulum with generalized coordinates θ_1 and θ_2. Determine its static equilibrium position when a horizontal force P is applied to m_2.

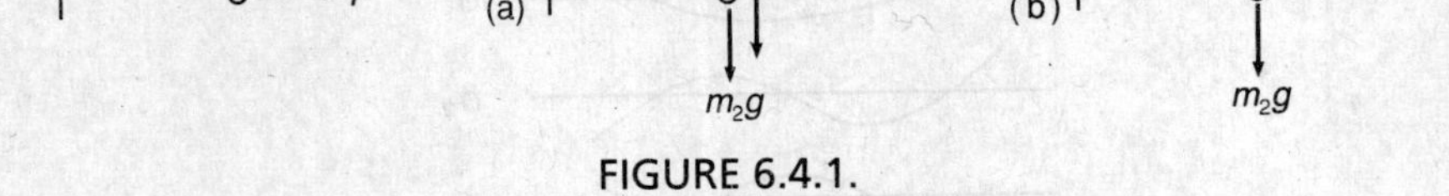

FIGURE 6.4.1.

With the system in its equilibrium position, give θ_2 a virtual displacement $\delta\theta_2$ [Fig. 6.4.1(a)] and write the equation for the virtual work δW of all the applied forces:

$$\delta W = -(m_2 g \sin\theta_2) l\, \delta\theta_2 + (P\cos\theta_2) l\, \delta\theta_2 = 0$$

From the equilibrium position (with $\delta\theta_2 = 0$), give θ_1 a virtual displacement $\delta\theta_1$, as in Fig. 6.4.1(b), and write the equation for δW:

$$\delta W = -(m_1 \sin\theta_1)l\delta\theta_1 - (m_2 g \sin\theta_1)l\delta\theta_1 + (P\cos\theta_1)l\delta\theta_1 = 0$$

These equations lead to the two equilibrium angles, given as

$$\tan\theta_2 = \frac{P}{m_2 g}$$

$$\tan\theta_1 = \frac{P}{(m_1 + m_2)g}$$

■

Example 6.4.2

Using the virtual work method, determine the equation of motion for the rigid beam of mass M loaded as shown in Fig. 6.4.2.

Solution Draw the beam in the displaced position θ and place the forces acting on it, including the inertia and damping forces. Give the beam a virtual displacement $\delta\theta$ and determine the work done by each force.

$$\text{Inertia force } \delta W = -\left(\frac{Ml^2}{3}\ddot{\theta}\right)\delta\theta$$

$$\text{Spring force } \delta W = -\left(k\frac{l}{2}\theta\right)\frac{l}{2}\,\delta\theta$$

$$\text{Damper force } \delta W = -(cl\dot{\theta})l\,\delta\theta$$

$$\text{Uniform load } \delta W = \int_0^l (p_0 f(t)dx)x\,\delta\theta = p_0 f(t)\frac{l^2}{2}\,\delta\theta$$

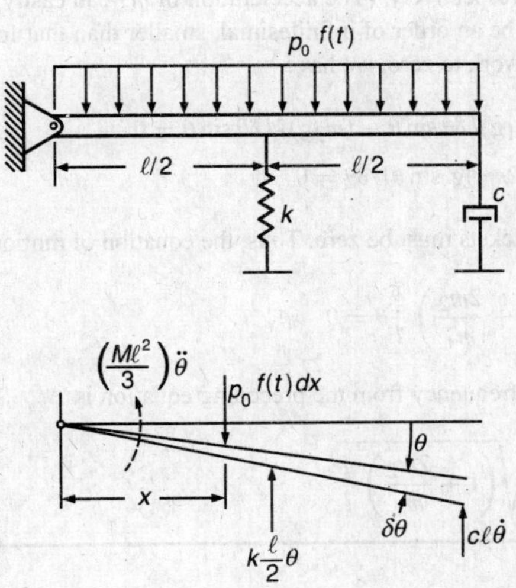

FIGURE 6.4.2.

Summing the virtual work and equating to zero gives the differential equation of motion:

$$\left(\frac{Ml^2}{3}\right)\ddot{\theta} + (cl^2)\dot{\theta} + k\frac{l^2}{4}\,\theta = p_0\frac{l^2}{2}f(t)$$

Example 6.4.3

Two simple pendulums are connected together with the bottom mass restricted to vertical motion in a frictionless guide, as shown in Fig. 6.4.3. Because only one coordinate θ is necessary, it represents an interconnected single-DOF system. Using the virtual work method, determine the equation of motion and its natural frequency.

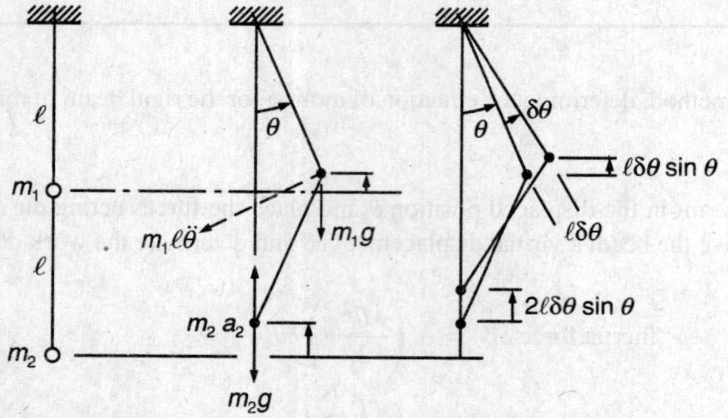

FIGURE 6.4.3. Virtual work of double pendulum with motion of m_2 restricted along vertical line.

Solution Sketch the system displaced by a small angle θ and place on it all forces, including inertia forces. Next give the coordinate θ a virtual displacement $\delta\theta$. Due to this displacement, m_1 and m_2 will undergo vertical displacements of $l\delta\theta\sin\theta$ and $2l\delta\theta\sin\theta$, respectively. (The acceleration of m_2 can easily be shown to be $2l(\ddot{\theta}\sin\theta + \dot{\theta}^2\cos\theta)$, and its virtual work will be an order of infinitesimal, smaller than that for the gravity force and can be neglected.) Equating the virtual work to zero, we have

$$\begin{aligned}\delta W &= -(m_1 l\ddot{\theta})l\,\delta\theta - (m_1 g)l\,\delta\theta\sin\theta - (m_2 g)2l\,\delta\theta\sin\theta = 0\\ &= -[m_1 l\ddot{\theta} + (m_1 + 2m_2)g\,\sin\theta]l\,\delta\theta = 0\end{aligned}$$

Because $\delta\theta$ is arbitrary, the quantity within the brackets must be zero. Thus, the equation of motion becomes

$$\ddot{\theta} + \left(1 + \frac{2m_2}{m_1}\right)\frac{g}{l}\theta = 0$$

where $\sin\theta \cong \theta$ has been substituted. The natural frequency from the preceding equation is

$$\omega_n = \sqrt{\left(1 + \frac{2m_2}{m_1}\right)\frac{g}{l}}$$

Example 6.4.4

Using the virtual work method, determine the equations of motion for the system shown in Fig. 6.4.4.

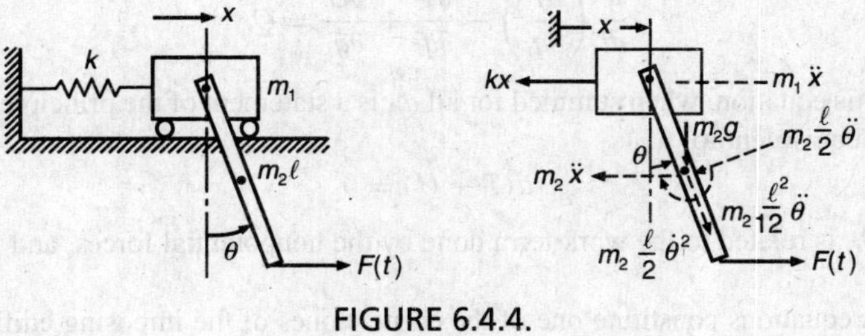

FIGURE 6.4.4.

Solution The generalized coordinates for the problem are x and θ. Sketch the system in the displaced position with all the active forces and inertia forces. Giving x a virtual displacement δx, the virtual work equation is

$$\delta W = -\left[(m_1 + m_2)\ddot{x} + kx\right]\delta x - \left(m_2 \frac{l}{2}\ddot{\theta}\cos\theta\right)\delta x$$
$$+\left(m_2 \frac{l}{2}\dot{\theta}^2 \sin\theta\right)\delta x + F(t)\delta x = 0$$

Because δx is arbitrary, the preceding equation leads to

$$(m_1 + m_2)\ddot{x} + m_2 \frac{l}{2}(\ddot{\theta}\cos\theta - \dot{\theta}^2 \sin\theta) + kx = F(t)$$

Next, allow a virtual displacement $\delta\theta$. δW is then

$$\delta W = -\left(m_2 \frac{l}{2}\ddot{\theta}\right)\frac{l}{2}\,\delta\theta - \left(m_2 \frac{l^2}{12}\ddot{\theta}\right)\delta\theta - (m_2 g \sin\theta)\frac{l}{2}\,\delta\theta$$
$$-(m_2 \ddot{x}\cos\theta)\frac{l}{2}\,\delta\theta + [F(t)\cos\theta]l\,\delta\theta = 0$$

from which we obtain

$$m_2 \frac{l^2}{3}\ddot{\theta} + m_2 \frac{l}{2}\ddot{x}\cos\theta + m_2 g \frac{l}{2}\sin\theta = F(t) l\cos\theta$$

These are nonlinear differential equations, which for small angles simplify to

$$(m_1 + m_2)\ddot{x} + m_2 \frac{l}{2}\ddot{\theta} + kx = F(t)$$
$$m_2 \frac{l^2}{3}\ddot{\theta} + m_2 \frac{l}{2}\ddot{x} + m_2 g \frac{l}{2}\theta = lF(t)$$

which can be expressed by the matrix equation

$$\begin{bmatrix} (m_1 + m_2) & m_2 \frac{l}{2} \\ m_2 \frac{l}{2} & m_2 \frac{l^2}{3} \end{bmatrix} \begin{Bmatrix} \ddot{x} \\ \ddot{\theta} \end{Bmatrix} + \begin{bmatrix} k & 0 \\ 0 & m_2 g \frac{l}{2} \end{bmatrix} \begin{Bmatrix} x \\ \theta \end{Bmatrix} = \begin{Bmatrix} F(t) \\ lF(t) \end{Bmatrix}$$

■

6.5 LAGRANGE'S EQUATION

Lagrange formulated a scalar procedure starting from the scalar quantities of kinetic energy, potential energy, and work expressed in terms of generalized coordinates. It is presented here as

$$\frac{d}{dt}\left(\frac{\partial T}{\partial \dot{q}_i}\right) - \frac{\partial T}{\partial q_i} + \frac{\partial U}{\partial q_i} = Q_i \tag{6.5.1}$$

The left side of this equation, when summed for all q_i, is a statement of the principle of conservation of energy, and is equivalent to

$$d(T + U) = 0$$

The right side, Q_i, is related to the work term done by the nonpotential forces, and will be taken up later.

Lagrange's equations constitute one of the cornerstones of the imposing edifice of analytical mechanics, which is dealt with at length in other volumes. Here our treatment is brief, but it is sufficient to introduce the fundamental merits of Lagrange's method to those who wish to appreciate its use.

Beginning with the case of a conservative system, where all external forces and all internal forces have a potential, the sum of the system's kinetic and potential energies is a constant.

$$T + U = E = \text{constant}$$

The total differential of E must then be zero.

$$dE = d(T + U) = dT + dU = 0 \tag{6.5.2}$$

The kinetic energy T is a function of the generalized coordinates q_i and the generalized velocity $\dot{q}_i$, whereas the potential energy U is a function only of q_i.

$$\begin{aligned} T &= T(q_1, q_2, \dots q_n; \dot{q}_1, \dot{q}_2, \dots \dot{q}_n) \\ U &= U(q_1, q_2, \dots q_n) \end{aligned} \tag{6.5.3}$$

The differential of T is

$$dT = \sum_{i=1}^{N} \frac{\partial T}{\partial q_i} dq_i + \sum_{i=1}^{N} \frac{\partial T}{\partial \dot{q}} d\dot{q}_i \tag{6.5.4}$$

To eliminate the second term with $d\dot{q}_i$, we start with the equation for kinetic energy

$$T = \frac{1}{2} \sum_{i=1}^{N} \sum_{j=1}^{N} m_{ij} \dot{q}_i \dot{q}_j \tag{6.5.5}$$

Differentiating this equation with respect to $\dot{q}_i$, multiplying by $\dot{q}_i$ and summing over i from 1 to N, we obtain the result equal to

$$\sum_{i=1}^{N} \frac{\partial T}{\partial \dot{q}_i} \dot{q}_i = \sum_{i=1}^{N} \sum_{j=1}^{N} m_{ij} \dot{q}_i \dot{q}_j = 2\,T$$

or

$$2\,T = \sum_{i=1}^{N} \frac{\partial T}{\partial \dot{q}_i} \dot{q}_i \tag{6.5.6}$$

We now form the differential of $2T$ from the preceding equation by using the product rule from calculus

$$2dT = \sum_{i=1}^{N} d\left(\frac{\partial T}{\partial \dot{q}_i}\right)\dot{q}_i + \frac{\partial T}{\partial \dot{q}_i} d\dot{q}_i \tag{6.5.7}$$

By subtracting Eq. (6.5.4) from this equation, the second term with $d\dot{q}_i$ is eliminated. By shifting the scalar quantity dt, the term $d(\frac{\partial T}{\partial \dot{q}_i})d\dot{q}_i$ becomes $\frac{d}{dt}(\frac{\partial T}{\partial \dot{q}_i})dq_i$, and the result is

$$dT = \sum_{i=1}^{N} \left[\frac{d}{dt}\left(\frac{\partial T}{\partial \dot{q}_i}\right) - \frac{\partial T}{\partial q_i}\right] dq_i \tag{6.5.8}$$

We now consider the term dU in Lagrange's equation. From Eq. (6.5.3), the differential of U is

$$dU = \sum_{i=1}^{N} \frac{\partial U}{\partial q_i} dq_i$$

Thus Eq. (6.5.3) for the invariance of the total energy becomes

$$d(T+U) = \sum_{i=1}^{N} \left[\frac{d}{dt}\left(\frac{\partial T}{\partial \dot{q}_i}\right) - \frac{\partial T}{\partial q_i} + \frac{\partial U}{\partial q_i}\right] dq_i = 0 \tag{6.5.9}$$

Because the N generalized coordinates are independent of one another, the dq_i can assume arbitrary values. Therefore the previous equation is satisfied only if

$$\frac{d}{dt}\left(\frac{\partial T}{\partial \dot{q}_i}\right) - \frac{\partial T}{\partial q_i} + \frac{\partial U}{\partial q_i} = 0 \quad i = 1, 2, \ldots N \tag{6.5.10}$$

This is Lagrange's equation for the case in which all the forces have a potential U. They can be somewhat modified by introducing the Lagrangian $L = (T - U)$. Because $\frac{\partial U}{\partial \dot{q}_i} = 0$, Eq. (6.5.10) can be written in terms of L as

$$\frac{d}{dt}\left(\frac{\partial L}{\partial \dot{q}_i}\right) - \frac{\partial L}{\partial q_i} = 0 \quad i = 1, 2, \ldots N \tag{6.5.11}$$

Nonconservative systems. The right side of Lagrange's equation (6.5.1) results from dividing the work term in the dynamical relationship $dT = dW$ into the work done by the potential and nonpotential forces as follows.

$$dT = dW_p + dW_{mp} \tag{6.5.12}$$

The work of the potential forces was shown earlier to be equal to $dW_p = -dU$, which is included in the left side of Lagrange's equation. The nonpotential work is equal to the work done by the nonpotential forces in a virtual displacement expressed in terms of the generalized coordinates. Thus, Lagrange's equation, Eq. (6.5.1) is the q_i component of the energy equation

$$d(T+U) = \delta W_{mp} \tag{6.5.13}$$

We can write the right side of this equation as

$$\delta W = \sum_{i=1}^{N} Q_i \delta q_i = Q_1 \delta q_1 + Q_2 \delta_2 + \cdots \tag{6.5.14}$$

The quantity Q_i is called the *generalized force*. In spite of its name Q_i can have units other than that of force; i.e., if δq_i is an angle, Q_i has the units of moment. The only requirement is that the product $Q_i \delta q_i$ be in the units of work. We now demonstrate the use of Lagrange's equation as applied to some simple examples.

Example 6.5.1

Using Lagrange's method, determine the equation of motion for the 3-DOF system shown in Fig. 6.5.1.

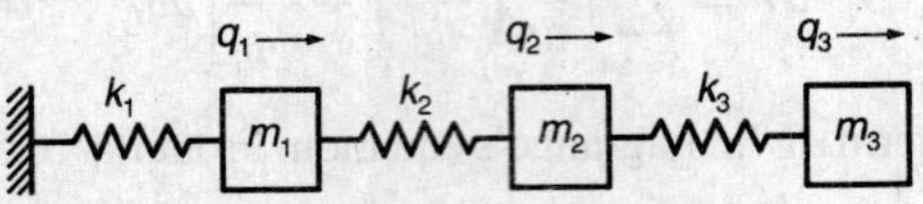

FIGURE 6.5.1.

Solution The kinetic energy here is not a function of q_i so that the term $\partial T/\partial q_i$ is zero. We have the following for the kinetic and potential energies:

$$T = \frac{1}{2}m_1\dot{q}_1^2 + \frac{1}{2}m_2\dot{q}_2^2 + \frac{1}{2}m_3\dot{q}_3^2$$

$$U = \frac{1}{2}k_1 q_1^2 + \frac{1}{2}k_2(q_2 - q_1)^2 + \frac{1}{2}k_3(q_3 - q_2)^2$$

and T for this problem is a function of only $\dot{q}_1$ and not of q_i.

By substituting into Lagrange's equation for $i = 1$,

$$\frac{\partial T}{\partial q_1} = m_1\dot{q}_1, \qquad \frac{d}{dt}\left(\frac{\partial T}{\partial \dot{q}_1}\right) = m_1\ddot{q}_1$$

$$\frac{\partial U}{\partial q_1} = k_1 q_1 - k_2(q_2 - q_1)$$

and the first equation is

$$m_1\ddot{q}_1 + (k_1 + k_2)q_1 - k_2 q_2 = 0$$

For $i = 2$, we have

$$\frac{\partial T}{\partial \dot{q}_2} = m_2\dot{q}_2 \qquad \frac{d}{dt}\left(\frac{\partial T}{\partial \dot{q}_2}\right) = m_2\ddot{q}_2$$

$$\frac{\partial U}{\partial q_2} = k_2(q_2 - q_1) - k_3(q_3 - q_2)$$

and the second equation becomes

$$m_2\ddot{q}_2 - k_2 q_1 + (k_2 + k_3)q_2 - k_3 q_3 = 0$$

Similarly for $i = 3$,

$$\frac{\partial T}{\partial q_3} = m_3\dot{q}_3 \qquad \frac{d}{dt}\left(\frac{\partial T}{\partial \dot{q}_3}\right) = m_3\ddot{q}_3$$

$$\frac{\partial U}{\partial q_3} = k_3(q_3 - q_2)$$

with the third equation

$$m_3\ddot{q}_3 - k_3 q_2 + k_3 q_3 = 0$$

These three equations can now be assembled into matrix form:

$$\begin{bmatrix} m_1 & 0 & 0 \\ 0 & m_2 & 0 \\ 0 & 0 & m_3 \end{bmatrix} \begin{Bmatrix} \ddot{q}_1 \\ \ddot{q}_2 \\ \ddot{q}_3 \end{Bmatrix} + \begin{bmatrix} (k_1 + k_2) & -k_2 & 0 \\ -k_2 & (k_2 + k_3) & -k_3 \\ 0 & -k_3 & k_3 \end{bmatrix} \begin{Bmatrix} q_1 \\ q_2 \\ q_3 \end{Bmatrix} = \begin{Bmatrix} 0 \\ 0 \\ 0 \end{Bmatrix}$$

We note from this example that the mass matrix results from the terms $(d/dt)(\partial T/\partial \dot{q}_i) - \partial T/\partial q_i$ and the stiffness matrix is obtained from $\partial U/\partial q_i$.

■

Example 6.5.2

Using Lagrange's method, set up the equations of motion for the system shown in Fig. 6.5.2.

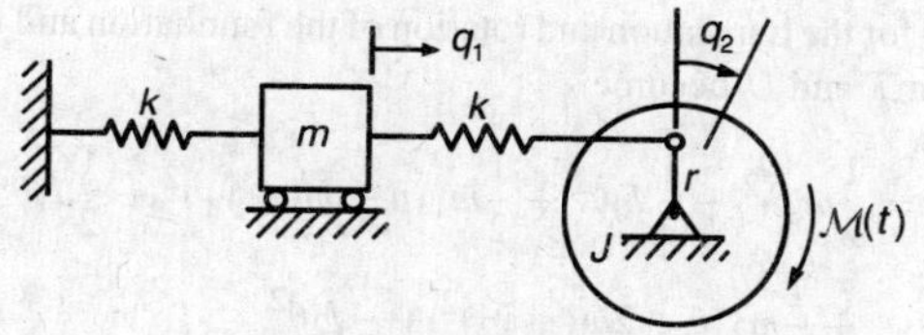

FIGURE 6.5.2.

Solution The kinetic and potential energies are

$$T = \frac{1}{2}m\dot{q}_1^2 + \frac{1}{2}J\dot{q}_2^2$$

$$U = \frac{1}{2}kq_1^2 + \frac{1}{2}K(rq_2 - q_1)^2$$

and from the work done by the external moment, the generalized force is

$$\delta W = \mathcal{M}(t)\delta q_2 \qquad \therefore Q_2 = \mathcal{M}(t)$$

Substituting into Lagrange's equation, the equations of motion are

$$m\ddot{q}_1 + 2kq_1 - krq_2 = 0$$

$$J\ddot{q}_2 - krq_1 + kr^2 q_2 = \mathcal{M}(t)$$

which can be rewritten as

$$\begin{bmatrix} m & 0 \\ 0 & J \end{bmatrix} \begin{Bmatrix} \ddot{q}_1 \\ \ddot{q}_2 \end{Bmatrix} + \begin{bmatrix} 2k & -kr \\ -kr & kr^2 \end{bmatrix} \begin{Bmatrix} q_1 \\ q_2 \end{Bmatrix} = \begin{Bmatrix} 0 \\ \mathcal{M}(t) \end{Bmatrix}$$

■

Example 6.5.3

Figure 6.5.3 shows a simplified model of a two-story building whose foundation is subject to translation and rotation. Determine T and U and the equations of motion.

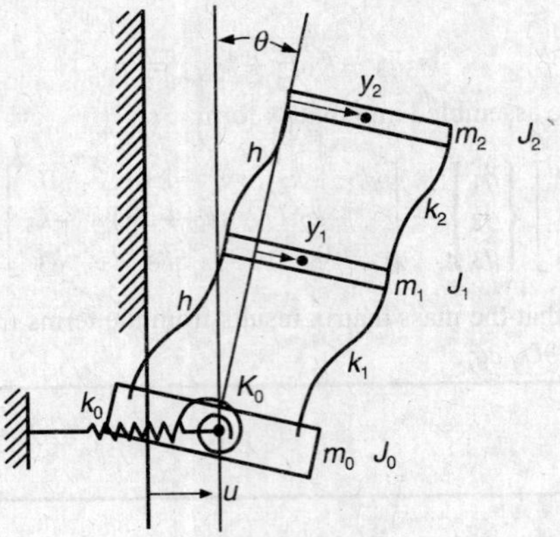

FIGURE 6.5.3.

Solution We choose u and θ for the translation and rotation of the foundation and y for the elastic displacement of the floors. The equations for T and U become

$$T = \frac{1}{2}m_0\dot{u}^2 + \frac{1}{2}J_0\dot{\theta}^2 + \frac{1}{2}m_1(\dot{u} + h\dot{\theta} + \dot{y}_1)^2 + \frac{1}{2}J_1\dot{\theta}^2$$
$$+ \frac{1}{2}m_2(\dot{u} + 2h\dot{\theta} + \dot{y}_2)^2 + \frac{1}{2}J_2\dot{\theta}^2$$
$$U = \frac{1}{2}k_0u^2 + \frac{1}{2}K_0\theta^2 + \frac{1}{2}k_1y_1^2 + \frac{1}{2}k_2(y_2 - y_1)^2$$

where u, θ, y_1, and y_2 are the generalized coordinates. Substituting into Lagrange's equation, we obtain, for example,

$$\frac{\partial T}{\partial \dot{\theta}} = (J_0 + J_1 + J_2)\dot{\theta} + m_1h(\dot{u} + h\dot{\theta} + y_1) + m_2 2h(\dot{u} + 2h\dot{\theta} + \dot{y}_2)$$
$$\frac{\partial U}{\partial \theta} = K_0$$

The four equations in matrix form become

$$\left[\begin{array}{cc|cc} (m_0 + m_1 + m_2) & (m_1 + 2m_2)h & m_1 & m_2 \\ (m_1 + 2m_2)h & (\sum J + m_1h^2 + 4m^2h^2) & m_1h & 2m_2h \\ \hline m_1 & m_1h & m_1 & 0 \\ m_2 & 2m_2h & 0 & m_2 \end{array}\right] \left\{\begin{array}{c} \ddot{u} \\ \ddot{\theta} \\ \hline \ddot{y}_1 \\ \ddot{y}_2 \end{array}\right\}$$
$$+ \left[\begin{array}{cc|cc} k_0 & 0 & 0 & 0 \\ 0 & K_0 & 0 & 0 \\ \hline 0 & 0 & (k_1 + k_2) & -k_2 \\ 0 & 0 & -k_2 & k_2 \end{array}\right] \left\{\begin{array}{c} u \\ \theta \\ \hline y_1 \\ y_2 \end{array}\right\} = \{0\}$$

It should be noted that the equation represented by the upper left corner of the matrices is that of rigid-body translation and rotation. ■

Example 6.5.4

Determine the generalized coordinates for the system shown in Fig. 6.5.4(a) and evaluate the stiffness and the mass matrices for the equations of motion.

Solution Figure 6.5.4(b) shows three generalized coordinates for which the stiffness matrix can be written as

$$\begin{Bmatrix} F_1 \\ M_1 \\ M_2 \end{Bmatrix} = \begin{bmatrix} k_{11} & k_{12} & k_{13} \\ k_{21} & k_{22} & k_{23} \\ k_{31} & k_{32} & k_{33} \end{bmatrix} \begin{Bmatrix} q_1 \\ q_2 \\ q_3 \end{Bmatrix}$$

The elements of each column of this matrix are the forces and moments required when the corresponding coordinate is given a value with all other coordinates equal to zero. The configurations for this determination are shown in Fig. 6.5.4(c), and the forces and moments necessary to maintain these deflections are obtained from the free-body diagrams of Fig. 6.5.4(d) with the aid of the equations shown in Fig. 11.4.2.

For q_1, we have

$$\begin{Bmatrix} F_1 \\ M_1 \\ M_2 \end{Bmatrix} = \begin{bmatrix} \frac{12EI_1}{l_1^3} & 0 & 0 \\ \frac{-6EI_1}{l_1^2} & 0 & 0 \\ 0 & 0 & 0 \end{bmatrix} \begin{Bmatrix} q_1 \\ 0 \\ 0 \end{Bmatrix}$$

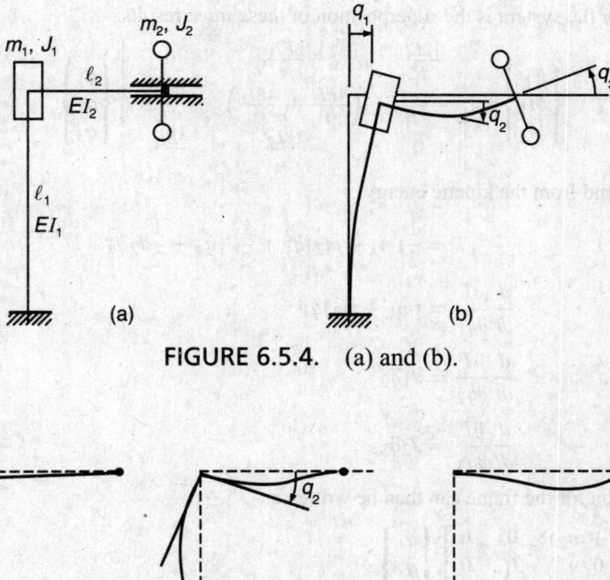

FIGURE 6.5.4. (a) and (b).

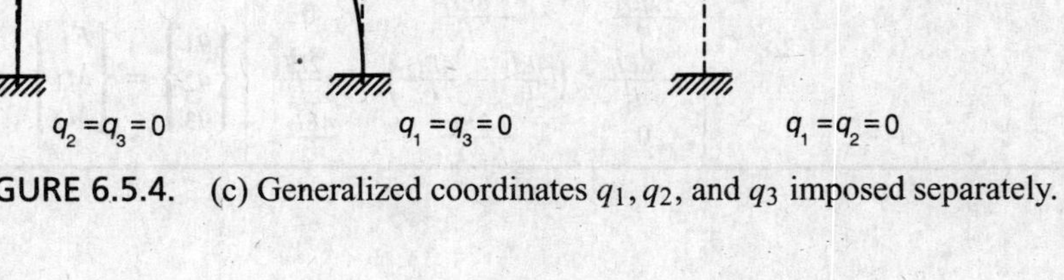

FIGURE 6.5.4. (c) Generalized coordinates q_1, q_2, and q_3 imposed separately.

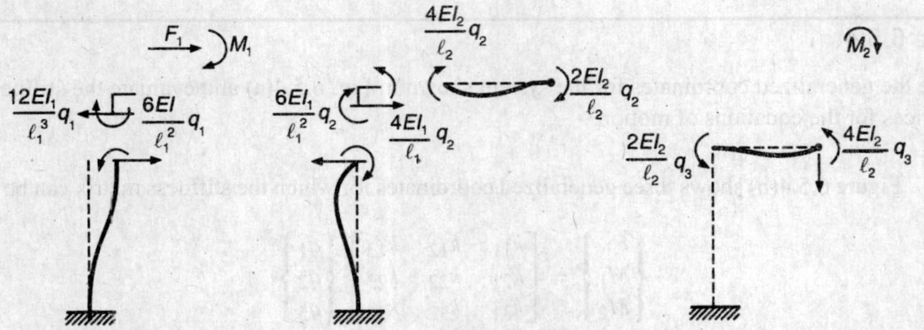

FIGURE 6.5.4. (d) Forces necessary to maintain equilibrium.

For q_2,

$$\begin{Bmatrix} F_1 \\ M_1 \\ M_2 \end{Bmatrix} = \begin{bmatrix} 0 & \dfrac{-6\,EI_1}{l_1^2} & 0 \\ 0 & \left(\dfrac{-4\,EI_1}{l_1} + \dfrac{-4\,EI_2}{l_2}\right) & 0 \\ 0 & \dfrac{2\,EI_2}{l_2} & 0 \end{bmatrix} \begin{Bmatrix} 0 \\ q_2 \\ 0 \end{Bmatrix}$$

For q_3,

$$\begin{Bmatrix} F_1 \\ M_1 \\ M_2 \end{Bmatrix} = \begin{bmatrix} 0 & 0 & 0 \\ 0 & 0 & \dfrac{-2EI_2}{l_2} \\ 0 & 0 & \dfrac{4EI_2}{l_2} \end{bmatrix} \begin{Bmatrix} 0 \\ 0 \\ q_3 \end{Bmatrix}$$

The stiffness matrix for the system is the superposition of these three results:

$$\begin{Bmatrix} F_1 \\ M_1 \\ M_2 \end{Bmatrix} = \begin{vmatrix} \dfrac{12EI_1}{l_1^3} & -\dfrac{6EI_1}{l_1^2} & 0 \\ -\dfrac{6EI_1}{l_1^2} & \left(\dfrac{4EI_1}{l_1} + \dfrac{4EI_2}{l_2}\right) & -\dfrac{2EI_2}{l_2} \\ 0 & -\dfrac{2EL_2}{l_2} & \dfrac{4EI_2}{l_2} \end{vmatrix} \begin{Bmatrix} q_1 \\ q_2 \\ q_3 \end{Bmatrix}$$

The mass matrix is found from the kinetic energy:

$$T = \frac{1}{2}(m_1 + m_2)\dot{q}_1^2 + \frac{1}{2}J_1\dot{q}_2^2 + \frac{1}{2}J_2\dot{q}_3^2$$

$$\frac{d}{dt}\frac{\partial T}{\partial \dot{q}_1} = (m_1 + m_2)\ddot{q}_1$$

$$\frac{d}{dt}\frac{\partial T}{\partial \dot{q}_2} = J_1\ddot{q}_2$$

$$\frac{d}{dt}\frac{\partial T}{\partial \dot{q}_3} = J_2\ddot{q}_3$$

The equations of motion for the frame can then be written as

$$\begin{bmatrix} (m_1 + m_2) & 0 & 0 \\ 0 & J_1 & 0 \\ 0 & 0 & J_2 \end{bmatrix} \begin{Bmatrix} \ddot{q}_1 \\ \ddot{q}_2 \\ \ddot{q}_3 \end{Bmatrix} + \begin{vmatrix} \dfrac{12EI_1}{l_1^3} & -\dfrac{6EI_1}{l_1^2} & 0 \\ -\dfrac{6EI_l}{l_1^2} & \left(\dfrac{4EI_1}{l_1} + \dfrac{4EI_2}{l_2}\right) & -\dfrac{2EI_2}{l_2} \\ 0 & -\dfrac{2EI_2}{l_2} & \dfrac{4EI_2}{l_2} \end{vmatrix} \begin{Bmatrix} q_1 \\ q_2 \\ q_3 \end{Bmatrix} = \begin{Bmatrix} F_1 \\ M_1 \\ M_2 \end{Bmatrix}$$

■

6.6 KINETIC ENERGY, POTENTIAL ENERGY, AND GENERALIZED FORCE IN TERMS OF GENERALIZED COORDINATE q

In the previous section, the use of Lagrange's equation was demonstrated for simple problems. We now discuss the quantities T, U, and Q from a more general point of view.

Kinetic energy. By representing the system by N particles, the instantaneous position of each particle can be expressed in terms of the N generalized coordinates

$$\mathbf{r}_j = \mathbf{r}_j(q_1, q_2, \ldots, q_N)$$

The velocity of the jth particle is

$$\mathbf{v}_j = \sum_{i=1}^{N} \frac{\partial \mathbf{r}_j}{\partial q_i} \dot{q}_i$$

and the kinetic energy of the system becomes

$$T = \frac{1}{2}\sum_{j=1}^{N} m_j \mathbf{v}_j \cdot \mathbf{v}_j = \frac{1}{2}\sum_{i=1}^{N}\sum_{j=1}^{N}\left(\sum_{i=1}^{N} m_i \frac{\partial \mathbf{r}_i}{\partial q_j} \cdot \frac{\partial \mathbf{r}_i}{\partial q_i}\right)\dot{q}_i\dot{q}_j$$

By defining the *generalized mass* as

$$m_{ij} = \sum_{i=1}^{N} m_i \frac{\partial \mathbf{r}_i}{\partial q_j} \cdot \frac{\partial \mathbf{r}_i}{\partial q_i}$$

the kinetic energy can be written as

$$\begin{aligned} T &= \frac{1}{2}\sum_{i=1}^{N}\sum_{j=1}^{N} m_{ij}\dot{q}_i\dot{q}_j \\ &= \frac{1}{2}[\dot{q}]^T[m]\{\dot{q}\} \end{aligned} \tag{6.6.1}$$

Potential energy. In a conservative system, the forces can be derived from the potential energy U, which is a function of the generalized coordinates q_j. Expanding U in a Taylor series about the equilibrium position, we have for a system of n degrees of freedom

$$U = U_0 + \sum_{j=1}^{n}\left(\frac{\partial U}{\partial q_j}\right)_0 q_j + \frac{1}{2}\sum_{j=1}^{n}\sum_{l=1}^{n}\left(\frac{\partial^2 U}{\partial q_j \partial q_l}\right)_0 q_j q_l + \cdots$$

In this expression, U_0 is an arbitrary constant that we can set equal to zero. The derivatives of U are evaluated at the equilibrium position 0 and are constants when the q_j's are small quantities equal to zero at the equilibrium position. Because U is a minimum in the equilibrium position, the first derivative $(\partial U/\partial q_j)_0$ is zero, which leaves only $(\partial^2 U/\partial q_j \partial q_l)_0$ and higher-order terms.

In the theory of small oscillations about the equilibrium position, terms beyond the second order are ignored and the equation for the potential energy reduces to

$$k_{jl} = \left(\frac{\partial^2 U}{\partial q_j \partial q_l}\right)_0$$

and the potential energy is written in terms of the *generalized stiffness* k_{jl} as

$$U = \frac{1}{2}\sum_{j=1}^{n}\sum_{l=1}^{n} k_{jl}q_j q_l$$

$$= \frac{1}{2}\{q\}^T[k]\{q\} \tag{6.6.2}$$

Generalized force. For the development of the generalized force, we start from the virtual displacement of the coordinate $\mathbf{r}_j$:

$$\delta \mathbf{r}_j = \sum_i \frac{\delta \mathbf{r}_j}{\delta q_i}\delta q_i$$

and the time t is not involved.

When the system is in equilibrium, the virtual work can now be expressed in terms of the generalized coordinates q_i:

$$\delta W = \sum_j \mathbf{F}_j \cdot \delta \mathbf{r}_j = \sum_j \sum_i \mathbf{F}_j \cdot \frac{\delta \mathbf{r}_j}{\delta q_i}\delta q_i$$

By interchanging the order of summation and letting

$$Q_i = \sum_j \mathbf{F}_j \cdot \frac{\delta \mathbf{r}_j}{\delta q_i}$$

be defined as the *generalized force*, the virtual work for the system, expressed in terms of the generalized coordinates, becomes

$$\delta W = \sum_i Q_i \delta q_i \tag{6.6.3}$$

6.7 ASSUMED MODE SUMMATION

When the displacement is expressed as the sum of shape functions $\phi_i(x)$ multiplied by the generalized coordinates $q_i(t)$, the kinetic energy, the potential energy, and the work equation lead to convenient expressions for the generalized mass, the generalized stiffness, and the generalized force.

Earlier in this chapter, a few distributed elastic systems were solved for the fundamental frequency using an assumed deflection shape and the energy method. For example, the deflection of a helical spring fixed at one end was assumed to be $(y/l)x$, and for the simply supported beam, the deflection curve $y = y_{\max}[3(x/l) - 4(x/l)^3]$, $(x/l) \le \frac{1}{2}$, was chosen. These assumptions when solved for the kinetic energy led to the effective mass and the natural frequency of a 1-DOF system. These assumed deflections can be expressed by the equation

$$u(x,t) = \phi(x)q_1(t)$$

where $q_1(t)$ is the single coordinate of the 1-DOF system.

For the multi-DOF system, this procedure can be expanded to

$$u(x,t) = \sum_i \phi_i(x)q_i(t)$$

where q_i is the generalized coordinate, and $\phi_i(x)$ is the assumed mode function. There are very few restrictions on these shape functions, which need only satisfy the geometric boundary conditions.

Generalized Mass

We assume the displacement at position x to be represented by the equation

$$
\begin{aligned}
r(x,t) &= \phi_1(x)q_1(t) + \phi_2(x)q_2(t) + \cdots + \phi_N(x)q_N(t) \\
&= \sum_{i=1}^{N} \phi_i(x)q_i(t)
\end{aligned}
\tag{6.7.1}
$$

where $\phi_i(x)$ are shape functions of only x.

The velocity is

$$
v(x) = \sum_{i=1}^{N} \phi_i(x)\dot{q}_i(t) \tag{6.7.2}
$$

and the kinetic energy becomes

$$
\begin{aligned}
T &= \frac{1}{2}\sum_{i=1}^{N}\sum_{j=1}^{N} \dot{q}_i\dot{q}_j \int \phi_i(x)\phi_j(x)\, dm \\
&= \frac{1}{2}\sum_{i=1}^{N}\sum_{j=1}^{N} m_{ij}\dot{q}_i\dot{q}_j
\end{aligned}
\tag{6.7.3}
$$

Thus, the generalized mass is

$$
m_{ij} = \int \phi_i(x)\phi_j(x)\, dm \tag{6.7.4}
$$

where the integration is carried out over the entire system. In case the system consists of discrete masses, m_{ij} becomes

$$
m_{ij} = \sum_{p=1}^{N} m_p\phi_i(x_p)\phi_j(x_p) \tag{6.7.5}
$$

Generalized Stiffness (Axial Vibration)

We again represent the displacement of the rod in terms of the assumed modes and the generalized coordinates:

$$
u(x,t) = \sum_{i=1}^{n} \varphi_i(x)q_i(t)
$$

The potential energy of the rod under axial stress is found from Hooke's law:

$$
\frac{P}{A} = E\frac{du}{dx}
$$

and the work done, which is,

$$
\begin{aligned}
dU &= \frac{1}{2}P\frac{du}{dx}dx = \frac{1}{2}EA\left(\frac{du}{dx}\right)^2 dx \\
U &= \frac{1}{2}\int AE\left(\frac{du}{dx}\right)^2 dx
\end{aligned}
\tag{6.7.6}
$$

Substituting for $u(x,t)$ gives

$$U = \frac{1}{2}\sum_i\sum_j q_i q_j \int AE\varphi_i'\varphi_j'\,dx$$
$$= \frac{1}{2}\sum_i\sum_j k_{ij}q_i q_j \qquad (6.7.7)$$

where the generalized stiffness is

$$k_{ij} = \int AE\varphi_i'\varphi_j'\,dx \qquad (6.7.8)$$

Example 6.7.1

Determine the equation of motion and the natural frequencies and normal modes of a fixed–free uniform rod of Fig. 6.7.1 using assumed modes $\varphi_1(x) = x/l$ and $\varphi_2(x) = (x/l)^2$.

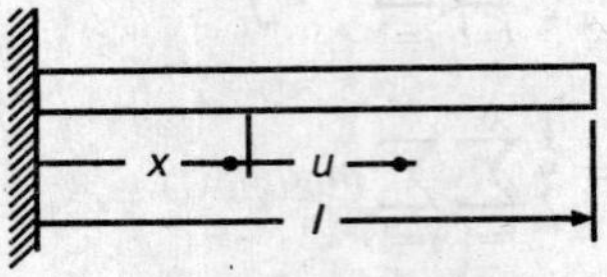

FIGURE 6.7.1.

The equation for the displacement of the rod is

$$u(x,t) = \varphi_1(x)q_1(t) + \varphi_2(x)q_2(t)$$
$$= \left(\frac{x}{l}\right)q_1 + \left(\frac{x}{l}\right)^2 q_2$$

Note that the assumed modes chosen satisfy the only geometric boundary condition of the problem, which is $u(0,t) = 0$. Thus, the generalized mass and the generalized stiffness are evaluated from

$$m_{ij} = \int_0^l \varphi_i(x)\varphi_j(x)m\,dx$$
$$k_{ij} = \int EA\varphi_i'(x)\varphi_j'(x)dx$$

$$m_{11} = m\int_0^l \left(\frac{x}{l}\right)^2 dx = \frac{1}{3}ml \qquad k_{11} = EA\int_0^l \frac{1}{l}\cdot\frac{1}{l}\,dx = \frac{EA}{l}$$
$$m_{12} = m_{21} = m\int_0^l \left(\frac{x}{l}\right)^3 dx = \frac{1}{4}ml \qquad k_{12} = k_{21} = EA\int_0^l \frac{1}{l}\cdot\frac{2x}{l^2}\,dx = \frac{EA}{l}$$
$$m_{22} = m\int_0^l \left(\frac{x}{l}\right)^4 dx = \frac{1}{5}ml \qquad k_{22} = EA\int_0^l \frac{4x^2}{l^4}\,dx = \frac{4EA}{3l}$$

which can be assembled into the following matrices:

$$M = ml\begin{bmatrix} \frac{1}{3} & \frac{1}{4} \\ \frac{1}{4} & \frac{1}{5} \end{bmatrix} \qquad K = \frac{EA}{l}\begin{bmatrix} 1 & 1 \\ 1 & \frac{4}{3} \end{bmatrix}$$

The equation of motion for the normal mode vibration then becomes

$$\left[-\omega^2 ml\begin{bmatrix}\frac{1}{3} & \frac{1}{4}\\ \frac{1}{4} & \frac{1}{5}\end{bmatrix}+\frac{EA}{l}\begin{bmatrix}1 & 1\\ 1 & \frac{4}{3}\end{bmatrix}\right]\begin{Bmatrix}q_1\\ q_2\end{Bmatrix}=\begin{Bmatrix}0\\ 0\end{Bmatrix}$$

By letting $\lambda = \omega^2 ml^2/EI$, the characteristic determinant

$$\begin{vmatrix}(1-\frac{1}{3}\lambda) & (1-\frac{1}{4}\lambda)\\ (1-\frac{1}{4}\lambda) & (\frac{4}{3}-\frac{1}{5}\lambda)\end{vmatrix}=0$$

reduces to the following polynomial equation for the eigenvalues:

$$\lambda^2 - 34.666\lambda + 79.999 = 0$$

Solving for λ, we have

$$\lambda = 17.333 \pm 14.847 = \begin{cases}2.486\\ 32.180\end{cases}$$

and the natural frequencies are

$$\omega_1 = 1.577\sqrt{\frac{EA}{ml^2}}$$

$$\omega_2 = 5.672\sqrt{\frac{EA}{ml^2}}$$

The exact values for this problem are

$$\omega_1 = \frac{\pi}{2}\sqrt{\frac{EA}{ml^2}} = 1.5708\sqrt{\frac{EA}{ml^2}}$$

$$\omega_2 = \frac{3\pi}{2}\sqrt{\frac{EA}{ml^2}} = 4.7124\sqrt{\frac{EA}{ml^2}}$$

which indicates good agreement for the first mode. The second mode frequency is 20.4 percent high, which is to be expected with only two modes.

From the first equation, the ratio of the amplitudes is

$$\frac{q_1}{q_2} = \frac{-(1-\frac{1}{4}\lambda)}{1-\frac{1}{3}\lambda}$$

By substituting $\lambda_1 = 2.486$, the first mode ratio is

$$\frac{q_1}{q_2} = \frac{-0.378}{0.171} = \frac{-1.0}{0.453}$$

For the second mode, we substitute $\lambda_2 = 32.18$ and obtain

$$\frac{q_1}{q_2} = \frac{-7.05}{9.73} = \frac{-1.0}{1.38}$$

The displacement equation for each mode can now be written as

$$u_1(x) = -\left(\frac{x}{l}\right) + 0.453\left(\frac{x}{l}\right)^2$$

$$u_2(x) = -\left(\frac{x}{l}\right) + 1.38\left(\frac{x}{l}\right)^2$$

■

Generalized Stiffness (Beams)

Determine the generalized stiffness for a beam of cross-sectional property EI when the displacement $y(x,t)$ is represented by the sum

$$y(x,t) = \sum_{i=1}^{n} \varphi_i(x)q_i(t) \tag{6.7.9}$$

The potential energy of a beam in bending is

$$U = \frac{1}{2}\int EI\left(\frac{d^2y}{dx^2}\right)^2 dx \tag{6.7.10}$$

Substituting for

$$\frac{d^2y}{dx^2} = \sum_{i=1}^{n} \varphi_i''(x)q_i(t)$$

we obtain

$$\begin{aligned} U &= \tfrac{1}{2}\sum_i\sum_j q_iq_j \int EI\varphi_i''\varphi_j''\,dx \\ &= \tfrac{1}{2}\sum_i\sum_j k_{ij}q_iq_j \end{aligned} \tag{6.7.11}$$

and the generalized stiffness is

$$k_{ij} = \int EI\varphi_i''\varphi_j''\,dx \tag{6.7.12}$$

Example 6.7.2 GENERALIZED FORCE

The frame of Fig. 6.3.3 with rigid members is acted upon by the forces and moments shown in Fig. 6.7.2. Determine the generalized forces.

Solution We let δq_1 be the virtual displacement of the upper left corner and δq_2 be the translation of the right support hinge. Due to δq_1, the virtual work done is

$$Q_1\delta q_1 = F_1\delta q_1 - F_2\frac{a}{l}\delta q_1 + (M_1 - M_2)\frac{1}{l}\delta q_1$$

$$\therefore Q_1 = F_1 - \frac{a}{l}F_2 + \frac{1}{l}(M_1 - M_2)$$

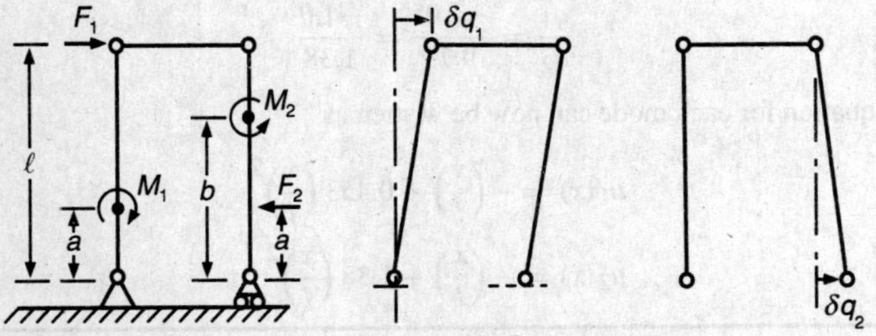

FIGURE 6.7.2.

The virtual work done due to δq_2 is

$$Q_2\delta q_2 = -F_2(l-a)\frac{\delta q_2}{l} + M_2\frac{\delta q_2}{l}$$

$$\therefore Q_2 = [-F_2(l-a) + M_2]\frac{1}{l}$$

It should be noted that the dimension of Q_1 and Q_2 is that of a force.

■

Example 6.7.3

In Fig. 6.7.3, three forces, F_1, F_2, and F_3, act at discrete points, x_1, x_2, and x_3, of a structure whose displacement is expressed by the equation

$$y(x,t) = \sum_{i=1}^{n} \varphi_i(x)q_i(t)$$

Determine the generalized force Q_i.

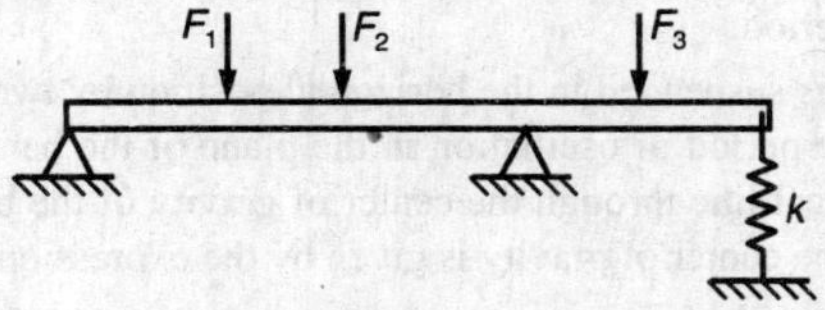

FIGURE 6.7.3.

Solution The virtual displacement is

$$\delta y = \sum_{i=1}^{n} \varphi_i(x)\delta q_i$$

and the virtual work due to this displacement is

$$\delta W = \sum_{j=1}^{3} F_j \cdot \left(\sum_{i=1}^{n} \varphi_i(x_j)\delta q_i\right)$$

$$= \sum_{i=1}^{n} \delta q_i \left(\sum_{j=1}^{3} F_j\varphi_i(x_j)\right) = \sum_{i=1}^{n} Q_i\delta q_i$$

The generalized force is then equal to $\delta W/\delta q_i$, or

$$Q_i = \sum_{j=1}^{3} F_j\varphi_i(x_j)$$

$$= F_1\varphi_i(x_1) + F_2\varphi_i(x_2) + F_3\varphi_i(x_3)$$

■

REFERENCES

[1] Rayleigh, L. and Strutt, J. W. *Theory of Sound*, Vol. 1, 2nd rev. ed., New York: Dover Publications, 1946.

[2] Goldstein, *Classical Mechanics*, Reading, Mass: Addison-Wesley, 1951.

[3] Lanczos, C. *The Variational Principles of Mechanics*, Toronto, Canada: The Univ. of Toronto Press, 1949.

PROBLEMS

6.1. A thin rectangular plate is bent into a semicircular cylinder, as shown in Fig. P6.1. Determine its period of oscillation if it is allowed to rock on a horizontal surface.

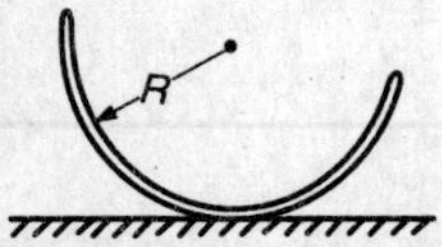

FIGURE P6.1.

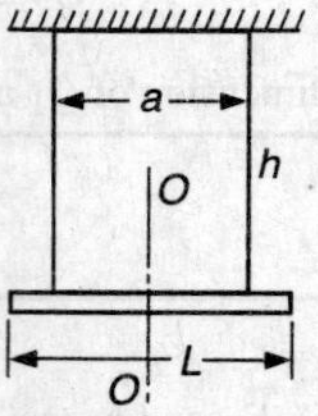

FIGURE P6.2.

6.2. A uniform bar of length L and weight W is suspended symmetrically by two strings, as shown in Fig. P6.2. Set up the differential equation of motion for small angular oscillations of the bar about the vertical axis O–O, and determine its period.

6.3. A uniform bar of length L is suspended in the horizontal position by two vertical strings of equal length attached to the ends. If the period of oscillation in the plane of the bar and strings is t_1 and the period of oscillation about a vertical line through the center of gravity of the bar is t_2, show that the radius of gyration of the bar about the center of gravity is given by the expression

$$k = \left(\frac{t_2}{t_1}\right)\frac{L}{2}$$

6.4. Using the energy method, show that the natural period of oscillation of the fluid in a U-tube manometer shown in Fig. P6.4 is

$$\tau = 2\pi\sqrt{\frac{l}{2g}}$$

where l is the length of the fluid column.

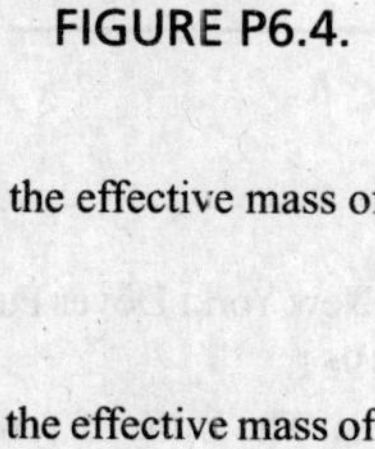

FIGURE P6.4.

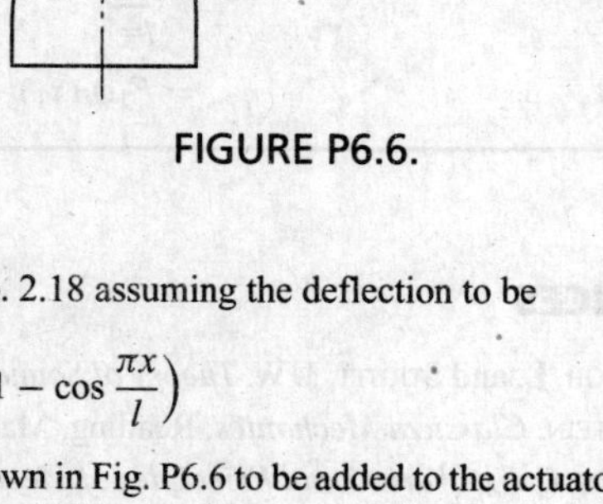

FIGURE P6.6.

6.5. Determine the effective mass of the columns of Prob. 2.18 assuming the deflection to be

$$y = \frac{1}{2}y_{\max}\left(1 - \cos\frac{\pi x}{l}\right)$$

6.6. Determine the effective mass of the rocket engine shown in Fig. P6.6 to be added to the actuator mass m_1.

6.7. The engine-valve system of Fig. P6.7 consists of a rocker arm of moment of inertia J, a valve of mass m_V and a spring of mass m_S. Determine its effective mass at A.

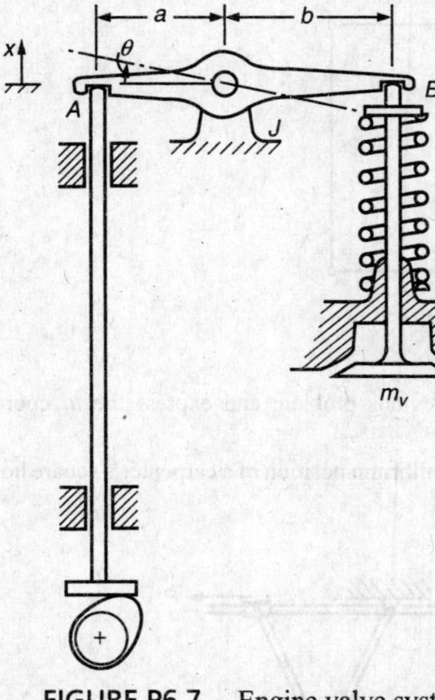

FIGURE P6.7. Engine valve system.

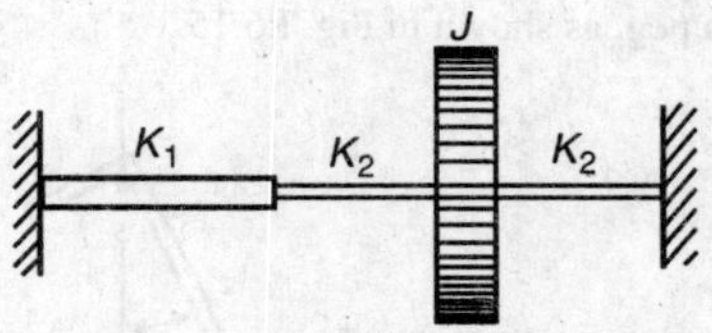

FIGURE P6.10.

6.8. A uniform cantilever beam of total mass ml has a concentrated mass M at its free end. Determine the effective mass of the beam to be added to M assuming the deflection to be that of a massless beam with a concentrated force at the end, and write the equation for its fundamental frequency.

6.9. Repeat Prob. 6.8 using the static deflection

$$y(x) = \frac{wl\,l^3}{24\,EI}\left[\left(\frac{x}{l}\right)^4 - 4\left(\frac{x}{l}\right) + 3\right]$$

for the uniformly loaded beam, and compare with previous result.

6.10. Determine the effective rotational stiffness of the shaft in Fig. P6.10 and calculate its natural period.

6.11. For purposes of analysis, it is desired to reduce the system of Fig. P6.11 to a simple linear spring-mass system of effective mass m_{eff} and effective stiffness k_{eff}. Determine m_{eff} and k_{eff} in terms of the given quantities.

6.12. Determine the effective mass moment of inertia for shaft 1 in the system shown in Fig. P6.12.

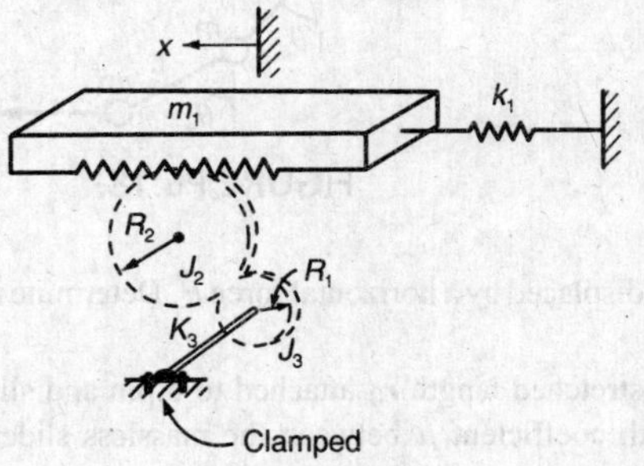

FIGURE P6.11.

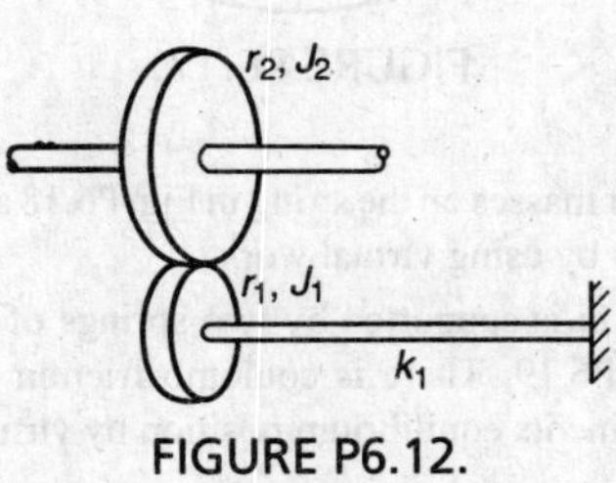

FIGURE P6.12.

6.13. List the displacement coordinates u_i for the plane frame of Fig. P6.13 and write the geometric constraint equations. State the number of degrees of freedom for the system.

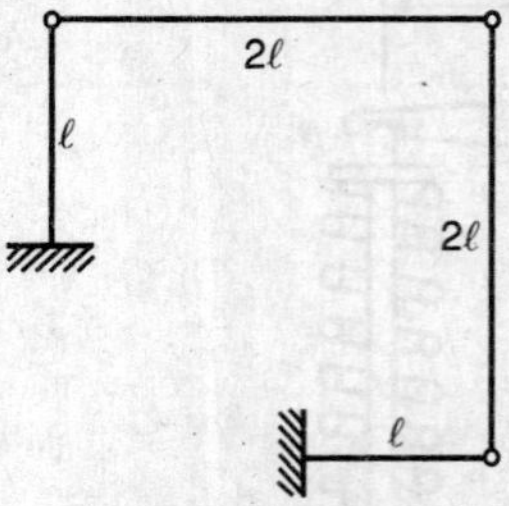

FIGURE P6.13.

6.14. Choose the generalized coordinates q_i for the previous problem and express the u_i coordinates in terms of q_i.

6.15. Using the method of virtual work, determine the equilibrium position of a carpenter's square hooked over a peg, as shown in Fig. P6.15.

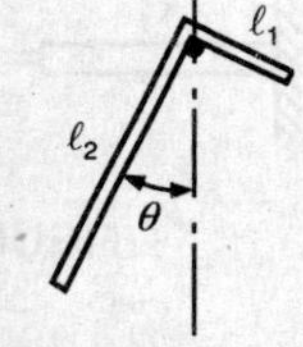

FIGURE P6.15.

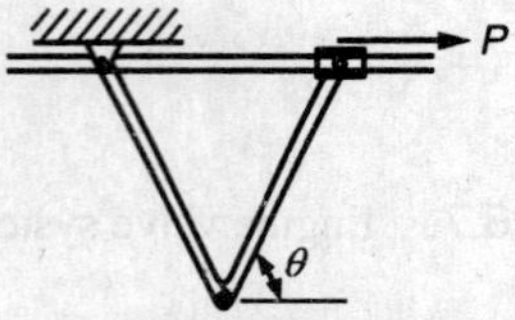

FIGURE P6.16.

6.16. Determine the equilibrium position of the two uniform bars shown in Fig. P6.16 when a force P is applied as shown. All surfaces are friction-free.

6.17. Determine the equilibrium position of two point masses m_1 and m_2 connected by a massless rod and placed in a smooth hemispherical bowl of radius R, as shown in Fig. P6.17.

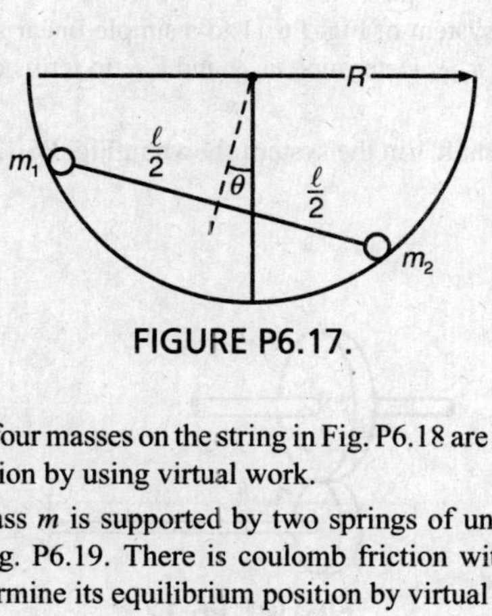

FIGURE P6.17.

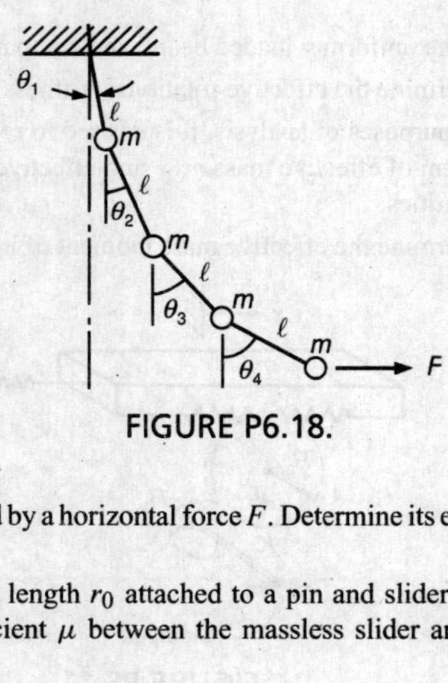

FIGURE P6.18.

6.18. The four masses on the string in Fig. P6.18 are displaced by a horizontal force F. Determine its equilibrium position by using virtual work.

6.19. A mass m is supported by two springs of unstretched length r_0 attached to a pin and slider, as shown in Fig. P6.19. There is coulomb friction with coefficient μ between the massless slider and the rod. Determine its equilibrium position by virtual work.

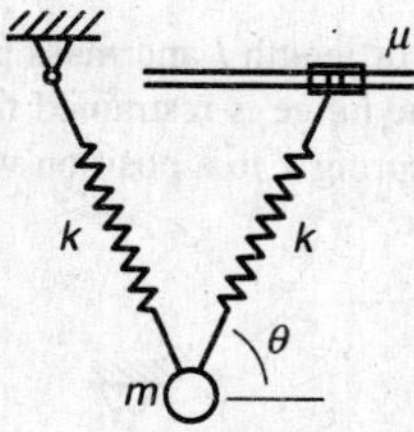

FIGURE P6.19.

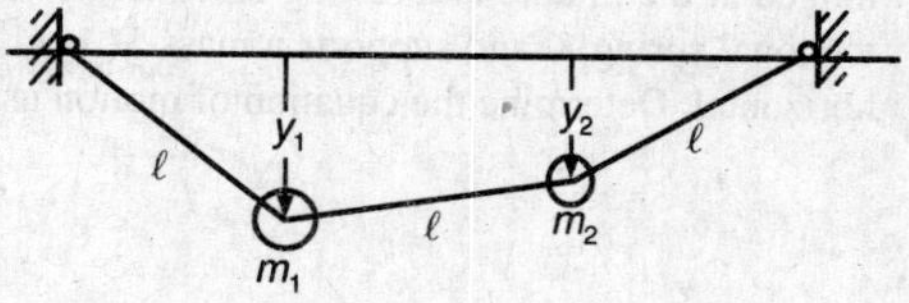

FIGURE P6.20.

6.20. Determine the equilibrium position of m_1 and m_2 attached to strings of equal length, as shown in Fig. P6.20.

6.21. A rigid uniform rod of length l is supported by a spring and a smooth floor, as shown in Fig. P6.21. Determine its equilibrium position by virtual work. The unstretched length of the spring is $h/4$.

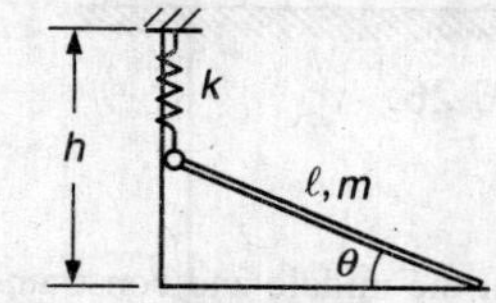

FIGURE P6.21.

6.22. Determine the equation of motion for small oscillation about the equilibrium position in Prob. 6.21.

6.23. A rigid uniform bar of mass m and length l is pinned at O and supported by a spring and viscous damper, as shown in Fig. P6.23. Measuring θ from the static equilibrium position, determine (a) the equation for small θ (the moment of inertia of the bar about O is $ml^2/3$), (b) the equation for the undamped natural frequency, and (c) the expression for critical damping. Use virtual work.

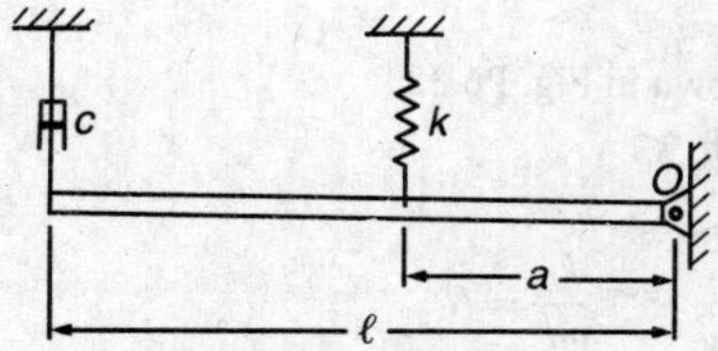

FIGURE P6.23.

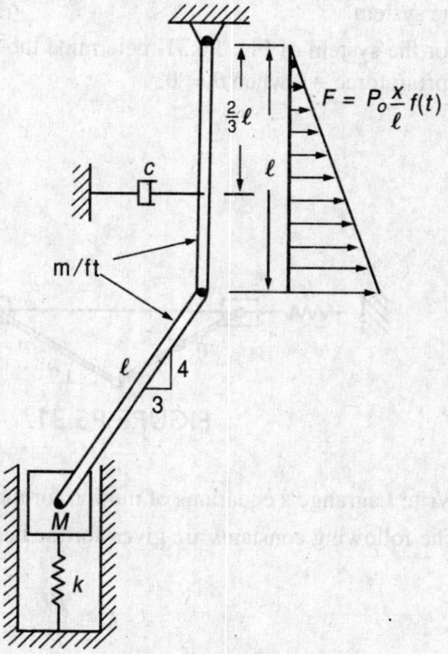

FIGURE P6.25.

6.24. Determine the equation of motion for Probs. 2.29 and 2.30 using virtual work.

6.25. Determine the differential equation of motion for free vibration of the system shown in Fig. P6.25, using virtual work.

6.26. The system shown in Fig. P6.26 has two rigid uniform beams of length l and mass per unit length m, hinged at the middle and resting on rollers at the test stand. The hinge is restrained from rotation by a torsional spring K and supports a mass M held up by another spring k to a position where the bars are horizontal. Determine the equation of motion using virtual work.

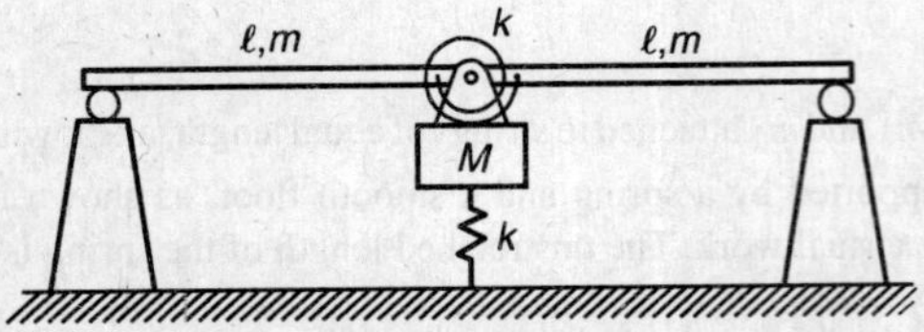

FIGURE P6.26.

FIGURE P6.27.

6.27. Two uniform stiff bars are hinged at the middle and constrained by a spring, as shown in Fig. P6.27. Using virtual work, set up the equation of motion for its free vibration.

6.28. The carpenter's square of Prob. 6.15 is displaced slightly from its equilibrium position and released. Determine its equation of oscillation.

6.29. Determine the equation of motion and the natural frequency of oscillation about its equilibrium position for the system in Prob. 6.17.

6.30. In Prob. 6.20, m_1 is given a small displacement and released. Determine the equation of oscillation for the system.

6.31. For the system of Fig. P6.31, determine the equilibrium position and its equation of vibration about it. Spring force = 0 when $\theta = 0$.

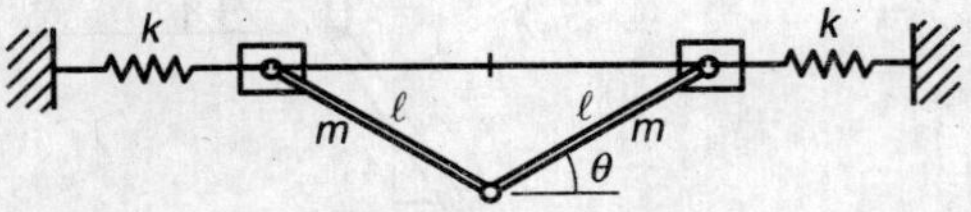

FIGURE P6.31.

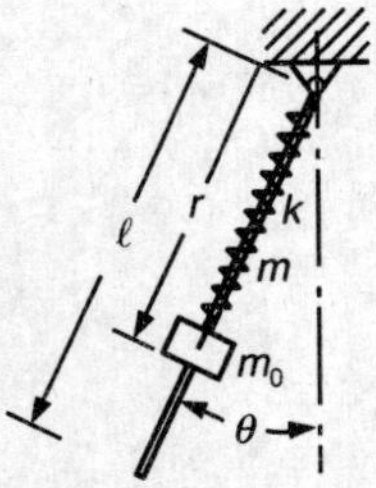

FIGURE P6.32.

6.32. Write Lagrange's equations of motion for the system shown in Fig. P6.32.

6.33. The following constants are given for the beam of Fig. P6.33:

$$k = \frac{EI}{l^3}, \qquad \frac{EI}{ml^4} = N, \qquad \frac{k}{ml} = N$$

$$K = 5\frac{EI}{l}, \qquad \frac{K}{ml^3} = 5N$$

Using the modes $\phi_1 = x/l$ and $\phi_2 = \sin(\pi x/l)$, determine the equation of motion by Lagrange's method, and determine the first two natural frequencies and mode shapes.

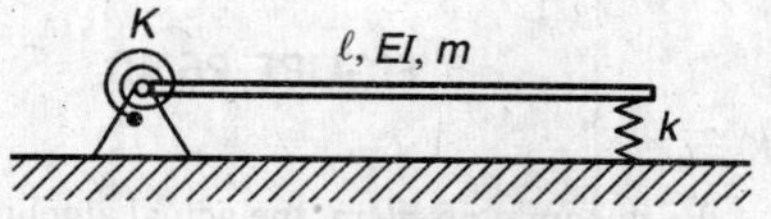

FIGURE P6.33.

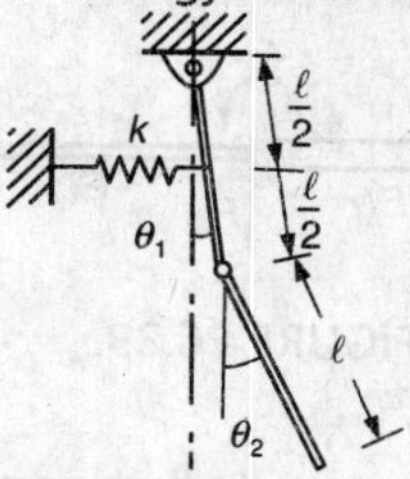

FIGURE P6.34.

6.34. Using Lagrange's method, determine the equations for the small oscillation of the bars shown in Fig. P6.34.

6.35. The rigid bar linkages of Example 6.3.1 are loaded by springs and masses, as shown in Fig. P6.35. Write Lagrange's equations of motion.

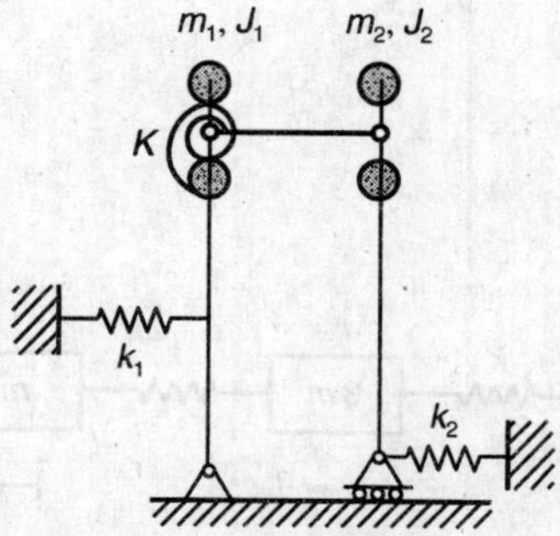

FIGURE P6.35.

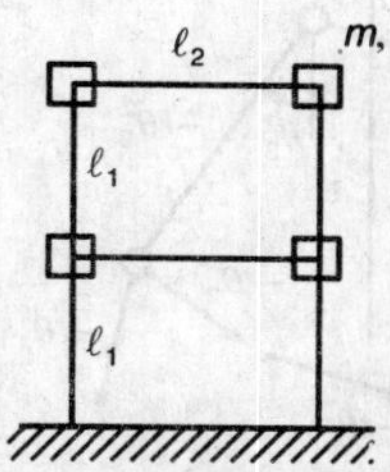

FIGURE P6.36.

6.36. Equal masses are placed at the corners of the frame of Example 6.3.2, as shown in Fig. P6.36. Determine the stiffness matrix and the matrix equation of motion. (Let $l_2 = l_1$.)

6.37. Determine the stiffness matrix for the frame shown in Fig. P6.37.

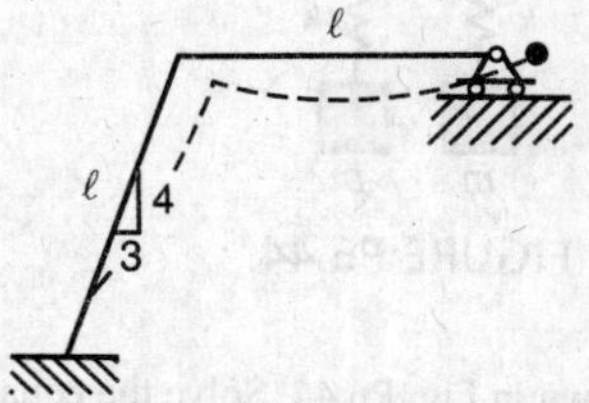

FIGURE P6.37.

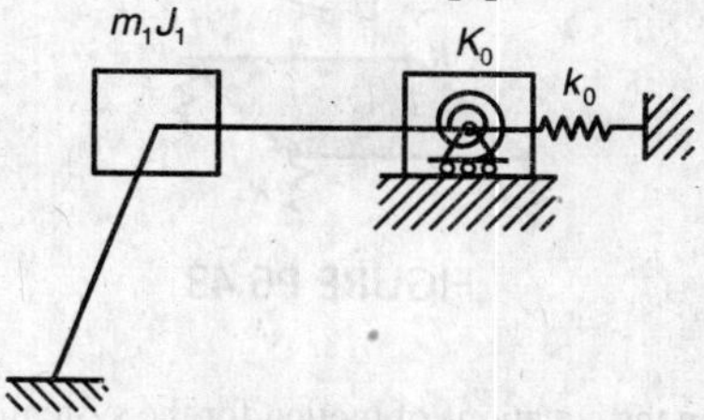

FIGURE P6.38.

6.38. The frame of Prob. 6.33 is loaded by springs and masses, as shown in Fig. P6.38. Determine the equations of motion and the normal modes of the system.

6.39. Using area moment and superposition, determine M_1 and R_2 for the beam shown in Fig. P6.39. Let $EI_1 = 2EI_2$.

6.40. With loads m and J placed as shown in Fig. P6.40, set up the equations of motion.

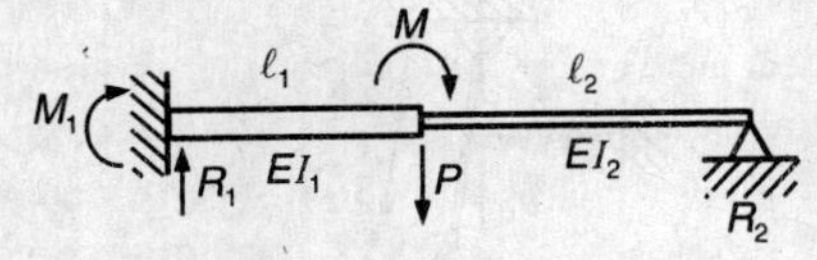

FIGURE P6.39.

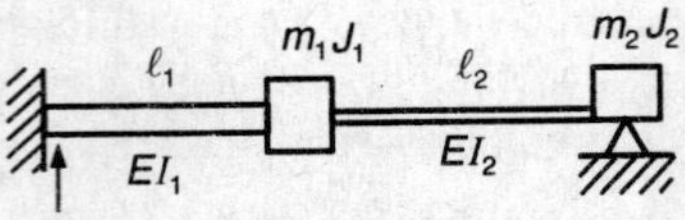

FIGURE P6.40.

6.41. For the extension of the double pendulum to the dynamic problem, the actual algebra can become long and tedious. Instead, draw the components of $-\ddot{r}$ as shown. By taking each $\delta\theta$ separately, the virtual work equation can be easily determined visually. Complete the equations of motion for the system in Fig. P6.41. Compare with Lagrange's derivation.

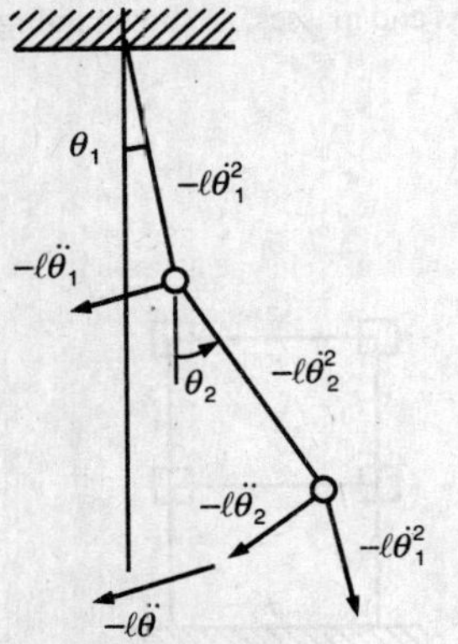

FIGURE P6.41.

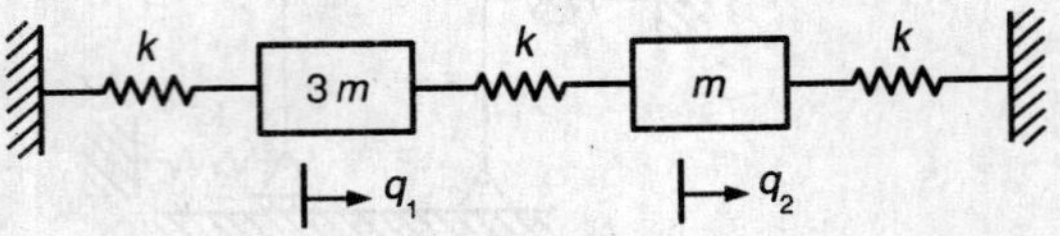

FIGURE P6.42.

6.42. Write the Lagrangian for the system shown in Fig. P6.42.

M **6.43.** Determine the equations of motion for the system shown in Fig. P6.43. Solve the equations numerically in MATLAB® for different initial conditions. (Assume the table does not rotate.)

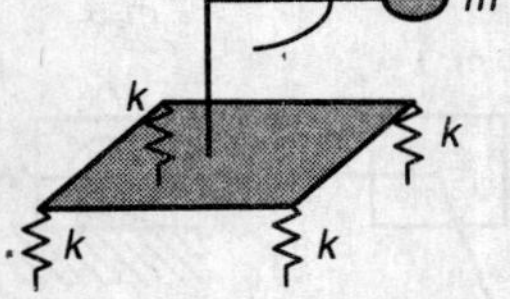

FIGURE P6.43.

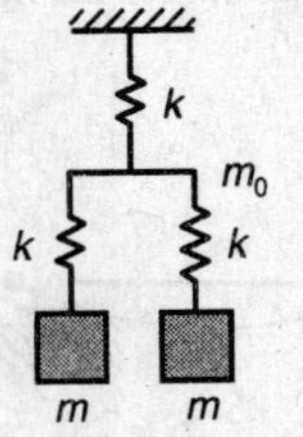

FIGURE P6.44.

M **6.44.** Determine the equations of motion for the system shown in Fig. P6.44. Solve the equations numerically in MATLAB® for different initial conditions. (Assume m_0 has no mass and it does not rotate.)

CHAPTER 7

Computational Methods

In the previous chapters, we have discussed the basic procedure for finding the eigenvalues and eigenvectors of a system. In this basic method, the eigenvalues of the system are found from the roots of the polynomial equation obtained from the characteristic determinant. Each of the roots (or eigenvalues) was then substituted, one at a time, into the equations of motion to determine the mode shape (or eigenvectors) of the system.

Although this method is applicable to any N-DOF system, for systems with DOF greater than 2, the characteristic equation results in an algebraic equation of degree 3 or higher and the digital computer is essential for the numerical work.

As an alternative to this procedure, there is an implicit method of transformation of coordinates coupled with an iteration procedure that results in all the eigenvalues and eigenvectors simultaneously. In this method, the equation of motion

$$[-\lambda M + K]X = 0 \tag{a}$$

must be converted to the standard eigenvalue form utilized in most of the computer programs. This standard form is

$$[\widetilde{A} - \lambda I]Y = 0 \tag{b}$$

where $\widetilde{A}$ is a square symmetric matrix, and Y is a new displacement vector transformed from X. Because these methods all involve the iteration procedure, we precede the transformation method with the computer application to the basic method and the method of matrix iteration.

7.1 ROOT SOLVING

Figure 7.1.1 shows a 3-DOF system for which the normal modes and natural frequencies are desired. The equation of motion for this system is

$$m\begin{bmatrix} 2 & & \\ & 1 & \\ & & 1 \end{bmatrix}\begin{Bmatrix} \ddot{x}_1 \\ \ddot{x}_2 \\ \ddot{x}_3 \end{Bmatrix} + k\begin{bmatrix} 3 & -1 & 0 \\ -1 & 2 & -1 \\ 0 & -1 & 1 \end{bmatrix}\begin{Bmatrix} x_1 \\ x_2 \\ x_3 \end{Bmatrix} = \begin{Bmatrix} 0 \\ 0 \\ 0 \end{Bmatrix}$$

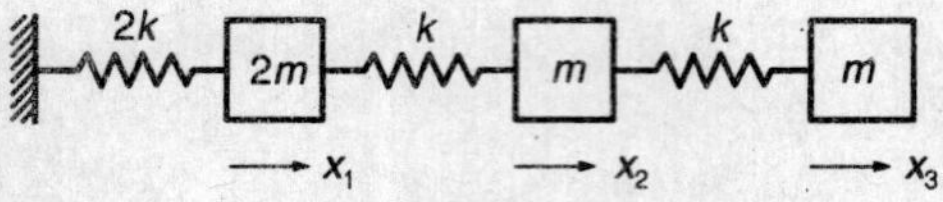

FIGURE 7.1.1.

or

$$\left(-\lambda\begin{bmatrix}2 & & \\ & 1 & \\ & & 1\end{bmatrix}+\begin{bmatrix}3 & -1 & 0\\ -1 & 2 & -1\\ 0 & -1 & 1\end{bmatrix}\right)\begin{Bmatrix}x_1\\ x_2\\ x_3\end{Bmatrix}=\begin{Bmatrix}0\\ 0\\ 0\end{Bmatrix} \tag{7.1.1}$$

where $\lambda = \omega^2 m/k$.

The eigenvalues of the system are found from the characteristic determinant equated to zero:

$$\begin{vmatrix}(3-2\lambda) & -1 & 0\\ -1 & (2-\lambda) & -1\\ 0 & -1 & (1-\lambda)\end{vmatrix}=0$$

This determinant reduces to a third-degree algebraic equation. Using the method of minors (see Appendix C) and choosing the elements of the first column as pivots, we have

$$(3-2\lambda)\begin{vmatrix}(2-\lambda) & -1\\ -1 & (1-\lambda)\end{vmatrix}+1\begin{vmatrix}-1 & 0\\ -1 & (1-\lambda)\end{vmatrix}=0$$

and the characteristic equation becomes

$$\lambda^3 - 4.50\lambda^2 + 5\lambda - 1 = 0$$

However, it is a simple matter to rewrite the above equation as

$$f(\lambda) = \lambda^3 - 4.50\lambda^2 + 5\lambda - 1 = 0$$

and plot it as a function of λ to find its zero crossings. This is done in Fig. 7.1.2 and one can see that one root is between [0,.5]; another between [1,1.5]; and a third root between [2.5,3]. By using straight lines between these points or Newton interpolation, the roots are found easily. Because the

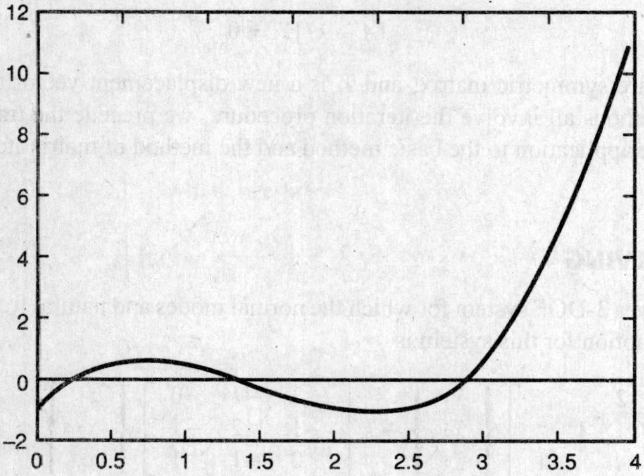

FIGURE 7.1.2.

computer can carry out thousands of calculations in a few seconds, $\Delta\lambda$ can be chosen very small, in which case, the interpolation can be minimized or even eliminated for the accuracy required.

As a further insight to the root location, we can assume the roots to be known as $\lambda_1, \lambda_2, \lambda_3$, and rewrite the polynomial in the factored form

$$f(\lambda) = (\lambda - \lambda_1)(\lambda - \lambda_2)(\lambda - \lambda_3) = 0$$

Multiplying out the factored form the above equation becomes

$$f(\lambda) = \lambda^3 - (\lambda_1 + \lambda_2 + \lambda_3)\lambda^2 + (\lambda_1\lambda_2 + \lambda_1\lambda_3 + \lambda_2\lambda_3)\lambda - \lambda_1\lambda_2\lambda_3 = 0$$

and one finds that the coefficient of the next to the highest power of λ is always the sum of the roots regardless of the degrees of freedom of the system. This additional information can be useful as a check on the roots found.

One can calculate the roots in MATLAB® using the command **roots(c)** where c is a vector that contains the coefficients of the polynomial in descending order. For our example, $c = [1, -4.5, 5, -1]$. The roots of this equation are given by roots(c) = 2.8892, 1.3554, .2554. The location of these roots agrees with the plot.

7.2 EIGENVECTORS BY GAUSS ELIMINATION

In solving for the mode shapes, the eigenvalues are substituted, one at a time, into the equation of motion. The Gauss method offers one way in which to solve for the ratio of amplitudes. Essentially, the Gauss procedure reduces the matrix equation to an upper triangular form that can be solved for the amplitudes starting from the bottom of the matrix equation.

Applying the Gauss method to the previous problem, we start with the equation of motion written in terms of λ:

$$\begin{bmatrix} (3-2\lambda_i) & -1 & 0 \\ -1 & (2-\lambda_i) & -1 \\ 0 & -1 & (1-\lambda_i) \end{bmatrix} \begin{Bmatrix} x_1 \\ x_2 \\ x_3 \end{Bmatrix}^{(i)} = \begin{Bmatrix} 0 \\ 0 \\ 0 \end{Bmatrix}$$

The eigenvalues solved for the problem were

$$\lambda = \omega^2 \frac{m}{k} = \begin{Bmatrix} 0.22536 \\ 1.3554 \\ 2.8892 \end{Bmatrix}$$

Substituting $\lambda_1 = 0.25536$ into the preceding equation, we have

$$\begin{bmatrix} 2.489 & -1 & 0 \\ -1 & 1.745 & -1 \\ 0 & -1 & 0.7446 \end{bmatrix} \begin{Bmatrix} x_1 \\ x_2 \\ x_3 \end{Bmatrix}^{(1)} = \begin{Bmatrix} 0 \\ 0 \\ 0 \end{Bmatrix}$$

In the Gauss method, the first step is to eliminate the terms of the first column in the second and third rows. Because the first column of the third row is already equal to zero, we need only to zero the first term of the second row. This is done by dividing the first row by 2.489 and adding it to the second row, which gives

$$\begin{bmatrix} 2.489 & -1 & 0 \\ 0 & 1.343 & -1 \\ 0 & -1 & 0.7446 \end{bmatrix} \begin{Bmatrix} x_1 \\ x_2 \\ x_3 \end{Bmatrix}^{(1)} = \begin{Bmatrix} 0 \\ 0 \\ 0 \end{Bmatrix}$$

Although it is not necessary to go further in this case, the procedure can be repeated to eliminate the -1 term of the third row by dividing the second row by 1.343 and adding it to the third row, which results in

$$\begin{bmatrix} 2.489 & -1 & 0 \\ 0 & 1.343 & -1 \\ 0 & 0 & 0 \end{bmatrix} \begin{Bmatrix} x_1 \\ x_2 \\ x_3 \end{Bmatrix}^{(1)} = \begin{Bmatrix} 0 \\ 0 \\ 0 \end{Bmatrix}$$

In either this equation or the previous one, the amplitude x_3 is assigned the value 1, which results in the first eigenvector or mode:

$$\phi_1 = \begin{Bmatrix} x_1 \\ x_2 \\ 1 \end{Bmatrix}^{(1)} = \begin{Bmatrix} 0.2992 \\ 0.7446 \\ 1.000 \end{Bmatrix}$$

By repeating the procedure with λ_2 and λ_3, the eigenvectors for the second and third modes can be found.

Eigenvectors can also be found by the method in Appendix C or by using the MATLAB® command **eig**, which will be discussed later in this chapter.

7.3 MATRIX ITERATION

With knowledge of orthogonality and the expansion theorem, we are in a position to discuss the somewhat different approach for finding the eigenvalues and eigenvectors of a multi-DOF system by the matrix iteration procedure. Although the method is applicable to the equations of motion formulated by either the flexibility or the stiffness matrices, we use the flexibility matrix for demonstration.

In terms of the flexibility matrix $[a] = K^{-1}$, the equation for the normal mode vibration is

$$\overline{A}X = \overline{\lambda}X \tag{7.3.1}$$

where

$$\overline{A} = [a][m] = K^{-1}M$$
$$\overline{\lambda} = 1/\omega^2$$

The iteration is started by assuming a set of amplitudes for the left column of Eq. (7.3.1) and performing the indicated operation, which results in a column of numbers. This is then normalized by making one of the amplitudes equal to unity and dividing each term of the column by the particular amplitude that was normalized. The procedure is then repeated with the normalized column until the amplitudes stabilize to a definite pattern. When the normalized column no longer differs from that of the previous iteration, it has converged to the eigenvector corresponding to the largest eigenvalue, which in this case is that of the smallest natural frequency ω_1.

Example 7.3.1

For the system shown in Fig. 7.3.1, write the matrix equation based on the flexibility and determine the lowest natural frequency by iteration.

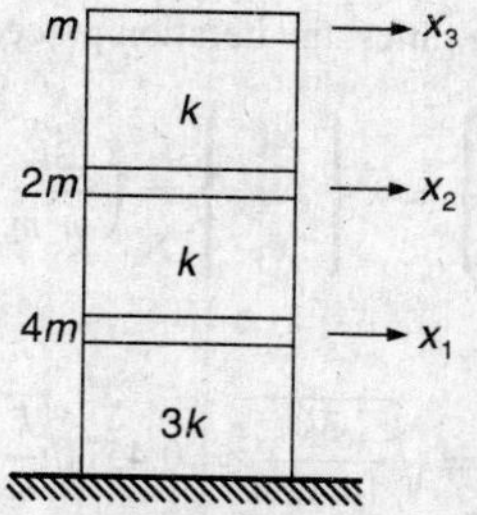

FIGURE 7.3.1.

Solution The mass and the flexibility matrices for the system are

$$[m] = m\begin{bmatrix} 4 & 0 & 0 \\ 0 & 2 & 0 \\ 0 & 0 & 1 \end{bmatrix} \qquad [a] = \frac{1}{3k}\begin{bmatrix} 1 & 1 & 1 \\ 1 & 4 & 4 \\ 1 & 4 & 7 \end{bmatrix}$$

and substituting into Eq. (7.3.1), we have

$$\begin{bmatrix} 1 & 1 & 1 \\ 1 & 4 & 4 \\ 1 & 4 & 7 \end{bmatrix}\begin{bmatrix} 4 & 0 & 0 \\ 0 & 2 & 0 \\ 0 & 0 & 1 \end{bmatrix}\begin{Bmatrix} x_1 \\ x_2 \\ x_3 \end{Bmatrix} = \left(\frac{3k}{\omega^2 m}\right)\begin{Bmatrix} x_1 \\ x_2 \\ x_3 \end{Bmatrix}$$

or

$$\begin{bmatrix} 4 & 2 & 1 \\ 4 & 8 & 4 \\ 4 & 8 & 7 \end{bmatrix}\begin{Bmatrix} x_1 \\ x_2 \\ x_3 \end{Bmatrix} = \bar{\lambda}\begin{Bmatrix} x_1 \\ x_2 \\ x_3 \end{Bmatrix}$$

To start the iteration, we arbitrarily assume

$$X_1 = \begin{Bmatrix} x_1 \\ x_2 \\ x_3 \end{Bmatrix} = \begin{Bmatrix} 0.2 \\ 0.6 \\ 1.0 \end{Bmatrix}$$

$$AX_1 = \begin{bmatrix} 4 & 2 & 1 \\ 4 & 8 & 4 \\ 4 & 8 & 7 \end{bmatrix}\begin{Bmatrix} 0.2 \\ 0.6 \\ 1.0 \end{Bmatrix} = \begin{Bmatrix} 3.0 \\ 9.6 \\ 12.6 \end{Bmatrix} = 12.6\begin{Bmatrix} 0.238 \\ 0.762 \\ 1.000 \end{Bmatrix}$$

By using the new normalized column for X_2, the second iteration yields

$$AX_2 = \begin{bmatrix} 4 & 2 & 1 \\ 4 & 8 & 4 \\ 4 & 8 & 7 \end{bmatrix}\begin{Bmatrix} 0.238 \\ 0.762 \\ 1.000 \end{Bmatrix} = \begin{Bmatrix} 3.476 \\ 11.048 \\ 14.048 \end{Bmatrix} = 14.048\begin{Bmatrix} 0.247 \\ 0.786 \\ 1.000 \end{Bmatrix}$$

In a similar manner, the third iteration gives

$$AX_3 = \begin{bmatrix} 4 & 2 & 1 \\ 4 & 8 & 4 \\ 4 & 8 & 7 \end{bmatrix}\begin{Bmatrix} 0.247 \\ 0.786 \\ 1.000 \end{Bmatrix} = \begin{Bmatrix} 3.560 \\ 11.276 \\ 14.276 \end{Bmatrix} = 14.276\begin{Bmatrix} 0.249 \\ 0.790 \\ 1.000 \end{Bmatrix}$$

By repeating this procedure a few more times, the iteration procedure converges to

$$14.324\begin{Bmatrix} 0.250 \\ 0.790 \\ 1.000 \end{Bmatrix} = \bar{\lambda}\begin{Bmatrix} x_1 \\ x_2 \\ x_3 \end{Bmatrix} = \left(\frac{3k}{\omega^2 m}\right)\begin{Bmatrix} 0.250 \\ 0.790 \\ 1.000 \end{Bmatrix}$$

Thus, the frequency of the lowest mode is

$$\omega_1 = \sqrt{\frac{3k}{14.32m}} = 0.457\sqrt{\frac{k}{m}}$$

with the mode shape

$$\phi_1 = \begin{Bmatrix} 0.250 \\ 0.790 \\ 1.000 \end{Bmatrix}$$

It should be mentioned here that if the equation of motion was formulated in terms of the stiffness matrix, the iteration equation would be

$$AX = \lambda X$$

$$[M^{-1}K]X = \omega^2 X$$

Because the iteration procedure always converges to the largest eigenvalue, the stiffness equation would converge to the highest mode. In vibration analysis, the lower modes are generally of greater interest than the higher modes, so that the matrix iteration procedure will find its use mainly for equations formulated in terms of flexibility where the eigenvalues are proportional to the reciprocal of ω^2.

■

7.4 CONVERGENCE OF THE ITERATION PROCEDURE

To show that the iteration procedure converges to the largest eigenvalue, which for the equation formulated in terms of flexibility is the lowest fundamental mode, the assumed trial vector X_1 is expressed in terms of the normal modes ϕ_i by the expansion theorem:

$$X_1 = c_1\phi_1 + c_2\phi_2 + c_3\phi_3 + \cdots + \tag{7.4.1}$$

where c_i are constants. Multiplying this equation by the dynamic matrix $\bar{A}$, we have

$$\bar{A}X_1 = X_2 = c_1\bar{A}\phi_1 + c_2\bar{A}\phi_2 + c_3\bar{A}\phi_3 + \cdots + \tag{7.4.2}$$

Because each normal mode satisfies the following equation

$$\bar{A}\phi_i = \bar{\lambda}_i\phi_i = \frac{1}{\omega_i^2}\phi_i \tag{7.4.3}$$

the right side of Eq. (7.4.2) becomes

$$X_2 = c_1\frac{1}{\omega_1^2}\phi_1 + c_2\frac{1}{\omega_2^2}\phi_2 + c_3\frac{1}{\omega_3^2}\phi_3 + \cdots +$$

which is the new displacement vector X_2. Again, premultiplying X_2 by the dynamic matrix and using Eq. (7.4.3), the result is

$$AX_2 = X_3 = c_1\frac{1}{\omega_1^4}\phi_1 + c_2\frac{1}{\omega_2^4}\phi_2 + c_3\frac{1}{\omega_3^4}\omega_3 + \cdots +$$

Thus, after several repetitions of the procedure, we obtain

$$AX_{n-1} = X_n = c_1 \frac{1}{\omega_1^{2n}} \phi_1 + c_2 \frac{1}{\omega_2^{2n}} \phi_2 + c_3 \frac{1}{\omega_3^{2n}} \phi_3 + \cdots + \tag{7.4.4}$$

Because $\omega_n^2 > \omega_{n-1}^2 > \cdots > \omega_2^2 > \omega_1^2$, the convergence is to the fundamental mode. For convergence to higher modes see Appendix G.

7.5 THE DYNAMIC MATRIX

The matrix equation for the normal mode vibration is generally written as

$$[-\lambda M + K]X = 0 \tag{7.5.1}$$

where M and K are both square symmetric matrices, and λ is the eigenvalue related to the natural frequency by $\lambda = \omega^2$. Premultiplying the preceding equation by M^{-1}, we have another form of the equation:

$$[-\lambda I + A]X = 0 \tag{7.5.2}$$

where $A = M^{-1}K$ and is called the *dynamic matrix*. In general $M^{-1}K$ is not symmetric.

If next we premultiply Eq. (7.5.1) by K^{-l}, we obtain

$$[\overline{A} - \overline{\lambda} I]X = 0 \tag{7.5.3}$$

where $\overline{A} = K^{-1}M$ is the dynamic matrix, and $\overline{\lambda} = 1/\omega^2 = 1/\lambda$ is the eigenvalue for the equation.

Although A and $\overline{A}$ are different, they are both called the dynamic matrix because the dynamic properties of the system are defined by A or $\overline{A}$. Again, matrix $\overline{A}$ is generally not symmetric.

If a given system is solved by either Eq. (7.5.2) or (7.5.3), the eigenvalues will be reciprocally related, but will result in the same natural frequencies. The eigenvectors for the two equations will also be identical.

7.6 TRANSFORMATION OF COORDINATES (STANDARD COMPUTER FORM)

In Eqs. (7.5.2) or (7.5.3), dynamic matrices A and $\overline{A}$ are usually unsymmetric. To obtain the standard form of the equation of motion for the computer, the following transformation of coordinates

$$X = U^{-1}Y \tag{7.6.1}$$

is introduced into the equation

$$[-\lambda M + K]X = 0$$

which results in the transformed equation

$$[-\lambda M U^{-1} + K U^{-l}]Y = 0$$

Premultiplying this equation by the transpose U^{-1}, which is designated as

$$[U^{-1}]^T = U^{-T}$$

we obtain the equation

$$[-\lambda U^{-T} M U^{-1} + U^{-T} K U^{-1}]Y = 0 \tag{7.6.2}$$

It is evident here that if we decompose either M or K into $U^T U$ in the preceding equation, we would obtain the standard form of the equation of motion.

With $M = U^T U$, Eq. (7.6.2) becomes

$$[-\lambda I + U^{-T} K U^{-1}]Y = 0 \quad \lambda = \omega^2 \tag{7.6.3}$$

whereas if $K = U^T U$, the equation is

$$[U^{-T} M U^{-1} - \overline{\lambda} I]Y = 0 \quad \overline{\lambda} = 1/\omega^2 \tag{7.6.4}$$

Both equations are in the standard form

$$[-\lambda I + \widetilde{A}]Y = 0$$

where the dynamic matrix $\widetilde{A}$ is symmetric.

To illustrate the use of the dynamic matrix and the standard computer form, we can use MATLAB® to calculate the eigenvalues and eigenvectors for the 3-DOF system shown in Fig. 7.1.1. First, we need to convert this problem to the standard eigenvalue problem by multiplying Eq. 7.1.1 by the inverse of the mass matrix. For this example, the dynamic matrix is given by

$$A = \begin{bmatrix} 1.5000 & -0.5000 & 0 \\ -1.0000 & 2.0000 & -1.0000 \\ 0 & -1.0000 & 1.0000 \end{bmatrix}$$

We can compute both the eigenvalues and eigenvectors in MATLAB® by typing the command **[U,D]=eig(A)**. The result of this command is two matrices, U and D. Matrix U contains the eigenvectors as column vectors and D is a diagonal matrix, which has the eigenvalues on the diagonal. Continuing with our example, we get the following two matrices

$$U = \begin{bmatrix} 0.7569 & 0.3031 & 0.2333 \\ 0.2189 & -0.8422 & 0.5808 \\ -0.6158 & 0.4458 & 0.7799 \end{bmatrix}$$

and

$$D = \begin{bmatrix} 1.3554 & 0 & 0 \\ 0 & 2.8892 & 0 \\ 0 & 0 & 0.2554 \end{bmatrix}$$

7.7 SYSTEMS WITH DISCRETE MASS MATRIX

For the lumped-mass system in which the coordinates are chosen at each of the masses, the mass matrix is diagonal and U is simply equal to the square root of each diagonal term. The inverse of U is then equal to the reciprocal of each term in U, so that we have

$$M = \begin{bmatrix} m_{11} & & \\ & m_{22} & \\ & & m_{33} \end{bmatrix} \qquad U = M^{1/2} = \begin{bmatrix} \sqrt{m_{11}} & & \\ & \sqrt{m_{22}} & \\ & & \sqrt{m_{33}} \end{bmatrix}$$

$$U^{-1} = U^{-T} = \begin{bmatrix} 1/\sqrt{m_{11}} & & \\ & 1/\sqrt{m_{22}} & \\ & & 1/\sqrt{m_{33}} \end{bmatrix}$$

Thus, the dynamic matrix $\widetilde{A} = U^{-T} K U^{-1}$ of Eq. (7.6.3) is simply determined.

Example 7.7.1

Consider the system of Example 5.7.1, which is shown again in Fig. 7.7.1. The mass and stiffness matrices for the problem are

$$M = m\begin{bmatrix} 2 & 0 \\ 0 & 1 \end{bmatrix} \quad K = k\begin{bmatrix} 3 & -1 \\ -1 & 1 \end{bmatrix}$$

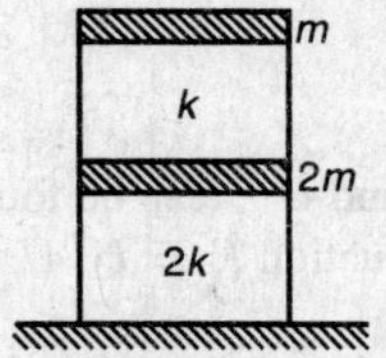

FIGURE 7.7.1.

We first decompose the mass matrix to $M = U^T U = M^{1/2}M^{1/2}$. Because M is diagonal, the matrix U is simply found from the square root of the diagonal terms. Its inverse is also found from the inverse of the diagonal terms, and its transpose is identical to the matrix itself.

$$U = M^{1/2} = \sqrt{m}\begin{bmatrix} \sqrt{2} & 0 \\ 0 & 1 \end{bmatrix} \quad U^{-1} = U^{-T} = \frac{1}{\sqrt{m}}\begin{bmatrix} 1/\sqrt{2} & 0 \\ 0 & 1 \end{bmatrix} = \frac{1}{\sqrt{m}}\begin{bmatrix} 0.7071 & 0 \\ 0 & 1 \end{bmatrix}$$

Thus, the terms of the standard equation become

$$U^{-T}MU^{-1} = U^{-T}U^{T}UU^{-1} = I$$

$$\tilde{A} = U^{-T}KU^{-1} = \frac{k}{m}\begin{bmatrix} 0.707 & 0 \\ 0 & 1 \end{bmatrix}\begin{bmatrix} 3 & -1 \\ -1 & 1 \end{bmatrix}\begin{bmatrix} 0.707 & 0 \\ 0 & 1 \end{bmatrix} = \frac{k}{m}\begin{bmatrix} 1.50 & -0.707 \\ -0.707 & 1.0 \end{bmatrix}$$

By letting $\lambda = \omega^2 m/k$, the equation of motion is then reduced to

$$\left[\begin{bmatrix} 1.50 & -0.707 \\ -0.707 & 1 \end{bmatrix} - \lambda\begin{bmatrix} 1 & 0 \\ 0 & 1 \end{bmatrix}\right]\begin{Bmatrix} y_1 \\ y_2 \end{Bmatrix} = \begin{Bmatrix} 0 \\ 0 \end{Bmatrix}$$

and its characteristic equation becomes

$$\begin{vmatrix} (1.50 - \lambda) & -0.707 \\ -0.707 & (1 - \lambda) \end{vmatrix} = 0 \text{ and } \lambda^2 - 2.50\lambda + 1 = 0$$

The eigenvalues and eigenvectors solved from these equations are

$$\lambda_1 = 0.50\begin{Bmatrix} y_1 \\ y_2 \end{Bmatrix}^{(1)} = \begin{Bmatrix} 0.707 \\ 1.000 \end{Bmatrix}$$

$$\lambda_2 = 2.00\begin{Bmatrix} y_1 \\ y_2 \end{Bmatrix}^{(2)} = \begin{Bmatrix} -1.414 \\ 1.000 \end{Bmatrix}$$

These are the modes in the y coordinates, and to obtain the normal nodes in the original x coordinates, we first assemble the previous modes into a modal matrix Y from which the modal matrix in the x coordinates is found.

$$Y = \begin{bmatrix} 0.707 & -1.414 \\ 1.000 & 1.000 \end{bmatrix}$$

$$X = U^{-1}Y = \begin{bmatrix} 0.707 & 0 \\ 0 & 1.0 \end{bmatrix} \begin{bmatrix} 0.707 & -1.414 \\ 1.00 & 1.00 \end{bmatrix} = \begin{bmatrix} 0.50 & -1.00 \\ 1.00 & 1.00 \end{bmatrix}$$

These results are in agreement with those found in Example 5.7.2.

7.8 CHOLESKY DECOMPOSITION

When matrix M or K is full, matrices U and U^{-1} can be found from the Cholesky decomposition. In this evaluation, we simply write the equation $K = U^T U$ (or $M = U^T U$) in terms of the upper triangular matrix for U and its transpose.

An example of a 4×4 stiffness matrix K is as follows:

$$\begin{bmatrix} u_{11} & 0 & 0 & 0 \\ u_{12} & u_{22} & 0 & 0 \\ u_{13} & u_{23} & u_{33} & 0 \\ u_{14} & u_{24} & u_{34} & u_{44} \end{bmatrix} \begin{bmatrix} u_{11} & u_{12} & u_{13} & u_{14} \\ 0 & u_{22} & u_{23} & u_{24} \\ 0 & 0 & u_{33} & u_{34} \\ 0 & 0 & 0 & u_{44} \end{bmatrix} = \begin{bmatrix} k_{11} & k_{12} & k_{13} & k_{14} \\ k_{21} & k_{22} & k_{23} & k_{24} \\ k_{31} & k_{32} & k_{33} & k_{34} \\ k_{41} & k_{42} & k_{43} & k_{44} \end{bmatrix}$$

Because the product matrix is also symmetric, only the upper triangular section is needed to evaluate U.

$$\begin{bmatrix} u_{11}^2 & u_{11}u_{12} & u_{11}u_{13} & u_{11}u_{14} \\ & (u_{12}^2 + u_{22}^2) & (u_{12}u_{13} + u_{22}u_{23}) & (u_{12}u_{14} + u_{22}u_{24}) \\ & & (u_{13}^2 + u_{23}^2 + u_{33}^2) & (u_{13}u_{14} + u_{23}u_{24} + u_{33}u_{34}) \\ & & & (u_{14}^2 + u_{24}^2 + u_{34}^2 + u_{44}^2) \end{bmatrix}$$

$$= \begin{bmatrix} k_{11} & k_{12} & k_{13} & k_{14} \\ & k_{22} & k_{23} & k_{24} \\ & & k_{33} & k_{34} \\ & & & k_{44} \end{bmatrix}$$

Equating term for term in the two matrices, we obtain from the first row

$$u_{11}^2 = k_{11}$$

$$u_{12} = k_{12}/u_{11}$$

$$u_{13} = k_{13}/u_{11}$$

$$u_{14} = k_{14}/u_{11}$$

From the second row, we have

$$u_{22}^2 = k_{22} - u_{12}^2$$

$$u_{13} = \frac{1}{u_{22}}(k_{23} - u_{12}u_{13})$$

$$u_{24} = \frac{1}{u_{22}}(k_{24} - u_{12}u_{14})$$

Similarly, the third and fourth rows yield

$$u_{33}^2 = k_{33} - u_{13}^2 - u_{23}^2$$

$$u_{34} = \frac{1}{u_{33}}(k_{34} - u_{13}u_{14} - u_{23}u_{24})$$

$$u_{44}^2 = k_{44} - u_{14}^2 - u_{24}^2 - u_{34}^2$$

We can now group these equations as follows from which we can write general expressions for an $n \times n$ matrix:

$$u_{22}^2 = k_{22} - u_{12}^2$$
$$u_{33}^2 = k_{33} - u_{13}^2 - u_{23}^2$$
$$u_{44}^2 = k_{44} - u_{14}^2 - u_{24}^2 - u_{34}^2$$
$$\vdots$$
$$u_{ii} = \left(k_{ii} - \sum_{l=1}^{i-1} u_{li}^2\right)^{1/2} \quad i = 2, 3, 4, \ldots, n$$

$$u_{23} = \frac{1}{u_{22}}(k_{23} - u_{12}u_{13})$$
$$u_{24} = \frac{1}{u_{22}}(k_{24} - u_{12}u_{14})$$
$$u_{34} = \frac{1}{u_{33}}(k_{34} - u_{13}u_{14} - u_{23}u_{24})$$
$$\vdots$$
$$u_{ij} = \frac{1}{u_{ii}}\left(k_{ij} - \sum_{l=1}^{i-1} u_{li}u_{lj}\right) i = 2, 3, 4, \ldots, n; \; j = i+1, i+2, \ldots, n$$

In MATLAB®, we can get the Cholesky factorization of a matrix, A, with the command **U = chol(A)**. The matrix U is an upper triangular matrix such that $U' * U = A$. As an example consider the matrix

$$A = \begin{bmatrix} 2 & -1 & 0 \\ -1 & 2 & -1 \\ 0 & -1 & 2 \end{bmatrix}$$

The Cholesky factorization is given by

$$U = \text{chol(A)}$$
$$= \begin{bmatrix} 1.4142 & -.7071 & 0 \\ 0 & 1.2247 & -.8165 \\ 0 & 0 & 1.1547 \end{bmatrix}$$

Inverse of U

The inverse of the triangular matrix U can be found from the equation:

$$
\underset{\text{(known)}}{U} \qquad \underset{\text{(unknown inverse)}}{U^{\tilde{n}1}} \qquad = \qquad \underset{\text{(unit matrix)}}{I}
$$

$$
\begin{bmatrix} u_{11} & u_{12} & u_{13} & u_{14} \\ 0 & u_{22} & u_{23} & u_{24} \\ 0 & 0 & u_{33} & u_{34} \\ 0 & 0 & 0 & u_{44} \end{bmatrix}
\begin{bmatrix} v_{11} & v_{12} & v_{13} & v_{14} \\ v_{21} & v_{22} & v_{23} & v_{24} \\ v_{31} & v_{32} & v_{33} & v_{34} \\ v_{41} & v_{42} & v_{43} & v_{44} \end{bmatrix}
=
\begin{bmatrix} 1 & 0 & 0 & 0 \\ 0 & 1 & 0 & 0 \\ 0 & 0 & 1 & 0 \\ 0 & 0 & 0 & 1 \end{bmatrix}
$$

Starting the multiplication of the two matrices on the left from the bottom row of U with the columns of v_{ij} and equating each term to the unit matrix, it will be found that $v_{ij} = 0$ for $i > j$, so that the inverse matrix U^{-1} is also an upper triangular matrix. The following sequence of multiplication will then yield the following results.

Row 4 × columns 1, 2, 3, and 4:

$$v_{44} = \frac{1}{u_{44}}$$

Row 3 × columns 1, 2, 3, and 4:

$$v_{33} = \frac{1}{u_{33}}$$

$$v_{34} = \frac{-1}{u_{33}}(u_{34}v_{44})$$

Row 2 × columns 1, 2, 3, and 4:

$$v_{22} = \frac{1}{u_{22}}$$

$$v_{23} = \frac{-1}{u_{22}}(u_{23}v_{33})$$

$$v_{24} = \frac{-1}{u_{22}}(u_{23}v_{34} + u_{24}v_{44})$$

Row 1 × columns 1, 2, 3, and 4:

$$v_{11} = \frac{1}{u_{11}}$$

$$v_{12} = \frac{-1}{u_{11}}(u_{12}v_{22})$$

$$v_{13} = \frac{-1}{u_{11}}(u_{12}v_{23} + u_{13}v_{33})$$

$$v_{14} = \frac{-1}{u_{11}}(u_{12}v_{24} + u_{13}v_{34} + u_{14}v_{44})$$

These results are then summarized by the following general equations:

$$v_{ij} = 0 \quad i > j$$

$$v_{ii} = \frac{1}{u_{ii}}$$

$$v_{ij} = \frac{-1}{u_{ii}}\left(\sum_{l=i+1}^{j} u_{il} + u_{lj}\right) \quad i < j$$

Example 7.8.1

Solve Example 7.7.1 by decomposing the stiffness matrix. The two matrices for the problem are

$$M = m\begin{bmatrix} 2 & 0 \\ 0 & 1 \end{bmatrix} \quad K = k\begin{bmatrix} 3 & -1 \\ -1 & 1 \end{bmatrix}$$

Solution For the 2 × 2 matrix, the algebraic work for the decomposition is small and we carry out all the steps.

Step 1:

$$U^T U = K$$

$$\begin{bmatrix} u_{11} & 0 \\ u_{12} & u_{22} \end{bmatrix}\begin{bmatrix} u_{11} & u_{12} \\ 0 & u_{22} \end{bmatrix} = \begin{bmatrix} u_{11}^2 & u_{11}u_{12} \\ u_{11}u_{12} & (u_{12}^2 + u_{22}^2) \end{bmatrix} = \begin{bmatrix} 3 & -1 \\ -1 & 1 \end{bmatrix}$$

$$u_{11} = \sqrt{3} = 1.732$$

$$u_{11}u_{12} = -1 \qquad \therefore u_{12} = -1/1.732 \qquad = -0.5774$$

$$u_{22}^2 = 1 - u_{12}^2 \qquad \therefore u_{22} = \sqrt{1 - (-0.5774)^2} \qquad = 0.8164$$

$$U = \begin{bmatrix} 1.732 & -0.5774 \\ 0 & 0.8162 \end{bmatrix}$$

Check by substituting back into $U^T U = K$.

Step 2: Find the inverse of U from $UU^{-1} = I$.

$$\begin{bmatrix} 1.732 & -0.5774 \\ 0 & 0.8162 \end{bmatrix}\begin{bmatrix} b_{11} & b_{12} \\ 0 & b_{22} \end{bmatrix} = \begin{bmatrix} 1.732b_{11} & (1.732b_{12} - 0.5774b_{22}) \\ 0 & 0.8164b_{22} \end{bmatrix} = \begin{bmatrix} 1 & 0 \\ 0 & 1 \end{bmatrix}$$

$$b_{11} = \frac{1}{1.732} = 0.5774 \quad b_{22} = \frac{1}{0.8164} = 1.2249$$

$$b_{12} = \frac{1}{1.732}(0.5774 \times 1.2249) = 0.4083$$

$$U^{-1} = \begin{bmatrix} 0.5774 & 0.4083 \\ 0 & 1.2249 \end{bmatrix}$$

Check by substituting back into $UU^{-1} = I$.

Step 3:

$$\tilde{A} = U^{-T}MU^{-1} = \begin{bmatrix} 0.5774 & 0 \\ 0.4083 & 1.2249 \end{bmatrix} \begin{bmatrix} 2 & 0 \\ 0 & 1 \end{bmatrix} \begin{bmatrix} 0.5774 & 0.4083 \\ 0 & 1.2249 \end{bmatrix}$$

$$= \begin{bmatrix} 0.6668 & 0.4715 \\ 0.4715 & 1.8338 \end{bmatrix}$$

Note that $\tilde{A}$ is symmetric.

Step 4: The equation of motion is now in standard form, but in y coordinates:

$$\left[\begin{bmatrix} 0.6668 & 0.4715 \\ 0.4715 & 1.8338 \end{bmatrix} - \bar{\lambda} \begin{bmatrix} 1 & 0 \\ 0 & 1 \end{bmatrix} \right] \begin{Bmatrix} y_1 \\ y_2 \end{Bmatrix} = \begin{Bmatrix} 0 \\ 0 \end{Bmatrix} \qquad \bar{\lambda} = \frac{k}{\omega^2 m}$$

Step 5: For this simple problem, the eigenvalues and eigenvectors in y coordinates are found from the usual procedure:

$$\begin{vmatrix} (0.6668 - \bar{\lambda}) & 0.4715 \\ 0.4715 & (1.8338 - \bar{\lambda}) \end{vmatrix} = 0$$

$$\bar{\lambda}^2 - 2.50\bar{\lambda} + 1.0 = 0$$

$$\bar{\lambda}_1 = 2.0 \qquad \begin{Bmatrix} y_1 \\ y_2 \end{Bmatrix}^{(1)} = \begin{Bmatrix} 0.3537 \\ 1.000 \end{Bmatrix}$$

$$\bar{\lambda}_2 = 0.50 \qquad \begin{Bmatrix} y_1 \\ y_2 \end{Bmatrix}^{(2)} = \begin{Bmatrix} -2.8267 \\ 1.000 \end{Bmatrix}$$

Step 6: Eigenvalues are not changed by the transformation of coordinates. The eigenvectors in the original x coordinates are found from the transformation equation.

$$\phi(x) = U^{-1}Y$$

$$\phi(x) = \begin{bmatrix} 0.5774 & 0.4083 \\ 0 & 1.2249 \end{bmatrix} \begin{bmatrix} 0.3537 & -2.8267 \\ 1.000 & 1.000 \end{bmatrix}$$

$$= \begin{bmatrix} 0.6125 & -1.2238 \\ 1.2249 & 1.2249 \end{bmatrix} \cong \begin{bmatrix} 0.50 & -1.00 \\ 1.00 & 1.00 \end{bmatrix}$$

$$\therefore \phi_1(x) = \begin{Bmatrix} x_1 \\ x_2 \end{Bmatrix}^{(1)} = \begin{Bmatrix} 0.50 \\ 1.00 \end{Bmatrix}$$

$$\therefore \phi_2(x) = \begin{Bmatrix} x_1 \\ x_2 \end{Bmatrix}^{(2)} = \begin{Bmatrix} -1.00 \\ 1.00 \end{Bmatrix}$$

■

Example 7.8.2

Figure 7.8.1 shows a 3-DOF model of a building for which the equation of motion is

$$\left[-\left(\frac{\omega^2 m}{k}\right) \begin{bmatrix} 4 & 0 & 0 \\ 0 & 2 & 0 \\ 0 & 0 & 1 \end{bmatrix} + \begin{bmatrix} 4 & -1 & 0 \\ -1 & 2 & -1 \\ 0 & -1 & 1 \end{bmatrix} \right] \begin{Bmatrix} x_1 \\ x_2 \\ x_3 \end{Bmatrix} = \begin{Bmatrix} 0 \\ 0 \\ 0 \end{Bmatrix}$$

Reduce the equation to the standard form by decomposing the stiffness matrix.

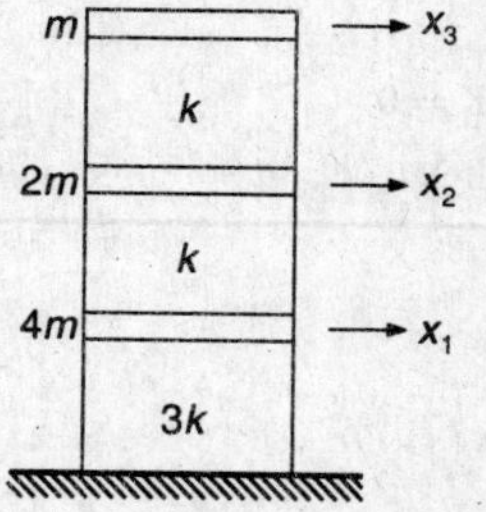

FIGURE 7.8.1.

Solution The transformation matrix is found from

$$U^T U = K$$

$$\begin{bmatrix} u_{11} & 0 & 0 \\ u_{12} & u_{22} & 0 \\ u_{13} & u_{23} & u_{33} \end{bmatrix} \begin{bmatrix} u_{11} & u_{12} & u_{13} \\ 0 & u_{22} & u_{23} \\ 0 & 0 & u_{33} \end{bmatrix} = \begin{bmatrix} 4 & -1 & 0 \\ -1 & 2 & -1 \\ 0 & -1 & 1 \end{bmatrix}$$

$$\begin{bmatrix} u_{11}^2 & u_{11}u_{12} & u_{11}u_{13} \\ u_{11}u_{12} & (u_{11}^2 + u_{22}^2) & (u_{12}u_{13} + u_{22}u_{23}) \\ u_{11}u_{13} & (u_{12}u_{13} + u_{23}u_{22}) & (u_{13}^2 + u_{23}^2 + u_{23}^2) \end{bmatrix} = \begin{bmatrix} 4 & -1 & 0 \\ -1 & 2 & -1 \\ 0 & -1 & 1 \end{bmatrix}$$

By equating the corresponding terms on each side, U is found:

$$U = \begin{bmatrix} 2 & -0.50 & 0 \\ 0 & 1.3228 & -0.7559 \\ 0 & 0 & 0.6547 \end{bmatrix}$$

For the inverse of U, we let $U^{-1} = [b_{ij}]$ and solve the equation

$$UU^{-1} = I$$

$$\begin{bmatrix} 2 & -0.50 & 0 \\ 0 & 1.3228 & -0.7559 \\ 0 & 0 & 0.6547 \end{bmatrix} \begin{bmatrix} b_{11} & b_{12} & b_{13} \\ 0 & b_{22} & b_{23} \\ 0 & 0 & b_{33} \end{bmatrix} = \begin{bmatrix} 1 & 0 & 0 \\ 0 & 1 & 0 \\ 0 & 0 & 1 \end{bmatrix}$$

Again, equating the terms of the two sides, we obtain

$$U^{-1} = [b_{ij}] = \begin{bmatrix} 0.50 & 0.1889 & 0.2182 \\ 0 & 0.7559 & 0.8726 \\ 0 & 0 & 1.5275 \end{bmatrix}$$

The dynamic matrix $\tilde{A}$ using the decomposed stiffness matrix is

$$\tilde{A} = U^{-T} M U^{-1}$$

$$= \begin{bmatrix} 0.50 & 0 & 0 \\ 0.1889 & 0.7559 & 0 \\ 1.2182 & 0.8726 & 1.5275 \end{bmatrix} \begin{bmatrix} 4 & 0 & 0 \\ 0 & 2 & 0 \\ 0 & 0 & 2 \end{bmatrix} \begin{bmatrix} 0.50 & 0.1889 & 0.2182 \\ 0 & 0.7559 & 0.8726 \\ 0 & 0 & 1.5275 \end{bmatrix}$$

$$= \begin{bmatrix} 1.00 & 0.3779 & 0.4364 \\ 0.3779 & 1.2857 & 1.4846 \\ 0.4363 & 1.4846 & 4.0476 \end{bmatrix}$$

The standard form is now

$$[-\bar{\lambda}I + \tilde{A}]Y = 0$$

where $\bar{\lambda} = k/\omega^2 m$ and $X = U^{-1}Y$.

■

7.9 JACOBI DIAGONALIZATION

In the section on orthogonality, Sec. 5.6 in Chapter 5, the assembling of the orthonormal eigenvectors $\tilde{\phi}$ into the modal matrix $\tilde{P}$ enabled the mass and the stiffness matrices to be expressed in the basic relationships:

$$\begin{aligned} \tilde{P}^T M \tilde{P} &= I \\ \tilde{P}^T K \tilde{P} &= \Lambda \end{aligned} \tag{7.9.1}$$

where I is a unit matrix, and Λ is a diagonal matrix of the eigenvalues. These relationships indicate that if the eigenvectors of the system are known, the eigenvalue problem is solved.

The Jacobi method is based on the principle that any real symmetric matrix $\tilde{A}$ has only real eigenvalues and can be diagonalized into the eigenvalue matrix $\Lambda = [\lambda_i]$ by an iteration method. In the Jacobi method, this is accomplished by several rotation matrices R by which the off-diagonal elements of $\tilde{A}$ are zeroed by repeated iterations until matrix $\tilde{A}$ is diagonalized. The method is developed for the standard eigenproblem equation:

$$(\tilde{A} - \lambda I)Y = 0 \tag{7.9.2}$$

and the major advantage of the procedure is that all of the eigenvalues and eigenvectors are found simultaneously.

In the standard eigenproblem, the M and K matrices have already been transposed into a single symmetric dynamic matrix $\tilde{A}$, which is more economical for iteration than two matrices. The kth iteration step is defined by the equations

$$\begin{aligned} R_k^T \tilde{A}_k R_k &= \tilde{A}_{k+1} \\ R_{k+1}^T \tilde{A}_{k+1} R_{k+1} &= \tilde{A}_{k+2}, \text{ etc.} \end{aligned} \tag{7.9.3}$$

where R_k is the rotation matrix.

Before discussing the general problem of diagonalizing the dynamic matrix $\tilde{A}$ of nth order, it will be helpful to demonstrate the Jacobi procedure with an elementary problem of a second-order matrix:

$$\tilde{A} = \begin{bmatrix} a_{11} & a_{12} \\ a_{12} & a_{22} \end{bmatrix}$$

The rotation matrix for this case is simply the orthogonal matrix

$$R = \begin{bmatrix} \cos\theta & -\sin\theta \\ \sin\theta & \cos\theta \end{bmatrix} \tag{7.9.4}$$

used in the transformation of coordinates to rotate the axes through an angle θ, as illustrated in Fig. 7.9.1.

Matrix R is orthonormal because it satisfies the relationship

$$R^T R = RR^T = I$$

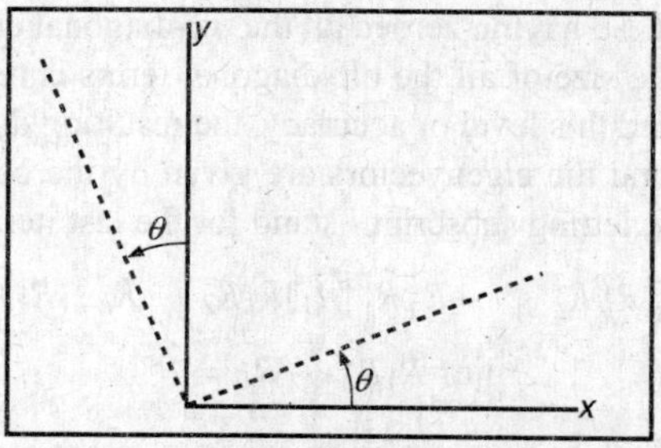

FIGURE 7.9.1.

In this case, there is only one off-diagonal element, a_{12}, and the eigenproblem is solved in a single step. We have

$$R_1^T\widetilde{A}_1R_1 = \begin{bmatrix} \cos\theta & \sin\theta \\ -\sin\theta & \cos\theta \end{bmatrix}\begin{bmatrix} a_{11} & a_{12} \\ a_{12} & a_{22} \end{bmatrix}\begin{bmatrix} \cos\theta & -\sin\theta \\ \sin\theta & \cos\theta \end{bmatrix} = \begin{bmatrix} \lambda_1 & 0 \\ 0 & \lambda_2 \end{bmatrix}$$

Equating the two sides of this equation, we obtain

$$\begin{aligned} \lambda_1 &= a_{11}\ \cos^2\theta + 2a_{12}\ \sin\theta\ \cos\theta + a_{22}\ \sin^2\theta \\ \lambda_2 &= a_{11}\ \sin^2\theta - 2a_{12}\ \sin\theta\ \cos\theta + a_{22}\ \cos^2\theta \\ 0 &= -(a_{11} - a_{22})\ \sin\theta\ \cos\theta + a_{12}(\cos^2\theta - sin^2\theta) \end{aligned} \tag{7.9.5}$$

From the last of Eqs (7.9.5), angle θ must satisfy the relation

$$\tan 2\theta = \frac{2a_{12}}{a_{11} - a_{22}} \tag{7.9.6}$$

The two eigenvalues are then obtained from the two remaining equations or directly from the diagonalized matrix. The eigenvectors corresponding to the two eigenvalues are represented by the two columns of the rotation matrix R1, which in this case is equal to $\widetilde{P}$.

For the previous problem there was only one diagonal term a_{ij} and no iteration was necessary. For the more general case of the nth-order matrix, the rotation matrix is a unit matrix with the rotation matrix superimposed to align with the (i, j) off-diagonal element to be zeroed. For example, to eliminate the element $a_{3,5}$ in a 6×6 matrix, the rotation matrix is

$$R = \begin{bmatrix} 1 & 0 & 0 & 0 & 0 & 0 \\ 0 & 1 & 0 & 0 & 0 & 0 \\ 0 & 0 & \cos\theta & 0 & -\sin\theta & 0 \\ 0 & 0 & 0 & 1 & 0 & 0 \\ 0 & 0 & \sin\theta & 0 & \cos\theta & 0 \\ 0 & 0 & 0 & 0 & 0 & 1 \end{bmatrix} \tag{7.9.7}$$

and θ is determined from the same equation as before.

$$\tan 2\theta = \frac{2a_{35}}{a_{33} - a_{55}} = \frac{2a_{ij}}{a_{ii} - a_{jj}} \tag{7.9.8}$$

If $a_{ii} = a_{jj}, 2\theta = \pm 90°$ and $\theta = \pm 45°$. Although 2θ can also be taken in the left half space, there is no loss of generality in restricting θ to the range $\pm 45°$. Due to the symmetry of matrix $\widetilde{A}$, this step reduces one pair of the off-diagonal terms to zero, and must be repeated for every pair of the off-diagonal terms of matrix $\widetilde{A}$. However, in reducing the next pair to zero, it introduces a small nonzero term to the previously zeroed element. So having zeroed all the off-diagonal elements, another sweep of the process must be made until the size of all the off-diagonal terms is reduced to the threshold of the specified value. Having reached this level of accuracy, the resulting diagonal matrix becomes equal to the eigenvalue matrix Λ, and the eigenvectors are given by the columns of the products of the rotation matrices. In summary, letting subscript l stand for the last iteration,

$$\begin{aligned}\tilde{A}_l &= R_l^T \cdots R_k^T R_{k-1}^T \cdots R_2^T R_1^T [\tilde{A}_1] R_1 R_2 \cdots R_{k-1} R_k \cdots R_l = \Lambda \\ &\lim_{l \to \infty} R_1 R_2 \cdots R_l = \tilde{P}\end{aligned} \tag{7.9.9}$$

Although the proof of convergence of the Jacobi iteration is beyond the scope of this text, experience has shown that rapid convergence is generally found, and usually acceptable results are obtained in less than five sweeps, and often in one or two sweeps when the off-diagonal elements in the original matrix are small in comparison to the diagonal elements. The number of calculations is also quite limited in that in spite of the size of the matrix, only two rows and two columns are involved for each iteration.

Example 7.9.1

When the mass matrix is decomposed in Fig. 7.8.1, the standard form of the equation of motion becomes

$$\left[-\lambda I + \begin{bmatrix} 1.0 & -0.3536 & 0 \\ -0.3536 & 1.0 & -0.7071 \\ 0 & -0.7071 & 1.0 \end{bmatrix}\right] \begin{Bmatrix} y_1 \\ y_2 \\ y_3 \end{Bmatrix} = \begin{Bmatrix} 0 \\ 0 \\ 0 \end{Bmatrix}$$

where $\lambda = \omega^2 m/k$. By using the Jacobi method, diagonalize the dynamic matrix, and determine the eigenvalues and the eigenvectors for the system.

Solution We first zero the largest off-diagonal term, which is $a_{23} = -0.7071$.

$$\tilde{A} = \begin{bmatrix} 1.0 & -0.3536 & 0 \\ -0.3536 & 1.0 & -0.7071 \\ 0 & -0.7071 & 1.0 \end{bmatrix}$$

$$R_1 = \begin{bmatrix} 1 & 0 & 0 \\ 0 & \cos\theta & -\sin\theta \\ 0 & \sin\theta & \cos\theta \end{bmatrix}$$

$$\tan 2\theta = \frac{2a_{23}}{a_{22} - a_{33}} = \frac{2(-0.7071)}{1 - 1} = \pm\infty$$

$$\therefore 2\theta = 90^\circ$$

$$\theta = 45^\circ$$

$$\sin 45^\circ = \cos 45^\circ = 0.7071$$

$$R_1 = \begin{bmatrix} 1 & 0 & 0 \\ 0 & 0.7071 & -0.7071 \\ 0 & 0.7071 & 0.7071 \end{bmatrix} \quad R_1^T = \begin{bmatrix} 1 & 0 & 0 \\ 0 & 0.7071 & 0.7071 \\ 0 & -0.7071 & 0.7071 \end{bmatrix}$$

$$\widetilde{A}_1 = R_1^T \widetilde{A} R_1$$

$$= \begin{bmatrix} 1 & 0 & 0 \\ 0 & 0.7071 & 0.7071 \\ 0 & -0.7071 & 0.7071 \end{bmatrix} \begin{bmatrix} 1.0 & -0.3536 & 0 \\ -0.3536 & 1.0 & -0.7071 \\ 0 & -0.7071 & 1.0 \end{bmatrix} \begin{bmatrix} 1 & 0 & 0 \\ 0 & 0.7071 & -0.7071 \\ 0 & 0.7071 & 0.7071 \end{bmatrix}$$

$$= \left[\begin{array}{cc:c} 1.0 & -0.250 & 0.250 \\ -0.250 & 0.2929 & 0 \\ \hdashline 0.250 & 0 & 1.7071 \end{array}\right]$$

We thus find that in zeroing the term $a_{23} = a_{32}$, we have introduced a new nonzero term $a_{13} = a_{31} = 0.250$. Next zero the term $a_{12} = -0.250$.

$$\tan 2\theta = \frac{2a_{12}}{a_{11} - a_{22}} = \frac{2(-0.250)}{1 - 0.2929} = -0.7071$$

$$2\theta = -35.26^\circ$$

$$\theta = -17.63^\circ$$

$$\sin\theta = -0.3029^\circ$$

$$\cos\theta = 0.9530$$

$$R_2 = \begin{bmatrix} 0.9530 & 0.3029 & 0 \\ -0.3029 & 0.9530 & 0 \\ 0 & 0 & 1 \end{bmatrix}$$

$$R_2^T \widetilde{A}_1 R_2 = \begin{bmatrix} 1.097 & 0 & 0.2383 \\ 0 & 0.2134 & 0.0757 \\ 0.2383 & 0.0757 & 1.7071 \end{bmatrix} = \widetilde{A}_2$$

To complete the first sweep of all the off-diagonal terms, we next zero the term a_{13}.

$$\tan\theta = \frac{2a_{13}}{a_{11} - a_{33}} = \frac{2(0.2383)}{1.097 - 1.7071} = -0.7812$$

$$2\theta = 37.996^\circ$$

$$\theta = -18.998^\circ$$

$$\sin\theta = -0.3255$$

$$\cos\theta = 0.9455$$

$$R_3 = \begin{bmatrix} 0.9455 & 0 & 0.3255 \\ 0 & 1 & 0 \\ -0.3255 & 0 & 0.9455 \end{bmatrix}$$

$$R_3^T \widetilde{A}_2 R_3 = \begin{bmatrix} 1.0147 & -0.0246 & -0.000 \\ -0.0246 & 0.2134 & 0.0717 \\ 0.000 & 0.0710 & 1.817 \end{bmatrix} = \widetilde{A}_3$$

To further reduce the size of the off-diagonal terms, the procedure should be repeated; however, we stop here and outline the procedure for determining the eigenvalues and eigenvectors of the problem. The eigenvalues are given by the diagonal elements of $\widetilde{A}$ and the eigenvectors of $\widetilde{A}$ are calculated from the products of the rotation matrices R_i as given by Eq. (7.9.9). These eigenvectors are of the transformed equation in the coordinates and must be converted to the eigenvectors of the original equation in the x coordinate by Eq. (7.6.1). It should also be noted that the eigenvalues are not always in the increasing order from 1 to n. In $\widetilde{A}_3, \lambda_1 = \omega_1^2 m/k$ is found in the middle of the diagonal.

λ FROM $\widetilde{A}_3$	COMPUTER VALUES
$\lambda_1 = 0.213$	$\lambda_2 = 0.2094$
$\lambda_2 = 1.014$	$\lambda_2 = 1.000$
$\lambda_3 = 1.817$	$\lambda_3 = 1.7905$

It is seen here that even with one sweep of the off-diagonal terms, the results are in fair agreement.

For the eigenvectors, we have

$$Y = R_1 R_2 R_3$$

$$= \begin{bmatrix} 1 & 0 & 0 \\ 0 & 0.7071 & -0.7071 \\ 0 & 0.7071 & 0.7071 \end{bmatrix} \begin{bmatrix} 0.9530 & 0.3029 & 0 \\ -0.3029 & 0.9530 & 0 \\ 0 & 0 & 1 \end{bmatrix} \begin{bmatrix} 0.9455 & 0 & 0.3255 \\ 0 & 1 & 0 \\ -0.3255 & 0 & 0.9455 \end{bmatrix}$$

$$= \begin{bmatrix} 0.9011 & 0.3029 & 0.3102 \\ 0.0276 & 0.6739 & -0.7383 \\ -0.4327 & 0.6739 & 0.5988 \end{bmatrix}$$

$$X = U^{-1} Y = \begin{bmatrix} 0.50 & 0 & 0 \\ 0 & 0.7071 & 0 \\ 0 & 0 & 1.00 \end{bmatrix} \begin{bmatrix} 0.9011 & 0.3029 & 0.3102 \\ 0.0276 & 0.6739 & -0.7383 \\ -0.4327 & 0.6739 & -0.5988 \end{bmatrix}$$

$$= \begin{bmatrix} 0.4006 & 0.1515 & 0.1551 \\ 0.0195 & 0.4765 & -0.5221 \\ -0.4327 & 0.6739 & 0.5988 \end{bmatrix}$$

When normalized to 1.0,

$$X = \begin{bmatrix} -0.940 & 0.225 & 0.259 \\ -0.045 & 0.707 & -0.872 \\ 1.00 & 1.00 & 1.00 \end{bmatrix} \quad \text{from } \widetilde{A}_3$$

mode 2 mode 1 mode 3

$$X = \begin{bmatrix} -1.0 & 0.25 & 0.25 \\ 0 & 0.79 & -0.79 \\ 1.00 & 1.00 & 1.00 \end{bmatrix} \quad \text{from the computer}$$

With the eigenvalues equal to $\lambda = \omega^2 m/k$, the three natural frequencies are found from

$$\omega_i = \sqrt{\lambda_i \frac{k}{m}}$$

$$\omega_1 = \sqrt{0.2094 \frac{k}{m}} = 0.4576 \sqrt{\frac{k}{m}}$$

$$\omega_2 = \sqrt{1.0 \frac{k}{m}} = 1.0 \sqrt{\frac{k}{m}}$$

$$\omega_3 = \sqrt{1.7905 \frac{k}{m}} = 1.3381 \sqrt{\frac{k}{m}}$$

■

7.10 *QR* METHOD FOR EIGENVALUE AND EIGENVECTOR CALCULATION

The MATLAB® command **eig(A)** computes the eigenvalues and eigenvectors of a matrix A using an iterative method based on decomposing the matrix A into an orthogonal matrix Q and an upper triangular matrix R. The basic idea behind this algorithm is to produce an upper triangular matrix which is similar to the original matrix A. Since similarity transformations preserve the eigenvalues of the original matrix, the eigenvalues can be read off the diagonal of the final matrix. The eigenvalues of the original matrix, the eigenvalues can be read off from the eigenvectors for the transformed matrix by multiplying these eigenvectors with the same matrices which were used to make A upper triangular.

The QR decomposition can be accomplished by the Householder transformation which will be discussed in detail. Once we know how to decompose a matrix into Q and R, we use an iteration procedure to produce an upper triangular matrix, which is similar to the original matrix. The QR decomposition allows one to write the matrix A as the product of two matrices (i.e., $A = Q * R$, where Q is orthogonal and R is upper triangular). These two matrices can be used to produce another matrix, A_1, which is similar to A and given by

$$\begin{aligned} A_1 &= R * Q \\ &= Q^{-1} * A * Q \\ &= Q * A * Q \end{aligned}$$

since $R = Q^{-1}A$ and $Q^{-1} = Q$. The new matrix A_1 is similar to A and hence it has the same eigenvalues as A but the eigenvectors have been changed by Q. The eigenvectors of A_1 satisfy the equation $A_1x = \lambda x$, which means that the eigenvectors of A can be obtained by multiplying the eigenvectors of A_1, by Q. This can be seen from the following equation $\lambda Qx = AQx$. The process is then repeated by decomposing A_1 into an orthogonal matrix Q_1 and an upper triangular matrix R_1 (i.e., $A_1 = Q_1 * R_1$). Again Q_1 and R_1 can be used to produce a matrix A_2 which is similar to A_1 (and consequently similar to A), by

$$\begin{aligned} A = R_1 * Q_1 \\ &= Q_1^{-1} * A_1 * Q_1 \\ &= Q_1^{-1} * Q^{-1} * A * Q * Q_1 \\ &= (Q * Q_1)^{-1} * A * (Q * Q_1) \\ &= (Q * Q_1) * A * (Q * Q_1) \end{aligned}$$

As before, A_2 has the same eigenvalues as A. If x is an eigenvector of A_2 (i.e., $A_2x = \lambda x$, then $Q * Q_1x$ is an eigenvector for A). This process can be continued to produce a series of similar matrices A_3, A_4, and so on. It can be shown that eventually this process will produce an upper triangular matrix which is similar to the original matrix (i.e., $A_n = (Q * Q_1 * Q_2 * \cdots * Q_{n-1})^{-1} AQ * Q_1 * Q_2 * \cdots * Q_{n-1})$, and A_n is upper triangular.

In order to speed up the convergence of the above iteration, it is customary to first convert the matrix A to a matrix which has zeros below the subdiagonal. This type of matrix is called a Hessenberg matrix. The following is an example of a 4 × 4 Hessenberg matrix:

$$H = \begin{bmatrix} 1 & 3 & 2 & 4 \\ 2 & 3 & 6 & 8 \\ 0 & 4 & 6 & 2 \\ 0 & 0 & 2 & 3 \end{bmatrix}$$

The general $n \times n$ Hessenberg matrix has the following general form

$$H = \begin{bmatrix} a_{11} & a_{12} & a_{13} & \cdots & a_{1n} \\ a_{21} & a_{22} & a_{23} & \cdots & a_{2n} \\ 0 & a_{32} & a_{33} & \cdots & a_{3n} \\ \vdots & \vdots & \vdots & & \vdots \\ 0 & 0 & \cdots & a_{nn-1} & a_{nn} \end{bmatrix}$$

As we will show next, the Householder transformation will produce a Hessenberg matrix which is similar to the original matrix.

A Householder matrix is given by

$$H = I - 2uu^t$$

for some unit vector u. Note that

$$\begin{aligned} H^t &= (I - 2uu^t) \\ &= I - 2u^t u \\ &= H \end{aligned}$$

and

$$\begin{aligned} HH &= (I - 2uu^t)(I - 2uu^t) \\ &= I - 2uu^t - 2uu^t + 4uu^t uu^t \\ &= I - 4uu^t + 4uu^t \\ &= I \end{aligned}$$

since $u^t u = 1$. This shows that H is symmetric and orthogonal; that is, $H = H^t = H^{-1}$. Given a matrix A, in order to construct H so that $H^{-1}AH$ produces a Hessenberg matrix, an iteration procedure can be used where each step zeros out the elements below the subdiagonal for one column. The procedure begins with the left-hand column. For example, if the first column is given by the vector $\vec{\mathbf{a}} = (a_1, a_2, a_3, \ldots a_n)^t$ then the Householder matrix H applied to a should produce the vector $\vec{\mathbf{r}} = (a_1, \alpha, 0, 0, \ldots, 0)^t$. In order for H to remain orthogonal, α is determined by the fact that $\|a\| = \|r\|$. The unit vector, u in the Householder transformation is given by $u = \frac{v}{\|v\|}$ where $v = a - r$. The remaining columns of the matrix can be handled in the same manner and the Householder matrix which takes the original matrix into Hessenberg form is given by the product of each intermediate matrix. The following example illustrates this procedure.

We want to convert the following matrix

$$A = \begin{bmatrix} 4 & 2 & 1 \\ 4 & 8 & 4 \\ 4 & 8 & 7 \end{bmatrix}$$

into upper Hessenberg form. This means that we want the Householder matrix to take the vector $\vec{\mathbf{a}} = (4, 4, 4)^t$ into the vector $\vec{\mathbf{r}} = (4, \alpha, 0)^t$. We need $a^t a = r^t r$ for the resulting matrix to be orthogonal. This determines α which for our example is such that $\alpha = \sqrt{32}$. The vector $v = a - r$ is given by $\vec{\mathbf{v}} = (0, -1.6569, 4)$. The length of the vector squared is 18.7452. This vector produces the Householder matrix

$$H = \begin{bmatrix} 1 & 0 & 0 \\ 0 & .7071 & .7071 \\ 0 & .7071 & -.7071 \end{bmatrix}$$

When this matrix is used to produce a matrix which is similar to A one gets the Hessenberg matrix

$$HAH = \begin{bmatrix} 4 & 2.1213 & .7071 \\ 5.6569 & 13.500 & 2.500 \\ 0 & -1.500 & 1.500 \end{bmatrix} \tag{7.10.1}$$

Because the matrix A is a 3×3, it only takes one iteration to convert it to Hessenberg form. For larger matrices this procedure would have to be repeated to clear the remaining columns.

At this point we want to describe the QR decomposition. Suppose we are given a matrix A, which we want to decompose into an orthogonal matrix, Q, and an upper triangular matrix, R. The orthogonal matrix is given by the Householder matrix which is designed so that when it is applied to the matrix A, the result is an upper triangular matrix (i.e., $H * A = R$). Since H is orthogonal and symmetric, $H * A = R$ implies $A = H * R$ which in turn implies that $A = Q * R$ where $Q = H$.

We will illustrate this procedure by continuing our example. We want to decompose the matrix in Eq. (7.10.1) into an orthogonal matrix and an upper triangular matrix. We do this first by constructing an orthogonal matrix which zeroes out the elements below the diagonal in the first column. The matrix which we need should take the vector $\vec{\mathbf{a}} = (4, 5.6560, 0)'$ to the vector $\vec{\mathbf{r}} = (-6.9282, 0, 0)'$. The vector $\mathbf{r}$ is determined by the condition $a'a = r'r$. One is free to choose the sign of r. This can be achieved by constructing the Householder matrix $Q_{11} = I - 2\frac{v*v'}{\|v\|^2}$, where $\vec{\mathbf{v}} = \vec{\mathbf{a}} - \vec{\mathbf{r}} = (2.9282, -5.6569, 0)$. For the matrix HAH we get

$$Q_{11} = \begin{bmatrix} -.5773 & -.8165 & 0 \\ -.8165 & .5774 & 0 \\ 0 & 0 & -1 \end{bmatrix}$$

When the matrix HAH is premultiplied by the matrix Q_{11}, we get

$$Q_{11} * HAH = \begin{bmatrix} -6.9282 & -12.2474 & -2.4495 \\ 0 & 6.0623 & -.8660 \\ 0 & 1.5000 & -1.5000 \end{bmatrix}$$

In order to complete the decomposition, we have to use the same procedure to clear the element below the diagonal in the second column of the matrix. The process results in a matrix Q_{12} which takes $\vec{\mathbf{a}}_2 = (-12.2474, 6.0623, 1.5000)$ to the vector $\vec{\mathbf{r}}_2 = (-12.2475, -6.245, 0)$. Again this comes from the condition $a'a = r'r$. The orthogonal matrix Q_1 which when applied to the matrix HAH produces an upper triangular matrix is given by the product of Q_{11} and Q_{12}, namely $Q_1 = Q_{12} * Q_{11}$. For our example, the QR decomposition is such that $HAH- = Q_1 * R_1$ where

$$Q_1 = \begin{bmatrix} -.5773 & .7936 & -.1961 \\ -.8165 & -.5604 & .1387 \\ 0 & .2402 & .9707 \end{bmatrix}$$

and

$$R_1 = \begin{bmatrix} -6.9282 & -12.2475 & -2.44495 \\ 0 & -6.2450 & -.4804 \\ 0 & 0 & 1.6641 \end{bmatrix}$$

We should point out at this point that the MATLAB® command **[Q, R] = qr(A)** produces the matrices Q and R for a matrix A.

Now that we know how to perform a QR decomposition, we would like to use the iteration procedure discussed at the beginning of this section to produce an upper triangular matrix. Continuing with our example, the first iteration produces a matrix, A_2 which is similar to HAH and it is given by

$$A_2 = R_1 * Q_1 = \begin{bmatrix} 14.0000 & .7844 & -2.7174 \\ 5.0990 & 3.3846 & -1.3323 \\ 0 & .3997 & 1.6154 \end{bmatrix}$$

Again one uses the QR decomposition on A_2, we write $A_2 = Q_2 * R_2$ and set $A_3 = R_2 * Q_2$. We QR decompose A_3 and so on. Continuing this iteration 15 times results in $Q_1, Q_2, \ldots Q_{15}$ and produces the following upper triangular matrix

$$U = \begin{bmatrix} 14.3246 & -5.0645 & 1.7655 \\ 0 & 3.000 & .4837 \\ 0 & 0 & 1.6754 \end{bmatrix}$$

where $U = (Q_1 * Q_2 * \cdots * Q_{15}) * (HAH) * (Q_1 * Q_2 \cdots * Q_{15})$. The eigenvalues for this matrix are the elements along the diagonal. These numbers agree with the eigenvalues which one gets by using the MATLAB® command **eig(A)**.

The algorithm which finds the eigenvectors of the original matrix starts by finding the eigenvectors of the upper triangular matrix and transforms them to the eigenvectors for HAH by multiplying them by the matrix $Q_1 * Q_2 * \ldots * Q_{15}$ as described previously. The eigenvectors for the upper triangular matrix can be found easily by backsubstitution. Backsubstitution works by computing the values of the vector from the bottom up. Consider the computation for the first eigenvector:

$$\begin{bmatrix} 14.3246 & -5.0645 & 1.7655 \\ 0 & 3.000 & .4837 \\ 0 & 0 & 1.6745 \end{bmatrix} \begin{bmatrix} x_{11} \\ x_{12} \\ x_{13} \end{bmatrix} = 14.3246 * \begin{bmatrix} x_{11} \\ x_{12} \\ x_{13} \end{bmatrix}$$

Using backsubstitution, one solves this system of equations for x_{13} first. The last equation implies that $x_{13} = 0$. Then one solves the second equation for x_{12} to find that $x_{12} = 0$. Finally, the first equation is solved for x_{13}. This gives $x_{13} = 1$. The eigenvector associated with the eigenvalue 14.3246 is (1, 0, 0). The other two eigenvectors can be found in the same way. The eigenvector associated with the eigenvalue 3 is (−.4082, −.9129, 0) and the eigenvector associated with the eigenvalue 1.6754 is (−.2593, −.3313, .9072). These eigenvectors can be converted into the ones for HAH by multiplying them by the matrix Q which is given by $Q = Q_1 * Q_2 * \ldots * Q_{15}$. These vectors can be converted into the one for the original matrix A by multiplying them by the matrix H. This process gives the eigenvectors for the matrix A as the column vectors of the following matrix:

$$E = \begin{bmatrix} -.1925 & -0.0701 & .1925 \\ -.6086 & 0.0000 & -.6086 \\ -.7698 & 0.7071 & .7698 \end{bmatrix} \tag{7.10.2}$$

In MATLAB®, one can compute the eigenvalues and eigenvectors by using the command **[U, D] = eig(A)**. The matrix U contains the eigenvectors as column vectors and the matrix D is a diagonal matrix which has the eigenvalues on the diagonal. The column vectors in Eq. (7.10.2) agree with the eigenvectors that one gets from MATLAB®.

Summary of the Algorithm. Given a matrix A, the following algorithm can be used to compute the eigenvalues and eigenvectors:

1. Convert the matrix A into Hessenberg form by the Householder matrix H (i.e., compute $A_1 = HAH$, where A_1 is a Hessenberg matrix).
2. QR decompose A_1 (i.e., $A_1 = Q_1 * R_1$).
3. Construct another matrix A_2 which is similar to A_1, $A_2 = R_1 * Q_1$.
4. Repeat steps 2 and 3 until A_n is an upper triangular matrix.
5. The eigenvalues for A are located on the diagonal of A_n.
6. Compute the eigenvectors for A_n using backsubstitution.
7. Multiply these vectors by the matrix $H * Q_1 * Q_2 * \ldots * Q_n$ to get the eigenvectors of A.

REFERENCES

[1] CRANDALL, S. H. *Engineering Analysis, A Survey of Numerical Procedures*. New York: McGraw-Hill Book Company, 1956.

[2] RALSTON, A., AND WILF, H. S. *Mathematical Methods for Digital Computers*, Vols. I and II, New York: John Wiley & Sons, 1968.

[3] SALVADORI, M. G., AND BARON, M. L. *Numerical Methods in Engineering*. Englewood Cliffs, N.J.: Prentice-Hall, 1952.

[4] BATHE, K.-J., AND WILSON, E. L. *Numerical Methods in Finite Element Analysis*. Englewood Cliffs, N.J.: Prentice-Hall, 1976.

[5] MEIROVITCH, L. *Computational Methods in Structural Dynamics*. Rockville, MD: Sijthoff & Noordhoff, 1980.

[6] MARTIN, R., AND WILKINSON, J. "Similarity Reduction of a General Matrix to Hessenberg Form." In *Handbook for Automatic Computation*, edited by BAUER, F., *et al.* Berlin: Springer-Verlag, 1971.

[7] MARTIN, R., PETERS, G., AND WILKINSON, J. "The *QR* algorithm for Real Hessenberg Matrice." In *Handbook for Automatic Computation*, edited by BAUER, F., *et al.* Berlin: Springer-Verlag, 1971.

PROBLEMS

M **7.1.** For the system shown in Fig. P7.1, the flexibility matrix is

$$[a] = \frac{1}{k}\begin{bmatrix} 0.5 & 0.5 & 0.5 \\ 0.5 & 1.5 & 1.5 \\ 0.5 & 1.5 & 2.5 \end{bmatrix}$$

Write the equation of motion in terms of the flexibility and derive the characteristic equation

$$\bar{\lambda}^3 - 9\bar{\lambda}^2 + 12\bar{\lambda} - 4 = 0$$

Use MATLAB® to solve for $\bar{\lambda}_i$ and ϕ_i.

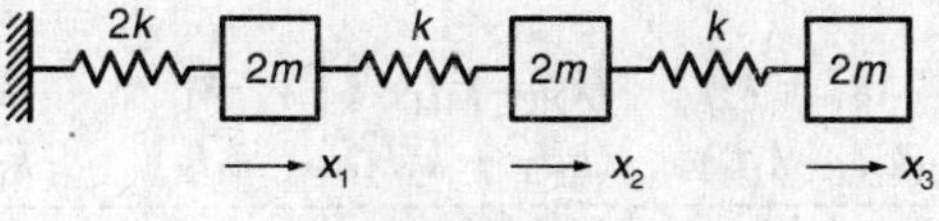

FIGURE P7.1.

7.2. For the system in Sec. 7.1, the eigenvector for the first mode was determined by the Gauss elimination method. Complete the problem of finding the second and third eigenvectors.

7.3. For Prob. 7.1 rewrite the characteristic determinant as

$$\left| -\lambda \begin{bmatrix} 2 & & \\ & 2 & \\ & & 2 \end{bmatrix} + \begin{bmatrix} 3 & -1 & 0 \\ -1 & 2 & -1 \\ 0 & -1 & 1 \end{bmatrix} \right| = 0$$

(See App. C.4.) Note that the new determinant is now not symmetric and that the sum of the diagonal, or trace, is 4.5, which is the sum of the eigenvalues. Determine the eigenvectors from the cofactors as in App. C.4. In the method of cofactors, App. C.4, the cofactors of the horizontal row, and not of the column, must be used. Explain why.

M **7.4.** Write the equations of motion for the 3-DOF system shown in Fig. P7.4, in terms of the stiffness matrix. By letting $m_1 = m_2 = m$ and $m_3 = 2m$ and $k_1 = k_2 = k_3 = k$, the roots of the characteristic equation are $\lambda_1 = 0.1267$, $\lambda_2 = 1.2725$, $\lambda_3 = 3.1007$. Using these results, calculate the eigenvectors by the method of Gauss elimination and check them against the eigenvectors obtained by the computer. Repeat the exercise starting with the flexibility equation.

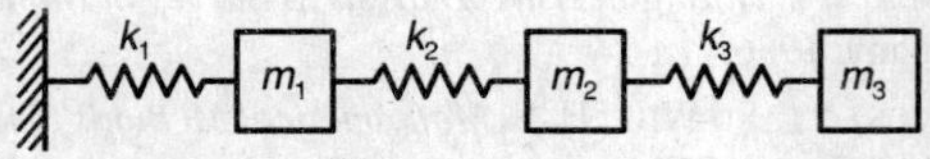

FIGURE P7.4.

M **7.5.** Determine the equation of motion for the system shown in Fig. P7.5 and show that its characteristic equation is (for equal k_s and m_s)

$$\lambda^4 - 9\lambda^3 + 25\lambda^2 - 21\lambda + 3 = 0$$

Solve for the eigenvalues and eigenvectors.

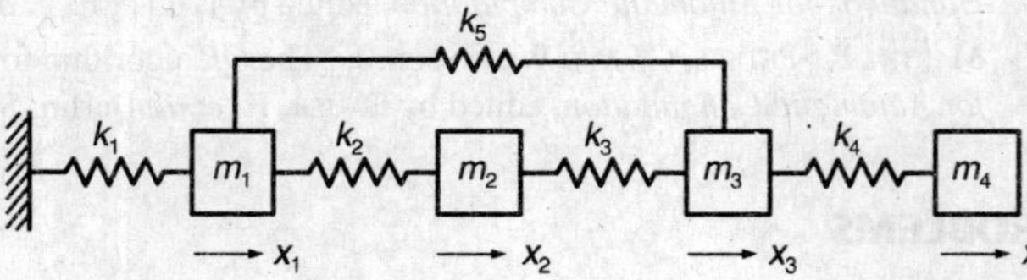

FIGURE P7.5.

7.6. Using the eigenvalues of Prob. 7.5, demonstrate the Gauss elimination method.

7.7. In Example 5.3.2, if the automobile wheel mass (m_0 for the two front wheels and the same for the two rear wheels) and tire stiffness (k_0 for the two front tires and the same for the two rear tires) are included, the 4-DOF equation of motion in matrix form becomes

$$\left[\begin{array}{cc|cc} m & & & \\ & J & & 0 \\ \hline & & m_0 & \\ 0 & & & m_0 \end{array}\right] \begin{Bmatrix} \ddot{x} \\ \ddot{\theta} \\ \ddot{x}_1 \\ \ddot{x}_2 \end{Bmatrix} +$$

$$\left[\begin{array}{cc|cc} (k_1 + k_2) & (k_2 l_2 - k_1 l_1) & -k_1 & -k_2 \\ (k_2 l_2 - k_1 l_1) & (k_1 l_1^2 + k_2 l_2^2) & k_1 l_1 & -k_2 l_2 \\ \hline -k_1 & k_1 l_1 & k_0 + k_1 & 0 \\ -k_2 & -k_2 l_2 & 0 & k_0 + k_2 \end{array}\right] \begin{Bmatrix} x \\ \theta \\ x_1 \\ x_2 \end{Bmatrix} = \{0\}$$

Draw the spring-mass diagram for the configuration and derive the foregoing equation.

M **7.8.** Additional data for Prob. 7.7 are $w_0 = m_0 g = 600\,\text{N}$ and $k_0 = 4 \times 10^5\,\text{N/m}$. Using a computer, determine the four natural frequencies and mode shapes.

M **7.9.** The uniform beam of Fig. P7.9 is free to vibrate in the plane shown and has two concentrated masses, $m_1 = \frac{w_1}{g} = 500\,\text{kg}$ and $m_2 = \frac{w_2}{g} = 100\,\text{kg}$. Determine the two natural frequencies and mode shapes. The flexibility influence coefficients for the problem are given as

$$a_{11} = \frac{l^3}{48\,EI} = \frac{1}{6}a_{22}, \quad a_{22} = \frac{l^3}{8\,EI},$$

$$a_{12} = a_{21} = \frac{l^3}{32EI} = \frac{1}{4}a_{22}$$

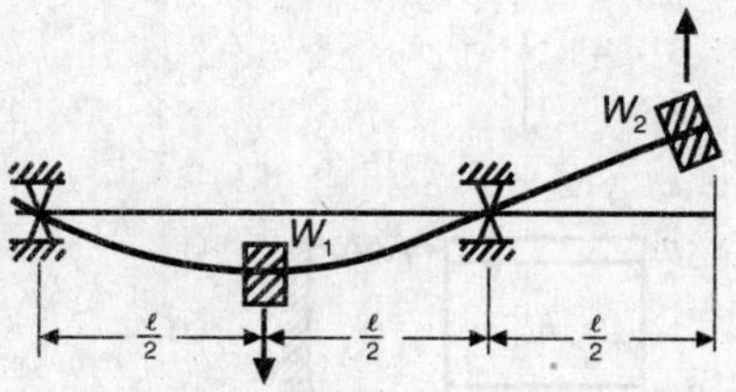

FIGURE P7.9.

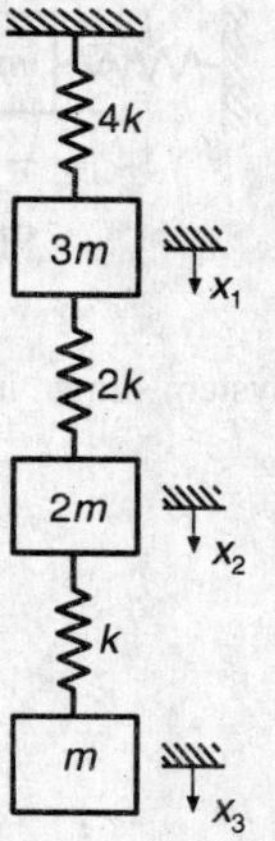

FIGURE P7.10.

M **7.10.** Determine the influence coefficients for the three-mass system of Fig. P7.10 and calculate the principal modes.

M **7.11.** Determine the three natural frequencies and modes for the cantilever beam of Fig. P7.11. *Note*: The flexibility matrix in Example 11.1.3 is for coordinates given in reverse order to above problem.

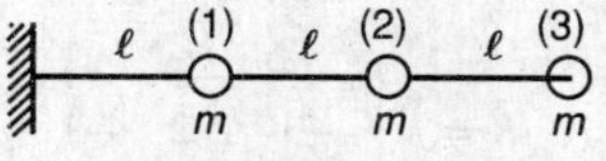

FIGURE P7.11.

M **7.12.** Determine the natural frequencies and mode shapes of the torsional system of Fig. P7.12.

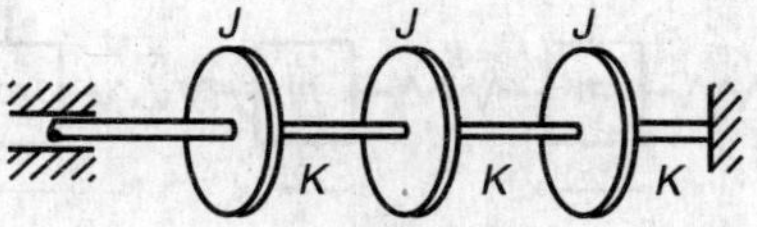

FIGURE P7.12.

M **7.13.** In Fig. P7.13 four masses are strung along strings of equal lengths. Assuming the tension to be constant, determine the natural frequencies and mode shapes.

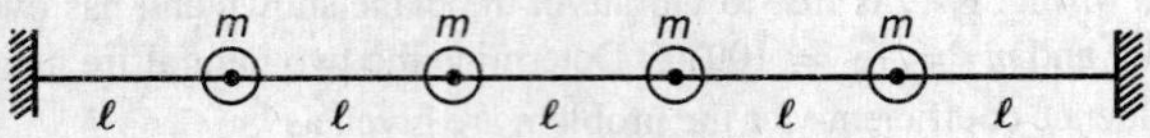

FIGURE P7.13.

M **7.14.** Decompose the stiffness matrix $K = U^T U$ for Fig. P7.14.

$$K = \begin{bmatrix} 2 & -1 \\ -1 & 4 \end{bmatrix}$$

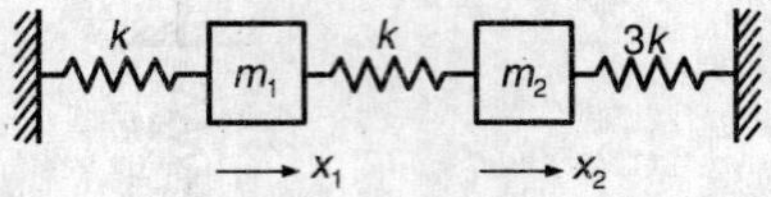

FIGURE P7.14.

M **7.15.** Repeat Prob. 7.14 for the system shown in Fig. P7.15.

$$K = \begin{bmatrix} 3 & -1 \\ -1 & 1 \end{bmatrix}$$

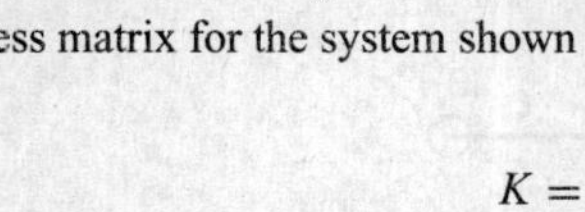

FIGURE P7.15.

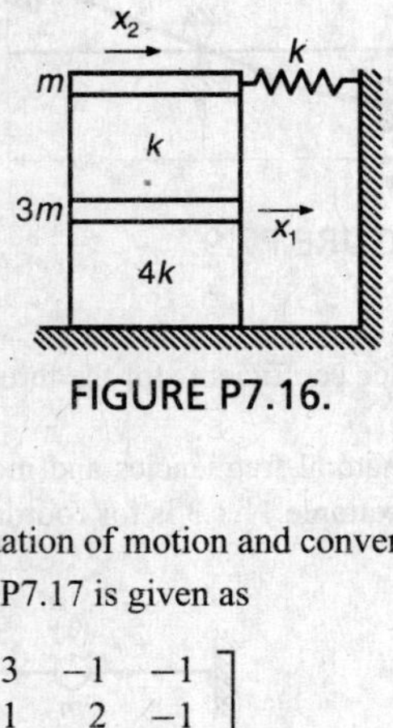

FIGURE P7.16.

7.16. For the system shown in Fig. P7.16, write the equation of motion and convert to the standard form.

M **7.17.** The stiffness matrix for the system shown in Fig. P7.17 is given as

$$K = k\begin{bmatrix} 3 & -1 & -1 \\ -1 & 2 & -1 \\ -1 & -1 & 2 \end{bmatrix}$$

Determine the Choleski decomposition U and U^{-1}.

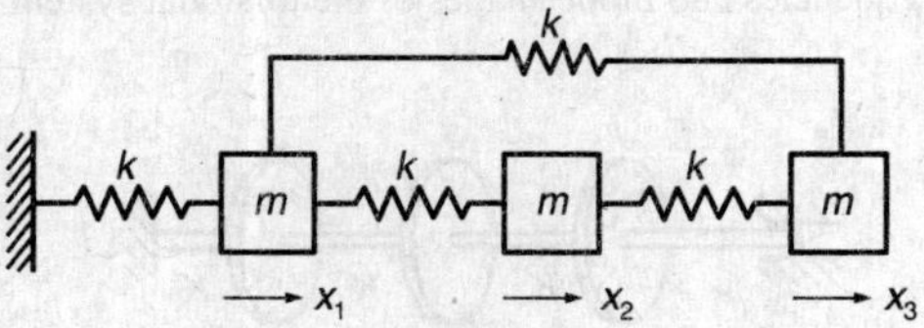

FIGURE P7.17.

M **7.18.** Given the mass and stiffness matrices

$$M = m\begin{bmatrix} 3 & 0 \\ 0 & 2 \end{bmatrix}, \quad K = k\begin{bmatrix} 3 & -1 \\ -1 & 2 \end{bmatrix}$$

determine the natural frequencies and mode shapes using the standard form.

M **7.19.** Repeat Example 7.9.1 by decomposing the stiffness matrix and compare the results with those given in the example.

M **7.20.** Express the following equation in standard form using Choleski decomposition of the mass matrix. Repeat by decomposing the stiffness matrix.

$$\left[\lambda\begin{bmatrix} 4 & 1 & 0 \\ 1 & 4 & 1 \\ 0 & 1 & 2 \end{bmatrix} + \begin{bmatrix} 2 & -1 & 0 \\ -1 & 2 & -1 \\ 0 & -1 & 1 \end{bmatrix}\right]\begin{Bmatrix} x_1 \\ x_2 \\ x_3 \end{Bmatrix} = \begin{Bmatrix} 0 \\ 0 \\ 0 \end{Bmatrix}$$

M **7.21.** Verify the equation of motion for the system of Fig. P7.21:

$$\begin{bmatrix} m_1 & 0 \\ 0 & m_2 \end{bmatrix}\begin{Bmatrix} \ddot{x}_1 \\ \ddot{x}_2 \end{Bmatrix} + \begin{bmatrix} (k_1 + k_2 + k_3) & -k_1 \\ -k_2 & (k_2 + k_4) \end{bmatrix}\begin{Bmatrix} x_1 \\ x_2 \end{Bmatrix} = \begin{Bmatrix} 0 \\ 0 \end{Bmatrix} \quad m_i = k_i = m \text{ and } k$$

Determine the eigenvalues and eigenvectors.

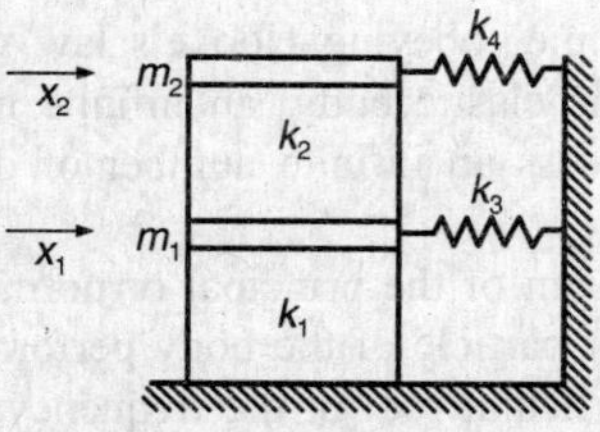

FIGURE P7.21.

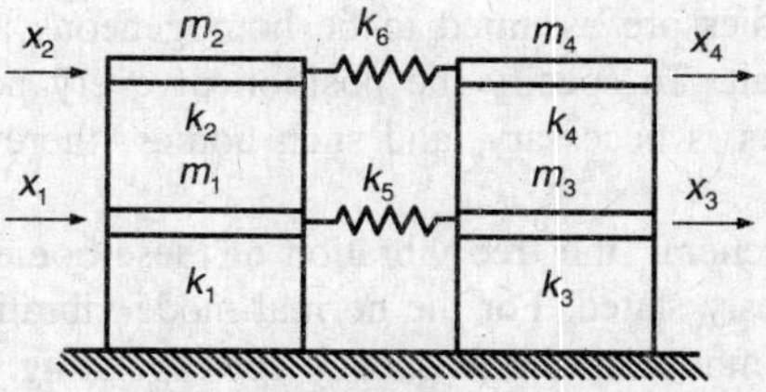

FIGURE P7.22.

M **7.22.** The equation of motion for the system shown in Fig. P7.22 is given as

$$\begin{bmatrix} m_1 & & & \\ & m_2 & & \\ & & m_3 & \\ & & & m_4 \end{bmatrix}\begin{Bmatrix} \ddot{x}_1 \\ \ddot{x}_2 \\ \ddot{x}_3 \\ \ddot{x}_4 \end{Bmatrix} + \begin{bmatrix} (k_1 + k_2 + k_5) & -k_2 & -k_5 & 0 \\ -k_2 & (k_2 + k_3) & 0 & -k_6 \\ -k_5 & 0 & (k_3 + k_4 + k_5) & -k_4 \\ 0 & -k_6 & -k_4 & (k_4 + k_6) \end{bmatrix}\begin{Bmatrix} x_1 \\ x_2 \\ x_3 \\ x_4 \end{Bmatrix} = \begin{Bmatrix} 0 \\ 0 \\ 0 \\ 0 \end{Bmatrix}$$

Determine its eigenvalues and eigenvectors when $m_i = m$ and $k_i = k$. Plot the mode shapes and discuss the action of springs k_5 and k_6.

CHAPTER 8

Vibration of Continuous Systems

The systems to be studied in this chapter have continuously distributed mass and elasticity. These bodies are assumed to be homogeneous and isotropic, obeying Hooke's law within the elastic limit. To specify the position of every point in the elastic body, an infinite number of coordinates is necessary, and such bodies, therefore, possess an infinite number of degrees of freedom.

In general, the free vibration of these bodies is the sum of the principal or normal modes, as previously stated. For the normal mode vibration, every particle of the body performs simple harmonic motion at the frequency corresponding to the particular root of the frequency equation, each particle passing simultaneously through its respective equilibrium position. If the elastic curve of the body under which the motion is started coincides exactly with one of the normal modes, only that normal mode will be produced. However, the elastic curve resulting from a blow or a sudden removal of forces seldom corresponds to that of a normal mode, and thus all modes are excited. In many cases, however, a particular normal mode can be excited by proper initial conditions.

For the forced vibration of the continuously distributed system, the mode summation method, previously touched upon, makes possible its analysis as a system with a finite number of degrees of freedom. Constraints are often treated as additional supports of the structure, and they alter the normal modes of the system. The modes used in representing the deflection of the system need not always be orthogonal, and a synthesis of the system using nonorthogonal functions is possible.

8.1 VIBRATING STRING

A flexible string of mass ρ per unit length is stretched under tension T. By assuming the lateral deflection y of the string to be small, the change in tension with deflection is negligible and can be ignored.

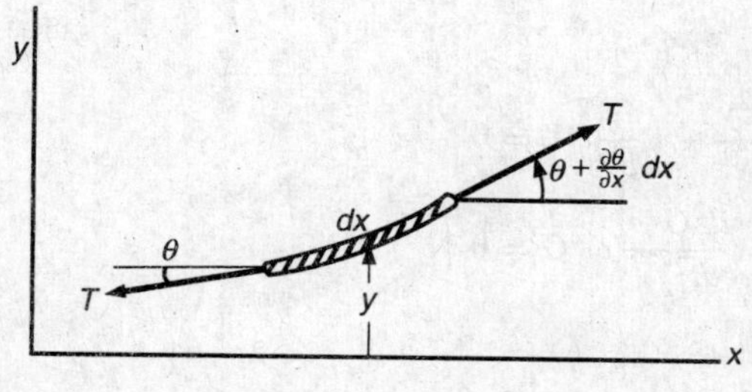

FIGURE 8.1.1. String element in lateral vibration.

In Fig. 8.1.1, a free-body diagram of an elementary length dx of the string is shown. By assuming small deflections and slopes, the equation of motion in the y-direction is

$$T\left(\theta + \frac{\partial \theta}{\partial x}dx\right) - T\theta = \rho\, dx \frac{\partial^2 y}{\partial t^2}$$

or

$$\frac{\partial \theta}{\partial x} = \frac{\rho}{T}\frac{\partial^2 y}{\partial t^2} \tag{8.1.1}$$

Because the slope of the string is $\theta = \partial y/\partial x$, the preceding equation reduces to

$$\frac{\partial^2 y}{\partial x^2} = \frac{1}{c^2}\frac{\partial^2 y}{\partial t^2} \tag{8.1.2}$$

where $c = \sqrt{T/\rho}$ can be shown to be the velocity of wave propagation along the string.

The general solution of Eq. (8.1.2) can be expressed in the form

$$y = F_1(ct - x) + F_2(ct + x) \tag{8.1.3}$$

where F_1 and F_2 are arbitrary functions. Regardless of the type of function F, the argument $(ct \pm x)$ upon differentiation leads to the equation

$$\frac{\partial^2 F}{\partial x^2} = \frac{1}{c^2}\frac{\partial^2 F}{\partial t^2} \tag{8.1.4}$$

and hence the differential equation is satisfied.

Considering the component $y = F_1(ct - x)$, its value is determined by the argument $(ct - x)$ and hence by a range of values of t and x. For example, if $c = 10$, the equation for $y = F_1(100)$ is satisfied by $t = 0$, $x = -100$; $t = 1$, $x = -90$; $t = 2$, $x = -80$; and so forth. Therefore, the wave profile moves in the positive x-direction with speed c. In a similar manner, we can show that $F_2(ct + x)$ represents a wave moving toward the negative x-direction with speed c. We therefore refer to c as the velocity of wave propagation.

One method of solving partial differential equations is that of separation of variables. In this method, the solution is assumed in the form

$$y(x, t) = Y(x)G(t) \tag{8.1.5}$$

By substitution into Eq. (8.1.2), we obtain

$$\frac{1}{Y}\frac{d^2 Y}{dx^2} = \frac{1}{c^2}\frac{1}{G}\frac{d^2 G}{dt^2} \tag{8.1.6}$$

Because the left side of this equation is independent of t, whereas the right side is independent of x, it follows that each side must be a constant. Letting this constant be $-(\omega/c)^2$, we obtain two ordinary differential equations:

$$\frac{d^2y}{dx^2} + \left(\frac{\omega}{c}\right)^2 Y = 0 \tag{8.1.7}$$

$$\frac{d^2G}{dt^2} + \omega^2 G = 0 \tag{8.1.8}$$

with the general solutions

$$Y = A \sin \frac{\omega}{c} x + B \cos \frac{\omega}{c} x \tag{8.1.9}$$

$$G = C \sin \omega t + D \cos \omega t \tag{8.1.10}$$

The arbitrary constants, A, B, C, and D depend on the boundary conditions and the initial conditions. For example, if the string is stretched between two fixed points with distance l between them, the boundary conditions are $y(0, t) = y(l, t) = 0$. The condition that $y(0, t) = 0$ will require that $B = 0$, so the solution will appear as

$$y = (C \sin \omega t + D \cos \omega t) \sin \frac{\omega}{c} x \tag{8.1.11}$$

The condition $y(l, t) = 0$ then leads to the equation

$$\sin \frac{\omega l}{c} = 0$$

or

$$\frac{\omega_n l}{c} = \frac{2\pi l}{\lambda} = n\pi, \quad n = 1, 2, 3, \ldots$$

and $\lambda = c/f$ is the wavelength and f is the frequency of oscillation. Each n represents a normal mode vibration with natural frequency determined from the equation

$$f_n = \frac{n}{2l} c = \frac{n}{2l} \sqrt{\frac{T}{\rho}}, \quad n = 1, 2, 3, \ldots \tag{8.1.12}$$

The mode shape is sinusoidal with distribution

$$Y = \sin n\pi \frac{x}{l} \tag{8.1.13}$$

In the more general case of free vibration initiated in any manner, the solution will contain many of the normal modes and the equation for the displacement can be written as

$$y(x, t) = \sum_{n=1}^{\infty} (C_n \sin \omega_n t + D_n \cos \omega_n t) \sin \frac{n\pi x}{l} \tag{8.1.14}$$

$$\omega_n = \frac{n\pi c}{l}$$

By fitting this equation to the initial conditions of $y(x, 0)$ and $\dot{y}(x, 0)$, the C_n and D_n can be evaluated.

Example 8.1.1

A uniform string of length l is fixed at the ends and stretched under tension T. If the string is displaced into an arbitrary shape $y(x, 0)$ and released, determine C_n and D_n of Eq. (8.1.14).

Solution At $t = 0$, the displacement and velocity are

$$y(x,0) = \sum_{n=1}^{\infty} D_n \sin \frac{n\pi x}{l}$$

$$\dot{y}(x,0) = \sum_{n=1}^{\infty} \omega_n C_n \sin \frac{n\pi x}{l} = 0$$

If we multiply each equation by $\sin k\pi x/l$ and integrate from $x = 0$ to $x = l$, all the terms on the right side will be zero, except the term $n = k$. Thus, we arrive at the result

$$D_k = \frac{2}{l}\int_0^l y(x,0)\sin\frac{k\pi x}{l}dx$$

$$C_k = 0, \quad k = 1, 2, 3, \ldots$$

■

8.2 LONGITUDINAL VIBRATION OF RODS

The rod considered in this section is assumed to be thin and uniform along its length. Due to axial forces, there will be displacements u along the rod that will be a function of both position x and time t. Because the rod has an infinite number of natural modes of vibration, the distribution of the displacements will differ with each mode.

Let us consider an element of this rod of length dx (Fig. 8.2.1). If u is the displacement at x, the displacement at $x + dx$ will be $u + (\partial u/\partial x)dx$. It is evident then that the element dx in the new position has changed in length by an amount $(\partial u/\partial x)dx$, and thus the unit strain is $\partial u/\partial x$. Because, from Hooke's law, the ratio of unit stress to unit strain is equal to the modulus of elasticity E, we can write

$$\frac{\partial u}{\partial x} = \frac{P}{AE} \tag{8.2.1}$$

where A is the cross-sectional area of the rod. By differentiating with respect to x,

$$AE\frac{\partial^2 u}{\partial x^2} = \frac{\partial P}{\partial x} \tag{8.2.2}$$

We now apply Newton's law of motion for the element and equate the unbalanced force to the product of the mass and acceleration of the element:

$$\frac{\partial P}{\partial x}dx = \rho A dx \frac{\partial^2 u}{\partial t^2} \tag{8.2.3}$$

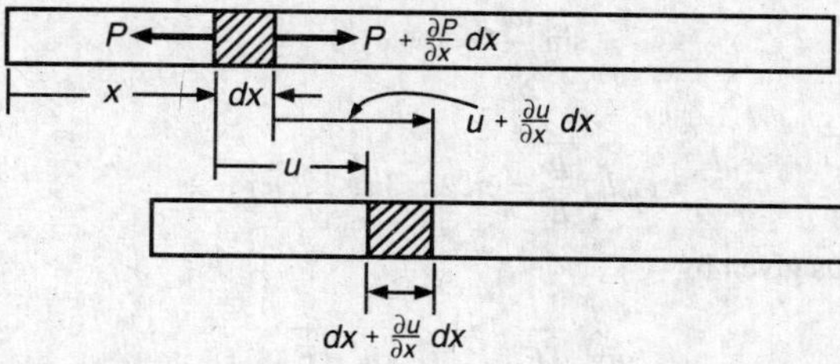

FIGURE 8.2.1. Displacement of rod element.

where ρ is the density of the rod, mass per unit volume. Eliminating $\partial P/\partial x$ between Eqs. (8.2.2) and (8.2.3), we obtain the partial differential equation

$$\frac{\partial^2 u}{\partial t^2} = \left(\frac{E}{\rho}\right)\frac{\partial^2 u}{\partial x^2} \tag{8.2.4}$$

or

$$\frac{\partial^2 u}{\partial x^2} = \frac{1}{c^2}\frac{\partial^2 u}{\partial t^2} \tag{8.2.5}$$

which is similar to that of Eq. (8.1.2) for the string. The velocity of propagation of the displacement or stress wave in the rod is then equal to

$$c = \sqrt{\frac{E}{\rho}} \tag{8.2.6}$$

and a solution or the form

$$u(x,t) = U(x)G(t) \tag{8.2.7}$$

will result in two ordinary differential equations similar to Eqs. (8.1.7) and (8.1.8), with

$$U(x) = A\sin\frac{\omega}{c}x + B\cos\frac{\omega}{c}x \tag{8.2.8}$$

$$G(t) = C\sin\omega t + D\cos\omega t \tag{8.2.9}$$

Example 8.2.1

Determine the natural frequencies and mode shapes of a free-free rod (a rod with both ends free).

Solution For such a bar, the stress at the ends must be zero. Because the stress is given by the equation $E\partial u/\partial x$, the unit strain at the ends must also be zero; that is,

$$\frac{\partial u}{\partial x} = 0 \quad \text{at } x = 0 \quad \text{and } x = l$$

The two equations corresponding to these boundary conditions are, therefore,

$$\left(\frac{\partial u}{\partial x}\right)_{x=0} = A\frac{\omega}{c}(C\sin\omega t + D\cos\omega t) = 0$$

$$\left(\frac{\partial u}{\partial x}\right)_{x=l} = \frac{\omega}{c}\left(A\cos\frac{\omega l}{c} - B\sin\frac{\omega l}{c}\right)(C\sin\omega t + D\cos\omega t) = 0$$

Because these equations must be true for any time t, A must be equal to zero from the first equation. Because B must be finite in order to have vibration, the second equation is satisfied when

$$\sin\frac{\omega l}{c} = 0$$

or

$$\frac{\omega_n l}{c} = \omega_n l\sqrt{\frac{\rho}{E}} = \pi, 2\pi, 3\pi, \ldots, n\pi$$

The frequency of vibration is thus given by

$$\omega_n = \frac{n\pi}{l}\sqrt{\frac{E}{\rho}}, \quad f_n = \frac{n}{2l}\sqrt{\frac{E}{\rho}}$$

where n represents the order of the mode. The solution of the free-free rod with zero initial displacement can then be written as

$$u = u_0 \cos \frac{n\pi}{l} x \sin \frac{n\pi}{l} \sqrt{\frac{E}{\rho}} t$$

The amplitude of the longitudinal vibration along the rod is, therefore, a cosine wave having n nodes.

8.3 TORSIONAL VIBRATION OF RODS

The equation of motion of a rod in torsional vibration is similar to that of longitudinal vibration of rods discussed in the preceding section.

By letting x be measured along the length of the rod, the angle of twist in any length dx of the ' due to torque T is

$$d\theta = \frac{T dx}{I_P G} \tag{8.3.1}$$

where $I_P G$ is the torsional stiffness given by the product of the polar moment of inertial I_P of the cross-sectional area and the shear modulus of elasticity G. The torque on the two faces of the element being T and $T + (\partial T/\partial x) dx$, as shown in Fig. 8.3.1, the net torque from Eq. (8.3.1) becomes

$$\frac{\partial T}{dx} dx = I_P G \frac{\partial^2 \theta}{\partial x^2} dx \tag{8.3.2}$$

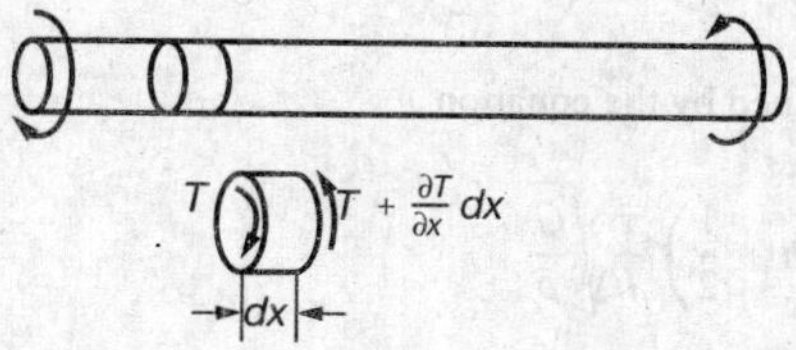

FIGURE 8.3.1. Torque acting on an element dx.

By equating this torque to the product of the mass moment of inertia $\rho I_P dx$ of the element and the angular acceleration $\partial^2\theta/\partial t^2$, where ρ is the density of the rod in mass per unit volume, the differential equation of motion becomes

$$\rho I_P dx \frac{\partial^2 \theta}{\partial t^2} = I_P G \frac{\partial^2 \theta}{dx^2} dx, \quad \frac{\partial^2 \theta}{\partial t^2} = \left(\frac{G}{\rho}\right) \frac{\partial^2 \theta}{\partial x^2} \tag{8.3.3}$$

This equation is of the same form as that of longitudinal vibration of rods, where θ and G/ρ replace u and E/ρ, respectively. The general solution hence can be written immediately by comparison as

$$\theta = \left(A \sin \omega \sqrt{\frac{\rho}{G}} x + B \cos \omega \sqrt{\frac{\rho}{G}} x \right) (C \sin \omega t + D \cos \omega t) \tag{8.3.4}$$

Example 8.3.1

Determine the equation for the natural frequencies of a uniform rod in torsional oscillation with one end fixed and the other end free, as in Fig. 8.3.2.

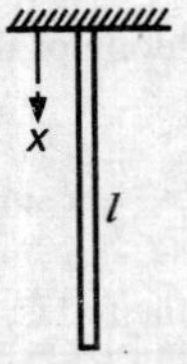

FIGURE 8.3.2.

Solution Starting with equation

$$\theta = (A \sin \omega \sqrt{\rho/G} x + B \cos \omega \sqrt{\rho/G} x) \sin \omega t$$

apply the boundary conditions, which are

(1) when $x = 0, v = 0$,
(2) when $x = l$, torque $= 0$, or

$$\frac{\partial \theta}{\partial x} = 0$$

Boundary condition (1) results in $B = 0$.
Boundary condition (2) results in the equation

$$\cos \omega \sqrt{\rho/G} l = 0$$

which is satisfied by the following angles

$$\omega_n \sqrt{\frac{\rho}{G}} l = \frac{\pi}{2}, \frac{3\pi}{2}, \frac{5\pi}{2}, \ldots, \left(n + \frac{1}{2}\right) \pi$$

The natural frequencies of the bar hence are determined by the equation

$$\omega_n = \left(n + \frac{1}{2}\right) \frac{\pi}{l} \sqrt{\frac{G}{\rho}}$$

where $n = 0, 1, 2, 3, \ldots$.

■

Example 8.3.2

The drill pipe of an oil well terminates at the lower end in a rod containing a cutting bit. Derive the expression for the natural frequencies, assuming the drill pipe to be uniform and fixed at the upper end of the rod and cutter to be represented by an end mass of moment of inertia J_0, as shown in Fig. 8.3.3.

Solution The boundary condition at the upper end is $x = 0, \theta = 0$, which requires B to be zero in Eq. (8.3.4).

For the lower end, the torque on the shaft is due to the inertia torque of the end disk, as shown by the free-body diagram of Fig. 8.3.3. The inertia torque of the disk is $-J_0(\partial^2\theta/\partial^2 t)_{x=l} = J_0\omega^2(\theta)_{x=l}$, whereas the shaft torque from Eq. (8.3.1) is $T_l = GI_P(d\theta/dx)_{x=l}$. Equating the two, we have

$$GI_P \left(\frac{d\theta}{dx}\right)_{x=l} = J_0 \omega^2 \theta_{x=l}$$

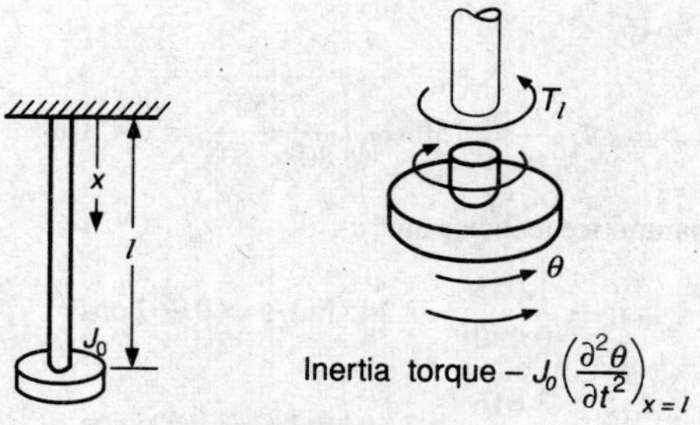

FIGURE 8.3.3.

By substituting from Eq. (8.3.4) with $B = 0$,

$$GI_P\omega\sqrt{\frac{\rho}{G}}\cos\omega\sqrt{\frac{\rho}{G}}l = J_0\omega^2\sin\omega\sqrt{\frac{\rho}{G}}l$$

$$\tan\omega l\sqrt{\frac{\rho}{G}} = \frac{I_P}{\omega J_0}\sqrt{G\rho} = \frac{I_P\rho l}{J_0\omega l}\sqrt{\frac{G}{\rho}} = \frac{J_{\text{rod}}}{J_0\omega l}\sqrt{\frac{G}{\rho}}$$

This equation is of the form

$$\beta\tan\beta = \frac{J_{\text{rod}}}{J_0} \qquad \beta = \omega l\sqrt{\frac{\rho}{G}}$$

which can be solved graphically or from tables.

Example 8.3.3

Using the frequency equation developed in the previous example, determine the first two natural frequencies of an oil-well drill pipe 1500 m long, fixed at the upper end and terminating at the lower end to a drill collar 36 m long. The average values for the drill pipe and drill collar are given as (assuming density $s = 7850\,\text{kg/m}^3$; and shear modulus $G = 80\,\text{GPa}$)

Drill pipe: outside diameter = 11 cm.

inside diameter = 9.7 cm.

$$I_P = 5.68\times10^{-6}\,\text{m}^4, \quad l = 1500\,\text{m}$$

$$J_{\text{rod}} = I_P\rho L = 5.68\times10^{-6}\times7850\times1500 = 66.9\,\text{kg m}^2$$

Drill collar: outside diameter = 19 cm

inside diameter = 5 cm

$$I_c = \frac{\pi}{32}(19^2 - 5^2) = 12732.87\,\text{cm}^4$$

$$J_o = I_c 3 l_c = 12732.87\times10^{-8}\times7850\times36 = 35.98\,\text{kg m}^2$$

Solution The equation to be solved is

$$\beta\tan\beta = \frac{J_{\text{rod}}}{J_0} = 1.86$$

Solving for β gives $\beta = 1.055, 3.616, \ldots$.

$$\beta = \omega l \sqrt{\frac{\rho}{G}} = 1500\,\omega \sqrt{\frac{7850}{80 \times 10^9}} = 0.470\,\omega$$

By solving for ω, the first two natural frequencies are

$$\omega_1 = \frac{1.055}{0.470} = 2.245 \text{ rad/s} = 0.357 \text{ cps}$$

$$\omega_2 = \frac{3.616}{0.470} = 7.694 \text{ rad/s} = 1.225 \text{ cps}$$

8.4 SUSPENSION BRIDGE AS CONTINUOUS SYSTEM

Due to its great flexibility, the Tacoma Narrows Bridge offers a unique example to demonstrate the applicability of the vibration theory of this section. Figure 8.4.1 shows the violent torsional oscillation of the Tacoma Narrows Bridge just prior to its collapse on November 7, 1940. The bridge had been plagued by a number of different modes of vibration under high winds since it was opened

FIGURE 8.4.1. Tacoma Narrows Bridge: Torsional oscillation. (*Courtesy Special Collections Division, University of Washington Libraries. Photo by F. B. Farquharson [Negative No. 4].*)

on July 1, 1940. During its short life of only four months, its unusual behavior had been observed and recorded by Professor F. B. Farquharson of the University of Washington.[1]

The catastrophic failure of the Tacoma Narrows Bridge has created considerable controversy and interest among engineers.[2] As in the flutter failure of aeroplane wings, flexible structures subjected to high aerodynamic excitation often develop self-excited oscillations with negative damping which lead to structural destruction.

Although simple resonance theory, itself, is insufficient to describe the failure of the Tacoma Narrows Bridge, the importance of creating simple vibrational models for its analysis must be recognized. The suspension bridge is a very flexible structure with distributed mass and stiffness. Although the floor of the bridge is generally uniform along its length, the supporting cables, which provide most of the stiffness, vary in slope and tension between the towers. The following data for the Tacoma Narrows Bridge were obtained from various sources.[3]

Data for the Tacoma Narrows Bridge

Geometric

$l = 850\,\text{m} =$ span between towers

$h = 71\,\text{m} =$ maximum sag of cables

$b = 12\,\text{m} =$ width between cables

$d = 0.4\,\text{m} =$ diameter of cables

$h/l = 0.083 = 1/12 =$ sag-to-span ratio

$b/l = 0.0139 = 1/72 =$ width-to-span ratio

Weights

$w_f = 62{,}750\,\text{N/m} =$ floor weight/ft along the bridge

$w_g = 4{,}700\,\text{N/m} =$ girder weight/cable/ft

$w_c = \frac{\pi}{4} \times (0.4)^2 \times 0.083 \times 7850 \times 9.81 = 789.2\,\text{N/m}$ of cable

$w_t = \frac{1}{2}(62{,}750) + 4{,}700 + 789.2 = 36{,}864.2\,\text{N/m} =$ total weight carried per cable

$\rho = w_t/g = 36864.2/9.81 = 3757.82\,\text{kg/m} =$ total mass/ft/cable

Assumptions and Calculated Quantities

Cable Tension. Figure 8.4.2 shows a free-body diagram of the cable between the tower and midspan. The cable at midspan is horizontal, which is also the horizontal component of the cable

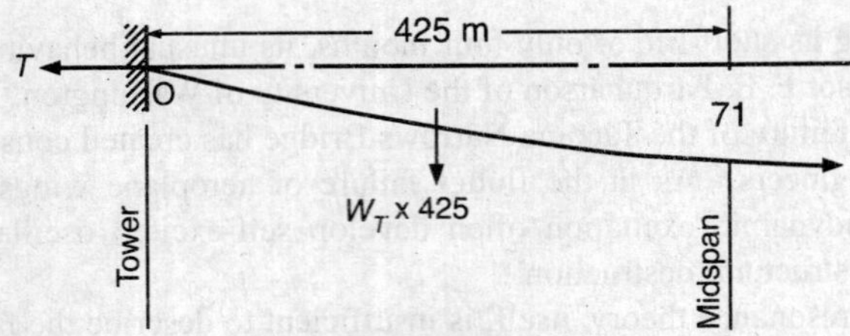

FIGURE 8.4.2.

tension at the tower. Equating the moment at the tower to zero, we have

$$\Sigma M_0 = 71T - 36864.2 \times 425 \times \tfrac{425}{2} = 0$$

$$\therefore T = 4.6 \times 10^7\ \text{N}$$

The vertical component of the cable tension at the tower is equal to the total downward force of $36{,}864.2 \times 425 = 1.56 \times 10^7$ N. Thus, the total cable tension at the tower is

$$T_0 = 10^7 \sqrt{(4.6)^2 + (1.56)^2} = 4.85 \times 10^7\ \text{N}.$$

We, therefore, can neglect the small variation of the cable tension along the span. Also, the small flexural stiffness of the floor in bending was considered negligible for this suspension bridge.

Torsional mass moment of inertia. Figure 8.4.3 shows the assumed equivalent cross section of the bridge for the polar mass moment of inertia calculation.

$$J \text{ for the floor} = mb^2/12 = \frac{62750 \times 12^2}{12} = 753000\ \text{Nm}$$

$$J \text{ for the girders plus cables} = 2 \times (4700 + 789.2) \times \left(\frac{12}{2}\right)^2 = 395222.4\ \text{Nm}$$

$$\text{Total } J = 1.15 \times 10^6\ \text{Nm} = 1.17 \times 10^5\ \text{kg} \cdot \text{m}^2$$

Torsional stiffness. For the Tacoma Narrows Bridge, the girders and the floor are both open sections, and the torsional stiffness provided by them is small in comparison to the torsional stiffness provided by the cables. Consider a pair of cables spaced b ft apart and under tension T. Let three consecutive stations, $i-1, i, i+1$, be equally spaced along the cable as shown in Fig. 8.4.4. Recalling the definition for the elements of the stiffness matrix in Sec. 11.3, Eq. (11.3.1), the stiffness at station i is equal to the lateral force F when displacement $y_i = 1.0$ with all other displacements, including $y_{i-1}, y_{i+1}, \ldots$, equal zero.

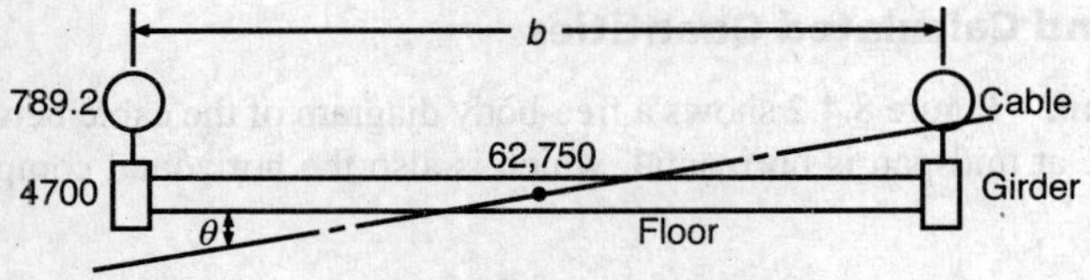

FIGURE 8.4.3.

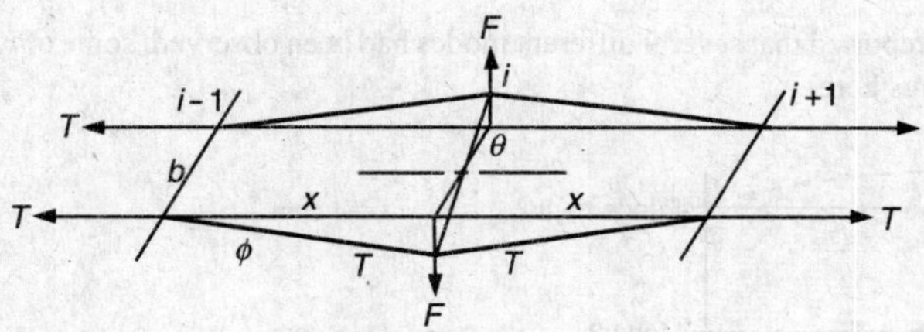

FIGURE 8.4.4.

Giving the cross section at i a small rotation, θ, we have $y_i = x\phi = (b/2)\theta$, and the vertical component of tension T is

$$F = 2T\phi = 2T\frac{b}{2x}\theta = \frac{Tb\theta}{x}$$

The torque of the cables is then $Fb = Tb^2\theta/x$ and the torsional stiffness of the cables, defined as the torque per unit length of the cables, is Tb^2 lb · ft/rad/ft.

$$Tb^2 = 4.850 \times 10^7 \times 12^2 = 984 \times 10^9 \text{ Nm}^2$$

Example 8.4.1 VERTICAL VIBRATION

With T and ρ constant, we can analyze the vertical vibration of the bridge as a flexible string of mass ρ per unit length stretched under tension T between two rigid towers that are l ft apart. With the boundary conditions $y(0, t) = y(l, t) = 0$, the general solution must satisfy the frequency equation

$$\sin\frac{\omega l}{c} = 0$$

as shown in Sec. 8.1. This equation is satisfied by

$$\frac{\omega l}{c} = \pi, 2\pi, 3\pi, \ldots, n\pi$$

or

$$f_n = \frac{n}{2l}\sqrt{\frac{T}{\rho}}, \quad n(\text{mode number}) = 1, 2, 3, \ldots$$

$$c = \sqrt{\frac{T}{\rho}} = \text{wave propagation velocity}$$

When $n = 1$, we have the fundamental mode; when $n = 2$, we have the second mode with a node at the center; etc., as shown in Fig. 8.4.5. Substituting numbers from the data, we have

$$f_n = \frac{n}{2 \times 850}\sqrt{\frac{4.6 \times 10^7}{3757.82}} = 0.0651n \text{ cps}$$

$$\cong 3.91n \text{ cpm} \cong 4n \text{ cpm}$$

F. B. Farquharson reported that several different modes had been observed, some of which can be identified with the computed results here.

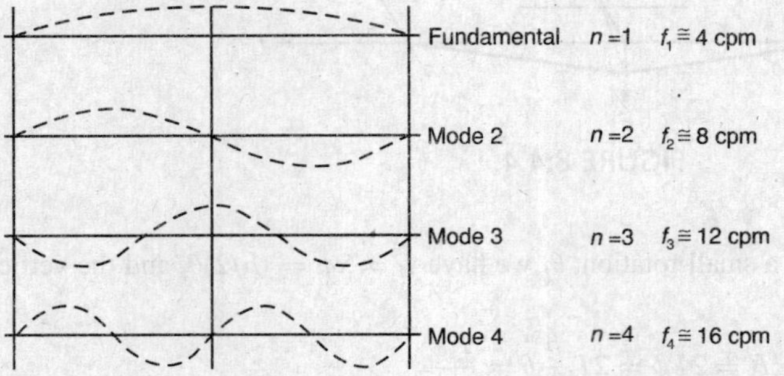

FIGURE 8.4.5.

Example 8.4.2 TORSIONAL VIBRATION

On the day of the Tacoma Narrows Bridge collapse, it was reported that high winds of 42 mph had excited several modes of vibration. The dominant mode was moving vertically with a node at midspan, which was calculated in the last section. This motion suddenly changed to torsional motion with a node at midspan and a period of 4 s, which built up to large amplitudes of nearly 45° before collapse.

Considering the bridge as an equivalent uniform rod, the torsional equation of motion can be rewritten as:

$$J\frac{\partial^2\theta}{\partial t^2} = K\frac{\partial^2\theta}{\partial x^2} \tag{8.4.1}$$

The solution is given by

$$\theta(x,t) = \left(A\sin\omega\sqrt{\frac{J}{K}}x + B\cos\omega\sqrt{\frac{J}{K}}x\right)(C\sin\omega t + D\cos\omega t) \tag{8.4.2}$$

where the term $(PI_P dx) = J$ is identified as the polar mass moment of inertia, and the term $(I_P G\, dx) = K$ is the torsional stiffness of length dx.

With the boundary conditions, $\theta(0,t) = \theta(l,t) = 0$, the natural frequencies are found from

$$\sin\omega\sqrt{\frac{J}{K}}l = 0$$

$$\omega\sqrt{\frac{J}{K}}l = \pi, 2\pi, \ldots, n\pi$$

For a node at midspan, $n = 2$:

$$2\pi f_2\sqrt{\frac{J}{K}}l = 2\pi$$

$$f_2 = \frac{1}{l}\sqrt{\frac{K}{J}}$$

$$\tau_2 = l\sqrt{\frac{J}{K}} = 850\sqrt{\frac{1.15\times 10^5}{6.984\times 10^9}}$$

$$= 3.48\ \text{s}$$

which agrees closely with the observed period of 4 s. Thus, with reasonable development of a simplified model, reliable calculations can be obtained.

8.5 EULER EQUATION FOR BEAMS

To determine the differential equation for the lateral vibration of beams, consider the forces and moments acting on an element of the beam shown in Fig. 8.5.1.

V and M are shear and bending moments, respectively, and $p(x)$ represents the loading per unit length of the beam.

By summing forces in the y-direction,

$$dV - p(x)dx = 0 \tag{8.5.1}$$

By summing moments about any point on the right face of the element,

$$dM - Vdx - \tfrac{1}{2}p(x)(dx)^2 = 0 \tag{8.5.2}$$

In the limiting process, these equations result in the following important relationships:

$$\frac{dV}{dx} = p(x) \qquad \frac{dM}{dx} = V \tag{8.5.3}$$

The first part of Eq. (8.5.3) states that the rate of change of shear along the length of the beam is equal to the loading per unit length, and the second states that the rate of change of the moment along the beam is equal to the shear.

From Eq. (8.5.3), we obtain the following:

$$\frac{d^2M}{dx^2} = \frac{dV}{dx} = p(x) \tag{8.5.4}$$

The bending moment is related to the curvature by the flexure equation, which, for the coordinates indicated in Fig. 8.5.1, is

$$M = EI\frac{d^2y}{dx^2} \tag{8.5.5}$$

Substituting this relation into Eq. (8.5.4), we obtain

$$\frac{d^2}{dx^2}\left(EI\frac{d^2y}{dx^2}\right) = p(x) \tag{8.5.6}$$

For a beam vibrating about its static equilibrium position under its own weight, the load per unit length is equal to the inertia load due to its mass and acceleration. Because the inertia force is in the same direction as $p(x)$, as shown in Fig. 8.5.1, we have, by assuming harmonic motion,

$$p(x) = \rho\omega^2 y \tag{8.5.7}$$

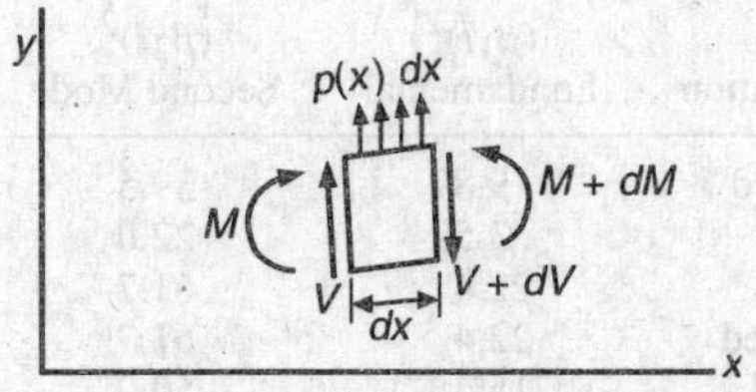

FIGURE 8.5.1.

where ρ is the mass per unit length of the beam. By using this relation, the equation for the lateral vibration of the beam reduces to

$$\frac{d^2}{dx^2}\left(EI\frac{d^2y}{dx^2}\right) - \rho\omega^2 y = 0 \tag{8.5.8}$$

In the special case where the flexural rigidity EI is a constant, the preceding equation can be written as

$$EI\frac{d^4y}{dx^4} - \rho\omega^2 y = 0 \tag{8.5.9}$$

On substituting

$$\beta^4 = \rho\frac{\omega^2}{EI} \tag{8.5.10}$$

we obtain the fourth-order differential equation

$$\frac{d^4y}{dx^4} - \beta^4 y = 0 \tag{8.5.11}$$

for the vibration of a uniform beam.

The general solution of Eq. (8.5.11) can be shown to be

$$y = A\cosh\beta x + B\sinh\beta x + C\cos\beta x + D\sin\beta x \tag{8.5.12}$$

To arrive at this result, we assume a solution of the form

$$y = e^{ax}$$

which will satisfy the differential equation when

$$a = \pm\beta, \quad \text{and} \quad a = \pm i\beta$$

Because

$$e^{\pm\beta x} = \cosh\beta x \pm \sinh\beta x$$
$$e^{\pm i\beta x} = \cos\beta x \pm i\sin\beta x$$

the solution in the form of Eq. (8.5.12) is readily established.

The natural frequencies of vibration are found from Eq. (8.5.10) to be

$$\omega_n = \beta_n^2\sqrt{\frac{EI}{\rho}} = (\beta_n l)^2\sqrt{\frac{EI}{\rho l^4}} \tag{8.5.13}$$

where the number β_n depends on the boundary conditions of the problem. Table 8.5.1 lists numerical values of $(\beta_n l)^2$ for typical end conditions.

TABLE 8.5.1

Beam Configuration	$(\beta_1 l)^2$ Fundamental	$(\beta_2 l)^2$ Second Mode	$(\beta_3 l)^2$ Third Mode
Simply supported	9.87	39.5	88.9
Cantilever	3.52	22.0	61.7
Free-free	22.4	61.7	121.0
Clamped-clamped	22.4	61.7	121.0
Clamped-hinged	15.4	50.0	104.0
Hinged-free	0	15.4	50.0

Example 8.5.1

Determine the natural frequencies of vibration of a uniform beam clamped at one end and free at the other.

Solution The boundary conditions are

$$\text{At } x = 0 \begin{cases} y = 0 \\ \dfrac{dy}{dx} = 0 \end{cases}$$

$$\text{At } x = l \begin{cases} M = 0 \quad \text{or} \quad \dfrac{d^2y}{dx^2} = 0 \\ V = 0 \quad \text{or} \quad \dfrac{d^3y}{dx^3} = 0 \end{cases}$$

Substituting these boundary conditions in the general solution, we obtain

$$(y)_{x=0} = A + C = 0, \quad \therefore A = -C$$

$$\left(\frac{dy}{dx}\right)_{x=0} = \beta[A \sinh \beta x + B \cosh \beta x - C \sin \beta x + D \cos \beta x]_{x=0} = 0$$

$$\beta[B + D] = 0, \quad \therefore B = -D$$

$$\left(\frac{d^2y}{dx^2}\right)_{x=l} = \beta^3[A \cosh \beta l + B \sinh \beta l - C \cos \beta l - D \sin \beta l] = 0$$

$$A(\cosh \beta l + \cos \beta l) + B(\sinh \beta l + \sin \beta l) = 0$$

$$\left(\frac{d^3y}{dx^3}\right)_{x=l} = \beta^3[A \sinh \beta l + \beta \cosh \beta l + C \sin \beta l - D \cos \beta l] = 0$$

$$A(\sinh \beta l - \sin \beta l) + B(\cosh \beta l + \cos \beta l) = 0$$

From the last two equations, we obtain

$$\frac{\cosh \beta l + \cos \beta l}{\sinh \beta l - \sin \beta l} = \frac{\sinh \beta l + \sin \beta l}{\cosh \beta l + \cos \beta l}$$

which reduces to

$$\cosh \beta l \cos \beta l + 1 = 0$$

This last equation is satisfied by a number of values of βl, corresponding to each normal mode of oscillation, which for the first and second modes are 1.875 and 4.695, respectively. The natural frequency for the first mode is hence given by

$$\omega_1 = \frac{(1.875)^2}{l^2} = \sqrt{\frac{EI}{\rho}} = \frac{3.515}{l^2}\sqrt{\frac{EI}{\rho}}$$

■

Example 8.5.2

Figure 8.5.2 shows a satellite boom in the process of deployment. The coiled portion, which is stored, is rotated and deployed out through straight guides to extend 31 m or more.

FIGURE 8.5.2. Satellite boom. (*Courtesy of Able Engineering, Santa Barbara, CA.*)

This particular boom has the following properties:

$$\text{Deployed diameter} = 317.5\,\text{mm}$$

$$\text{Bay length} = 185\,\text{mm}$$

$$\text{Boom weight} = 4.85\,\text{N/m of length}$$

$$\text{Bending stiffness, } EI = 43.1 \times 10^9\ \text{Nmm}^2 \text{ about the neutral axis}$$

$$\text{Torsional stiffness, } GA = 15.78 \times 10^8\ \text{Nmm}^2$$

Determine the natural frequencies in bending and in its free unloaded state if its length is 6.2 m. The boom can be represented as a uniform beam.

Solution The natural frequencies in bending can be found from the equation

$$\omega_n = (\beta_n l)^2 \sqrt{\frac{EI}{\rho l^4}}$$

From Table 8.5.1, the first natural frequency becomes

$$\omega_1 = 3.52 \sqrt{\frac{43.1 \times 10^9 \times (10^{-3})^2}{\dfrac{4.85}{9.81}(6.2)^4}} = 27.04\,\text{rad/s}$$

$$= 4.30\,\text{cps.}$$

8.6 SYSTEM WITH REPEATED IDENTICAL SECTIONS

Repeated identical sections are often encountered in engineering structures. They represent a lumped-mass approximation to the continous structure, such as, the Nstorey high-rise building is often built with identical floors of mass m and lateral shear stiffness of k lb/in., as modeled in Fig. 8.6.1. By applying the method of difference equations to such structures, simple analytical equations for the natural frequencies and mode shapes can be found.

By referring to Fig. 8.6.1; the equation of motion for the nth mass is

$$m\ddot{x}_n = k(x_{n+1} - x_n) - k(x_n - x_{n-1}) \tag{8.6.1}$$

which for harmonic motion can be represented in terms of the amplitudes as

$$X_{n+1} - 2\left(1 - \frac{\omega^2 m}{2k}\right)X_n + X_{n-1} = 0 \tag{8.6.2}$$

The solution to this equation is found by substituting

$$X_n = e^{i\beta n} \tag{8.6.3}$$

which leads to the relationship

$$1 - \frac{\omega^2 m}{2\,k} = \frac{e^{i\beta} + e^{-i\beta}}{2} = \cos\beta$$

$$\frac{\omega^2 m}{k} = 2(1 - \cos\beta) = 4\sin^2\frac{\beta}{2} \tag{8.6.4}$$

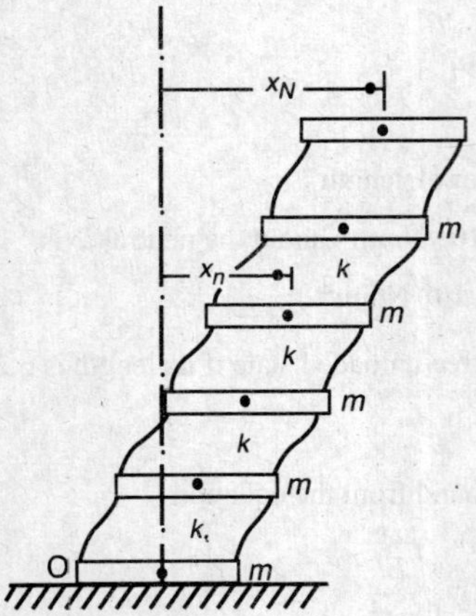

FIGURE 8.6.1. Repeated structure for difference equation analysis.

The general solution for X_n is

$$X_n = A \cos \beta n + B \sin \beta n \tag{8.6.5}$$

where A and B are evaluated from the boundary conditions.

Boundary conditions. The difference equation (8.6.2) is restricted to $1 \leqslant n \leqslant (N-1)$ and must be extended to $n = 0$ and $n = N$ by the boundary conditions.

At the ground, the amplitude of motion is zero, $X_0 = 0$. Equation (8.6.2) for mass m_1 then becomes

$$X_2 - 2\left(1 - \frac{m\omega^2}{2k}\right) X_1 = 0 \tag{8.6.6}$$

Substituting Eqs. (8.6.4) and (8.6.5) into the previous equation, we obtain

$$(A \cos 2\beta + B \sin 2\beta) - 2 \cos \beta (A \cos \beta + B \sin \beta) = 0$$

$$A(\cos 2\beta - 2 \cos^2 \beta) + B(\sin 2\beta - 2 \sin \beta \cos \beta) = 0$$

Because $\cos 2\beta - 2 \cos^2 \beta = 1$ and $\sin 2\beta - 2 \sin \beta \cos \beta = 0$, we have

$$A(1) + B(0) = 0$$

$$\therefore A = 0$$

and the general solution for the amplitude reduces to

$$X_n = B \sin \beta n \tag{8.6.7}$$

At the top, the boundary equation is

$$m_N \ddot{x}_N = -k(x_N - x_{N-1})$$

Because the sections at the two boundaries of the system are outside the domain of the difference equation, the choice for the value of m_N is arbitrary. However, we will soon see that the choice $m_N = m/2$ simplifies the boundary equation at the top. In terms of the amplitudes, the previous

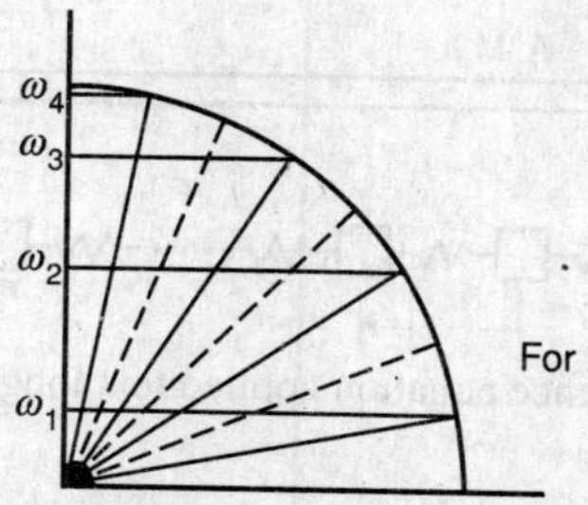

FIGURE 8.6.2. Natural frequencies of a repeated structure with $N = 4$.

equation becomes

$$X_{N-1} = \left(1 - \frac{\omega^2 m}{2k}\right) X_N \tag{8.6.8}$$

Substituting from Eqs. (8.6.4) and (8.6.7), we obtain the following equation for evaluating the quantity β:

$$\sin \beta(N-1) + \cos \beta \sin \beta N$$

This equation then reduces to

$$\sin \beta \cos \beta N = 0$$

which is satisfied by

$$\cos \beta N = 0$$

$$\frac{\beta}{2} = \frac{\pi}{4N}, \frac{3\pi}{4N}, \frac{5\pi}{4N}, \ldots, \frac{(2i-1)\pi}{4N}$$

The natural frequencies are then available from Eq. (8.6.4) as

$$\omega_i = 2\sqrt{\frac{k}{m}} \sin \frac{\beta_i}{2}$$

$$= 2\sqrt{\frac{k}{m}} \sin \frac{(2i-1)\pi}{4N} \tag{8.6.9}$$

If the top mass is m instead of $\frac{1}{2}m$, the boundary equation results in a slightly different equation

$$\frac{\beta}{2} = \frac{(2-1)\pi}{2(2N+1)}$$

and

$$\omega_i = 2\sqrt{\frac{k}{m}} \sin \frac{(2i-1)\pi}{2(2N+1)}$$

Figure 8.6.2 shows a graphical representation of these natural frequencies when $N = 4$.

The method of difference equation presented here is applicable to many other dynamical systems where repeating sections are present. The natural frequencies are always given by Eq. (8.6.9); however, the quantity β must be established for each problem from its boundary conditions.

Example 8.6.1

Figure 8.6.3 shows a fixed-free rod modeled by N repeated spring-mass sections. Because the difference equation solution of the N-story building is applicable here, express the natural frequency equation in terms of the parameters of the rod for longitudinal vibration.

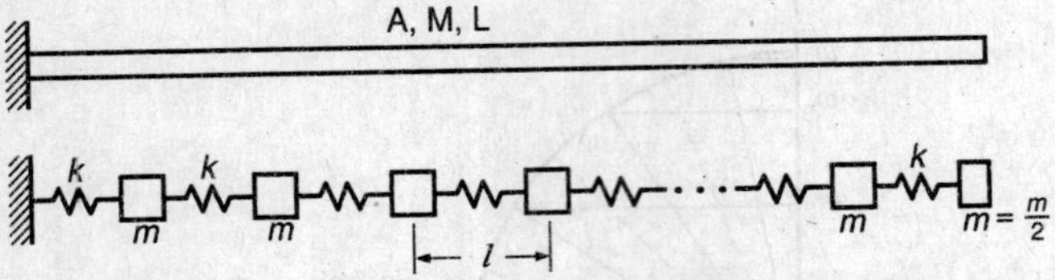

FIGURE 8.6.3. Difference equation applied to a longitudinal system.

Solution By letting $l = L/N$ for the repeating section, the spring stiffness for the section is $k = AE/l$ and the mass is $m = M/N$. Substituting into Eq. (8.6.9), we obtain

$$\omega_i = 2\sqrt{\frac{AEN^2}{ML}}\sin\frac{(2i-1)\pi}{4N} \tag{a}$$

If N is very large, the angle $\pi/4N$ is small and

$$\sin\frac{(2i-1)\pi}{4N} \cong \frac{(2i-1)\pi}{4N}$$

for the lower frequencies. The previous equation can then be approximated by

$$\omega_i \cong (2i-1)\frac{\pi}{2}\sqrt{\frac{AE}{ML}}, \quad i \ll N \tag{b}$$

which is the exact equation for the longitudinal vibration of the uniform rod. For higher frequencies, the assumption $\sin\theta = \theta$ will not be valid (see Fig. 8.6.2), and Eq. (a) for the discrete mass system must be used. ∎

REFERENCES

[1] F. B. FARQUHARSON, Aerodynamic Stability of Suspension Bridges, *University of Washington Engineering Experiment Station Bulletin*, No. 116, Part 1 (1950).

[2] K. Y. BILLAH, and R. H. SCANLAN, "Resonance, Tacoma Narrows Bridge Failure, and Undergraduate Physics Textbooks," *Amer. J. Physics*, Vol. 59, No. 2, pp. 118–124 (Feb. 1991).

[3] W. T. THOMSON, "Vibration Periods at Tacoma Narrows," *Engineering News Record*, Vol. P477, pp. 61–62 (March 27, 1941).

PROBLEMS

8.1. Derive the equation for the natural frequencies of a uniform cord of length l fixed at the two ends. The cord is stretched to a tension T and its mass per unit length is ρ.

8.2. A cord of length l and mass per unit length ρ is under tension T with the left end fixed and the right end attached to a spring-mass system, as shown in Fig. P8.2. Determine the equation for the natural frequencies.

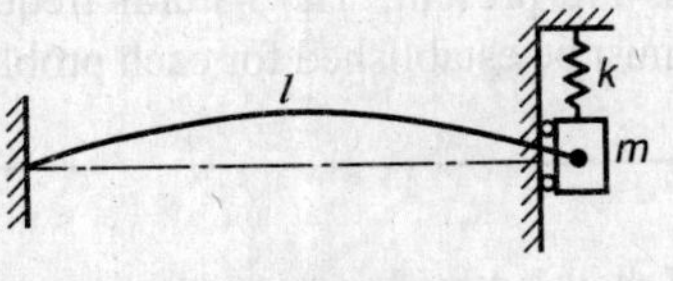

FIGURE P8.2.

8.3. Find the wave velocity along a rope whose mass is 0.372 kg/m when stretched to a tension of 444 N.

8.4. Shown in Fig. P8.4 is a flexible cable supported at the upper end and free to oscillate under the influence of gravity. Show that the equation of lateral motion is

$$\frac{\partial^2 y}{\partial t^2} = g\left(x\frac{\partial^2 y}{\partial x^2} + \frac{\partial y}{\partial x}\right)$$

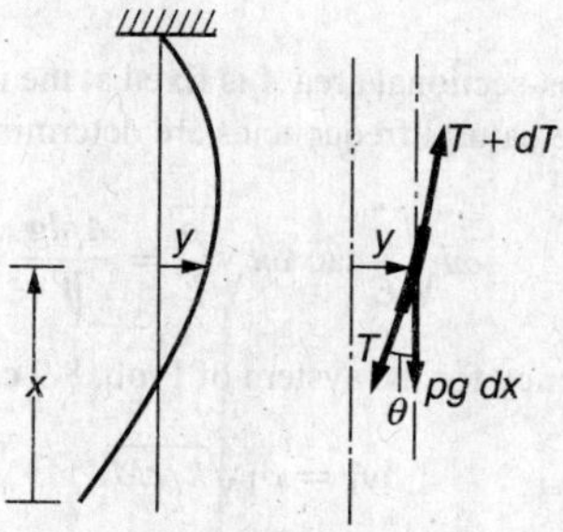

FIGURE P8.4.

8.5. In Prob. 8.4, assume a solution of the form $y = Y(x)\ cos\ \omega\pm$ and show that $Y(x)$ can be reduced to a Bessel's differential equation

$$\frac{d^2Y(z)}{dz^2} + \frac{1}{z}\frac{dY(x)}{dz} + Y(z) = 0$$

with solution

$$Y(z) = J_0(z) \quad \text{or}$$

$$Y(x) = J_0\left(2\omega\sqrt{\frac{x}{g}}\right)$$

by a change in variable $z^2 = 4\omega^2 x/g$.

8.6. A harmonic vibration has an amplitude that varies as a cosine function along the *x*-direction such that

$$y = a\ \cos\ kx \cdot \sin\ \omega t$$

Show that if another harmonic vibration of same frequency and equal amplitude displaced in space phase and time phase by a quarter wavelength is added to the first vibration, the resultant vibration will represent a traveling wave with a propagation velocity equal to $c = \omega/k$.

8.7. A particular satellite consists of two equal masses of m each, connected by a cable of length $2l$ and mass density ρ, as shown in Fig. P8.7. The assembly rotates in space with angular speed ω_0. Show that if the variation in the cable tension is neglected, the differential equation of lateral motion of the cable is

$$\frac{\partial^2 y}{\partial x^2} = \frac{\rho}{m\omega_0^2 l}\left(\frac{\partial^2 y}{\partial t^2} - \omega_0^2 y\right)$$

and that its fundamental frequency of oscillation is

$$\omega^2 = \left(\frac{\pi}{2l}\right)^2\left(\frac{m\omega_0 l}{\rho}\right) - \omega_0^2$$

8.8. Find the velocity of longitudinal waves along a thin steel bar. The modulus of elasticity and mass per unit volume of steel are $200 \times 10^9\ \text{N/m}^2$ and $7810\ \text{kg/m}^3$, respectively.

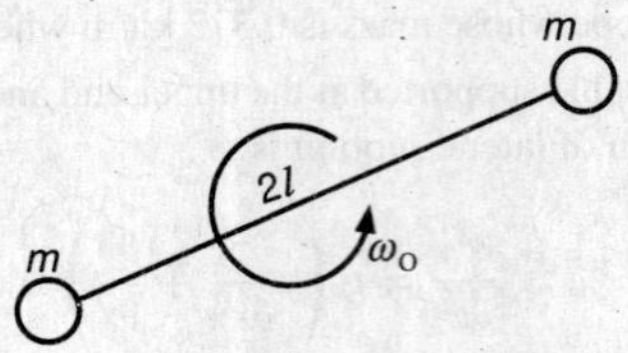

FIGURE P8.7.

8.9. A uniform rod of length l and cross-sectional area A is fixed at the upper end and is loaded with a weight W on the other end. Show that the natural frequencies are determined from the equation

$$\omega l\sqrt{\frac{\rho}{E}}\tan \omega l\sqrt{\frac{\rho}{E}} = \frac{A\rho lg}{W}$$

8.10. Show that the fundamental frequency for the system of Prob. 8.9 can be expressed in the form

$$\omega_1 = \beta_1\sqrt{k/rM}$$

where

$$n_1 l = \beta_1, \quad r = \frac{M_{\text{rod}}}{M}$$

$$k = \frac{AE}{l}, \quad M = \text{end mass}$$

Reducing this system to a spring k and an end mass equal to $M + \frac{1}{3}M_{\text{rod}}$, determine an appropriate equation for the fundamental frequency. Show that the ratio of the approximate frequency to the exact frequency found is

$$(1/\beta_1)\sqrt{3r/(3+r)}$$

8.11 A uniform bar of length l is fixed at one end and free at the other end. Show that the frequencies of normal longitudinal vibrations are $f = (n + \frac{1}{2})c/2l$, where $c = \sqrt{E/\rho}$ is the velocity of longitudinal waves in the bar, and $n = 0, 1, 2, \ldots$

8.12. The equation for the longitudinal oscillations of a slender rod with viscous damping is

$$m\frac{\partial^2 u}{\partial t^2} = AE\frac{\partial^2 u}{\partial x^2} - \alpha\frac{\partial u}{\partial t} + \frac{p_0}{l}p(x)f(t)$$

where the loading per unit length is assumed to be separable. Letting $u = \sum_i \phi_i(x)q_i(t)$ and $p(x) = \sum_i b_i\phi_i(x)$ show that

$$u = \frac{p_0}{ml\sqrt{1-\zeta^2}}\sum\frac{b_k\phi_j}{\omega_j}\int_0^t f(t-\tau)e^{-\zeta\omega_k\tau}\sin\omega_j\sqrt{1-\zeta^2}\,\tau\,d\tau$$

$$b_j = \frac{1}{l}\int_0^l p(x)\phi_j(x)\,dx$$

Derive the equation for the stress at any point x.

8.13. The frequency of magnetostriction oscillators is determined by the length of the nickel alloy rod, which generates an alternating voltage in the surrounding coils equal to the frequency of longitudinal vibration of the rod, as shown in Fig. P8.13. Determine the proper length of the rod clamped at the middle for a frequency of 20 kcps if the modulus of elasticity and density are given as $E = 200$ GPa and $\rho = 7800\ \text{kg/m}^3$, respectively.

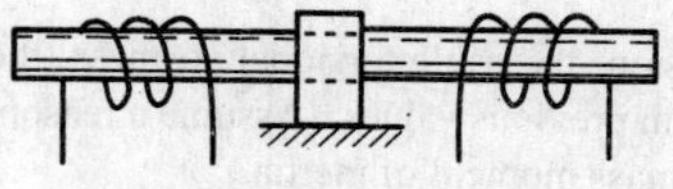

FIGURE P8.13.

8.14. Determine the expression for the natural frequencies of torsional oscillations of a uniform rod of length l clamped at the middle and free at the two ends.

8.15. A uniform bar has these specifications: length l, mass density per unit volume ρ, and torsional stiffness $I_P G$, where I_P is the polar moment of inertia of the cross section and G the shear modulus. The end $x = 0$ is fastened to a torsional spring of stiffness K Nm rad and the end l is fixed, as shown in Fig. P8.15. Determine the transcendental equation from which natural frequencies can be established. Verify the correctness of this equation by considering special cases for $K = 0$ and $K = \infty$.

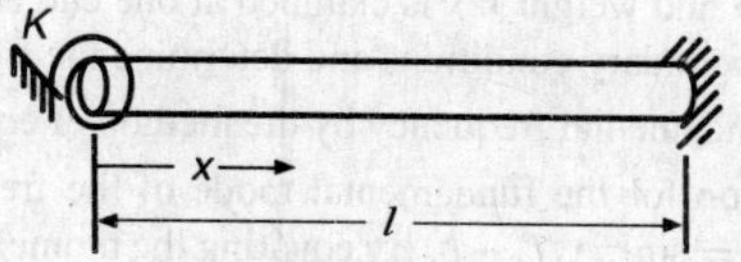

FIGURE P8.15.

8.16. Show that $c = \sqrt{G/\rho}$ is the velocity of propagation of torsional strain along the rod. What is the numerical value of c for steel?

8.17. Determine the natural frequencies of a torsional system consisting of a uniform shaft of mass moment inertia J_s with a disk of inertia J_0 attached to each end. Check the fundamental frequency by reducing the uniform shaft to a torsional spring with end masses.

8.18. The following data on the Golden Gate Bridge was obtained from reports provided by the district engineer for the bridge:

$$l = 1400\,\text{m}$$

$$h = 155\,\text{m}$$

$$b = 30\,\text{m}$$

$$\omega_t = 3 \times 10^5\ \text{N/m (total weight per linear meter, including cables)}$$

Determine the cable stiffness Tb^2 in torsion and compare with the old stiffness of the Tacoma Narrows Bridge.

8.19. For a 1-DOF model of an airplane wing, assume an equation of the form

$$J_0\ddot{\theta} + c\dot{\theta} + k\theta = f_1(v, \theta) + f_2(v, \dot{\theta})$$

where θ is the angle of attack and v is the wind velocity. Discuss the possibility of negative damping and the importance of the aerodynamic characteristics of the floor and stiffness girders for suspension bridges.

8.20. The new Tacoma Narrows Bridge, reopened on October 14, 1950, has the following data:

$$l = 940\,\text{m (between towers)}$$

$$b = 20\,\text{m (width between cables)}$$

$$k = 93\,\text{m (maximum sag of cables)}$$

$$w_t = 10^5\,\text{N/m}$$

$$J_0 = \frac{\omega_t}{g}\rho^2 \text{(rotational mass moment of inertia)}$$

Calculate the new cable tension, the cable torsional stiffness, the new vertical and torsional vibration frequencies, and compare with previous values. (Assume a reasonable value for the radius of gyration ρ in determining the torsional mass moment of inertia.)

8.21. Name some of the factors not accounted for in the method presented in Sec. 8.4 for the calculation of the natural frequencies of suspension bridges.

8.22. Determine the natural frequencies of a uniform beam of length l clamped at both ends.

8.23. Determine the natural frequencies of a uniform beam of length l, clamped at one end and pinned at the other end.

8.24. Determine the expression for the natural frequencies of a free-free bar in lateral vibration.

8.25. A concrete test beam 50 × 50 × 300 mm, supported at two points $0.224l$ from the ends, was found to resonate at 1690 cps. If the density of concrete is 2450 kg/m^3, determine the modulus of elasticity, assuming the beam to be slender.

8.26. A uniform beam of length l and weight W_b is clamped at one end and carries a concentrated weight W_0 at the other end. State the boundary conditions and determine the frequency equation.

8.27. Solve Prob. 8.26 for the fundamental frequency by the method of equivalent mass placed at the free end.

8.28. Determine the node position for the fundamental mode of the free-free beam by Rayleigh's method, assuming the curve to be $y = \sin(\pi x/l) - b$. By equating the momentum to zero, determine b. Substitute this value of b to find ω_1.

8.29. The pinned end of a pinned-free beam is given a harmonic motion of amplitude y_0 perpendicular to the beam. Show that the boundary conditions result in the equation

$$\frac{y_0}{y_l} = \frac{\sinh \beta l \cos \beta l - \cosh \beta l \sin \beta l}{\sinh \beta l - \sin \beta l}$$

which, for $y_0 \to 0$, reduces to

$$\tanh \beta l = \tan \beta l$$

8.30. A simply supported beam has an overhang of length l_2, as shown in Fig. P8.30. If the end of the overhang is free, show that boundary conditions require the deflection equation for each span to be

$$\phi_1 = C\left(\sin \beta x - \frac{\sin \beta l_1}{\sinh \beta l_1} \sinh \beta x\right)$$

$$\phi_2 = A\left[\cos \beta x + \cosh \beta x - \left(\frac{\cos \beta l_2 + \cosh \beta l_2}{\sin \beta l_2 + \sinh \beta l_2}\right)(\sin \beta x + \sinh \beta x)\right]$$

where x is measured from the left and right ends.

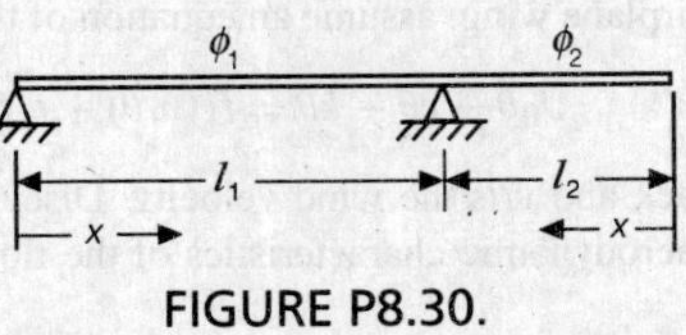

FIGURE P8.30.

8.31. If a satellite boom of uniform weight W_b is loaded with concentrated load W_1 at $x = x_1$ and an end load W_0, show that its fundamental frequency can be obtained from the equation

$$\omega_1 = \sqrt{\frac{3EIg}{l^3 \overline{W}}}$$

where

$$\overline{W} = W_0 + 0.237\, W_b + W_1 \left\{\frac{y(x_1)}{y(l)}\right\}^2$$

8.32. Write the difference equations for the spring-mass system shown in Fig. P8.32 and find the natural frequencies of the system.

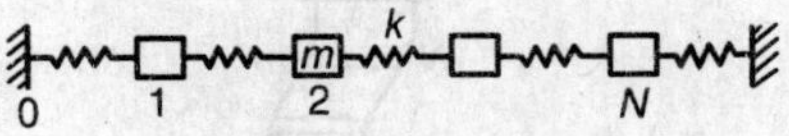

FIGURE P8.32.

8.33. An N-mass pendulum is shown in Fig. P8.33. Determine the difference equations, boundary conditions, and the natural frequencies.

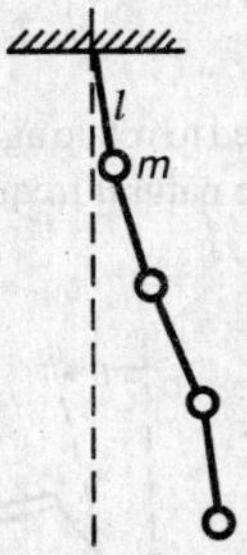

FIGURE P8.33.

8.34. Set up the difference equations for N equal masses on a string with tension T, as shown in Fig. P8.34. Determine the boundary equations and the natural frequencies.

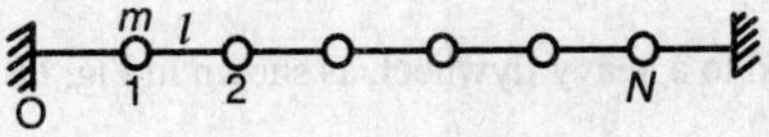

FIGURE P8.34.

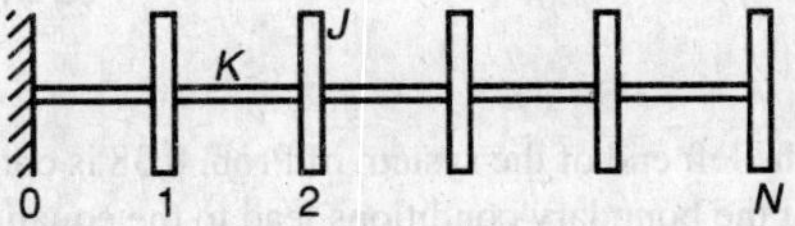

FIGURE P8.35.

8.35. Set up the difference equations for the torsional system shown in Fig. P8.35. Determine the boundary equations and solve for the natural frequencies.

8.36. If the top story of a building is restrained by a spring or stiffness K_N, as shown in Fig. P8.36, determine the natural frequencies of the N-story building.

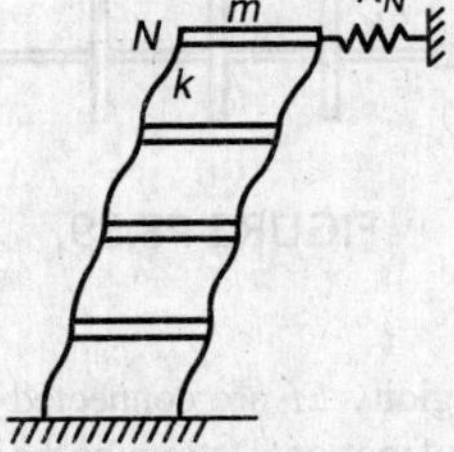

FIGURE P8.36.

8.37. A ladder-type structure is fixed at both ends, as shown in Fig. P8.37. Determine the natural frequencies.

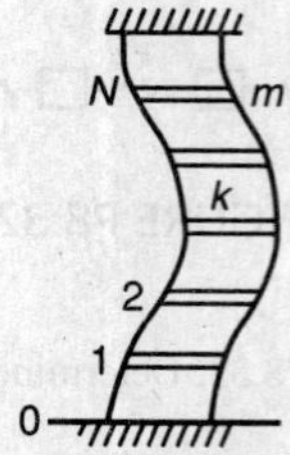

FIGURE P8.37.

8.38. If the base of an N-story building is allowed to rotate against a resisting spring K_θ, as shown in Fig. P8.38, determine the boundary equations and the natural frequencies.

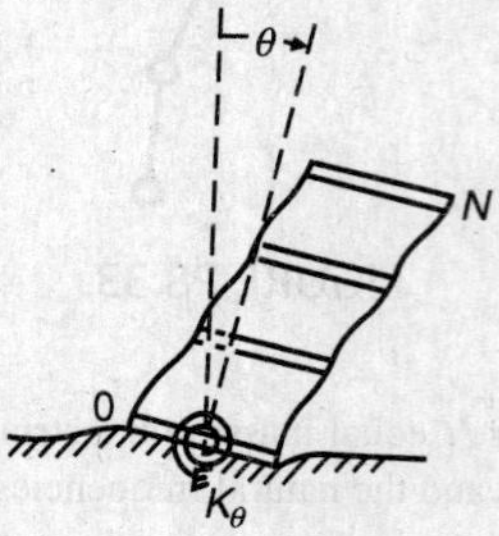

FIGURE P8.38.

8.39. If the left end of the system of Prob. 8.38 is connected to a heavy flywheel, as shown in Fig. P8.39, show that the boundary conditions lead to the equation

$$(-\sin N\beta \cos\beta + \sin N\beta)\left(1 + 4\frac{K}{K_a}\frac{J_a}{J}\sin^2\frac{\beta}{2}\right) = -2\frac{J_a}{J}\sin^2\frac{\beta}{2}\sin\beta\cos N\beta$$

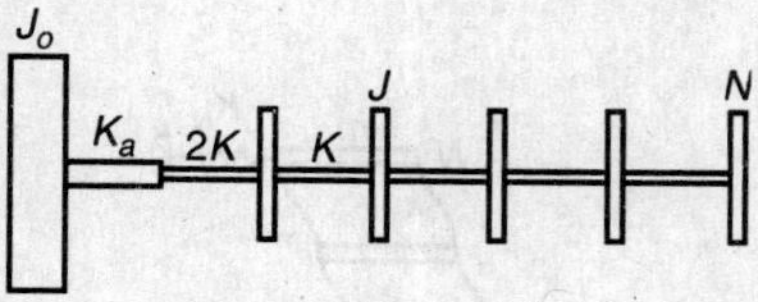

FIGURE P8.39.

8.40. Two beams of the same flexural rigidity EI are connected by a spring of stiffness k as shown in the Fig. P8.40. Determine the equations of motion. Determine the fundamental frequency of the antisymmetric mode (i.e., where $y_1 = -y_2$).

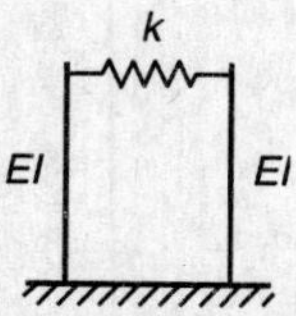

FIGURE P8.40.

8.41. A ball hits the baseball bat at its end at time $t = 0$ with the speed of $v\ m/s$. The speed of the bat at that moment is $v\ m/s$ in the direction opposite to that of the ball. Assuming that the player is holding the bat tightly at one end which is not moving, determine the natural frequency of the first mode.

8.42. The natural frequencies and normal modes presented for the 10-DOF system of Example 5.9.1 were obtained from the eigenvalue-eigenvector computer program. Verify these numbers by the use of Eq. 8.6.9 for ω_n and $X_n = B \sin \beta n$ for the amplitude.

C H A P T E R 9

Mode-Summation Procedures for Continuous Systems (Beams)

Structures made up of beams are common in engineering.* They constitute systems of an infinite number of degrees of freedom, and the mode-summation methods make possible their analysis as systems of a finite number of degrees of freedom. Constraints are often found as additional supports of the structure, and they alter the normal modes of the system. In the use of the mode-summation method, convergence of the series is of importance, and the mode-acceleration method offers a varied approach. The modes used in representing the deflection of a system need not always be orthogonal. The synthesis of a system using nonorthogonal functions is illustrated.

Large structures such as space stations are generally composed of continuous sections which can be analyzed by the mode participation methods. Shown in Fig. 9.1.1 is one such design, parts of which offer opportunities for challenging analysis.

9.1 MODE-SUMMATION METHOD

In Sec. 5.7, the equations of motion were decoupled by the modal matrix to obtain the solution of forced vibration in terms of the normal coordinates of the system. In this section, we apply a similar technique to continuous systems by expanding the deflection in terms of the normal modes of the system.

Consider, for example, the general motion of a beam loaded by a distributed force $p(x, t)$, whose equation of motion is

$$[EIy''(x, t)]'' + m(x)\ddot{y}(x, t) = p(x, t) \tag{9.1.1}$$

*The Olympus Satellite, shown in Fig. 9.1.1, is one of several configurations proposed for deployment in space. The large panels of solar cells are deployed by lightweight booms of glass fiber, ingeniously designed to extend the panels for hundreds of feet.

FIGURE 9.1.1. Olympus satellite and deployment boom. (*Courtesy of Astro Aerospace, Carpinteria, California.*)

The normal modes $\phi_i(x)$ of such a beam must satisfy the equation

$$(EI\phi_i'')'' - \omega_i^2 m(x)\phi_i = 0 \tag{9.1.2}$$

and its boundary conditions. The normal modes $\phi_i(x)$ are also orthogonal functions satisfying the relation

$$\int_0^l m(x)\phi_i\phi_j dx = \begin{cases} 0 & \text{for } j \neq i \\ M_i & \text{for } j = i \end{cases} \tag{9.1.3}$$

By representing the solution to the general problem in terms of $\phi_i(x)$

$$y(x,t) = \sum_i \phi_i(x) q_i(t) \tag{9.1.4}$$

the generalized coordinate $q_i(t)$ can be determined from Lagrange's equation by first establishing the kinetic and potential energies.

Recognizing the orthogonality relation, Eq. (9.1.3), the kinetic energy is

$$T = \frac{1}{2}\int_0^l \dot{y}^2(x,t)m(x)\,dx = \frac{1}{2}\sum_i\sum_j \dot{q}_i\dot{q}_j \int_0^l \phi_i\phi_j m(x)\,dx$$

$$= \frac{1}{2}\sum_i M_i \dot{q}_i^2 \tag{9.1.5}$$

where the generalized mass M_i is defined as

$$M_i = \int_0^l \phi_i^2(x)m(x)\,dx \tag{9.1.6}$$

Similarly, the potential energy is

$$U = \frac{1}{2}\int_0^l EIy''^2(x,t)\,dx = \frac{1}{2}\sum_i\sum_j q_i q_j \int_0^l EI\phi_i''\phi_j''\,dx$$

$$= \frac{1}{2}\sum_i K_i q_i^2 = -\frac{1}{2}\sum \omega_i^2 M_i q_i^2 \tag{9.1.7}$$

where the generalized stiffness is

$$K_i = \int_0^l EI[\phi_i''(x)]^2\,dx \tag{9.1.8}$$

In addition to T and U, we need the generalized force Q_i, which is determined from the work done by the applied force $p(x,t)dx$ in the virtual displacement δq_i.

$$\delta W = \int_0^l p(x,t)\left(\sum_i \phi_i \delta q_i\right) dx$$

$$= \sum_i \delta q_i \int_0^l p(x,t)\phi_i(x)\,dx \tag{9.1.9}$$

where the generalized force is

$$Q_i = \int_0^l p(x,t)\phi_i(x)\,dx \tag{9.1.10}$$

Substituting into Lagrange's equation,

$$\frac{d}{dt}\left(\frac{\partial T}{\partial \dot{q}_i}\right) - \frac{\partial T}{\partial q_i} + \frac{\partial U}{\partial q_i} = Q_i \tag{9.1.11}$$

we find the differential equation for $q_i(t)$ to be

$$\ddot{q}_i + \omega_i^2 q_i = \frac{1}{M_i}\int_0^l p(x,t)\phi_i(x)\,dx \tag{9.1.12}$$

It is convenient at this point to consider the case when the loading per unit length $p(x,t)$ is separable in the form

$$p(x,t) = \frac{P_0}{l}p(x)f(t) \tag{9.1.13}$$

Equation (9.1.12) then reduces to

$$\ddot{q}_i + \omega_i^2 q_i = \frac{P_0}{M_i}\Gamma_i f(t) \tag{9.1.14}$$

where

$$\Gamma_i = \frac{1}{l}\int_0^l p(x)\phi_i(x)\,dx \tag{9.1.15}$$

is defined as the *mode participation factor* for mode i. The solution of Eq. (9.1.14) is then

$$\begin{aligned} q_i(t) &= q_i(0)\cos\omega_i t + \frac{1}{\omega_i}\dot{q}_i(0)\sin\omega_i t \\ &+ \left(\frac{P_0\Gamma_i}{M_i\omega_i^2}\right)\omega_i\int_0^t f(\xi)\sin\omega_i(t-\xi)\,d\xi \end{aligned} \tag{9.1.16}$$

Because the ith mode statical deflection [with $\ddot{q}_i(t) = 0$] expanded in terms of $\phi_i(x)$ is $P_0\Gamma_i/M_i\omega_i^2$, the quantity

$$D_i(t) = \omega_i\int_0^t f(\xi)\sin\omega_i(t-\xi)\,d\xi \tag{9.1.17}$$

can be called the *dynamic load factor* for the ith mode.

Example 9.1.1

A simply supported uniform beam of mass M_0 is suddenly loaded by the force shown in Fig. 9.1.2. Determine the equation of motion.

Solution The normal modes of the beam are

$$\phi_n(x) = \sqrt{2}\sin\frac{n\pi x}{l}$$

$$\omega_n = (n\pi)^2\sqrt{EI/M_0 l^3}$$

and the generalized mass is

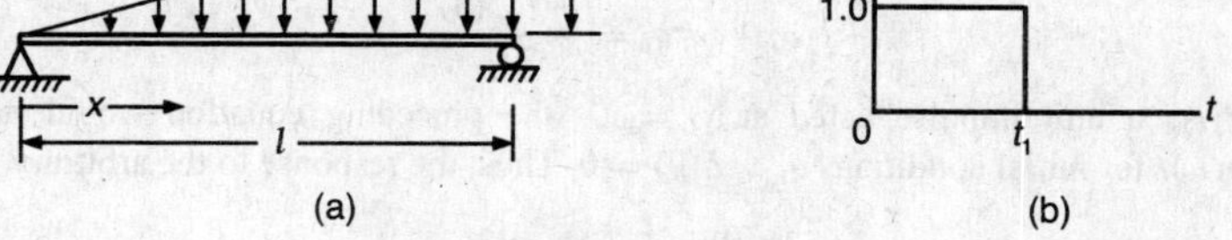

FIGURE 9.1.2.

$$M_n = \frac{M_0}{l}\int_0^l 2\sin^2\frac{n\pi x}{l}\,dx = M_0$$

The generalized force is

$$\int_0^l p(x,t)\phi_n(x)\,dx = g(t)\int_0^l \frac{w_0 x}{l}\sqrt{2}\sin\frac{n\pi x}{l}\,dx$$

$$= g(t)\frac{w_0\sqrt{2}}{l}\left[\frac{\sin(n\pi x/l)}{(n\pi/l)^2} - \frac{x\cos(n\pi x/l)}{n\pi/l}\right]_0^l$$

$$= -g(t)\frac{w_0\sqrt{2}l}{n\pi}\cos n\pi$$

$$= -\frac{\sqrt{2}lw_0}{n\pi}g(t)(-1)^n$$

where $g(t)$ is the time history of the load. The equation for q_n is then

$$\ddot{q}_n + \omega_n^2 q_n = \frac{-\sqrt{2}lw_0}{n\pi M_0}(-1)^n g(t)$$

which has the solution

$$q_n(t) = \frac{-\sqrt{2}lw_0}{n\pi M_0}\frac{(-1)^n}{\omega_n^2}(1-\cos\omega t) \quad 0 \le t \le t_1$$

$$= \frac{-\sqrt{2}lw_0}{n\pi M_0}\frac{(-1)^n}{\omega_n^2}(1-\cos\omega_n t)$$

$$+ \frac{2\sqrt{2}lw_0(-1)^n}{n\pi M_0\omega_n^2}[1-\cos\omega_n(t-t_1)] \quad t_1 \le t \le \infty$$

Thus, the deflection of the beam is expressed by the summation

$$y(x,t) = \sum_{n=1}^{\infty} q_n(t)\sqrt{2}\sin\frac{\pi n x}{l}$$

■

Example 9.1.2

A missile in flight is excited longitudinally by the thrust $F(t)$ of its rocket engine at the end $x = 0$. Determine the equation for the displacement $u(x,t)$ and the acceleration $\ddot{u}(x,t)$.

Solution We assume the solution for the displacement to be

$$u(x,t) = \sum q_i(t)\varphi_i(x)$$

where $\varphi_i(x)$ are normal modes of the missile in longitudinal oscillation. The generalized coordinate q_i satisfies the differential equation

$$\ddot{q}_i + \omega_i^2 q_i = \frac{F(t)\varphi(0)}{M_i}$$

If, instead of $F(t)$, a unit impulse acted at $x = 0$, the preceding equation would have the solution $[\varphi(0)/(M_i\omega_i)]\sin\omega_i t$ for initial conditions $q_i = \dot{q}(0) = 0$. Thus, the response to the arbitrary force $F(t)$ is

$$q_i(t) = \frac{\varphi_i(0)}{M_i\omega_i}\int_0^t F(\xi)\sin\omega_i(t-\xi)\,d\xi$$

and the displacement at any point x is

$$u(x,t) = \sum_i \frac{\varphi_i(x)\varphi_i(0)}{M_i\omega_i} \int_0^t F(\xi) \sin \omega_i(t-\xi)\, d\xi$$

The acceleration $\ddot{q}_i(t)$ of mode i can be determined by rewriting the differential equation and substituting the former solution for $q_i(t)$:

$$\ddot{q}_i(t) = \frac{F(t)\varphi_i(0)}{M_i} - \omega_i^2 q_i(t)$$
$$= \frac{F(t)\varphi_i(0)}{M_i} - \frac{\varphi_i(0)\omega_i}{M_i} \int_0^t F(\xi) \sin \omega_i(t-\xi)\, d\xi$$

Thus, the equation for the acceleration of any point x is found as

$$\ddot{u}(x,t) = \sum_i \ddot{q}_i(t)\varphi_i(x)$$
$$= \sum_i \left[\frac{F(t)\varphi_i(0)\varphi_i(x)}{M_i} - \frac{\varphi_i(0)\varphi_i(x)\omega_i}{M_i} \int_0^t F(\xi) \sin \omega_i(t-\xi)\, d\xi \right]$$

Example 9.1.3

Determine the response of a cantilever beam when its base is given a motion $y_b(t)$ normal to the beam axis, as shown in Fig. 9.1.3.

Solution The differential equation for the beam with base motion is

$$[EIy''(x,t)]'' + m(x)[\ddot{y}_b(t) + \ddot{y}(x,t)] = 0$$

which can be rearranged to

$$[EIy''(x,t)]'' + m(x)\ddot{y}(x,t) = -m(x)\ddot{y}_b(t)$$

Thus, instead of the force per unit length $F(x,t)$ we have the inertial force per unit length $-m(x)\ddot{y}_b(t)$. By assuming the solution in the form

$$y(x,t) = \sum_i q_i(t)\varphi_i(x)$$

the equation for the generalized coordinate q_i becomes

$$\ddot{q}_i + \omega_i^2 q_i = -\ddot{y}_b(t)\frac{1}{M_i}\int_0^l \varphi_i(x)\, dx$$

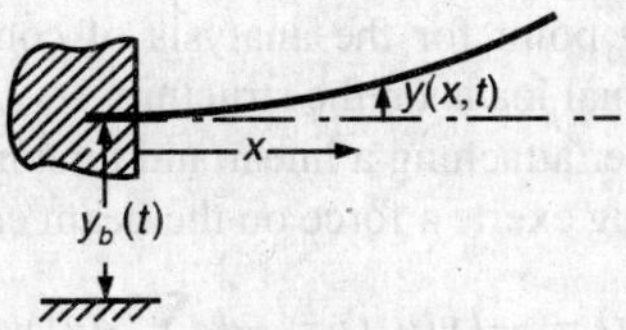

FIGURE 9.1.3.

The solution for q_i then differs from that of a simple oscillator only by the factor $-(1/M_i)\int_0^l \varphi_i(x)\,dx$ so that for the initial conditions $y(0) = \dot{y}(0) = 0$:

$$q_i(t) = \left[-\frac{1}{M_i}\int_0^l \varphi_i(x)\,dx\right]\frac{1}{\omega_i}\int_0^t \ddot{y}_b(\xi)\sin\omega_i(t-\xi)\,d\xi$$

■

9.2 NORMAL MODES OF CONSTRAINED STRUCTURES

When a structure is altered by the addition of a mass or a spring, we refer to it as a *constrained structure*. For example, a spring tends to act as a constraint on the motion of the structure at the point of its application, and possibly increases the natural frequencies of the system. An added mass, on the other hand, can decrease the natural frequencies of the system. Such problems can be formulated in terms of generalized coordinates and the mode-summation technique.

Consider the forced vibration of any one-dimensional structure (i.e., the points on the structure defined by one coordinate x) excited by a force per unit length $f(x,t)$ and moment per unit length $M(x,t)$. If we know the normal modes of the structure, ω_i and $\varphi_i(x)$, its deflection at any point x can be represented by

$$y(x,t) = \sum_i q_i(t)\varphi_i(x) \tag{9.2.1}$$

where the generalized coordinate q_i must satisfy the equation

$$\ddot{q}_i(t) + \omega_i^2 q_i(t) = \frac{1}{M_i}\left[\int f(x,t)\varphi_i(x)\,dx + \int M(x,t)\varphi_i'(x)\,dx\right] \tag{9.2.2}$$

The right side of this equation is $1/M_i$ times the generalized force Q_i, which can be determined from the virtual work of the applied loads as $Q_i = \delta W/\delta q_i$.

If, instead of distributed loads, we have a concentrated force $F(a,t)$ and a concentrated moment $M(a,t)$ at some point $x = a$, the generalized force for such loads is from

$$\begin{aligned}\delta W &= F(a,t)\delta y(a,t) + M(a,t)\delta y'(a,t)\\ &= F(a,t)\sum_i \varphi_i(a)\delta q_i + M(a,t)\sum_i \varphi_i'(a)\delta q_i\end{aligned} \tag{9.2.3}$$

$$Q_i = \frac{\delta W}{\delta q_i} + F(a,t)\varphi_i(a) + M(a,t)\varphi_i'(a)$$

Then, instead of Eq. (9.1.14), we obtain the equation

$$\ddot{q}_i(t) + \omega_i^2 q_i(t) = \frac{1}{M_i}[F(a,t)\varphi_i(a) + M(a,t)\varphi_i'(a)] \tag{9.2.4}$$

These equations form the starting point for the analysis of constrained structures, provided the constraints are expressible as external loads on the structure.

As an example, let us consider attaching a linear and torsional spring to the simply supported beam of Fig. 9.2.1. The linear spring exerts a force on the beam equal to

$$F(a,t) = -ky(a,t) = -k\sum_j q_j(t)\varphi_j(a) \tag{9.2.5}$$

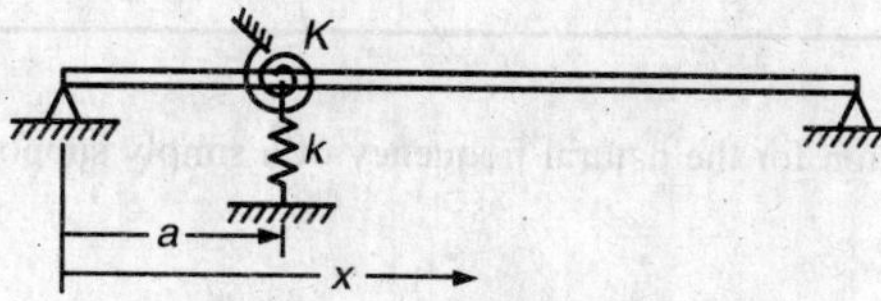

FIGURE 9.2.1.

whereas the torsional spring exerts a moment

$$M(a,t) = -Ky'(a,t) = -K\sum_j q_j(t)\varphi_j'(a) \tag{9.2.6}$$

Substituting these equations into Eq. (9.2.4), we obtain

$$\ddot{q}_i + \omega_i^2 q_i = \frac{1}{M_i}\left[-k\varphi_i(a)\sum_j q_j\varphi_j(a) - K\varphi_i'(a)\sum_j q_j\varphi_j'(a)\right] \tag{9.2.7}$$

The normal modes of the constrained modes are also harmonic and so we can write

$$q_i = \overline{q_i}^{e^{i\omega t}}$$

The solution to the ith equation is then

$$\overline{q}_i = \frac{1}{M_i(\omega_i^2 - \omega^2)}\left[-k\varphi_i(a)\sum_j \overline{q}_j\varphi_j(a) - K\varphi_i'(a)\sum_j \overline{q}_j\varphi_j'(a)\right] \tag{9.2.8}$$

If we use n modes, there will be n values of $\overline{q}_j$ and n equations such as the preceding one. The determinant formed by the coefficients of the $\overline{q}_j$ will then lead to the natural frequencies of the constrained modes, and the mode shapes of the constrained structure are found by substituting the $\overline{q}_j$ into Eq. (9.2.1).

If, instead of springs, a mass m_0 is placed at a point $x = a$, as shown in Fig. 9.2.2, the force exerted by m_0 on the beam is

$$F(a,t) = -m_0\ddot{y}(a,t) = -m_0\sum_j \ddot{q}_j\varphi_j(a) \tag{9.2.9}$$

Thus, in place of Eq. (9.2.8), we obtain the equation

$$\overline{q}_i = \frac{1}{M_i(\omega_i^2 - \omega^2)}\left[\omega^2 m_0\varphi_i(a)\sum_j \overline{q}_j\varphi_j(a)\right] \tag{9.2.10}$$

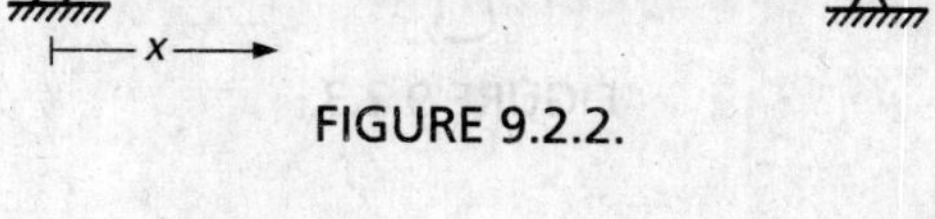

FIGURE 9.2.2.

Example 9.2.1

Give a single-mode approximation for the natural frequency of a simply supported beam when a mass m_0 is attached to it at $x = l/3$.

Solution When only a single mode is used, Eq. (9.2.10) reduces to

$$M_1(\omega_1^2 - \omega^2) = \omega^2 m_0 \varphi_1^2(a)$$

Solving for ω^2, we obtain

$$\left(\frac{\omega}{\omega_1}\right)^2 = \frac{1}{1 + \dfrac{m_0}{M_1}\varphi_1^2(a)}$$

For the first mode of the unconstrained beam, we have

$$\omega_1 = \pi^2\sqrt{\frac{EI}{Ml^3}}, \qquad \varphi_1(x) = \sqrt{2}\sin\frac{\pi x}{l}$$

$$\varphi_1\left(\frac{l}{3}\right) = \sqrt{2}\sin\frac{\pi}{3} = \sqrt{2}\times 0.866$$

$$M_1 = M = \text{mass of the beam}$$

Thus, its substitution into the preceding equation gives the value for the one-mode approximation for the constrained beam of

$$\left(\frac{\omega}{\omega_1}\right)^2 = \frac{1}{1 + 1.5\dfrac{m_0}{M}}$$

■

Example 9.2.2

A missile is constrained in a test stand by linear and torsional springs, as shown in Fig. 9.2.3. Formulate the inverse problem of determining its free-free modes from the normal modes of the constrained missile, which are designated as and Φ_i and Ω_i.

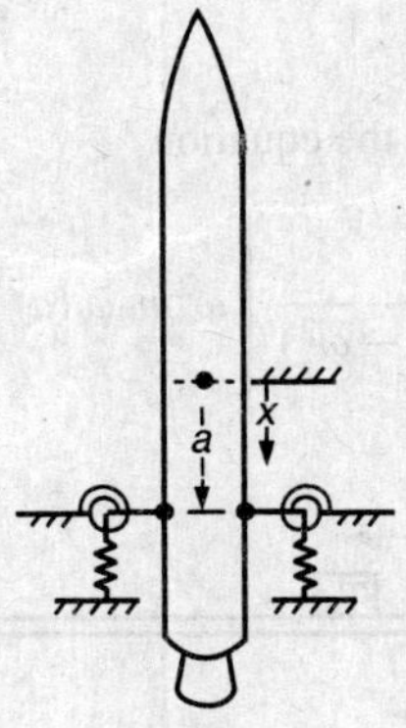

FIGURE 9.2.3.

Solution The problem is approached in a manner similar to that of the direct problem in which, in place of φ_i and ω_i, we use Φ_i and Ω_i. We now relieve the constraints at the supports by introducing opposing forces $-F(a)$ and $-M(a)$ equal to $ky(a)$ and $Ky'(a)$.

To carry out this problem in greater detail, we start with the equation

$$\bar{q}_i = \frac{-F(a)\Phi_i(a) - M(a)\Phi_i'(a)}{M_i\Omega_i^2[1-(\Omega/\Omega_i)^2]}$$

which replaces Eq. (9.2.8). Letting $D_i(\omega) = M_i\Omega_i^2[1-(\omega/\Omega_i)^2]$, the displacement at $x = a$ is

$$y(a) = \sum_i \Phi_i(a)\bar{q}_i = \sum_i \frac{-F(a)\Phi_i^2(a) - M(a)\Phi_i'(a)\Phi_i(a)}{D_i(\omega)}$$

We now replace $-F(a)$ and $-M(a)$ with $ky(a)$ and $Ky'(a)$ and write

$$y(a) = \sum_i \frac{ky(a)\Phi_i^2(a) + Ky'(a)\Phi_i'(a)\Phi_i(a)}{D_i(\omega)}$$

$$y'(a) = \sum_i \frac{ky(a)\Phi_i'(a)\Phi_i(a) + Ky'(a)\Phi_i'^2(a)}{D_i(\omega)}$$

These equations can now be rearranged as

$$y(a)\left[1 - k\sum_i \frac{\Phi_i^2(a)}{D_i(\omega)}\right] = y'(a)K\sum_i \frac{\Phi_i'(a)\Phi_i(a)}{D_i(\omega)}$$

$$y(a)k\sum_i \frac{\Phi_i'(a)\Phi_i(a)}{D_i(\omega)} = y'(a)\left[1 - K\sum_i \frac{\Phi_i'^2(a)}{D_i(\omega)}\right]$$

The frequency equation then becomes

$$\left[1 - k\sum_i \frac{\Phi_i^2(a)}{D_i(\omega)}\right]\left[1 - K\sum_i \frac{\Phi_i'^2(a)}{D_i(\omega)}\right] - kK\left[\sum_i \frac{\Phi_i'(a)\Phi_i(a)}{D_i(\omega)}\right]^2 = 0$$

The slope-to-deflection ratio at $x = a$ is

$$\frac{y'(a)}{y(a)} = \frac{1 - k\sum_i \frac{\Phi_i^2(a)}{D_i(\omega)}}{K\sum_i \frac{\Phi_i'(a)\Phi_i(a)}{D_i(\omega)}}$$

The free-free mode shape is then given by

$$\frac{y(x)}{y(a)} = \sum_i \frac{k\Phi_i(a)\Phi_i(x) + K\frac{y'(a)}{y(a)}\Phi_i'(a)\Phi_i(x)}{D_i(\omega)}$$

■

Example 9.2.3

Determine the constrained modes of the missile of Fig. 9.2.3, using only the first free-free mode $\phi_1(x), \omega_1$, together with translation $\phi_T = 1, \Omega_T = 0$ and rotation $\varphi_R = x, \Omega_R = 0$, where x is measured positively toward the tail of the missile.

Solution The generalized mass for each of the three modes is

$$M_T = \int dm = M$$

$$M_R = \int x^2 dm = I = M\rho^2$$

$$M_1 = \int \varphi_1^2 \, dm = M$$

where the $\rho_1(x)$ mode was normalized such that $M_1 = M$ = actual mass.

The frequency dependent factors D_i are

$$D_T = -M_T\omega^2 = -M\omega^2 = -M\omega_1^2\lambda$$

$$D_R = -M\rho^2\omega^2 = -M\rho^2\omega_1^2\lambda$$

$$D_1 = M\omega_1^2\left[1 - \left(\frac{\omega}{\omega_1}\right)^2\right] = M\omega_1^2(1-\lambda)$$

$$\left(\frac{\omega}{\omega_1}\right)^2 = \lambda$$

The frequency equation for this problem is the same as that of Example 9.2.2, except that the minus k's are replaced by positive k's and $\varphi(x)$ and ω replace $\Phi(x)$ and Ω. Substituting the previous quantities into the frequency equation, we have

$$\left\{1 - \frac{k}{M\omega_1^2}\left[\frac{1}{\lambda} + \frac{a^2}{\rho^2\lambda} - \frac{\varphi_1^2(a)}{1-\lambda}\right]\right\}\left\{1 - \frac{K}{M\omega_1^2}\left[\frac{1}{\rho^2\lambda} - \frac{\varphi_1'^2(a)}{1-\lambda}\right]\right\}$$

$$-\frac{kK}{M^2\omega_1^4}\left\{\frac{-a}{\rho^2\lambda} + \frac{\varphi_1'(a)\varphi_1(a)}{1-\lambda}\right\}^2 = 0$$

which can be simplified to

$$\lambda^2(1-\lambda) + \left(\frac{k}{M\omega_1^2}\right)\left[\varphi_1^2(a) + \frac{K}{k}\varphi_1'^2(a)\right]\lambda^2$$

$$-\left(\frac{k}{M\omega_1^2}\right)\left(1 + \frac{a^2}{\rho^2} + \frac{K}{k\rho^2}\right)\lambda(1-\lambda) + \left(\frac{k}{M\omega_1^2}\right)^2\frac{K}{k\rho^2}(1-\lambda)$$

$$-\left(\frac{k}{M\omega_1^2}\right)^2\frac{K}{k}\lambda\left\{\varphi_1'^2(a) + \frac{1}{\rho^2}[\varphi_1(a) - a\varphi_1'(a)]^2\right\} = 0$$

A number of special cases of the preceding equation are of interest, and we mention one of these. If $K = 0$, the frequency equation simplifies to

$$\lambda^2 - \left\{1 + \left(\frac{k}{M\omega_1^2}\right)\left[1 + \frac{a^2}{\rho^2} + \varphi_1^2(a)\right]\right\}\lambda + \left(\frac{k}{M\omega_1^2}\right)\left(1 + \frac{a^2}{\rho^2}\right) = 0$$

Here $x = a$ might be taken negatively so that the missile is hanging by a spring. ■

9.3 MODE-ACCELERATION METHOD

One of the difficulties encountered in any mode-summation method has to do with the convergence of the procedure. If this convergence is poor, a large number of modes must be used, thereby increasing the order of the frequency determinant. The mode-acceleration method tends to overcome this difficulty by improving the convergence so that a fewer number of normal modes is needed.

The mode-acceleration method starts with the same differential equation for the generalized coordinate q_i but rearranged in order. For example, we can start with Eq. (9.2.4) and write it in the order

$$q_i(t) = \frac{F(a,t)\varphi_i(a)}{M_i\omega_i^2} + \frac{M(a,t)\varphi_i'(a)}{M_i\omega_i^2} - \frac{\ddot{q}_i(t)}{\omega_i^2} \tag{9.3.1}$$

Substituting this into Eq. (9.2.1), we obtain

$$\begin{aligned} y(x,t) &= \sum_i q_i(t)\varphi_i(x) \\ &= F(a,t)\sum_i \frac{\varphi_i(a)\varphi_i(x)}{M_i\omega_i^2} + M(a,t)\sum_i \frac{\varphi_i'(a)\varphi_i(x)}{M_i\omega_i^2} \\ &\quad - \sum_i \frac{\ddot{q}_i(t)\varphi_i(x)}{\omega_i^2} \end{aligned} \tag{9.3.2}$$

We note here that if $F(a,t)$ and $M(a,t)$ were static loads, the last term containing the acceleration would be zero. Thus, the terms

$$\begin{aligned} \sum_i \frac{\varphi_i(a)\varphi_i(x)}{M_i\omega_i^2} &= \alpha(a,x) \\ \sum \frac{\varphi_i'(a)\varphi_i(x)}{M_i\omega_i^2} &= \beta(a,x) \end{aligned} \tag{9.3.3}$$

must represent influence functions, where $\alpha(a,x)$ and $\beta(a,x)$ are the deflections at x due to a unit load and unit moment at a, respectively. We can, therefore, rewrite Eq. (9.3.2) as

$$y(x,t) = F(a,t)\alpha(a,x) + M(a,t)\beta(a,x) - \sum \frac{\ddot{q}(t)\varphi_i(x)}{\omega_i^2} \tag{9.3.4}$$

Because of ω_i^2 in the denominator of the terms summed, the convergence is improved over the mode-summation method.

In the forced-vibration problem in which $F(a,t)$ and $M(a,t)$ are excitations, Eq. (9.2.4) is first solved for $q_i(t)$ in the conventional manner, and then substituted into Eq. (9.3.4) for the deflection. For the normal modes of constrained structures, $F(a,t)$ and $M(a,t)$ are again the forces and moments exerted by the constraints, and the problem is treated in a manner similar to those of Sec. 9.2. However, because of the improved convergence, fewer number of modes will be found to be necessary.

Example 9.3.1

Using the mode-acceleration method, solve the problem of Fig. 9.2.2 of a concentrated mass m_0 attached to the structure.

Solution By assuming harmonic oscillations.

$$F(a,t) = \overline{F}(a)e^{i\omega t}$$
$$q_i(t) = \overline{q}_i e^{i\omega t}$$
$$y(x,t) = y(x)e^{i\omega t}$$

By substituting these equations into Eq. (9.3.4) and letting $x = a$,

$$\overline{y}(a) = \overline{F}(a)\alpha(a,a) + \omega^2 \sum_j \frac{\overline{q}_j \varphi_j(a)}{\omega_j^2}$$

Because the force exerted by m_0 on the structure is

$$\overline{F}(a) = m_0 \omega^2 \overline{y}(a)$$

we can eliminate $\overline{y}(a)$ between the previous two equations, obtaining

$$\frac{\overline{F}(a)}{m_0\omega^2} = \overline{F}(a)x(a,a) + \omega^2 \sum_j \frac{\overline{q}_j \varphi_j(a)}{\omega_j^2}$$

or

$$\overline{F}(a) = \frac{\omega^2 \sum_j \frac{\overline{q}_j \varphi_j(a)}{\omega_j^2}}{\frac{1}{m_0\omega^2} - \alpha(a,a)}$$

If we now substitute this equation into Eq. (9.2.4) and assume harmonic motion, we obtain the equation

$$(\omega_i^2 - \omega^2)\overline{q}_i = \frac{\overline{F}(a)\varphi_i(a)}{M_i} = \frac{\omega^2 \varphi_i(a) \sum_j \overline{q}_j \frac{\varphi_j(a)}{\omega_j^2}}{M_i \left[\frac{1}{m_0\omega^2} - \alpha(a,a)\right]}$$

Rearranging, we have

$$[1 - m_0\omega^2 \alpha(a,a)](\omega_i^2 - \omega^2)\overline{q_i} = \frac{\omega^4 m_0 \varphi_i(a)}{M_i} \sum_j \frac{q_i \varphi_j(a)}{\omega_j^2}$$

which represents a set of linear equations in $\overline{q}_k$. The series represented by the summation will, however, converge rapidly because of ω_j^2 in the denominator. Offsetting this advantage of smaller number modes is the disadvantage that these equations are now quartic rather than quadratic in ω.

■

9.4 COMPONENT-MODE SYNTHESIS

We discuss here another mode-summation procedure, in which the deflection of each structural subcomponent is represented by the sum of the polynomials instead of normal modes. These mode functions themselves need not be orthogonal or satisfy the junction conditions of displacement and force as long as their combined sum allows these conditions to be satisfied. Lagrange's equation, and in particular the method of superfluous coordinates, forms the basis for the synthesis process.

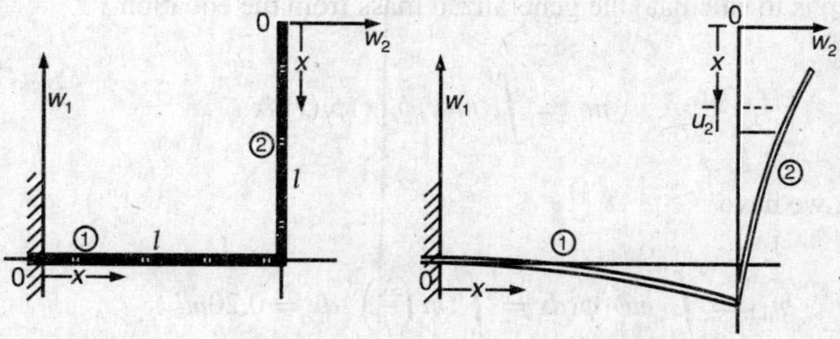

FIGURE 9.4.1. Beam sections 1 and 2 with their coordinates.

To present the basic ideas of the method of modal synthesis, we consider a simple beam with a 90° bend, an example that was used by W. Hurty.[1] The beam, shown in Fig. 9.4.1, is considered to vibrate only in the plane of the paper.

We separate the beam into two sections, ① and ②, whose coordinates are shown as w_1, x; w_2, x; and u_2, x. For Part ①, assume the deflection to be

$$\begin{aligned} w_1(x,t) &= \phi_1(x)p_1(t) + \phi_2(x)p_2(t) + \cdots \\ &= \left(\frac{x}{l}\right)^2 p_1 + \left(\frac{x}{l}\right)^3 p_2 \end{aligned} \tag{9.4.1}$$

Note that the two mode functions satisfy the geometric and force conditions at the boundaries of section ① as follows:

$$\begin{aligned} &w_1 = (0) && w_1(l) = p_1 + p_2 \\ &w_1'(0) = 0 && w_1'(l) = \frac{2}{l}p_1 + \frac{3}{l}p_3 \\ &w_1''(0) = \frac{M(0)}{EI} = \frac{2}{l^2}p_1 && w_1''(l) = \frac{M(l)}{EI} = \frac{2}{l^2}p_1 + \frac{6}{l^2}p_2 \\ &w_1'''(0) = \frac{V(0)}{EI} = \frac{6}{l^3}p_2 && w_1'''(l) = \frac{V(l)}{EI} = \frac{6}{l^3}p_2 \end{aligned} \tag{9.4.2}$$

Next consider part ② with the origin of the coordinates w_2, x at the free end. The following functions satisfy the boundary conditions of beam section ②:

$$\begin{aligned} w_2(x,t) &= \phi_3(x)p_3(t) + \phi_4(x)p_4(t) + \phi_5(x)p_5(t) + \cdots \\ &= 1p_3 + \left(\frac{x}{l}\right)p_4 + \left(\frac{x}{l}\right)^4 p_5 \end{aligned} \tag{9.4.3}$$

$$\begin{aligned} u_2(x,t) &= \phi_6(x)p_6(t) + \cdots \\ &= 1p_6 \end{aligned} \tag{9.4.4}$$

where $u_2(x,t)$ is the displacement in the x-direction.

The next step is to calculate the generalized mass from the equation

$$m_{ij} = \int_0^l m(x)\phi_i(x)\phi_j(x)dx$$

For subsection ①, we have

$$m_{11} = \int_0^l m\phi_1\phi_1 dx = \int_0^l m\left(\frac{x}{l}\right)^4 dx = 0.20ml$$

$$m_{12} = \int_0^l m\phi_1\phi_2 dx = \int_0^l m\left(\frac{x}{l}\right)^5 dx = 0.166ml = m_{21}$$

$$m_{22} = \int_0^l m\phi_2\phi_2 dx = \int_0^l m\left(\frac{x}{l}\right)^6 dx = 0.1428ml$$

The generalized mass for subsection ② is computed in a similar manner using ϕ_3 to ϕ_6:

$$m_{33} = 1.0ml$$

$$m_{34} = 0.50ml = m_{43}$$

$$m_{35} = 0.20ml = m_{53}$$

$$m_{44} = 0.333ml$$

$$m_{45} = 0.166ml = m_{54}$$

$$m_{55} = 0.111ml$$

$$m_{66} = 1.0ml$$

Because there is no coupling between the longitudinal displacement u_2 and the lateral displacement $w_2, m_{63} = m_{64} = m_{65} = 0$.

The generalized stiffness is found from the equation

$$k_{ij} = \int_0^l EI\phi_i''\phi_j'' dx$$

Thus,

$$k_{11} = EI\int_0^l \phi_1''\phi_1'' dx = EI\int_0^l \left(\frac{2}{l^2}\right)^2 dx = 4\frac{EI}{l^3}$$

$$k_{12} = k_{21} = EI\int_0^l \left(\frac{2}{l^2}\right)\left(\frac{6x}{l^3}\right) dx = 6\frac{EI}{l^3}$$

$$k_{22} = 12\frac{EI}{l^3}$$

$$k_{55} = 28.8\frac{EI}{l^3}$$

All other k_{ij} are zero.

The results computed for m_{ij} and k_{ij} can now be arranged in the mass and stiffness matrices partitioned as follows:

$$[m] = ml \left[\begin{array}{cc:ccc:c} 0.2000 & 0.1666 & 0 & 0 & 0 & 0 \\ 0.1666 & 0.1428 & 0 & 0 & 0 & 0 \\ \hdashline 0 & 0 & 1.0000 & 0.5000 & 0.2000 & 0 \\ 0 & 0 & 0.5000 & 0.3333 & 0.1666 & 0 \\ 0 & 0 & 0.2000 & 0.1666 & 0.1111 & 0 \\ \hdashline 0 & 0 & 0 & 0 & 0 & 1.0000 \end{array}\right] \tag{9.4.5}$$

$$[k] = \frac{EI}{l^3} \left[\begin{array}{cc:ccc:c} 4 & 6 & 0 & 0 & 0 & 0 \\ 6 & 12 & 0 & 0 & 0 & 0 \\ \hdashline 0 & 0 & 0 & 0 & 0 & 0 \\ 0 & 0 & 0 & 0 & 0 & 0 \\ 0 & 0 & 0 & 0 & 28.8 & 0 \\ \hdashline 0 & 0 & 0 & 0 & 0 & 0 \end{array}\right] \tag{9.4.6}$$

where the upper left matrix refers to section ① and the remainder to section ②.

At the junction between sections ① and ②, we have the following constraint equations:

$$w_1(l) + u_2(l) = 0 \qquad \text{or} \qquad p_1 + p_2 + p_6 = 0$$

$$w_2(l) = 0 \qquad\qquad p_3 + p_4 + p_5 = 0$$

$$w_1'(l) - w_2'(l) = 0 \qquad\qquad 2p_1 + 3p_2 - p_4 - 4p_5 = 0$$

$$EI[w_1''(l) + w_2''(l)] = 0 \qquad\qquad 2p_1 + 6p_2 + 12p_5 = 0$$

Arranged in matrix form, these are

$$\begin{bmatrix} 1 & 1 & 0 & 0 & 0 & 1 \\ 0 & 0 & 1 & 1 & 1 & 0 \\ 2 & 3 & 0 & -1 & -4 & 0 \\ 2 & 6 & 0 & 0 & 12 & 0 \end{bmatrix} \begin{Bmatrix} p_1 \\ p_2 \\ p_3 \\ p_4 \\ p_5 \\ p_6 \end{Bmatrix} = 0 \tag{9.4.7}$$

Because the total number of coordinates used is 6 and there are four constraint equations, the number of generalized coordinates for the system is 2 (i.e., there are four superfluous coordinates corresponding to the four constraint equations; see Sec. 6.3). We can thus choose any two of the coordinates to be the generalized coordinates q. Let $p_1 = q_1$ and $p_6 = q_6$ be the generalized coordinates and express $p_1, \ldots, p_6$ in terms of q_1 and q_6. This is accomplished in the following steps.

Rearrange Eq. (9.4.7) by shifting columns 1 and 6 to the right side:

$$\begin{bmatrix} 1 & 0 & 0 & 0 \\ 0 & 1 & 1 & 1 \\ 3 & 0 & -1 & -4 \\ 6 & 0 & 0 & 12 \end{bmatrix} \begin{Bmatrix} p_2 \\ p_3 \\ p_4 \\ p_5 \end{Bmatrix} = \begin{bmatrix} -1 & -1 \\ 0 & 0 \\ -2 & 0 \\ -2 & 0 \end{bmatrix} \begin{Bmatrix} q_1 \\ q_6 \end{Bmatrix} \tag{9.4.8}$$

In abbreviated notations, the preceding equation is

$$[s]\{p_{2-5}\} = [Q]\{q_{1,6}\}$$

Premultiply by $[s]^{-1}$ to obtain

$$\{p_{2-5}\} = [s]^{-1}[Q]\{q_{1,6}\}$$

Supply the identity of $p_1 = q_1$ and $p_6 = q_6$ as follows:

$$\{p_{1-6}\} = [C]\{q_{1,6}\}$$

This constraint equation is now in terms of the generalized coordinates q_1 and q_6 as follows:

$$\begin{Bmatrix} p_1 \\ p_2 \\ p_3 \\ p_4 \\ p_5 \\ p_6 \end{Bmatrix} = \begin{bmatrix} 1 & 0 \\ -1 & -1 \\ 2 & 4.50 \\ -2.333 & -5.0 \\ 0.333 & 0.50 \\ 0 & 1 \end{bmatrix} \begin{Bmatrix} q_1 \\ q_6 \end{Bmatrix} = [C] \begin{Bmatrix} q_1 \\ q_6 \end{Bmatrix} \tag{9.4.9}$$

Returning to the Lagrange equation for the system, which is

$$ml[m]\{\ddot{p}\} + \frac{EI}{l^3}[k]\{p\} = 0 \tag{9.4.10}$$

substitute for $\{p\}$ in terms of $\{q\}$ from the constraint equation (9.4.9)

$$ml[m][C]\{\ddot{q}\} + \frac{EI}{l^3}[k][C]\{q\} = 0$$

Premultiply by the transpose $[C]'$:

$$ml[C]'[m][C]\{\ddot{q}\} + \frac{EI}{l^3}[C]'[k][C]\{q\} = 0 \tag{9.4.11}$$

Comparing Eqs. (9.4.10) and (9.4.11), we note that in Eq. (9.4.10), the mass and stiffness matrices are 6×6 [see Eqs. (9.4.5) and (9.4.6)], whereas the matrices $[C]'[m][C]$ and $[C]'[k][C]$ in Eq. (9.4.11) are 2×2. Thus, we have reduced the size of the system from a 6×6 to a 2×2 problem.

By letting $\{\ddot{q}\} = -\omega^2\{q\}$, Eq. (9.4.11) is in the form

$$\left[\omega^2 ml \begin{bmatrix} a_{11} & a_{12} \\ a_{21} & a_{22} \end{bmatrix} + \frac{EI}{l^3} \begin{bmatrix} b_{11} & b_{12} \\ b_{21} & b_{22} \end{bmatrix}\right] \begin{Bmatrix} q_1 \\ q_6 \end{Bmatrix} = 0 \tag{9.4.12}$$

The numerical values of the matrix $[a_{ij}]$ and $[b_{ij}]$ from Eqs. (9.4.5), (9.4.6), and (9.4.9) are

$$A = [a_{ij}] = [C]'[m][C] = \begin{bmatrix} 1.1774 & 2.6614 \\ 2.6614 & 7.3206 \end{bmatrix}$$

$$B = [b_{ij}] = [C]'[k][C] = \begin{bmatrix} 7.200 & 10.800 \\ 10.800 & 19.200 \end{bmatrix}$$

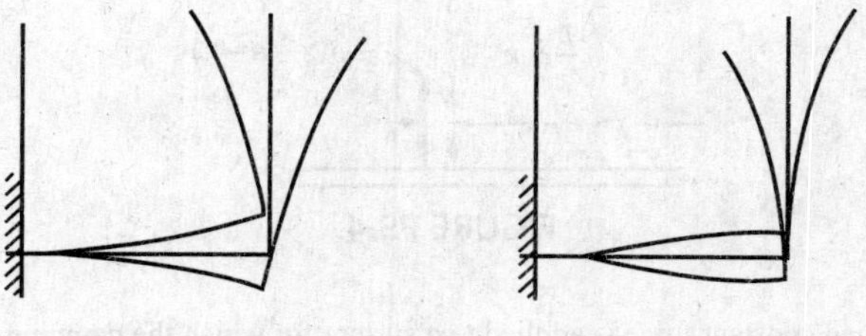

FIGURE 9.4.2. First and second mode shapes.

By using MATLAB®, we find the two natural frequencies of the system from Eq. (9.4.12). This is done by first computing the dynamic matrix, which is given by $D = A^{-1} * B$. Then the square root of the eigenvalues of D are computed which results in the following

$$\omega_1 = 1.172\sqrt{\frac{EI}{ml^4}}$$

$$\omega_2 = 3.198\sqrt{\frac{EI}{Ml^4}}$$

Figure 9.4.2 shows the mode shapes corresponding to these frequencies. Since Eq. (9.4.12) enables the solution of the eigenvectors only in terms of an arbitrary reference, q_6 can be solved with $q_1 = 1.0$. The coordinates p are then found from Eq. (9.4.9), and the mode shapes are obtained from Eqs. (9.4.1), (9.4.3), and (9.4.4).

REFERENCE

[1] WALTER C. HURTY, "Vibrations of Structural Systems by Component Synthesis," *J. Eng. Mech. Div., Proc. ASCE* (August 1960) pp. 51–69.

PROBLEMS

9.1. Determine the mode participation factor for a uniformly distributed force.

9.2. Show that the dynamic load factor for a suddenly applied force reaches a maximum value of 2.0.

9.3. If a concentrated force acts at $x = a$, the loading per unit length corresponding to it can be represented by a delta function $l\delta(x - a)$. Show that the mode-participation factor then becomes $K_i = \varphi_i(a)$ and the deflection is expressible as

$$y(x,t) = \frac{P_0 l^3}{EI} \sum_i \frac{\varphi_i(a)\varphi_i(x)}{(\beta_i l)^4} D_i(t)$$

where $\omega_i^2 = (\beta_i l)^4 (EI/Ml^3)$ and $(\beta_i l)$ is the eigenvalue of the normal mode equation.

9.4. For a couple of moment M_0 acting at $x = a$, show that the loading $p(x)$ is the limiting case of two delta functions shown in Fig. P9.4 as $\epsilon \to 0$. Show also that the mode-participation factor for this case is

$$K_i = l\frac{d\varphi_i(x)}{dx}\bigg|_{x=a} = (\beta_i l)\varphi_i'(x)_{x=a}$$

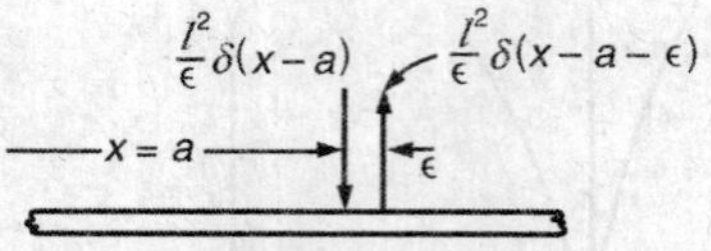

FIGURE P9.4.

9.5. If a suddenly applied constant force is applied to a system for which the damping factor of the ith mode is $\zeta = c/c_{cr}$, show that the dynamic load factor is given approximately by the equation

$$D_i = 1 - e^{-\zeta\omega_i t}\cos\omega_i t$$

9.6. A simply supported uniform beam has suddenly applied to it the load distribution shown in Fig. P9.6, where the time variation is a step function. Determine the response $y(x, t)$ in terms of the normal modes of the beam. Indicate what modes are absent and write down the first two existing modes.

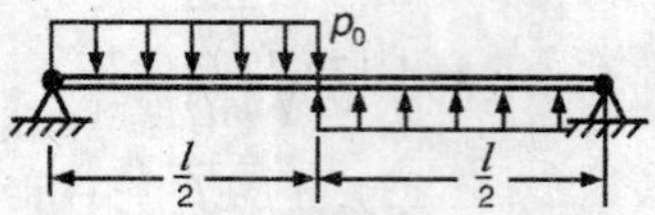

FIGURE P9.6.

9.7. A concentrated force $P_0 f(t)$ is applied to the center of a simply supported uniform beam, as shown in Fig. P9.7. Show that the deflection is given by

$$y(x,t) = \frac{P_0 l^3}{EI}\sum_i \frac{K_i\varphi_i(x)}{(\beta_i l)^4}D_i$$

$$= \frac{2P_0 l^3}{EI}\left[\frac{\sin\left(\pi\frac{x}{l}\right)}{\pi^4}D_1(t) - \frac{\sin\left(3\pi\frac{x}{l}\right)}{(3\pi)^4}D_3(t) + \frac{\sin\left(5\pi\frac{x}{l}\right)}{(5\pi)^4}D_5(t) - \cdots\right]$$

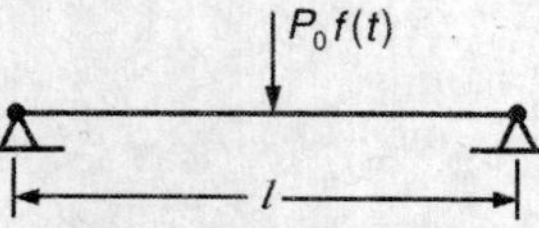

FIGURE P9.7.

FIGURE P9.8.

9.8. A couple of moment M_0 is applied at the center of the beam of Prob. 9.7, as shown in Fig. P9.8. Show that the deflection at any point is given by the equation

$$y(x,t) = \frac{M_0 l^2}{EI}\sum_i \frac{\varphi_i'(a)\varphi_i(x)}{(\beta_i l)^3}D_i(t)$$

$$= \frac{2M_0 l^2}{EI}\left[\frac{\sin\left(2\pi\frac{x}{l}\right)}{(2\pi)^3}D_2(t) + \frac{\sin\left(4\pi\frac{x}{l}\right)}{(4\pi)^3}D_4(t) - \frac{\sin\left(6\pi\frac{x}{l}\right)}{(6\pi)^3}D_6(t) + \cdots\right]$$

9.9. Consider a uniform beam of mass M and length l supported on equal springs of total stiffness k, as shown in Fig. P9.9a. Assume the deflection to be

$$y(x,t) = \varphi_1(x)q_1(t) + \varphi_2(x)q_2(t)$$

and choose $\varphi_1 = \sin(\pi x/l)$ and $\varphi_2 = 1.0$. Using Lagrange's equation, show that

$$\ddot{q}_1 + \frac{4}{\pi}\ddot{q}_2 + \omega_{11}^2 q_1 = 0$$

$$\frac{2}{\pi}\ddot{q}_1 + \ddot{q}_2 + \omega_{22}^2 q_2 = 0$$

where

$$\omega_{11}^2 = \pi^4(EI/Ml^3)$$

= natural frequency of beam on rigid supports

$$\omega_{22}^2 = k/M$$

= natural frequency of rigid beam on springs

Solve these equations and show that

$$\omega^2 = \omega_{22}^2 \frac{\pi^2}{2}\left[\frac{(R+1) \pm \sqrt{(R-1)^2 + \frac{32}{\pi^2}R}}{\pi^2 - 8}\right]$$

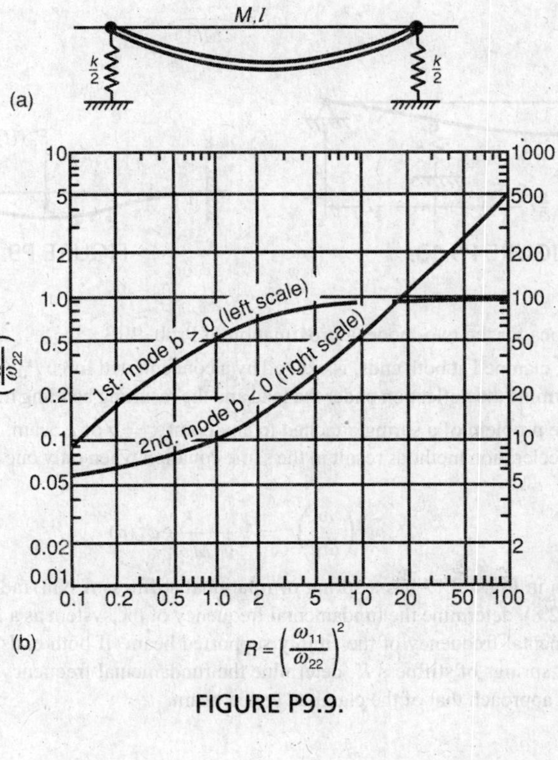

FIGURE P9.9.

Let $y(x,t) = [b + \sin \pi(x/l)]q$ and use Rayleigh's method to obtain

$$\frac{q_2}{q_1} = b = \frac{\pi}{8}\left[(R-1) \mp \sqrt{(R-1)^2 + \frac{32}{\pi^2}R}\right]$$

$$R = \left(\frac{\omega_{11}}{\omega_{22}}\right)^2$$

A plot of the natural frequencies of the system is shown in Fig. P9.9b.

9.10. A slender rod of length l, free at $x = 0$ and fixed at $x = l$, is struck longitudinally by a time-varying force concentrated at the end $x = 0$. Show that all modes are equally excited (i.e., that the mode-participation factor is independent of the mode number), the complete solution being

$$u(x,t) = \frac{2F_0 l}{AE}\left[\frac{\cos\left(\frac{\pi}{2}\frac{x}{l}\right)}{\left(\frac{\pi}{2}\right)^2}D_1(t) + \frac{\cos\left(\frac{3\pi}{2}\frac{x}{l}\right)}{\left(\frac{3\pi}{2}\right)^2}D_3(t) + \cdots\right]$$

9.11. If the force of Prob. 9.10 is concentrated at $x = l/3$, determine which modes will be absent in the solution.

9.12. In Prob. 9.11, determine the participation factor of the modes present and obtain a complete solution for an arbitrary time variation of the applied force.

9.13. A spring of stiffness k is attached to a uniform beam, as shown in Fig. P9.13. Show that the one-mode approximation results in the frequency equation

$$\left(\frac{\omega}{\omega_1}\right)^2 = 1 + 1.5\left(\frac{k}{M}\right)\left(\frac{Ml^3}{\pi^4 EI}\right)$$

where

$$\omega_1^2 = \frac{\pi^4 EI}{Ml^3}$$

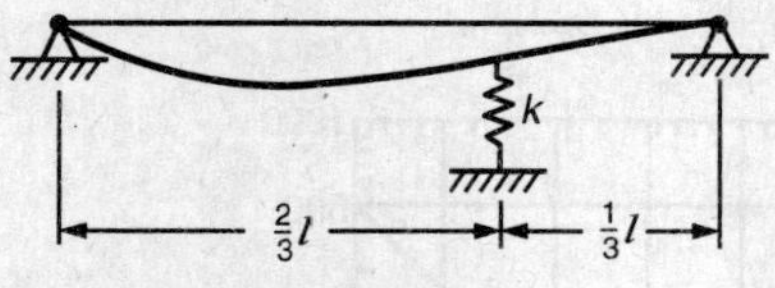

FIGURE P9.13.

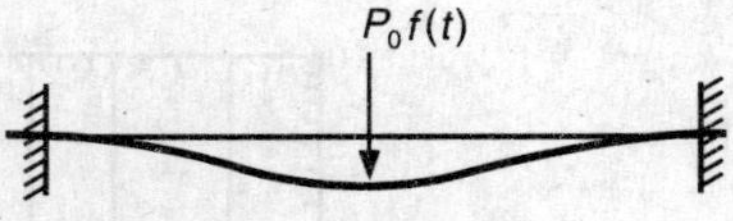

FIGURE P9.15.

9.14. Write the equations for the two-mode approximation of Prob. 9.13.

9.15. A uniform beam, clamped at both ends, is excited by a concentrated force $P_0 f(t)$ at midspan, as shown in Fig. P9.15. Determine the deflection under the load and the resulting bending moment at the clamped ends.

9.16. Show that for the problem of a spring attached to any point $x = a$ of a beam, both the constrained-mode and the mode-acceleration methods result in the same equation when only one mode is used, this equation being

$$\left(\frac{\omega}{\omega_1}\right)^2 = 1 + \frac{k}{M\omega_1^2}\varphi_1^2(a)$$

9.17. The beam shown in Fig. P9.17 has a spring of rotational stiffness K Nm/rad at the left end. Using two modes in Eq. (9.2.8), determine the fundamental frequency of the system as a function of $K/M\omega_1^2$, where ω_1 is the fundamental frequency of the simply supported beam. If both ends of the beam of Fig. P9.17 are restrained by springs of stiffness K, determine the fundamental frequency. As K approaches infinity, the result should approach that of the clamped ended beam.

FIGURE P9.17.

9.18. Repeat Prob. 9.14 using the mode-acceleration method.

9.19. An airplane is idealized to a simplified model of a uniform beam of length l and mass per unit length m with a lumped mass at M_0 at its center, as shown in Fig. P9.19. Using the translation of M_0 as one of the generalized coordinates, write the equations of motion and establish the natural frequency of the symmetric mode. Use the first cantilever mode for the wing. For the system determine the antisymmetric mode by using the rotation of the fuselage as one of the generalized coordinates.

FIGURE P9.19.

9.20. If wing tip tanks of mass M_1 are added to the system of Prob. 9.19, determine the new frequency.

9.21. Using the method of constrained modes, show that the effect of adding a mass m_1 with moment of inertia J_1 to a point x_1 on the structure changes the first natural frequency ω_1 to

$$\omega_1' = \frac{\omega_1}{\sqrt{1 + \frac{m_1}{M_1}\varphi_1^2(x_1) + \frac{J_1}{M_1}\varphi_1'^2(x_1)}}$$

and the generalized mass and damping to

$$M_1' = M_1\left[1 + \frac{m_1\varphi_1^2(x_1)}{M_1} + \frac{J_1}{M_1}\varphi_1'^2(x)\right]$$

$$\zeta_1' = \frac{\zeta_1}{\sqrt{1 + \frac{m_1}{M_1}\varphi_1^2(x_1) + \frac{J_1}{M_1}\varphi_1'^2(x_1)}}$$

where a one-mode approximation is used for the inertia forces.

9.22. Formulate the vibration problem of the frame shown in Fig. P9.22 by the component-mode synthesis. Assume the corners to remain at 90°.

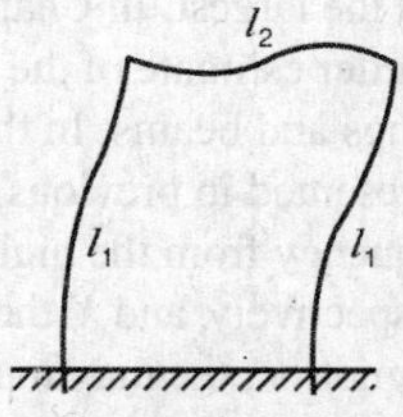

FIGURE P9.22.

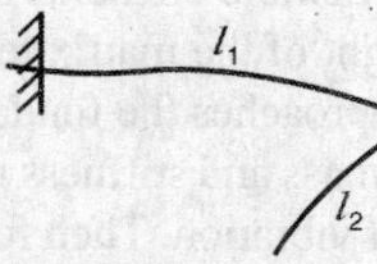

FIGURE P9.23.

9.23. A rod of circular section is bent at right angles in a horizontal plane as shown in Fig. P9.23. Using a component-mode synthesis, set up the equations for the vibration perpendicular to the plane of the rod. Note that member 1 is in flexure and torsion. Assume that it is bending only in the vertical plane.

CHAPTER 10

Classical Methods

The exact analysis for the vibration of systems of many degrees of freedom is generally difficult and its associated calculations are laborious. Even with high-speed digital computers that can solve equations of many DOF, the results beyond the first few normal modes are often unreliable and meaningless. In many cases, all the normal modes of the system are not required, and an estimate of the fundamental and a few of the lower modes is sufficient. For this purpose, Rayleigh's method and Dunkerley's equation are of great value and importance.

In many vibrational systems, we can consider the mass to be lumped. A shaft transmitting torque for several pulleys along its length is an example. Holzer devised a simple procedure for the calculation of the natural frequencies of such a system. Holzer's method was extended to beam vibration by Myklestad and both methods have been matricized into a transfer matrix procedure by Pestel. Many of these procedures were developed in the early years and may be considered as classical methods. They are now routinely processed by digital computer; however, a basic understanding of each of these methods is essential.

10.1 RAYLEIGH METHOD

The fundamental frequency of multi-DOF systems is often of greater interest than its higher natural frequencies because its forced response in many cases is the largest. In Chapter 2, under the energy method, Rayleigh's method was introduced to obtain a better estimate of the fundamental frequency of systems that contained flexible elements such as springs and beams. In this section, we examine the Rayleigh method in light of the matrix techniques presented in previous chapters and show that the Rayleigh frequency approaches the fundamental frequency from the high side.

Let M and K be the mass and stiffness matrices, respectively, and X the assumed displacement vector for the amplitude of vibration. Then for harmonic motion, the maximum kinetic and potential energies can be written as

$$T_{\max} = \frac{1}{2}\omega^2 X^T M X \tag{10.1.1}$$

and

$$U_{\max} = \frac{1}{2} X^T K X \tag{10.1.2}$$

Equating the two and solving for ω^2, we obtain the Rayleigh quotient:

$$\omega^2 = \frac{X^T K X}{X^T M X} \tag{10.1.3}$$

This quotient approaches the lowest natural frequency (or fundamental frequency) from the high side, and its value is somewhat insensitive to the choice of the assumed amplitudes. To show these qualities, we express the assumed displacement curve in terms of the normal modes X_i as follows

$$X = X_1 + C_2 X_2 + C_3 X_3 + \cdots \tag{10.1.4}$$

Then

$$X^T K X = X_1^T K X_1 + C_2^2 X_2^T K X_2 + C_3^2 X_3^T K X_3 + \cdots$$

and

$$X^T M X = X_1^T M X_1 + C_2^2 X_2^T M X_2 + C_3^2 X_3^T M X_3 + \cdots$$

where cross terms of the form $X_i^T K X_j$ and $X_i^T M X_j$ have been eliminated by the orthogonality conditions.

Noting that

$$X_i^T K X_i = \omega_i^2 X_i^T M X_i \tag{10.1.5}$$

the Rayleigh quotient becomes

$$\omega^2 = \omega_1^2 \left[1 + C_2^2 \left(\frac{\omega_2^2}{\omega_1^2} - 1 \right) \frac{X_2^T M X_2}{X_1^T M X_1} + \cdots \right] \tag{10.1.6}$$

If $X_i' M X_i$ is normalized to the same number, this equation reduces to

$$\omega^2 = \omega_1^2 \left[1 + C_2^2 \left(\frac{\omega_2^2}{\omega_1^2} - 1 \right) + \cdots \right] \tag{10.1.7}$$

It is evident, then, that ω^2 is greater than ω_1^2 because $\omega_2^2/\omega_1^2 > 1$. Because C_2 represents the deviation of the assumed amplitudes from the exact amplitudes X_1, the error in the computed frequency is only proportional to the square of the deviation of the assumed amplitudes from their exact values.

This analysis shows that if the exact fundamental deflection (or mode) X_1 is assumed, the fundamental frequency found by this method will be the correct frequency, because C_2, C_3, and so on, will then be zero. For any other curve, the frequency determined will be higher than the fundamental. This fact can be explained on the basis that any deviation from the natural curve requires additional constraints, a condition that implies greater stiffness and higher frequency. In general, the use of the static deflection curve of the elastic body results in a fairly accurate value of the fundamental frequency. If greater accuracy is desired, the approximate curve can be repeatedly improved.

In our previous discussion of the Rayleigh method, the potential energy was determined by the work done by the static weights in the assumed deformation. This work is, of course, stored in the flexible manner as strain energy. For beams, the elastic strain energy can be calculated in terms of its flexural rigidity EI.

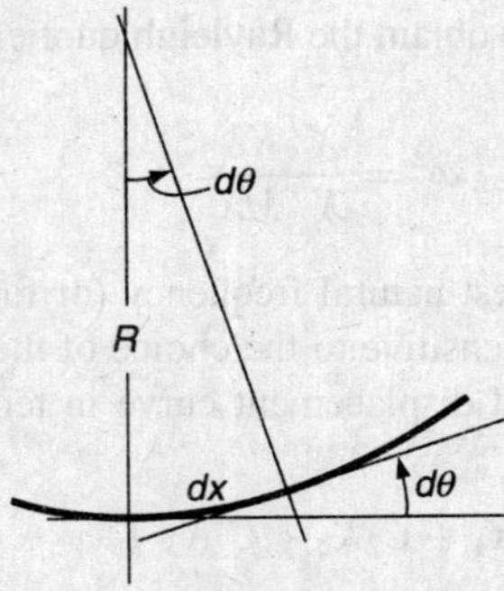

FIGURE 10.1.1.

By letting M be the bending moment and θ the slope of the elastic curve, the strain energy stored in an infinitesimal beam element is

$$dU = \frac{1}{2} M d\theta \tag{10.1.8}$$

Because the deflection in beams is generally small, the following geometric relations are assumed to hold (see Fig. 10.1.1):

$$\theta = \frac{dy}{dx} \quad \frac{1}{R} = \frac{d\theta}{dx} = \frac{d^2y}{dx^2}$$

In addition, we have, from the theory of beams, the flexure equation:

$$\frac{1}{R} = \frac{M}{EI} \tag{10.1.9}$$

where R is the radius of curvature. By substituting for $d\theta$ and $1/R$, U can be written as

$$U_{\max} = \frac{1}{2}\int \frac{M^2}{EI} dx = \frac{1}{2}\int EI \left(\frac{d^2y}{dx^2}\right)^2 dx \tag{10.1.10}$$

where the integration is carried out over the entire beam.

The kinetic energy is simply

$$T_{\max} = \frac{1}{2}\int \dot{y}^2 dm = \frac{1}{2}\omega^2 \int y^2 dm \tag{10.1.11}$$

where y is the assumed deflection curve. Thus, by equating the kinetic and potential energies, an alternative equation for the fundamental frequency of the beam is

$$\omega^2 = \frac{\int EI \left(\dfrac{d^2y}{dx^2}\right)^2 dx}{\int y^2 dm} \tag{10.1.12}$$

Example 10.1.1

In applying this procedure to a simply supported beam of uniform cross section, shown in Fig. 10.1.2, we assume the deflection to be represented by a sine wave as follows:

$$y = \left(y_0 \sin \frac{\pi x}{l}\right) \sin \omega t$$

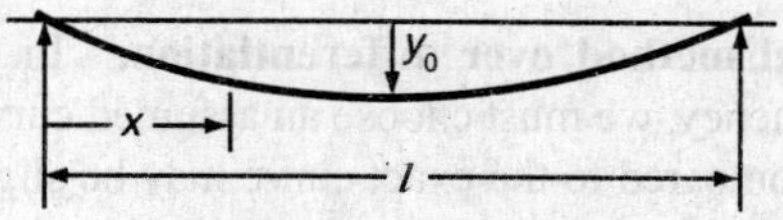

FIGURE 10.1.2.

where y_0 is the maximum deflection at midspan. The second derivative then becomes

$$\frac{d^2y}{dx^2} = -\left(\frac{\pi x}{l}\right)^2 y_0 \sin\frac{\pi x}{l} \sin\omega t$$

Substituting into Eq. (10.1.12), we obtain

$$\omega^2 = \frac{EI\left(\frac{\pi}{l}\right)^4 \int_0^l \sin^2\frac{\pi x}{l}dx}{m\int_0^l \sin^2\frac{\pi x}{l}dx} = \pi^4\frac{EI}{ml^4}$$

The fundamental frequency, therefore, is

$$\omega_1 = \pi^2\sqrt{\frac{EI}{ml^4}}$$

In this case, the assumed curve happened to be the natural vibration curve, and the exact frequency is obtained by Rayleigh's method. Any other curve assumed for the case can be considered to be the result of additional constraints, or stiffness, which result in a constant greater than π^2 in the frequency equation.

■

Example 10.1.2

If the distance between the ends of the beam of Fig. 10.1.2 is rigidly fixed, a tensile stress σ will be developed by the lateral deflection. Account for this additional strain energy in the frequency equation.

Solution Due to the lateral deflection, the length dx of the beam is increased by an amount

$$\left[\sqrt{1+(dy/dx)^2} - 1\right] dx \cong \frac{1}{2}\left(\frac{dy}{dx}\right)^2 dx$$

The additional strain energy in element dx is

$$dU = \frac{1}{2}\sigma A\epsilon\, dx = \frac{1}{2}EA\epsilon^2\, dx$$

where A is the cross-sectional area, σ is the stress due to tension and $\epsilon = \frac{1}{2}(dy/dx)^2$ is the unit strain.

Equating the kinetic energy to the total strain of bending and tension, we obtain

$$\frac{1}{2}\omega^2\int y^2 dm = \frac{1}{2}\int EI\left(\frac{d^2y}{dx^2}\right)^2 dx + \frac{1}{2}\int\frac{EA}{4}\left(\frac{dy}{dx}\right)^4 dx$$

The preceding equation then leads to the frequency equation:

$$\omega_1^2 = \frac{\int EI\left(\frac{d^2y}{dx^2}\right)^2 dx + \int\frac{EA}{4}\left(\frac{dy}{dx}\right)^4 dx}{\int y^2 dm}$$

which contains an additional term due to tension.

■

Accuracy of the integral method over differentiation. In using Rayleigh's method of determing the fundamental frequency, we must choose an assumed curve. Although the deviation of this assumed deflection curve compared to the exact curve may be slight, its derivative could be in error by a large amount and hence the strain energy computed from the equation

$$U = \frac{1}{2}\int EI\left(\frac{d^2y}{dx^2}\right)^2 dx$$

may be inaccurate. To avoid this difficulty, the following integral method for evaluating U is recommended for some beam problems.

We first recognize that the shear V is the integral of the inertia loading $m\omega^2 y$ from the free end of the beam, as indicated by both Figs. 10.1.3 and 10.1.4.

$$V(\xi) = \omega^2 \int_{\xi}^{l} m(\xi)y(\xi)d\xi \tag{10.1.13}$$

Because bending moment is related to the shear by the equation

$$\frac{dM}{dx} = V \tag{10.1.14}$$

the moment at x is found from the integral

$$M(x) = \int_{x}^{l} V(\xi)d\xi \tag{10.1.15}$$

The strain energy of the beam is then found from

$$U = \frac{1}{2}\int_0^l \frac{M(x)^2}{EI} dx \tag{10.1.16}$$

which avoids any differentiation of the assumed deflection curve.

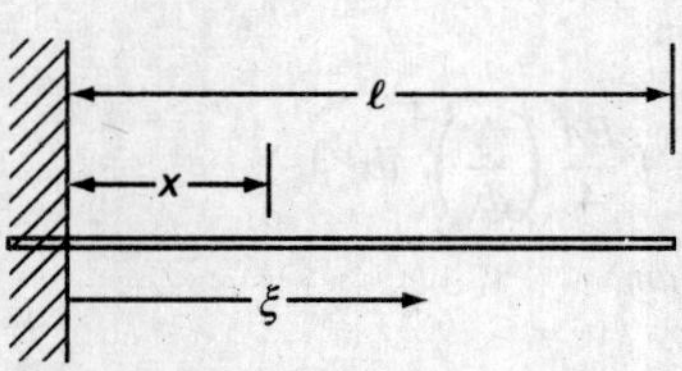

FIGURE 10.1.3.

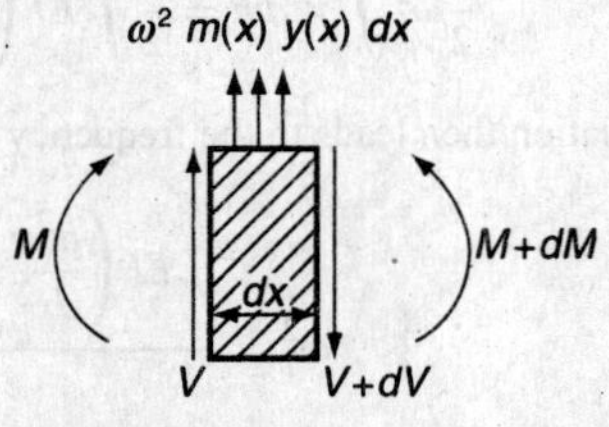

FIGURE 10.1.4. Free-body diagram of the beam element.

Example 10.1.3

Determine the fundamental frequency of the uniform cantilever beam shown in Fig. 10.1.5 using the simple curve $y = cx^2$.

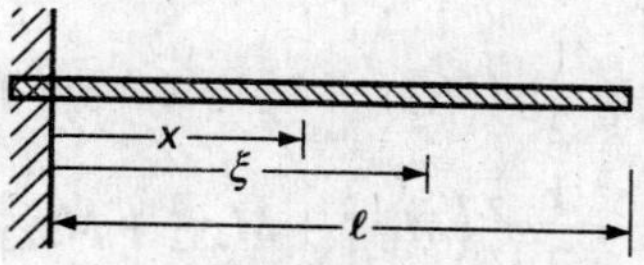

FIGURE 10.1.5.

Solution If we use Eq. (10.1.12), we find the result to be very much in error because the previous curve does not satisfy the boundary conditions at the free end. By using Eq. (10.1.12), we obtain

$$\omega = 4.47\sqrt{\frac{EI}{ml^4}}$$

whereas the exact value is

$$\omega_1 = 3.52\sqrt{\frac{EI}{ml^4}}$$

Acceptable results using the given curve can be found by the procedure outlined in the previous section.

$$V(\xi) = \omega^2 \int_\xi^l mc\xi^2 d\xi = \frac{\omega^2 mc}{3}(l^3 - \xi^3)$$

and the bending moment becomes

$$M(x) = \int_x^l V(\xi)d\xi \frac{\omega^2 mc}{3} \int_x^l (l^3 - \xi^3)d\xi$$

$$= \frac{\omega^2 mc}{12}(3l^4 - 4l^3x + x^4)$$

The maximum strain energy is found by substituting $M(x)$ and $U_{\max}$:

$$U_{\max} = \frac{1}{2EI}\left(\frac{\omega^2 mc}{12}\right)^2 \int_0^l (3l^4 - 4l^3x + x^4)^2 dx$$

$$= \frac{\omega^4}{2EI}\frac{m^2c^2}{144}\frac{312}{135}l^9$$

The maximum kinetic energy is

$$T_{\max} = \frac{1}{2}\int_0^l \dot{y}^2 m\, dx = \frac{1}{2}c^2\omega^2 m \int_0^l x^4 dx = \frac{1}{2}c^2\omega^2 m \frac{l^5}{5}$$

By equating these results, we obtain

$$\omega_1 = \sqrt{\frac{12.47EI}{ml^4}} = 3.53\sqrt{\frac{EI}{ml^4}}$$

which is very close to the exact result. ■

Lumped masses. The Rayleigh method can be used to determine the fundamental frequency of a beam or shaft represented by a series of lumped masses. At a first approximation, we assume a static deflection curve due to loads M_1g, M_2g, M_3g, and so on, with corresponding deflections $y_1, y_2, y_3, \ldots$. The strain energy stored in the beam is determined from the work done by these loads, and the maximum potential and kinetic energies become

$$U_{\max} = \frac{1}{2}g\left(M_1y_1 + M_2y_2 + M_3y_3 + \cdots\right) \tag{10.1.17}$$

$$T_{\max} = \frac{1}{2}\omega^2\left(M_1y_1^2 + M_2y_2^2 + M_3y_3^2 + \cdots\right) \tag{10.1.18}$$

By equating the two, the frequency equation is established as

$$\omega_1^2 = \frac{g\Sigma_i M_i y_i}{\Sigma_i M_i y_i^2} \tag{10.1.19}$$

Example 10.1.4

Calculate the first approximation to the fundamental frequency of lateral vibration for the system shown in Fig. 10.1.6.

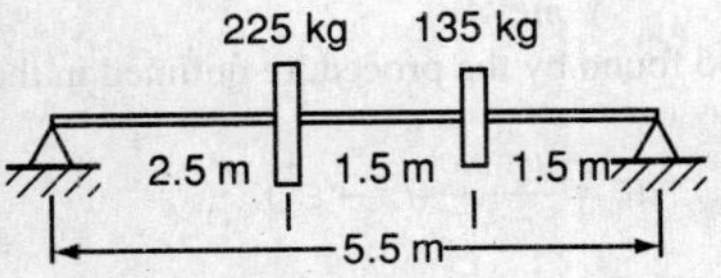

FIGURE 10.1.6.

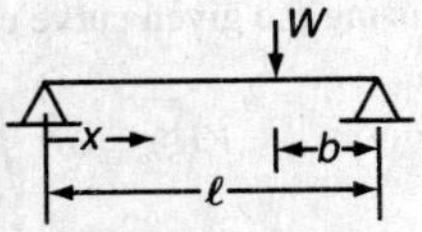

FIGURE 10.1.7.

Solution Referring to the table at the end of Chapter 2, we see that the deflection of the beam at any point x (see Fig. 10.1.7) from the left end due to a single load W at a distance b from the right end is

$$y(x) = \frac{Wbx}{6EIl}(l^2 - x^2 - b^2) \quad x \le (l - b)$$

The deflections at the loads can be obtained from the superposition of the deflections due to each load acting separately.

Due to the 135-kg mass, we have

$$y_1' = \frac{(9.81 \times 135) \times 1.5 \times 2.5}{6 \times 5.5EI}\left[(5.5)^2 - (2.5)^2 - (1.5)^2\right] = 3.273 \times \frac{10^3}{EI}m$$

$$y_2' = \frac{(9.81 \times 135) \times 1.5 \times 4}{6 \times 5.5EI}\left[(5.5)^2 - (4.0)^2 - (1.5)^2\right] = 2.889 \times \frac{10^3}{EI}m$$

Due to the 225-kg mass, the deflection at the corresponding points are

$$y_1'' = \frac{(9.81 \times 225) \times 2.5 \times 3.0}{6 \times 5.5EI}\left[(5.5)^2 - (3.0)^2 - (2.5)^2\right] = 7.524 \times \frac{10^3}{EI}m$$

$$y_2'' = \frac{(9.81 \times 225) \times 2.5 \times 1.5}{6 \times 5.5EI}\left[(5.5)^2 - (1.5)^2 - (2.5)^2\right] = 5.455 \times \frac{10^3}{EI}m$$

By adding y' and y'', the deflections at 1 and 2 become

$$y_1 = 10.797 \times \frac{10^3}{EI} m \quad y_2 = 8.344 \times \frac{10^3}{EI} m$$

By substituting into Eq. (10.1.19), the first approximation to the fundamental frequency is

$$\omega_1 = \sqrt{\frac{9.81(225 \times 10.797 + 135 \times 8.344)EI}{\left[225 \times (10.797)^2 + 135 \times (8.344)^2\right] 10^3}}$$
$$= 0.03129\sqrt{EI} \text{ rad/s}$$

If further accuracy is desired, a better approximation to the dynamic curve can be made by using the dynamic loads $m\omega^2 y$. Because the dynamic loads are proportional to the deflection y, we can recalculate the deflection with the modified loads gm_1 and $gm_2(y_2/y_1)$.

10.2 DUNKERLEY'S EQUATION

The Rayleigh method, which gives the upper bound to the fundamental frequency, can now be complemented by Dunkerley's[1] equation, which results in a lower bound to the fundamental frequency. For the basis of the Dunkerley equation, we examine the characteristic equation formulated from the flexibility coefficients, which is

$$\begin{vmatrix} \left(a_{11}m_1 - \frac{1}{\omega^2}\right) & a_{12}m_2 & a_{13}m_3 \\ a_{21}m_1 & \left(a_{22}m_2 - \frac{1}{\omega^2}\right) & a_{23}m_3 \\ a_{31}m_1 & a_{32}m_2 & \left(a_{33}m_3 - \frac{1}{\omega^2}\right) \end{vmatrix} = 0$$

Expanding this determinant, we obtain the third-degree equation in $1/\omega^2$.

$$\left(\frac{1}{\omega^2}\right)^3 - (a_{11}m_1 + a_{22}m_2 + a_{33}m_3)\left(\frac{1}{\omega^2}\right)^2 + \cdots = 0 \tag{10.2.1}$$

If the roots of this equation are $1/\omega_1^2, 1/\omega_2^2$, and $1/\omega_3^2$, the previous equation can be factored into the following form:

$$\left(\frac{1}{\omega^2} - \frac{1}{\omega_1^2}\right)\left(\frac{1}{\omega^2} - \frac{1}{\omega_2^2}\right)\left(\frac{1}{\omega^2} - \frac{1}{\omega_3^2}\right) = 0$$

or

$$\left(\frac{1}{\omega^2}\right)^3 - \left(\frac{1}{\omega_1^2} + \frac{1}{\omega_2^2} + \frac{1}{\omega_3^2}\right)\left(\frac{1}{\omega^2}\right)^2 + \cdots = 0 \tag{10.2.2}$$

As is well known in algebra, the coefficient of the second highest power is equal to the sum of the roots of the characteristic equation. It is also equal to the sum of the diagonal terms of matrix A^{-1}, which is called the *trace* of the matrix (see Appendix C):

$$\text{trace } A^{-1} = \sum_{i=1}^{3}\left(\frac{1}{\omega_i^2}\right)$$

These relationships are true for n greater than 3, and we can write for an n-DOF system the following equation:

$$\frac{1}{\omega_1^2}+\frac{1}{\omega_2^2}+\cdots+\frac{1}{\omega_n^2}=a_{11}m_1+a_{22}m_2+\cdots+a_{nn}m_n \tag{10.2.3}$$

The estimate to the fundamental frequency is made by recognizing that $\omega_2, \omega_3, \ldots$ are natural frequencies of higher modes and hence $1/\omega_2^2, 1/\omega_3^2, \ldots$ can be neglected in the left side of Eq. (10.2.3). The term $1/\omega_1^2$ is consequently larger than the true value, and therefore ω_1 is smaller than the exact value of the fundamental frequency. Dunkerley's estimate of the fundamental frequency is then made from the equation

$$\frac{1}{\omega_1^2}<(a_{11}m_1+a_{22}m_2+\cdots+a_{nn}m_n) \tag{10.2.4}$$

Because the left side of the equation has the dimension of the reciprocal of the frequency squared, each term on the right side must also be of the same dimension. Each term on the right side must then be considered to be the contribution to $1/\omega_1^2$ in the absence of all other masses, and, for convenience, we let $a_{ii}m_i = 1/\omega_{ii}^2$, or

$$\frac{1}{\omega_1^2}<\left(\frac{1}{\omega_{11}^2}+\frac{1}{\omega_{22}^2}+\cdots+\frac{1}{\omega_{nn}^2}\right) \tag{10.2.5}$$

Thus, the right side becomes the sum of the effect of each mass acting in the absence of all other masses.

Example 10.2.1

Dunkerley's equation is useful for estimating the fundamental frequency of a structure undergoing vibration testing. Natural frequencies of structures are often determined by attaching an eccentric mass exciter to the structure and noting the frequencies corresponding to the maximum amplitude. The frequencies so measured represent those of the structure plus exciter and can deviate considerably from the natural frequencies of the structure itself when the mass of the exciter is a substantial percentage of the total mass. In such cases, the fundamental frequency of the structure by itself can be determined by the following equation:

$$\frac{1}{\omega_1^2}=\frac{1}{\omega_{11}^2}+\frac{1}{\omega_{22}^2} \tag{a}$$

where ω_1 = fundamental frequency of structure plus exciter
ω_{11} = fundamental frequency of the structure by itself
ω_{22} = natural frequency of exciter mounted on the structure in the absence of other masses.

It is sometimes convenient to express the equation in another form, for instance,

$$\frac{1}{\omega_1^2}=\frac{1}{\omega_{11}^2}+a_{22}m_2 \tag{b}$$

where m_2 is the mass of the concentrated weight or exciter, and a_{22} the influence coefficient of the structure at the point of attachment of the exciter.

■

Example 10.2.2

An airplane rudder tab showed a resonant frequency of 30 cps when vibrated by an eccentric mass shaker of mass 0.69 kg. By attaching an additional mass of 0.69 kg to the shaker, the resonant frequency was lowered to 24 cps. Determine the true natural frequency of the tab.

Solution The measured resonant frequencies are those due to the total mass of the tab and shaker. Letting f_{11} be the true natural frequency of the tab and substituting into Eq. (b) of Example 10.2.1, we obtain

$$\frac{1}{(2\pi \times 30)^2} = \frac{1}{(2\pi f_{11})^2} + 0.69a_{22}$$
$$\frac{1}{(2\pi \times 24)^2} = \frac{1}{(2\pi f_{11})^2} + 1.38a_{22}$$

By eliminating a_{22}, the true natural frequency is

$$f_{11} = 45.4 \text{ cps}$$

The rigidity of stiffness of the tab at the point of attachment of the shaker can be determined from $1/a_{22}$, which from the same equations is found to be.

$$k_2 = \frac{1}{a_{22}} = \frac{1}{2.3 \times 10^{-5}} = 43466 \text{ N/m}$$

■

Example 10.2.3

Determine the fundamental frequency of a uniformly loaded cantilever beam with a concentrated mass M at the end, equal to the mass of the uniform beam (see Fig. 10.2.1).

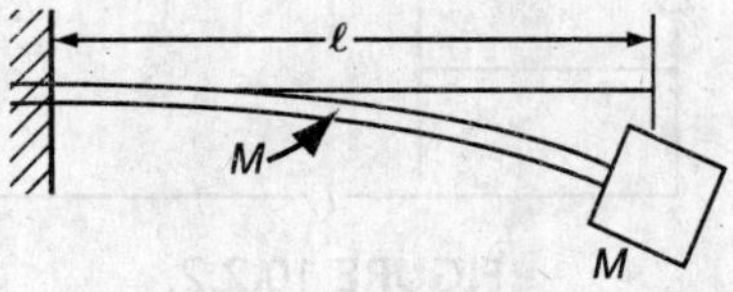

FIGURE 10.2.1.

Solution The frequency equation for the uniformly loaded beam by itself is

$$\omega_{11}^2 = 3.515^2 \left(\frac{EI}{Ml^3}\right)$$

For the concentrated mass by itself attached to a weightless cantilever beam, we have

$$\omega_{22}^2 = 3.00 \left(\frac{EI}{Ml^3}\right)$$

By substituting into Dunkerley's formula rearranged in the following form, the natural frequency of the system is determined as

$$\omega_1^2 = \frac{\omega_{11}^2 \omega_{22}^2}{\omega_{11}^2 + \omega_{22}^2} = \frac{(3.515)^2 \times 3.0}{(3.515)^2 + 3.0} \left(\frac{EI}{Ml^3}\right) = 2.41 \left(\frac{EI}{Ml^3}\right)$$

This result can be compared to the frequency equation obtained by Rayleigh's method, which is

$$\omega_1^2 = \frac{3EI}{\left(1 + \dfrac{33}{140}\right) Ml^3} = 2.43 \left(\frac{EI}{Ml^3}\right)$$

■

Example 10.2.4

The natural frequency of a given airplane wing in torsion is 1600 cpm. What will be the new torsional frequency if a 4500 N fuel tank is hung at a position one-sixth of the semispan from the center line of the airplane such that its moment of inertia about the torsional axis is 200 kg m^2? The torsional stiffness of the wing at this point is 6.78×10^6 Nm/rad.

Solution The frequency of the tank attached to the weightless wing is

$$f_{22} = \frac{1}{2\pi}\sqrt{\frac{6.78 \times 10^6}{200}} = 29.31 \text{ cps} = 1758 \text{ cpm}$$

The new torsional frequency with the tank, from Eq. (a) of Example 10.2.1, then becomes

$$\frac{1}{f_1^2} = \frac{1}{(1600)^2} + \frac{1}{(1758)^2}; \quad f_1 = 1183 \text{ cpm}$$

■

Example 10.2.5

The fundamental frequency of a uniform beam of mass M, simply supported as in Fig. 10.2.2, is equal to $\pi^2\sqrt{EI/Ml^3}$. If a lumped mass m_0 is attached to the beam at $x = l/3$, determine the new fundamental frequency.

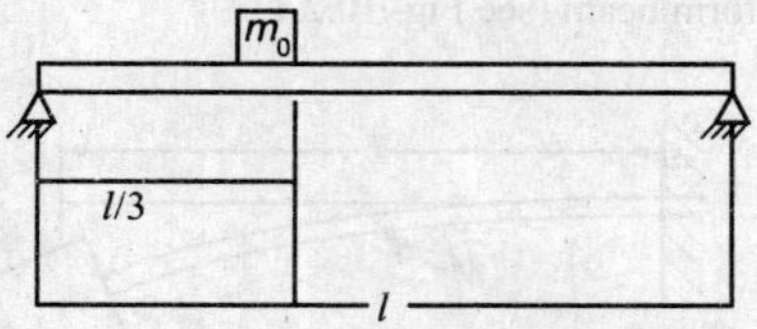

FIGURE 10.2.2.

Solution Starting with Eq. (b) of Example 10.2.1, we let ω_{11} be the fundamental frequency of the uniform beam and ω_1 the new fundamental frequency with m_0 attached to the beam. Multiplying through Eq. (b) by ω_1^2, we have

$$1 = \left(\frac{\omega_1}{\omega_{11}}\right)^2 + a_{22}m_0\omega_{11}^2\left(\frac{\omega_1}{\omega_{11}}\right)^2$$

or

$$\left(\frac{\omega_1}{\omega_{11}}\right)^2 = \frac{1}{1 + a_{22}m_0\omega_{11}^2}$$

The quantity a_{22} is the influence coefficient at $x = l/3$ due to a unit load applied at the same point. It can be found from the beam formula in Example 10.1.4 to be

$$a_{22} = \frac{8}{6 \times 81}\frac{l^3}{EI}$$

Substituting $\omega_{11}^2 = \pi^4 EI/Ml^3$ together with a_{22}, we obtain the convenient equation

$$\left(\frac{\omega_1}{\omega_{11}}\right)^2 = \frac{1}{1 + \dfrac{8\pi^4}{6 \times 81}\dfrac{m_0}{M}} = \frac{1}{1 + 1.6\dfrac{m_0}{M}}$$

■

Example 10.2.6

Determine the fundamental frequency of the three-story building shown in Fig. 10.2.3, where the foundation is capable of translation.

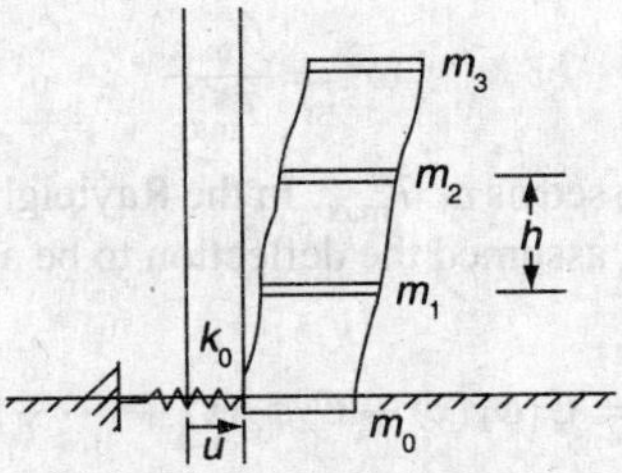

FIGURE 10.2.3.

Solution If a unit force is placed at each floor, the influence coefficients are

$$a_{00} = \frac{1}{k_0}$$

$$a_{11} = \frac{1}{k_0} + \frac{h^3}{24EI_1}$$

$$a_{22} = \frac{1}{k_0} + \frac{h^3}{24EI_1} + \frac{h^3}{24EI_2}$$

$$a_{33} = \frac{1}{k_0} + \frac{h^3}{24EI_1} + \frac{h^3}{24EI_2} + \frac{h^3}{24EI_3}$$

The Dunkerley equation then becomes

$$\frac{1}{\omega_1^2} = \frac{m_0}{k_0} + \left(\frac{1}{k_0} + \frac{h^3}{24EI_1}\right) m_1 = \left(\frac{1}{k_0} + \frac{h^3}{24EI_1} + \frac{h^3}{24EI_2}\right) m_2 + \left(\frac{1}{k_0} + \frac{h^3}{24EI_1} + \frac{h^3}{24EI_2} + \frac{h^3}{24EI_3}\right) m_3$$

If the columns are of equal stiffness, the preceding equation reduces to

$$\frac{1}{\omega_1^2} = \frac{1}{k_0}(m_0 + m_1 + m_2 + m_3) + m_1 \frac{h^3}{24EI} + m_2 \frac{2h^3}{24EI} + m_3 \frac{3h^3}{24EI}$$

■

10.3 RAYLEIGH–RITZ METHOD

W. Ritz developed a method that is an extension of Rayleigh's method. It not only provides a means of obtaining a more accurate value for the fundamental frequency, but it also gives approximations to the higher frequencies and mode shapes.

The Ritz method is essentially the Rayleigh method in which the single shape function is replaced by a series of shape functions multiplied by constant coefficients. The coefficients are adjusted by minimizing the frequency with respect to each of the coefficients, which results in n algebraic equations in ω^2. The solutions of these equations then gives the natual frequencies and mode shapes of the system. As in Rayleigh's method, the success of the method depends on the choice of the shape funcions that should satisfy the geometric boundary conditions of the problem.

The method should also be differentiable, at least to the order of the derivatives appearing in the energy equations. The functions, however, can disregard discontinuities such as those of shear due to concentrated masses that involve third derivatives in beams.

We now outline in a general manner the procedure of the Rayleigh–Ritz method, starting with Rayleigh's equation:

$$\omega^2 = \frac{U_{\max}}{T^*_{\max}} \tag{10.3.1}$$

where the kinetic energy is expressed as $\omega^2 T^*_{\max}$. In the Rayleigh method, a single function is chosen for the deflection; Ritz, however, assumed the deflection to be a sum of several functions multiplied by constants, as follows:

$$y(x) = C_1\phi_1(x) + C_2\phi_2(x) + \cdots + C_n\phi_n(x) \tag{10.3.2}$$

where $\phi_i(x)$ are any admissible functions satisfying the boundary conditions. $U_{\max}$ and $T_{\max}$ are expressible in the form of Eqs. (6.6.1) and (6.6.2):

$$\begin{aligned} U &= \frac{1}{2}\sum_i\sum_j k_{ij}C_iC_j \\ T^* &= \frac{1}{2}\sum_i\sum_j m_{ij}C_iC_j \end{aligned} \tag{10.3.3}$$

where k_{ij} and m_{ij} depend on the type of problem. For example, for the beam, we have

$$k_{ij} = \int EI\phi_i''\phi_j''\,dx \quad \text{and} \quad m_{ij} = \int m\phi_i\phi_j dx$$

whereas for the longitudinal oscillation of slender rods,

$$k_{ij} = \int EA\phi_i'\phi_j' dx \quad \text{and} \quad m_{ij} = \int m\phi_i\phi_j dx$$

We now minimize ω^2 by differentiating it with respect to each of the constants. For example, the derivative of ω^2 with respect to C_i is

$$\frac{\partial\omega^2}{\partial C_i} = \frac{\partial}{\partial C_i}\left(\frac{U_{\max}}{T^*_{\max}}\right) = \frac{T^*_{\max}\dfrac{\partial U_{\max}}{\partial C_i} - U_{\max}\dfrac{\partial T^*_{\max}}{\partial C_i}}{T^{*2}_{\max}} = 0 \tag{10.3.4}$$

which is satisfied by

$$\frac{\partial U_{\max}}{\partial C_i} - \frac{U_{\max}}{T^*_{\max}}\frac{\partial T^*_{\max}}{\partial C_i} = 0$$

or because $U_{\max}/T^*_{\max} = \omega^2$,

$$\frac{\partial U_{\max}}{\partial_i C_i} - \omega^2\frac{\partial T^*_{\max}}{\partial C_i} = 0 \tag{10.3.5}$$

The two terms in this equation are then

$$\frac{\partial U_{\max}}{\partial C_i} = \sum_i^n k_{ij}C_j \quad \text{and} \quad \frac{\partial T^*_{\max}}{\partial C_i} = \sum_j^n m_{ij}C_j$$

and so Eq. (10.3.5) becomes

$$C_1(k_{i1} - \omega^2 m_{i1}) + C_2(k_{i2} - \omega^2 m_{i2}) + \cdots + C_n(k_{in} - \omega^2 m_{in}) = 0 \tag{10.3.6}$$

With i varying from 1 to n, there will be n such equations, which can be arranged in matrix form as

$$\begin{bmatrix} (k_{11}-\omega^2 m_{11}) & (k_{12}-\omega^2 m_{12}) & \dots & (k_{1n}-\omega^2 m_{1n}) \\ (k_{21}-\omega^2 m_{21}) & \dots & & \\ \vdots & & & \vdots \\ (k_{n1}-\omega^2 m_{n1}) & \dots & & (k_{nn}-\omega^2 m_{nn}) \end{bmatrix} \begin{Bmatrix} C_1 \\ C_2 \\ \vdots \\ C_n \end{Bmatrix} = 0 \qquad (10.3.7)$$

The determinant of this equation is an n-degree algebraic equation in ω^2, and its solution results in the n natural frequencies. The mode shape is also obtained by solving for the C's for each natural frequency and substituting into Eq. (10.3.2) for the deflection.

Example 10.3.1

Figure 10.3.1 shows a wedge-shaped plate of constant thickness fixed into a rigid wall. Determine the first two natural frequencies and mode shapes in longitudinal oscillation by using the Rayleigh–Ritz method.

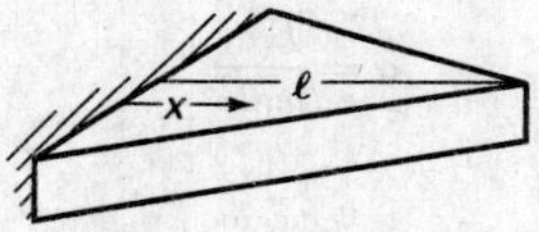

FIGURE 10.3.1.

Solution For the displacement function, we choose the first two longitudinal modes of a uniform rod clamped at one end.

$$\begin{aligned} u(x) &= C_1 \sin\frac{\pi x}{2l} + C_2 \sin\frac{3\pi x}{2l} \\ &= C_1\phi_1(x) + C_2\phi_2(x) \end{aligned} \qquad \text{(a)}$$

The mass per unit length and the stiffness at x are

$$m(x) = m_0\left(1-\frac{x}{l}\right) \quad \text{and} \quad EA(x) = EA_0\left(1-\frac{x}{l}\right)$$

The k_{ij} and the m_{ij} for the longitudinal modes are calculated from the equations

$$\begin{aligned} k_{ij} &= \int_0^l EA(x)\phi_i'\phi_j' dx \\ m_{ij} &= \int_0^l m(x)\phi_i\phi_j dx \\ k_{11} &= \frac{\pi^2}{4l^2}EA_0 \int_0^l \left(1-\frac{x}{l}\right)\cos^2\frac{\pi x}{2l}dx = \frac{EA_0}{2l}\left(\frac{\pi^2}{8}+\frac{1}{2}\right) \\ &= 0.86685\frac{EA_0}{l} \\ k_{12} &= \frac{3\pi^2}{4l^2}EA_0 \int_0^l \left(1-\frac{x}{l}\right)\cos\frac{\pi x}{2l}\cos\frac{3\pi x}{2l}dx = 0.750\frac{EA_0}{l} \\ k_{22} &= \frac{9\pi^2}{4l^2}EA_0 \int_0^l \left(1-\frac{x}{l}\right)\cos^2\frac{3\pi x}{2l}dx = \frac{EA_0}{2l}\left(\frac{9\pi^2}{8}+\frac{1}{2}\right) \\ &= 5.80165\frac{EA_0}{l} \end{aligned} \qquad \text{(b)}$$

$$
\begin{aligned}
m_{11} &= m_0 \int_0^l \left(1-\frac{x}{l}\right)\sin^2\frac{\pi x}{2l}\,dx = m_0 l\left(\frac{1}{4}-\frac{1}{\pi^2}\right) = 0.148679 m_0 l \\
m_{12} &= m_0 \int_0^l \left(1-\frac{x}{l}\right)\sin\frac{\pi x}{2l}\sin\frac{3\pi x}{2l}\,dx = m_0 l\left(\frac{1}{\pi^2}\right) = 0.101321 m_0 l \\
m_{22} &= m_0 \int_0^l \left(1-\frac{x}{l}\right)\sin^2\frac{3\pi x}{2l}\,dx = m_0 l\left(\frac{1}{4}-\frac{1}{9\pi^2}\right) = 0.238742 m_0 l
\end{aligned}
$$

Substituting into Eq. (10.3.7), we obtain

$$
\begin{bmatrix}
\left(0.86685\dfrac{EA_0}{l} - 0.14868 m_0 l\omega^2\right) & \left(0.750\dfrac{EA_0}{l} - 0.10132 m_0 l\omega^2\right) \\
\left(0.750\dfrac{EA_0}{l} - 0.10132 m_0 l\omega^2\right) & \left(5.80165\dfrac{EA_0}{l} - 0.23874 m_0 l\omega^2\right)
\end{bmatrix}
\begin{Bmatrix} C_1 \\ C_2 \end{Bmatrix} = 0 \tag{c}
$$

Setting the determinant of the preceding equation to zero, we obtain the frequency equation

$$\omega^4 - 36.3676\alpha\omega^2 + 177.0377\alpha^2 = 0 \tag{d}$$

where

$$\alpha = \frac{EA_0}{m_0 l^2} \tag{e}$$

The two roots of this equation are

$$\omega_1^2 = 5.7898\alpha \quad \text{and} \quad \omega_2^2 = 30.5778\alpha$$

Using these results in Eq. (c), we obtain

$$
\begin{aligned}
C_2 &= 0.03689 C_1 && \text{for mode 1} \\
C_1 &= -0.63819 C_2 && \text{for mode 2}
\end{aligned}
$$

The two natural frequencies and mode shapes are then

$$
\begin{aligned}
\omega_1 &= 2.4062\sqrt{\frac{EA_0}{m_0 l^2}} \qquad u_1(x) = 1.0\sin\frac{\pi x}{2l} + 0.03689\sin\frac{3\pi x}{2l} \\
\omega_1 &= 5.5297\sqrt{\frac{EA_0}{m_0 l^2}} \qquad u_2(x) = -0.63819\sin\frac{\pi x}{2l} + 1.0\sin\frac{3\pi x}{2l}
\end{aligned}
$$

■

10.4 HOLZER METHOD

When an undamped system is vibrating freely at any one of its natural frequencies, no external force, torque, or moment is necessary to maintain the vibration. Also, the amplitude of the mode shape is immaterial to the vibration. Recognizing these facts, Holzer[2] proposed a method of calculation for the natural frequencies and mode shapes of torsional systems by assuming a frequency and starting with a unit amplitude at one end of the system and progressively calculating the torque and angular displacement to the other end. The frequencies that result in zero external torque or compatible boundary conditions at the other end are the natural frequencies of the system. The method can be applied to any lumped-mass system, linear spring-mass systems, beams modeled by discrete masses and beam springs, and so on.

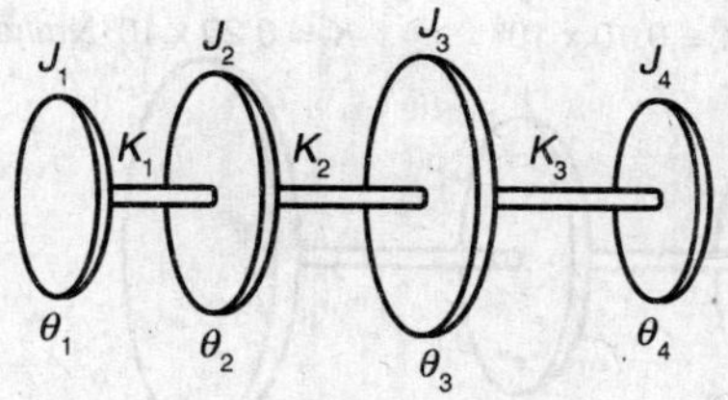

FIGURE 10.4.1.

Holzer's procedure for torsional systems. Figure 10.4.1 shows a torsional system represented by a series of disks connected by shafts. By assuming a frequency ω and amplitude $\theta_1 = 1$, the inertia torque of the first disk is

$$-J_1\ddot{\theta}_1 = J_1\omega^2\theta_1 = J_1\omega^2 1$$

where harmonic motion is implied. This torque acts through shaft 1 and twists it by

$$\frac{J_1\omega^2}{K_1} = \theta_1 - \theta_2 = 1 - \theta_2$$

or

$$\theta_2 = 1 - \frac{J_1\omega^2}{K_1}$$

With θ_2 known, the inertia torque of the second disk is calculated as $J_2\omega^2\theta_2$. The sum of the first two intertia torques acts through the shaft K_2, causing it to twist by

$$\frac{J_1\omega^2 + J_2\omega^2\theta_2}{K_2} = \theta_2 - \theta_3$$

In this manner, the amplitude and torque at every disk can be calculated. The resulting torque at the far end,

$$T_{\text{ext}} = \sum_{i=1}^{4} J_i\omega^2\theta_i$$

can then be plotted for the chosen ω. By repeating the calculation with other values of ω, the natural frequencies are found when $T_{\text{ext}} = 0$. The angular displacements θ_i corresponding to the natural frequencies are the mode shapes.

Example 10.4.1

Determine the natural frequencies and mode shapes of the system shown in Fig. 10.4.2.

Solution Table 10.4.1 defines the parameters of the system and the sequence of calculations, which can be easily carried out. Presented are calculations for $\omega = 20$ and 40. The quantity T_3 is the torque to the right of disk 3, which must be zero at the natural frequencies. Figure 10.4.3 shows a plot of T_3 versus ω. Several

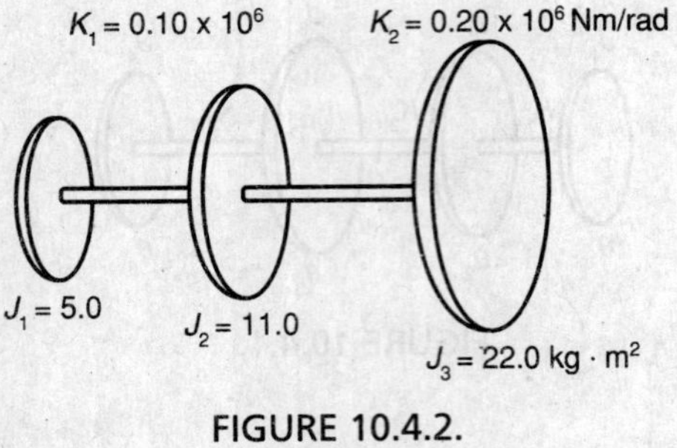

FIGURE 10.4.2.

TABLE 10.4.1

Parameters of the System			
	Station 1	Station 2	Station 3
	$J_1 = 5$	$J_2 = 11$	$J_3 = 22$
	$K_1 = 0.10 \times 10^6$	$K_2 = 0.20 \times 10^6$	$K_3 = 0$
Calculation Program			
ω	$\theta_1 = 1.0$	$\theta_2 = 1 - T_1/k_1$	$\theta_3 = \theta_2 - T_2/k_2$
ω^2	$T_1 = \omega^2\theta_1 J_1$	$T_2 = T_1 + \omega^2\theta_2 J_2$	$T_3 = T_2 + \omega^2\theta_3 J_3$
20	1.0	0.980	.9484
400	2.0×10^3	6.312×10^3	14.66×10^3
40	1.0	0.920	0.799
1600	8.0×10^3	24.19×10^3	52.32×10^3

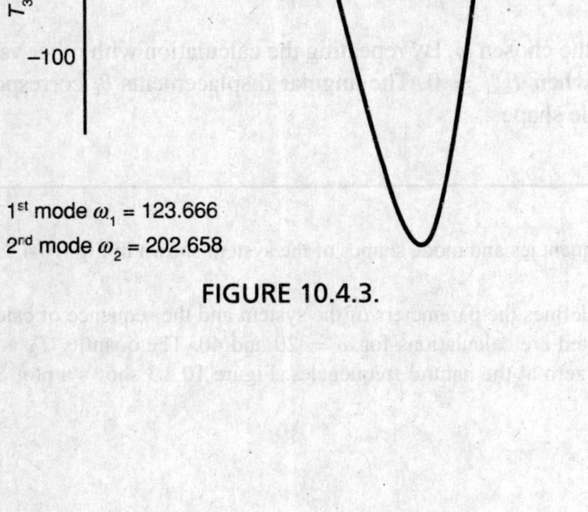

FIGURE 10.4.3.

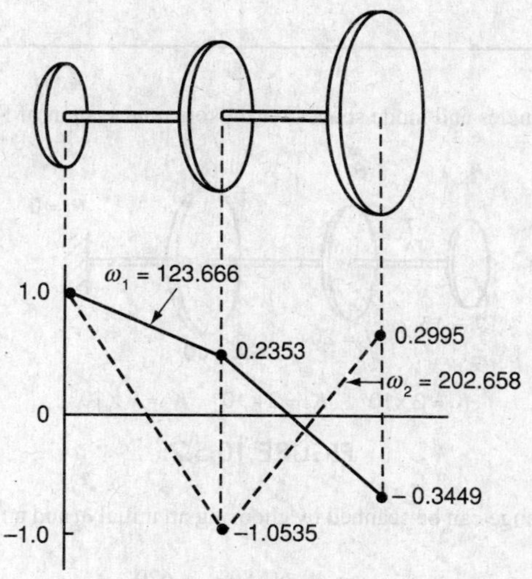

FIGURE 10.4.4.

frequencies in the vicinity of $T_3 = 0$ were input to obtain accurate values of the first and second shapes displayed in Fig. 10.4.4.

■

10.5 DIGITAL COMPUTER PROGRAM FOR THE TORSIONAL SYSTEM

The calculations for the Holzer problem can be greatly speeded up by using a high-speed digital computer. The problem treated is the general torsional system of Fig. 10.5.1. The program is written in such a manner that by changing the data, it is applicable to any other torsional system.

The quantities of concern here are the torsional displacement θ of each disk and the torque T carried by each shaft. We adopt two indexes: N to define the position along the structure and I for the frequency used.

The equations relating the displacement and torque at the Nth and $(N+1)$st stations are

$$\theta(I, N+1) = \theta(I, N) - T(I, N)/K(N) \tag{10.5.1}$$

$$T(I, N+1) = T(I, N) + \lambda(I) * J(N+1) * \theta(I, N+1) \tag{10.5.2}$$

where $\lambda = \omega^2, \theta(I, 1) = 1, T(I, 1) = \lambda(I) * J(1)$.

By starting at $N = 1$, these two equations are to be solved for θ and T at each point N of the structure for various values of λ. At the natural frequencies, θ must be zero at the fixed end or T must be zero at the free end.

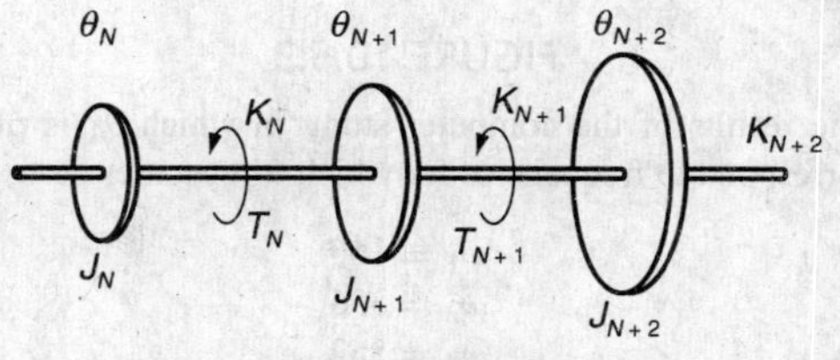

FIGURE 10.5.1.

Example 10.5.1

Determine the natural frequencies and mode shapes for the torsional system of Fig. 10.5.2.

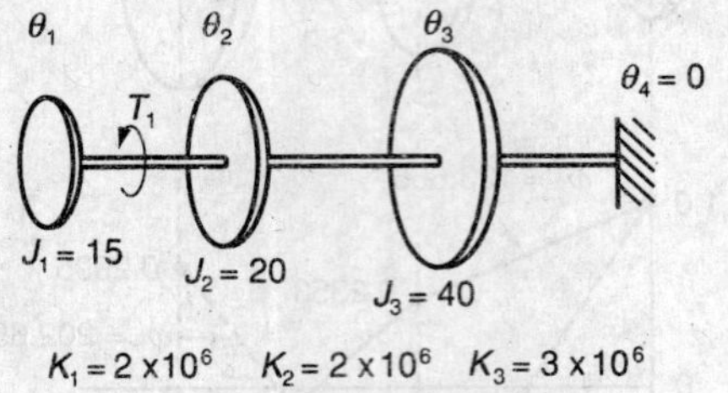

FIGURE 10.5.2.

Solution The frequency range can be scanned by choosing an initial ω and an increment $\Delta\omega$. We choose for this problem the frequencies

$$\omega = 40, 60, 80, \ldots, 620$$

which can be programmed as

$$\omega(I) = 40 + (I - 1) * 20 \quad I = 1 \text{ to } 30$$

The corresponding $\lambda(I)$ is computed as

$$\lambda(I) = \omega(I)^2$$

The computation is started with the boundary conditions $N = 1$:

$$\theta(I, 1) = 1$$
$$T(I, 1) = \lambda(I) * J(1)$$

Equations (10.5.1) and (10.5.2) then give the values of θ and T at the next station $M = N + 1 = 2$. This loop is repeated until $M = 4$, at which time I is advanced an integer to the next frequency. The process is then repeated.

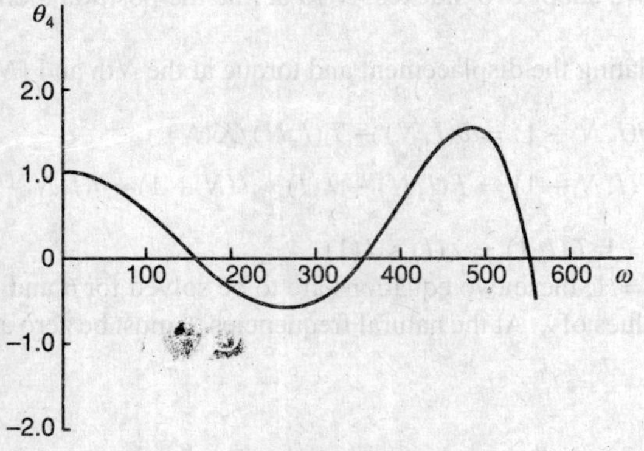

FIGURE 10.5.3.

Figure 10.5.3 shows the results of the computer study in which θ_4 is plotted against ω. The natural frequencies of the system correspond to frequencies for which θ_4 becomes zero, which are approximately

$$\omega_1 = 160$$
$$\omega_2 = 356$$
$$\omega_3 = 552$$

The mode shapes can be found by printing θ_N for each of the preceding frequencies.

10.6 MYKLESTAD'S METHOD FOR BEAMS

When a beam is replaced by lumped masses connected by massless beam sections, a method developed by N. O. Myklestad[3,4] can be used to progressively compute the deflection, slope, moment, and shear from one section to the next, in a manner similar to the Holzer method.

Uncoupled flexural vibration. Figure 10.6.1 shows a typical section of an idealized beam with lumped masses. By taking the free-body section in the manner indicated, it will be possible to write equations for the shear and moment at $i+1$ entirely in terms of quantities at i. These can then be substituted into the geometric equations for θ and y.

From equilibrium considerations, we have

$$V_{i+1} = V_i - m_i\omega^2 y_i \tag{10.6.1}$$

$$M_{i+1} = M_i - V_{i+1}l_i \tag{10.6.2}$$

From geometric considerations, using influence coefficients of uniform beam sections, we have

$$\theta_{i+1} = \theta_i + M_{i+1}\left(\frac{l}{EI}\right)_i + V_{i+1}\left(\frac{l^2}{2EI}\right)_i \tag{10.6.3}$$

$$y_{i+1} = y_i + \theta_i l_i + M_{i+1}\left(\frac{l^2}{2EI}\right)_i + V_{i+1}\left(\frac{l^3}{3EI}\right)_i \tag{10.6.4}$$

where

$(l/EI)_i$ = slope at $i+1$ measured from a tangent at i due to a unit moment at $i+1$;
$(l^2/2EI)_i$ = slope at $i+1$ measured from a tangent at i due to a unit shear at $i+1$
= deflection at $i+1$ measured from a tangent at i due to a unit moment at $i+1$;
$(l^3/3EI)_i$ = deflection at $i+1$ measured from a tangent at i due to a unit shear at $i+1$.

Thus, Eqs. (10.6.1) through (10.6.4) in the sequence given enable the calculations to proceed from i to $i+1$.

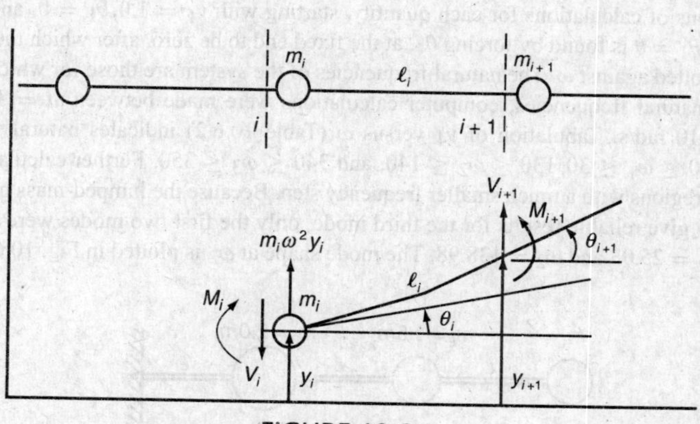

FIGURE 10.6.1.

Boundary conditions. Of the four boundary conditions at each end, two are generally known. For example, a cantilever beam with $i = 1$ at the free end would have $V_1 = M_1 = 0$. Because the amplitude is arbitrary, we can choose $y_1 = 1.0$. Having done so, the slope θ_1 is fixed to a value that is yet to be determined. Because of the linear character of the problem, the four quantities at the far end will be in the form

$$\begin{aligned} V_n &= a_1 + b_1\theta_1 \\ M_n &= a_2 + b_2\theta_1 \\ \theta_n &= a_3 + b_3\theta_1 \\ y_n &= a_4 + b_4\theta_1 \end{aligned}$$

where a_i, b_i are constants and θ_1 is unknown. Thus, the frequencies that satisfy the boundary condition $\theta_n = y_n = 0$ for the cantilever beam will establish θ_1 and the natural frequencies of the beam, i.e., $\theta_1 = -a_3/b_3$ and $y_n = a_4 - (a_3/b_3)b_4 = 0$. Hence, by plotting y_n versus ω, the natural frequencies of the beam can be found.

Example 10.6.1

To illustrate the computational procedure, we determine the frequencies of the cantilever beam shown in Fig. 10.6.2. The massless beam sections are assumed to be identical so that the influence coefficients for each section are equal. The numerical constants for the problem are given as

$$m_1 = 100\,\text{kg} \qquad \frac{1}{EI} = 5 \times 10^{-6}\frac{1}{Nm}$$

$$l = 0.5\,\text{m} \qquad \frac{l^2}{2EI} = 1.25 \times 10^{-6}\frac{1}{N}$$

$$EI = 0.10 \times 10^{+6}\,\text{N}\cdot\text{m}^2 \qquad \frac{l^3}{3EI} = 0.41666 \times 10^{-6}\frac{m}{N}$$

The computation is started at 1. Because each of the quantities V, M, θ, and y will be in the form $a+b$, they are arranged into two columns, each of which can be computed separately. The calculation for the left column is started with $V_1 = 0$, $M_1 = 0$, $\theta_1 = 0$, and $y_1 = 1.0$. The right columns, which are proportional to θ, are started with the initial values of $V_1 = 0$, $M_1 = 0$, $\theta_1 = 1\theta$, and $y_1 = 0$.

Table 10.6.1 shows how the computation for Eqs. (10.6.1) through (10.6.4) can be carried out with any programmable calculator. The frequency chosen for this table is $\omega = 10$.

To start the computation, we note that the moment and shear at station 1 are zero. We can choose the deflection at station 1 to be 1.0, in which case the slope at this point becomes an unknown θ. We, therefore, carry out two columns of calculations for each quantity, starting with $y_1 = 1.0, \theta_1 = 0$, and $y_1 = 0, \theta_1 = 0$. The unknown slope $\theta_1 = \theta$ is found by forcing θ_4, at the fixed end to be zero, after which the deflection y_4 can be calculated and plotted against ω. The natural frequencies of the system are those for which $y_4 = 0$.

To search the natural frequencies, computer calculations were made between $\omega = 10$ to $\omega = 400$ at frequency steps of 10 rad/s. Tabulation of y_4 versus ω (Table 10.6.2) indicates natural frequencies in the frequency regions $20 \le \omega_1 \le 30$, $130 \le \omega_2 \le 140$, and $340 \le \omega_3 \le 350$. Further calculations were carried out in each of these regions with a much smaller frequency step. Because the lumped-mass model of only three masses could hardly give reliable results for the third mode, only the first two modes were recomputed; these were found to be $\omega_1 = 25.03$ and $\omega_2 = 138.98$. The mode shape at ω_2 is plotted in Fig. 10.6.3.

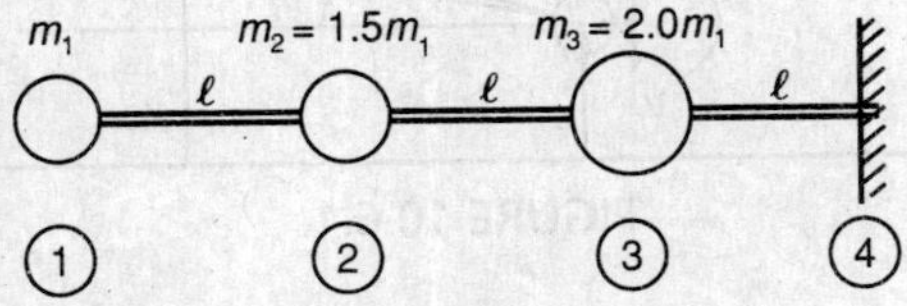

FIGURE 10.6.2.

TABLE 10.6.1

	Ω = 10				Ω2 = 100			
i	*V (Newton)*		*M (Newton · meter)*		*θ (Radians)*		*y (Meter)*	
1	0	0	0	0	0	θ	1.0	0
2	−10,000	0	5000	0	0.0125	1.0θ	1.002084	0.5θ
3	−25,031	-7500θ	17515	3750θ	0.06879	1.00937θ	1.0198	1.001563θ
4	−45,427	-27532θ	40228	17516θ	0.21315	1.0625θ	1.08555	1.5167θ

$\theta_4 = 0.21315 + 1.0625\theta = 0 \quad \theta_1 = -0.2006117$

$y_4 = 1.08555 + 1.5167(-0.2006117) = 0.78128$ plot vs. $\omega = 10$

TABLE 10.6.2

ω	y_4		ω	y_4	
10	0.7813		210	1.6170	
20	0.2659	$\leftarrow \omega_1$	220	1.7619	
30	−0.2922		230	1.8749	
40	−0.7372		240	1.9531	
50	−1.0285		250	1.9936	
60	−1.1800		260	1.9941	
70	−1.1292		270	1.9522	
80	−1.1719		280	1.8661	
90	−1.0589		290	1.7340	
100	−0.8964		300	1.5544	
110	−0.6972		310	1.3258	
120	−0.4714		320	1.0472	
130	−0.2278	$\leftarrow \omega_2$	330	0.7177	
140	0.0264		340	0.3363	$\leftarrow \omega_3$
150	0.2844		350	−0.0975	
160	0.5405		360	−0.5844	
170	0.7892		370	−1.1247	
180	1.0256		380	−1.7187	
190	1.2451		390	−2.3666	
200	1.4436		400	−3.0685	

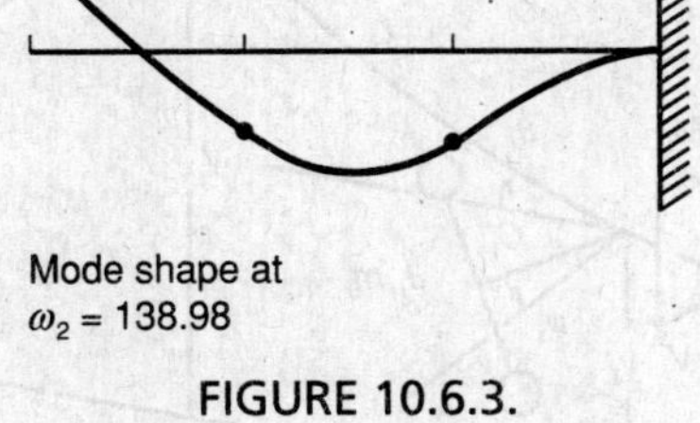

FIGURE 10.6.3.

10.7 COUPLED FLEXURE–TORSION VIBRATION

Natural modes of vibration of airplane wings and other beam structures are often coupled flexure–torsion vibration, which for higher modes differs considerably from those of uncoupled modes. To treat such problems, we must model the beam as shown in Fig. 10.7.1. The elastic axis of the beam about which the torsional rotation takes place is assumed to be initially straight. It is able to twist, but its bending displacement is restricted to the vertical plane. The principal axes of bending for all cross sections are parallel in the undeformed state. Masses are lumped at each station with its center of gravity at distance c_i from the elastic axis and J_i is the mass moment of intertia of the section about the elastic axis, i.e., $J_i = J_{cg} + m_i c_i^2$.

Figure 10.7.2 shows the ith section, from which the following equations can be written:

$$V_{i+1} = V_i - m_i\omega^2(y_i + c_i\varphi_i) \tag{10.7.1}$$

$$M_{i+1} = M_i - V_{i+1}l_i \tag{10.7.2}$$

$$T_{i+1} = T_i + J_i\omega^2\varphi_i + m_ic_i\omega^2y_i \tag{10.7.3}$$

$$\theta_{i+1} = \theta_i + V_{i+1}\left(\frac{l^2}{2EI}\right)_i + M_{i+1}\left(\frac{l}{EI}\right)_i \tag{10.7.4}$$

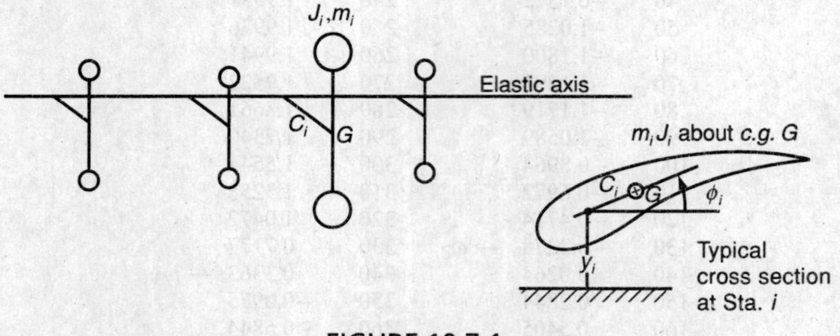

FIGURE 10.7.1.

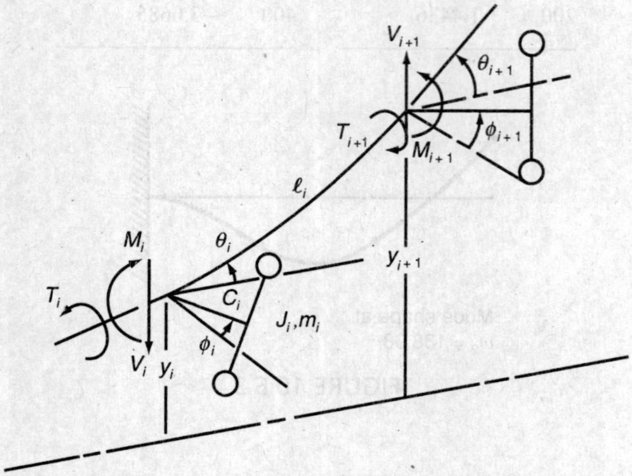

FIGURE 10.7.2.

$$y_{i+1} = y_i + \theta_i l_i + V_{i+1}\left(\frac{l^3}{3EI}\right)_i + M_{i+1}\left(\frac{l^2}{2EI}\right)_i \tag{10.7.5}$$

$$\varphi_{i+1} = \varphi_i + T_{i+1} h_i \tag{10.7.6}$$

where T = the torque
h = the torsional influence coefficient = l/GI_P
φ = the torsional rotation of elastic axis

For free-ended beams, we have the following boundary conditions to start the computation:

$$V_1 = M_1 = T_1 = 0$$
$$\theta_1 = \theta \quad y_1 = 1.0 \quad \varphi_1 = \varphi$$

Here again, the quantities of interest at any station are linearly related to θ_1 and φ_1 and can be expressed in the form

$$a + b\theta_1 + c\varphi_1 \tag{10.7.7}$$

Natural frequencies are established by the satisfaction of the boundary conditions at the other end. Often, for symmetric beams such as the airplane wing, only one-half the beam need be considered. The satisfaction of the boundary conditions for the symmetric and antisymmetric modes enables sufficient equations for the solution.

10.8 TRANSFER MATRICES

The Holzer and Myklestad methods can be recast in terms of transfer matrices.[5] The transfer matrix defines the geometric and dynamic relationships of the element between the two stations and allows the state vector for the force and displacement to be transferred from one station to the next station.

Torsional system. Signs are often a source of confusion in rotating systems, and it is necessary to clearly define the sense of positive quantities. The coordinate along the rotational axis is considered positive toward the right. If a cut is made along the shaft, the face with the outward normal toward the positive coordinate direction is called the *positive face*. Positive torques and positive angular displacements are indicated on the positive face by arrows pointing positively according to the right-hand screw rule, as shown in Fig. 10.8.1.

With the stations numbered from left to right, the nth element is represented by the massless shaft of torsional stiffness K_n and the mass of polar moment of inertia J_n, as shown in Fig. 10.8.2.

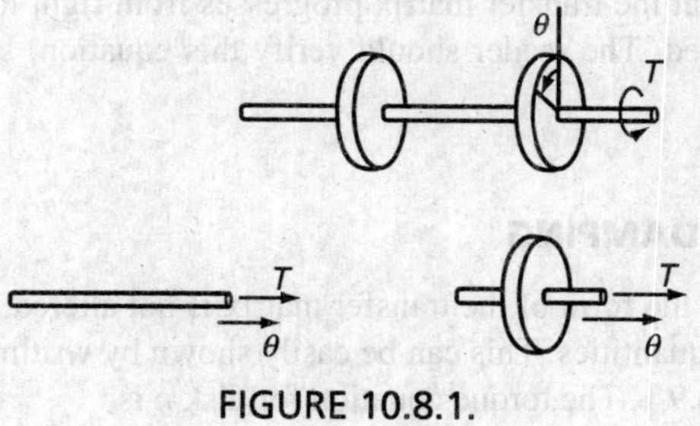

FIGURE 10.8.1.

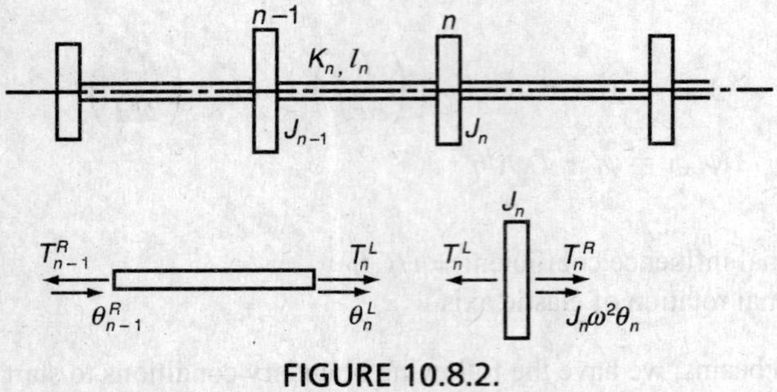

FIGURE 10.8.2.

Separating the shaft from the rotating mass, we can write the following equations and express them in matrix form. Superscripts L and R represent the left and right sides of the members.

For the mass:

$$\left.\begin{aligned} \theta_n^R &= \theta_n^L \\ T_n^R - T_n^L &= -\omega^2 J_n \theta_n \end{aligned}\right\} \begin{Bmatrix} \theta \\ T \end{Bmatrix}_n^R = \begin{bmatrix} 1 & 0 \\ -\omega^2 J & 1 \end{bmatrix}_n \begin{Bmatrix} \theta \\ T \end{Bmatrix}_n^L \tag{10.8.1}$$

For the shaft:

$$\left.\begin{aligned} K_n(\theta_n^L - \theta_{n-1}^R) &= T_{n-1}^R \\ T_n^L &= T_{n-1}^R \end{aligned}\right\} \begin{Bmatrix} \theta \\ T \end{Bmatrix}_n^L = \begin{bmatrix} 1 & \frac{1}{K} \\ 0 & 1 \end{bmatrix}_n \begin{Bmatrix} \theta \\ T \end{Bmatrix}_{n-1}^R \tag{10.8.2}$$

The matrix pertaining to the mass is called the *point matrix* and the matrix associated with the shaft, the *field matrix*. The two can be combined to establish the transfer matrix for the nth element, which is

$$\begin{Bmatrix} \theta \\ T \end{Bmatrix}_n^R \underset{\rightarrow}{=} \begin{bmatrix} 1 & -\dfrac{1}{K} \\ -\omega^2 J & \left(1 - \dfrac{\omega^2 J}{K}\right) \end{bmatrix}_n \begin{Bmatrix} \theta \\ T \end{Bmatrix}_{n-1}^R \tag{10.8.3}$$

In the development so far, the stations were numbered in increasing order from left to right with the transfer matrix also progressing to the right. The arrow under the equal sign indicates this direction of progression. In some problems, it is convenient to proceed with the transfer matrix in the opposite direction, in which case we need only to invert Eq. (10.8.3). We then obtain the relationship

$$\begin{Bmatrix} \theta \\ T \end{Bmatrix}_{n-1}^R \underset{\leftarrow}{=} \begin{bmatrix} \left(1 - \dfrac{\omega^2 J}{K}\right) & \dfrac{1}{K} \\ \omega^2 J & 1 \end{bmatrix} \begin{Bmatrix} \theta \\ T \end{Bmatrix}_n^R \tag{10.8.4}$$

The arrow now indicates that the transfer matrix progresses from right to left with the order of the station numbering unchanged. The reader should verify this equation, starting with the free-body development.

10.9 SYSTEMS WITH DAMPING

When damping is included, the form of the transfer matrix is not altered, but the mass and stiffness elements become complex quantities. This can be easily shown by writing the equations for the nth subsystem shown in Fig. 10.9.1. The torque equation for disk n is

$$-\omega^2 J_n \theta_n = T_n^R - T_n^L - i\omega c_n \theta_n$$

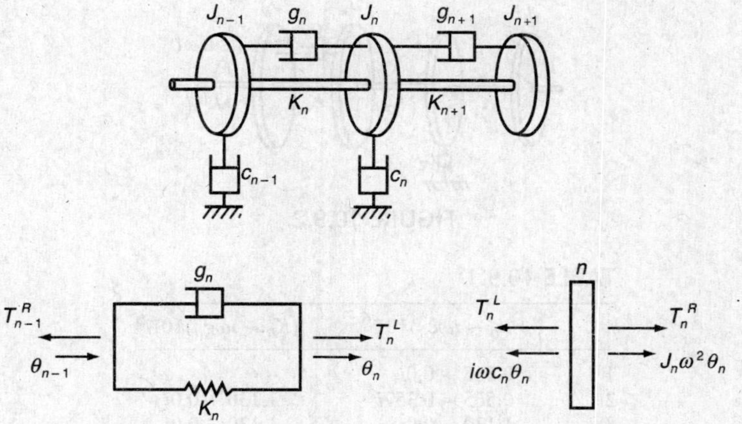

FIGURE 10.9.1. Torsional system with damping.

or

$$(i\omega c_n - \omega^2 J_n)\theta_n = T_n^R - T_n^L \tag{10.9.1}$$

The elastic equation for the nth shaft is

$$\begin{aligned} T_n^L &= K_n(\theta_n - \theta_{n-1}) + i\omega g_n(\theta_n - \theta_{n-1}) \\ &= (K_n + i\omega g_n)(\theta_n - \theta_{n-1}) \end{aligned} \tag{10.9.2}$$

Thus, the point matrix and the field matrix for the damped system become

$$\begin{Bmatrix} \theta \\ T \end{Bmatrix}_n^R = \begin{bmatrix} 1 & 0 \\ (i\omega c - \omega^2 J) & 1 \end{bmatrix}_n \begin{Bmatrix} \theta \\ T \end{Bmatrix}_n^L \tag{10.9.3}$$

$$\begin{Bmatrix} \theta \\ T \end{Bmatrix}_n^L = \begin{bmatrix} 1 & \dfrac{1}{K + i\omega g} \\ 0 & 1 \end{bmatrix}_n \begin{Bmatrix} \theta \\ T \end{Bmatrix}_{n-1}^R \tag{10.9.4}$$

which are identical to the undamped case except for the mass and stiffness elements; these elements are now complex.

Example 10.9.1

The torsional system of Fig. 10.9.2 is excited by a harmonic torque at a point to the right of disk 4. Determine the torque–frequency curve and establish the first natural frequency of the system.

$$\begin{aligned} J_1 &= J_2 = 57.15 \text{ Nms}^2 \\ J_3 &= J_4 = 114.30 \text{ Nms}^2 \\ K_2 &= K_3 = K_4 = 114300 \text{ Nm/rad} \\ c_2 &= 1143 \text{ Nms/rad} \\ g_4 &= 2286 \text{ Nms/rad} \end{aligned}$$

Solution The numerical computations for $\omega^2 = 1000$ are shown in Table 10.9.1. The complex mass and stiffness terms are first tabulated for each station n. By substituting into the point and field matrices, i.e., Eqs. (10.9.3) and (10.9.4), the complex amplitude and torque for each station are found, as Table 10.9.2.

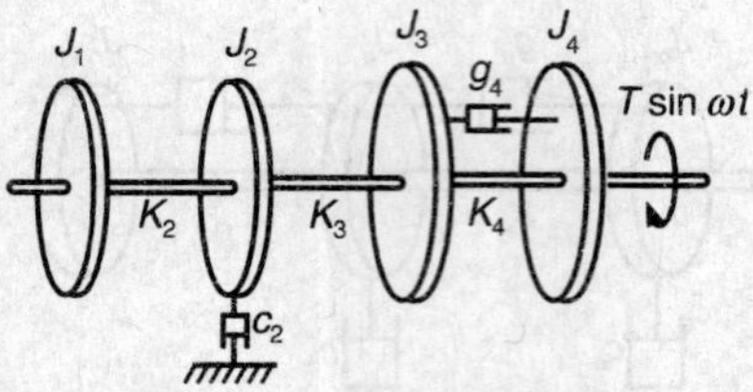

FIGURE 10.9.2.

TABLE 10.9.1

n	$(\omega^2 J_n - i\omega c_n)10^{-6}$	$(K_n + i\omega g_n)10^{-6}$
1	$0.565 + 0.0i$	–
2	$0.565 - 0.357i$	$1.130 + 0.0i$
3	$1.130 - 0.0i$	$1.130 + 0.0i$
4	$1.130 + 0.0i$	$1.130 + 0.715i$

TABLE 10.9.2

n	θ_n	T_n^R (for $\omega^2 = 1000$) $\times 10^{-5}$
1	$1.0 + 0.0i$	$-0.565 + 0.0i$
2	$0.50 + 0.0i$	$-0.848 + 0.179i$
3	$-0.250 + 0.158i$	$-0.565 + 0.0i$
4	$-0.607 + 0.384i$	$0.121 - 0.434i$

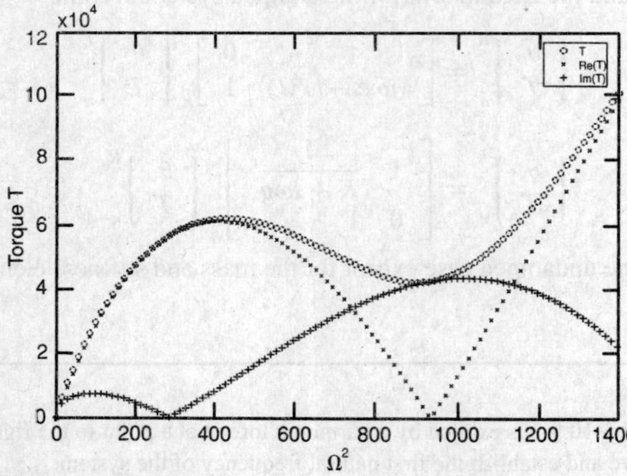

FIGURE 10.9.3. Torsion–frequency curve for the damped torsional system of Fig. 10.9.2.

These computations are repeated for a sufficient number of frequencies to plot the torque–frequency curve of Fig. 10.9.3. The plot shows the real and imaginary parts of T_4^R as well as their resultant, which in this problem is the exciting torque. For example, the resultant torque at $\omega^2 = 1000$ is $10^6\sqrt{(0.121)^2 + (0.434)^2} = 0.451 \times 10^5$ Nm. The first natural frequency of the system from this diagram is found to be approximately $\omega = \sqrt{930} = 30.5$ rad/s, where the natural frequency is defined as that frequency of the undamped system that requires no torque to sustain the motion.

■

Example 10.9.2

In Fig. 10.9.2, if $T = 225$ Nm and $\omega = 31.6$ rad/s, determine the amplitude of the second disk.

Solution Table 10.9.2 indicates that a torque of 4.51×10^4 Nm produces an amplitude of $\theta_2 = 0.50$ rad. Because amplitude is proportional to torque, the amplitude of the second disk for the specified torque is $0.50 \times (225/4.51 \times 10^4) = 0.0025$ rad.

■

10.10 GEARED SYSTEM

Consider the geared torsional system of Fig. 10.10.1, where the speed ratio of shaft 2 to shaft 1 is n. The system can be reduced to an equivalent single shaft system as follows.

With the speed of shaft 2 equal to $\dot{\theta}_2 = n\dot{\theta}_1$, the kinetic energy of the system is

$$T = \frac{1}{2}J_1\dot{\theta}_1^2 + \frac{1}{2}J_2 n^2 n^2 \dot{\theta}_1^2 \tag{10.10.1}$$

Thus, the equivalent inertia of disk 2 referred to shaft 1 is $n^2 J_2$.

To determine the equivalent stiffness of shaft 2 referred to shaft 1, clamp disks 1 and 2 and apply a torque to gear 1, rotating it through an angle θ_1. Gear 2 will then rotate through the angle $\theta_2 = n\theta_1$, which will also be the twist in shaft 2. The potential energy of the system is then

$$U = \frac{1}{2}K_1\theta_1^2 + \frac{1}{2}K_2\theta_1^2 \tag{10.10.2}$$

and the equivalent stiffness of shaft 2 referred to shaft 1 is $n^2 K_2$.

The rule for geared systems is thus quite simple: *Multiply all stiffness and inertias of the geared shaft by* n^2, where n is the speed ratio of the geared shaft to the reference shaft.

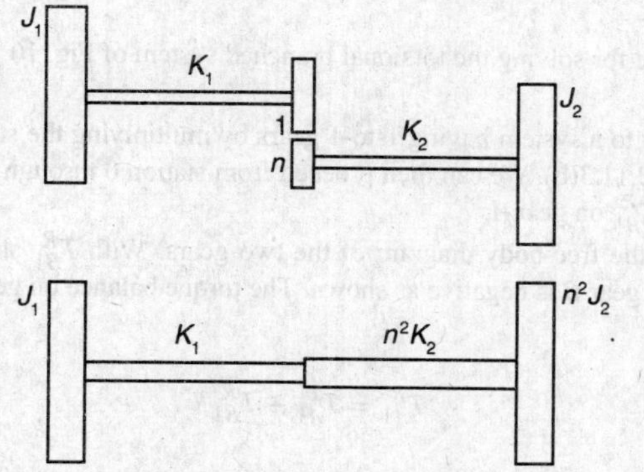

FIGURE 10.10.1. Geared system and its equivalent single-shaft system.

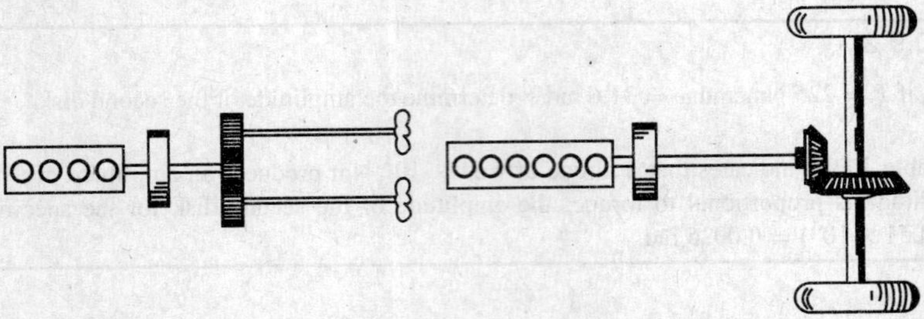

FIGURE 10.11.1. Examples of branched torsional systems.

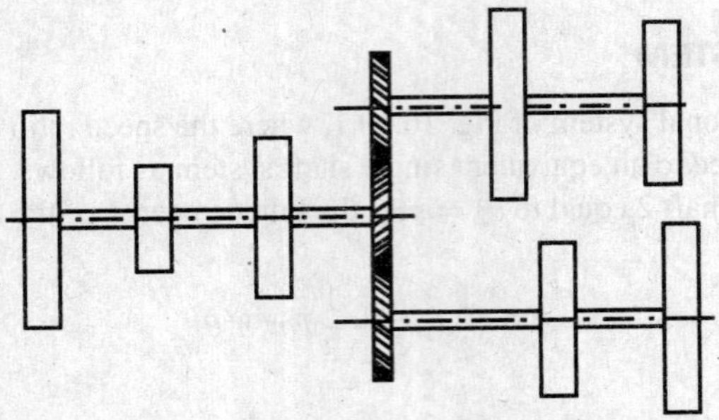

FIGURE 10.11.2. Branched system reduced to common speeds by 1-to-1 gears.

10.11 BRANCHED SYSTEMS

Branched systems are frequently encountered; some common examples are the dual propeller system of a marine installation and the drive shaft and differential of an automobile, which are shown in Fig. 10.11.1.

Such systems can be reduced to the form with 1-to-1 gears shown in Fig. 10.11.2 by multiplying all the inertias and stiffnesses of the branches by the square of their speed ratios.

Example 10.11.1

Outline the matrix procedure for solving the torsional branched system of Fig. 10.11.3.

Solution We first convert to a system having 1-to-1 gears by multiplying the stiffness and inertia of branch B by n^2, as shown in Fig. 10.11.3(b). We can then proceed from station 0 through to station 3, taking note that gear B introduces a torque T_{B1}^R on gear A.

Figure 10.11.4 shows the free-body diagram of the two gears. With T_{B1}^R shown as positive torque, the torque exerted on gear A by gear B is negative as shown. The torque balance on gear A is then

$$T_{A1}^R = T_{A1}^L + T_{B1}^R \tag{a}$$

and we need now to express T_{B1}^R in terms of the angular displacement θ_1 of shaft A.

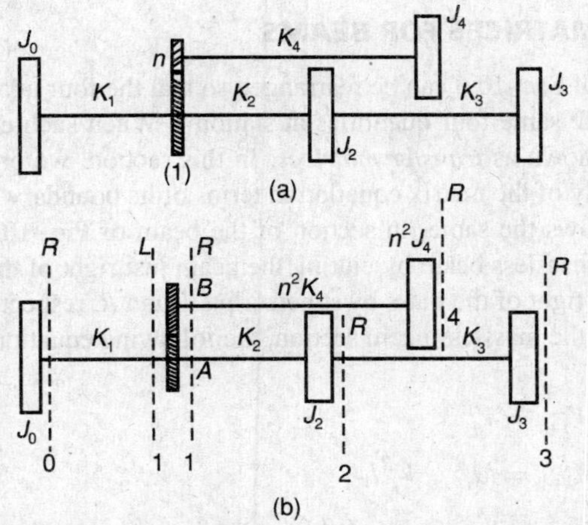

FIGURE 10.11.3. Branched system and reduced system.

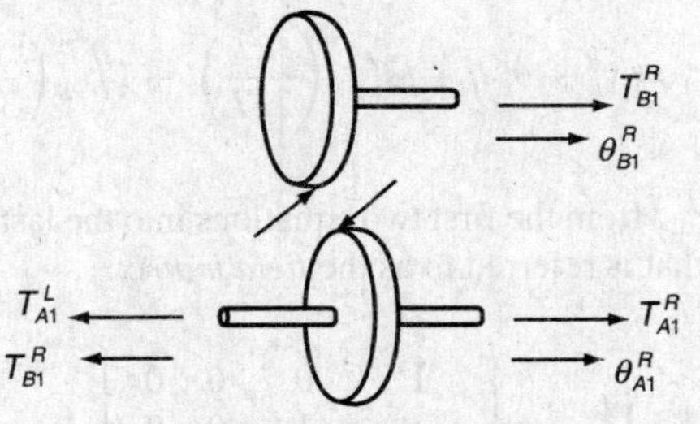

FIGURE 10.11.4.

Using Eq. (10.8.4) and noting that $T^R_{B4} = 0$, we have for shaft B

$$\begin{Bmatrix} \theta_B \\ T_B \end{Bmatrix}^R_1 = \begin{bmatrix} \left(1 - \dfrac{\omega^2 n^2 J_4}{n^2 K_4}\right) & \dfrac{-1}{n^2 K_4} \\ \omega^2 n^3 J_4 & 1 \end{bmatrix} \begin{Bmatrix} \theta_B \\ 0 \end{Bmatrix}^R_4 \tag{b}$$

Because $\theta^R_{B1} = -\theta^L_{A1} = -\theta^R_{A1}$, we obtain

$$\theta^R_{B1} = \left(1 - \frac{\omega^2 J_4}{K_4}\right)\theta^R_{B4} = -\theta^L_{A1} \tag{c}$$

$$T^R_{B1} = \omega^2 n^2 J_4 \theta^R_{B4} \tag{d}$$

By eliminating θ^R_{B4},

$$T^R_{B1} = \frac{-\omega^2 n^2 J_4}{1 - \omega^2 J_4/K_4}\theta^L_{A1} \tag{e}$$

By substituting Eq. (e) into Eq. (a), the transfer function of shaft A across the gears becomes

$$\begin{Bmatrix} \theta_A \\ T_A \end{Bmatrix}^R_1 \underset{\rightarrow}{=} \begin{bmatrix} 1 & 0 \\ -\omega^2 J_4/(1 - \omega^2 J_4/K_4) & 1 \end{bmatrix} \begin{Bmatrix} \theta_A \\ T_A \end{Bmatrix}^L_1 \tag{f}$$

It is now possible to proceed along shaft A from $1R$ to $3R$ in the usual manner.

■

10.12 TRANSFER MATRICES FOR BEAMS

The algebraic equation of Sec. 10.6 can be rearranged so that the four quantities at station $i+1$ are expressed in terms of the same four quantities at station i. When such equations are presented in matrix form, they are known as *transfer matrices*. In this section, we present a procedure for the formulation and assembly of the matrix equation in terms of its boundary conditions.

Figure 10.12.1 shows the same ith section of the beam of Fig. 10.6.1 broken down further into a point mass and a massless beam by cutting the beam just right of the mass. We designate the quantities to the left and right of the mass by superscripts L and R, respectively.

Considering, first, the massless beam section, the following equations can be written:

$$\begin{aligned}
V_{i+i}^L &= V_i^R \\
M_{i+1}^L &= M_i^R - V_i^R l_i \\
\theta_{i+1}^L &= \theta_i^R + M_{i+1}^L\left(\frac{l}{EI}\right)_i + V_{i+1}^L\left(\frac{l^2}{2EI}\right)_i \\
y_{i+1}^L &= y_i^R + \theta_i^R l_i + M_{i+1}^L\left(\frac{l^2}{2EI}\right)_i + V_{i+1}^L\left(\frac{l^3}{3EI}\right)_i
\end{aligned} \tag{10.12.1}$$

Substituting for V_{i+1}^L and M_{i+1}^L from the first two equations into the last two and arranging the results in matrix form, we obtain what is referred to as the *field matrix*:

$$\begin{Bmatrix} -V \\ M \\ \theta \\ y \end{Bmatrix}_{i+1}^L = \begin{bmatrix} 1 & 0 & 0 & 0 \\ l & 1 & 0 & 0 \\ \dfrac{l^2}{2EI} & \dfrac{l}{EI} & 1 & 0 \\ \dfrac{l^3}{6EI} & \dfrac{l^2}{2EI} & l & 1 \end{bmatrix} \begin{Bmatrix} -V \\ M \\ \theta \\ y \end{Bmatrix}_i^R. \tag{10.12.2}$$

In this equation, a minus sign has been inserted for V in order to make the elements of the field matrix all positive.

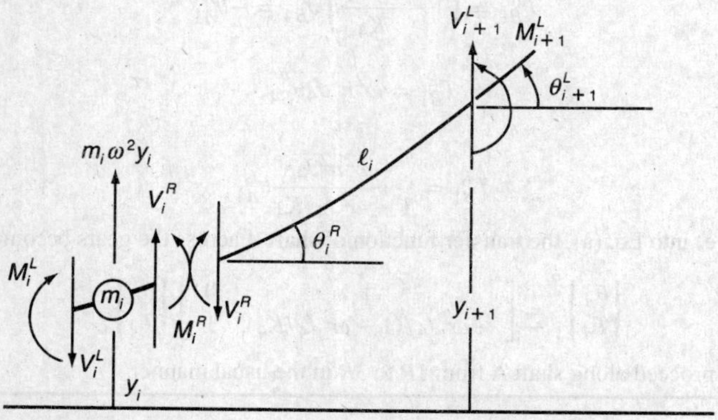

FIGURE 10.12.1. Beam sections for transfer matrices.

Next, consider the point mass for which the following equations can be written:

$$\begin{aligned} V_i^R &= V_i^L - m_i\omega^2 y_i \\ M_i^R &= M_i^L \\ \theta_i^R &= \theta_i^L \\ y_i^R &= y_i^L \end{aligned} \tag{10.12.3}$$

In matrix form, these equations become

$$\begin{Bmatrix} -V \\ M \\ \theta \\ y \end{Bmatrix}_i^R = \begin{bmatrix} 1 & 0 & 0 & m\omega^2 \\ 0 & 1 & 0 & 0 \\ 0 & 0 & 1 & 0 \\ 0 & 0 & 0 & 1 \end{bmatrix} \begin{Bmatrix} -V \\ M \\ \theta \\ y \end{Bmatrix}_i^L \tag{10.12.4}$$

which is known as the *point matrix*.

Substituting Eq. (10.12.4) into Eq. (10.12.2) and multiplying, we obtain the assembled equation for the ith section:

$$\begin{Bmatrix} -V \\ M \\ \theta \\ y \end{Bmatrix}_{i+1}^R = \begin{bmatrix} 1 & 0 & 0 & m\omega^2 \\ l & 1 & 0 & m\omega^2 l \\ \dfrac{l^2}{2EI} & \dfrac{l}{EI} & 1 & m\omega^2 \dfrac{l^2}{2EI} \\ \dfrac{l^3}{6EI} & \dfrac{l^2}{2EI} & l & \left(1 + \dfrac{m\omega^2 l^3}{6EI}\right) \end{bmatrix} \begin{Bmatrix} -V \\ M \\ \theta \\ y \end{Bmatrix}_i^L \tag{10.12.5}$$

The square matrix in this equation is called the *transfer matrix*, because the state vector at i is transferred to the state vector at $i + 1$ through this matrix. It is evident then that it is possible to progress through the structure so that the state vector at the far end is related to the state vector at the starting end by an equation of the form

$$\begin{Bmatrix} -V \\ M \\ \theta \\ y \end{Bmatrix}_n = \begin{bmatrix} u_{11} & u_{12} & - & u_{14} \\ - & - & - & - \\ - & - & - & - \\ u_{41} & u_{42} & - & u_{44} \end{bmatrix} \begin{Bmatrix} -V \\ M \\ \theta \\ y \end{Bmatrix}_1 \tag{10.12.6}$$

where matrix $[u]$ is the product of all the transfer matrices of the structure.

The advantage of the transfer matrix lies in the fact that the unknown quantity at 1, i.e., θ_1, for the cantilever beam, need not be carried through each station as in the algebraic set of equations. The multiplication of the 4×4 matrices by the digital computer is a routine problem. Also, the boundary equations are clearly evident in the matrix equation. For example, the assembled equation for the cantilever beam is

$$\begin{Bmatrix} -V \\ M \\ 0 \\ 0 \end{Bmatrix}_n = \begin{bmatrix} - & - & - & - \\ - & - & - & - \\ - & - & u_{33} & u_{34} \\ - & - & u_{43} & u_{44} \end{bmatrix} \begin{Bmatrix} 0 \\ 0 \\ \theta \\ 1 \end{Bmatrix}_1 \tag{10.12.7}$$

and the natural frequencies must satisfy the equations

$$0 = u_{33}\theta + u_{34}$$

$$0 = u_{43}\theta + u_{44}$$

or

$$y_n = -\frac{u_{34}}{u_{33}} \cdot u_{43} + u_{44} = 0 \tag{10.12.8}$$

In a plot of y_n vs. ω, the natural frequencies correspond to the zeros of the curve.

REFERENCES

[1] S. Dunkerley, "On the Whirling and Vibration of Shafts," *Phil. Trans. Roy. Soc.*, Vol. 185 (1895), pp. 269–360.

[2] H. Holzer, *Die Berechnung der Drehschwingungen* (Berlin: Springer-Verlag, 1921).

[3] N. O. Myklestad, "A New Method of Calculating Natural Modes of Uncoupled Bending Vibration of Airplane Wings and Other Types of Beams," *J. Aero. Sci.* (April 1944), pp. 153–162.

[4] N. O. Myklestad, "Vibration Analysis" (New York: McGraw-Hill, 1944).

[5] E. C. Pestel and F. A. Leckie, "Matrix Methods in Elastomechanics" (New York: McGraw-Hill, 1963).

PROBLEMS

10.1. Using Rayleigh's method, estimate the fundamental frequency of the lumped-mass system shown in Fig. P10.1.

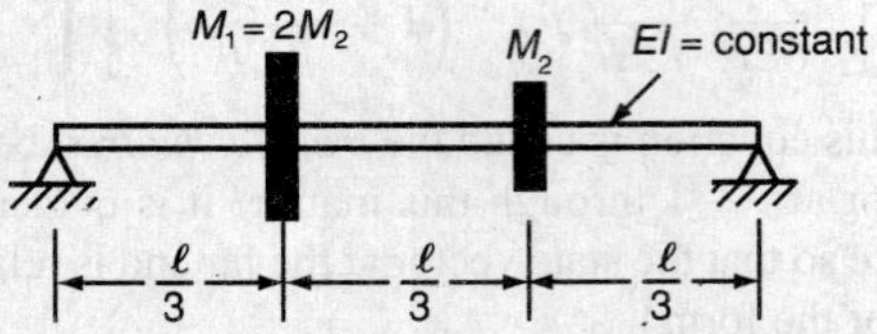

FIGURE P10.1.

10.2. Estimate the fundamental frequency of the lumped-mass cantilever beam shown in Fig. P10.2.

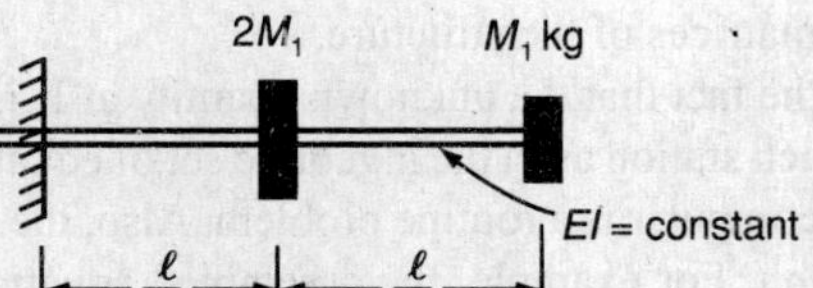

FIGURE P10.2.

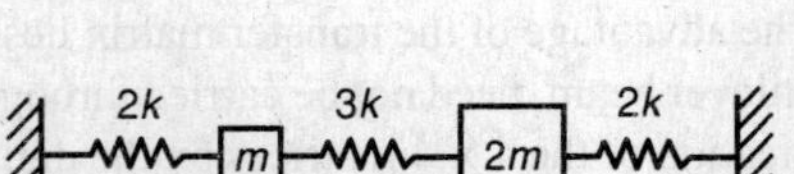

FIGURE P10.3.

10.3. Write the kinetic and potential energy expressions for the system of Fig. P10.3 and determine the equation for ω^2 by equating the two energies. Letting $x_2/x_1 = n$, plot ω^2 versus n. Pick the maximum and minimum values of ω^2 and the corresponding values of n, and show that they represent the two natural modes of the system.

10.4. Using the curve

$$y(x) = \frac{l^3}{3EI}\left(\frac{x}{l}\right)^2$$

solve Prob. 10.2 by using the method of integration. *Hint:* Draw shear and moment diagrams based on inertia loads.

10.5. Another form of Rayleigh's quotient for the fundamental frequency can be obtained by starting from the equation of motion based on the flexibility influence coefficient

$$X = aM\ddot{X}$$
$$= \omega^2 aMX$$

Premultiplying by $X^T M$, we obtain

$$X^T MX = \omega^2 X^T MaMX$$

and the Rayleigh quotient becomes

$$\omega^2 = \frac{X^T MX}{X^T MaMX}$$

Solve for ω_1 in Example 10.1.4 by using the foregoing equation.

10.6. Using the deflection

$$y(x) = y_{\max} \sin(\pi x/l),$$

determine the fundamental frequency of the beam shown in Fig. P10.6 (a) if $EI_2 = EI_1$ and (b) if $EI_2 = 4EI_1$.

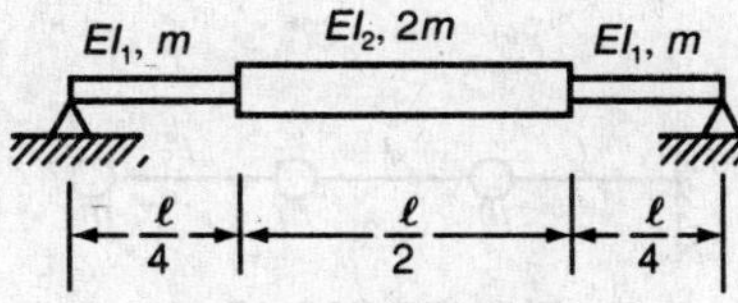

FIGURE P10.6.

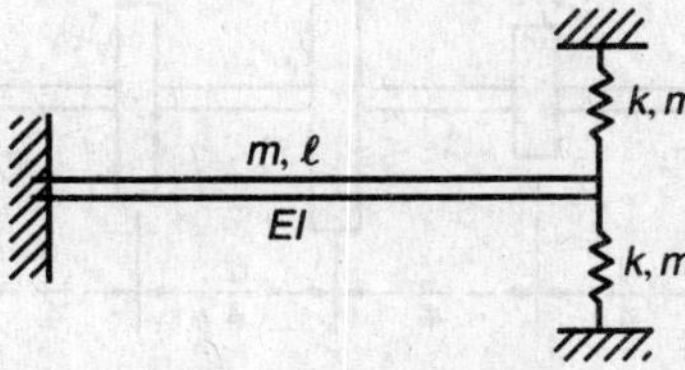

FIGURE P10.8.

10.7. Repeat Prob. 10.6, but use the curve

$$y(x) = y_{\max}\frac{4x}{l}\left(1 - \frac{x}{l}\right)$$

10.8. A uniform cantilever beam of mass m per unit length has its free end pinned to two springs of stiffness k and mass m_0 each, as shown in Fig. P10.8. Using Rayleigh's method, find its natural frequency ω_1.

10.9. A uniform beam of mass M and stiffness $K = EI/l^3$, shown in Fig. P10.9, is supported on equal springs with total vertical stiffness of k lb/in. Using Rayleigh's method with the deflection $y_{\max} = \sin(\pi x/l) + b$, show that the frequency equation becomes

$$\omega^2 = \frac{2k}{M}\left[\frac{\frac{K}{k}\frac{\pi^4}{4} + \frac{b^2}{2}}{\frac{1}{2} + \frac{4b}{\pi} + b^2}\right]$$

By $\partial\omega^2/\partial b = 0$, show that the lowest frequency results when

$$b = -\frac{\pi}{4}\left(\frac{1}{2} - \frac{K\pi^4}{2k}\right) \pm \sqrt{\left[\frac{\pi}{2}\left(\frac{1}{2} - \frac{K\pi^4}{2k}\right)\right]^2 + \frac{\pi^4 K}{2k}}$$

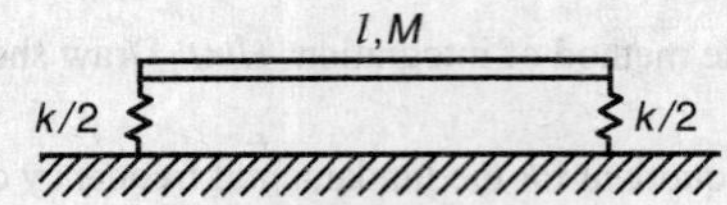

FIGURE P10.9.

10.10. Assuming a static deflection curve

$$y(x) = y_{max}\left[3\left(\frac{x}{l}\right) - 4\left(\frac{x}{l}\right)^3\right], \qquad 0 \leqslant x \leqslant \frac{1}{2}$$

determine the lowest natural frequency of a simply supported beam of constant EI and a mass distribution of

$$m(x) = m_0\frac{x}{l}\left(1 - \frac{x}{l}\right)$$

by the Rayleigh method.

10.11. Using Dunkerley's equation, determine the fundamental frequency of the beam shown in Fig. P10.11.

$$W_1 = W, \quad W_2 = 4W, \quad W_3 = 2W$$

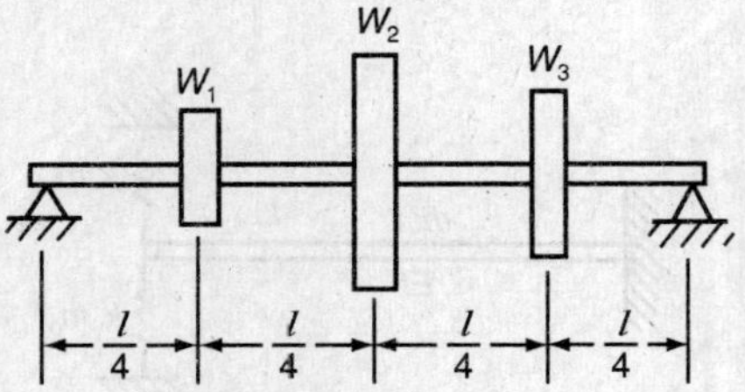

FIGURE P10.11.

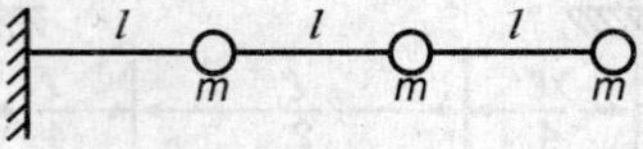

FIGURE P10.13.

10.12. A load of 500 N at the wing tip of a fighter plane produced a corresponding deflection of 20 mm. If the fundamental bending frequency of the same wing is 622 cpm, approximate the new bending frequency when a 150 kg fuel tank (including fuel) is attached to the wing tip.

10.13. Using Dunkerley's equation, determine the fundamental frequency of the three-mass cantilever beam shown in Fig. P10.13.

10.14. A given beam was vibrated by an eccentric mass shaker of mass 5.44 kg at the midspan, and resonance was found at 435 cps. With an additional mass of 4.52 kg, the resonant frequency was lowered to 398 cps. Determine the natural frequency of the beam.

10.15. For the wedge-shaped plate of Example 10.3.1, determine the first two natural frequencies and mode shapes for bending vibration by using the Ritz deflection function $y = C_1x^2 + C_2x^3$.

10.16. Using the Rayleigh–Ritz method, determine the first two natural frequencies and mode shapes for the longitudinal vibration of a uniform rod with a spring of stiffness k_0 attached to the free end, as shown in Fig. P10.16. Use the first two normal modes of the fixed-free rod in longitudinal motion.

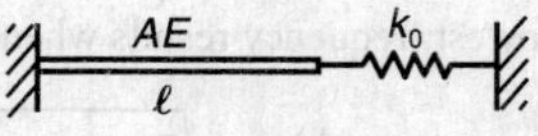

FIGURE P10.16.

10.17. Using the Rayleigh–Ritz method and assuming modes x/l and $\sin(\pi x/l)$, determine the two natural frequencies and modes of a uniform beam pinned at the right end and attached to a spring of stiffness k at the left end (Fig. P10.17).

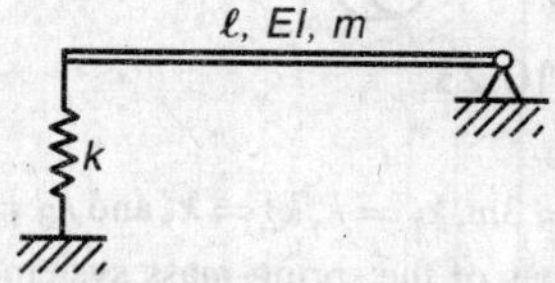

FIGURE P10.17.

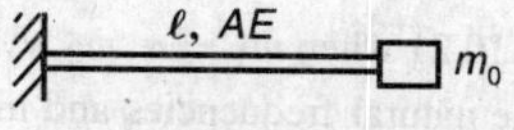

FIGURE P10.18.

10.18. Repeat Prob. 10.16, but this time, the spring is replaced by a mass m_0, as shown in Fig. P10.18.

10.19. For the simply supported variable mass beam of Prob. 10.10, assume the deflection to be made up of the first two modes of the uniform beam and solve for the two natural frequencies and mode shapes by the Rayleigh–Ritz method.

10.20. A uniform rod hangs freely from a hinge at the top. Using the three modes $\phi_1 = x/l$, $\phi_2 = \sin(\pi x/l)$, and $\phi_3 = \sin(2\pi x/l)$, determine the characteristic equation by using the Rayleigh–Ritz method.

M **10.21.** Determine the natural frequencies and mode shapes of the three-story building of Fig. P10.21 by using Holzer's method for all $m_s = m$ and all $k_s = k$.

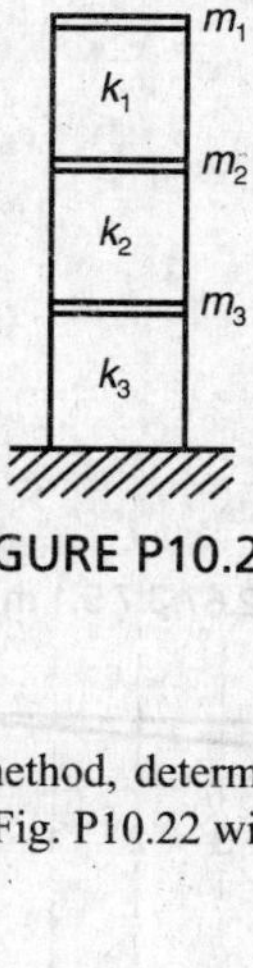

FIGURE P10.21.

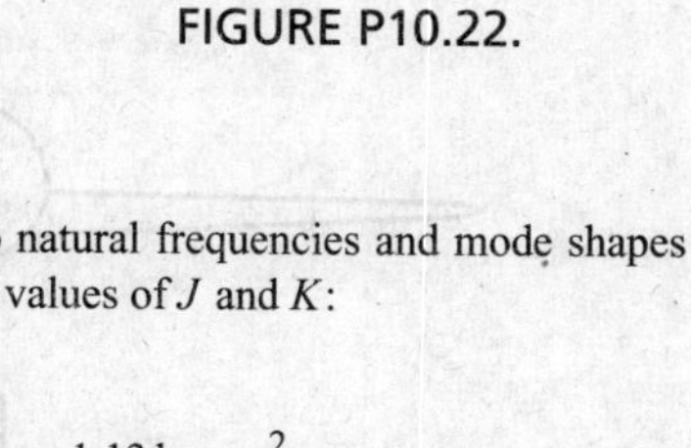

FIGURE P10.22.

M **10.22.** Using Holzer's method, determine the first two natural frequencies and mode shapes of the torsional system shown in Fig. P10.22 with the following values of J and K:

$$J_1 = J_2 = J_3 = 1.13\,\text{kg}\cdot\text{m}^2$$
$$J_4 = 2.26\,\text{kg}\cdot\text{m}^2$$
$$K_1 = K_2 = 0.169 \times 10^6\,\text{Nm/rad}$$
$$K_3 = 0.226 \times 10^6\,\text{Nm/rad}$$

M **10.23.** Using Holzer's method, determine the natural frequencies and mode shapes of the torsional system of Fig. P10.23 when $J = 5\,\text{kg}\cdot\text{m}^2$ and $K = 20 \times 10^6\,\text{Nm/rad}$.

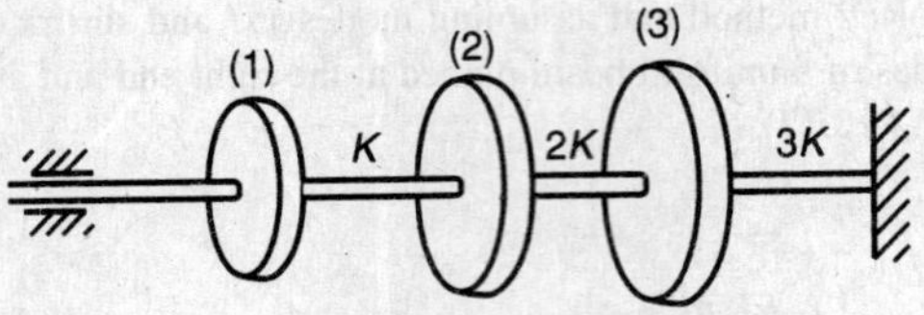

FIGURE P10.23.

M **10.24.** Repeat Prob. 10.21 when $m_1 = m, m_2 = 2m, m_3 = 3m, k_1 = k, k_2 = k$, and $k_3 = 2k$.

M **10.25.** Determine the natural frequencies and mode shapes of the spring-mass system of Fig. P10.25 by the Holzer method when all masses are equal and stiffnesses are equal.

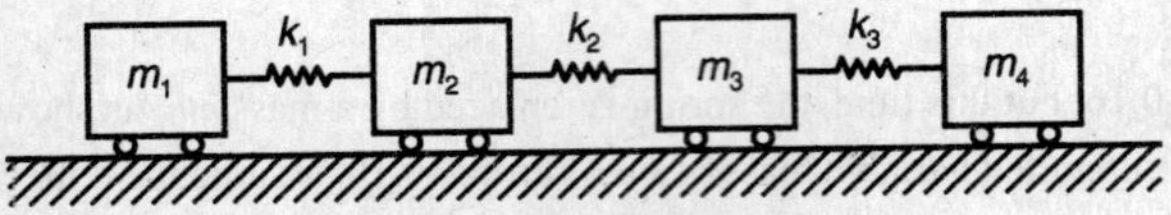

FIGURE P10.25.

M **10.26.** A fighter-plane wing is reduced to a series of disks and shafts for Holzer's analysis, as shown in Fig. P10.26. Determine the first two natural frequencies for symmetric and antisymmetric torsional oscillations of the wings, and plot the torsional mode corresponding to each.

n	J kg · m^2	K Nm/rad
1	5.65	1.7×10^6
2	15.58	3.4
3	16.37	2.5
4	20.44	4.1
5	29.35	13.6
6	$\frac{1}{2} \times 15{,}806$	

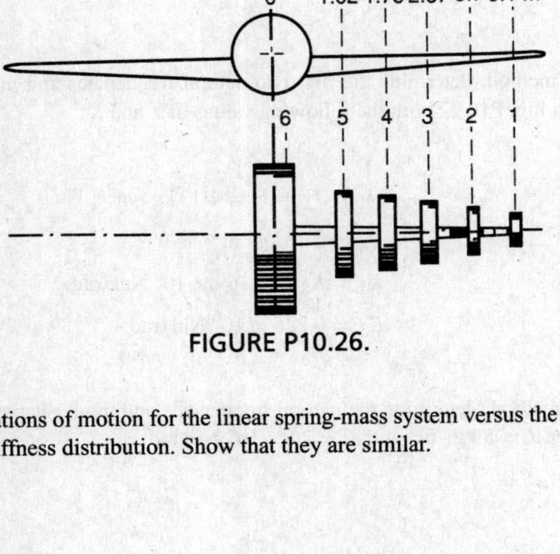

FIGURE P10.26.

10.27. Compare the equations of motion for the linear spring-mass system versus the torsional system with the same mass and stiffness distribution. Show that they are similar.

10.28. Determine the natural modes of the simplified model of an airplane shown in Fig. P10.28 where $M/m = n$ and the beam length l is uniform.

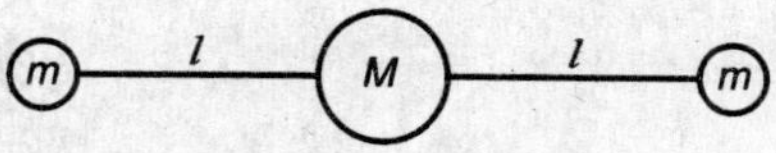

FIGURE P10.28.

10.29. Using Myklestad's method, determine the boundary equations for the simply supported beam of Fig. P10.29.

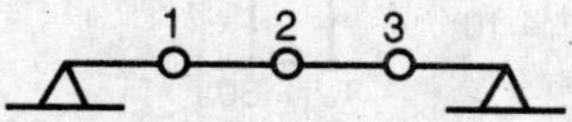

FIGURE P10.29.

M **10.30.** Determine the first two natural frequencies and mode shapes of the three-mass cantilever of Fig. P10.30.

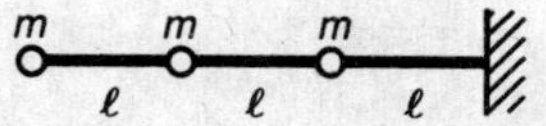

FIGURE P10.30.

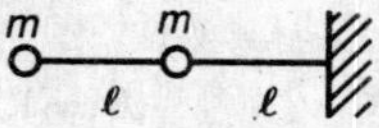

FIGURE P10.31.

10.31. Using Myklestad's method, determine the natural frequencies and mode shapes of the two-lumped-mass cantilever beam of Fig. P10.31. Compare with previous results by using influence coefficients.

10.32. For the beam of Fig. P10.32, check that the boundary condition of zero deflection at the left end is satisfied for these natural frequencies when Myklestad's method is used. That is, check the deflection for change in sign when frequencies above and below the natural frequency are used.

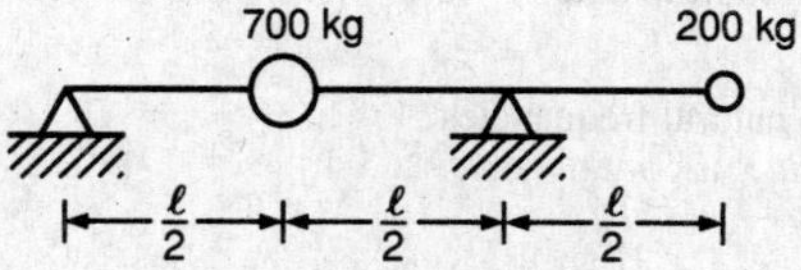

FIGURE P10.32.

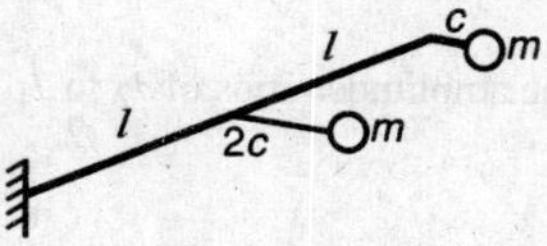

FIGURE P10.33.

10.33. Determine the flexure–torsion vibration for the system shown in Fig. P10.33.

M **10.34.** A torsional system with a torsional damper is shown in Fig. P10.34. Determine the torque–frequency curve for the system.

M **10.35.** Shown in Fig. P10.35 is a linear system with damping between masses 1 and 2. Carry out a computer analysis for numerical values assigned by the instructor, and determine the amplitude and phase of each mass at a specified frequency.

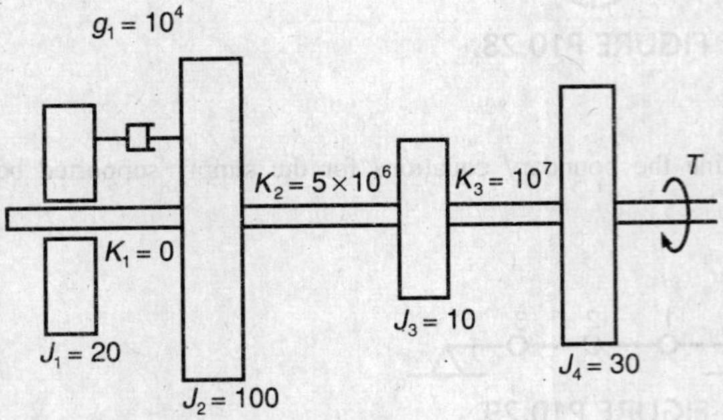

FIGURE P10.34.

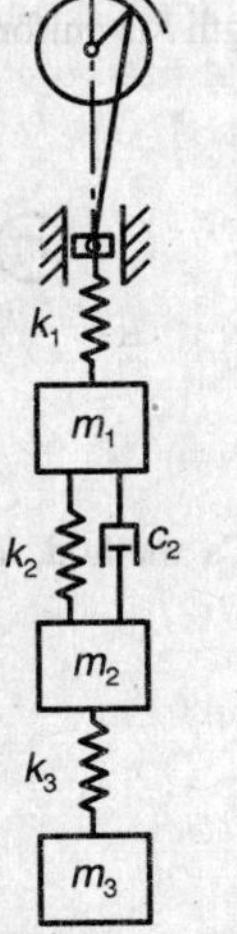

FIGURE P10.35.

10.36. Determine the lowest natural frequencies of the torsional system shown in Fig. P10.36 for the following values of J, K, and n:

$$J_1 = 1.7 \text{ kgm}^2$$
$$K_1 = 2.26 \times 10^5 \text{ Nm/rad}$$
$$J_2 = 1.1 \text{ kgm}^2$$
$$K_2 = 1.81 \times 10^5 \text{ Nm/rad}$$
$$J_3 = 2 \text{ kgm}^2$$
$$K_3 = 1.13 \times 10^5 \text{ Nm/rad}$$
$$J_4 = 0.7 \text{ kgm}^2$$
$$K_4 = 4.52 \times 10^5 \text{ Nm/rad}$$

Speed ratio of the drive shaft to axle = 4 to 1

What are the amplitude ratios of J_2 to J_1 at the natural frequencies?

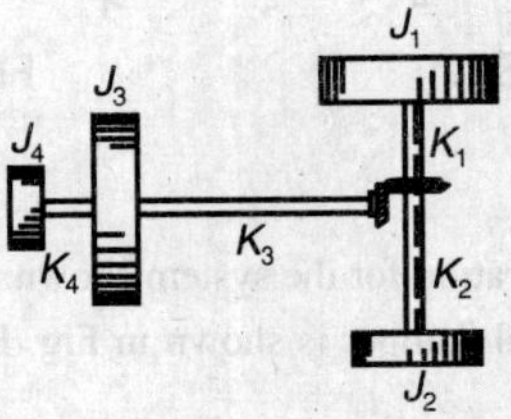

FIGURE P10.36.

10.37. Reduce the torsional system of the automobile shown in Fig. P10.37(a) to the equivalent torsional system shown in Fig. P10.37(b). The necessary information is as follows:

J of each rear wheel = 1.04 kgm ^{2}
J of flywheel = 1.39 kgm ^{2}
Transmission of speed ratio (drive shaft of engine speed) = 1.0 to 3.0
Differential speed ratio (axle to drive shaft) = 1.0 to 3.5
Axle dimensions = 31.75 mm diameter, 635 mm long (each)
Drive shaft dimensions = 38 mm diameter, 1880 mm long
Stiffness of crankshaft between cylinders, measured experimentally = 6.9×10^5 Nm/rad
Stiffness of crankshaft between cylinder 4 and flywheel = 5.1×10^5 Nm/rad

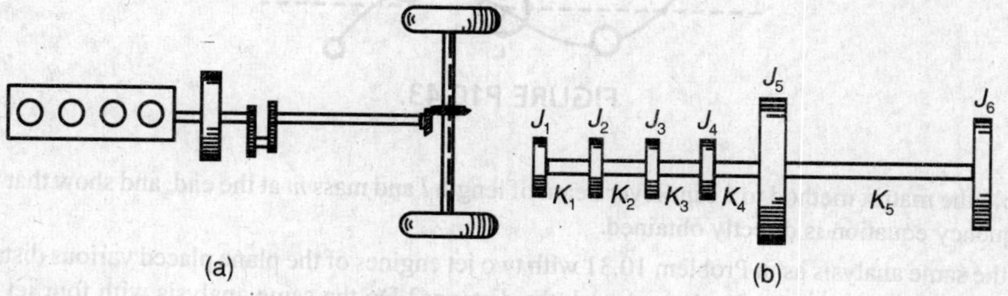

FIGURE P10.37.

10.38. Determine the equivalent torsional system for the geared system shown in Fig. P10.38 and find its natural frequency.

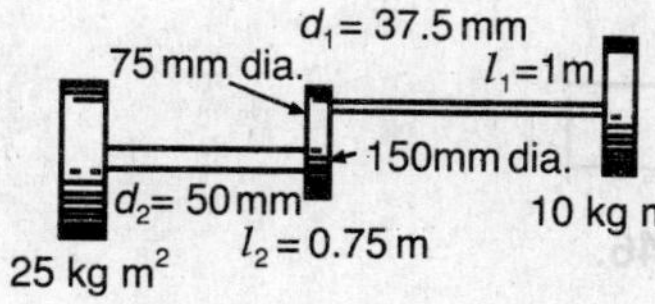

FIGURE P10.38.

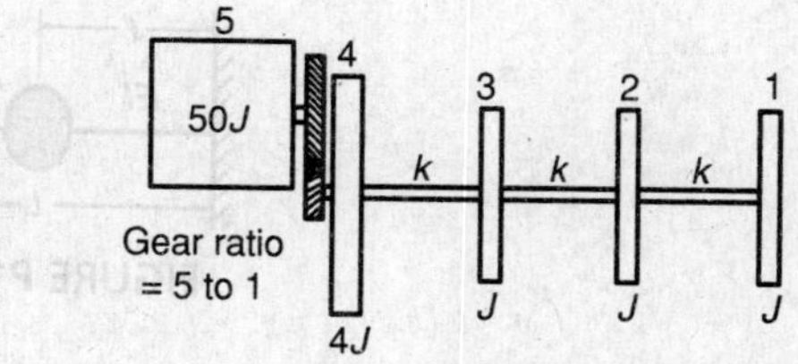

FIGURE P10.41.

10.39. If the small and large gears of Prob. 10.38 have the inertias $J' = 2$ and $J'' = 6$, determine the equivalent single shaft system and establish the natural frequencies.

M **10.40.** Assume that the J of each cylinder of Prob. 10.37 = 0.0225 kg m^2 and determine the natural frequencies of the system.

10.41. Determine the equations for the torsional system shown in Fig. P10.41. Solve for the principal modes of oscillation.

10.42. Apply the matrix method to a cantilever beam with two equal masses spaced equally at distance l. Show that the boundary conditions of zero slope and deflection lead to the equation

$$\theta_1 = \frac{\frac{1}{2}m\omega^2 lK\left(5 + \frac{1}{6}m\omega^2 l^2 K\right)}{1 + \frac{1}{2}l^2 Km\omega^2}$$

$$= \frac{1 + \frac{3}{2}m\omega^2 l^2 K + \left(\frac{1}{6}m\omega^2 l^2 K\right)^2}{2l + \frac{1}{6}m\omega^2 l^3 K}$$

where $K = l/EI$. Obtain the frequency equation from the foregoing relationship and determine the two natural frequencies.

10.43. Using the matrix formulation, establish the boundary conditions for the symmetric and antisymmetric bending modes for the system shown in Fig. P10.43. Plot the boundary determinant against the frequency ω to establish the natural frequencies, and draw the first two mode shapes.

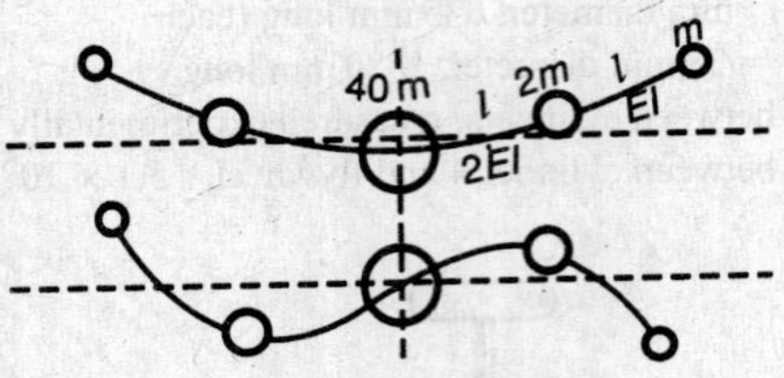

FIGURE P10.43.

10.44. Apply the matrix method to a cantilever beam of length l and mass m at the end, and show that the natural frequency equation is directly obtained.

10.45. Do the same analysis as in Problem 10.31 with two jet engines of the plane placed various distances from the body. How do the results depend on l, the distance? Do the same analysis with four jet engines of the plane placed symmetrically about the body. The first pair is placed an arbitrary distance l_1 from the body and the second pair is placed at the distance l_2 from the first. How do the results depend on l_1, l_2?

10.46. Determine the fundamental frequency for the problem shown in Fig. P10.46 using the Rayleigh method. Plot the dependency of the frequency on l.

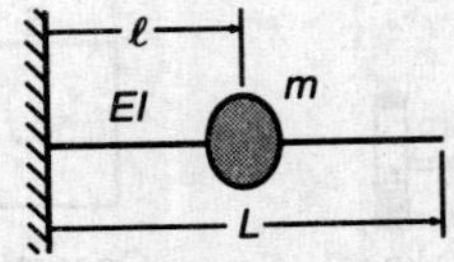

FIGURE P10.46.

10.47. Determine the fundamental frequency for the problem shown in Fig. P10.47 using Dunkerley's equation. Plot the dependency of the frequency on l_1 and l_2.

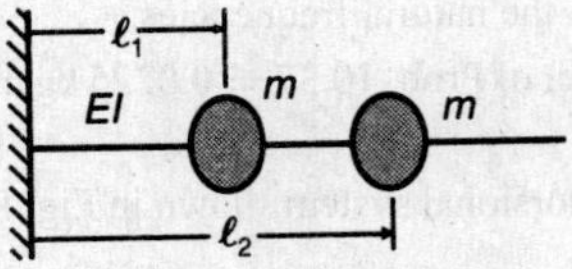

FIGURE P10.47.

10.48. Estimate the fundamental frequency for the two previous problems using the Rayleigh–Ritz method.

CHAPTER 11

Introduction to the Finite Element Method

Before discussing the finite element method, we determine the stiffness matrix of simple frame structures by considering the structure as an assemblage of structural elements. With the forces and moments at the ends of the elements known from structural theory, the joints between the elements are matched for compatibility of displacements and the forces and moments at the joints are established by imposing the condition of equilibrium.

In the finite element method, the same procedure is followed, but in a more systematic way for computer calculation. Although structures with few elements can be analyzed simply by the method outlined initially, the "bookkeeping" for a large structure of many elements would soon overcome the patience of the analyst. In the finite element method, element coordinates and forces are transformed into global coordinates and the stiffness matrix of the entire structure is presented in a global system of common orientation.

The accuracy obtainable from the finite element method depends on being able to duplicate the vibration mode shapes. Using only one finite element between structural joints or corners gives good results for the first lowest mode because the static deflection curve is a good approximation to the lowest dynamic mode shape. For higher modes, several elements are necessary between structural joints. This leads to large matrices for which a computer is essential in solving for the eigenvalues and eigenvectors of the system.

This chapter introduces the reader to the basic ideas of the finite element method and also includes the development of the corresponding mass matrix to complete the equations of motion for the dynamic problem. Only structural elements for the axial and beam elements are discussed here. For the treatment of plates and shells, the reader is referred to other texts.

11.1 FLEXIBILITY INFLUENCE COEFFICIENTS

The elastic behavior of a system can be expressed either in terms of the stiffness or the flexibility. So far, we have written the equations of motion for the normal mode vibration in terms of the stiffness K:

$$(-\omega^2[M] + [K])\{X\} = \{0\} \tag{11.1.1}$$

In the stiffness formulation, the force is expressed in terms of the displacement:

$$\{F\} = [K]\{X\} \tag{11.1.2}$$

The flexibility is the inverse of the stiffness. The displacement is here written in terms of the force:

$$\begin{aligned}\{X\} &= [K]^{-1}\{F\} \\ &= [a]\{F\}\end{aligned} \tag{11.1.3}$$

The equation of motion in terms of the flexibility is easily determined by premultiplying Eq. (11.1.1) by $[K]^{-1} = [a]$:

$$(-\omega^2[a][M] + I)\{X\} = \{0\} \tag{11.1.4}$$

where $K^{-1}K = \mathrm{I} =$ unit matrix.

The choice as to which approach to adopt depends on the problem. Some problems are more easily pursued on the basis of stiffness, and for others, the flexibility approach is desirable. The inverse property of one or the other is an important concept that is used throughout the theory of vibration.

The flexibility matrix written in terms of its coefficients a_{ij} is

$$\begin{Bmatrix} x_1 \\ x_2 \\ x_3 \end{Bmatrix} = \begin{bmatrix} a_{11} & a_{12} & a_{13} \\ a_{21} & a_{22} & a_{23} \\ a_{31} & a_{32} & a_{33} \end{bmatrix} \begin{Bmatrix} f_1 \\ f_2 \\ f_3 \end{Bmatrix} \tag{11.1.5}$$

The *flexibility influence coefficient* a_{ij} is defined as the displacement at i due to a unit force applied at j with all other forces equal to zero. Thus, the first column of the foregoing matrix represents the displacements corresponding to $f_1 = 1$ and $f_2 = f_3 = 0$. The second column is equal to the displacements for $f_2 = 1$ and $f_1 = f_3 = 0$, and so on.

Example 11.1.1

Determine the flexibility matrix for the three-spring system of Fig. 11.1.1.

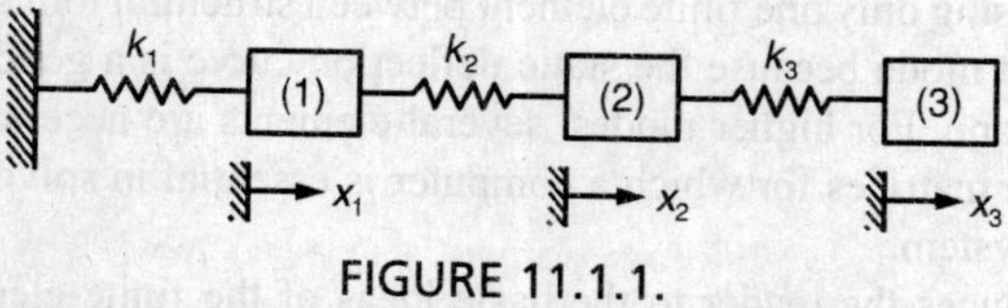

FIGURE 11.1.1.

Solution By applying a unit force $f_1 = 1$ at (1) with $f_2 = f_3 = 0$, the displacements, x_1, x_2, and x_3, are found for the first column of the flexibility matrix

$$\begin{Bmatrix} x_1 \\ x_2 \\ x_3 \end{Bmatrix} = \begin{bmatrix} \hat{a}/k_1 & 0 & 0 \\ 1/k_1 & 0 & 0 \\ 1/k_1 & 0 & 0 \end{bmatrix} \begin{Bmatrix} f_1 = 1 \\ 0 \\ 0 \end{Bmatrix}$$

Here springs k_2 and k_3 are unstretched and are displaced equally with station (1).

Next, apply forces $f_1 = 0$, $f_2 = 1$, and $f_3 = 0$, to obtain

$$\begin{Bmatrix} x_1 \\ x_2 \\ x_3 \end{Bmatrix} = \begin{bmatrix} 0 & \frac{1}{k_1} & 0 \\ 0 & \left(\frac{1}{k_1} + \frac{1}{k_2}\right) & 0 \\ 0 & \left(\frac{1}{k_1} + \frac{1}{k_2}\right) & 0 \end{bmatrix} \begin{Bmatrix} 0 \\ 1 \\ 0 \end{Bmatrix}$$

In this case, the unit force is transmitted through k_1 and k_2, and k_3 is unstretched.

In a similar manner, for $f_1 = 0$, $f_2 = 0$, and $f_3 = 1$, we have

$$\begin{Bmatrix} x_1 \\ x_2 \\ x_3 \end{Bmatrix} = \begin{bmatrix} 0 & 0 & \frac{1}{k_1} \\ 0 & 0 & \frac{1}{k_1} + \frac{1}{k_2} \\ 0 & 0 & \frac{1}{k_1} + \frac{1}{k_2} + \frac{1}{k_3} \end{bmatrix} \begin{Bmatrix} 0 \\ 0 \\ 1 \end{Bmatrix}$$

The complete flexibility matrix is now the sum of the three prior matrices:

$$\begin{Bmatrix} x_1 \\ x_2 \\ x_3 \end{Bmatrix} = \begin{bmatrix} \frac{1}{k_1} & \frac{1}{k_1} & \frac{1}{k_1} \\ \frac{1}{k_1} & \frac{1}{k_1} + \frac{1}{k_2} & \frac{1}{k_1} + \frac{1}{k_2} \\ \frac{1}{k_1} & \frac{1}{k_1} + \frac{1}{k_2} & \frac{1}{k_1} + \frac{1}{k_2} + \frac{1}{k_3} \end{bmatrix} \begin{Bmatrix} f_1 \\ f_2 \\ f_3 \end{Bmatrix}$$

Note the symmetry of the matrix about the diagonal.

■

Example 11.1.2

Determine the flexibility matrix for the system shown in Fig. 11.1.2.

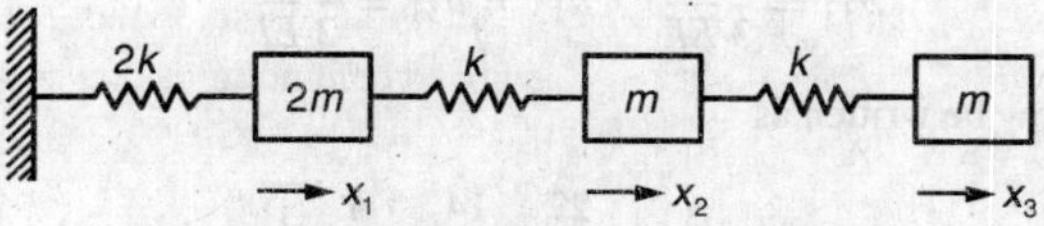

FIGURE 11.1.2.

Solution We have here $k_1 = 2k$, $k_2 = k$, and $k_3 = k$, and the flexibility matrix from Example 11.1.1 becomes

$$[\mathbf{a}] = \frac{1}{k}\begin{bmatrix} 0.5 & 0.5 & 0.5 \\ 0.5 & 1.5 & 1.5 \\ 0.5 & 1.5 & 2.5 \end{bmatrix}$$

■

Example 11.1.3

Determine the flexibility influence coefficients for stations (1), (2), and (3) of the uniform cantilever beam shown in Fig. 11.1.3.

Solution The influence coefficients can be determined by placing unit loads at (1), (2), and (3) as shown, and calculating the deflections at these points. By using the area moment method,[1] the deflection at the various stations is equal to the moment of the M/EI area about the position in question. For example, the value of $a_{21} = a_{12}$ is found from Fig. 11.1.3 as follows:

$$a_{12} = \frac{1}{EI}\left[\frac{1}{2}(2l)^2 \times \frac{7}{3}l\right] = \frac{14}{3}\frac{l^3}{EI}$$

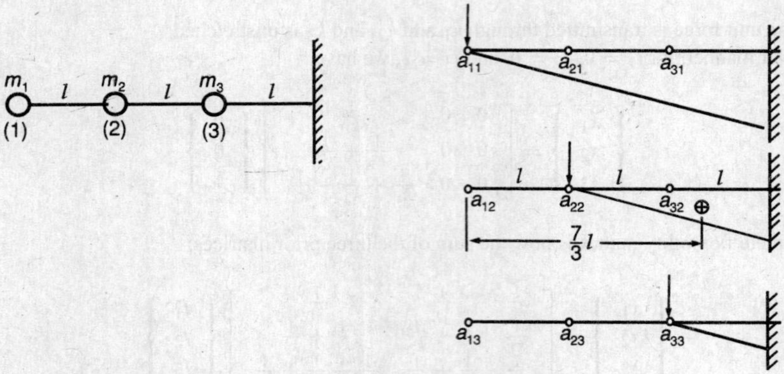

FIGURE 11.1.3.

The other values (determined as before) are

$$a_{11} = \frac{27}{3}\frac{l^3}{EI} \qquad a_{21} = a_{12} = \frac{14}{3}\frac{l^3}{EI}$$
$$a_{22} = \frac{8}{3}\frac{l^3}{EI} \qquad a_{23} = a_{32} = \frac{2.5}{3}\frac{l^3}{EI}$$
$$a_{33} = \frac{1}{3}\frac{l^3}{EI} \qquad a_{13} = a_{31} = \frac{4}{3}\frac{l^3}{EI}$$

The flexibility matrix can now be written as

$$a = \frac{l^3}{3EI}\begin{bmatrix} 27 & 14 & 4 \\ 14 & 8 & 2.5 \\ 4 & 2.5 & 1 \end{bmatrix}$$

and the symmetry about the diagonal should be noted. ■

Example 11.1.4

The flexibility influence coefficients can be used to set up the equations of a flexible shaft supported by a rigid bearing at one end with a force P and a moment M at the other end, as shown in Fig. 11.1.4.

The deflection and slope at the free end is

$$\begin{aligned} y &= a_{11}P + a_{12}M \\ \theta &= a_{21}P + a_{22}M \end{aligned} \tag{11.1.6}$$

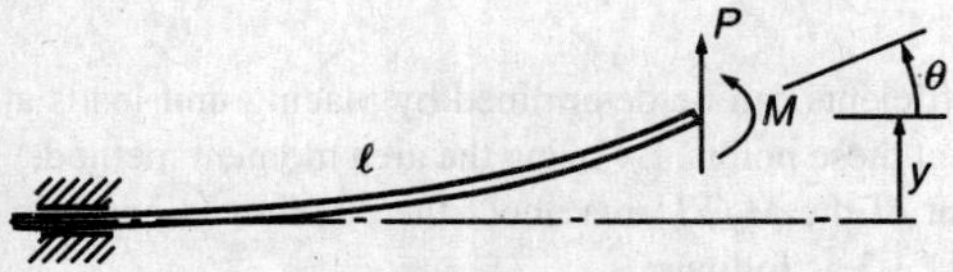

FIGURE 11.1.4.

FIGURE 11.1.5.
Demonstration gyroscope. (*Courtesy of UCSB Mechanical Engineering Undergraduate Laboratory.*)

which can be expressed by the matrix equation

$$\begin{Bmatrix} y \\ \theta \end{Bmatrix} = \begin{bmatrix} a_{11} & a_{12} \\ a_{21} & a_{22} \end{bmatrix} \begin{Bmatrix} P \\ M \end{Bmatrix} \tag{11.1.7}$$

The influence coefficients in this equation are

$$a_{11} = \frac{l^3}{3EI}, \quad a_{12} = a_{21} = \frac{l^3}{2EI}, \quad a_{22} = \frac{l}{EI} \tag{11.1.8}$$

■

The equation presented here could offer a basis for solving the problem of the gyroscopic whirl of a spinning wheel fixed to the end of an overhanging shaft. P and M in this case would be replaced by the inertia force and the gyroscopic moment of the spinning wheel. By including the flexibility of the supporting bearing, a still more general problem can be examined (see Prob. 5.59).

Figure 11.1.5 shows a demonstration gyroscope in gimbals. The mass distribution of the wheel is adjustable to obtain general moment of inertia configuration other than that of the symmetric wheel resulting in the simple inertia force P and the gyroscopic moment M shown in Fig. 11.1.4.

11.2 RECIPROCITY THEOREM

The reciprocity theorem states that in a linear system, $a_{ij} = a_{ji}$. For the proof of this theorem, we consider the work done by forces f_i and f_j, where the order of loading is i followed by j and then by its reverse. Reciprocity results when we recognize that the work done is independent of the order of loading.

By applying f_i, the work done is $\frac{1}{2}f_i^2 a_{ii}$. By applying f_j, the work done by f_j is $\frac{1}{2}f_j^2 a_{jj}$. However, i undergoes further displacement, $a_{ij}f_j$, and the additional work done by f_i becomes $a_{ij}f_j f_i$. Thus, the total work done is

$$W = \frac{1}{2}f_i^2 a_{ii} + \frac{1}{2}f_j^2 a_{jj} + a_{ij}f_j f_i$$

We now reverse the order of loading, in which case the total work done is

$$W = \frac{1}{2}f_j^2 a_{jj} + \frac{1}{2}f_i^2 a_{ii} + a_{ji}f_i f_j$$

Because the work done in the two cases must be equal, we find that

$$a_{ij} = a_{ji}$$

Example 11.2.1

Figure 11.2.1 shows an overhanging beam with P first applied at 1 and then at 2. In Fig. 11.2.1(a), the deflection at 2 is

$$y_2 = a_{21}P$$

In Fig. 11.2.1(b), the deflection at 1 is

$$y_1 = a_{12}P$$

Because $a_{12} = a_{21}, y_1$ will equal y_2, i.e., for a linear system, the deflection at 2, due to a load at 1, is equal to the deflection at 1 when the same load is applied at 2.

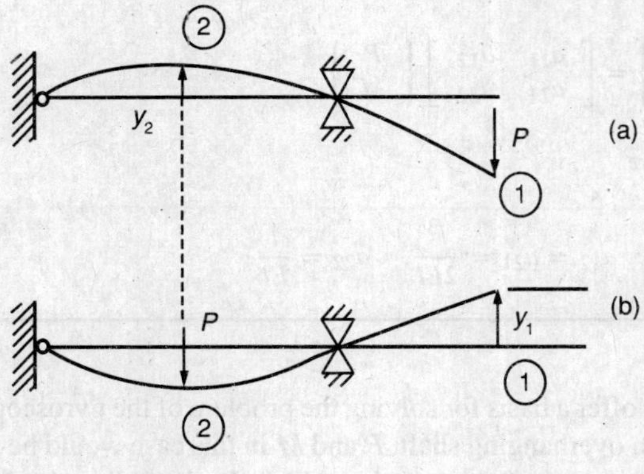

FIGURE 11.2.1.

11.3 STIFFNESS INFLUENCE COEFFICIENTS

The stiffness matrix written in terms of the influence coefficients k_{ij} is

$$\begin{Bmatrix} f_1 \\ f_2 \\ f_3 \end{Bmatrix} = \begin{bmatrix} k_{11} & k_{12} & k_{13} \\ k_{21} & k_{22} & k_{23} \\ k_{31} & k_{32} & k_{33} \end{bmatrix} \begin{Bmatrix} x_1 \\ x_2 \\ x_3 \end{Bmatrix} \tag{11.3.1}$$

The elements of the stiffness matrix have the following interpretation. If $x_1 = 1.0$ and $x_2 = x_3 = 0$, the forces at 1, 2, and 3 that are required to maintain this displacement according to Eq. (11.3.1) are k_{11}, k_{21}, and k_{31} in the first column. Similarly, the forces f_1, f_2, and f_3 required to maintain the displacement configuration $x_1 = 0, x_2 = 1.0$, and $x_3 = 0$ are k_{12}, k_{22}, and k_{32} in the second column. Thus, the general rule for establishing the stiffness elements of any column is to set the displacement corresponding to that column to unity with all other displacements equal to zero and measure the forces required at each station.

Example 11.3.1

Figure 11.3.1 shows a 3-DOF system. Determine the stiffness matrix and write its equation of motion.

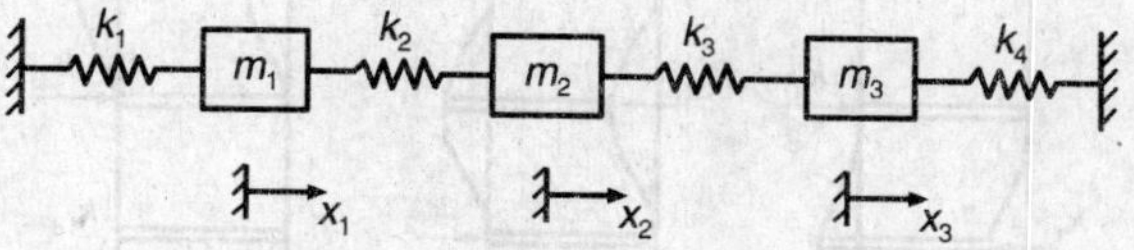

FIGURE 11.3.1.

Solution Let $x_1 = 1.0$ and $x_2 = x_3 = 0$. The forces required at 1, 2, and 3, considering forces to the right as positive, are

$$f_1 = k_1 + k_2 = k_{11}$$

$$f_2 = -k_2 = k_{21}$$

$$f_3 = 0 = k_{31}$$

Repeat with $x_2 = 1$, and $x_1 = x_3 = 0$. The forces are now

$$f_1 = -k_2 = k_{12}$$

$$f_2 = k_2 + k_3 = k_{22}$$

$$f_3 = -k_3 = k_{32}$$

For the last column of k's, let $x_3 = 1$ and $x_1 = x_2 = 0$. The forces are

$$f_1 = 0 = k_{13}$$

$$f_2 = -k_3 = k_{23}$$

$$f_3 = k_3 + k_4 = k_{33}$$

The stiffness matrix can now be written as

$$K = \begin{bmatrix} (k_1 + k_2) & -k_2 & 0 \\ -k_2 & (k_2 + k_3) & -k_3 \\ 0 & -k_3 & (k_3 + k_4) \end{bmatrix}$$

and its equation of motion becomes

$$\begin{bmatrix} m_1 & 0 & 0 \\ 0 & m_2 & 0 \\ 0 & 0 & m_3 \end{bmatrix} \begin{Bmatrix} \ddot{x}_1 \\ \ddot{x}_2 \\ \ddot{x}_3 \end{Bmatrix} + \begin{bmatrix} (k_1 + k_2) & -k_2 & 0 \\ -k_2 & (k_2 + k_3) & -k_3 \\ 0 & -k_3 & (k_3 + k_4) \end{bmatrix} \begin{Bmatrix} x_1 \\ x_2 \\ x_3 \end{Bmatrix} = \begin{Bmatrix} f_1 \\ f_2 \\ f_3 \end{Bmatrix}$$

■

Example 11.3.2

Consider the four-story building with rigid floors shown in Fig. 11.3.2. Show diagramatically the significance of the terms of the stiffness matrix.

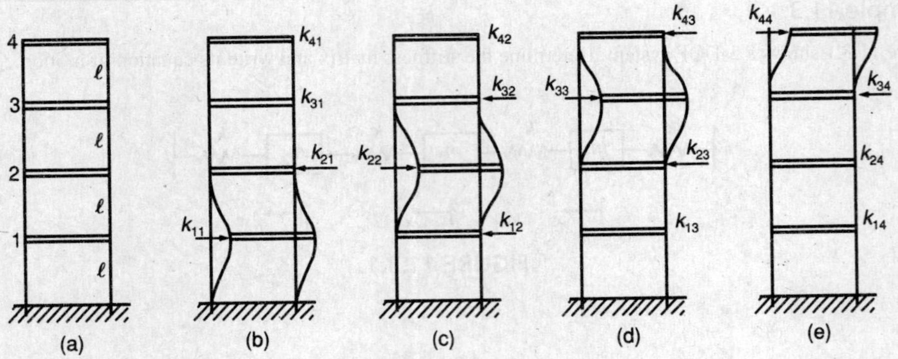

FIGURE 11.3.2.

Solution The stiffness matrix for the problem is a 4 × 4 matrix. The elements of the first column are obtained by giving station 1 a unit displacement with the displacement of all other stations equal to zero, as shown in Fig. 11.3.2(b). The forces required for this configuration are the elements of the first column. Similarly, the elements of the second column are the forces necessary to maintain the configuration shown in Fig. 11.3.2(c).

It is evident from these diagrams that $k_{11} = k_{22} = k_{33}$ and that they can be determined from the deflection of a fixed–fixed beam of length $2l$, which is

$$k_{11} = k_{22} = k_{33} = \frac{192EI}{(2l)^3} = 24\frac{EI}{l^3}$$

The stiffness matrix is then easily found as

$$[k] = \frac{EI}{l^3}\begin{bmatrix} 24 & -12 & 0 & 0 \\ -12 & 24 & -12 & 0 \\ 0 & -12 & 24 & -12 \\ 0 & 0 & -12 & 12 \end{bmatrix}$$

■

Example 11.3.3

Determine the stiffness matrix for Example 11.1.2 by inverting the flexibility matrix:

$$[a] = \frac{1}{k}\begin{bmatrix} 0.5 & 0.5 & 0.5 \\ 0.5 & 1.5 & 1.5 \\ 0.5 & 1.5 & 2.5 \end{bmatrix}$$

Solution Although the stiffness matrix of this system is easily found by summing forces on each mass in Fig. 11.1.2, we demonstrate the use of the mathematical equation

$$[a]^{-1} = \frac{1}{|a|}\text{adj } [a]$$

of Appendix C. The determinant of $[a]$ is found from the minors using the first column.

$$|a| = \frac{1}{k}\left\{0.5\begin{vmatrix}1.5 & 1.5\\ 1.5 & 2.5\end{vmatrix} - 0.5\begin{vmatrix}0.5 & 0.5\\ 1.5 & 2.5\end{vmatrix} + 0.5\begin{vmatrix}0.5 & 0.5\\ 1.5 & 1.5\end{vmatrix}\right\}$$

$$= \frac{0.5}{k}\{1.5 - 0.5 + 0\} = \frac{1}{2k}$$

For the adjoint matrix, we have (see Appendix C)

$$\text{adj }[a] = \begin{bmatrix}1.5 & -0.5 & 0\\ -0.5 & 1.0 & -0.5\\ 0 & -0.5 & 0.5\end{bmatrix}$$

Thus, the inverse of $[a]$ is

$$[a]^{-1} = [k] = 2k\begin{bmatrix}1.5 & -0.5 & 0\\ -0.5 & 1.0 & -0.5\\ 0 & -0.5 & 0.5\end{bmatrix} = k\begin{bmatrix}3 & -1 & 0\\ -1 & 2 & -1\\ 0 & -1 & 1\end{bmatrix}$$

which is the stiffness matrix.

Example 11.3.4

By using the stiffness matrix developed in Example 11.3.3, determine the equation of motion, its characteristic determinant, and the characteristic equation.

Solution The equation of motion for the normal modes is

$$-\omega^2 m\begin{bmatrix}2 & 0 & 0\\ 0 & 1 & 0\\ 0 & 0 & 1\end{bmatrix}\begin{Bmatrix}x_1\\ x_2\\ x_3\end{Bmatrix} + k\begin{bmatrix}3 & -1 & 0\\ -1 & 2 & -1\\ 0 & -1 & 1\end{bmatrix}\begin{Bmatrix}x_1\\ x_2\\ x_3\end{Bmatrix} = \begin{Bmatrix}0\\ 0\\ 0\end{Bmatrix}$$

from which the characteristic determinant with $\lambda = \omega^2 m/k$ becomes

$$\begin{vmatrix}(3-2\lambda) & -1 & 0\\ -1 & (2-\lambda) & -1\\ 0 & -1 & (1-\lambda)\end{vmatrix} = 0$$

The characteristic equation from this determinant is

$$\lambda^3 - 4.5\lambda^2 + 5\lambda - 1 = 0$$

The roots of this equation can be found in MATLAB® by typing the command **roots(c)** where c is the vector containing the coefficients of the polynomial in descending order. For this example $c = [1, -4.5, 5, -1]$. The roots are given by

$$2.8892, 1.3554, 0.2554$$

Alternatively, one can compute these numbers by computing the eigenvalues of the dynamic matrix $A = M^{-1} * K$. Once the matrices M and K have been input into MATLAB®, the dynamic matrix is computed by using the following command:

$$A = \text{inv}(M) * K$$

The result is

$$A = \begin{bmatrix}1.5000 & -0.5000 & 0\\ -1.000 & 2.000 & -1.0000\\ 0 & -1.0000 & 1.0000\end{bmatrix}$$

The eigenvalues can now be computed using

$$D = \text{eig}(A).$$

The result is

$$D = \begin{Bmatrix} 1.3554 \\ 2.8892 \\ 0.2554 \end{Bmatrix}$$

Both of these approaches give the same values for the eigenvalues for the normal modes.

■

11.4 STIFFNESS MATRIX OF BEAM ELEMENTS

Engineering structures are generally composed of beam elements. If the ends of the elements are rigidly connected to the adjoining structure instead of being pinned, the element will act like a beam with moments and lateral forces acting at the ends. For the most part, the relative axial displacements will be small compared to the lateral displacements of the beam and we will assume them to be zero for now.

Figure 11.4.1 shows a uniform beam with arbitrary end displacements, v_1, θ_1 and v_2, θ_2, taken in the positive sense. These displacements can be considered in terms of the superposition of four displacements taken separately, as shown in Fig. 11.4.2. Shown also are the end forces and moments required to maintain the equilibrium of the separate displacements, which can be simply determined by the area-moment method. They relate to the following stiffness matrix:

$$\begin{Bmatrix} F_1 \\ M_1 \\ F_2 \\ M_2 \end{Bmatrix} = \begin{bmatrix} k_{11} & k_{12} & k_{13} & k_{14} \\ k_{21} & k_{22} & k_{23} & k_{24} \\ k_{31} & k_{32} & k_{33} & k_{34} \\ k_{41} & k_{42} & k_{43} & k_{44} \end{bmatrix} \begin{Bmatrix} u_1 \\ \theta_1 \\ u_2 \\ \theta_2 \end{Bmatrix}$$

where each column represents the force and moment required for each of the displacements taken separately. The positive sense of these coordinates is arbitrary; however, the configuration shown in Fig. 11.4.1 conforms to that generally used in the finite element method, to be presented shortly.

Also presented here are force and moment relationships for a pinned beam. Although the pinned beam does not conform to the usual definition of beam stiffness, its force and moment relationships are often convenient, and are presented here in Figure 11.4.2(a).

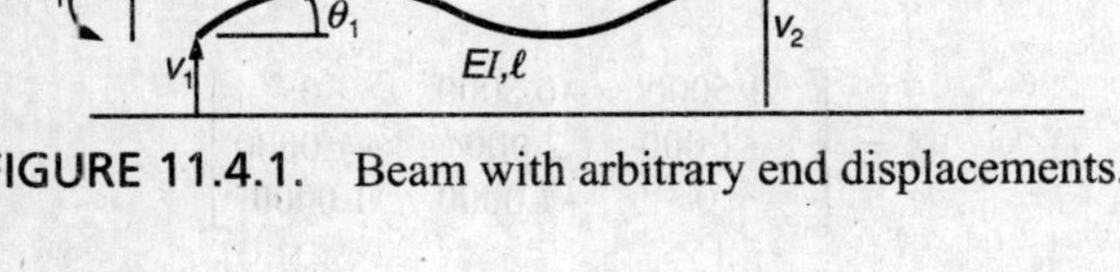

FIGURE 11.4.1. Beam with arbitrary end displacements.

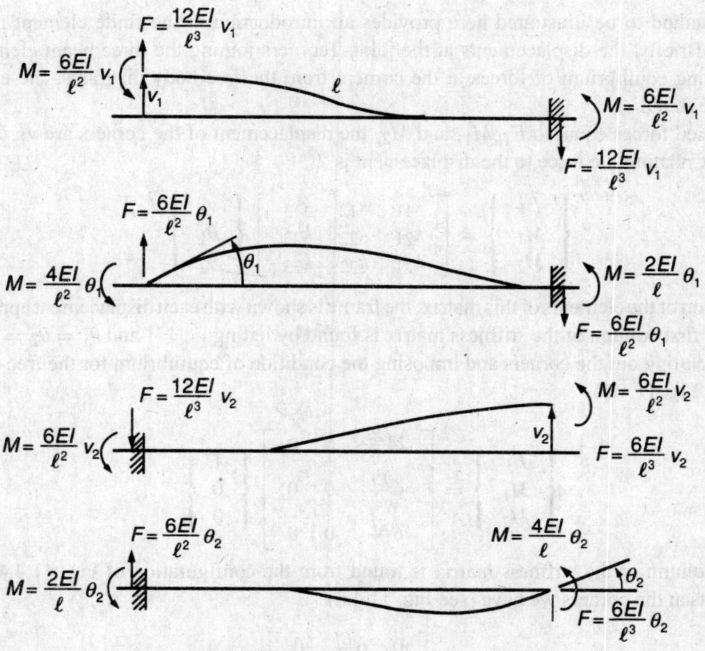

FIGURE 11.4.2. Stiffness of beam element.

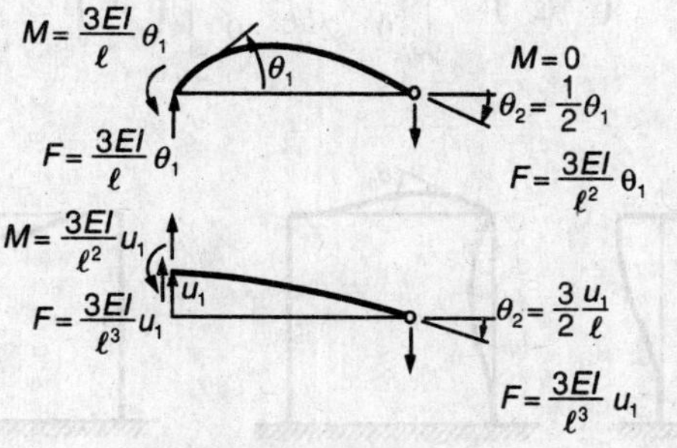

FIGURE 11.4.2(a).

Example 11.4.1

Determine the stiffness matrix for the square frame of Fig. 11.4.3. Assume the corners to remain at 90°.

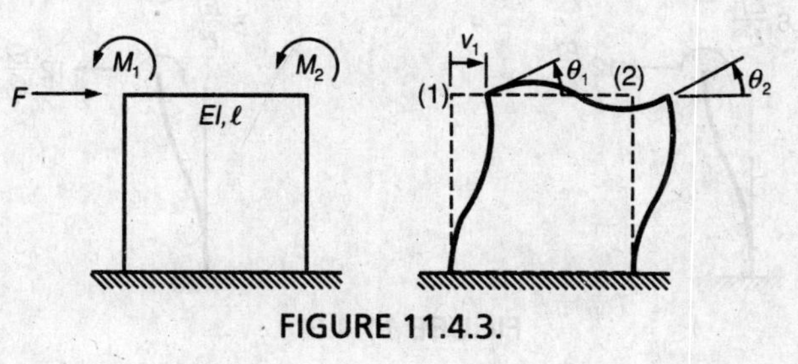

FIGURE 11.4.3.

Solution The method to be illustrated here provides an introduction to the finite element method, which is discussed later. Briefly, the displacements at the joints (corners joining the three beam elements) must be compatible. Ensuring equilibrium of forces at the corners from the free-body diagrams, the elements of the stiffness matrix are found.

With the applied forces equal to F_1, M_1, and M_2, the displacement of the corners are v_1, θ_1, and θ_2, and the stiffness matrix relating the force to the displacement is

$$\begin{Bmatrix} F_1 \\ M_1 \\ M_2 \end{Bmatrix} = \begin{bmatrix} k_{11} & k_{12} & k_{13} \\ k_{21} & k_{22} & k_{23} \\ k_{31} & k_{32} & k_{33} \end{bmatrix} \begin{Bmatrix} v_1 \\ \theta_1 \\ \theta_2 \end{Bmatrix}$$

For the determination of the elements of this matrix, the frame is shown with each displacement applied separately in Fig. 11.4.4. The first column of the stiffness matrix is found by letting $v_1 = 1$ and $\theta_1 = \theta_2 = 0$, as shown in Fig. 11.4.4(a). By cutting out the corners and imposing the condition of equilibrium for the free-body diagram, the results are (see Fig. 11.4.5)

$$\begin{Bmatrix} F_1 \\ M_1 \\ M_2 \end{Bmatrix} = \begin{bmatrix} 24\frac{EI}{l^2} & 0 & 0 \\ 6\frac{EI}{l^2} & 0 & 0 \\ 6\frac{EI}{l^2} & 0 & 0 \end{bmatrix} \begin{Bmatrix} 1 \\ 0 \\ 0 \end{Bmatrix}$$

The second column of the stiffness matrix is found from the configuration of Fig. 11.4.4(b). Summing forces and moments at the corners we have (see Fig. 11.4.6)

$$\begin{Bmatrix} F_1 \\ M_1 \\ M_2 \end{Bmatrix} = \begin{bmatrix} 0 & 6\frac{EI}{l^2} & 0 \\ 0 & 8\frac{EI}{l} & 0 \\ 0 & 2\frac{EI}{l} & 0 \end{bmatrix} \begin{Bmatrix} 0 \\ 1 \\ 0 \end{Bmatrix}$$

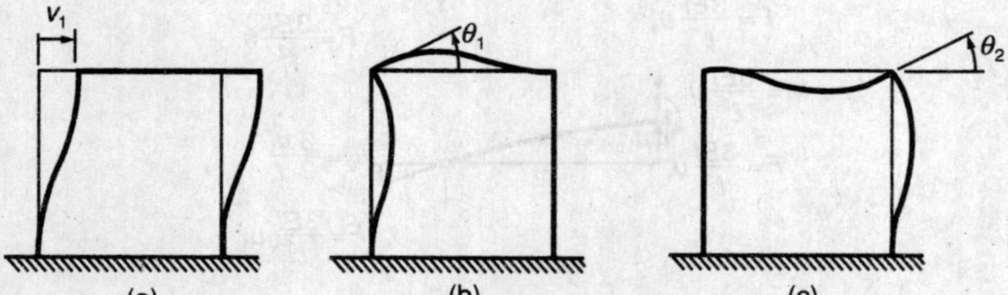

FIGURE 11.4.4.

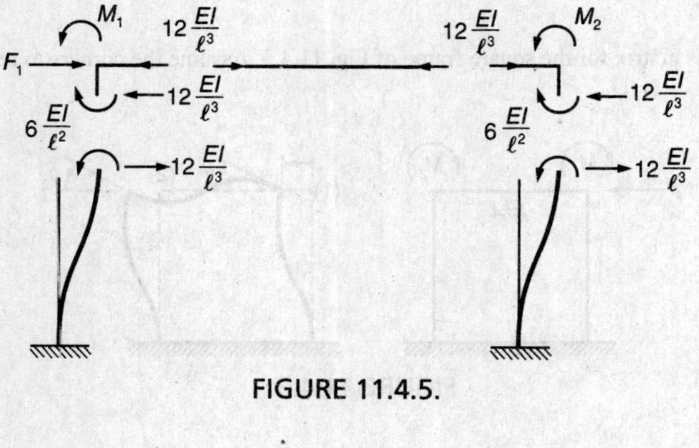

FIGURE 11.4.5.

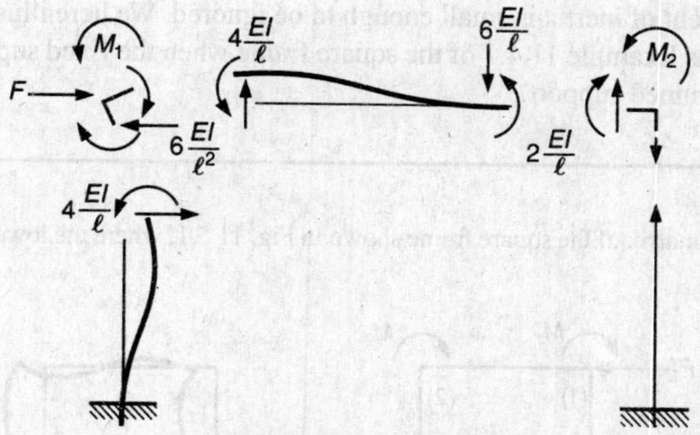

FIGURE 11.4.6.

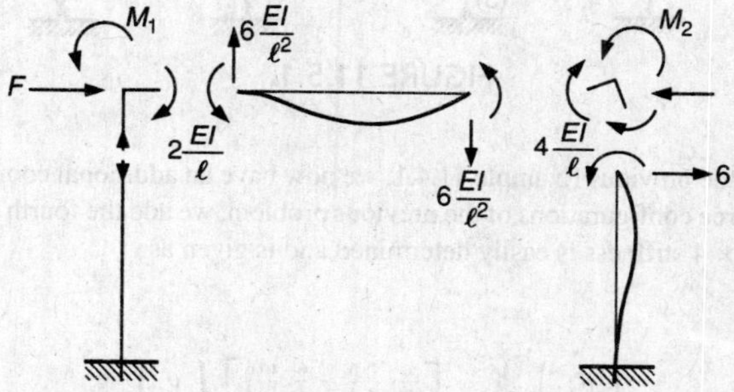

FIGURE 11.4.7.

In like manner, the third column of the stiffness matrix is found from the configuration of Fig. 11.4.4(c) (see Fig. 11.4.7).

$$\begin{Bmatrix} F_1 \\ M_1 \\ M_2 \end{Bmatrix} = \begin{bmatrix} 0 & 0 & 6\frac{EI}{l^2} \\ 0 & 0 & 2\frac{EI}{l} \\ 0 & 0 & 8\frac{EI}{l} \end{bmatrix} \begin{Bmatrix} 0 \\ 0 \\ 1 \end{Bmatrix}$$

By superpositioning the preceding three configurations, the stiffness matrix for the square frame with fixed legs is

$$\begin{Bmatrix} F_1 \\ M_1 \\ M_2 \end{Bmatrix} = \frac{EI}{l} \begin{bmatrix} \frac{24}{l^2} & \frac{6}{l} & \frac{6}{l} \\ \frac{6}{l} & 8 & 2 \\ \frac{6}{l} & 2 & 8 \end{bmatrix} \begin{Bmatrix} v_1 \\ \theta_1 \\ \theta_2 \end{Bmatrix}$$

■

11.5 STATIC CONDENSATION FOR PINNED JOINTS

For pinned joints where the moment is zero, the size of the stiffness matrix can be reduced by a procedure called *static condensation.*[2] The procedure can also be used in discrete mass systems where the mass moment of inertia is small enough to be ignored. We here illustrate the procedure by applying it to previous Example 11.4.1 of the square frame when the fixed support of the lower right leg is replaced by a pinned support.

Example 11.5.1

Determine the stiffness matrix of the square frame shown in Fig. 11.5.1, where the lower right support is pinned.

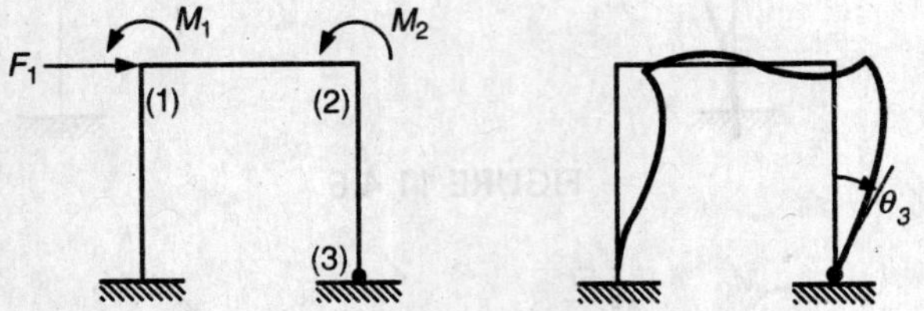

FIGURE 11.5.1.

Solution Compared to the previous Example 11.4.1, we now have an additional coordinate θ_3, which results in a 4×4 matrix. To the three configurations of the previous problem, we add the fourth configuration, as shown in Fig. 11.5.2. The new 4×4 stiffness is easily determined and is given as

$$\begin{Bmatrix} F_1 \\ M_1 \\ M_2 \\ \hdashline M_3 \end{Bmatrix} = \frac{EI}{l} \left[\begin{array}{ccc:c} \frac{24}{l^2} & \frac{6}{l} & \frac{6}{l} & \frac{6}{l} \\ \frac{6}{l} & 8 & 2 & 0 \\ \frac{6}{l} & 2 & 8 & 2 \\ \hdashline \frac{6}{l} & 0 & 2 & 4 \end{array}\right] \begin{Bmatrix} v_1 \\ \theta_1 \\ \theta_2 \\ \theta_3 \end{Bmatrix}$$

which we partition by the dotted lines and relabel as

$$\begin{Bmatrix} \mathcal{F} \\ \hdashline \mathcal{M} \end{Bmatrix} = \left[\begin{array}{c:c} K_{11} & K_{12} \\ \hdashline K_{21} & K_{22} \end{array}\right] \begin{Bmatrix} V \\ \hdashline \Theta \end{Bmatrix} \tag{11.5.1}$$

Note here that K_{11} is the stiffness matrix of the previous problem. Multiplying out the new matrix, we obtain

$$\begin{aligned} \mathcal{F} &= K_{11}V + K_{12}\Theta \\ \mathcal{M} &= K_{21}V + K_{22}\Theta \end{aligned} \tag{11.5.2}$$

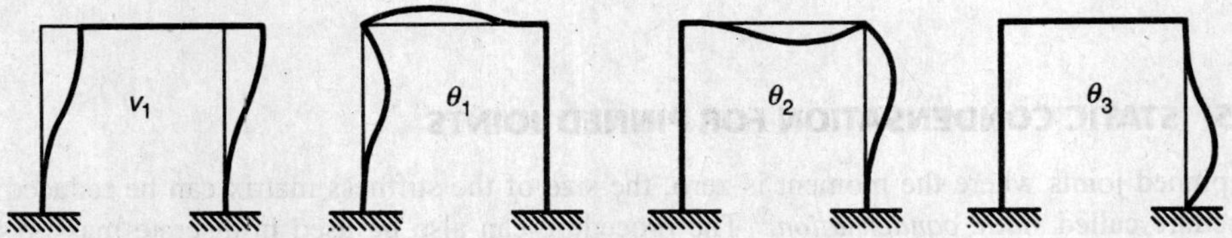

FIGURE 11.5.2.

Because for the pinned end, the moment is zero, we let $\mathcal{M} = 0$ and solve for Θ in terms of the other coordinates, thus reducing the size of the 4×4 matrix to a 3×3 matrix.

$$\Theta = -K_{22}^{-1} K_{21} V \tag{11.5.3}$$

Substituting this into the first equation, we have

$$\mathcal{F} = (K_{11} - K_{12} K_{22}^{-1} K_{21}) V \tag{11.5.4}$$

Because the first term of this equation is that of the previous example, we need only to determine the second term, which is

$$K_{12} K_{22}^{-1} K_{21} = \frac{EI}{l} \begin{bmatrix} \frac{6}{l} \\ 0 \\ 2 \end{bmatrix} \begin{bmatrix} \frac{1}{4} \end{bmatrix} \begin{bmatrix} \frac{6}{l} & 0 & 2 \end{bmatrix}$$

$$= \frac{EI}{4l} \begin{bmatrix} \frac{6}{l} \\ 0 \\ 2 \end{bmatrix} \begin{bmatrix} \frac{6}{l} & 0 & 2 \end{bmatrix} = \frac{EI}{l} \begin{bmatrix} \frac{9}{l^2} & 0 & \frac{3}{l} \\ 0 & 0 & 0 \\ \frac{3}{l} & 0 & 1 \end{bmatrix}$$

Subtracting this from K_{11}, we obtain the reduced 3×3 stiffness matrix for the square frame with one pinned end.

$$\begin{Bmatrix} F_1 \\ M_1 \\ M_2 \end{Bmatrix} = \frac{EI}{l} \begin{bmatrix} \frac{15}{l^2} & \frac{6}{l} & \frac{3}{l} \\ \frac{6}{l} & 8 & 2 \\ \frac{3}{l} & 2 & 7 \end{bmatrix} \begin{Bmatrix} v_1 \\ \theta_1 \\ \theta_2 \end{Bmatrix}$$

Note that the middle column and row remain untouched.

■

11.6 AXIAL FINITE ELEMENT STIFFNESS AND MASS MATRICES

Axial element. An element with pinned ends can support only axial forces and hence will act like a spring. Figure 11.6.1 shows a spring and a uniform rod pinned to a stationary wall and subjected to a force F. The force–displacement relationships for the two cases are simply

$$\begin{array}{ll} \text{Spring} & f = ku \\ \text{Uniform rod} & F = \left(\frac{EA}{l}\right) u \end{array} \tag{11.6.1}$$

In general, these axial elements can be a part of a pin-connected structure that allows displacement of both ends. In the finite element method, the displacement and force at each end of the element must be accounted for with proper sign. Figure 11.6.2 shows an axial element labeled with displacements u_1, u_2, and forces F_1, F_2, all in the positive sense. If we write the force–displacement relationship in terms of the stiffness matrix, the equation is

$$\begin{Bmatrix} F_1 \\ F_2 \end{Bmatrix} = \begin{bmatrix} k_{11} & k_{12} \\ k_{21} & k_{22} \end{bmatrix} \begin{Bmatrix} u_1 \\ u_2 \end{Bmatrix} \tag{11.6.2}$$

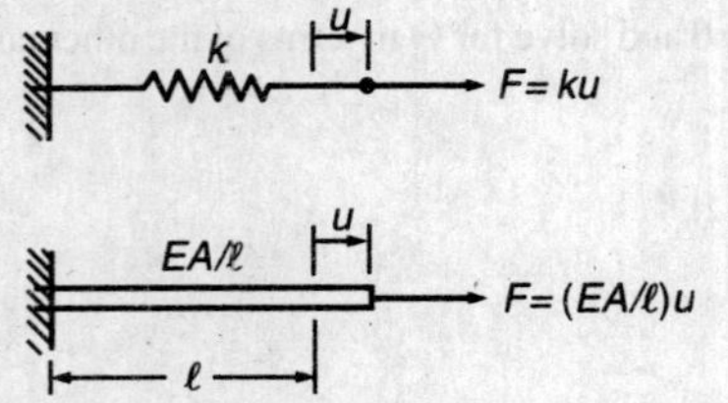

FIGURE 11.6.1.

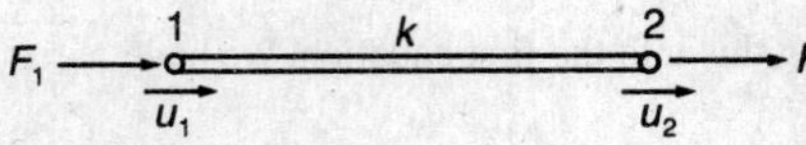

FIGURE 11.6.2.

The elements of the first column of the stiffness matrix represent the forces at the two ends when $u_1 = 1$ and $u_2 = 0$, as shown in Fig. 11.6.3. Thus, $F_1 = ku_1$ and $F_2 = -ku_1$.

Similarly, by letting $u_2 = 1$ and $u_1 = 0$, we obtain, as in Fig. 11.6.4, $F_1 = -ku_2$ and $F_2 = ku_2$. Thus, Eq. (11.6.2) becomes

$$\begin{Bmatrix} F_1 \\ F_2 \end{Bmatrix} = k \begin{bmatrix} 1 & -1 \\ -1 & 1 \end{bmatrix} \begin{Bmatrix} u_1 \\ u_2 \end{Bmatrix} \tag{11.6.2$'$}$$

If the spring is replaced by a uniform rod, $k = AE/l$ and the equation becomes

$$\begin{Bmatrix} F_1 \\ F_2 \end{Bmatrix} = \frac{EA}{l} \begin{bmatrix} 1 & -1 \\ -1 & 1 \end{bmatrix} \begin{Bmatrix} u_1 \\ u_2 \end{Bmatrix} \tag{11.6.3}$$

These equations thus define the stiffness matrix for axial elements in terms of axial coordinates u_i and axial forces F_i, regardless of the orientation of the axial member.

Mode shape and mass matrix for axial element. With the two ends of the axial member displaced by u_1 and u_2, the displacement at any point $\xi = x/l$ is assumed to be a straight line, as shown in Fig. 11.6.5(a). The displacement is, therefore, the superposition of the two mode shapes shown in Fig. 11.6.5(b). The normalized mode shapes are then

$$\varphi_1 = (1 - \xi) \quad \text{and} \quad \varphi_2 = \xi \tag{11.6.4}$$

The mass matrix is found by expressing u as the sum of the two mode shapes:

$$u = (1 - \xi)u_1 + \xi u_2 \tag{11.6.5}$$

and writing the equation for the kinetic energy. We here assume uniform mass distribution m per unit length.

$$\begin{aligned} T &= \frac{1}{2}\int_0^l \dot{u}^2 m\, dx = \frac{1}{2} m \int_0^1 [(1-\xi)\dot{u}_1 + \xi \dot{u}_2]^2 l\, d\xi \\ &= \frac{1}{2} ml \left(\frac{1}{2}\dot{u}_1^2 + \frac{1}{3}\dot{u}_1 \dot{u}_2 + \frac{1}{3}\dot{u}_2^2 \right) \end{aligned} \tag{11.6.6}$$

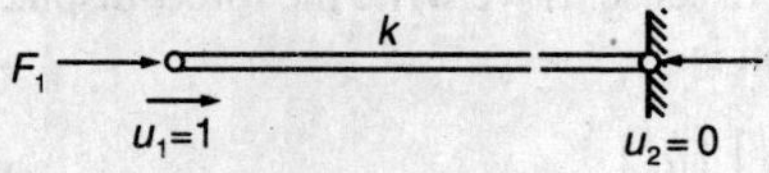

FIGURE 11.6.3.

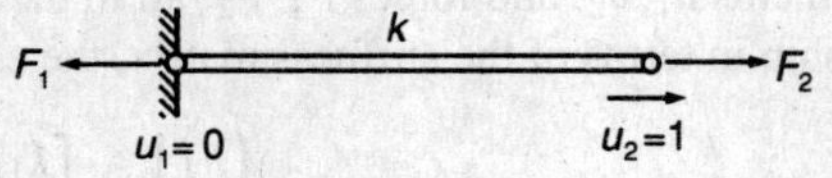

FIGURE 11.6.4.

$$\frac{d}{dt}\frac{\partial T}{\partial \dot{u}_i}$$

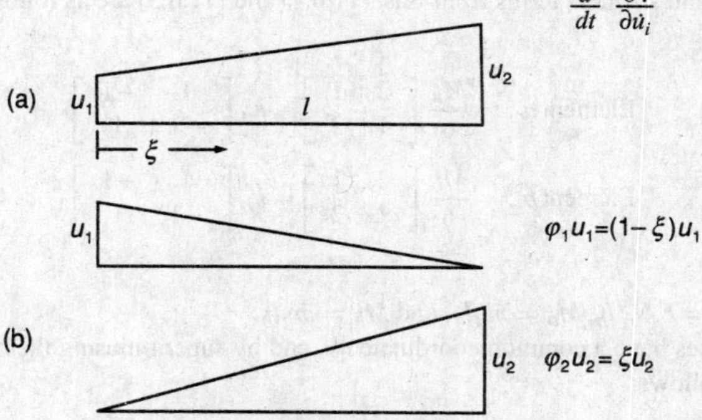

FIGURE 11.6.5.

Because the generalized mass from Lagrange's equation is

$$\frac{d}{dt}\frac{\partial T}{\partial \dot{u}_i}$$

we find

$$\frac{d}{dt}\frac{\partial T}{\partial \dot{u}_1} = ml\left(\frac{1}{3}\ddot{u}_1 + \frac{1}{6}\ddot{u}_2\right)$$

$$\frac{d}{dt}\frac{\partial T}{\partial \dot{u}_2} = ml\left(\frac{1}{6}\ddot{u}_1 + \frac{1}{3}\ddot{u}_2\right)$$

which establishes the mass matrix for the axial element as

$$\frac{ml}{6}\begin{bmatrix} 2 & 1 \\ 1 & 2 \end{bmatrix} \tag{11.6.7}$$

The terms of the mass matrix are also available from

$$m_{ij} = \int \varphi_1 \varphi_j \, dm$$

Example 11.6.1

Determine the equation of motion for the longitudinal vibration of the two-section bar shown in Fig. 11.6.6.

Solution Numbering the joints as 1, 2, and 3, we have two axial elements, 1–2, and 2–3, with displacements u_1, u_2, and u_3. Although u_1 is zero, we at first allow it to be unrestrained and later impose its zero value.

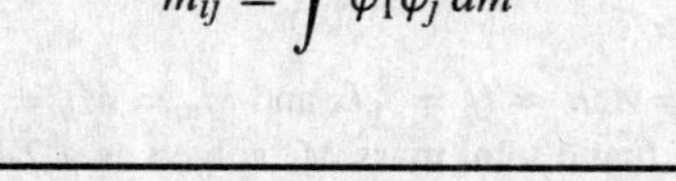

FIGURE 11.6.6.

The element mass and stiffness terms from Eqs. (11.6.7) and (11.6.3) are as follows:

$$\text{Element } a: \quad \frac{M_a}{6}\begin{bmatrix} 2 & 1 \\ 1 & 2 \end{bmatrix} \quad k_a\begin{bmatrix} 1 & -1 \\ -1 & 1 \end{bmatrix}$$

$$\text{Element } b: \quad \frac{M_b}{6}\begin{bmatrix} 2 & 1 \\ 1 & 2 \end{bmatrix} \quad k_b\begin{bmatrix} 1 & -1 \\ -1 & 1 \end{bmatrix}$$

where $k_a = EA_a/l_a, k_b = EA_b/l_b, M_a = m_a l_a$, and $M_b = m_b l_b$.

The element matrices have a common coordinate u_2, and by superimposing them, they can be assembled into a 3 × 3 matrix as follows:

$$\text{Mass matrix} \quad \frac{1}{6}\begin{bmatrix} 2M_a & M_a & 0 \\ M_a & 2M_a + 2M_b & M_b \\ 0 & M_b & 2M_b \end{bmatrix}\begin{Bmatrix} \ddot{u}_1 \\ \ddot{u}_2 \\ \ddot{u}_3 \end{Bmatrix} \tag{11.6.8}$$

$$\text{Stiffness matrix} \quad \begin{bmatrix} k_a & -k_a & 0 \\ -k_a & k_a + k_b & -k_b \\ 0 & -k_b & k_b \end{bmatrix}\begin{Bmatrix} u_1 \\ u_2 \\ u_3 \end{Bmatrix} \tag{11.6.9}$$

We note here that the stiffness matrix is singular and does not have an inverse. This is to be expected because no limitations have been placed on the displacements. The first and third rows of the stiffness matrix, as it stands, result in $k_a(u_1 - u_2) = k_b(u_2 - u_3) = 0$, which indicates that no relative motion between coordinates takes place, a situation corresponding to rigid-body translation.

If we fix point 1 so that $u_1 = 0$, then the first column of the matrices can be deleted. The second and third rows then result in the following equation for the longitudinal vibration of the two-section bar:

$$\frac{1}{6}\begin{bmatrix} 2(M_a + M_b) & M_b \\ M_b & 2M_b \end{bmatrix}\begin{Bmatrix} \ddot{u}_2 \\ \ddot{u}_3 \end{Bmatrix} + \begin{bmatrix} (k_1 + k_b) & -k_b \\ -k_b & k_b \end{bmatrix}\begin{Bmatrix} u_2 \\ u_3 \end{Bmatrix} = \begin{Bmatrix} 0 \\ 0 \end{Bmatrix}$$

Special case. If $A_a = A_b = A, l_a = l_b = \frac{1}{2}L$, and $M_a = M_b = \frac{1}{2}M$, the previous problem becomes that of a uniform bar of total length L and total mass M, solved as a 2-DOF system with coordinates at the midpoint and the free end. The equation of the previous problem then becomes

$$\frac{M}{12}\begin{bmatrix} 4 & 1 \\ 1 & 2 \end{bmatrix}\begin{Bmatrix} \ddot{u}_2 \\ \ddot{u}_3 \end{Bmatrix} + \frac{2EA}{\text{L}}\begin{bmatrix} 2 & -1 \\ -1 & 1 \end{bmatrix}\begin{Bmatrix} u_2 \\ u_3 \end{Bmatrix} = \begin{Bmatrix} 0 \\ 0 \end{Bmatrix}$$

If we let $\lambda = \omega^2 ML/24EA$, the characteristic equation for the natural frequencies becomes

$$\begin{vmatrix} (2 - 4\lambda) & -(1 + \lambda) \\ -(1 + \lambda) & (1 - 2\lambda) \end{vmatrix} = 0$$

or

$$\lambda^2 - \frac{10}{7}\lambda - \frac{1}{7} = 0$$

Its solution results in

$$\lambda = \begin{cases} 0.1082 \\ 1.3204 \end{cases} \qquad \omega = \begin{cases} 1.6115\sqrt{\dfrac{EA}{ML}} \\ 5.6293\sqrt{\dfrac{EA}{ML}} \end{cases}$$

The natural frequencies of the uniform bar in longitudinal vibration are known and are given by the equation $\omega_i = (2n+1)(\pi/2)\sqrt{EA/ML}$. Results computed from this equation for the first two modes are

$$\omega = \begin{cases} 1.5708\sqrt{\dfrac{EA}{ML}} \\ 4.7124\sqrt{\dfrac{EA}{ML}} \end{cases}$$

Comparison between the two indicates that the agreement between the results of the 2-DOF finite element model and that of the continuous model is 2.6 percent high for the first mode and 19.5 percent high for the second mode. A three-element model will of course be expected to give closer agreement.

■

Variable properties. One simple approach to problems of variable properties is to use many elements of short length. The variation of mass or stiffness over each element is then small and can be neglected. The problem then becomes one of constant mass and stiffness for each element that simplifies the problem considerably because these terms can be placed outside of the integrals. Of course, the larger numbers of elements will lead to equations of larger DOF.

Computer program. The program **bar.m** is a MATLAB® script file which computes the natural frequencies as determined by a finite element method for a cantilever bar. Since it allows the elements to have different properties, this program can be used to model bars that have variable properties. This program prompts the user to input the length of the bar; the number of elements desired; the mass of each element; the elastic modulus of each element; and the cross-sectional area of each element. It then constructs the mass matrix and the stiffness matrix for the model. For the 3 × 3 cases these matrices are given in Eqs. (11.1.8) and (11.1.9). From these it constructs the dynamic matrix. The natural frequencies are determined from the eigenvalues of the dynamic matrix. See Appendix F for more information about this program.

11.7 STIFFNESS AND MASS MATRICES FOR THE BEAM FINITE ELEMENT

Beam stiffness. If the ends of the element are rigidly connected to the adjoining structure instead of being pinned, the element will act like a beam with moments and lateral forces acting at the joints. In general, the relative axial displacement $u_2 - u_1$ will be small compared to the lateral displacement v of the beam and can be assumed to be zero. When axial forces as well as beam forces and moments must be considered, it is a simple matter to make additions to the beam stiffness matrix, as we show later.

The local coordinates for the beam element are the lateral displacements and rotations at the two ends. We consider only the planar structure in this discussion, so that each joint will have a lateral displacement v and a rotation θ, resulting in four coordinates, v_1, θ_1 and v_2, θ_2. The positive sense of these coordinates is arbitrary, but for computer bookkeeping purposes, the diagram of Fig. 11.7.1 is the one accepted by most structural engineers. Positive senses of the forces and moments also follow the same diagram.

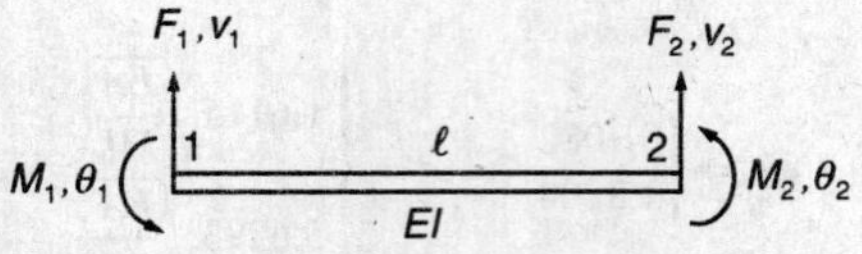

FIGURE 11.7.1. Positive sense of beam displacement and forces.

The preceding displacements can be considered to be the superposition of the four shapes, labeled $\varphi_1(x), \varphi_2(x), \varphi_3(x)$, and $\varphi_4(x)$, shown in Fig. 11.7.2. The forces and moments required at the two ends were found in Section 11.4 and are shown in Fig. 11.7.3 with the factor EI/l^3 omitted. The diagram immediately leads to the force–stiffness equation:

$$\begin{Bmatrix} F_1 \\ M_1 \\ F_2 \\ M_2 \end{Bmatrix} = \frac{EI}{l^3}\left[\begin{array}{cc|cc} 12 & 6l & -12 & 6l \\ 6l & 4l^2 & -6l & 2l^2 \\ \hline -12 & -6l & 12 & -6l \\ 6l & 2l^2 & -6l & 4l^2 \end{array}\right]\begin{Bmatrix} v_1 \\ \theta_1 \\ v_2 \\ \theta_2 \end{Bmatrix} \tag{11.7.1}$$

Equation (11.7.1) for the stiffness was obtained from the given forces and moments shown in Fig. 11.7.3. The stiffness matrix as well as the mass matrix can also be determined from the potential and kinetic energy, provided the shape functions $\varphi_i(x)$ of the beam are known.

For the development of the general equation of the beam, which is a cubic polynomial, the deflection is expressed in the form

$$v(x) = p_1 + p_2\xi + p_3\xi^2 + p_4\xi^3 \tag{11.7.2}$$

where

$$\xi = \frac{x}{l} \quad \text{and} \quad p_i = \text{constants}$$

Differentiating yields the slope equation

$$l\theta(x) = p_2 + 2p_3\xi + 3p_4\xi^2 \tag{11.7.3}$$

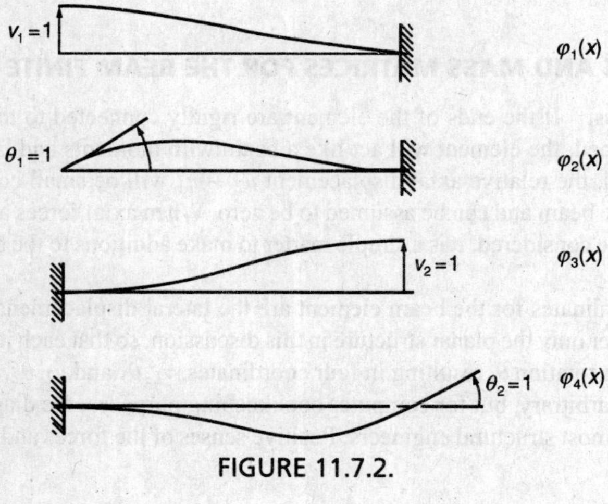

FIGURE 11.7.2.

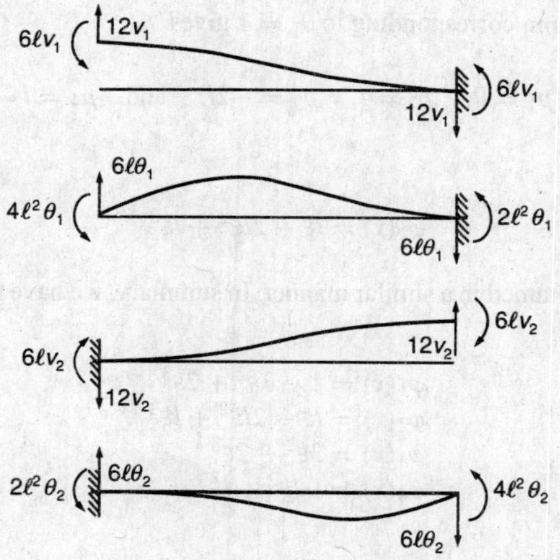

FIGURE 11.7.3.

If we apply the boundary conditions $\xi = 0$ and $\xi = 1$, the boundary equations can be expressed by the following matrix equation:

$$\begin{Bmatrix} v_1 \\ l\theta_1 \\ \hline v_2 \\ l\theta_2 \end{Bmatrix} = \left[\begin{array}{cc|cc} 1 & 0 & 0 & 0 \\ 0 & 1 & 0 & 0 \\ \hline 1 & 1 & 1 & 1 \\ 0 & 1 & 2 & 3 \end{array}\right] \begin{Bmatrix} p_1 \\ p_2 \\ p_3 \\ p_4 \end{Bmatrix} \tag{11.7.4}$$

With the matrix partitioned as shown, it is evident that p_1 and p_2 are related to v_1 and $l\theta_1$ by a unit matrix. After substituting $p_1 = v_1$ and $p_2 = l\theta_1$, we can easily solve the last two rows of the matrix for p_3 and p_4. The desired inverse of Eq. (11.7.4) then becomes

$$\begin{Bmatrix} p_1 \\ p_2 \\ \hline p_3 \\ p_4 \end{Bmatrix} = \left[\begin{array}{cc|cc} 1 & 0 & 0 & 0 \\ 0 & 1 & 0 & 0 \\ \hline -3 & -2 & 3 & -1 \\ 2 & 1 & -2 & 1 \end{array}\right] \begin{Bmatrix} v_1 \\ l\theta_1 \\ \hline v_2 \\ l\theta_2 \end{Bmatrix} \tag{11.7.5}$$

This equation enables the determination of the p_i for each of the displacements equated to unity with all the others equal to zero. That is, for $v_1(x) = 1$ with all other displacements equal to zero, the first column of Eq. (11.7.5) gives

$$p_1 = 1, \quad p_2 = 0, \quad p_3 = -3, \quad \text{and} \quad p_4 = 2$$

Substituting these into Eq. (11.7.2) gives the shape function for the first configuration of Fig. 11.7.2 of

$$\varphi_1(x) = 1 - 3\xi^2 + 2\xi^3$$

Similarly, the second column corresponding to $\theta_1 = 1$ gives

$$p_1 = 0, \quad p_2 = l, \quad p_3 = -2l, \quad \text{and} \quad p_4 = l$$

and

$$\varphi_2(x) = l\xi - 2l\xi^2 + l\xi^3$$

The other two $\varphi_i(x)$ are obtained in a similar manner. In summary, we have the following for the four beam shape functions:

$$\begin{aligned} \varphi_1(x) &= 1 - 3\xi^2 + 2\xi^3 \\ \varphi_2(x) &= l\xi - 2l\xi^2 + l\xi^3 \\ \varphi_3(x) &= 3\xi^2 - 2\xi^3 \\ \varphi_4(x) &= -l\xi^2 + l\xi^3 \end{aligned} \tag{11.7.6}$$

Generalized mass and generalized stiffness. By considering the displacement in general to be the superposition of the four shape functions shown in Fig. (11.7.2), we have

$$\begin{aligned} y(x) &= \varphi_1 v_1 + \varphi_2 \theta_1 + \varphi_3 v_2 + \phi_4 \theta_2 \\ &= \varphi_1 q_1 + \varphi_2 q_2 + \varphi_3 q_3 + \varphi_4 q_4 \end{aligned} \tag{11.7.7}$$

where q_i has been substituted for the end displacements.

To determine the generalized mass, the preceding equation is substituted into the equation for the kinetic energy.

$$\begin{aligned} T &= \frac{1}{2}\int \dot{y}^2 m\, dx = \frac{1}{2}\sum_i \sum_j \dot{q}_i \dot{q}_j \int \varphi_i \varphi_j m\, dx \\ &= \frac{1}{2}\sum_i \sum_j m_{ij} \dot{q}_i \dot{q}_j \end{aligned} \tag{11.7.8}$$

Thus, the generalized mass m_{ij}, which forms the elements of the mass matrix, is equal to

$$m_{ij} = \int_0^l \varphi_i \varphi_j m\, dx \tag{11.7.9}$$

Substituting the four beam functions into Eq. (11.7.9), the mass matrix for the uniform beam element is expressed in terms of the end displacements:

$$\frac{ml}{420}\left[\begin{array}{cc|cc} 156 & 22l & 54 & -13l \\ 22l & 4l^2 & 13l & -3l^2 \\ \hline 54 & 13l & 156 & -22l \\ -13l & -3l^2 & -22l & 4l^2 \end{array}\right] \tag{11.7.10}$$

The matrix is called *consistent mass*, because it is based on the same beam functions used for the stiffness matrix.[3]

11.8 TRANSFORMATION OF COORDINATES (GLOBAL COORDINATES)

In determining the stiffness matrix of the entire structure in terms of local elements, it is necessary first to match the displacements of the adjacent elements to ensure compatibility. In Chapter 6, this was done by examination of each joint, taking account of the orientations of the adjoining members at each joint.

In the finite element method, this requirement for displacement compatibility is simplified by resolving the element displacements and forces into a common coordinate system known as *global coordinates*.

Consider again a planar structure and examine a local element ①, ② at an angle α with the global coordinates $\bar{u}$, $\bar{v}$, which will be assumed in the horizontal and vertical directions, as shown in Fig. 11.8.1(a).

The displacement $\mathbf{r}_1$ of joint ① to ①′ must be the same in both the local and global coordinates. This requirement can be expressed by the equation

$$\mathbf{r}_1 = u_1\mathbf{i} + v_1\mathbf{j} = \bar{u}_1\bar{\mathbf{i}} + \bar{v}_1\bar{\mathbf{j}}$$

where $\mathbf{i}$, $\mathbf{j}$ and $\bar{\mathbf{i}}$, $\bar{\mathbf{j}}$ are unit vectors for the two coordinate systems. Forming the dot product for the preceding equation with $\mathbf{i}$, we obtain

$$u_1(\mathbf{i}\cdot\mathbf{i}) + v_1(\mathbf{j}\cdot\mathbf{i}) = \bar{u}_1(\bar{\mathbf{i}}\cdot\mathbf{i}) + \bar{v}_1(\bar{\mathbf{j}}\cdot\mathbf{i})$$

or

$$u_1 + 0 = \bar{u}_1 \cos\alpha + \bar{v}_1 \sin\alpha$$

Next taking the dot product with $\mathbf{j}$, we obtain

$$0 + v_1 = -\bar{u}_1 \sin\alpha + \bar{v}_1 \cos\alpha$$

Thus, we can express these results by the matrix equation

$$\begin{Bmatrix} u_1 \\ v_1 \end{Bmatrix} = \begin{bmatrix} \cos\alpha & \sin\alpha \\ -\sin\alpha & \cos\alpha \end{bmatrix} \begin{Bmatrix} \bar{u}_1 \\ \bar{v}_1 \end{Bmatrix} \tag{11.8.1}$$

The preceding equation expresses the local coordinates u_1, v_1 in terms of the global coordinates $\bar{u}_1, \bar{v}_1$. These results are readily confirmed geometrically from Fig. 11.8.1(b).

Similarly, the displacement at joint ② in local coordinates can be expressed in terms of the global coordinates by the same transformation equation. The rotation angle for the two coordinate

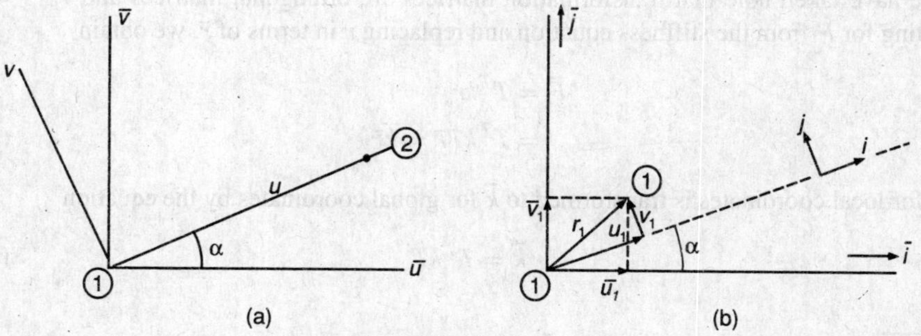

FIGURE 11.8.1.

systems must be, of course, the same, so that $\theta = \overline{\theta}$. We can then include θ in the transformation matrix as

$$\begin{Bmatrix} u \\ v \\ \theta \end{Bmatrix}_i = \begin{bmatrix} \cos\alpha & \sin\alpha & 0 \\ -\sin\alpha & \cos\alpha & 0 \\ 0 & 0 & 2 \end{bmatrix} \begin{Bmatrix} \overline{u} \\ \overline{v} \\ \overline{\theta} \end{Bmatrix}_i \qquad i = 1,2 \tag{11.8.2}$$

Thus, the transformation matrix for any element making an angle α measured counterclockwise from the horizontal is

$$\begin{Bmatrix} u_1 \\ v_1 \\ \theta_1 \\ \hline u_2 \\ v_2 \\ \theta_2 \end{Bmatrix} = \left[\begin{array}{ccc|ccc} c & s & 0 & & & \\ -s & c & 0 & & 0 & \\ 0 & 0 & 1 & & & \\ \hline & & & c & s & 0 \\ & 0 & & -s & c & 0 \\ & & & 0 & 0 & 1 \end{array}\right] \begin{Bmatrix} \overline{u}_1 \\ \overline{v}_1 \\ \overline{\theta}_1 \\ \hline \overline{u}_2 \\ \overline{v}_2 \\ \overline{\theta}_2 \end{Bmatrix} \tag{11.8.3}$$

where $c = \cos\alpha$ and $s = \sin\alpha$. It is easily seen that the transformation matrix developed for displacements also applies for the force vector.

In shorter notation, we can rewrite the transformation equations from local to global coordinates as

$$\begin{aligned} r &= T\overline{r} \\ F &= T\overline{F} \end{aligned} \tag{11.8.4}$$

where T is the transformation matrix, and r, F and $\overline{r}, \overline{F}$ are the displacement and force in the local and global coordinates, respectively. We add to this the relationships between r and F, which is the stiffness matrix:

$$F = kr \tag{11.8.5}$$

and which we wish to write in the global system as $\overline{F} = \overline{k}\overline{r}$. From Eq. (11.8.4), we have

$$\overline{F} = T^{-1}F = T^T F \tag{11.8.6}$$

Here we have taken note that transformation matrices are orthogonal matrices and $T^{-1} = T^T$.* Substituting for F from the stiffness equation and replacing r in terms of $\overline{r}$, we obtain

$$\begin{aligned} \overline{F} &= T^T kr \\ &= T^T kT\overline{r} = \overline{k}\overline{r} \end{aligned} \tag{11.8.7}$$

Thus, k for local coordinates is transformed to $\overline{k}$ for global coordinates by the equation

$$\overline{k} = T^T kT \tag{11.8.8}$$

*See Appendix C.

11.9 ELEMENT STIFFNESS AND ELEMENT MASS IN GLOBAL COORDINATES

Axial elements. For axial elements, the end moments are zero and the end forces and displacements are collinear with the element length. Thus, for systems involving only axial elements, the 6 × 6 transformation matrix reduces to the following 4 × 4 matrix:

$$T = \left[\begin{array}{cc:cc} c & s & 0 & \\ -s & c & & \\ \hdashline 0 & & c & s \\ & & -s & c \end{array}\right] \tag{11.9.1}$$

We note here that the stiffness and mass matrices for the axial element are of order 2 × 2 and, therefore, must be rewritten as a 4 × 4 matrix as follows:

$$\begin{Bmatrix} F_1 \\ F_2 \end{Bmatrix} = \frac{EA}{l}\begin{bmatrix} 1 & -1 \\ -1 & 1 \end{bmatrix}\begin{Bmatrix} u_1 \\ u_2 \end{Bmatrix} = \frac{EA}{l}\left[\begin{array}{cc:cc} 1 & 0 & -1 & 0 \\ 0 & 0 & 0 & 0 \\ \hdashline -1 & 0 & 1 & 0 \\ 0 & 0 & 0 & 0 \end{array}\right]\begin{Bmatrix} u_1 \\ v_1 \\ u_2 \\ v_2 \end{Bmatrix}$$

$$\begin{Bmatrix} F_1 \\ F_2 \end{Bmatrix} = \frac{ml}{6}\begin{bmatrix} 2 & 1 \\ 1 & 2 \end{bmatrix}\begin{Bmatrix} \ddot{u}_1 \\ \ddot{u}_2 \end{Bmatrix} = \frac{ml}{6}\left[\begin{array}{cc:cc} 2 & 0 & 1 & 0 \\ 0 & 0 & 0 & 0 \\ \hdashline 1 & 0 & 2 & 0 \\ 0 & 0 & 0 & 0 \end{array}\right]\begin{Bmatrix} \ddot{u}_1 \\ \ddot{v}_1 \\ \ddot{u}_2 \\ \ddot{v}_2 \end{Bmatrix} \tag{11.9.2}$$

These 4 × 4 matrices can then be substituted into Eq. (11.8.8) in order to convert them to the global coordinates:

$$\bar{k} = T^T k T = \frac{EA}{l}\left[\begin{array}{cc:cc} c^2 & cs & -c^2 & -cs \\ cs & s^2 & -cs & -s^2 \\ \hdashline -c^2 & -cs & c^2 & cs \\ -cs & -s^2 & cs & s^2 \end{array}\right] \tag{11.9.3}$$

$$\bar{m} = T^T m T = \frac{ml}{6}\left[\begin{array}{cc:cc} 2c^2 & 2cs & c^2 & -cs \\ 2cs & 2s^2 & cs & s^2 \\ \hdashline c^2 & cs & 2c^2 & 2cs \\ cs & s^2 & 2cs & 2s^2 \end{array}\right] \tag{11.9.4}$$

Example 11.9.1

Determine the stiffness matrix for the 3, 4, 5 oriented pinned truss of Fig. 11.9.1.

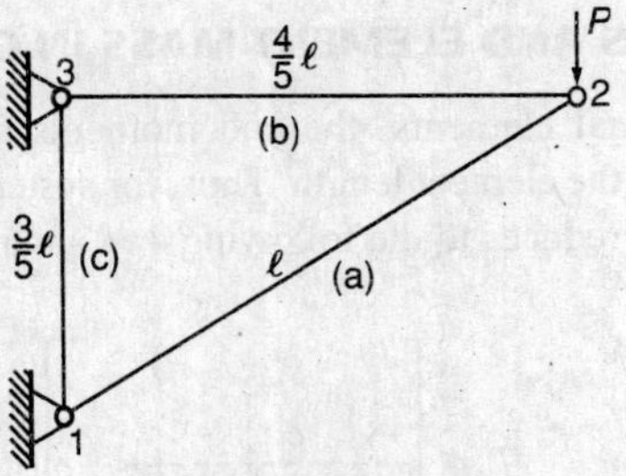

FIGURE 11.9.1.

Solution The structure is composed of three pinned members a, b, c with joints 1, 2, 3. Each joint has 2 DOF in the global system, and the six forces and displacements are related by the following equation:

$$\begin{Bmatrix} \bar{F}_{1x} \\ \bar{F}_{1y} \\ \bar{F}_{2x} \\ \bar{F}_{2y} \\ \bar{F}_{3x} \\ \bar{F}_{3y} \end{Bmatrix} = [\bar{K}] \begin{Bmatrix} \bar{u}_1 \\ \bar{v}_1 \\ \bar{u}_2 \\ \bar{v}_2 \\ \bar{u}_3 \\ \bar{v}_3 \end{Bmatrix}$$

The global stiffness of each element is determined from Eq. (11.9.3) by substituting sin α and cos α for the particular member.

Element a (1 to 2):

$$c = \frac{4}{5}, \quad s = \frac{3}{5}$$

$$\bar{k}_a \bar{r}_a = \frac{1}{25}\left(\frac{EA}{l}\right)\left[\begin{array}{cc|cc} 16 & 12 & -16 & -12 \\ 12 & 9 & -12 & -9 \\ \hline -16 & -12 & 16 & 12 \\ -12 & -9 & 12 & 9 \end{array}\right]\begin{Bmatrix} \bar{u}_1 \\ \bar{v}_1 \\ \bar{u}_2 \\ \bar{v}_2 \end{Bmatrix}$$

Element b (2 to 3):

$$c = -1, \; s = 0$$

$$\bar{k}_b \bar{r}_b = \left(\frac{5EA}{4l}\right)\left[\begin{array}{cc|cc} 1 & 0 & -1 & 0 \\ 0 & 0 & 0 & 0 \\ \hline -1 & 0 & 1 & 0 \\ 0 & 0 & 0 & 0 \end{array}\right]\begin{Bmatrix} \bar{u}_2 \\ \bar{v}_2 \\ \bar{u}_3 \\ \bar{v}_3 \end{Bmatrix}$$

$$= \frac{1}{25}\left(\frac{EA}{l}\right)\left[\begin{array}{cc|cc} \frac{125}{4} & 0 & -\frac{125}{4} & 0 \\ 0 & 0 & 0 & 0 \\ \hline -\frac{125}{4} & 0 & \frac{125}{4} & 0 \\ 0 & 0 & 0 & 0 \end{array}\right]\begin{Bmatrix} \bar{u}_2 \\ \bar{v}_2 \\ \bar{u}_3 \\ \bar{v}_3 \end{Bmatrix}$$

Element c (3 to 1):

$$c = 0, \; s = -1$$

$$\bar{k}_c\bar{r}_c = \frac{5EA}{3l}\begin{bmatrix} 0 & 0 & 0 & 0 \\ 0 & 1 & 0 & -1 \\ 0 & 0 & 0 & 0 \\ 0 & -1 & 0 & 1 \end{bmatrix}\begin{Bmatrix} \bar{u}_3 \\ \bar{v}_3 \\ \bar{u}_1 \\ \bar{v}_1 \end{Bmatrix}$$

$$= \frac{1}{25}\left(\frac{EA}{l}\right)\begin{bmatrix} 0 & 0 & 0 & 0 \\ 0 & \frac{125}{3} & 0 & -\frac{125}{3} \\ 0 & 0 & 0 & 0 \\ 0 & -\frac{125}{3} & 0 & \frac{125}{3} \end{bmatrix}\begin{Bmatrix} \bar{u}_3 \\ \bar{v}_3 \\ \bar{u}_1 \\ \bar{v}_1 \end{Bmatrix}$$

These must now be assembled for the 6 × 6 stiffness equation. The matrices for a and b have a common displacement $\begin{Bmatrix} \bar{u}_2 \\ \bar{v}_2 \end{Bmatrix}$, and it is easily seen that they fit together with an overlap of the section associated with the common displacement:

$$\left(\frac{EA}{25l}\right)\begin{bmatrix} 16 & 12 & -16 & -12 & & \\ 12 & 9 & -12 & -9 & & \\ -16 & -12 & 16+\frac{125}{4} & 12 & -\frac{125}{4} & 0 \\ -12 & -9 & 12 & 9 & 0 & 0 \\ & & -\frac{125}{4} & 0 & \frac{125}{4} & 0 \\ & & 0 & 0 & 0 & 0 \end{bmatrix}\begin{Bmatrix} \bar{u}_1 \\ \bar{v}_1 \\ \bar{u}_2 \\ \bar{v}_2 \\ \bar{u}_3 \\ \bar{v}_3 \end{Bmatrix}$$

In order to find the proper location for k_C, it can be separated into four 2 × 2 matrices, which can be arranged as

$$\left(\frac{EA}{25l}\right)\begin{bmatrix} 0 & 0 & & & 0 & 0 \\ 0 & \frac{125}{3} & & & 0 & -\frac{125}{3} \\ & & & & & \\ & & & & & \\ 0 & 0 & & & 0 & 0 \\ 0 & -\frac{125}{3} & & & 0 & \frac{125}{3} \end{bmatrix}\begin{Bmatrix} \bar{u}_1 \\ \bar{v}_1 \\ \\ \\ \bar{u}_3 \\ \bar{v}_3 \end{Bmatrix}$$

Superimposing these three matrices, we see that the stiffness matrix for the truss is

$$\begin{Bmatrix} \bar{F}_{1x} \\ \bar{F}_{1y} \\ \bar{F}_{2x} \\ \bar{F}_{2y} \\ \bar{F}_{3x} \\ \bar{F}_{3y} \end{Bmatrix} = \left(\frac{EA}{25l}\right)\begin{bmatrix} 16 & 12 & -16 & -12 & 0 & 0 \\ 12 & 9+\frac{125}{3} & -12 & -9 & 0 & -\frac{125}{3} \\ -16 & -12 & 16+\frac{125}{4} & 12 & -\frac{125}{4} & 0 \\ -12 & -9 & 12 & 9 & 0 & 0 \\ 0 & 0 & -\frac{125}{4} & 0 & \frac{125}{4} & 0 \\ 0 & -\frac{125}{3} & 0 & 0 & 0 & \frac{125}{3} \end{bmatrix}\begin{Bmatrix} \bar{u}_1 \\ \bar{v}_1 \\ \bar{u}_2 \\ \bar{v}_2 \\ \bar{u}_3 \\ \bar{v}_3 \end{Bmatrix}$$

We now impose the condition of zero displacement for joints 1 and 3, which wipes out columns 1, 2, 5, and 6, leaving the equation

$$\begin{Bmatrix} \bar{F}_{1x} \\ \bar{F}_{1y} \\ \hdashline 0 \\ -P \\ \hdashline \bar{F}_{3x} \\ \bar{F}_{3y} \end{Bmatrix} = \left(\frac{EA}{25l}\right) \begin{bmatrix} -16 & -12 \\ -12 & -9 \\ \hdashline 16 + 31.25 & 12 \\ 12 & 9 \\ \hdashline -31.25 & 0 \\ 0 & 0 \end{bmatrix} \begin{Bmatrix} \bar{u}_2 \\ \bar{v}_2 \end{Bmatrix}$$

The middle two rows are

$$\begin{Bmatrix} 0 \\ -P \end{Bmatrix} = \left(\frac{EA}{25l}\right) \begin{bmatrix} 47.25 & 12 \\ 12 & 9 \end{bmatrix} \begin{Bmatrix} \bar{u}_2 \\ \bar{v}_2 \end{Bmatrix}$$

which can be inverted to

$$\begin{Bmatrix} \bar{u}_2 \\ \bar{v}_2 \end{Bmatrix} = \left(\frac{25l}{EA}\right) \frac{1}{281.25} \begin{bmatrix} 9 & -12 \\ -12 & 47.25 \end{bmatrix} \begin{Bmatrix} 0 \\ -P \end{Bmatrix}$$

Thus, the horizontal and vertical deflections of joint 2 are

$$\bar{u}_2 = \left(\frac{25l}{281.25EA}\right)(12P) = 1.066\frac{Pl}{EA}$$

$$\bar{v}_2 = \left(\frac{25l}{281.25EA}\right)(-47.25P) = -4.200\frac{Pl}{EA}$$

With these values, the reaction forces at pins 1 and 3 are

$$\bar{F}_{1x} = \left(\frac{EA}{25l}\right)\left[-16 \times 1.066\frac{Pl}{EA} + 12 \times 4.200\frac{Pl}{EA}\right] = 1.333P$$

$$\bar{F}_{1y} = 1.000P$$

$$\bar{F}_{3x} = -1.333P$$

$$\bar{F}_{3y} = 0$$

Of course, these reactions are easily found by taking moments about the fixed pins; however, this example illustrates the general procedure to be followed for a more complex structure.

■

Beam element. The stiffness and mass matrices for the beam element are of order 4×4, whereas the transformation matrix is 6×6. Thus, to transform these matrices for the global coordinates, we need to modify them by adding the axial components rearranged as follows:

$$\frac{EA}{l}\left[\begin{array}{ccc:ccc} 1 & 0 & 0 & -1 & 0 & 0 \\ 0 & 0 & 0 & 0 & 0 & 0 \\ 0 & 0 & 0 & 0 & 0 & 0 \\ \hdashline -1 & 0 & 0 & 1 & 0 & 0 \\ 0 & 0 & 0 & 0 & 0 & 0 \\ 0 & 0 & 0 & 0 & 0 & 0 \end{array}\right]\begin{array}{c} u_1 \\ v_1 \\ \theta_1 \\ u_2 \\ v_2 \\ \theta_2 \end{array}$$

$$\frac{ml}{6}\left[\begin{array}{ccc:ccc} 2 & 0 & 0 & 1 & 0 & 0 \\ 0 & 0 & 0 & 0 & 0 & 0 \\ 0 & 0 & 0 & 0 & 0 & 0 \\ \hdashline 1 & 0 & 0 & 2 & 0 & 0 \\ 0 & 0 & 0 & 0 & 0 & 0 \\ 0 & 0 & 0 & 0 & 0 & 0 \end{array}\right]$$

The element matrices to be used in the transformation then become

$$k = \frac{EI}{l^3}\left[\begin{array}{ccc:ccc} R & 0 & 0 & -R & 0 & 0 \\ 0 & 12 & 6l & 0 & -12 & 6l \\ 0 & 6l & 4l^2 & 0 & -6l & 2l^2 \\ \hdashline -R & 0 & 0 & R & 0 & 0 \\ 0 & -12 & -6l & 0 & 12 & -6l \\ 0 & 6l & 2l^2 & 0 & -6l & 4l^2 \end{array}\right] \tag{11.9.5}$$

where $R = \left(\frac{EA}{l}\right)\left(\frac{l^3}{EI}\right) = \frac{Al^2}{I}$

$$m = \frac{ml}{420}\left|\begin{array}{ccc:ccc} N & 0 & 0 & \frac{1}{2}N & 0 & 0 \\ 0 & 156 & 22l & 0 & 54 & -13l \\ 0 & 22l & 4l^2 & 0 & 13l & -3l^2 \\ \hdashline \frac{1}{2}N & 0 & 0 & N & 0 & 0 \\ 0 & 54 & 13l & 0 & 156 & -22l \\ 0 & -13l & -3l^2 & 0 & -22l & 4l^2 \end{array}\right| \tag{11.9.6}$$

where $N = \left(\frac{ml}{3}\right)\left(\frac{420}{ml}\right) = 140$

These 6 × 6 element matrices are transformed to global coordinates (with bars over the letters) by the equations $\bar{k} = T^T kT$ and $\bar{m} = T^T mT$:

$$\bar{k} = \frac{EI}{l^3}\left[\begin{array}{ccc:ccc} (Rc^2+12s^2) & (R-12)cs & -6ls & (-Rc^2-12s^2) & (-R+12)cs & -6ls \\ (R-12)cs & (Rs^2+12c^2) & 6lc & (-R+12)cs & (-Rs^2-12c^2) & 6lc \\ -6ls & 6lc & 4l^2 & 6ls & -6lc & 2l^2 \\ \hdashline (-Rc^2-12s^2) & (-R+12)cs & 6ls & (Rc^2+12s^2) & (R-12)cs & 6ls \\ (-R+12)cs & (-Rs^2-12c^2) & -6lc & (R-12)cs & (Rs^2+12c^2) & -6lc \\ -6ls & 6lc & 2l^2 & 6ls & -6lc & 4l^2 \end{array}\right] \begin{array}{c} \bar{u} \\ \bar{v} \\ \theta \\ \\ \\ \\ \end{array} \tag{11.9.7}$$

$$\bar{m} = \frac{ml}{420}\left[\begin{array}{ccc:ccc} (Nc^2+156s^2) & (N-156)cs & -22ls & (\frac{1}{2}Nc^2+54s^2) & (\frac{1}{2}N-54)cs & 13ls \\ (N-156)cs & (Ns^2+156c^2) & 22lc & (\frac{1}{2}N-54)cs & (\frac{1}{2}Ns^2+54c^2) & -13lc \\ -22ls & 22lc & 4l^2 & -13ls & 13lc & -3l^2 \\ \hdashline (\frac{1}{2}Nc^2+54s^2) & (\frac{1}{2}N-54)cs & -13ls & (Nc^2+156s^2) & (N-156)cs & 22ls \\ (\frac{1}{2}N-54)cs & (\frac{1}{2}Ns^2+54c^2) & 13lc & (N-156)cs & (Ns^2+156c^2) & -22lc \\ 13ls & -13lc & -3l^2 & 22ls & -22lc & 4l^2 \end{array}\right] \tag{11.9.8}$$

11.10 VIBRATIONS INVOLVING BEAM ELEMENTS

To illustrate the finite element method for beams, we consider some of the problems solved earlier in this chapter. The object here is, first, to show how to assemble the system equation using two elements and, second, to reduce the degrees of freedom of the equation by elimination of rotational coordinates.

Example 11.10.1

The beam in Fig. 11.10.1 is considered as two equal elements of length $l/2$, whose stiffness and mass matrices are given by Eqs. (11.7.1) and (11.7.10). With $l/2$ substituted for l, the element matrices are as follows:

Element a:

$$\text{Stiffness}\ \left(\frac{8EI}{l^3}\right)\left[\begin{array}{cc:cc} 12 & 3l & -12 & 3l \\ 3l & l^2 & -3l & 0.5l^2 \\ \hdashline -12 & -3l & 12 & -3l \\ 3l & 0.5l^2 & -3l & l^2 \end{array}\right] \qquad \text{Displacement vector} \begin{Bmatrix} v_1 \\ \theta_1 \\ v_2 \\ \theta_2 \end{Bmatrix}$$

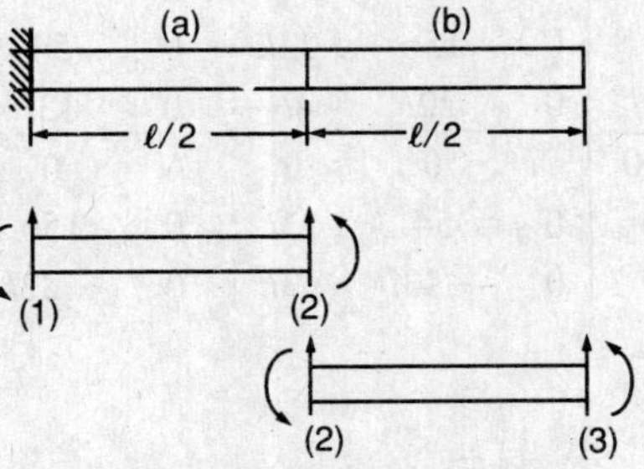

FIGURE 11.10.1. Uniform cantilever beam.

$$\text{Mass}\left(\frac{ml}{840}\right)\left[\begin{array}{cc:cc} 156 & 11l & 54 & -6.5l \\ 11l & l^2 & 6.5l & -0.75\,l^2 \\ \hdashline 54 & 6.5l & 156 & -11l \\ -6.5l & -0.75\,l^2 & -11l & l^2 \end{array}\right]$$

Element *b*: Element *b* is the same as element *a* except for the displacement vector, which is

$$\begin{Bmatrix} v_2 \\ \theta_2 \\ v_3 \\ \theta_3 \end{Bmatrix}$$

With the global coordinates coinciding with the beam axis, the assembly of the system matrix is simply that of superimposing the preceding matrices for elements *a* and *b* into a 6×6 matrix. That is, for the stiffness matrix, we have

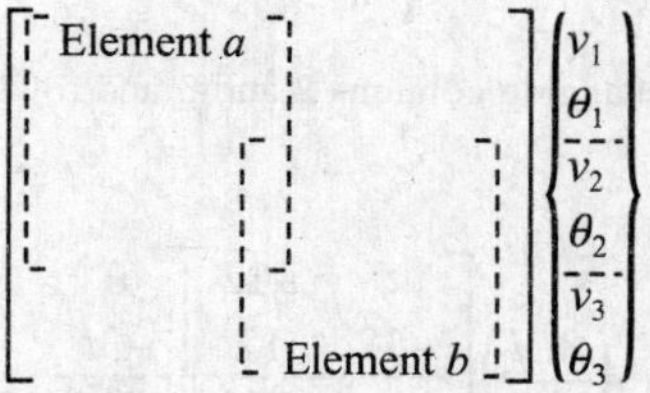

Because $v_1 = \theta_1 = 0$ due to the constraint of the wall, the first two columns can be ignored. Also, we are not concerned with the force and moment, F_1 and M_1, respectively, in the vibration problem. We can, therefore, strike out the first two rows as well as the first two columns, leaving the equation

$$\frac{ml}{840}\left[\begin{array}{cc:cc} 312 & 0 & 54 & -6.5l \\ 0 & 2l^2 & 6.5l & -0.75l^2 \\ \hdashline 54 & 6.5l & 156 & -11l \\ -6.5l & -0.75l^2 & -11l & l^2 \end{array}\right]\begin{Bmatrix} \ddot{v}_2 \\ \ddot{\theta}_2 \\ \ddot{v}_3 \\ \ddot{\theta}_3 \end{Bmatrix}$$

$$+\left(\frac{8\,EI}{l^3}\right)\left[\begin{array}{cc:cc} 24 & 0 & -12 & 3l \\ 0 & 2l^2 & -3l & 0.5l^2 \\ \hdashline -12 & -3l & 12 & -3l \\ 3l & 0.5l^2 & -3l & l^2 \end{array}\right]\begin{Bmatrix} \ddot{v}_2 \\ \ddot{\theta}_2 \\ \ddot{v}_3 \\ \ddot{\theta}_3 \end{Bmatrix} = \begin{Bmatrix} F_2 \\ M_2 \\ F_3 \\ M_3 \end{Bmatrix} \tag{11.10.1}$$

To solve for the free vibration of the beam, the force vector is made equal to zero and the acceleration vector is replaced by $-\omega^2$ times the displacement.

■

Computer program. The program **beam.m** is a MATLAB® script file which computes the natural frequencies as determined by a finite element model for the cantilever beam. After prompting the user to input the length of the beam; the number of elements desired; the mass of the beam; the elastic modulus of the beam; and the moment of inertia of the beam, the program constructs the mass and stiffness matrices for the model. For a beam composed of two equal elements, these matrices can be found in Eq. (11.10.1). The dynamic matrix is then constructed from these two matrices.

The eigenvalues of the dynamic matrix are computed and are used to determine the natural frequencies of the model. For more information about the program, see Appendix F.

Coordinate reduction

Example 11.10.2

The solution of the preceding equation requires an eigenvalue–eigenvector computer program. However, we consider a simpler problem of replacing the uniformly distributed mass by lumped masses at joints 2 and 3. The mass matrix is then a series of 0s except for elements m_{22} and m_{33}. This suggests rearranging the preceding equation so that the displacement vector is in the rearranged order

$$\begin{Bmatrix} v_2 \\ v_3 \\ \theta_2 \\ \theta_3 \end{Bmatrix}$$

This is simply accomplished by interchanging columns 2 and 3 and rows 2 and 3, resulting in the following equation:

$$\left[\begin{array}{cc|c} m_2 & 0 & 0 \\ 0 & m_3 & \\ \hline 0 & & 0 \end{array}\right]\begin{Bmatrix} \ddot{v}_2 \\ \ddot{v}_3 \\ \ddot{\theta}_2 \\ \ddot{\theta}_3 \end{Bmatrix} + \left(\frac{8EI}{l^3}\right)\left[\begin{array}{cc|cc} 24 & -12 & 0 & 3l \\ -12 & 12 & -3l & -3l \\ \hline 0 & -3l & 2l^2 & 0.5l^2 \\ 3l & -3l & 0.5l^2 & l^2 \end{array}\right]\begin{Bmatrix} v_2 \\ v_3 \\ \theta_2 \\ \theta_3 \end{Bmatrix} = \begin{Bmatrix} 0 \\ 0 \\ 0 \\ 0 \end{Bmatrix}$$

The equation is now in the form

$$\left[\begin{array}{c|c} M_{11} & 0 \\ \hline 0 & 0 \end{array}\right]\begin{Bmatrix} \ddot{V} \\ \ddot{\theta} \end{Bmatrix} + \left[\begin{array}{c|c} K_{11} & K_{12} \\ \hline K_{21} & K_{22} \end{array}\right]\begin{Bmatrix} V \\ \theta \end{Bmatrix} = \begin{Bmatrix} 0 \\ 0 \end{Bmatrix} \tag{11.10.2}$$

which can be written as

$$M_{11}\ddot{V} + K_{11}V + K_{12}\theta = 0$$
$$K_{21}V + K_{22}\theta = 0$$

From the second equation, θ can be expressed in terms of V:

$$\theta = -K_{22}^{-1}K_{21}V$$

Substituting into the first equation, we have

$$M_{11}\ddot{V} + (K_{11} - K_{12}K_{22}^{-1}K_{21})V = 0 \tag{11.10.3}$$

which in terms of the original quantities becomes

$$\begin{bmatrix} m_2 & 0 \\ 0 & m_3 \end{bmatrix}\begin{Bmatrix} \ddot{v}_2 \\ \ddot{v}_3 \end{Bmatrix} + \left(\frac{8EI}{l^3}\right)\left[\begin{bmatrix} 24 & -12 \\ -12 & 12 \end{bmatrix} - \begin{bmatrix} 0 & 3l \\ -3l & -3l \end{bmatrix}\begin{bmatrix} 2l^2 & 0.5l^2 \\ 0.5l^2 & l^2 \end{bmatrix}^{-1}\begin{bmatrix} 0 & -3l \\ 3l & -3l \end{bmatrix}\right]\begin{Bmatrix} v_2 \\ v_3 \end{Bmatrix} = \begin{Bmatrix} 0 \\ 0 \end{Bmatrix}$$

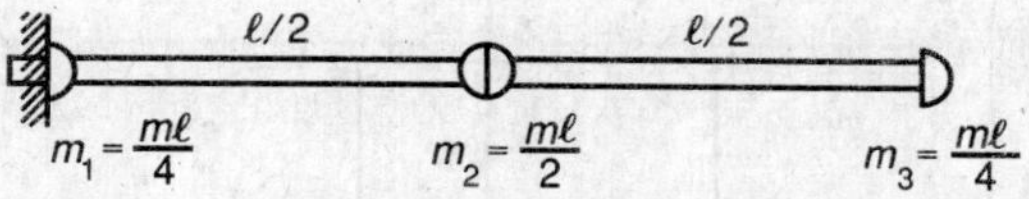

FIGURE 11.10.2. Two-element discrete mass model of a uniform cantilever beam.

The term

$$K_{11} - K_{12}K_{22}^{-1}K_{21} \tag{11.10.4}$$

is the *reduced stiffness*, and its value when multiplied out is

$$\frac{8EI}{7l^3}\begin{vmatrix} 96 & -30 \\ -30 & 12 \end{vmatrix} = \frac{48EI}{7l^3}\begin{vmatrix} 16 & -5 \\ -5 & 2 \end{vmatrix}$$

Thus, the original 4 × 4 equation has been reduced to a 2 × 2 equation, the final form being

$$\begin{bmatrix} m_2 & 0 \\ 0 & m_3 \end{bmatrix}\begin{Bmatrix} \ddot{v}_2 \\ \ddot{v}_3 \end{Bmatrix} + \left(\frac{48EI}{7l^3}\right)\begin{bmatrix} 16 & -5 \\ -5 & 2 \end{bmatrix}\begin{Bmatrix} v_2 \\ v_3 \end{Bmatrix} = \begin{Bmatrix} 0 \\ 0 \end{Bmatrix}$$

An acceptable discrete mass distribution is one in which the mass of each element is divided into half at each end of the element. Thus, if the total mass of the uniform beam of length l is ml, the mass of each element is $ml/2$ and $m_2 = 2(ml/4) = ml/2$ and $m_3 = ml/4$, as shown in Fig. 11.10.2.

The equation of motion and solution then becomes

$$\left[-\lambda\begin{bmatrix} 2 & 0 \\ 0 & 1 \end{bmatrix} + \begin{bmatrix} 16 & -5 \\ -5 & 2 \end{bmatrix}\right]\begin{Bmatrix} v_2 \\ v_3 \end{Bmatrix} = \begin{Bmatrix} 0 \\ 0 \end{Bmatrix}$$

where

$$\lambda = \frac{\omega^2 ml}{4} \cdot \frac{7l^3}{48EI} = \omega^2 \frac{7}{192}\left(\frac{ml^4}{EI}\right)$$

$$\lambda_1 = 0.3632 \quad \omega_1 = 3.516 \quad \text{exact value} = 3.516$$

$$\lambda_2 = 9.637 \quad \omega_2 = 22.033 \quad \text{exact value} = 22.034$$

$$\phi_1 = \begin{Bmatrix} 0.327 \\ 1.000 \end{Bmatrix} \qquad \phi_2 = \begin{Bmatrix} -1.527 \\ 1.000 \end{Bmatrix}$$

■

Example 11.10.3

Determine the equation of free vibration of the portal frame with identical elements.

Solution By labeling the joints as shown in Fig. 11.10.3, the stiffness and mass for each element are available from Eqs. (11.9.7) and (11.9.8). Because joints 0 and 3 have zero displacements, we write only the terms corresponding to joints 1 and 2.

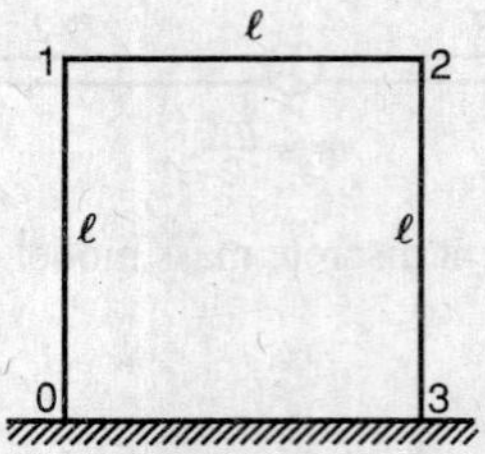

FIGURE 11.10.3.

Element 0–1, $\alpha = 90°, c = 0, s = 1$:

$$\overline{k}_{0-1} = \frac{EI}{l^3}\left[\begin{array}{c|ccc} & -12 & 0 & -6l \\ & 0 & -R & 0 \\ & 6l & 0 & 2l^2 \\ \hline & 12 & 0 & 6l \\ & 0 & R & 0 \\ & 6l & 0 & 4l^2 \end{array}\right]\begin{array}{c} \\ \\ \\ \overline{u}_1 \\ \overline{v}_1 \\ \overline{\theta}_1 \end{array}$$

$$\overline{m}_{0-1} = \frac{ml}{420}\left[\begin{array}{c|ccc} & 54 & 0 & 13l \\ & 0 & \frac{1}{2}N & 0 \\ & -13l & 0 & -3l^2 \\ \hline & 156 & 0 & 22l \\ & 0 & 0 & 0 \\ & 22l & 0 & 4l^2 \end{array}\right]$$

Element 1–2, $\alpha = 0°, c = 1, s = 0$:

$$\overline{k}_{1-2} = \frac{EI}{l^3}\left[\begin{array}{ccc|ccc} R & 0 & 0 & -R & 0 & 0 \\ 0 & 12 & 6l & 0 & -12 & 6l \\ 0 & 6l & 4l^2 & 0 & -6l & 2l^2 \\ \hline -R & 0 & 0 & R & 0 & 0 \\ 0 & -12 & -6l & 0 & 12 & -6l \\ 0 & 6l & 2l^2 & 0 & -6l & 4l^2 \end{array}\right]\begin{array}{c} \overline{u}_1 \\ \overline{v}_1 \\ \overline{\theta}_1 \\ \overline{u}_2 \\ \overline{v}_2 \\ \overline{\theta}_2 \end{array}$$

$$\overline{m}_{1-2} = \frac{ml}{420}\left[\begin{array}{ccc|ccc} N & 0 & 0 & \frac{1}{2}N & 0 & 0 \\ 0 & 156 & 22l & 0 & 54 & -13l \\ 0 & 22l & 4l^2 & 0 & 13l & -3l^2 \\ \hline \frac{1}{2}N & 0 & 0 & N & 0 & 0 \\ 0 & 54 & 13l & 0 & 156 & -22l \\ 0 & -13l & -3l^2 & 0 & -22l & 4l^2 \end{array}\right]$$

Element 2–3, $\alpha = 270°, c = 0, s = -1$:

$$\bar{k}_{2-3} = \frac{EI}{l^3}\left[\begin{array}{ccc|ccc} 12 & 0 & 6l & & & \\ 0 & R & 0 & & & \\ 6l & 0 & 4l^2 & & & \\ \hline -12 & 0 & -6l & & & \\ 0 & -R & 0 & & & \\ 6l & 0 & 2l^2 & & & \end{array}\right]\begin{matrix} \bar{u}_2 \\ \bar{v}_2 \\ \bar{\theta}_2 \\ \bar{u}_3 \\ \bar{v}_3 \\ \bar{\theta}_3 \end{matrix}$$

$$\bar{m}_{2-3} = \frac{ml}{420}\left[\begin{array}{ccc|ccc} 156 & 0 & 22l & & & \\ 0 & N & 0 & & & \\ 22l & 0 & 4l^2 & & & \\ \hline & 0 & & & & \\ & & & & & \\ & & & & & \end{array}\right]$$

Assembling these matrices, we have

$$\frac{EI}{l^3}\left[\begin{array}{ccc|ccc} (12+R) & 0 & 6l & -R & 0 & 0 \\ 0 & (12+R) & 6l & 0 & -12 & 6l \\ 6l & 6l & 8l^2 & 0 & -6l & 2l^2 \\ \hline -R & 0 & 0 & (12+R) & 0 & 6l \\ 0 & -12 & -6l & 0 & (12+R) & -6l \\ 0 & 6l & 2l^2 & 6l & -6l & 8l^2 \end{array}\right]\begin{matrix} \bar{u}_1 \\ \bar{v}_1 \\ \bar{\theta}_1 \\ \bar{u}_2 \\ \bar{v}_2 \\ \bar{\theta}_2 \end{matrix} \quad \text{(a)}$$

$$\frac{ml}{420}\left[\begin{array}{ccc|ccc} (156+N) & 0 & 22l & \frac{1}{2}N & 0 & 0 \\ 0 & 156 & 22l & 0 & 54 & -13l \\ 22l & 22l & 8l^2 & 0 & 13l & -3l^2 \\ \hline \frac{1}{2}N & 0 & 0 & (156+N) & 0 & 22l \\ 0 & 54 & 13l & 0 & (156+N) & -22l \\ 0 & -13l & -3l^2 & 22l & -22l & 8l^2 \end{array}\right] \quad \text{(b)}$$

We next note that $v_1 = v_2 = 0$, which eliminates columns 2 and 5 as well as rows 2 and 5. The equation for free vibration with $N = 140$ substituted then becomes

$$-\frac{\omega^2 ml}{420}\left[\begin{array}{cc|cc} 296 & 22l & 70 & 0 \\ 22l & 8l^2 & 0 & -3l^2 \\ \hline 70 & 0 & 296 & 22l \\ 0 & -3l^2 & 22l & 8l^2 \end{array}\right]\begin{Bmatrix} \bar{u}_1 \\ \bar{\theta}_1 \\ \bar{u}_2 \\ \bar{\theta}_2 \end{Bmatrix} \quad \text{(c)}$$

$$+\frac{EI}{l^3}\left[\begin{array}{cc|cc} (12+R) & 6l & -R & 0 \\ 6l & 8l^2 & 0 & 2l^2 \\ \hline -R & 0 & (12+R) & 6l \\ 0 & 2l^2 & 6l & 8l^2 \end{array}\right]\begin{Bmatrix} \bar{u}_1 \\ \bar{\theta}_1 \\ \bar{u}_2 \\ \bar{\theta}_2 \end{Bmatrix} = \begin{Bmatrix} 0 \\ 0 \\ 0 \\ 0 \end{Bmatrix}$$

■

Example 11.10.4

Figure 11.10.4 shows the lowest antisymmetric and the lowest symmetric modes of free vibration for the portal frame. Determine the natural frequencies for the given modes.

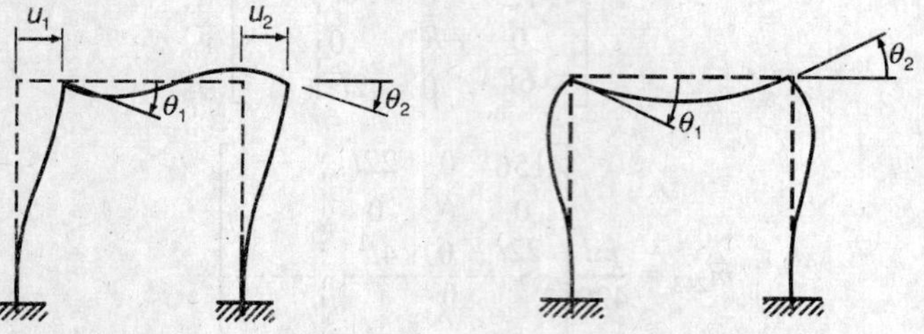

FIGURE 11.10.4.

Solution *Antisymmetric Mode.* The deflection and slope of stations 1 and 2 are identical, i.e., $\bar{u}_1 = \bar{u}_2$ and $\bar{\theta}_1 = \bar{\theta}_2$. These conditions are imposed on the preceding equation by adding column 3 to column 1 and column 4 to column 2. This results in identical equations for $\begin{Bmatrix} \bar{u}_1 \\ \bar{\theta}_1 \end{Bmatrix}$ and $\begin{Bmatrix} \bar{u}_2 \\ \bar{\theta}_2 \end{Bmatrix}$:

$$\left[-\frac{\omega^2 ml}{420} \begin{bmatrix} 366 & 22l \\ 22l & 5l^2 \end{bmatrix} + \frac{EI}{l^3} \begin{bmatrix} 12 & 6l \\ 6l & 10l^2 \end{bmatrix} \right] \begin{Bmatrix} \bar{u}_1 \\ \bar{\theta}_1 \end{Bmatrix} = \begin{Bmatrix} 0 \\ 0 \end{Bmatrix}$$

By letting $\lambda = \omega^2 ml^4/420EI$, the determinant* of this equation

$$\begin{vmatrix} (12 - 366\lambda) & (6 - 22\lambda)l \\ (6 - 22\lambda)l & (10 - 5\lambda)l^2 \end{vmatrix} = 0$$

results in two roots:

$$\lambda_1 = 0.0245 \qquad \omega_1 = 3.21\sqrt{\frac{EI}{ml^4}}$$

$$\lambda_2 = 2.543 \qquad \omega_2 = 32.68\sqrt{\frac{EI}{ml^4}}$$

The lowest natural frequency corresponds to the simple shape displayed in Fig. 11.10.4(a) and is of acceptable accuracy. However, the second antisymmetric mode would be of more complex shape and ω_2 computed with the few stations used in this example would not be accurate. Several more stations would be necessary to adequately represent the higher modes.

Symmetric Mode: For the symmetric mode, we have $u_1 = u_2 = 0$ and $\theta_2 = -\theta_1$. Deleting columns 1 and 3 and subtracting column 4 from column 2, we obtain just one equation for θ_1:

$$\left[-\frac{\omega^2 ml}{420}(11l^2) + \frac{EI}{l^3}(6l^2) \right] \theta_1 = 0$$

---

*When the determinant is multiplied out, l^2 becomes a factor that cancels out. Thus, we can let $l = 1.0$ in the matrices of the frequency equation without altering the values of λ_1 and λ_2.

λ and ω are then

$$\lambda = \frac{6}{11} \qquad \omega = 15.14\sqrt{\frac{EI}{ml^4}}$$

■

Example 11.10.5

Figure 11.10.5 shows external loads acting on the portal frame. Examine the boundary condition and determine the stiffness matrix in terms of the coordinates given.

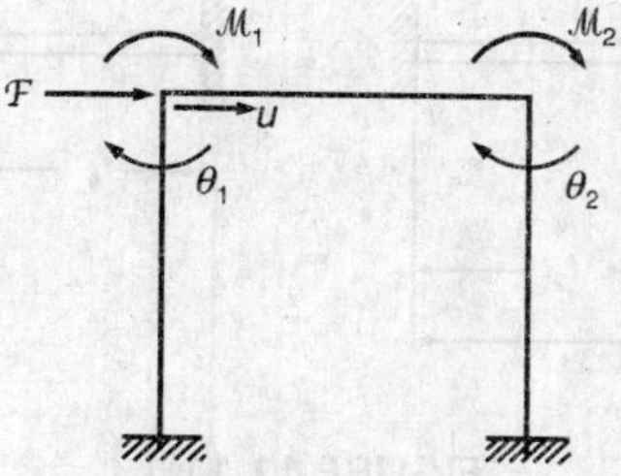

FIGURE 11.10.5.

Solution The condition of no extension of members $\overline{u}_1 = \overline{u}_2$ is satisfied by adding column 3 to column 1 in Eq. (c), Example 11.10.3. This eliminates the extension term R. We can also add row 3 to row 1 and rewrite the stiffness matrix as a 3×3 matrix:

$$\begin{Bmatrix} \overline{F}_{1x} + \overline{F}_{2x} \\ \overline{M}_1 \\ \overline{M}_2 \end{Bmatrix} = \frac{EI}{l^3}\begin{bmatrix} 24 & 6l & 6l \\ 6l & 8l^2 & 2l^2 \\ 6l & 2l^2 & 8l^2 \end{bmatrix}\begin{Bmatrix} \overline{u}_1 \\ \overline{\theta}_1 \\ \overline{\theta}_2 \end{Bmatrix}$$

Comparing the external loads of Fig. 11.10.5 with those of the global system, we have

$$\begin{Bmatrix} \overline{F}_{1x} + \overline{F}_{2x} \\ \overline{M}_1 \\ \overline{M}_2 \end{Bmatrix} = \begin{Bmatrix} \mathcal{F} \\ -\mathcal{M}_1 \\ -\mathcal{M}_2 \end{Bmatrix} \qquad \begin{Bmatrix} \overline{u}_1 \\ \overline{\theta}_1 \\ \overline{\theta}_2 \end{Bmatrix} = \begin{Bmatrix} u \\ -\theta_1 \\ -\theta_2 \end{Bmatrix}$$

With $\overline{F}_{2x} = 0$ and $\overline{F}_{1x} = \mathcal{F}$, the stiffness matrix in terms of the given coordinates and given loads is

$$\begin{Bmatrix} \mathcal{F} \\ \mathcal{M}_1 \\ \mathcal{M}_2 \end{Bmatrix} = \frac{EI}{l^3}\begin{bmatrix} 24 & -6l & -6l \\ -6l & 8l^2 & 2l^2 \\ -6l & 2l^2 & 8l^2 \end{bmatrix}\begin{Bmatrix} u \\ \theta_1 \\ \theta_2 \end{Bmatrix}$$

■

11.11 SPRING CONSTRAINTS ON STRUCTURE

In Chapter 8, spring constraints were treated by virtual work as generalized forces. The same concept applies in the finite element approach. The point of application of the spring must be chosen here as a joint station. Thus, the load on the original structure in global coordinates is supplemented by the spring force.

Because the spring force is always opposite to the displacement, the force or moment at the joint is decreased by $-kv_i$ or $-K\theta_i$. Thus, the terms, when shifted to the other side of the equation, become additions to the corresponding stiffness term.

Example 11.11.1

Determine the stiffness matrix for the uniform beam with a linear and rotational spring, as shown in Fig. 11.11.1(a).

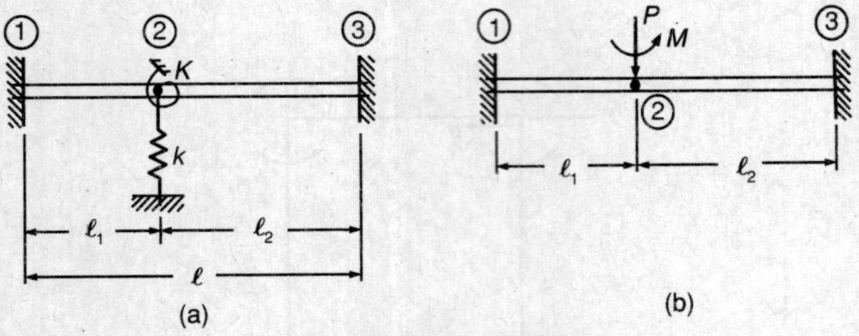

FIGURE 11.11.1.

Solution We first establish the stiffness matrix of the beam without the springs [Fig. 11.11.1(b)], but with loads P and M acting at station 2. The stiffness matrix for each section 1–2 and 2–3 can be assembled from the beam element matrix, Eq. (11.7.1). Noting that $v_1 = \theta_1 = v_3 = \theta_3 = 0$, we need only evaluate the portion of the matrix associated with the coordinates v_2 and θ_2, which becomes

$$\begin{Bmatrix} \overline{F}_2 \\ \overline{M}_2 \end{Bmatrix} = EI \begin{bmatrix} 12\left(\dfrac{1}{l_1^3} + \dfrac{1}{l_2^3}\right) & -6\left(\dfrac{1}{l_1^2} - \dfrac{1}{l_2^2}\right) \\ -6\left(\dfrac{1}{l_1^2} - \dfrac{1}{l_2^2}\right) & 4\left(\dfrac{1}{l_1} + \dfrac{1}{l_2}\right) \end{bmatrix} \begin{Bmatrix} \overline{v}_2 \\ \overline{\theta}_2 \end{Bmatrix}$$

With the springs acting at station 2, the force vector is replaced by

$$\begin{Bmatrix} \overline{F}_2 & - & k\overline{v}_2 \\ \overline{M}_2 & - & K\overline{\theta}_2 \end{Bmatrix}$$

Shifting the spring forces to the right side of the equation, we obtain

$$\begin{Bmatrix} \overline{F}_2 \\ \overline{M}_2 \end{Bmatrix} = EI \begin{bmatrix} 12\left(\dfrac{1}{l_1^3} + \dfrac{1}{l_2^3}\right) + \dfrac{k}{EI} & -6\left(\dfrac{1}{l_1^2} - \dfrac{1}{l_2^2}\right) \\ -6\left(\dfrac{1}{l_1^2} - \dfrac{1}{l_2^2}\right) & 4\left(\dfrac{1}{l_1} + \dfrac{1}{l_2}\right) + \dfrac{K}{EI} \end{bmatrix} \begin{Bmatrix} \overline{v}_2 \\ \overline{\theta}_2 \end{Bmatrix}$$

Because the force $\overline{F}_2$ in the global system is positive in the upward direction, and $\overline{M}_2$ is positive counterclockwise, the previous equation can be rearranged to

$$\begin{Bmatrix} -P \\ M \end{Bmatrix} = \frac{EI}{l^3} \begin{bmatrix} 12\left(\dfrac{l^3}{l_1^3} + \dfrac{l^3}{l_2^3}\right) + \dfrac{kl^3}{EI} & -6l\left(\dfrac{l^2}{l_1^2} - \dfrac{l^2}{l_2^2}\right) \\ -6l\left(\dfrac{l^2}{l_1^2} - \dfrac{l^2}{l_2^2}\right) & 4l^2\left(\dfrac{l}{l_1} + \dfrac{l}{l_2}\right) + \dfrac{Kl^3}{EI} \end{bmatrix} \begin{Bmatrix} \overline{v}_2 \\ \overline{\theta}_2 \end{Bmatrix}$$

which defines the stiffness matrix for the beam with the spring constraints.

The equation indicates that the system is decoupled for $l_1 = l_2 = l/2$, in which case the equation reduces to

$$\begin{Bmatrix} -P \\ M \end{Bmatrix} = \frac{EI}{l^3} \begin{bmatrix} \left(192 + \frac{kl^3}{EI}\right) & \\ & \left(16l^2 + \frac{Kl^3}{EI}\right) \end{bmatrix} \begin{Bmatrix} \bar{v}_2 \\ \bar{\theta}_2 \end{Bmatrix}$$

The deflection at the center is then

$$\bar{v}_2 = \frac{-(Pl^3/EI)}{192 + kl^3/EI} \qquad \theta_2 = \frac{Ml^3/EI}{16l^2 + Kl^3/EI}$$

■

Example 11.11.2

Determine the natural frequencies of the constrained beam of Example 11.11.1 when $l_1 = l_2 = l/2$.

Solution For this determination, we need the mass matrix, which can be assembled from Eq. (11.7.10) as

$$\left(\frac{m}{420}\right)\begin{bmatrix} 156(l_1 + l_2) & -22(l_1^2 - l_2^2) \\ -22(l_1^2 - l_2^2) & 4(l_1^3 + l_2^3) \end{bmatrix} = \left(\frac{ml}{420}\right)\begin{bmatrix} 156 & 0 \\ 0 & l^2 \end{bmatrix}$$

The equation of motion then becomes

$$\left[-\frac{\omega^2 ml}{420}\begin{bmatrix} 156 & 0 \\ 0 & l^2 \end{bmatrix} + \frac{EI}{l^3}\begin{bmatrix} \left(192 + \frac{kl^3}{EI}\right) & 0 \\ 0 & \left(16l^2 + \frac{Kl^3}{EI}\right) \end{bmatrix}\right] \begin{Bmatrix} \bar{v}_2 \\ \bar{\theta}_2 \end{Bmatrix} = \begin{Bmatrix} 0 \\ 0 \end{Bmatrix}$$

Again, coordinates $\bar{v}_2$ and $\bar{\theta}_2$ are decoupled. By letting $\lambda = \omega^2 ml^4/420EI$, the equation for $\bar{v}_2$ gives

$$\lambda = \frac{1}{156}\left(192 + \frac{kl^3}{EI}\right) = 1.231 + 0.00641\frac{kl^3}{EI}$$

and the natural frequency for this mode is

$$\omega_1 = 22.73\sqrt{\frac{EI}{ml^4}}\sqrt{1 + 0.00521\left(\frac{kl^3}{EI}\right)}$$

Similarly, the equation for θ_2 results in

$$\lambda = 16 + \frac{Kl}{EI}$$

and

$$\omega_2 = 81.98\sqrt{\frac{EI}{ml^4}}\sqrt{1 + 0.0625\left(\frac{kl}{EI}\right)}$$

Thus, both natural frequencies are increased by the constraining springs. If $k = K = 0$, the exact natural frequencies for the beam with fixed ends are

$$\omega_1 = 22.37\sqrt{\frac{EI}{ml^4}} \qquad \omega_2 = 61.67\sqrt{\frac{EI}{ml^4}}$$

so that the error in the finite element approach is 1.61 percent for the first mode and 33.9 percent for the second mode. Dividing the beam into shorter elements reduces these errors.

■

11.12 GENERALIZED FORCE FOR DISTRIBUTED LOAD

As discussed in Chapter 6, the generalized force is found from the virtual work of the applied forces. With the displacement expressed as

$$y(x) = \phi_1(x)v_1 + \phi_2(x)\theta_1 + \phi_3(x)v_2 + \phi_4(x)\theta_2 \tag{11.12.1}$$

the virtual work of the applied distributed force $p(x)$ is

$$\begin{aligned} \delta W &= \int_0^l p(x)\,\delta y(x)\,dx \\ &= \delta v_1 \int_0^l p(x)\phi_1(x)\,dx + \delta\theta_1 \int_0^l p(x)\phi_2(x)\,dx \\ &\quad + \delta v_2 \int_0^l p(x)\phi_3(x)\,dx + \delta\theta_2 \int_0^l p(x)\phi_4(x)\,dx \end{aligned} \tag{11.12.2}$$

The integrals in Eq. (11.12.2) are the generalized forces.

If the same procedure is applied to the end forces, F_1, M_1, F_2, and M_2, the virtual work is

$$\delta W = F_1 \delta v_1 + M_1\,\delta\theta_1 + F_2\,\delta v_2 + M_2\,\delta\theta_2 \tag{11.12.3}$$

Equating the virtual work in the previous two cases, we obtain the following relationships:

$$\begin{aligned} F_1 &= \int_0^l p(x)\phi_1(x)\,dx \qquad F_2 = \int_0^l p(x)\phi_3(x)\,dx \\ M_1 &= \int_0^l p(x)\phi_2(x)\,dx \quad\ M_2 = \int_0^l p(x)\phi_4(x)\,dx \end{aligned} \tag{11.12.4}$$

Thus, for the distributed load, the equivalent finite element loads are the generalized forces just given.

Example 11.12.1

Figure 11.12.1 shows a cantilever beam of length l_1 with a uniform load $p(x) = p$ N/m. over the outer half of the beam. Determine the deflection and slope at the free end using the method of this section.

Solution We use a single element ①–② and first determine the inverse of the stiffness matrix. Because $v_1 = \theta_1 = 0$, the stiffness equation from Eq. (11.7.1) is

$$\begin{Bmatrix} F_2 \\ M_2 \end{Bmatrix} = \frac{EI}{l_1^3}\begin{bmatrix} 12 & -6l_1 \\ -6l_1 & 4l_1^2 \end{bmatrix}\begin{Bmatrix} v_2 \\ \theta_2 \end{Bmatrix}$$

Its inverse, using the adjoint method, is

$$\begin{Bmatrix} v_2 \\ \theta_2 \end{Bmatrix} = \frac{l_1^3}{EI}\frac{1}{12l_1^2}\begin{bmatrix} 4l_1^2 & 6l_1 \\ 6l_1 & 12 \end{bmatrix}\begin{Bmatrix} F_2 \\ M_2 \end{Bmatrix}$$

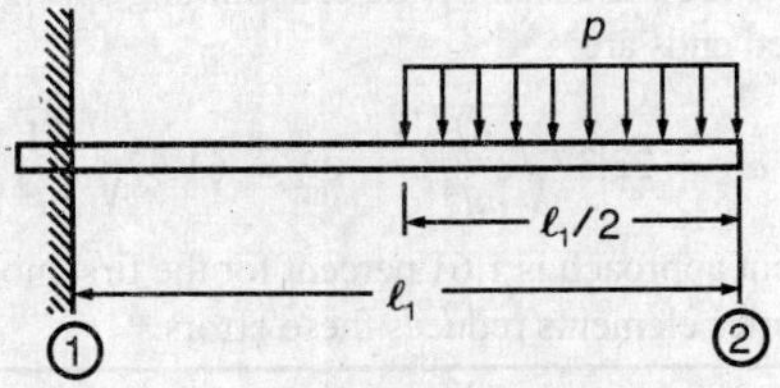

FIGURE 11.12.1.

The equivalent finite element forces, from Eq. (11.12.4), are

$$F_2 = \int_{l_2}^{l_1} -p\phi_3(x)dx = -p\int_{1/2}^{1} \phi_3(\xi)l_1 d\xi = -pl_1 \int_{1/2}^{1} (3\xi^2 - 2\xi^3)d\xi = -\frac{13}{32}pl_1$$

$$M_2 = \int_{1/2}^{1} -p\phi_4(\xi)l_1 d\xi = -pl_1^2 \int_{1/2}^{1} (-\xi^2 + \xi^3)d\xi = \frac{88}{1536}pl_1^2$$

Substituting these values into the inverted equation, we have

$$\begin{Bmatrix} v_2 \\ \theta_2 \end{Bmatrix} = \frac{l_1}{12EI}\begin{bmatrix} 4l_1^2 & 6l_1 \\ 6l_1 & 12 \end{bmatrix}\begin{Bmatrix} -\frac{13}{32}pl_1 \\ \frac{88}{1536}pl_1^2 \end{Bmatrix}$$

$$= \frac{pl_1^4}{12EI}\begin{Bmatrix} -\frac{52}{32} + \frac{528}{1536} \\ -\frac{78}{32l_1} + \frac{1056}{1536l_1} \end{Bmatrix} = \frac{-pl_1^4}{48EI}\begin{Bmatrix} 5.125 \\ \frac{7.000}{l_1} \end{Bmatrix}$$

These results agree with those calculated from the area–moment method.

■

11.13 GENERALIZED FORCE PROPORTIONAL TO DISPLACEMENT

When the generalized force is proportional to the displacement, it can be transferred to the left side of the equation of motion to combine with the stiffness matrix for the free vibration. Presented in this section are two cases: (1) for distributed forces normal to the beam, and (2) for distributed forces parallel to the beam.

Case 1: The term $p(x)$ in the virtual work equation (11.12.2) is replaced by $f(x)y(x)$, which results in the equation

$$\delta W = \int_0^l f(x)y(x)\delta y(x)dx \tag{11.13.1}$$

With $y(x) = \sum_i \phi_i q_i$, where ϕ_i are the beam functions, and q_i are the element end deflections as in Eq. (11.12.1), the virtual work is

$$\delta W = \sum_i \sum_j q_j \delta q_i \int_0^l f(x)\phi_i\phi_j dx \tag{11.13.2}$$

and the generalized force becomes

$$Q_i = \frac{\delta W}{\delta q_i} = \sum_j q_j \int_0^l f(x)\phi_i\phi_j dx \tag{11.13.3}$$

which is proportional to the displacement.

Example 11.13.1

Figure 11.13.1 shows a cantilever beam with elastic foundation under the outer half of the beam. The stiffness of the foundation is $-ky$ N/m, so that $f(x) = -k$, a constant. The equation of motion then takes the form

$$\frac{ml}{840}[m_{ij}]\begin{Bmatrix}\ddot{v}_2\\ \ddot{\theta}_2\\ \ddot{v}_3\\ \ddot{\theta}_3\end{Bmatrix} + \frac{8EI}{l^3}[k_{ij}]\begin{Bmatrix}v_2\\ \theta_2\\ v_3\\ \theta_3\end{Bmatrix} = \begin{Bmatrix}Q_1\\ Q_2\\ Q_3\\ Q_4\end{Bmatrix}$$

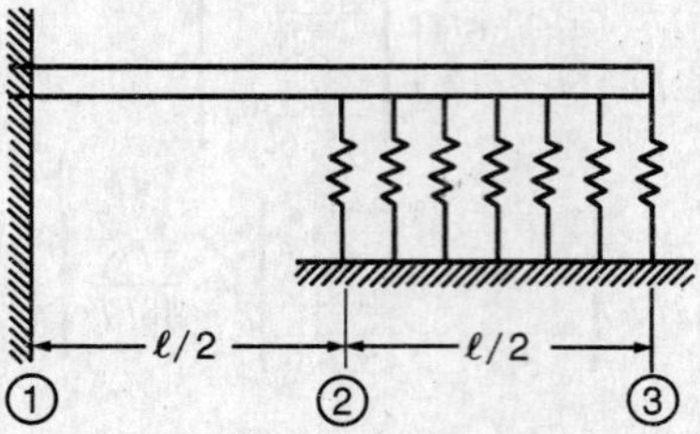

FIGURE 11.13.1.

Evaluating the integral in Eq. (11.13.3) for an element of length l, we have

$$\{Q_i\} = -kl\begin{bmatrix} 0.3714 & 0.524l & 0.1286 & -0.03095l \\ & 0.009524l^2 & 0.03905l & -0.007143l^2 \\ & & 0.3714 & -0.05238l \\ & & & 0.009524l^2 \end{bmatrix}\begin{Bmatrix}v_2\\ \theta_2\\ v_3\\ \theta_3\end{Bmatrix}$$

When applied to this problem with $l = l/2$ and transferred to the left side of the equation, the stiffness of the beam is increased.

■

Case 2: A distributed force $p(x)dx$ parallel to the beam will do virtual work $p(x)dx \cdot \delta u(x)$, where $u(x)$ is the horizontal displacement due to deflection $y(x)$. Displacement $u(x)$ is equal to the difference between the horizontal projection of the deflected beam and x:

$$u(x) = \int_0^x (ds - dx) = \int_0^x \left[dx\sqrt{1 + \left(\frac{dy}{dx}\right)^2} - dx \right] = \int_0^x \frac{1}{2}y'^2 dr$$

where r is a dummy variable for x, and $y' = dy/dr$. The virtual displacement of x is then equal to

$$\delta u(x) = \int_0^x \frac{1}{2}\delta y'^2 dr$$

where the integrand is interpreted as follows:

$$\frac{1}{2}\delta y'^2 = \frac{1}{2}\left[(y' + \delta y')^2 - y'^2\right] = y'\delta y'$$

Thus, the virtual work for the distributed force becomes

$$\delta W = -\int_0^l p(x)\int_0^x y'\delta y' drdx \qquad (11.13.4)$$

Substituting for y' in terms of the beam functions, we have

$$\delta W = -\sum_i \sum_j q_j \delta q_i \int_0^l p(x) \int_0^x \phi_i' \phi_j' \, dr dx \tag{11.13.5}$$

$$Q_i = \frac{\delta W}{\delta q_i} = -\sum_j q_j \int_0^l p(x) \int_0^x \phi_i' \phi_j' \, dr dx \tag{11.13.6}$$

Example 11.13.2

Rotational element. An example of interest here is the helicopter blade whirling with angular speed Ω, as shown in Fig. 11.13.2. For the first beam element, the loading is $\Omega^2 xm\,dx$ and Eq. (11.13.6) applies without change. For subsequent elements, coordinate x must be measured from the beginning of the new element to conform to that of the beam functions. The load for the element is simply $\Omega^2(l_i + x)m\,dx$, where l_i is the distance from the rotation axis to the beginning of the new element. Presented here is the generalized force associated with the load $\Omega^2 xm\,dx$, which is applicable to the first element.

$$\{Q_i\} = -m\Omega^2 l \begin{bmatrix} 0.4286 & 0.01429l & -0.4286 & 0.06429l \\ & 0.05714l^2 & -0.01429l & -0.009524l^2 \\ & & 0.4286 & -0.06429l \\ & & & 0.02381l^2 \end{bmatrix} \begin{Bmatrix} v_1 \\ \theta_1 \\ v_2 \\ \theta_2 \end{Bmatrix}$$

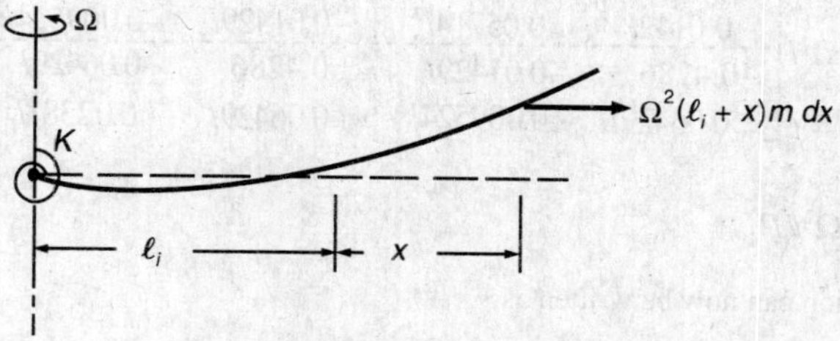

FIGURE 11.13.2.

■

Example 11.13.3

Using one element, determine the equation of motion of the helicopter blade of length l rotating at speed Ω. Assume the blade to be rigidly fixed to the rotor shaft.

Solution The mass and stiffness terms for the single element of length l are

$$\frac{ml}{420}\left[\begin{array}{cc:cc} 156 & 22l & 54 & -13l \\ 22l & 4l^2 & 13l & -3l^2 \\ \hdashline 54 & 13l & 156 & -22l \\ -13l & -3l & -22l & 4l^2 \end{array}\right] \begin{Bmatrix} \ddot{v}_1 \\ \ddot{\theta}_1 \\ \ddot{v}_2 \\ \ddot{\theta}_2 \end{Bmatrix} = \frac{ml}{420} M\ddot{V}$$

$$\frac{EI}{l^3}\left[\begin{array}{cc|cc} 12 & 6l & -12 & 6l \\ 6l & 4l^2 & -6l & 2l^2 \\ \hline -12 & -6l & 12 & -6l \\ 6l & 2l^2 & -6l & 4l^2 \end{array}\right]\begin{Bmatrix} v_1 \\ \theta_1 \\ v_2 \\ \theta_2 \end{Bmatrix} = \frac{EI}{l^3}KV$$

The term due to rotation is found from the generalized force Q given in Eq. (11.13.6). For its evaluation, the integral involved is

$$m\Omega^2 l\int_0^l x\int_0^x \varphi_i'\varphi_j' dr \cdot dx = m\Omega^2 l\int_0^1 \xi\left[\int_0^\xi \varphi_i'\varphi_j' l d\xi\right] l d\xi$$

where

$$\varphi_1' = (-6\xi + 6\xi^2)\frac{1}{l}$$

$$\varphi_2' = 1 - 4\xi + 3\xi^2$$

$$\varphi_3' = (6\xi - 6\xi^2)\frac{1}{l}$$

$$\varphi_4' = -2\xi + 3\xi^2$$

Substituting these into the previous integral, we obtain the result

$$Q = -m\Omega^2 l\left[\begin{array}{cc|cc} 0.4286 & 0.01429l & -0.4286 & 0.6429l \\ 0.0142l & 0.05714l^2 & -0.01429l & -0.009524l^2 \\ \hline -0.4286 & -0.01429l & 0.4286 & -0.06429l \\ 0.06429l & -0.009524l^2 & -0.06429l & 0.02381l^2 \end{array}\right]\begin{Bmatrix} v_1 \\ \theta_1 \\ v_2 \\ \theta_2 \end{Bmatrix}$$

$$= -m\Omega^2 lHV$$

The equation of motion can now be written as

$$\left[-\frac{\omega^2 ml}{420}M + \frac{EI}{l^3}K\right]V = -m\Omega^2 lHV$$

By multiplying and dividing the right hand term by EI/l^3 and transferring it to the left side, we obtain

$$-\frac{\omega^2 ml}{420}MV + \frac{EI}{l^3}\left[K + \frac{m\Omega^2 l^4}{EI}H\right]V = 0$$

or

$$M - \bar{\lambda}\left[K + \frac{\Omega^2 ml^4}{EI}H\right] = 0$$

where

$$\bar{\lambda} = \frac{420EI}{\omega^2 ml^4}$$

With the boundary conditions $v_1 = \theta_1 = 0$, we need only to maintain the lower right quadrant of the matrices. Also by remembering that the l_s inside the matrices all cancel in the solution for the eigenvalues and eigenvectors, we can let $l = 1.0$. The final equation of motion is then

$$\left[\begin{bmatrix} 156 & -22 \\ -22 & 4 \end{bmatrix} - \bar{\lambda}\left(\begin{bmatrix} 12 & -6 \\ -6 & 4 \end{bmatrix} + \left(\frac{\Omega^2 ml^4}{EI}\right)\begin{bmatrix} 0.4286 & -0.06429 \\ -0.06429 & -0.02381 \end{bmatrix}\right)\right]\begin{Bmatrix} v_2 \\ \theta_2 \end{Bmatrix} = \begin{Bmatrix} 0 \\ 0 \end{Bmatrix}$$

This equation can be solved for the eigenvalues $\overline{\lambda}$ by assuming a number for the rotation parameter. If we choose $\Omega^2 ml^4/EI = 1.0$, we obtain

$$\left(\begin{bmatrix} 156 & -22 \\ -22 & 4 \end{bmatrix} - \overline{\lambda}\begin{bmatrix} 12.43 & -6.064 \\ -6.064 & 4.024 \end{bmatrix}\right)\begin{Bmatrix} v_2 \\ \theta_2 \end{Bmatrix} = \begin{Bmatrix} 0 \\ 0 \end{Bmatrix}$$

$$\begin{vmatrix} (156 - 12.43\overline{\lambda}) & -(22 - 6.064\overline{\lambda}) \\ -(22 - 6.064\overline{\lambda}) & (4 - 4.024\overline{\lambda}) \end{vmatrix} = 0$$

The eigenvalues and natural frequencies from the determinant are

$$\overline{\lambda}_1 = 30.65 \qquad \omega_1 = 3.70\sqrt{\frac{EI}{ml^4}}$$

$$\overline{\lambda}_2 = 0.345 \qquad \omega_2 = 34.89\sqrt{\frac{EI}{ml^4}}$$

and the associated eigenvectors and modes are

$$\phi_1 = \begin{Bmatrix} v_2 \\ \theta_2 \end{Bmatrix}^{(1)} = \begin{Bmatrix} 0.545 \\ 0.749 \end{Bmatrix} \qquad \phi_2 = \begin{Bmatrix} v_2 \\ \theta_2 \end{Bmatrix}^{(2)} = \begin{Bmatrix} 0.0807 \\ 0.615 \end{Bmatrix}$$

For $\Omega = 0$, the natural frequencies for the single element analysis are

$$\omega_1 = 3.53\sqrt{\frac{EI}{ml^4}}$$

$$\omega_2 = 34.81\sqrt{\frac{EI}{ml^4}}$$

For comparison, the exact values for $\Omega = 0$ are

$$\omega_1 = 3.515\sqrt{\frac{EI}{ml^4}}$$

$$\omega_2 = 22.032\sqrt{\frac{EI}{ml^4}}$$

which indicates that the single-element analysis results in unacceptable accuracy for the second mode. The eigenvectors for the single-element analysis, which are deflection and slope at the free end, cannot be compared to the more conventional eigenvectors that display deflection along the beam.

■

Example 11.13.4 TWO-ELEMENT BEAM

If we divide the beam into two equal sections, then l is replaced by $l/2$, and the rotational force over the second element must be changed to

$$p_2(x) = \left(\frac{l}{2} + x\right) m\Omega^2 dx$$

The generalized force is now

$$Q = m\Omega^2 l \int_0^{l/2} \left(\frac{l}{2} + x\right) \int_0^x \varphi_i' \varphi_j' dr dx$$

$$= m\Omega^2 l \left\{ \int_0^{l/2} \frac{l}{2} \int_0^x \varphi_i' \varphi_j' dr dx + \int_0^{l/2} x \int_0^x \varphi_i' \varphi_j' dr dx \right\}$$

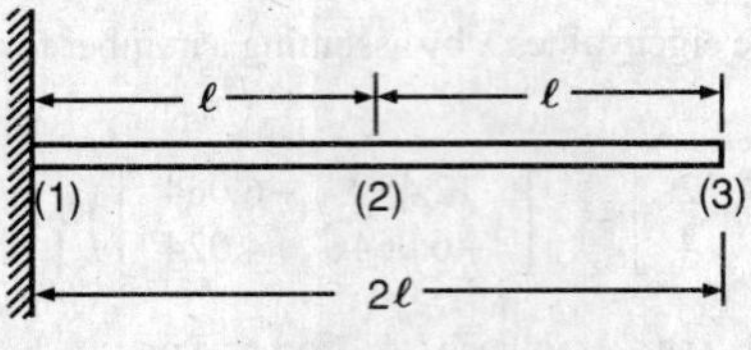

FIGURE 11.13.3.

The last integral in this expression is the same as that for the one-element beam, except for l replaced by $l/2$. The first integral now needs evaluating. In formulating the equation of motion, this now requires changing all l's in the matrices to $l/2$.

We now suggest a different approach of leaving the length of each element equal to l, so that the total length of the beam is $2l$. This results in great savings in computation because the matrices for each element will remain the same as that for the one-element beam and all the l's inside the matrices can remain as l, which can be assigned as unity for the eigenvalue computation as before; i.e., we now solve the problem shown in Fig. 11.13.3. After the eigenvalues are determined, we let l in the expression for the eigenvalues be replaced by $l/2$.
The new integral to be evaluated is

$$m\Omega^2 l \int_0^l l \int_0^x \varphi_i' \varphi_j' drdx$$

which has been carried out and is equal to

$$\Pi = m\Omega^2 l \begin{bmatrix} 0.600 & 0 & -0.600 & 0.100l \\ & 0.100l^2 & 0 & -0.0166l^2 \\ & & 0.600 & -0.100l \\ & & & 0.0333l \end{bmatrix}$$

■

Assembling Matrices for Two-Element Beam

For the two-element team, the assembled matrices are 6×6. However, because $v_1 = \theta_1 = 0$, the first two columns and rows are eliminated and we obtain a 4×4 matrix.

Mass

$$\frac{ml}{420} \left[\begin{array}{cc:cc:cc} 156 & 22 & 54 & -13 & & \\ 22 & 4 & 13 & -3 & & \\ \hdashline 54 & 13 & 156 & -22 & 54 & -13 \\ & & 156 & 22 & & \\ -13 & -3 & -22 & 4 & 13 & -3 \\ \hdashline & & 54 & 13 & 156 & -22 \\ & & -13 & -3 & -22 & 4 \end{array}\right] \begin{Bmatrix} v_1 = 0 \\ \theta_1 = 0 \\ v_2 \\ \theta_2 \\ v_3 \\ \theta_3 \end{Bmatrix}$$

$$= \frac{ml}{420} \begin{bmatrix} 312 & 0 & 54 & -13 \\ 0 & 8 & 13 & -3 \\ 54 & 13 & 156 & -22 \\ -13 & -3 & -22 & 4 \end{bmatrix} \begin{Bmatrix} v_2 \\ \theta_2 \\ v_3 \\ \theta_3 \end{Bmatrix}$$

Stiffness

$$\frac{EI}{l^3}\begin{bmatrix} 24 & 0 & -12 & 6 \\ 0 & 8 & -6 & 2 \\ -12 & -6 & 12 & -6 \\ 6 & 2 & -6 & 4 \end{bmatrix}\begin{Bmatrix} v_2 \\ \theta_2 \\ v_3 \\ \theta_3 \end{Bmatrix}$$

Generalized force. From the first integral for Q, we have

$$-\Omega^2 ml\begin{bmatrix} 0.8572 & -0.0500 & -0.4286 & 0.06429 \\ -0.0500 & 0.0810 & -0.01429 & -0.009524 \\ -0.4286 & -0.01429 & 0.4286 & -0.06429 \\ 0.06429 & -0.009524 & -0.06429 & 0.02391 \end{bmatrix}$$

From the second integral for Q,

$$-\Omega^2 ml\begin{bmatrix} 1.200 & -0.100 & -0.600 & 0.100 \\ -0.100 & 0.133 & 0 & -0.0166 \\ -0.600 & 0 & 0.600 & -0.100 \\ 0.100 & -0.0166 & -0.100 & 0.0333 \end{bmatrix}$$

By adding the two matrices, the generalized force becomes

$$-\frac{EI}{l}\left(\frac{\Omega^2 ml^4}{EI}\right)\begin{vmatrix} 2.057 & -0.150 & -1.029 & 0.10643 \\ -0.150 & 0.2143 & -0.01429 & -0.0262 \\ -1.029 & -0.01429 & 1.0286 & -0.1643 \\ 0.1064 & -0.02612 & -0.1643 & 0.0571 \end{vmatrix}\begin{Bmatrix} v_2 \\ \theta_2 \\ v_3 \\ \theta_3 \end{Bmatrix}$$

$$= -\frac{EI}{l^3}\left(\frac{\Omega^2 ml^4}{EI}\right)HV$$

It is now necessary to choose a numerical value for the rotation parameter $\Omega^2 ml^4/EI$ and combine the previous equation with the stiffness matrix. This was done for rotation parameters 0, 1, 2, and 4 to obtain the computer results for the eigenvalues and eigenvectors. Because the previous matrices fed into the computer are those for the two-element beam with each element of length l, the eigenvalues are those for a beam of length $2l$.

Examination of the eigenvalue expression indicates that for a beam of length l with each element of length $l/2$, the length l must be replaced by $l/2$ in the equation for ω_i.

$$\lambda = \left(\frac{\omega^2 ml^4}{420EI}\right) \qquad \omega_i = \sqrt{\lambda_i \frac{420EI}{m(l/2)^4}} = 4\sqrt{\frac{420\lambda_i EI}{ml^4}}$$

With this change, the computer results for λ_i and the natural frequencies of a two-element beam of length l are shown in Table 11.13.1. The case for $\Omega = 0$ is compared to exact values, which shows that the results are quite good for the first two modes.

TABLE 11.13.1 Computer Results for Two-Element Rotating Beam of Length l

$\frac{\Omega^2 ml^4}{EI}$	i	λ_i for Beam of Length $2l$	$\omega_i \Big/ 4\sqrt{\frac{420EI\lambda_i}{ml^4}}$	Exact
0	1	0.001841	3.51	3.515
	2	0.07348	22.22	22.034
	3	0.84056	75.15	61.697
	4	7.08106	215.1	120.9
1	1	0.0035169	4.861	
	2	0.08445	23.82	
	3	0.86754	76.35	
	4	7.13759	219.0	
2	1	0.0049532	5.77	
	2	0.095627	25.35	
	3	0.8947349	77.54	
	4	7.19323	219.8	
4	1	0.0103809	8.35	
	2	0.158008	32.58	
	3	1.04317	83.72	
	4	7.83817	229.5	

FIGURE 11.13.4. Robinson Helicopter Model R22: Blades 18.3 cm. wide and 3.84 m long; cantilever period of approximately 1 s; gross weight of 6094 N loaded; tip speed of blades 183 m/s.

Shown in Figs. 11.13.4 and 11.13.5 are two helicopters of different size. The Robinson Helicopter, Model R22, shown in Fig. 11.13.4 is a small two-seater vehicle used mainly for pleasure flying. The descriptive data accompanying the photo indicates some of its specifications and size.

In contrast, the commercial helicopter, shown in Fig. 11.13.5, used for hauling material and workers between shore and oil platforms is a large vehicle capable of transporting a maximum load of 26,689 N. As in all helicopters, the rotor blades are very flexible. Their rotational speed is governed by the requirement of keeping the tip speed below the speed of sound.

FIGURE 11.13.5. Commercial helicopter for oil platform service: Blades 61 cm wide and 7.32 m long, 890 N each; cantilever compliance of 0.004 m/N load at the tip; total weight of the helicopter is 31,138 N empty and 57,827 N loaded.

SUGGESTED READING

[1] COOK, R. D. *Concepts and Applications of Finite Element Analysis*. New York: John Wiley & Sons, 1974.

[2] GALLAGHER, R. H. *Finite Element Analysis Fundamentals*. Englewood Cliffs, NJ: Prentice-Hall, 1975.

[3] ROCKEY, K. C., EVANS, H. R., GRIFFITH, D. W. AND NETHEROOT, D. A. *The Finite Element Method*. New York: Halsted Press Book, John Wiley & Sons, 1975.

[4] YANG, T. Y., *Finite Element Structural Analysis*. Englewood Cliffs, NJ: Prentice-Hall, 1986.

[5] WEAVER, W. AND JOHNSTON, P. R. *Structural Dynamics by Finite Elements*. Englewood Cliffs, NJ: Prentice-Hall, 1987.

[6] CLOUGH, R. W. AND PENZIEN, J. *Dynamics of Structures*. New York: McGraw-Hill, 1975.

[7] CRAIG, R. R. Jr. *Structural Dynamics*. John Wiley & Sons, 1981.

REFERENCES

[1] E. P. POPOV, *Introduction to Mechanics of Solids* (Englewood Cliffs, NJ: Prentice-Hall, 1968), p. 411.

[2] L. MEIROVITCH, *Computational Methods in Structural Dynamics* (Rockville, MD: Sidthoff & Noordhoff, 1990), p. 369.

[3] J. S. ARCHER, "Consistent Mass Matrix for Distributed Mass Systems," *J. Struct. Div. ASCE*, Vol. 89, No. STA4 (August 1963), pp. 161–178.

PROBLEMS

11.1. Three equal springs of stiffness k N/m. are joined at one end, the other ends being arranged symmetrically at 120° from each other, as shown in Fig. P11.1. Prove that the influence coefficients of the junction in a direction making an angle θ with any spring is independent of θ and equal to $1/1.5k$.

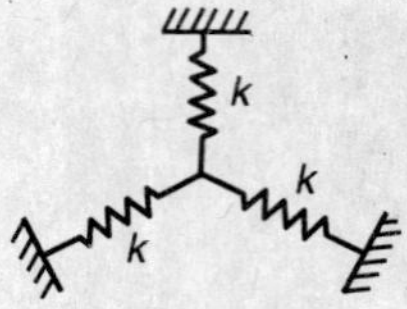

FIGURE P11.1.

11.2. Determine the flexibility matrix for the spring-mass system shown in Fig. P11.2.

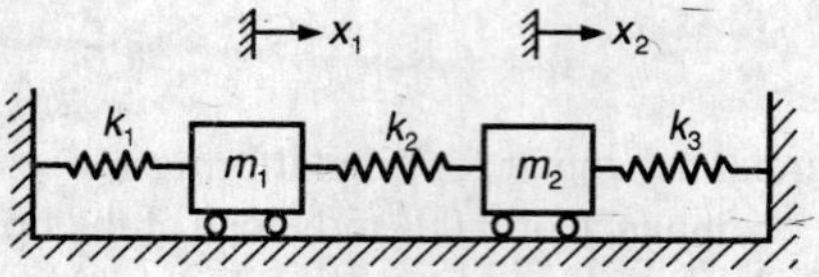

FIGURE P11.2.

11.3. A simply supported uniform beam of length l is loaded with weights at positions $0.3l$ and $0.7l$. Determine the flexibility influence coefficients for these positions.

11.4. Determine the influence coefficients for the triple pendulum shown in Fig. P11.4.

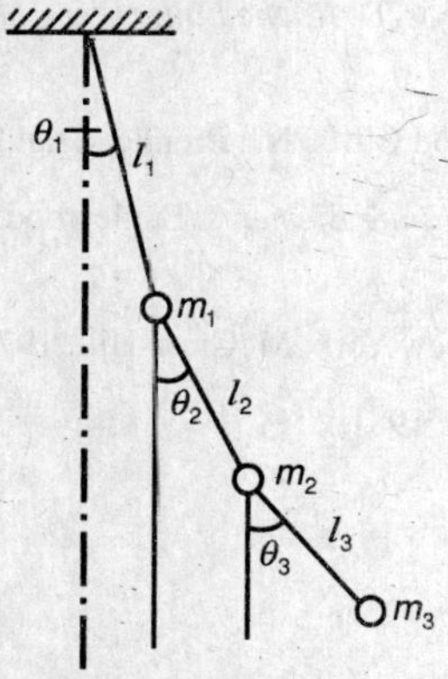

FIGURE P11.4.

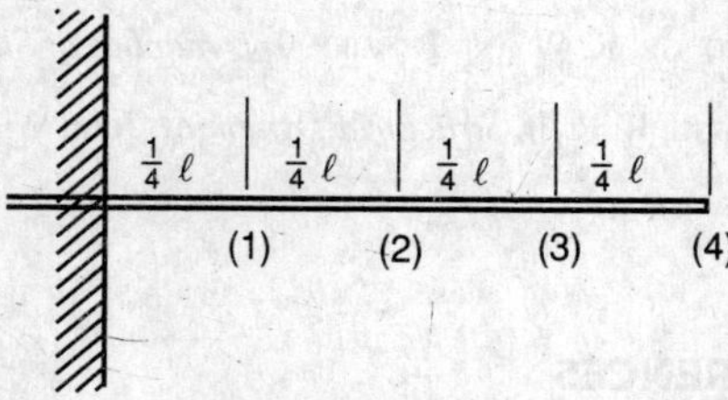

FIGURE P11.5.

11.5. Determine the flexibility matrix for the cantilever beam shown in Fig. P11.5 and calculate the stiffness matrix from its inverse.

11.6. Determine the flexibility matrix for the uniform beam of Fig. P11.6 by using the area–moment method.

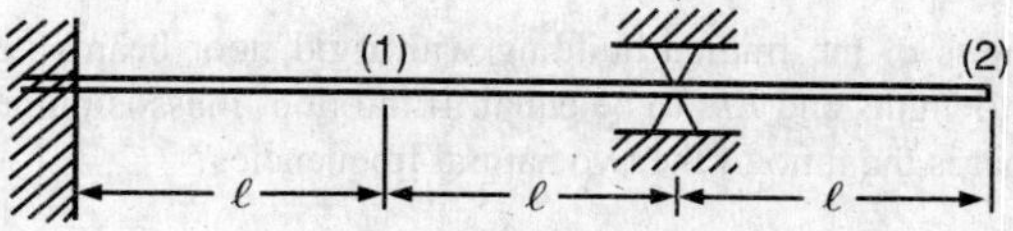

FIGURE P11.6.

11.7. Determine the stiffness matrix for the system shown in Fig. P11.7 and establish the flexibility matrix by its inverse.

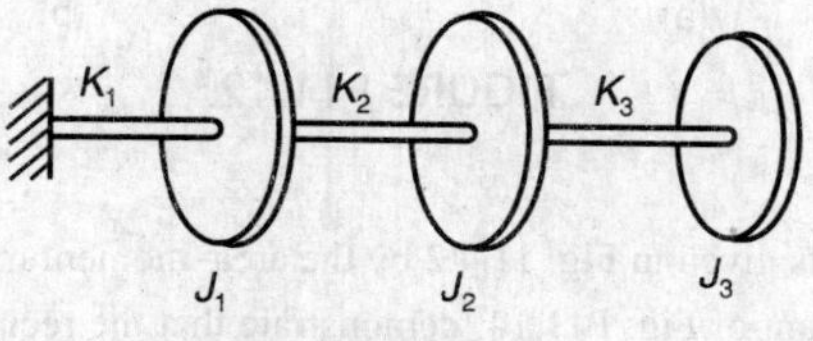

FIGURE P11.7.

11.8. Consider a system with n springs in series as presented in Fig. P11.8 and show that the stiffness matrix is a band matrix along the diagonal.

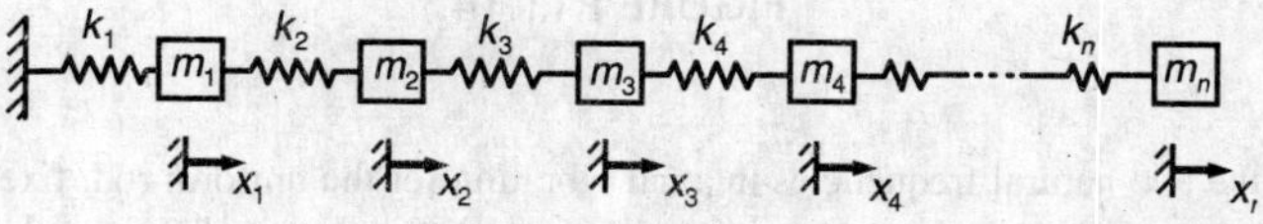

FIGURE P11.8.

11.9. Determine the flexibility matrix for the four-story building of Fig. 11.3.2 and invert it to arrive at the stiffness matrix given in the text.

11.10. The rectangular frame of Fig. P11.10 is fixed in the ground. Determine the stiffness matrix for the force system shown.

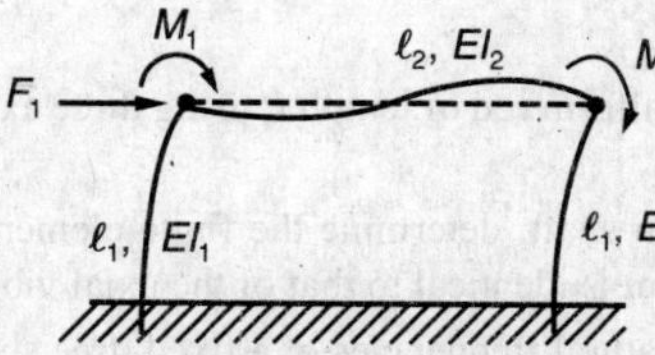

FIGURE P11.10.

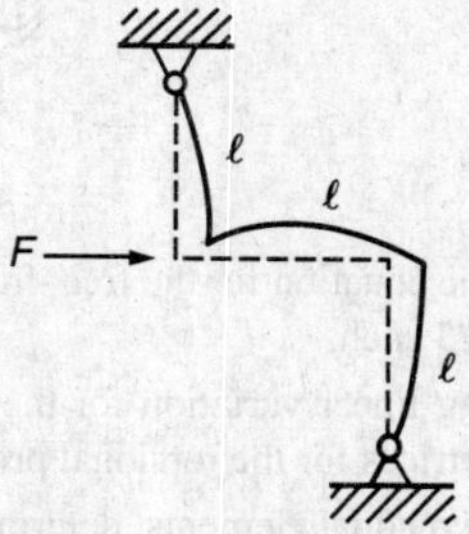

FIGURE P11.11.

11.11. Determine the stiffness against the force F for the frame of Fig. P11.11, which is pinned at the top and bottom.

11.12. Compare the stiffness of the framed building with rigid floor beams versus that with flexible floor beams. Assume all lengths and EIs to be equal. If the floor mass is pinned at the corners as shown in Fig. P11.12(b), what is the ratio of the two natural frequencies?

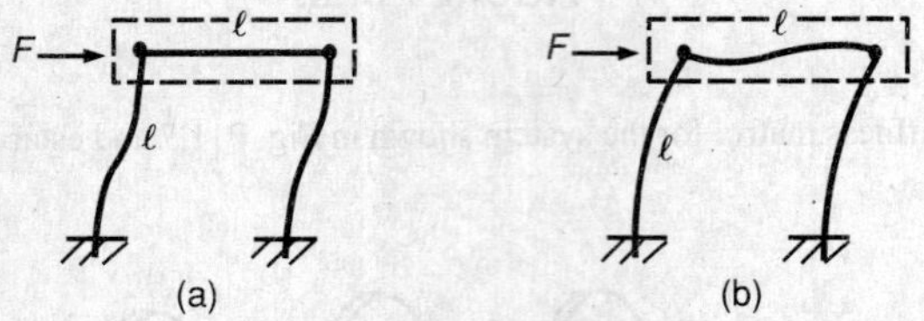

FIGURE P11.12.

11.13. Verify each of the results given in Fig. 11.4.2 by the area–moment method and superposition.

11.14. Using the cantilever beam of Fig. P11.14, demonstrate that the reciprocity theorem holds for moment loads as well as forces.

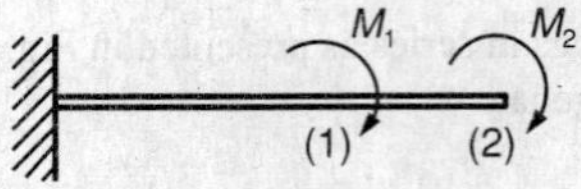

FIGURE P11.14.

11.15. Determine the two natural frequencies in axial vibration for the uniform rod, fixed at one end and free at the other end, using two elements with the intermediate station at $l/3$ from the fixed end. Compare results with those when the station is chosen at midlength. What conclusions do you come to regarding choice of station location?

11.16. A tapered rod is modeled as two uniform sections, as shown in Fig. P11.16, where $EA_1 = 2EA_2$ and $m_1 = 2m_2$. Determine the two natural frequencies of longitudinal vibration.

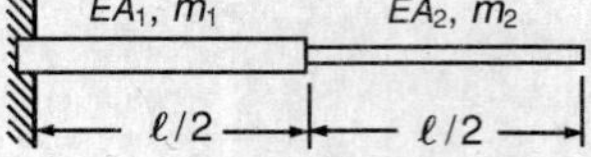

FIGURE P11.16.

11.17. Set up the equation for the free–free vibration of a uniform rod of length l, using three axial elements of length $l/3$ each.

11.18. Assuming linear variation for the twist of a uniform shaft, determine the finite element stiffness and mass matrices for the torsional problem. The problem is identical to that of the axial vibration.

11.19. Using two equal elements, determine the first two natural frequencies of a fixed–free shaft in torsional oscillation.

11.20. Using two uniform sections in torsional vibration, describe the finite element relationship to the 2-DOF lumped-mass torsional system.

11.21. Figure P11.21 shows a conical tube of constant thickness fixed at the large end and free at the other end. Using one element, determine the equation for its longitudinal vibration.

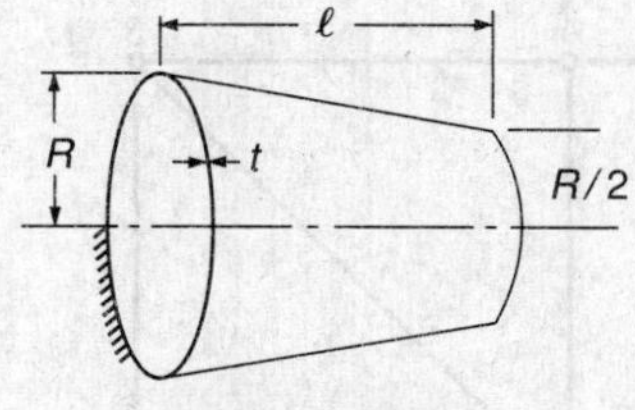

FIGURE P11.21.

11.22. Treat the tube of Fig. P11.21 as a two-element problem of equal length in longitudinal vibration.

11.23. Determine the equation for the tube of Fig. P11.21 in torsional vibration using (a) two elements and (b) N-stepped uniform elements.

11.24. The simple frame of Fig. P11.24 has pinned joints. Determine its stiffness matrix.

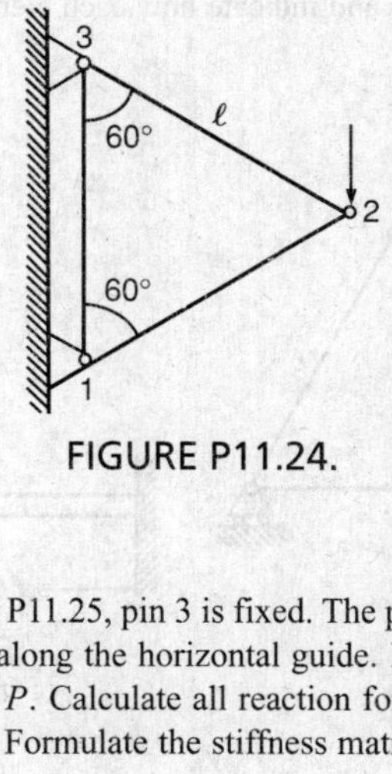

FIGURE P11.24.

11.25. In the pinned truss shown in Fig. P11.25, pin 3 is fixed. The pin at 1 is free to move in a vertical guide, and the pin at 2 can only move along the horizontal guide. If a force P is applied at pin 2 as shown, determine u_2 and v_1 in terms of P. Calculate all reaction forces at pins 1, 2, and 3, and check to see whether equilibrium is satisfied. Formulate the stiffness matrix with factor EA/l by the finite element method.

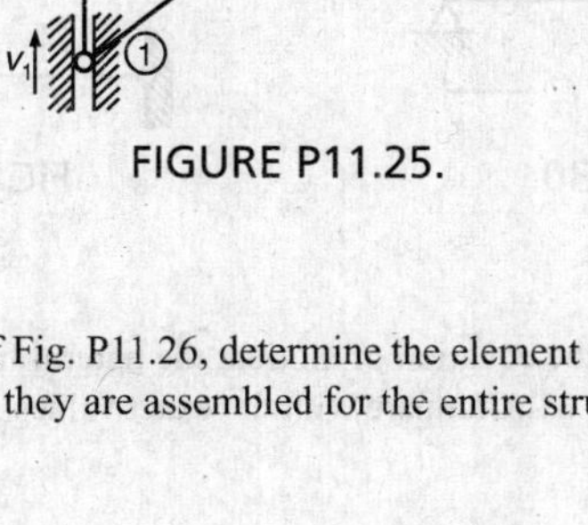

FIGURE P11.25.

11.26. For the pinned square truss of Fig. P11.26, determine the element stiffness and mass matrices in global coordinates and indicate how they are assembled for the entire structure.

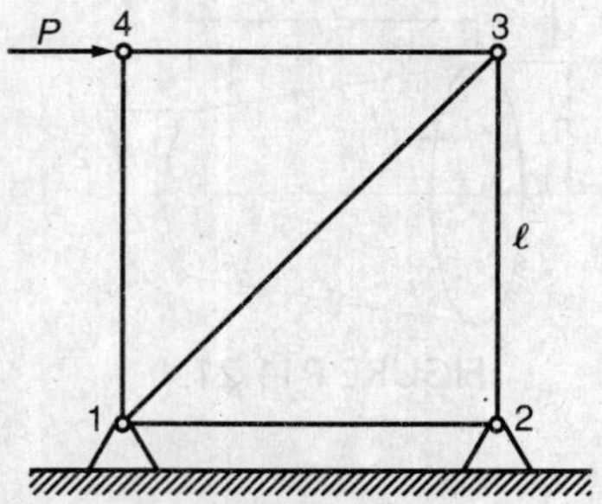

FIGURE P11.26.

Construct the dynamic matrix. Use this to complete the frequencies of the free vibrations for this structure.

11.27. For the pinned truss of Fig. P11.27, there are just three orientations of the elements. Determine the stiffness matrix for each orientation and indicate how each element matrix is assembled in the global system.

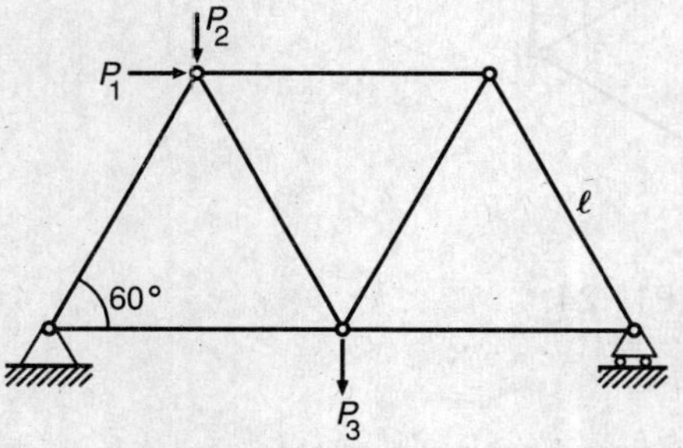

FIGURE P11.27.

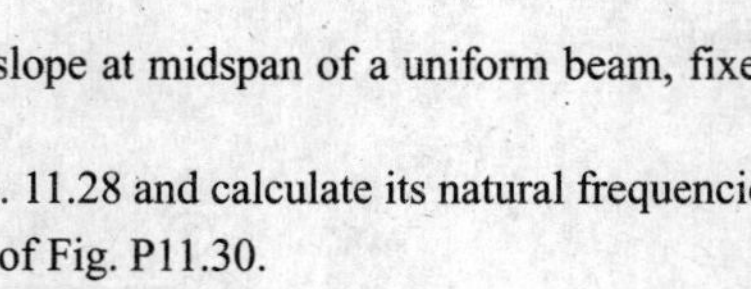

FIGURE P11.28.

11.28. Using two elements, determine the deflection and slope at midspan of a uniform beam, fixed at both ends, when loaded as shown in Fig. P11.28.

11.29. Determine the consistent mass for the beam of Prob. 11.28 and calculate its natural frequencies.

11.30. Determine the free-vibration equation for the beam of Fig. P11.30.

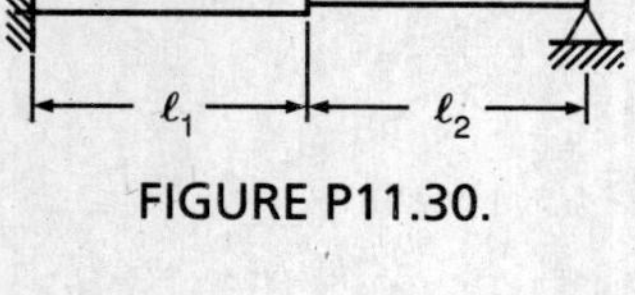

FIGURE P11.30.

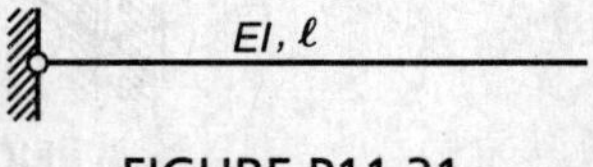

FIGURE P11.31.

M **11.31.** Using one element, determine the equation of motion, the natural frequencies, and the mode shapes of a pinned–free beam of Fig. P11.31. Compare with the exact values.

M **11.32.** Repeat Prob. 11.31 using two elements and six elements. Does the agreement with the exact values improve with a larger number of elements?

11.33. Determine the stiffness matrix for the frame of Fig. P11.33. The upper right end is restricted from rotating but is free to slide in and out.

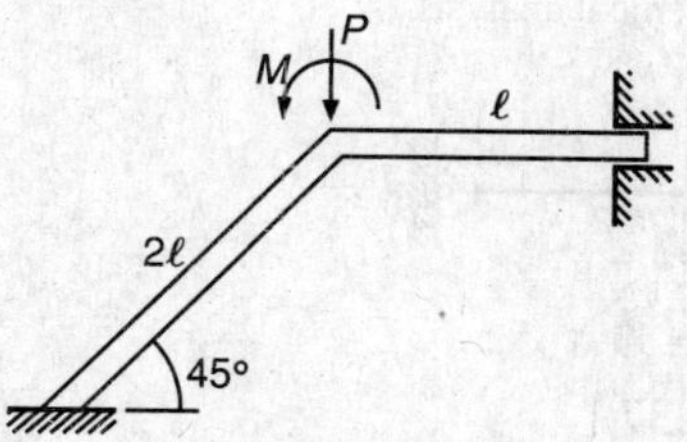

FIGURE P11.33.

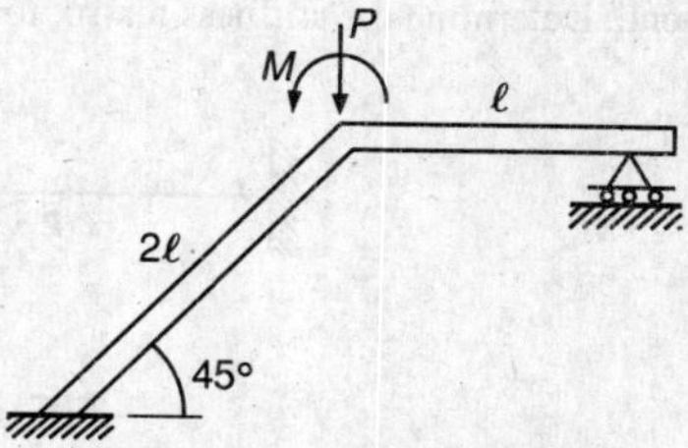

FIGURE P11.34.

11.34. The frame of Fig. P11.34 is free to rotate and translate at the upper right end. Determine its stiffness matrix.

11.35. Determine the deflection and slope at the load for the frames of Fig. P11.35. Consider the corners to be rigid.

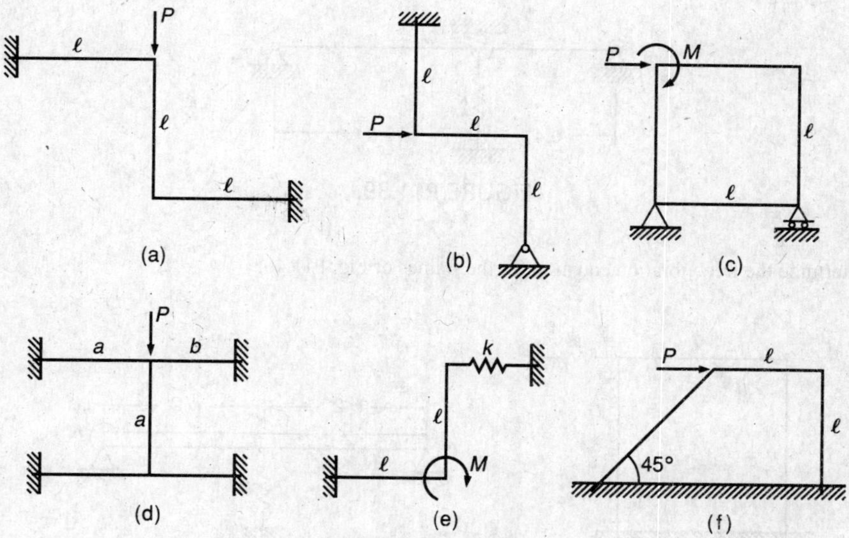

FIGURE P11.35.

M **11.36.** The pinned–free beam of Prob. 11.31 is restrained by a spring of torsional stiffness K Nm/rad at the pin, as shown in Fig. P11.36. Choose the numerical value of K so that under its static weight, the beam rotates 1/10 rad, and make the calculations as in Prob. 11.32. (Use one and two elements and let $5mgl^3/EI = 1.0$.)

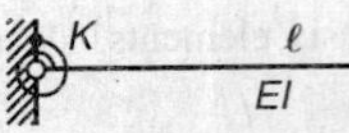

FIGURE P11.36.

11.37. Figure P11.37 shows a pin-ended beam with a linear spring k at midspan and a torsional spring K at the right end. Determine the stiffness matrix for a two-element analysis.

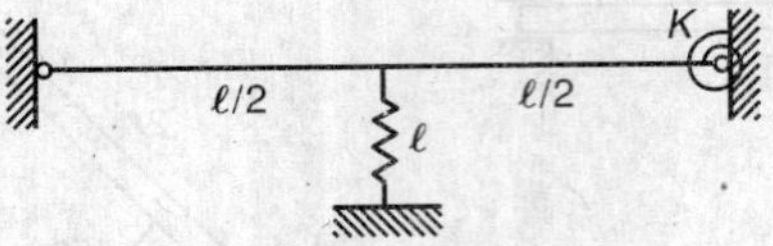

FIGURE P11.37.

M **11.38.** Determine the mass matrix for the beam of Prob. 11.37 and find all its natural frequencies and mode shapes when

$$\frac{kl^3}{EI} = \frac{1}{4} \quad \text{and} \quad \frac{Kl^3}{EI} = \frac{1}{2}l^2$$

Check the solution of Prob. 11.37 by letting $k = K = 0$. The eigenvalues should agree with those of a pinned–pinned beam.

M **11.39.** For the beam of Fig. P11.39, determine the finite element equation of motion. Determine the eigenvalues and eigenvectors of the beam when $kl^3/8EI = 1.0$ and $Kl^3/EI = 2l^2$.

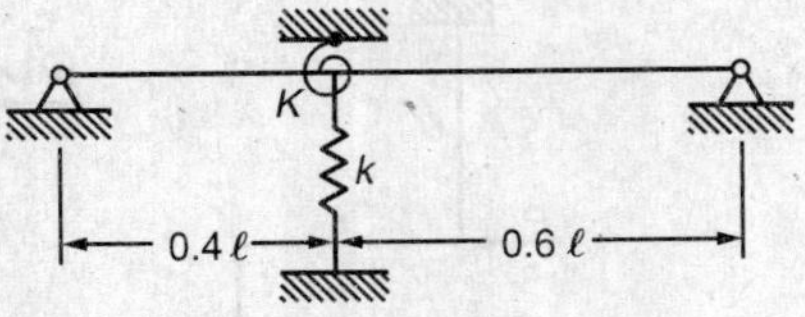

FIGURE P11.39.

11.40. Determine the free vibration equation for the frames of Fig. P11.40.

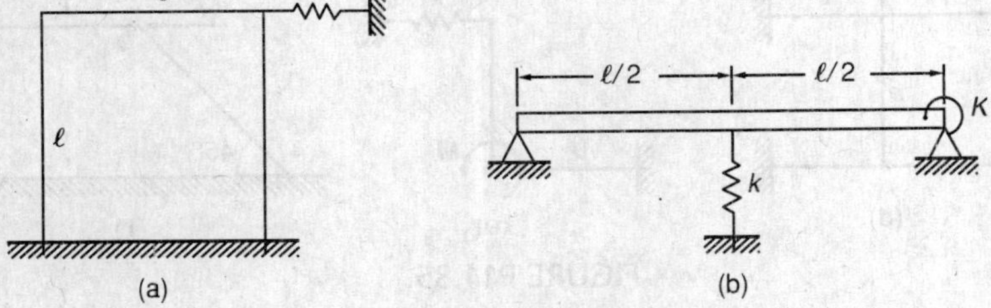

FIGURE P11.40.

11.41. Using two elements, determine the equivalent junction loads for the distributed forces for the span in Fig. P11.41(a). For the span of Fig. P11.41(b), determine the deflection and slope at midspan.

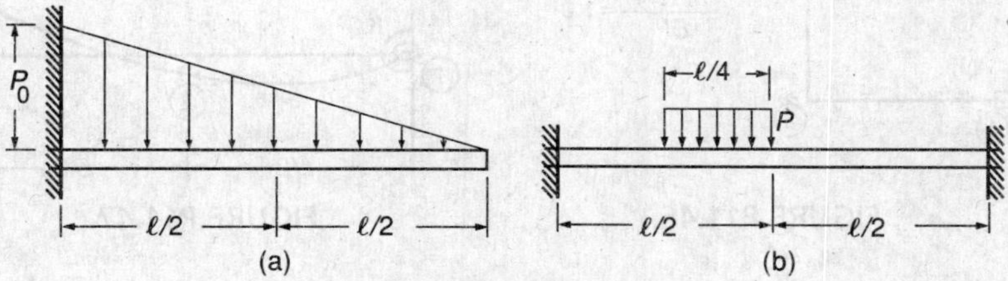

FIGURE P11.41.

M **11.42.** Set up the two-element equations for the system of Fig. P11.42 in terms of the six coordinates shown and solve the eigenvalues and eigenvectors. Show that the symmetric mode for free vibration reduces to a 3×3 equation. Determine the mass and stiffness matrices for this problem and calculate the natural frequencies and mode shapes.

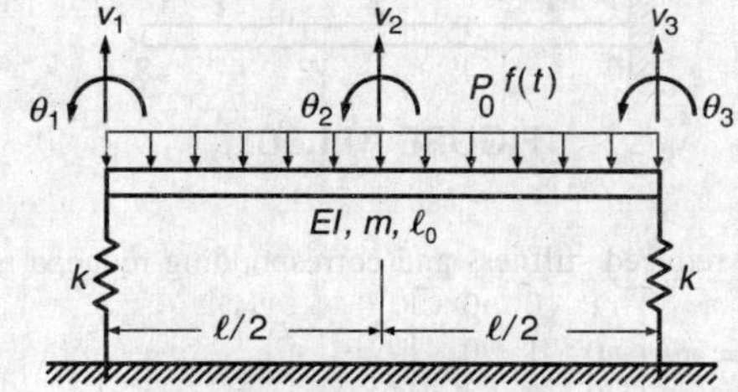

FIGURE P11.42.

M **11.43.** Solve for the eigenvalues and eigenvectors for the 4×4 beam in Example 11.10.1.

M **11.44.** The uniform beam of Fig. P11.44 is supported on an elastic foundation that exerts a restraining force per unit length of $-ky(x)$ over the right half of the beam. Using two elements, develop the equations of motion. With $kl^3/8EI = 10$, determine the natural frequencies and compare with those without the elastic foundation. Plot the mode shapes for the first two modes.

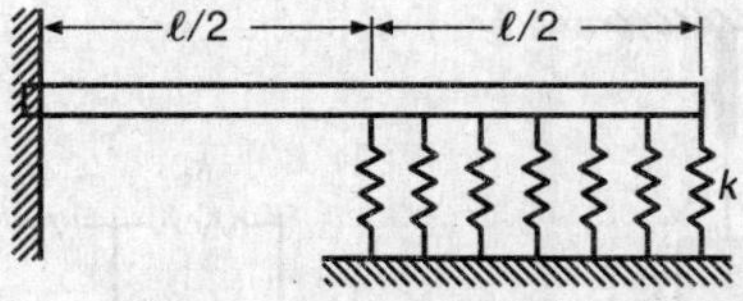

FIGURE P11.44.

M **11.45.** Repeat Prob. 11.44 assuming the left end is pinned instead of fixed.

M **11.46.** Figure P11.46 shows one of the "ell" beams of a centrifuge that whirls around the vertical axis O–O with angular speed Ω rad/s. Using the stations indicated, determine the equation of motion and its natural frequencies. Compare with the case $\Omega = 0$.

11.47. If the pinned-free beam with a torsional spring is rotated about the vertical axis, as shown in Fig. P11.47, determine the new stiffness matrix for the first element of length $l/2$.

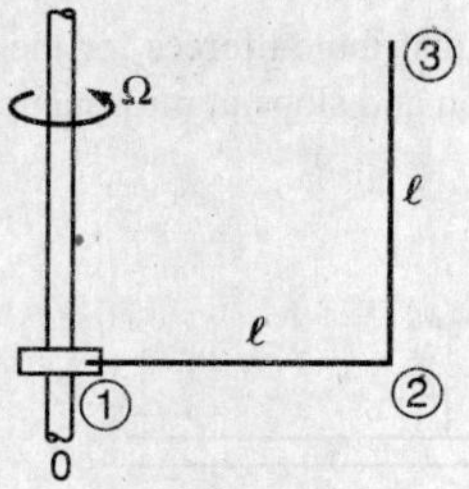

FIGURE P11.46.

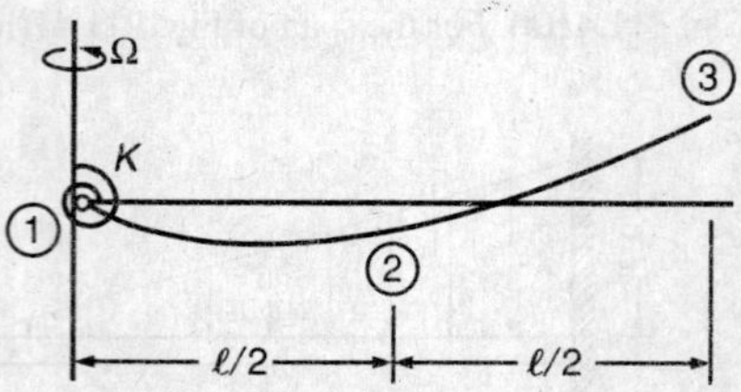

FIGURE P11.47.

11.48. For the helicopter blade of Fig. P11.47, determine the stiffness equation for the outer half of the blade.

M **11.49.** Write the complete equation for the two-element blade of Fig. P11.47 and solve for the natural frequencies and mode shapes.

M **11.50.** For the uniform cantilever beam modeled by three elements shown in Fig. P11.50 the stiffness matrix is of order 6 × 6. Rearrange the stiffness matrix, determine the 3 × 3 reduced stiffness matrix K^* and compute the eigenvalues and eigenvectors. Compare the results with those of Prob. 7.11.

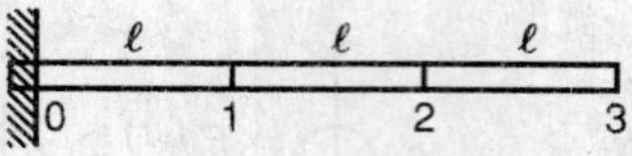

FIGURE P11.50.

M **11.51.** Repeat Prob. 11.50 with reduced stiffness and corresponding reduced mass. Compare with assumed 3 × 3 mass matrix of $M = ml \begin{bmatrix} 1 & 0 & 0 \\ 0 & 1 & 0 \\ 0 & 0 & .5 \end{bmatrix}$

M **11.52.** Repeat Prob. 11.16 with the following values: $A_2 = 1, E = 1, l = 1$, and $m_2 = 1$. Consider each of the two elements as a uniform bar. Model each of these with four elements. Compute the natural frequencies in the longitudinal vibration.

M **11.53.** Compute the free vibrations for the beam in Example 11.10.1 with the following values: $l = 12$, $m = 1$, $E = 1$, and $I = 1$. Repeat this calculation using six uniformly spaced elements.

11.54. Consider a two-section bar with a mass at its end and a spring-damper system attached to the mass as in Fig. P11.54. Determine the equations of motion for the longitudinal vibration.

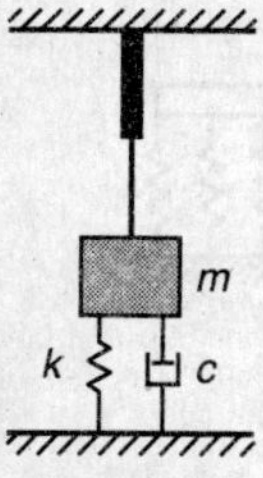

FIGURE P11.54.

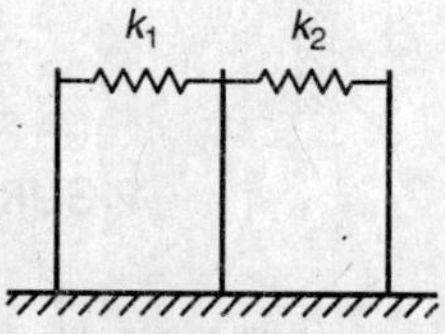

FIGURE P11.55.

11.55. Determine the equations of motion for the system shown in Fig. P11.55. The flexural rigidity of the beam in the center is different from that of the other two beams. Is the solution $y_1 = y_2 = y_3$ possible? What are the conditions for its existence?

CHAPTER 12

Random Vibrations

The types of functions we have considered up to now can be classified as deterministic, i.e., mathematical expressions can be written that will determine their instantaneous values at any time t. There are, however, a number of physical phenomena that result in nondeterministic data for which future instantaneous values cannot be predicted in a deterministic sense. As examples, we can mention the noise of a jet engine, the heights of waves in a choppy sea, ground motion during an earthquake, and pressure gusts encountered by an airplane in flight. These phenomena all have one thing in common: the unpredictability of their instantaneous value at any future time. Nondeterministic data of this type are referred to as *random time functions*.

12.1 RANDOM PHENOMENA

A sample of a typical random time function is shown in Fig. 12.1.1. In spite of the irregular character of the function, many random phenomena exhibit some degree of statistical regularity, and certain averaging procedures can be applied to establish gross characteristics useful in engineering design.

In any statistical method, a large amount of data is necessary to establish reliability. For example, to establish the statistics of the pressure fluctuation due to air turbulence over a certain air route, an airplane may collect hundreds of records of the type shown in Fig. 12.1.2.

Each record is called a *sample*, and the total collection of samples is called the *ensemble*. We can compute the ensemble average of the instantaneous pressures in each sample at time t_1. We can also multiply the instantaneous pressures in each sample at times t_1 and $t_1 + \tau$, and average these results for the ensemble. If such averages do not differ as we choose different values of t_1, then the random process described by this ensemble is said to be *stationary*.

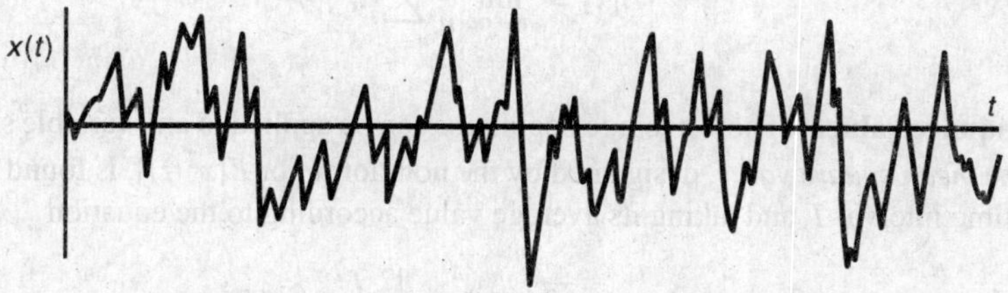

FIGURE 12.1.1. A record of random time functions.

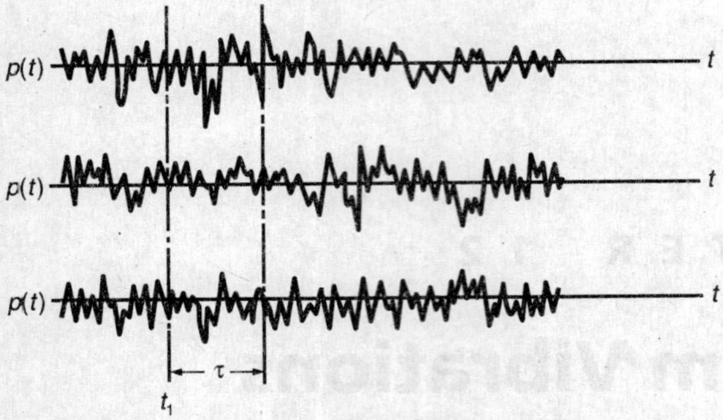

FIGURE 12.1.2. An ensemble of random time functions.

If the ensemble averages are replaced next by time averages, and if the results computed from each sample are the same as those of any other sample and equal to the ensemble average, then the random process is said to be *ergodic*.

Thus, for a stationary ergodic random phenomenon, its statistical properties are available from a single time function of a sufficiently long time period. Although such random phenomena may exist only theoretically, its assumption greatly simplifies the task of dealing with random variables. This chapter treats only this class of stationary ergodic random functions.

12.2 TIME AVERAGING AND EXPECTED VALUE

Expected value. In random vibrations, we repeatedly encounter the concept of time averaging over a long period of time. The most common notation for this operation is defined by the following equation in which $x(t)$ is the variable.

$$\overline{x(t)} = \langle x(t) \rangle = \lim_{T\to\infty} \frac{1}{T} \int_0^T x(t)\,dt \tag{12.2.1}$$

This number is also equal to the *expected value* of $x(t)$, which is written as

$$E[x(t)] = \lim_{T\to\infty} \frac{1}{T} \int_0^T x(t)\,dt \tag{12.2.2}$$

It is the average or mean value of a quantity sampled over a long time. In the case of discrete variables x_i, the expected value is given by the equation

$$E[x] = \lim_{n\to\infty} \frac{1}{n} \sum_{i=1}^{n} x_i \tag{12.2.3}$$

Mean square value. These average operations can be applied to any variable such as $x^2(t)$ or $x(t) \cdot y(t)$. The *mean square value*, designated by the notation $\overline{x^2}$ or $E[x^2(t)]$, is found by integrating $x^2(t)$ over a time interval T and taking its average value according to the equation

$$E[x^2(t)] = \overline{x^2} = \lim_{T\to\infty} \frac{1}{T} \int_0^T x^2\,dt \tag{12.2.4}$$

Variance and standard deviation. It is often desirable to consider the time series in terms of the mean and its fluctuation from the mean. A property of importance describing the fluctuation is the *variance* σ^2, which is the mean square value about the mean, given by the equation

$$\sigma^2 = \lim_{T\to\infty} \frac{1}{T}\int_0^T (x - \bar{x})^2\, dt \tag{12.2.5}$$

By expanding the above equation, it is easily seen that

$$\sigma^2 = \overline{x^2} - (\bar{x})^2 \tag{12.2.6}$$

so that the variance is equal to the mean square value minus the square of the mean. The positive square root of the variance is the *standard deviation*, σ.

Fourier series. Generally, random time functions contain oscillations of many frequencies, which approach a continuous spectrum. Although random time functions are generally not periodic, their representations by Fourier series, in which the periods are extended to a large value approaching infinity, offers a logical approach.

In Chapter 1, the exponential form of the Fourier series was shown to be

$$x(t) = \sum_{-\infty}^{\infty} c_n e^{in\omega_1 t} = c_0 + \sum_{n=1}^{\infty}(c_n e^{in\omega_1 t} + c_n^* e^{-in\omega_1 t}) \tag{12.2.7}$$

This series, which is a real function, involves a summation over negative and positive frequencies, and it also contains a constant term c_0. The constant term c_0 is the average value of $x(t)$ and because it can be dealt with separately, we exclude it in future considerations. Moreover, actual measurements are made in terms of positive frequencies, and it would be more desirable to work with the equation

$$x(t) = \text{Re}\sum_{n=1}^{\infty} C_n e^{in\omega_1 t} \tag{12.2.8}$$

The one-sided summation in the previous equation is complex and, hence, the real part of the series must be stipulated for $x(t)$ real. Because the real part of a vector is one-half the sum of the vector and its conjugate [see Eq. (1.1.9)],

$$x(t) = \text{Re}\sum_{n=1}^{\infty} C_n e^{in\omega_1 t} = \frac{1}{2}\sum_{n=1}^{\infty}(C_n e^{in\omega_1 t} + C_n^* e^{-in\omega_1 t})$$

By comparison with Eq. (1.2.6), we find

$$\begin{aligned} C_n = 2c_n &= \frac{2}{T}\int_{-T/2}^{T/2} x(t) e^{-in\omega_1 t}\, dt \\ &= a_n - ib_n \end{aligned} \tag{12.2.9}$$

Example 12.2.1

Determine the mean square value of a record of random vibration $x(t)$ containing many discrete frequencies.

Solution Because the record is periodic, we can represent it by the real part of the Fourier series:

$$x(t) = \text{Re} \sum_{n=1}^{\infty} C_n e^{in\omega_0 t}$$
$$= \frac{1}{2} \sum_{n=1}^{\infty} (C_n e^{in\omega_0 t} + C_n^* e^{-in\omega_0 t})$$

where C_n is a complex number, and C_n^* is its complex conjugate. [See Eq. (12.2.9).] Its mean square value is

$$\overline{x^2} = \lim_{T\to\infty} \frac{1}{T} \int_0^T \frac{1}{4} \sum_{n=1}^{\infty} (C_n e^{in\omega_0 t} + C_n^* e^{-in\omega_0 t})^2 \, dt$$
$$= \lim_{T\to\infty} \sum_{n=1}^{\infty} \frac{1}{4} \left(\frac{C_n^2 e^{i2n\omega_0 t}}{i2n\omega_0 T} + 2C_n C_n^* + \frac{C_n^{*2} e^{-i2n\omega_0 t}}{-i2n\omega_0 T} \right)_0^T$$
$$= \sum_{n=1}^{\infty} \frac{1}{2} C_n C_n^* = \sum_{n=1}^{\infty} \frac{1}{2} |C_n|^2 = \sum_{n=1}^{\infty} \overline{C_n^2}$$

In this equation, $e^{\pm i2n\omega_0 t}$, for any t, is bounded between ± 1, and due to $T \to \infty$ in the denominator, the first and last terms become zero. The middle term, however, is independent of T. Thus, the mean square value of the periodic function is simply the sum of the mean square value of each harmonic component present.

12.3 FREQUENCY RESPONSE FUNCTION

In any linear system, there is a direct linear relationship between the input and the output. This relationship, which also holds for random functions, is represented by the block diagram of Fig. 12.3.1.

In the time domain, the system behavior can be determined in terms of the system impulse response $h(t)$ used in the convolution integral of Eq. (4.2.1).

$$y(t) = \int_0^t x(\xi) h(t - \xi) d\xi \tag{12.3.1}$$

A much simpler relationship is available for the frequency domain in terms of the frequency response function $H(\omega)$, which we can define as the ratio of the output to the input under steady-state conditions, with the input equal to a harmonic time function of unit amplitude. The transient solution is thus excluded in this consideration. In random vibrations, the initial conditions and the phase have little meaning and are therefore ignored. We are mainly concerned with the average energy, which we can associate with the mean square value.

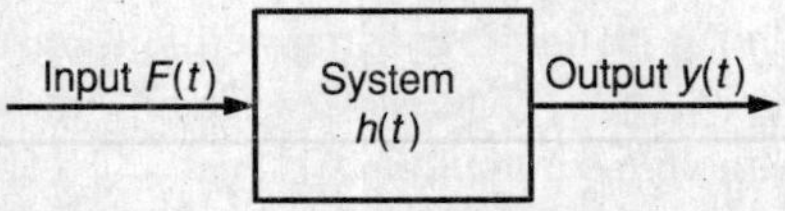

FIGURE 12.3.1. Input–output relationship of a linear system.

Applying this definition to a single-DOF system,

$$m\ddot{y} + c\dot{y} + ky = x(t) \tag{12.3.2}$$

let the input be $x(t) = e^{i\omega t}$. The steady-state output will then be $y = H(\omega)e^{i\omega t}$, where $H(\omega)$ is a complex function. Substituting these into the differential equation and canceling $e^{i\omega t}$ from each side, we obtain

$$(-m\omega^2 + ic\omega + k)H(\omega) = 1$$

The frequency response function is then

$$\begin{aligned} H(\omega) &= \frac{1}{k - m\omega^2 + ic\omega} \\ &= \frac{1}{k}\frac{1}{1 - (\omega/\omega_n)^2 + i2\zeta(\omega/\omega_n)} \end{aligned} \tag{12.3.3}$$

As mentioned in Chapter 3, we will absorb the factor $1/k$ in with the force. $H(\omega)$ is then a nondimensional function of ω/ω_n and the damping factor ζ.

The input–output relationship in terms of the frequency-response function can be written as

$$y(t) = H(\omega)F_0e^{i\omega t} \tag{12.3.4}$$

where $F_0e^{i\omega t}$ is a harmonic function.

For the mean square response, we follow the procedure of Example 12.2.1 and write

$$y = \frac{1}{2}F_0(He^{i\omega t} + H^*e^{-i\omega t}) \tag{12.3.5}$$

Thus, by squaring and substituting into Eq. (12.2.4), we find the mean square value of y is

$$\begin{aligned} \overline{y^2} &= \frac{F_0^2}{4}\lim_{T\to\infty}\frac{1}{T}\int_0^T (H^2e^{i2\omega t} + 2HH^* + H^*e^{-i2\omega t})\,dt \\ &= \frac{F_0^2}{2}H(\omega)H^*(\omega) = \overline{F_0^2}|H(\omega)|^2 \end{aligned} \tag{12.3.6}$$

In the preceding equation, the first and last terms become zero because of $T \to \infty$ in the denominator, whereas the middle term is independent of T. Equation (12.3.6) indicates that the mean square value of the response is equal to the mean square excitation multiplied by the square of the absolute values of the frequency response function. For excitations expressed in terms of Fourier series with many frequencies, the response is the sum of terms similar to Eq. (12.3.6).

Example 12.3.1

A single-DOF system with natural frequency $\omega_n = \sqrt{k/m}$ and damping $\zeta = 0.20$ is excited by the force

$$\begin{aligned} F(t) &= F\cos\frac{1}{2}\omega_n t + F\cos\omega_n t + F\cos\frac{3}{2}\omega_n t \\ &= \sum_{m=1/2,1,3/2} F\cos m\omega_n t \end{aligned}$$

Determine the mean square response and compare the output spectrum with that of the input.

Solution The response of the system is simply the sum of the response of the single-DOF system to each of the harmonic components of the exciting force.

$$x(t) = \sum_{m=1/2,1,3/2} |H(m\omega)|F \cos(m\omega_n t - \phi_m)$$

where

$$\left|H\left(\frac{1}{2}\omega_n\right)\right| = \frac{1/k}{\sqrt{9/16 + (0.20)^2}} = \frac{1.29}{k}$$

$$|H(\omega_n)| = \frac{1/k}{\sqrt{4(0.20)^2}} = \frac{2.50}{k}$$

$$\left|H\left(\frac{3}{2}\omega_n\right)\right| = \frac{1/k}{\sqrt{25/16 + (0.20)^2}} = \frac{0.72}{k}$$

$$\phi_{1/2} = \tan^{-1}\frac{4\zeta}{3} = 0.083\pi$$

$$\phi_1 = \tan^{-1}\infty = 0.50\pi$$

$$\phi_{3/2} = \tan^{-1}\frac{-12\zeta}{5} = -0.142\pi$$

Substituting these values into $x(t)$, we obtain the equation

$$\begin{aligned} x(t) = \frac{F}{k}[&1.29\cos(0.5\omega_n t - 0.083\pi) \\ &+ 2.50\cos(\omega_n t - 0.50\pi) \\ &+ 0.72\cos(1.5\omega_n t - 0.142\pi)] \end{aligned}$$

The mean square response is then

$$\overline{x^2} = \frac{F^2}{2k^2}[(1.29)^2 + (2.50)^2 + (0.72)^2]$$

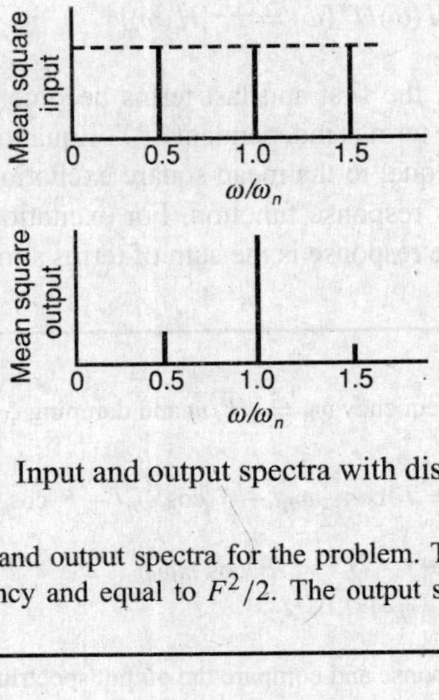

FIGURE 12.3.2. Input and output spectra with discrete frequencies.

Figure 12.3.2 shows the input and output spectra for the problem. The components of the mean square input are the same for each frequency and equal to $F^2/2$. The output spectrum is modified by the system frequency-response function.

■

12.4 PROBABILITY DISTRIBUTION

By referring to the random time function of Fig. 12.4.1, what is the probability of its instantaneous value being less than (more negative than) some specified value x_1? To answer this question, we draw a horizontal line at the specified value x_1 and sum the time intervals Δt_i during which $x(t)$ is less than x_1. This sum divided by the total time then represents the fraction of the total time that $x(t)$ is less than x_1, which is the probability that $x(t)$ will be found less than x_1.

$$\begin{aligned} P(x_1) &= \text{Prob}[x(t) < x_1] \\ &= \lim_{t\to\infty} \frac{1}{t} \sum \Delta t_i \end{aligned} \tag{12.4.1}$$

If a large negative number is chosen for x_1, none of the curve will extend negatively beyond x_1, and, hence, $P(x_1 \to -\infty) = 0$. As the horizontal line corresponding to x_1 is moved up, more of $x(t)$ will extend negatively beyond x_1, and the fraction of the total time in which $x(t)$ extends below x_1 must increase, as shown in Fig. 12.4.2(a). As $x \to \infty$, all $x(t)$ will lie in the region less than $x = \infty$, and, hence, the probability of $x(t)$ being less than $x = \infty$ is certain, or $P(x = \infty) = 1.0$. Thus, the curve of Fig. 12.4.2(a), which is cumulative toward positive x, must increase monotonically from 0 at $x = -\infty$ to 1.0 at $x = +\infty$. The curve is called the cumulative probability distribution function $P(x)$.

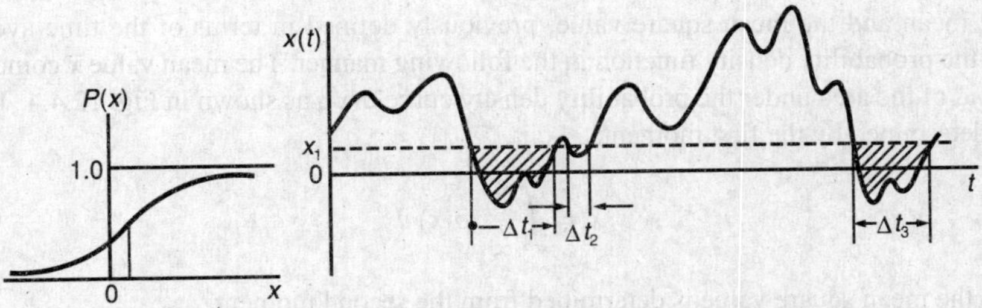

FIGURE 12.4.1. Calculation of cumulative probability.

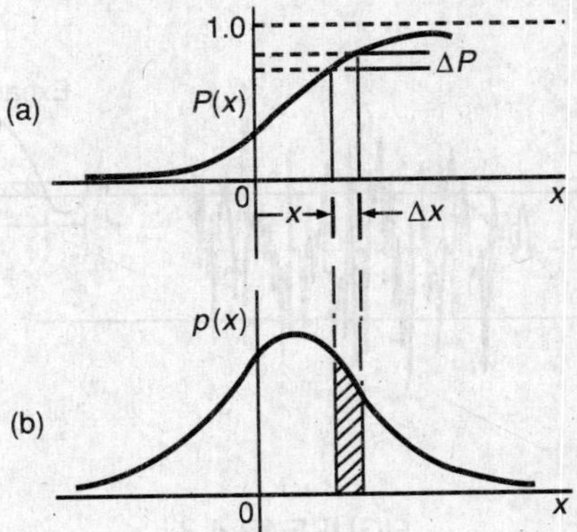

FIGURE 12.4.2. (a) Cumulative probability, (b) Probability density.

If next we wish to determine the probability of $x(t)$ lying between the values x_1 and $x_1 + \Delta x$, all we need to do is subtract $P(x_1)$ from $P(x_1 + \Delta x)$, which is also proportional to the time occupied by $x(t)$ in the zone x_1 to $x_1 + \Delta x$.

We now define the *probability density function* $p(x)$ as

$$p(x) = \lim_{\Delta x \to 0} \frac{P(x + \Delta x) - P(x)}{\Delta x} = \frac{dP(x)}{dx} \tag{12.4.2}$$

and it is evident from Fig. 12.4.2(b) that $p(x)$ is the slope of the cumulative probability distribution $P(x)$. From the preceding equation, we can also write

$$P(x_1) = \int_{-\infty}^{x_1} p(x)\,dx \tag{12.4.3}$$

The area under the probability density curve of Fig. 12.4.2(b) between two values of x represents the probability of the variable being in this interval. Because the probability of $x(t)$ being between $x = \pm\infty$ is certain,

$$P(\infty) = \int_{-\infty}^{+\infty} p(x)\,dx = 1.0 \tag{12.4.4}$$

and the total area under the $p(x)$ curve must be unity. Figure 12.4.3 again illustrates the probability density $p(x)$ which is the fraction of the time occupied by $x(t)$ in the interval x to $x + dx$.

The mean and the mean square value, previously defined in terms of the time average, are related to the probability density function in the following manner. The mean value $\bar{x}$ coincides with the centroid of the area under the probability density curve $p(x)$, as shown in Fig. 12.4.4. Therefore, it can be determined by the first moment:

$$\bar{x} = \int_{-\infty}^{\infty} xp(x)\,dx \tag{12.4.5}$$

Likewise, the mean square value is determined from the second moment

$$\overline{x^2} = \int_{-\infty}^{\infty} x^2 p(x)\,dx \tag{12.4.6}$$

which is analogous to the moment of inertia of the area under the probability density curve about $x = 0$.

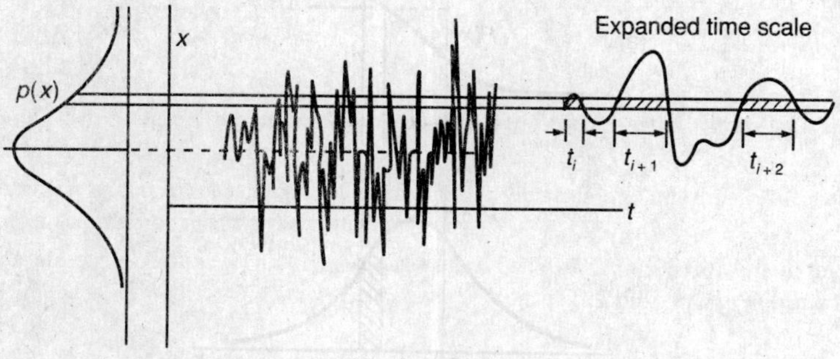

FIGURE 12.4.3.

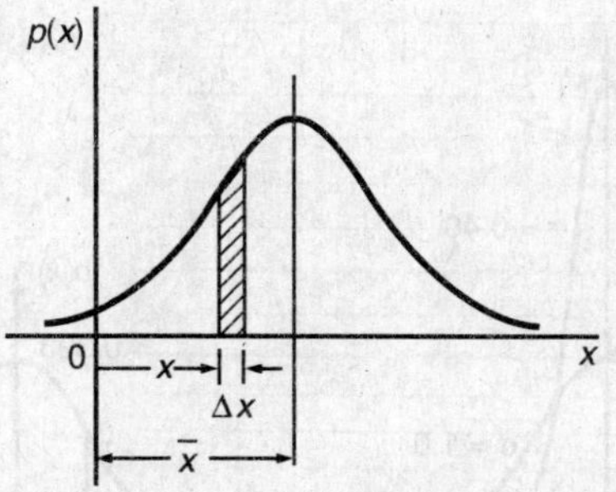

FIGURE 12.4.4. First and second moments of $p(x)$.

The *variance* σ^2, previously defined as the mean square value about the mean, is

$$\begin{aligned}\sigma^2 &= \int_{-\infty}^{\infty} (x-\bar{x})^2 p(x)\,dx \\ &= \int_{-\infty}^{\infty} x^2 p(x)\,dx - 2\bar{x}\int_{-\infty}^{\infty} xp(x)\,dx + (\bar{x})^2 \int_{-\infty}^{\infty} p(x)\,dx \\ &= \overline{x^2} - 2(\bar{x})^2 + (\bar{x})^2 \\ &= \overline{x^2} - (\bar{x})^2\end{aligned} \tag{12.4.7}$$

The *standard deviation* σ is the positive square root of the variance. When the mean value is zero, $\sigma = \sqrt{\overline{x^2}}$, and the standard deviation is equal to the root-mean-square (rms) value.

Gaussian and Rayleigh distributions. Certain distributions that occur frequently in nature are the *Gaussian* (or normal) distribution and the *Rayleigh* distribution, both of which can be expressed mathematically. The Gaussian distribution is a bell-shaped curve, symmetric about the mean value (which will be assumed to be zero) with the following equation:

$$p(x) = \frac{1}{\sigma\sqrt{2\pi}} e^{-x^2/2\sigma^2} \tag{12.4.8}$$

The standard deviation σ is a measure of the spread about the mean value; the smaller the value of σ, the narrower the $p(x)$ curve (remember that the total area = 1.0), as shown in Fig. 12.4.5(a).

In Fig. 12.4.5(b), the Gaussian distribution is plotted nondimensionally in terms of x/σ. The probability of $x(t)$ being between $\pm\lambda\sigma$, where λ is any positive number, is found from the equation

$$\text{Prob}[-\lambda\sigma \le x(t) \le \lambda\sigma] = \frac{1}{\sigma\sqrt{2\pi}} \int_{-\lambda\sigma}^{\lambda\sigma} e^{-x^2/2\sigma^2}\,dx \tag{12.4.9}$$

The following table presents numerical values associated with $\lambda = 1, 2,$ and 3.

λ	$\text{Prob}[-\lambda\sigma \le x(t) \le \lambda\sigma]$	$\text{Prob}[\lvert x\rvert > \lambda\sigma]$
1	68.3%	31.7%
2	95.4%	4.6%
3	99.7%	0.3%

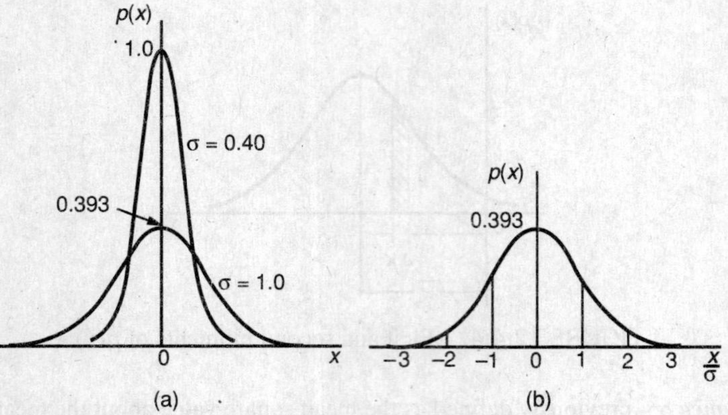

FIGURE 12.4.5. Normal distribution.

The probability of $x(t)$ lying outside $\pm\lambda\sigma$ is the probability of $|x|$ exceeding $\lambda\sigma$, which is 1.0 minus the preceding values, or the equation

$$\text{Prob}[|x| > \lambda\sigma] = \frac{2}{\sigma\sqrt{2\pi}}\int_{\lambda\sigma}^{\infty} e^{-x^2/2\sigma^2}\,dx = erfc\left(\frac{\lambda}{\sqrt{2}}\right) \tag{12.4.10}$$

Random variables restricted to positive values, such as the absolute value A of the amplitude, often tend to follow the Rayleigh distribution, which is defined by the equation

$$p(A) = \frac{A}{\sigma^2}e^{-A^2/2\sigma^2} \qquad A > 0 \tag{12.4.11}$$

The probability density $p(A)$ is zero here for $A < 0$ and has the shape shown in Fig. 12.4.6.

The mean and mean square values for the Rayleigh distribution can be found from the first and second moments to be

$$\begin{aligned} \overline{A} &= \int_0^{\infty} Ap(A)\,dA = \int_0^{\infty}\frac{A^2}{\sigma^2}e^{-A^2/2\sigma^2}\,dA = \sqrt{\frac{\pi}{2}}\sigma \\ \overline{A^2} &= \int_0^{\infty} A^2p(A)\,dA = \int_0^{\infty}\frac{A^3}{\sigma^2}e^{-A^2/2\sigma^2}\,dA = 2\sigma^2 \end{aligned} \tag{12.4.12}$$

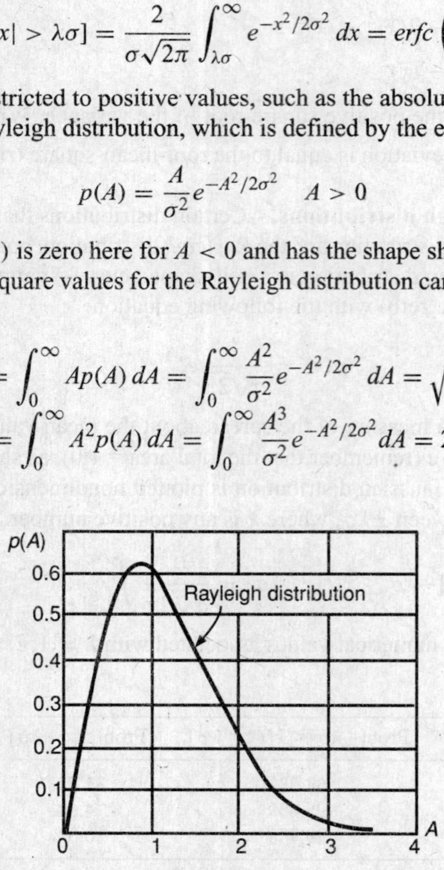

FIGURE 12.4.6. Rayleigh distribution.

The variance associated with the Rayleigh distribution is

$$\sigma_A^2 = \overline{A^2} - (\overline{A})^2 = \left(\frac{4-\pi}{2}\right)\sigma^2$$
$$\therefore \sigma_A \cong \frac{2}{3}\sigma \qquad (12.4.13)$$

Also, the probability of A exceeding a specified value $\lambda\sigma$ is

$$\text{Prob}[A > \lambda\sigma] = \int_{\lambda\sigma}^{\infty} \frac{A}{\sigma^2} e^{-A^2/2\sigma^2}\, dA \qquad (12.4.14)$$

which has the following numerical values:

λ	$P[A > \lambda\sigma]$
0	100%
1	60.7%
2	13.5%
3	1.2%

Three important examples of time records frequently encountered in practice are shown in Fig. 12.4.7, where the mean value is arbitrarily chosen to be zero. The cumulative probability distribution for the sine wave is easily shown to be

$$P(x) = \frac{1}{2} + \frac{1}{\pi}\sin^{-1}\frac{x}{A}$$

and its probability density, by differentiation, is

$$p(x) = \frac{1}{\pi\sqrt{A^2 - x^2}} \qquad |x| < A$$
$$= 0 \qquad |x| > A$$

For the wide-band record, the amplitude, phase, and frequency all vary randomly and an analytical expression is not possible for its instantaneous value. Such functions are encountered in

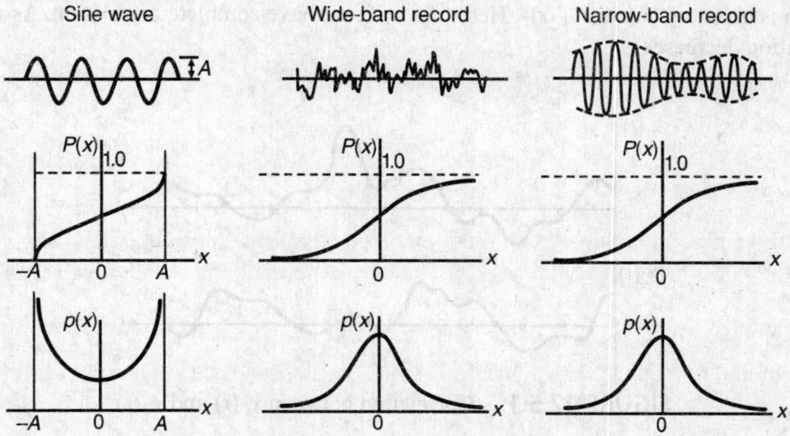

FIGURE 12.4.7. Probability functions for three types of records.

radio noise, jet engine pressure fluctuation, atmospheric turbulence, and so on, and a most likely probability distribution for such records is the *Gaussian distribution*.

When a wide-band record is put through a narrow-band filter, or a resonance system in which the filter bandwidth is small compared to its central frequency f_0, we obtain the third type of wave, which is essentially a constant-frequency oscillation with slowly varying amplitude and phase. The probability distribution for its instantaneous values is the same as that for the wide-band random function. However, the absolute values of its peaks, corresponding to the envelope, will have a Rayleigh distribution.

Another quantity of great interest is the distribution of the peak values. Rice[1] shows that the distribution of the peak values depends on a quantity $N_0/2M$, where N_0 is the number of zero crossings, and $2M$ is the number of positive and negative peaks. For a sine wave or a narrow band, N_0 is equal to $2M$, so that the ratio $N_0/2M = 1$. For a wide-band random record, the number of peaks will greatly exceed the number of zero crossings, so that $N_0/2M$ tends to approach zero. When $N_0/2M = 0$, the probability density distribution of peak values turns out to be Gaussian, whereas when $N_0/2M = 1$, as in the narrow-band case, the probability density distribution of the peak values tends to a *Rayleigh distribution*.

12.5 CORRELATION

Correlation is a measure of the similarity between two quantities. As it applies to vibration waveforms, correlation is a time-domain analysis useful for detecting hidden periodic signals buried in measurement noise, propagation time through the structure, and for determining other information related to the structure's spectral characteristics, which are better discussed under Fourier transforms.

Suppose we have two records, $x_1(t)$ and $x_2(t)$, as shown in Fig. 12.5.1. The *correlation* between them is computed by multiplying the ordinates of the two records at each time t and determining the average value $\langle(x_1(t)x_2(t)\rangle$ by dividing the sum of the products by the number of products. It is evident that the correlation so found will be largest when the two records are similar or identical. For dissimilar records, some of the products will be positive and others will be negative, so their sum will be smaller.

Next, consider the case in which $x_2(t)$ is identical to $x_1(t)$ but shifted to the left by a time τ, as shown in Fig. 12.5.2. Then, at time (t), when x_1 is $x(t)$, the value of x_2 is $x(t+\tau)$, and the correlation is given by $\langle x(t)x(t+\tau)\rangle$. Here, if $\tau = 0$, we have complete correlation. As τ increases, the correlation decreases.

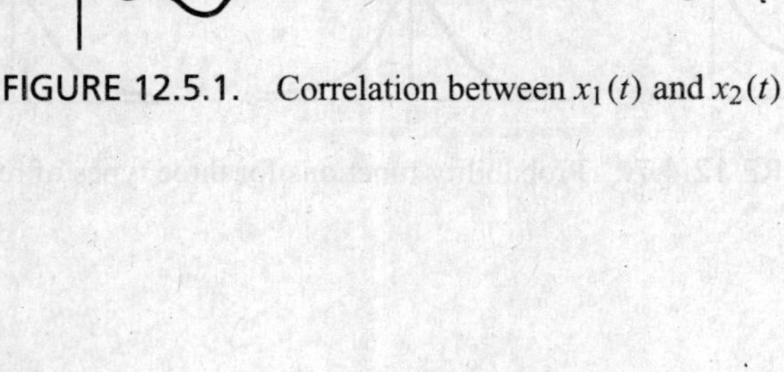

FIGURE 12.5.1. Correlation between $x_1(t)$ and $x_2(t)$.

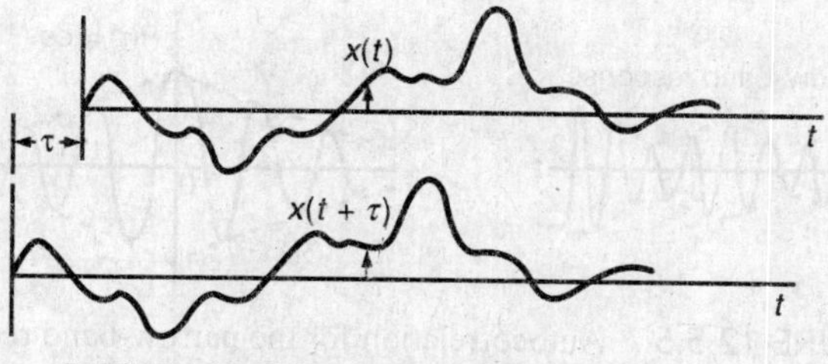

FIGURE 12.5.2. Function $x(t)$ shifted by τ.

It is evident that this result can be computed from a single record by multiplying the ordinates at time t and $t+\tau$ and determining the average. We then call this result the *autocorrelation* and designate it by $R(\tau)$. It is also the expected value of the product $x(t)x(t+\tau)$, or

$$\begin{aligned} R(\tau) &= E[x(t)x(t+\tau)] = \langle x(t)x(t+\tau)\rangle \\ &= \lim_{T\to\infty}\frac{1}{T}\int_{-T/2}^{T/2} x(t)x(t+\tau)\,dt \end{aligned} \tag{12.5.1}$$

When $\tau = 0$, this definition reduces to the mean square value:

$$R(0) = \overline{x^2} = \sigma^2 \tag{12.5.2}$$

Because the second record of Fig. 12.5.2 can be considered to be delayed with respect to the first record, or the first record advanced with respect to the second record, it is evident that $R(\tau) = R(-\tau)$ is symmetric about the origin $\tau = 0$ and is always less than $R(0)$.

Highly random functions, such as the wide-band noise shown in Fig. 12.5.3, soon lose their similarity within a short time shift. Its autocorrelation, therefore is a sharp spike at $\tau = 0$ that drops off rapidly with $\pm\tau$ as shown. It implies that wide-band random records have little or no correlation except near $\tau = 0$.

For the special case of a periodic wave, the autocorrelation must be periodic of the same period, because shifting the wave one period brings the wave into coincidence again. Figure 12.5.4 shows a sine wave and its autocorrelation.

For the narrow-band record shown in Fig. 12.5.5, the autocorrelation has some of the characteristics found for the sine wave in that it is again an even function with a maximum at

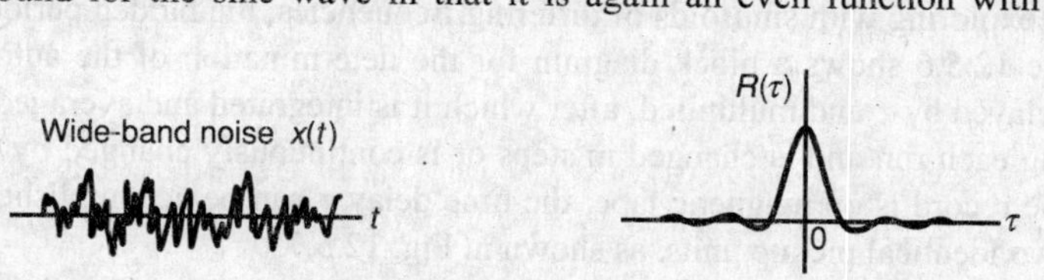

FIGURE 12.5.3. Highly random function and its autocorrelation.

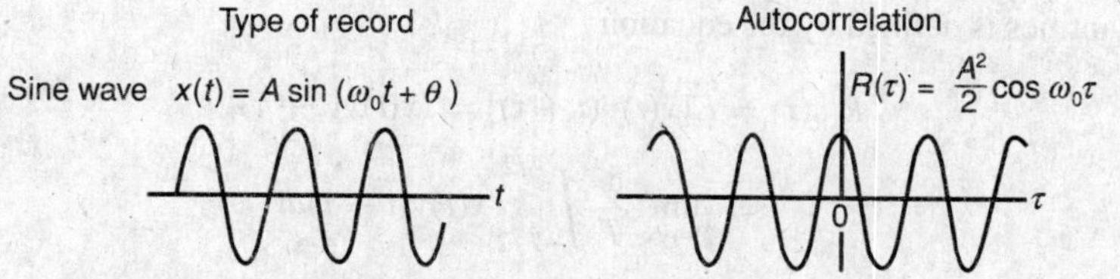

FIGURE 12.5.4. Sine wave and its autocorrelation.

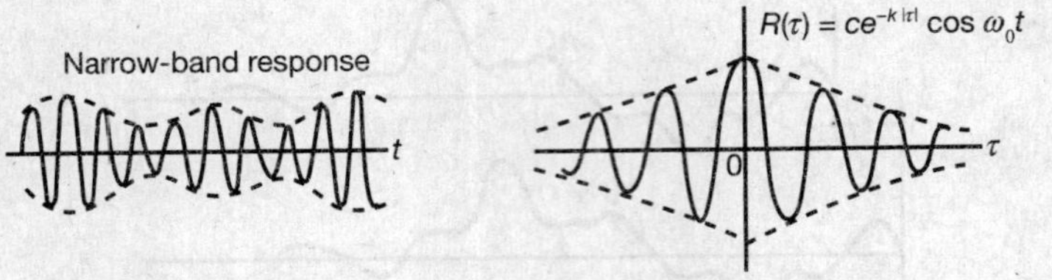

FIGURE 12.5.5. Autocorrelation for the narrow-band record.

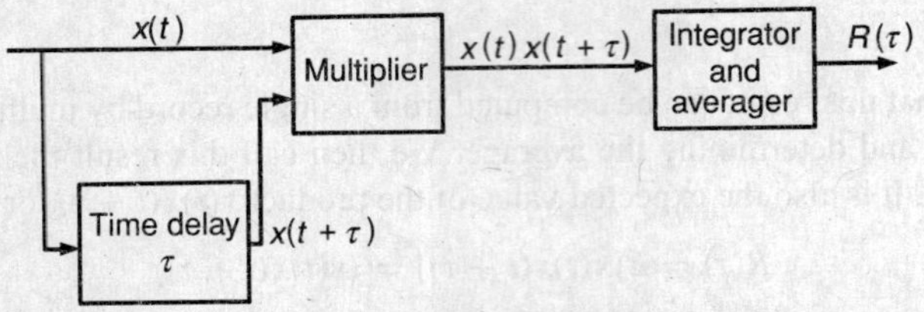

FIGURE 12.5.6. Block diagram of the autocorrelation analyzer.

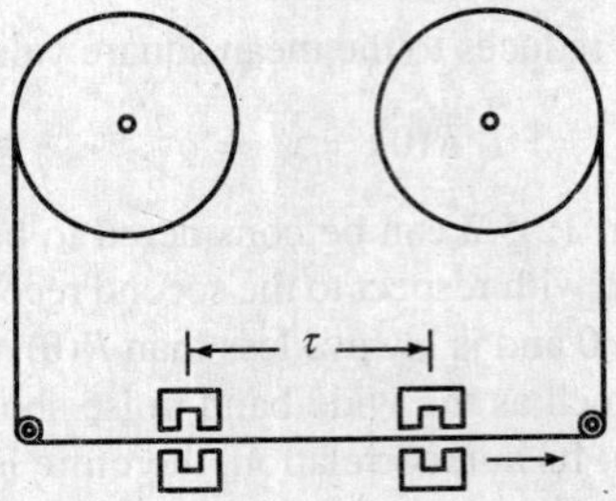

FIGURE 12.5.7. Time delay for autocorrelation.

$\tau = 0$ and frequency ω_0 corresponding to the dominant or central frequency. The difference appears in the fact that $R(\tau)$ approaches zero for large τ for the narrow-band record. It is evident from this discussion that hidden periodicities in a noisy random record can be detected by correlating the record with a sinusoid. There will be almost no correlation between the sinusoid and the noise that will be suppressed. By exploring with sinusoids of differing frequencies, the hidden periodic signal can be detected. Figure 12.5.6 shows a block diagram for the determination of the autocorrelation. The signal $x(t)$ is delayed by τ and multiplied, after which it is integrated and averaged. The delay time τ is fixed during each run and is changed in steps or is continuously changed by a slow sweeping technique. If the record is on magnetic tape, the time delay τ can be accomplished by passing the tape between two identical pickup units, as shown in Fig. 12.5.7.

Cross correlation. Consider two random quantities $x(t)$ and $y(t)$. The correlation between these two quantities is defined by the equation

$$\begin{aligned} R_{xy}(\tau) &= E[x(t)y(t+\tau)] = \langle x(t)y(t+\tau)\rangle \\ &= \lim_{T\to\infty}\frac{1}{T}\int_{-T/2}^{T/2} x(t)y(t+\tau)dt \end{aligned} \tag{12.5.3}$$

which can also be called the *cross correlation* between the quantities x and y.

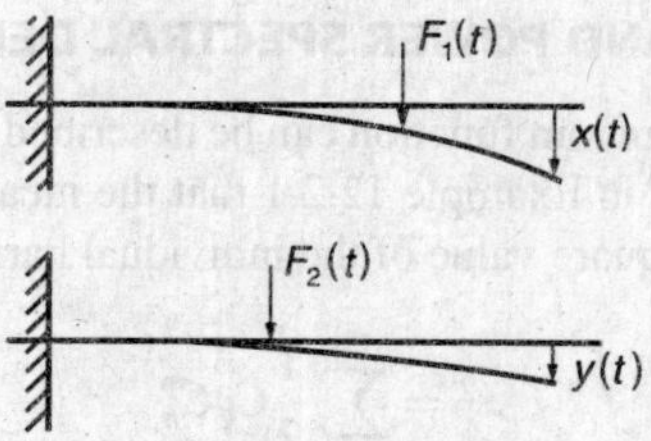

FIGURE 12.5.8.

Such quantities often arise in dynamical problems. For example, let $x(t)$ be the deflection at the end of a beam due to a load $F_1(t)$ at some specified point. $y(t)$ is the deflection at the same point, due to a second load $F_2(t)$ at a different point than the first, as illustrated in Fig. 12.5.8. The deflection due to both loads is then $z(t) = x(t) + y(t)$, and the autocorrelation of $z(t)$ as a result of the two loads is

$$\begin{aligned} R_z(\tau) &= \langle z(t)z(t+\tau)\rangle \\ &= \langle [x(t)+y(t)][x(t+\tau)+y(t+\tau)]\rangle \\ &= \langle x(t)x(t+\tau)\rangle + \langle x(t)y(t+\tau)\rangle \\ &\quad + \langle y(t)x(t+\tau)\rangle + \langle y(t)y(t+\tau)\rangle \\ &= R_x(\tau) + R_{xy}(\tau) + R_{yx}(\tau) + R_y(\tau) \end{aligned} \tag{12.5.4}$$

Thus, the autocorrelation of a deflection at a given point due to separate loads $F_1(t)$ and $F_2(t)$ cannot be determined simply by adding the autocorrelations $R_x(\tau)$ and $R_y(\tau)$ resulting from each load acting separately. $R_{xy}(\tau)$ and $R_{yx}(\tau)$ are here referred to as *cross correlation*, and, in general, they are not equal.

Example 12.5.1

Show that the autocorrelation of the rectangular gating function shown in Fig. 12.5.9 is a triangle.

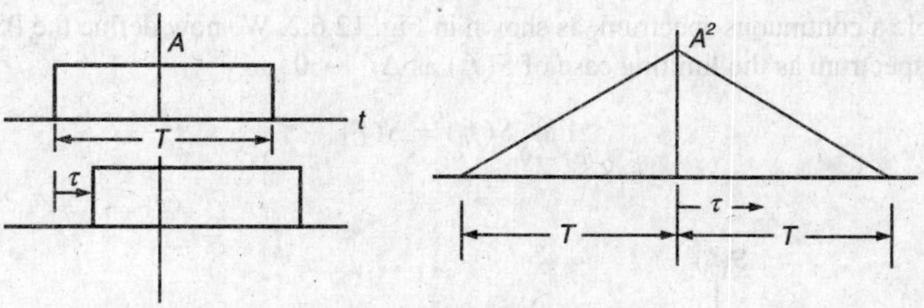

FIGURE 12.5.9. Autocorrelation of a rectangle is a triangle.

Solution If the rectangular pulse is shifted in either direction by τ, its product with the original pulse is $A^2(T-\tau)$. It is easily seen then that starting with $\tau = 0$, the autocorrelation curve is a straight line that forms a triangle with height A^2 and base equal to $2T$. ■

12.6 POWER SPECTRUM AND POWER SPECTRAL DENSITY

The frequency composition of a random function can be described in terms of the spectral density of the mean square value. We found in Example 12.2.1 that the mean square value of a periodic time function is the sum of the mean square value of the individual harmonic component present.

$$\overline{x^2} = \sum_{n=1}^{\infty} \frac{1}{2} C_n C_n^*$$

Thus $\overline{x^2}$ is made up of discrete contributions in each frequency interval Δf.

We first define the contribution to the mean square in the frequency interval Δf as the *power spectrum* $G(f_n)$:

$$G(f_n) = \frac{1}{2} C_n C_n^* \tag{12.6.1}$$

The mean square value is then

$$\overline{x^2} = \sum_{n=1}^{\infty} G(f_n) \tag{12.6.2}$$

We now define the discrete *power spectral density* $S(f_n)$ as the power spectrum divided by the frequency interval Δf:

$$S(f_n) = \frac{G(f_n)}{\Delta f} = \frac{C_n C_n^*}{2\Delta f} \tag{12.6.3}$$

The mean square value can then be written as

$$\overline{x^2} = \sum_{n=1}^{\infty} S(f_n)\Delta f \tag{12.6.4}$$

The power spectrum and the power spectral density will hereafter be abbreviated as PS and PSD, respectively.

An example of discrete PSD is shown in Fig. 12.6.1. When $x(t)$ contains a very large number of frequency components, the lines of the discrete spectrum become closer together and they more nearly resemble a continuous spectrum, as shown in Fig. 12.6.2. We now define the PSD, $S(f)$, for a continuous spectrum as the limiting case of $S(f_n)$ as $\Delta f \to 0$.

$$\lim_{\Delta f \to 0} S(f_n) = S(f) \tag{12.6.5}$$

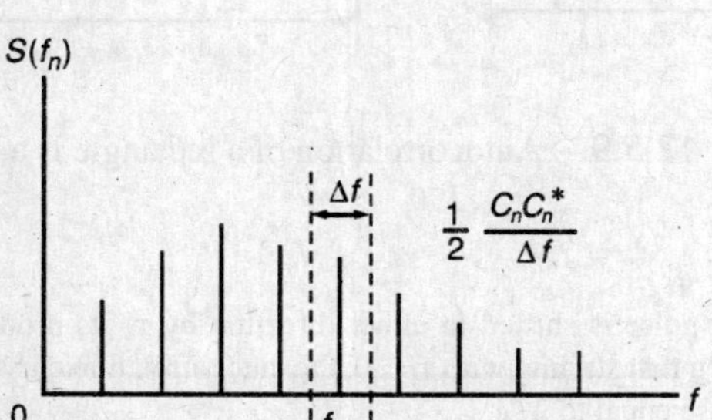

FIGURE 12.6.1. Discrete spectrum.

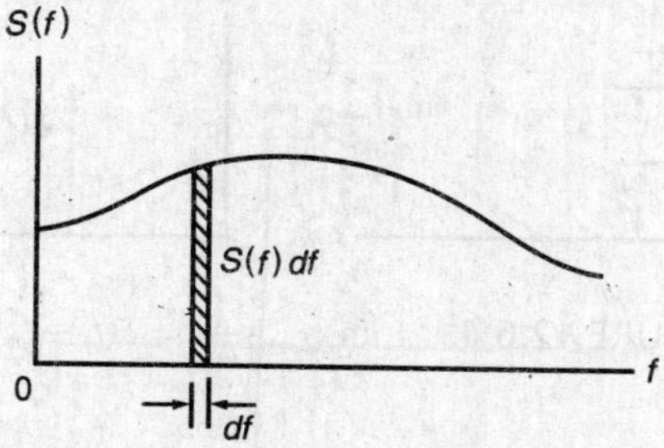

FIGURE 12.6.2. Continuous spectrum.

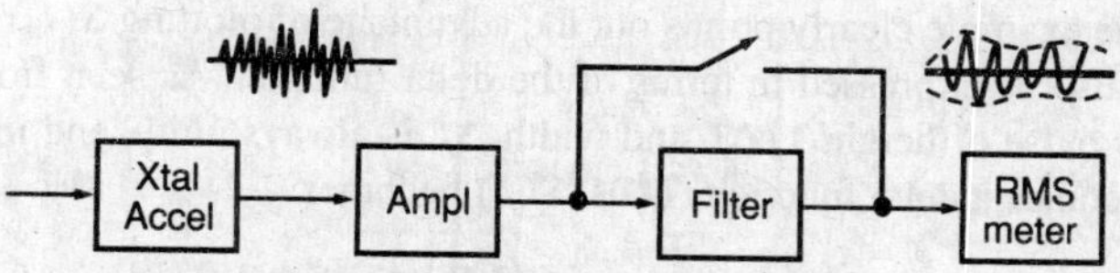

FIGURE 12.6.3. Measurement of random data.

The mean square value is then

$$\overline{x^2} = \int_0^\infty S(f)df \tag{12.6.6}$$

To illustrate the meaning of PS and PSD, the following experiment is described. A Xtal accelerometer is attached to a shaker, and its output is amplified, filtered, and read by a rms voltmeter, as shown by the block diagram of Fig. 12.6.3. The rms voltmeter should have a long time constant, which corresponds to a long averaging time.

We excite the shaker by a wide-band random input that is constant over the frequency range 0 to 2000 Hz. If the filter is bypassed, the rms voltmeter will read the rms vibration in the entire frequency spectrum. By assuming an ideal filter that will pass all vibrations of frequencies within the passband, the output of the filter represents a narrow-band vibration.

We consider a central frequency of 500 Hz and first set the upper and lower cutoff frequencies at 580 and 420 Hz, respectively. The rms meter will now read only the vibration within this 160-Hz band. Let us say that the reading is $8g$. The mean square value is then $G(f_n) = 64g^2$, and its spectral density is $S(f_n) = 64g^2/160 = 0.40g^2/\text{Hz}$.

We next reduce the passband to 40 Hz by setting the upper and lower filter frequencies to 520 and 480 Hz, respectively. The mean square value passed by the filter is now one-quarter of the previous value, or $16g^2$, and the rms meter reads $4g$.

By reducing the passband further to 10 Hz, between 505 Hz and 495 Hz, the rms meter reading becomes $2g$, as shown in the following tabulation:

Frequencies	Bandwidth	RMS Meter Reading	Filtered Mean Square	Spectral Density
f	Δf	$\sqrt{\delta(\overline{x^2})}$	$G(f_n) = \Delta(\overline{x^2})$	$S(f_n) = \frac{\Delta(\overline{x^2})}{\Delta f}$
580–420	160	$8g$	$64g^2$	$0.40g^2/\text{Hz}$
520–480	40	$4g$	$16g^2$	$0.40g^2/\text{Hz}$
505–495	10	$2g$	$4g^2$	$0.40g^2/\text{Hz}$

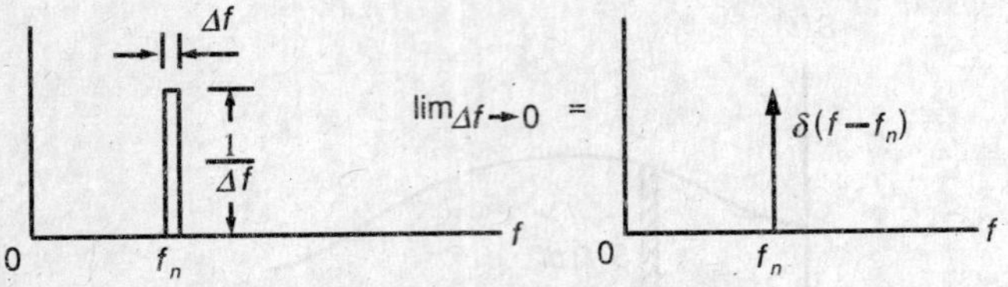

FIGURE 12.6.4. $\text{Lim}_{\Delta f\to 0}\frac{1}{\Delta f} = \delta(f - f_n)$.

Note that as the bandwidth is reduced, the mean square value passed by the filter, or $G(f_n)$, is reduced proportionally. However, by dividing by the bandwidth, the density of the mean square value, $S(f_n)$, remains constant. The example clearly points out the advantage of plotting $S(f_n)$ instead of $G(f_n)$.

The PSD can also be expressed in terms of the delta function. As seen from Fig. 12.6.4, the area of a rectangular pulse of height $1/\Delta f$ and width Δf is always unity, and in the limiting case, when $\Delta f \to 0$, it becomes a delta function. Thus, $S(f)$ becomes

$$S(f) = \lim_{\Delta f\to 0} S(f_n) = \lim_{\Delta f\to 0} \frac{G(f_n)}{\Delta f} = G(f)\delta(f - f_n)$$

Typical spectral density functions for two common types of random records are shown in Figs. 12.6.5 and 12.6.6. The first is a wide-band noise-type of record that has a broad spectral density function. The second is a narrow-band random record that is typical of a response of a sharply resonant system to a wide-band input. Its spectral density function is concentrated around the frequency of the instantaneous variation within the envelope.

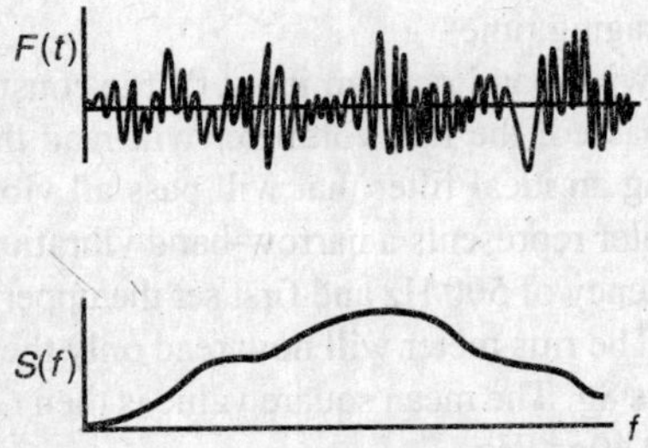

FIGURE 12.6.5. Wide-band record and its spectral density.

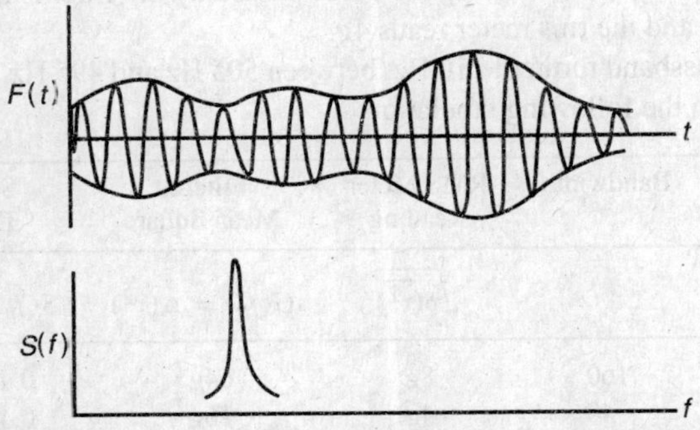

FIGURE 12.6.6. Narrow-band record and its spectral density.

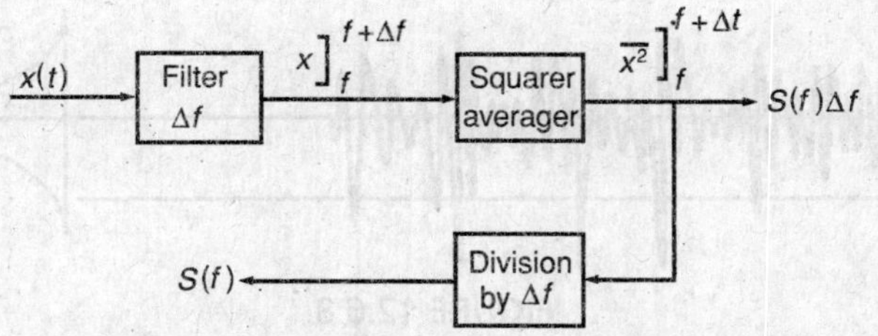

FIGURE 12.6.7. Power spectral density analyzer.

The spectral density of a given record can be measured electronically by the circuit of Fig. 12.6.7. Here the spectral density is noted as the contribution of the mean square value in the frequency interval Δf which is divided by Δf.

$$S(f) = \lim_{\Delta f \to 0} \frac{\Delta(\overline{x^2})}{\Delta f} \tag{12.6.7}$$

The band-pass filter of passband $B = \Delta f$ passes $x(t)$ in the frequency interval f to $f + \Delta f$, and the output is squared, averaged, and divided by Δf.

For high resolution, Δf should be made as narrow as possible; however, the passband of the filter cannot be reduced indefinitely without losing the reliability of the measurement. Also, a long record is required for the true estimate of the mean square value, but actual records are always of finite length. It is evident now that a parameter of importance is the product of the record length and the bandwidth, $2BT$, which must be sufficiently large.[2]

Example 12.6.1

A random signal has a spectral density that is a constant

$$S(f) = 0.004 \text{ cm}^2/\text{cps}$$

between 20 and 1200 cps and that is zero outside this frequency range. Its mean value is 2.0 cm. Determine its rms value and its standard deviation.

Solution The mean square value is found from

$$\overline{x^2} = \int_0^{\infty} S(f)\,df = \int_{20}^{1200} 0.004\,df = 4.72$$

and the rms value is

$$\text{rms} = \sqrt{\overline{x^2}} = \sqrt{4.72} = 2.17 \text{ cm}$$

The variance σ^2 is defined by Eq. (12.2.6):

$$\begin{aligned}\sigma^2 &= \overline{x^2} - (\bar{x})^2 \\ &= 4.72 - 2^2 = 0.72\end{aligned}$$

and the standard deviation becomes

$$\sigma = \sqrt{0.72} = 0.85 \text{ cm}$$

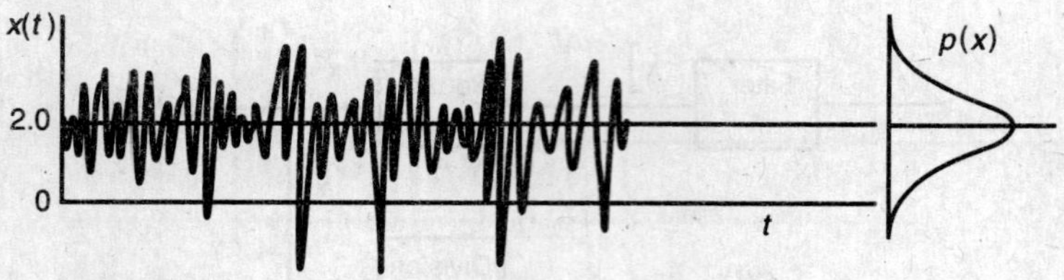

FIGURE 12.6.8.

The problem is graphically displayed by Fig. 12.6.8, which shows the time variation of the signal and its probability distribution.

Example 12.6.2

Determine the Fourier coefficients C_n and the power spectral density of the periodic function shown in Fig. 12.6.9.

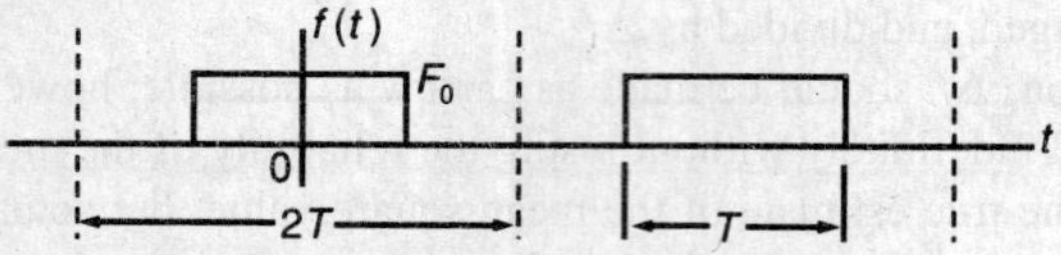

FIGURE 12.6.9.

Solution The period is $2T$ and C_n are

$$C_0 = \frac{2}{2T}\int_{-T/2}^{T/2} F_0\,d\xi = F_0$$

$$C_n = \frac{2}{2T}\int_{-T/2}^{T/2} F_0 e^{-in\omega_0\xi}\,d\xi = F_0\left[\frac{\sin(n\pi/2)}{n\pi/2}\right]$$

Numerical values of C_n are computed as in the following table and plotted in Fig. 12.6.10.

n	$\frac{n\pi}{2}$	$\sin\frac{n\pi}{2}$	$\frac{1}{2}C_n$
0	0	0	$\frac{F_0}{2} = 1.0\frac{F_0}{2}$
1	$\frac{\pi}{2}$	1	$\left(\frac{2}{\pi}\right)\frac{F_0}{2} = 0.636\frac{F_0}{2}$
2	π	0	0
3	$\frac{3\pi}{2}$	-1	$\left(-\frac{2}{3\pi}\right)\frac{F_0}{2} = 0.212\frac{F_0}{2}$
4	2π	0	0
5	$\frac{5\pi}{2}$	1	$\left(\frac{2}{5\pi}\right)\frac{F_0}{2} = 0.127\frac{F_0}{2}$

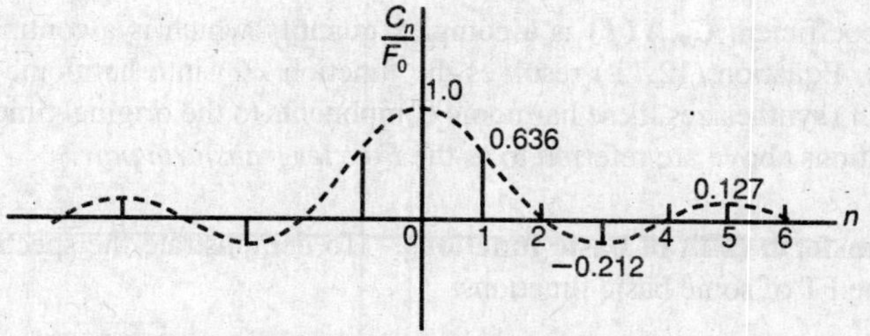

FIGURE 12.6.10. Fourier coefficients versus n.

The mean square value is determined from the equation

$$\begin{aligned}\overline{x^2} &= \lim_{T\to\infty}\frac{1}{2T}\int_{-T}^{T} x^2(t)\,dt\\ &= \lim_{T\to\infty}\frac{1}{2T}\int_{T}^{-T}\frac{1}{4}\left[\sum_n (C_n e^{in\omega_0 t} + C_n^* e^{-in\omega_0 t}\right]^2 dt\\ &= \sum_{n=1}^{\infty}\frac{C_nC_n^*}{2}\end{aligned}$$

and because $\overline{x^2} = \int_{\infty}^{0} S_f(\omega)d\omega$ the spectral density function can be represented by a series of delta functions:

$$S_f(\omega) = \sum_{n=1}^{\infty}\frac{C_nC_n^*}{2}\delta(\omega - n\omega_0)$$

12.7 FOURIER TRANSFORMS

The discrete frequency spectrum of periodic functions becomes a continuous one when the period T is extended to infinity. Random vibrations are generally not periodic and the determination of its continuous frequency spectrum requires the use of the Fourier integral, which can be regarded as a limiting case of the Fourier series as the period approaches infinity.

The Fourier transform has become the underlying operation for the modern time series analysis. In many of the modern instruments for spectral analysis, the calculation performed is that of determining the amplitude and phase of a given record.

The *Fourier integral* is defined by the equation

$$x(t) = \int_{-\infty}^{\infty} X(f)e^{i2\pi ft}\,df \tag{12.7.1}$$

In contrast to the summation of the discrete spectrum of sinusoids in the Fourier series, the Fourier integral can be regarded as a summation of the continuous spectrum of sinusoids. The quantity $X(f)$ in the previous equation is called the *Fourier transform* of $x(t)$, which can be evaluated from the equation

$$X(f) = \int_{-\infty}^{\infty} x(t)e^{-i2\pi ft}\,dt \tag{12.7.2}$$

Like the Fourier coefficient $C_n, X(f)$ is a complex quantity which is a continuous function of f from $-\infty$ to $+\infty$. Equation (12.7.2) resolves the function $x(t)$ into harmonic components $X(f)$ whereas Eq. (12.7.1) synthesizes these harmonic components to the original time function $x(t)$. The two previous equations above are referred to as the *Fourier transform pair*.

Fourier transform (FT) of basic functions. To demonstrate the spectral character of the FT, we consider the FT of some basic functions.

Example 12.7.1

$$x(t) = Ae^{i2\pi f_n t} \tag{a}$$

From Eq. (12.7.1), we have

$$Ae^{i2\pi f_n t} = \int_{-\infty}^{\infty} X(f)e^{i2\pi ft}\,df$$

Recognizing the properties of a delta function, this equation is satisfied if

$$X(f) = A\delta(f - f_n) \tag{b}$$

Substituting into Eq. (12.7.2), we obtain

$$\delta(f - f_n) = \int_{-\infty}^{\infty} e^{-i2\pi(f-f_n)t}\,dt$$

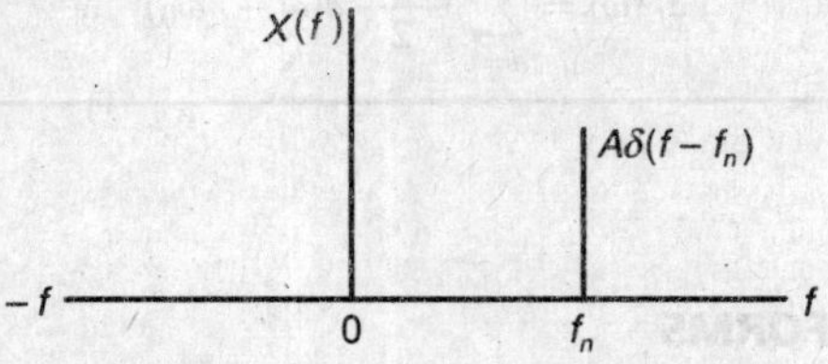

FIGURE 12.7.1. FT of $Ae^{i2\pi f_n t}$.

The FT of $x(t)$ is displayed in Fig. 12.7.1, which demonstrates its spectral character. ■

Example 12.7.2

$$x(t) = a_n \cos(2\pi f_n t) \tag{a}$$

Because

$$\cos 2\pi f_n t = \frac{1}{2}(e^{i2\pi f_n t} + e^{-i2\pi f_n t})$$

the result of Example 12.7.1 immediately gives

$$X(f) = \frac{a_n}{2}[\delta(f - f_n) - \delta(f + f_n)] \tag{b}$$

Figure 12.7.2 shows that $X(f)$ is a two-sided function of f.

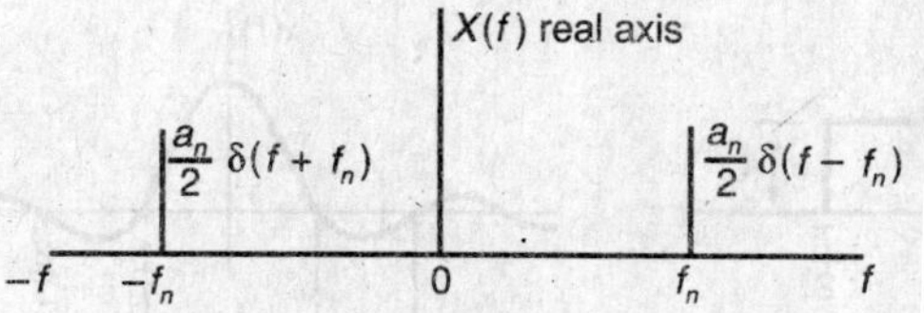

FIGURE 12.7.2. FT of $a_n \cos 2\pi f_n t$.

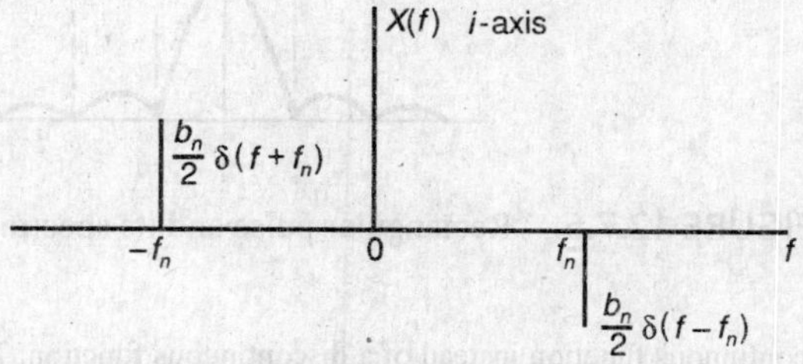

FIGURE 12.7.3. FT of $b_n \sin 2\pi f_n t$.

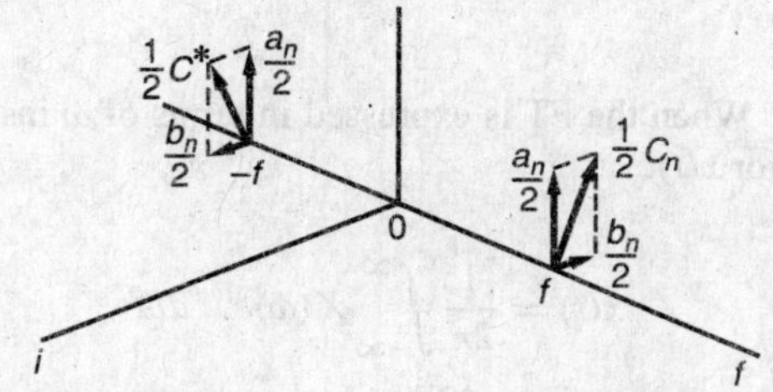

FIGURE 12.7.4. FT of $a_n \cos 2\pi f_n t + b_n \sin 2\pi f_n t$.

In a similar manner, the FT of $b_n \sin 2\pi f_n t$ is

$$X(f) = -i\frac{b_n}{2}[\delta(f - f_n) - \delta(f + f_n)]$$

which is shown on the imaginary plane of Fig. 12.7.3.

If we put the two FTs together in perpendicular planes, as shown in Fig. 12.7.4, we obtain the complex conjugate coefficients $C_n = a_n - ib_n$ and $C_n^* = a_n + ib_n$. Thus, the product

$$\frac{C_n C_n^*}{4} = \frac{1}{4}(a_n^2 + b_n^2) = c_n c_n^*$$

is the square of the magnitude of the Fourier series, which is generally plotted at $\pm f$.

Example 12.7.3

We next determine the FT of a rectangular pulse, which is an example of an aperiodic function. (See Fig. 12.7.5.) Its FT is

$$X(f) = \int_{-\infty}^{\infty} x(t)e^{-i2\pi ft}\,dt = \int_{-T/2}^{T/2} Ae^{-i2\pi ft}\,dt = AT\left(\frac{\sin \pi fT}{\pi fT}\right)$$

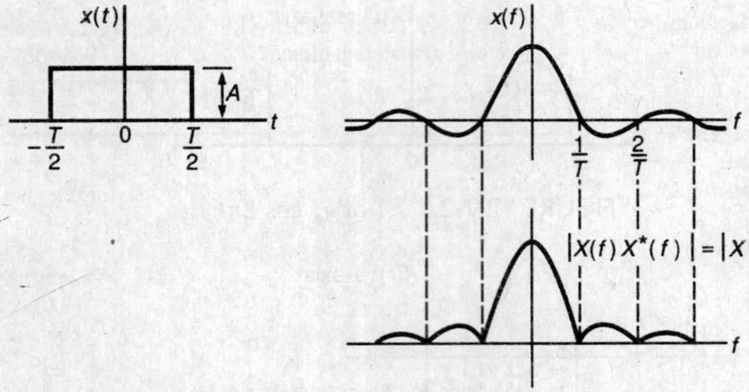

FIGURE 12.7.5. Rectangular pulse and its spectra.

Note that the FT is now a continuous function instead of a discontinuous function. The product XX^*, which is a real number, is also plotted here. Later it will be shown to be equal to the spectral density function.

■

FTs of derivatives. When the FT is expressed in terms of ω instead of f, a factor $1/2\pi$ is introduced in the equation for $x(t)$:

$$x(t) = \frac{1}{2\pi}\int_{-\infty}^{\infty} X(\omega)e^{i\omega t}d\omega \tag{12.7.3}$$

$$X(\omega) = \int_{-\infty}^{\infty} x(t)e^{-i\omega t}dt \tag{12.7.4}$$

This form is sometimes preferred in developing mathematical relationships. For example, if we differentiate Eq. (12.7.3) with respect to t, we obtain the FT pair:

$$\dot{x}(t) = \frac{1}{2\pi}\int_{-\infty}^{\infty} [i\omega X(\omega)]e^{i\omega t}d\omega$$

$$i\omega X(\omega) = \int_{-\infty}^{\infty} \dot{x}(t)e^{-i\omega t}\,dt$$

Thus, the FT of a derivative is simply the FT of the function multiplied by $i\omega$:

$$FT[\dot{x}(t)] = i\omega FT[x(t)] \tag{12.7.5}$$

Differentiating again, we obtain

$$FT[\ddot{x}(t)] = -\omega^2 FT[x(t)] \tag{12.7.6}$$

These equations enable one to conveniently take the FT of differential equations. For example, if we take the FT of the differential equation

$$m\ddot{y} + c\dot{y} + ky = x(t)$$

we obtain

$$(-m\omega^2 + i\omega c + k)Y(\omega) = X(\omega)$$

where $X(\omega)$ and $Y(\omega)$ are the FT of $x(t)$ and $Y(t)$, respectively.

Parseval's theorem. Parseval's theorem is a useful tool for converting time integration into frequency integration. If $X_1(f)$ and $X_2(f)$ are Fourier transforms of real time functions $x_1(t)$ and $x_2(t)$, respectively, Parseval's theorem states that

$$\begin{aligned}\int_{-\infty}^{\infty} x_1(t)x_2(t)\,dt &= \int_{-\infty}^{\infty} X_1(f)X_2^*(f)\,df \\ &= \int_{-\infty}^{\infty} X_1^*(f)X_2(f)\,df\end{aligned} \tag{12.7.7}$$

This relationship may be proved using the Fourier transform as follows:

$$x_1(t)x_2(t) = x_2(t)\int_{-\infty}^{\infty} X_1(f)e^{i2\pi ft}\,df$$

$$\begin{aligned}\int_{-\infty}^{\infty} x_1(t)x_2(t)\,dt &= \int_{-\infty}^{\infty} x_2(t)\int_{-\infty}^{\infty} X_1(f)e^{i2\pi ft}df\,dt \\ &= \int_{-\infty}^{\infty} X_1(f)\left[\int_{-\infty}^{\infty} x_2(t)e^{i2\pi ft}\,dt\right]df \\ &= \int_{-\infty}^{\infty} X_1(f)X_2^*(f)\,df\end{aligned}$$

All the previous formulas for the mean square value, autocorrelation, and cross correlation can now be expressed in terms of the Fourier transform by Parseval's theorem.

Example 12.7.4

Express the mean square value in terms of the Fourier transform. Letting $x_1(t) = x_2(t) = x(t)$, and averaging over T, which is allowed to go to ∞, we obtain

$$\overline{x^2} = \lim_{T\to\infty}\frac{1}{T}\int_{-T/2}^{T/2} x^2(t)\,dt = \int_{-\infty}^{\infty}\lim_{T\to\infty}\frac{1}{T}X(f)X^*(f)\,df$$

Comparing this with Eq. (12.6.6), we obtain the relationship

$$S(f_{\pm}) = \lim_{T\to\infty}\frac{1}{T}X(f)X^*(f) \tag{12.7.8}$$

where $S(f_{\pm})$ is the spectral density function over positive and negative frequencies.

■

Example 12.7.5

Express the autocorrelation in terms of the Fourier transform. We begin with the Fourier transform of $x(t+\tau)$:

$$x(t+\tau) = \int_{-\infty}^{\infty} X(f)e^{i2\pi f(t+\tau)}\,df$$

Substituting this into the expression for the autocorrelation, we obtain

$$\begin{aligned}
R(\tau) &= \lim_{T\to\infty}\frac{1}{T}\int_{-\infty}^{\infty} x(t)x(t+\tau)\,dt \\
&= \lim_{T\to\infty}\frac{1}{T}\int_{-\infty}^{\infty} x(t)\int_{-\infty}^{\infty} X(f)e^{i2\pi ft}e^{i2\pi f\tau}\,df\,dt \\
&= \int_{-\infty}^{\infty}\frac{1}{T}\left[\int_{-\infty}^{\infty} x(t)e^{i2\pi ft}\,dt\right]X(f)e^{i2\pi f\tau}\,df \\
&= \int_{-\infty}^{\infty}\left[\lim_{T\to\infty}\frac{1}{T}X^*(f)X(f)\right]e^{i2\pi f\tau}\,df
\end{aligned}$$

By substituting from Eq. (12.7.8) the preceding equation becomes

$$R(\tau) = \int_{-\infty}^{\infty} S(f)e^{i2\pi f\tau}\,df \tag{12.7.9}$$

The inverse of the preceding equation is also available from the Fourier transform:

$$S(f) = \int_{-\infty}^{\infty} R(\tau)e^{-i2\pi f\tau}\,d\tau \tag{12.7.10}$$

Because $R(\tau)$ is symmetric about $\tau = 0$, the last equation can also be written as

$$S(f) = 2\int_{0}^{\infty} R(\tau)\cos 2\pi f\tau\,d\tau \tag{12.7.11}$$

These are the *Wiener–Khintchine* equations, and they state that the spectral density function is the FT of the autocorrelation function.

As a parallel to the Wiener–Khintchine equations, we can define the cross correlation between two quantities $x(t)$ and $y(t)$ as

$$\begin{aligned}
R_{xy}(\tau) = \langle x(t)y(t+\tau)\rangle &= \lim_{T\to\infty}\frac{1}{T}\int_{-T/2}^{T/2} x(t)y(t+\tau)\,dt \\
&= \int_{-\infty}^{\infty}\lim_{T\to\infty}\frac{1}{T}X^*(f)Y(f)e^{i2\pi f\tau}\,df
\end{aligned} \tag{12.7.12}$$

$$R_{xy}(\tau) = \int_{-\infty}^{\infty} S_{xy}(f)e^{i2\pi f\tau}\,df$$

where the cross-spectral density is defined as

$$\begin{aligned}
S_{xy}(f) &= \lim_{T\to\infty}\frac{1}{T}X^*(f)Y(f) \qquad -\infty \leqslant f \leqslant \infty \\
&= \lim_{T\to\infty}\frac{1}{T}X(f)Y^*(f) \\
&= S^*_{xy}(f) = S_{xy}(-f)
\end{aligned} \tag{12.7.13}$$

Its inverse from the Fourier transform is

$$S_{xy}(f) = \int_{-\infty}^{\infty} R_{xy}(\tau)e^{-i2\pi f\tau}\,d\tau \tag{12.7.14}$$

which is parallel to Eq. (12.7.10). Unlike the autocorrelation, the cross-correlation and the cross-spectral density functions are, in general, not even functions; hence, the limits $-\infty$ to $+\infty$ are retained.

■

Example 12.7.6

Using the relationship

$$S(f) = 2\int_0^\infty R(\tau)\cos 2\pi f\tau\, d\tau$$

and the results of Example 12.5.1,

$$R(\tau) = A^2(T-\tau)$$

find $S(f)$ for the rectangular pulse.

Solution Because $R(\tau) = 0$ for τ outside $\pm T$, we have

$$\begin{aligned}
S(f) &= 2\int_0^T A^2(T-\tau)\cos 2\pi f\tau\, d\tau \\
&= 2A^2T\int_0^T \cos 2\pi f\tau\, d\tau - 2A^2\int_0^T \tau\cos 2\pi f\tau\, dt \\
&= 2A^2T\left.\frac{\sin 2\pi f\tau}{2\pi f}\right|_0^T - 2A^2\left[\frac{\cos 2\pi f\tau}{(2\pi f)^2} + \frac{\tau}{2\pi f}\sin 2\pi f\tau\right]_0^T \\
&= \frac{2A^2}{(2\pi f)^2}(1-\cos 2\pi fT) = A^2T^2\left(\frac{\sin\pi fT}{\pi fT}\right)^2
\end{aligned}$$

Thus, the power spectral density of a rectangular pulse using Eq. (12.7.11) is

$$S(f) = A^2T^2\left(\frac{\sin\pi fT}{\pi fT}\right)^2$$

Note from Example 12.7.3 that this is also equal to $X(f)X^*(f) = |X(f)|^2$.

■

Example 12.7.7

Show that the frequency response function $H(\omega)$ is the Fourier transform of the impulse response function $h(t)$.

Solution From the convolution integral, Eq. (4.2.1), the response equation in terms of the impulse response function is

$$x(t) = \int_{-\infty}^t f(\xi)h(t-\xi)\, d\xi$$

where the lower limit has been extended to $-\infty$ to account for all past excitations. By letting $\tau = (t-\xi)$, the last integral becomes

$$x(t) = \int_0^\infty f(t-\tau)h(\tau)\, d\tau$$

For a harmonic excitation $f(t) = e^{i\omega t}$, the preceding equation becomes

$$\begin{aligned}
x(t) &= \int_0^\infty e^{i\omega(t-\tau)}h(\tau)\, d\tau \\
&= e^{i\omega t}\int_0^\infty h(\tau)e^{-i\omega\tau}\, d\tau
\end{aligned}$$

Because the steady-state output for the input $y(t) = e^{i\omega t}$ is $x = H(\omega)e^{i\omega t}$, the frequency-response function is

$$H(\omega) = \int_0^{\infty} h(\tau)e^{-i\omega\tau}d\tau = \int_{-\infty}^{\infty} h(\tau)e^{i\omega\tau}d\tau$$

which is the FT of the impulse response function $h(t)$. The lower limit in the preceding integral has been changed from 0 to $-\infty$ because $h(t) = 0$ for negative t.

12.8 FTS AND RESPONSE

In engineering design, we often need to know the relationship between different points in the system. For example, how much of the roughness of a typical road is transmitted through the suspension system to the body of an automobile? (Here the term transfer function* is often used for the frequency-response function.) Furthermore, it is often not possible to introduce a harmonic excitation to the input point of the system. It may be necessary to accept measurements $x(t)$ and $Y(f)$ at two different points in the system for which the frequency response function is desired. The frequency response function for these points can be obtained by taking the FT of the input and output. The quantity $H(\omega)$ is then available from

$$H(\omega) = \frac{Y(\omega)}{X(\omega)} = \frac{\text{FT of output}}{\text{FT of input}} \tag{12.8.1}$$

where $X(\omega)$ and $Y(\omega)$ are the FT of $x(t)$ and $y(t)$.

If we multiply and divide this equation by the complex conjugate $X^*(\omega)$, the result is

$$H(\omega) = \frac{Y(\omega)X^*(\omega)}{X(\omega)X^*(\omega)} \tag{12.8.2}$$

The denominator $X(\omega)X^*(\omega)$ is now a real quantity. The numerator is the cross spectrum $Y(\omega)X^*(\omega)$ between the input and the output and is a complex quantity. The phase of $H(\omega)$ is then found from the real and imaginary parts of the cross spectrum, which is simply

$$|Y(\omega)|\underline{/\phi_y} \cdot |X^*(\omega)|\underline{/\phi_x} = |Y(\omega)X^*(\omega)|\underline{/\phi_y - \phi_x} \tag{12.8.3}$$

Another useful relationship can be found by multiplying $H(\omega)$ by its conjugate $H^*(\omega)$. The result is

$$H(\omega)H^*(\omega) = \frac{Y(\omega)Y^*(\omega)}{X(\omega)X^*(\omega)}$$

or

$$Y(\omega)Y^*(\omega) = |H(\omega)|^2 X(\omega)X^*(\omega) \tag{12.8.4}$$

Thus, the output power spectrum is equal to the square of the system transfer function multiplied by the input power spectrum. Obviously, each side of the previous equation is real and the phase does not enter in.

*Strictly speaking, the transfer function is the ratio of the Laplace transform of the output to the Laplace transform of the input. In the frequency domain, however, the real part of $s = \alpha + i\omega$ is zero, and the LT becomes the FT.

We wish now to examine the mean square value of the response. From Eq. (12.7.8), the mean square value of the input $x(t)$ is

$$\overline{x^2} = \int_{-\infty}^{\infty} S_x(f_\pm)\,df = \int_{-\infty}^{\infty} \lim_{T\to\infty} \frac{1}{T} X(f)X^*(f)\,df$$

The mean square value of the output $y(t)$ is

$$\overline{y^2} = \int_{-\infty}^{\infty} S_y(f_\pm)\,df = \int_{-\infty}^{\infty} \lim_{T\to\infty} \frac{1}{T} Y(f)Y^*(f)\,df$$

Substituting $YY^* = |H(f)|^2 XX^*$, we obtain

$$\begin{aligned}\overline{y^2} &= \int_{-\infty}^{\infty} |H(f)|^2 \left[\lim_{T\to\infty} \frac{1}{T} X(f)X^*(f)\right] df \\ &= \int_{-\infty}^{\infty} |H(f)|^2 S_x(f_\pm)\,df\end{aligned} \tag{12.8.5}$$

which is the mean square value of the response in terms of the system response function and the spectral density of the input.

In these expressions, $S(f_\pm)$ are the two-sided spectral density functions over both the positive and negative frequencies. Also, $S(f_\pm)$ are even functions. In actual practice, it is desirable to work with spectral densities over only the positive frequencies. Equation (12.8.5) can then be written as

$$\overline{y^2} = \int_{0}^{\infty} |H(f)|^2 S_x(f_+)\,df \tag{12.8.6}$$

and because the two expressions must result in the same value for the mean square value, the relationship between the two must be

$$S(f_+) = S(f) = 2S(f_\pm) \tag{12.8.7}$$

Some authors also use the expression

$$\overline{y^2} = \int_{0}^{\infty} |H(\omega)|^2 S_x(\omega)\,d\omega \tag{12.8.8}$$

Again, the equations must result in the same mean square value so that

$$2\pi S(\omega) = S(f) \tag{12.8.9}$$

For a single-DOF system, we have

$$H(f) = \frac{1/k}{[1-(f/f_n)^2] + i[2\zeta(f/f_n)]} \tag{12.8.10}$$

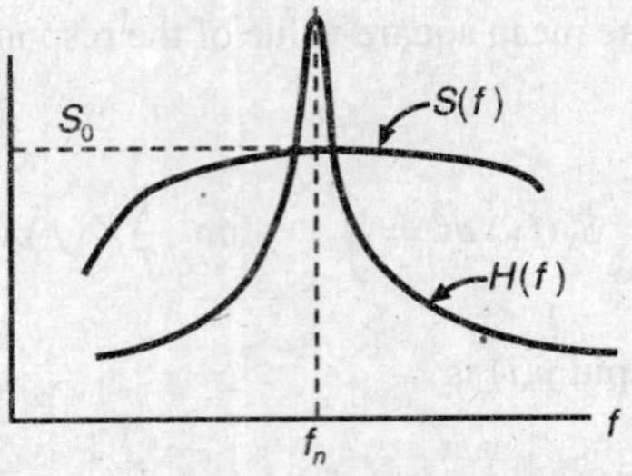

FIGURE 12.8.1. $S(f)$ and $H(f)$ leading to $\overline{y^2}$ of Equation 12.7.9.

If the system is lightly damped, the response function $H(f)$ is peaked steeply at resonance, and the system acts like a narrow-band filter. If the spectral density of excitation is broad, as in Fig. 12.8.1, the mean square response for the single-DOF system can be approximated by the equation

$$\overline{y^2} \cong \frac{f_n}{k^2} S_x(f_n) \frac{\pi}{4\zeta} \tag{12.8.11}$$

where

$$\frac{\pi}{4\zeta} = \int_0^\infty \frac{d(f/f_n)}{[1-(f/f_n)^2]^2 + [2\zeta(f/f_n)^2]}$$

and $S_x(f_n)$ is the spectral density of the excitation at frequency f_n.

Example 12.8.1

The response of any structure to a single-point random excitation can be computed by a simple numerical procedure, provided the spectral density of the excitation and the frequency response curve of the structure are known. For example, consider the structure of Fig. 12.8.2(a), whose base is subjected to a random acceleration input with the power spectral density function shown in Fig. 12.8.2(b). It is desired to compute the response of the point p and establish the probability of exceeding any specified acceleration.

The frequency response function $H(f)$ for the point p can be obtained experimentally by applying to the base a variable frequency sinusoidal shaker with a constant acceleration input a_0, and measuring the acceleration response at p. Dividing the measured acceleration by a_0, $H(f)$ may appear as in Fig. 12.8.2(c).

The mean square response $\overline{a_p^2}$ at p is calculated numerically from the equation

$$\overline{a_p^2} = \sum_i S(f_i)|H(f_i)|^2 \Delta f_i$$

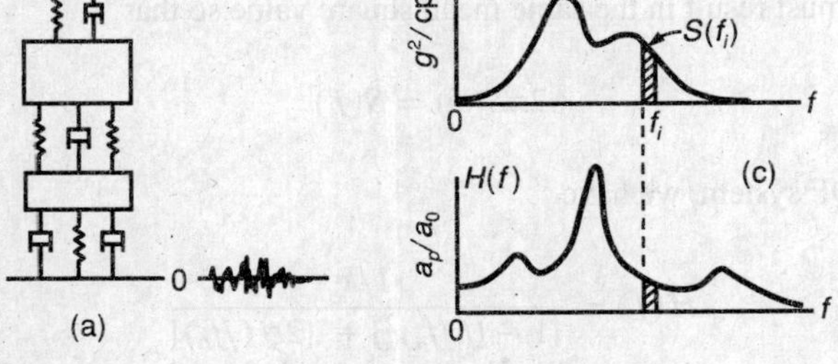

FIGURE 12.8.2.

TABLE 12.8.1 Numerical Example

f (cps)	Δf (cps)	$S(f_i)$ (g^2/cps)	$\lvert H(F_i)\rvert$ (Nondimensional)	$\lvert H(f_i)\rvert^2 \Delta f$ (cps)	$S(f_i)\lvert H(f_i)\rvert^2 \Delta f$ (g^2 units)
0	10	0	1.0	10.0	0
10	10	0	1.0	10.0	0
20	10	0.2	1.1	12.1	2.4
30	10	0.6	1.4	19.6	11.8
40	10	1.2	2.0	40.0	48.0
50	10	1.8	1.3	16.9	30.5
60	10	1.8	1.3	16.9	30.5
70	10	1.1	2.0	40.0	44.0
80	10	0.9	3.7	137.0	123.0
90	10	1.1	5.4	291.0	320.0
100	10	1.2	2.2	48.4	57.7
110	10	1.1	1.3	16.9	18.6
120	10	0.8	0.8	6.4	5.1
130	10	0.6	0.6	3.6	2.2
140	10	0.3	0.5	2.5	0.8
150	10	0.2	0.6	3.6	0.7
160	10	0.2	0.7	4.9	0.1
170	10	0.1	1.3	16.9	1.7
180	10	0.1	1.1	12.1	1.2
190	10	0.5	0.7	4.9	2.3
200	10	0	0.5	2.5	0
210	10	0	0.4	1.6	0
					$\overline{a^2} = 700.6g^2$
					$\sigma = \sqrt{700.6g^2} = 26.6g$

Table 12.8.1 illustrates the computational procedure.

The probability of exceeding specified accelerations are

$$p[|a| > 26.6g] = 31.7\%$$

$$p[a_{\text{peak}} > 26.6g] = 60.7\%$$

$$p[|a| > 79.8g] = 0.3\%$$

$$p[a_{\text{peak}} > 79.8g] = 1.2\%$$

■

SUGGESTED READING

[1] BENDAT, J. S. *Principles and Applications of Random Noise Theory.* New York: John Wiley & Sons, 1958.

[2] BLACKMAN, R. B. AND TUKEY, J. W. *The Measurement of Power Spectra.* New York: Dover Publications, 1958.

[3] CLARKSON, B. L. "The Effect of Jet Noise on Aircraft Structures," *Aeronautical Quarterly*, Vol. 10, Part 2, May 1959.

[4] CRAMER, H. *The Elements of Probability Theory*. New York: John Wiley & Sons, 1955.

[5] CRANDALL, S. H. *Random Vibration.* Cambridge, Mass.: The Technology Press of M.I.T., 1948.

[6] CRANDALL, S. H. *Random Vibration*, Vol. 2. Cambridge, Mass.: The Technology Press of M.I.T., 1963.

[7] ROBSON, J. D. *Random Vibration.* Edinburgh: Edinburgh University Press, 1964.

[8] THOMSON, W. T. AND BARTON, M. V. "The Response of Mechanical Systems to Random Excitation," *J. Appl. Mech.*, June 1957, pp. 248–251.

REFERENCES

[1] S.O. RICE, *Mathematical Analysis of Random Noise* (New York: Dover Publications, 1954).

[2] See J. S. BENDAT, and A. G. PIERSOL, *Random Data* (New York: John Wiley & Sons, 1971), p. 96.

PROBLEMS

12.1. Give examples of random data and indicate classifications for each example.

12.2. Discuss the differences between nonstationary, stationary, and ergodic data.

12.3. Throw a coin 50 times, recording 1 for head and 0 for tail. Determine the probability of obtaining heads by dividing the cumulative heads by the number of throws and plot this number as a function of the number of throws. The curve should approach 0.5.

12.4. Discuss what we mean by the expected value. What is the expected number of heads when eight coins are thrown 100 times; 1000 times? What is the probability for tails?

12.5. A sine wave with a steady component has the equation

$$x = A_0 + A_1 \sin \omega t$$

Determine the expected values $E(x)$ and $E(x^2)$.

12.6. Determine the mean and mean square values for the rectified sine wave.

12.7. For the series of triangular waves shown in Fig. P12.7, determine the mean and the mean square values.

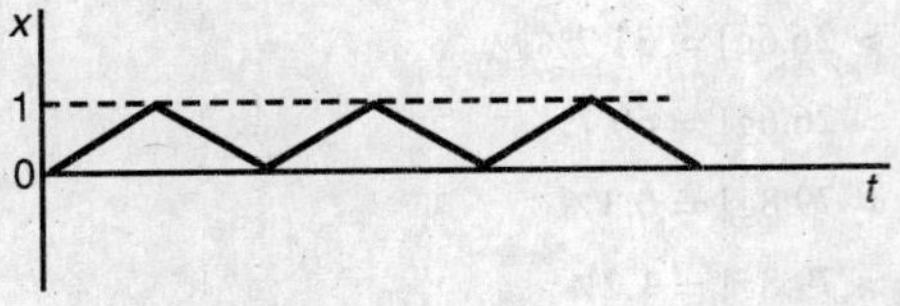

FIGURE P12.7.

12.8. Show that for the Gaussian probability distribution $p(x)$, the central moments are given by

$$E(x^n) = \int_{-\infty}^{\infty} x^n p(x)\,dx$$

$$= \begin{cases} 0 & \text{for } n \text{ odd} \\ 1 \cdot 3 \cdot 5 \cdots (n-1)\sigma^n & \text{for } n \text{ even} \end{cases}$$

12.9. Discuss why the probability distribution of the peak values of a random function should follow the Rayleigh distribution or one similar in shape to it.

12.10. What would the cumulative probability and the probability density curves look like for the rectangular wave shown in Fig. P12.10?

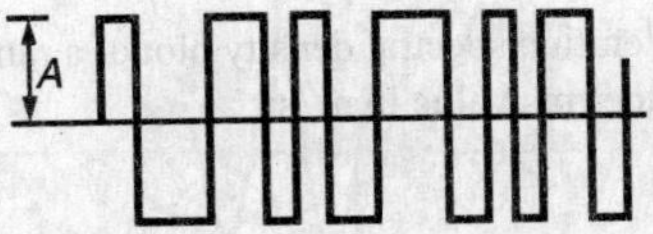

FIGURE P12.10.

12.11. Derive the equations for the cumulative probability and the probability density functions of the sine wave. Plot these results.

12.12. Determine the autocorrelation of the rectangular pulse and plot it against τ.

12.13. Determine the autocorrelation of the triangular wave shown in Fig. P12.13.

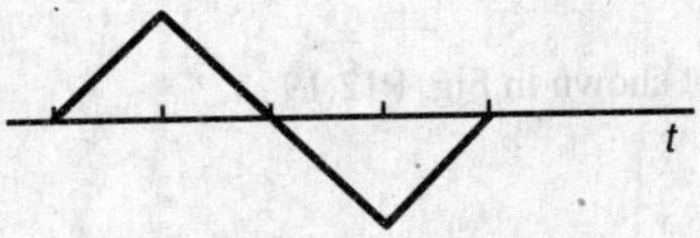

FIGURE P12.13.

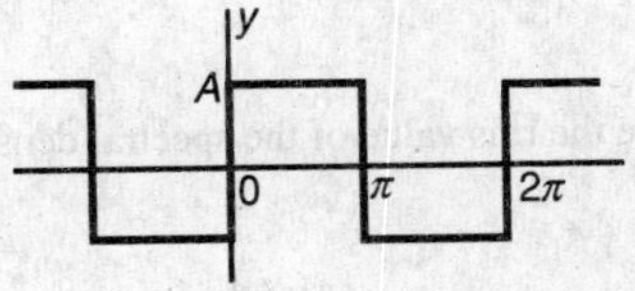

FIGURE P12.15.

12.14. Determine the autocorrelation of a cosine wave $x(t) = A \cos t$, and plot it against τ.

12.15. Determine the autocorrelation of the rectangular wave shown in Fig. P12.15.

12.16. Determine the autocorrelation of the binary sequence shown in Fig. P12.16. *Suggestion*: Trace the wave on transparent graph paper and shift it through τ.

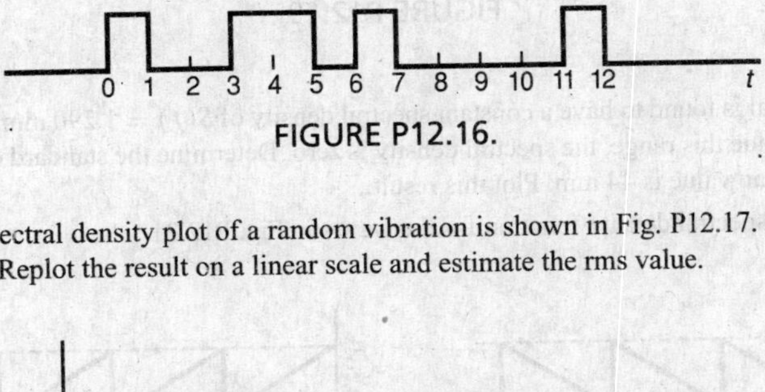

FIGURE P12.16.

12.17. The power spectral density plot of a random vibration is shown in Fig. P12.17. The slopes represent a 6-dB/octave. Replot the result on a linear scale and estimate the rms value.

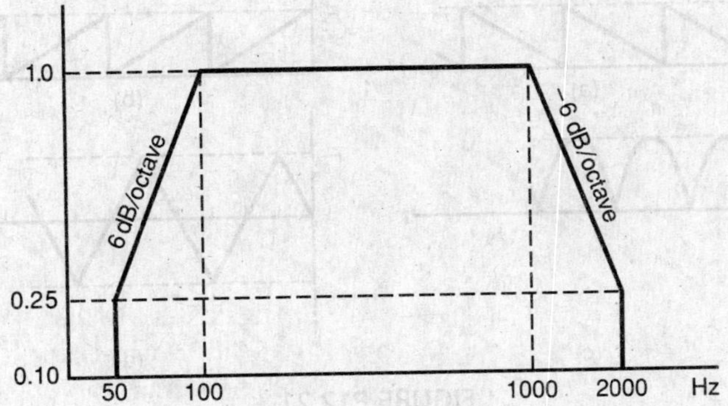

FIGURE P12.17.

12.18. Figure P12.18 shows the acceleration spectral density plot of a random vibration. Approximate the area by a rectangle and determine the rms value in m/s^2.

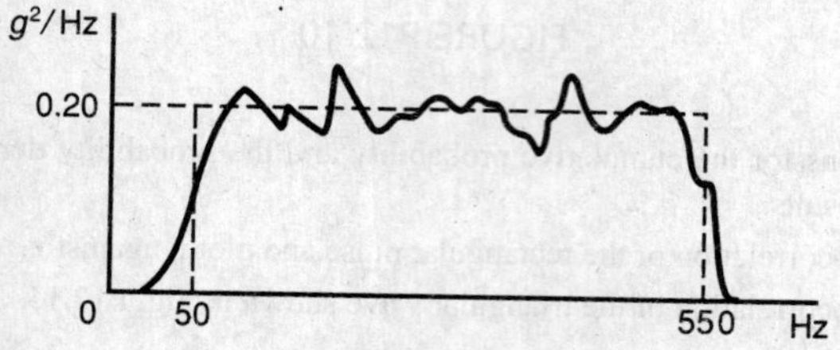

FIGURE P12.18.

12.19. Determine the rms value of the spectral density plot shown in Fig. P12.19.

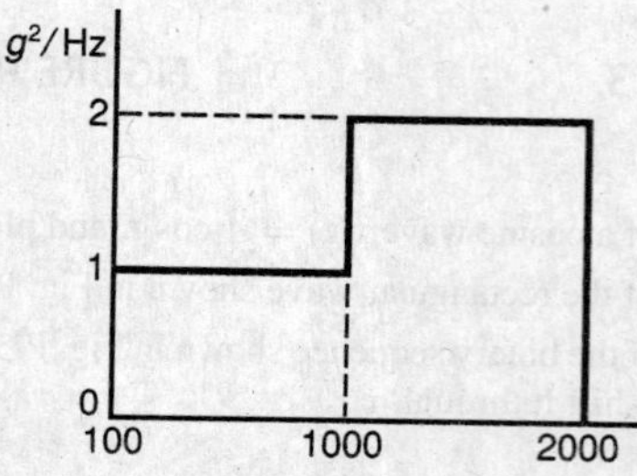

FIGURE P12.19.

12.20. A random signal is found to have a constant spectral density of $S(f) = 1.290$ mm^2/cps between 20 and 2000 cps. Outside this range, the spectral density is zero. Determine the standard deviation and the rms value if the mean value is 44 mm. Plot this result.

12.21. Determine the spectral density function for the waves in Fig. P12.21.

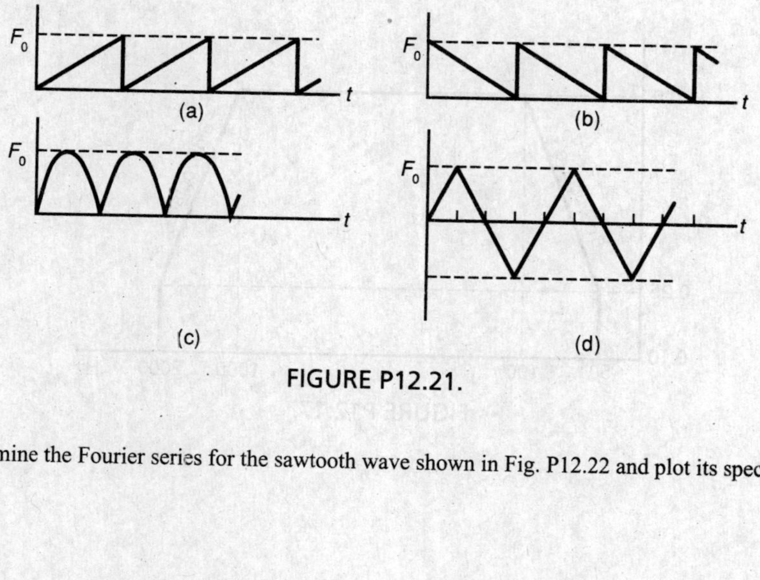

FIGURE P12.21.

12.22. Determine the Fourier series for the sawtooth wave shown in Fig. P12.22 and plot its spectral density.

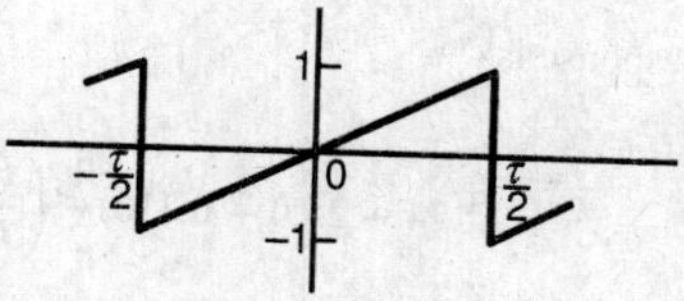

FIGURE P12.22.

12.23. Derive the equation for the coefficients C_n of the periodic function

$$f(t) = \text{Re} \sum_{n=0}^{\infty} C_n e^{in\omega_0 t}$$

12.24. Show that for Prob. 12.23, $C_{-n} = C_n^*$, and that $f(t)$ can be written as

$$f(t) = \sum_{n=-\infty}^{\infty} C_n e^{in\omega_0 t}$$

12.25. Determine the complex form of the Fourier series for the rectangular wave shown in Fig. P12.15 and plot its spectral density.

12.26. Determine the complex form of the Fourier series for the wave shown in Fig. P12.26 and plot its spectral density.

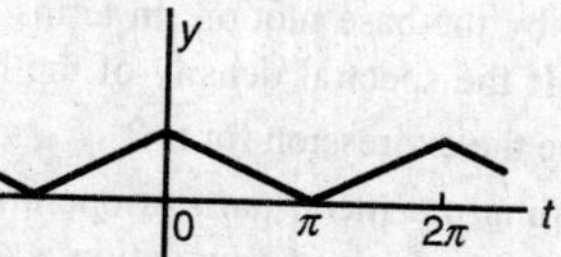

FIGURE P12.26.

12.27. The differential equation of a system with structural damping is given as

$$m\bar{x} + k(1 + iy)x = F(t)$$

Determine the frequency-response function.

12.28. The sharpness of the frequency-response curve near resonance is often expressed in terms of $Q = \frac{1}{2}\zeta$. Points on either side of resonance where the response falls to a value $1/\sqrt{2}$ are called half-power points. Determine the respective frequencies of the half-power points in terms of ω_n and Q.

12.29. Show that

$$\int_0^{\infty} \frac{d\eta}{(1-\eta^2)^2 + (2\zeta\eta)^2} = \frac{\pi}{4\zeta} \quad \text{for } \zeta \ll 1$$

12.30. In Example 12.7.3, what is the probability of the instantaneous acceleration exceeding a value 53.2g? Of the peak value exceeding this value?

12.31. A single-DOF system with natural frequency ω_n and damping factor $\zeta = 0.10$ is excited by the force

$$F(t) = F\cos(0.5\omega_n t - \theta_1) + F\cos(\omega_n t - \theta^2) + F\cos(2\omega_n t - \theta_3)$$

Show that the mean square response is

$$\overline{y^2} = (1.74 + 25.0 + 0.110)\frac{1}{2}\left(\frac{F}{k}\right)^2$$
$$= 13.43\left(\frac{F}{k}\right)^2$$

12.32. For a single-DOF system, the substitution of Eq. (12.8.10) into Eq. (12.8.6) results in

$$\overline{y^2} = \int_0^\infty S_x(f_+)\frac{1}{k^2}\frac{df}{[1-(f/f_n)^2]^2 + [2\zeta(f/f_n)]^2}$$

where $S_x(f_+)$ is the spectral density of the excitation force. When the damping ζ is small and the variation of $S_x(f_+)$ is gradual, the last equation becomes

$$\overline{y^2} \cong S_x(f_n)\frac{f_n}{k^2}\int_0^\infty \frac{d(f/f_n)}{[1-(f/f_n)^2]^2 + [2\zeta(f/f_n)]^2}$$
$$= S_x(f_n)\frac{f_n}{k^2}\frac{\pi}{4\zeta}$$

which is Eq. (12.8.11). Derive a similar equation for the mean square value of the relative motion z of a single-DOF system excited by the base motion, in terms of the spectral density $S_y(f_+)$ of the base acceleration. (See Sec. 3.6.) If the spectral density of the base acceleration is constant over a given frequency range, what must be the expression for $\overline{z^2}$?

12.33. A large hydraulic press stamping out metal parts is operating under a series of forces approximated by Fig. P12.33. The mass of the press on its foundation is 40 kg and its natural frequency is 2.20 Hz. Determine the Fourier spectrum of the excitation and the mean square value of the response.

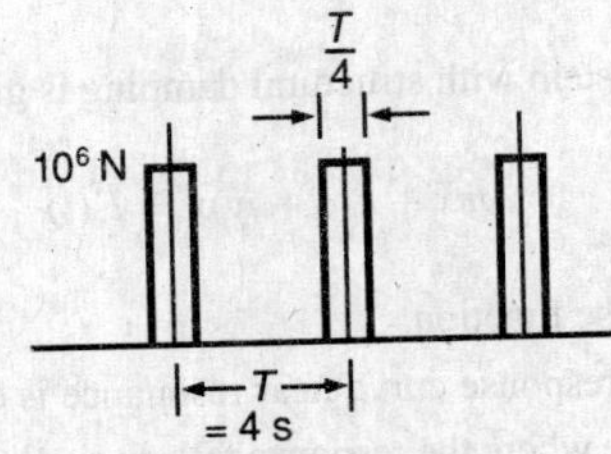

FIGURE P12.33.

12.34. An SDF system with viscous damping $\zeta = 0.03$ is excited by white-noise excitation $F(t)$ having a constant power spectral density of $5 \times 10^6\ N^2/Hz$. The system has a natural frequency of $\omega_n = 30$ rad/s and a mass of 1500 kg. Determine σ. Assuming Rayleigh distribution for peaks, determine the probability that the maximum peak response will exceed 0.037 m.

12.35. A jet engine with a mass of 272 kg is tested on a stand, which results in a natural frequency of 26 Hz. The spectral density of the jet force under test is shown in Fig. P12.35. Determine the probability of the vibration amplitude in the axial direction of the jet thrust exceeding 0.012 m. Assume $\zeta = 0.10$.

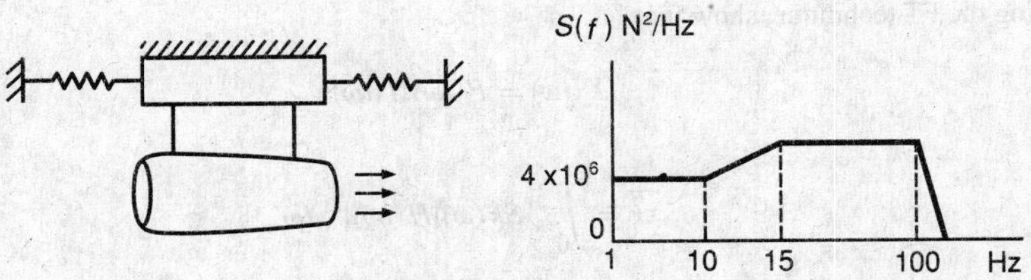

FIGURE P12.35.

M **12.36.** Referring to Sec. 3.6, we can write the equation for the absolute acceleration of the mass undergoing base excitation as

$$\ddot{x} = \frac{k + i\omega c}{k - m\omega^2 + i\omega c} \cdot \ddot{y}$$

Determine the equation for the mean square acceleration $\overline{\ddot{x}^2}$. Establish a numerical integration technique for the computer evaluation of $\overline{\ddot{x}^2}$.

12.37. A radar dish with a mass of 60 kg is subject to wind loads with the spectral density shown in Fig. P12.37. The dish-support system has a natural frequency of 4 Hz. Determine the mean square response and the probability of the dish exceeding a vibration amplitude of 0.132 m. Assume $\zeta = 0.05$.

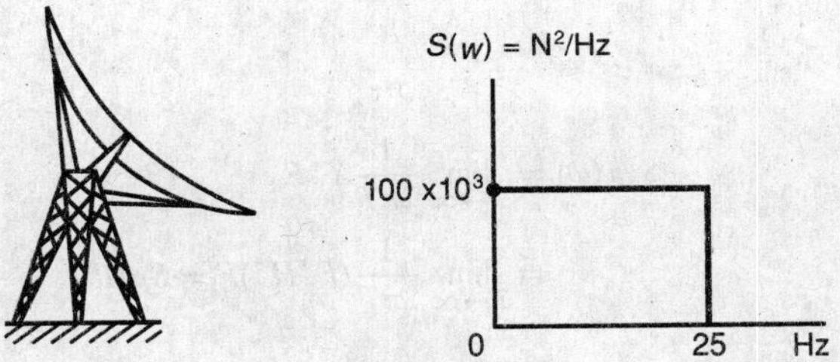

FIGURE P12.37.

12.38. Find the frequency spectrum of the rectangular pulse shown in Fig. P12.38.

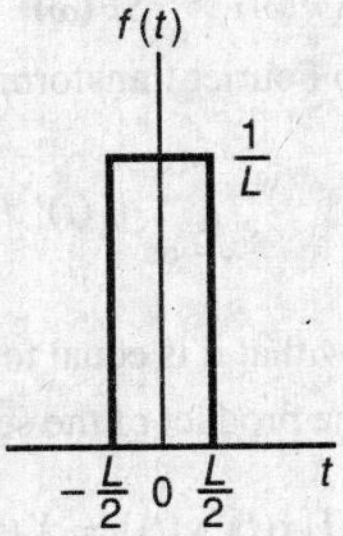

FIGURE P12.38.

12.39. Starting with the relationship

$$x(t) = \int_0^\infty f(t - \xi)h(\xi)\,d\xi$$

and using the FT technique, show that

$$X(i\omega) = F(i\omega)H(i\omega)$$

and

$$\overline{x^2} = \int_0^{\infty} S_F(\omega)|H(i\omega)|^2\, d\omega$$

where

$$S_F(\omega) = \lim_{T\to\infty} \frac{1}{2\pi T} F(i\omega)F^*(i\omega)$$

12.40. Starting with the relationship

$$H(i\omega) = |H(i\omega)|e^{i\phi(\omega)}$$

show that

$$\frac{H(i\omega)}{H^*(i\omega)} = e^{i2\phi(\omega)}$$

12.41. Starting with the equations

$$\begin{aligned} S_{FX}(\omega) &= \lim_{T\to\infty} \frac{1}{2\pi T} F^*(i\omega)X(i\omega) \\ &= \lim_{T\to\infty} \frac{1}{2\pi T} F(FH) = S_F H \end{aligned}$$

and

$$\begin{aligned} S_{XF}(\omega) &= \lim_{T\to\infty} \frac{1}{2\pi T} X^* F \\ &= \lim_{T\to\infty} \frac{1}{2\pi T} (F^* H^*)F = S_F H^* \end{aligned}$$

show that

$$\frac{S_{FX}(\omega)}{S_{XF}(\omega)} = e^{i2\phi(\omega)}$$

and

$$\frac{S_F(\omega)}{S_{XF}(\omega)} = \frac{S_{FX}(\omega)}{S_F(\omega)} = H(i\omega)$$

12.42. Show that the unit step function has no Fourier transform. *Hint:* Examine

$$\int_{-\infty}^{\infty} |f(t)|\, dt$$

12.43. Determine the FT of $x(t - t_0)$ and show that it is equal to $e^{-i2\pi f t_0}X(f)$, where $X(f) = \text{FT}[x(t)]$.

12.44. Prove that the FT of a convolution is the product of the separate FT.

$$\text{FT}[x(t)^* y(t)] = X(f)Y(f)$$

12.45. Using the derivative theorem, show that the FT of the derivative of a rectangular pulse is a sine wave.

12.46. The differential equation for the longitudinal motion of a uniform slender rod is

$$\frac{\partial^2 u}{\partial t^2} = c^2 \frac{\partial^2 u}{\partial x^2}$$

Show that for an arbitrary axial force at the end $x = 0$, with the other end $x = l$ free, the Laplace transform of the response is

$$\bar{u}(x, s) = \frac{-c\bar{F}(s)e^{-s(l/c)}}{sAE(1 - e^{-2s(l/c)})}\left[e^{(s/c)(x-l)} + e^{-(s/c)(s-l)}\right]$$

12.47. If the force in Prob. 12.46 is harmonic and equal to $F(t) = F_0 e^{i\omega t}$, show that

$$u(x, t) = \frac{cF_0 e^{i\omega t}\cos[(\omega l/c)(x/l - l)]}{\omega AE \sin(\omega l/c)}$$

and

$$\sigma(x, t) = \frac{-\sin[(\omega l/c)(x/l - 1)]}{\sin(\omega l/c)}\frac{F_0}{A}e^{i\omega t}$$

where σ is the stress.

12.48. With $S(\omega)$ as the spectral density of the excitation stress at $x = 0$, show that the mean square stress in Prob. 12.46 is

$$\overline{\sigma^2} \cong \frac{2\pi}{\gamma}\sum_n \frac{c}{n\pi l}S(\omega_n)\sin^2 n\pi\frac{x}{l}$$

where structural damping is assumed. The normal modes of the problem are

$$\varphi_n(x) = \sqrt{2}\cos n\pi\left(\frac{x}{l} - 1\right),$$

$$\omega_n = n\pi\left(\frac{c}{l}\right), \quad c = \sqrt{\frac{AE}{m}}$$

12.49. The ski-lift system of Prob. 5.89 is forced by wind on the mass. The force has white-noise characteristics, and $\sigma = 0.5$. Determine the probability that the maximum peak response will exceed 10°.

12.50. For some random variables the integral in Eq. (12.4.4) does not converge. Consider a function given by

$$p(x) = \frac{a}{b + x^2}$$

For which values of a and b is this a probability density function? The resulting probability distribution is called the Cauchy distribution. Does it have finite variance?

12.51. The exponential distribution is given by $P(x) = 1 - \exp(-\lambda x)$. Derive its probability density function, mean and the variance. This distribution often occurs in practice as a description of the time elapsing between unpredictable events.

CHAPTER 13

Nonlinear Vibrations

Linear system analysis serves to explain much of the behavior of oscillatory systems. However, there are a number of oscillatory phenomena that cannot be predicted or explained by the linear theory.

In the linear systems that we have studied, cause and effect are related linearly; i.e., if we double the load, the response is doubled. In a nonlinear system, this relationship between cause and effect is no longer proportional. For example, the center of an oil can may move proportionally to the force for small loads, but at a certain critical load, it will snap over to a large displacement. The same phenomenon is also encountered in the buckling of columns, electrical oscillations of circuits containing inductance with an iron core, and vibration of mechanical systems with nonlinear restoring forces.

The differential equation describing a nonlinear oscillatory system can have the general form

$$\ddot{x} + f(\dot{x}, x, t) = 0$$

Such equations are distinguished from linear equations in that the principle of superposition does not hold for their solution.

Analytical procedures for the treatment of nonlinear differential equations are difficult and require extensive mathematical study. Exact solutions that are known are relatively few, and a large part of the progress in the knowledge of nonlinear systems comes from approximate and graphical solutions and from studies made on computing machines. Much can be learned about a nonlinear system, however, by using the state space approach and studying the motion presented in the phase plane.

13.1 PHASE PLANE

In an *autonomous* system, time t does not appear explicitly in the differential equation of motion. Thus, only the differential of time, dt, appears in such an equation.

We first study an autonomous system with the differential equation

$$\ddot{x} + f(x, \dot{x}) = 0 \tag{13.1.1}$$

where $f(x, \dot{x})$ can be a nonlinear function of x and $\dot{x}$. In the method of *state space*, we express the last equation in terms of two first-order equations as follows:

$$\begin{aligned} \dot{x} &= y \\ \dot{y} &= -f(x, y) \end{aligned} \tag{13.1.2}$$

If x and y are Cartesian coordinates, the xy-plane is called the *phase plane*. The *state* of the system is defined by the coordinate x and $y = \dot{x}$, which represents a point on the phase plane. As the state of the system changes, the point on the phase plane moves, thereby generating a curve that is called the *trajectory*.

Another useful concept is the *state speed* V defined by the equation

$$V = \sqrt{\dot{x}^2 + \dot{y}^2} \tag{13.1.3}$$

When the state speed is zero, an *equilibrium state* is reached in that both the velocity of $\dot{x}$ and the acceleration $\dot{y} = \ddot{x}$ are zero.

Dividing the second of Eq. (13.1.2) by the first, we obtain the relation

$$\frac{dy}{dx} = \frac{-f(x,y)}{y} = \phi(x,y) \tag{13.1.4}$$

Thus, for every point x, y in the phase plane for which $\phi(x,y)$ is not indeterminate, there is a unique slope of the trajectory.

If $y = 0$ (i.e., points along the x-axis) and $f(x,y) \neq 0$, the slope of the trajectory is infinite. Thus, all trajectories corresponding to such points must cross the x-axis at right angles.

If $y = 0$ and $f(x,y) = 0$, the slope is indeterminate. We define such points as *singular points*. Singular points correspond to a state of equilibrium in that both the velocity $y = \dot{x}$ and the force $\ddot{x} = \dot{y} = -f(x,y)$ are zero. Further discussion is required to establish whether the equilibrium represented by the singular point is stable or unstable.

Example 13.1.1

Determine the phase plane of a single-DOF oscillator:

$$\ddot{x} + \omega^2 x = 0$$

Solution With $y = \dot{x}$, this equation is written in terms of two first-order equations:

$$\dot{y} = -\omega^2 x$$
$$\dot{x} = y$$

Dividing, we obtain

$$\frac{dy}{dx} = -\frac{\omega^2 x}{y}$$

Separating variables and integrating

$$y^2 + \omega^2 x^2 = C$$

which is a series of ellipses, the size of which is determined by C. The preceding equation is also that of conservation of energy:

$$\frac{1}{2} m\dot{x}^2 + \frac{1}{2} kx^2 = C'$$

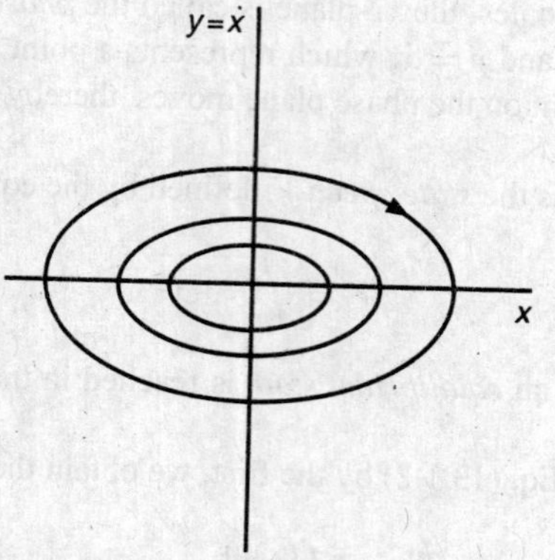

FIGURE 13.1.1.

Because the singular point is at $x = y = 0$, the phase plane plot appears as in Fig. 13.1.1. If y/ω is plotted in place of y, the ellipses of Fig. 13.1.1 reduce to circles.

13.2 CONSERVATIVE SYSTEMS

In a conservative system the total energy remains constant. Summing the kinetic and potential energies per unit mass, we have

$$\frac{1}{2}\dot{x}^2 + U(x) = E = \text{constant} \tag{13.2.1}$$

Solving for $y = \dot{x}$, the ordinate of the phase plane is given by the equation

$$y = \dot{x} = \pm\sqrt{2[E - U(x)]} \tag{13.2.2}$$

It is evident from this equation that the trajectories of a conservative system must be symmetric about the x-axis.

The differential equation of motion for a conservative system can be shown to have the form

$$\ddot{x} = f(x) \tag{13.2.3}$$

Because $\ddot{x} = \dot{x}(d\dot{x}/dx)$, the last equation can be written as

$$\dot{x}\,d\dot{x} - f(x)\,dx = 0 \tag{13.2.4}$$

Integrating, we have

$$\frac{\dot{x}^2}{2} - \int_0^x f(x)\,dx = E \tag{13.2.5}$$

and by comparison with Eq. (13.2.1) we find

$$U(x) = -\int_0^x f(x)\,dx$$
$$f(x) = -\frac{dU}{dx} \tag{13.2.6}$$

Thus, for a conservative system, the force is equal to the negative gradient of the potential energy.

With $y = \dot{x}$, Eq. (13.2.4) in the state space becomes

$$\frac{dy}{dx} = \frac{f(x)}{y} \tag{13.2.7}$$

We note from this equation that singular points correspond to $f(x) = 0$ and $y = \dot{x} = 0$, and hence are equilibrium points. Equation (13.2.6) then indicates that at the equilibrium points, the slope of the potential energy curve $U(x)$ must be zero. It can be shown that the minima of $U(x)$ are stable equilibrium positions, whereas the saddle points corresponding to the maxima of $U(x)$ are positions of unstable equilibrium.

Stability of equilibrium. By examining Eq. (13.2.2), the value of E is determined by the initial conditions of $x(0)$ and $y(0) = \dot{x}(0)$. If the initial conditions are large, E will also be large. For every position x, there is a potential $U(x)$; for motion to take place, E must be greater than $U(x)$. Otherwise, Eq. (13.2.2) shows that the velocity $y = \dot{x}$ is imaginary.

Figure 13.2.1 shows a general plot of $U(x)$ and the trajectory y vs. x for various values of E computed in Table 13.2.1 from Eq. (13.2.2).

For $E = 7$, $U(x)$ lies below $E = 7$ only between $x = 0$ to 1.2, $x = 3.8$ to 5.9, and $x = 7$ to 8.7. The trajectories corresponding to $E = 7$ are closed curves and the period associated with them can be found from Eq. (13.2.2) by integration:

$$\tau = 2\int_{x_1}^{x_2} \frac{dx}{\sqrt{2[E - U(x)]}}$$

where x_1 and x_2 are extreme points of the trajectory on the x-axis.

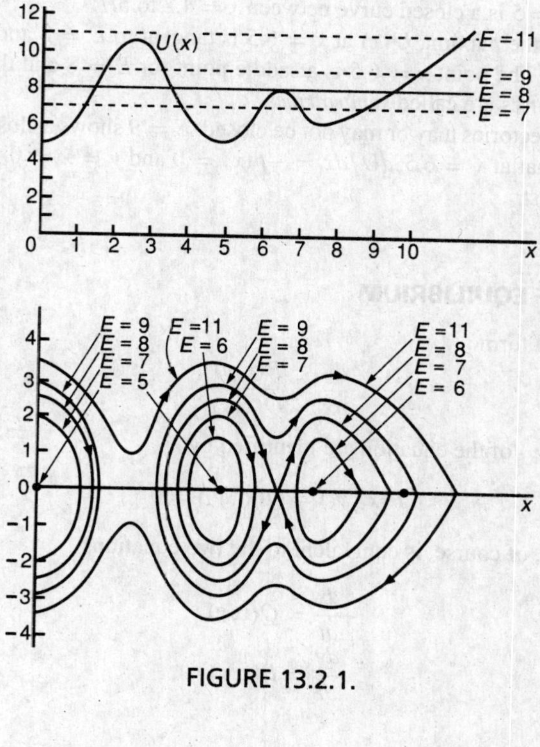

FIGURE 13.2.1.

TABLE 13.2.1 Computation of Phase Plane for $U(x)$ Given in Fig. 13.2.1

		$y = \pm\sqrt{2[E - U(x)]}$			
x	$U(x)$	$\pm y$ at $E = 7$	$\pm y$ at $E = 8$	$\pm y$ at $E = 9$	$\pm y$ at $E = 11$
0	5.0	2.0	2.45	2.83	3.46
1.0	6.3	1.18	1.84	2.32	
1.5	8.0	imag	0	1.41	2.45
2.0	9.6	imag	imag	imag	
3.0	10.0	imag	imag	imag	1.41
3.5	8.0	imag	0	1.41	2.45
4.0	6.5	1.0	1.73	2.24	
5.0	5.0	2.0	2.45	2.83	3.46
5.5	5.7	1.61	2.24	2.57	
6.0	7.2	imag	1.26	1.90	
6.5	8.0	imag	0	1.41	2.45
7.0	7.0	0	1.41	2.0	
7.5	6.0	1.41	2.0	2.45	3.16
8.0	6.3	1.18	1.84	2.32	
9.0	7.4	imag	1.09	1.79	
9.5	8.0	imag	0	1.41	
10.0	8.8	imag	imag	0.63	
11.5					0

For smaller initial conditions, these closed trajectories become smaller. For $E = 6$, the trajectory about the equilibrium points $x = 7.5$ contracts to a point, whereas the trajectory about the equilibrium point $x = 5$ is a closed curve between $x = 4.2$ to 5.7.

For $E = 8$ one of the maxima $U(x)$ at $x = 6.5$ is tangent to $E = 8$ and the trajectory at this point has four branches. The point $x = 6.5$ is a saddle point for $E = 8$ and the motion is unstable. The saddle point trajectories are called *separatrices*.

For $E > 8$, the trajectories may or may not be closed. $E = 9$ shows a closed trajectory between $x = 3.3$ to 10.2. Note that at $x = 6.5, dU/dx = -f(x) = 0$ and $y = \dot{x} \neq 0$ for $E = 9$, and hence equilibrium does not exist.

13.3 STABILITY OF EQUILIBRIUM

Expressed in the general form

$$\frac{dy}{dx} = \frac{P(x,y)}{Q(x,y)} \tag{13.3.1}$$

the singular points (x_s, y_s) of the equation are identified by

$$P(x_s, y_s) = Q(x_s, y_s) = 0 \tag{13.3.2}$$

Equation (13.3.1), of course, is equivalent to the two equations

$$\begin{aligned} \frac{dx}{dt} &= Q(x,y) \\ \frac{dy}{dt} &= P(x,y) \end{aligned} \tag{13.3.3}$$

from which the time dt has been eliminated. A study of these equations in the neighborhood of the singular point provides us with answers as to the stability of equilibrium.

Recognizing that the slope dy/dx of the trajectories does not vary with translation of the coordinate axes, we translate the u, v axis to one of the singular points to be studied, as shown in Fig. 13.3.1. We then have

$$x = x_s + u$$
$$y = y_x + v \qquad (13.3.4)$$
$$\frac{dy}{dx} = \frac{dv}{du}$$

If $P(x,y)$ and $Q(x,y)$ are now expanded in terms of the Taylor series about the singular point (x_s, y_s), we obtain for $Q(x,y)$

$$Q(x,y) = Q(x_s, y_s) + \left(\frac{\partial Q}{\partial u}\right)_s u + \left(\frac{\partial Q}{\partial v}\right)_s v + \left(\frac{\partial^2 Q}{\partial u^2}\right)_s u^2 + \cdots \qquad (13.3.5)$$

and a similar equation for $P(x,y)$. Because $Q(x_s, y_s)$ is zero and $(\partial Q/\partial u)_s$ and $(\partial Q/\partial v)_s$ are constants, Eq. (13.3.1) in the region of the singularity becomes

$$\frac{dv}{du} = \frac{cu + ev}{au + bv} \qquad (13.3.6)$$

where the higher-order derivatives of P and Q have been omitted. Thus, a study of the singularity at (x_s, y_s) is possible by studying Eq. (13.3.6) for small u and v.

Returning to Eq. (13.3.3) and taking note of Eqs. (13.3.4) and (13.3.5), Eq. (13.3.6) is seen to be equivalent to

$$\frac{du}{dt} = au + bv$$
$$\frac{dv}{dt} = cu + ev \qquad (13.3.7)$$

which can be rewritten in matrix form:

$$\begin{Bmatrix} \dot{u} \\ \dot{v} \end{Bmatrix} = \begin{bmatrix} a & b \\ c & e \end{bmatrix} \begin{Bmatrix} u \\ v \end{Bmatrix} \qquad (13.3.8)$$

It was shown in Sec. 5.6 that if the eigenvalues and eigenvectors of a matrix equation such as Eq. (13.3.8) are known, a transformation

$$\begin{Bmatrix} u \\ v \end{Bmatrix} + [P] \begin{Bmatrix} \xi \\ \eta \end{Bmatrix} = \left[\begin{Bmatrix} u_1 \\ v_1 \end{Bmatrix} \begin{Bmatrix} u_2 \\ v_2 \end{Bmatrix} \right] \begin{Bmatrix} \xi \\ \eta \end{Bmatrix} \qquad (13.3.9)$$

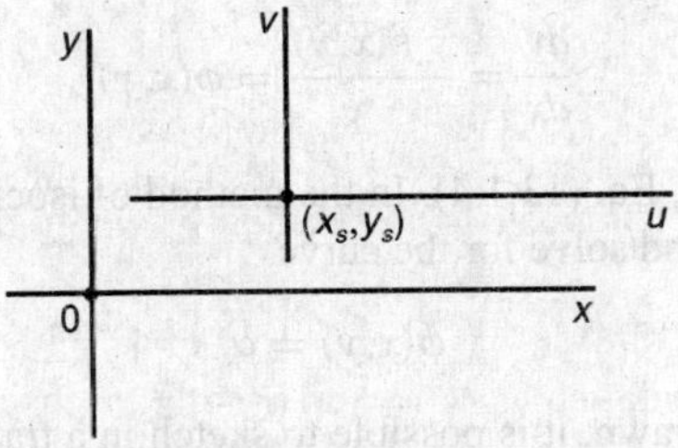

FIGURE 13.3.1.

where $[P]$ is a modal matrix of the eigenvector columns, will decouple the equation to the form

$$\begin{Bmatrix} \dot{\xi} \\ \dot{\eta} \end{Bmatrix} = [\Lambda] \begin{Bmatrix} \xi \\ \eta \end{Bmatrix} = \begin{bmatrix} \lambda_1 & 0 \\ 0 & \lambda_2 \end{bmatrix} \begin{Bmatrix} \xi \\ \eta \end{Bmatrix} \tag{13.3.10}$$

Because Eq. (13.3.10) has the solution

$$\begin{aligned} \xi &= e^{\lambda_1 t} \\ \eta &= e^{\lambda_2 t} \end{aligned} \tag{13.3.11}$$

the solution for u and v are

$$\begin{aligned} u &= u_1 e^{\lambda_1 t} + u_2 e^{\lambda_2 t} \\ v &= v_1 e^{\lambda_1 t} + v_2 e^{\lambda_2 t} \end{aligned} \tag{13.3.12}$$

It is evident, then, that the stability of the singular point depends on the eigenvalues λ_1 and λ_2 determined from the characteristic equation

$$\begin{vmatrix} (a-\lambda) & b \\ c & (e-\lambda) \end{vmatrix} = 0$$

or

$$\lambda_{1,2} = \left(\frac{a+e}{2}\right) \pm \sqrt{\left(\frac{a+e}{2}\right)^2 - (ae - bc)} \tag{13.3.13}$$

Thus

if $(ae - bc) > \left(\frac{a+e}{2}\right)^2$, the motion is oscillatory;
if $(ae - bc) < \left(\frac{a+e}{2}\right)^2$, the motion is aperiodic;
if $(a + e) > 0$, the system is unstable;
if $(a + e) < 0$, the system is stable.

The type of trajectories in the neighborhood of the singular point can be determined by first examining Eq. (13.3.10) in the form

$$\frac{d\xi}{d\eta} = \frac{\lambda_1}{\lambda_2}\frac{\xi}{\eta} \tag{13.3.14}$$

which has the solution

$$\xi = (\eta)^{\lambda_1/\lambda_2}$$

we use the transformation of Eq. (13.3.9) to plot v vs. u.

13.4 METHOD OF ISOCLINES

Consider the autonomous system with the equation

$$\frac{dy}{dx} = -\frac{f(x,y)}{y} = \phi(x,y) \tag{13.4.1}$$

that was discussed in Sec. 13.1, Eq. (13.1.4). In the method of isoclines, we fix the slope dy/dx by giving it a definite number α, and solve for the curve

$$\phi(x,y) = \alpha \tag{13.4.2}$$

With a family of such curves drawn, it is possible to sketch in a trajectory starting at any point x, y as shown in Fig. 13.4.1.

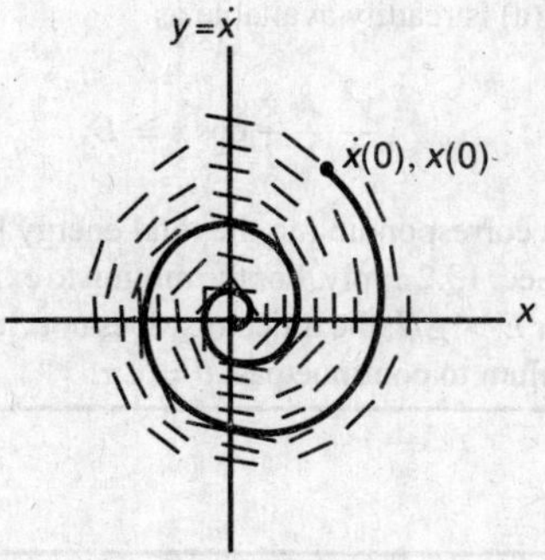

FIGURE 13.4.1.

Example 13.4.1

Determine the isoclines for the simple pendulum.

Solution The equation for the simple pendulum is

$$\ddot{\theta} + \frac{g}{l}\sin\theta = 0 \tag{a}$$

Letting $x = \theta$ and $y = \dot{\theta} = \dot{x}$, we obtain

$$\frac{dy}{dx} = -\frac{g}{l}\frac{\sin x}{y} \tag{b}$$

Thus, for $dy/dx = \alpha$, a constant, the equation for the isocline, Eq. (13.4.2), becomes

$$y = -\left(\frac{g}{l\alpha}\right)\sin x \tag{c}$$

It is evident from Eq. (b) that the singular points lie along the x-axis at $x = 0, \pm\pi, \pm 2\pi$, and so on. Figure 13.4.2 shows isoclines in the first quadrant that correspond to negative values of α. By starting at an arbitrary point $x(0), y(0)$, the trajectory can be sketched by proceeding tangentially to the slope segments.

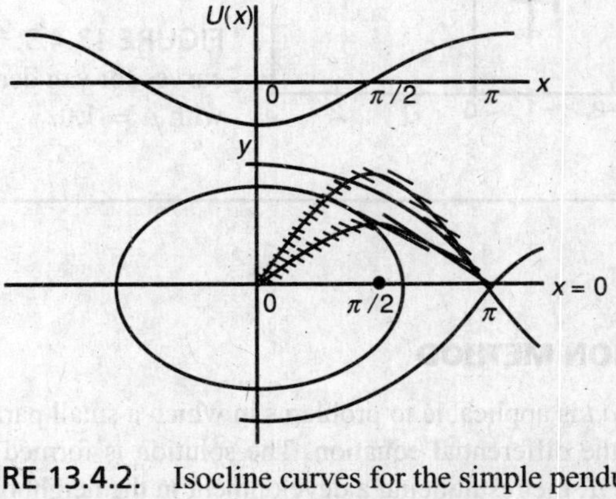

FIGURE 13.4.2. Isocline curves for the simple pendulum.

In this case the integral of Eq. (a) is readily available as

$$\frac{y^2}{2} - \frac{g}{l}\cos x = E$$

where E is a constant of integration corresponding to the total energy [see Eq. (13.2.1)]. We also have $U(x) = -(g/l)\cos x$ and the discussions of Sec. 13.2 apply. For the motion to exist, E must be greater than $-g/l$. $E = g/l$ corresponds to the separatrix, and for $E > g/l$, the trajectory does not close. This means that the initial conditions are large enough to cause the pendulum to continue past $\theta = 2\pi$.

Example 13.4.2

One of the interesting nonlinear equations that has been studied extensively is the *van der Pol equation*:

$$\ddot{x} - \mu\dot{x}(1 - x^2) + x = 0$$

The equation somewhat resembles that of free vibration of a spring-mass system with viscous damping; however, the damping term of this equation is nonlinear in that it depends on both the velocity and the displacement. For small oscillations ($x < 1$), the damping is negative, and the amplitude increases with time. For $x > 1$, the damping is positive, and the amplitude diminishes with time. If the system is initiated with $x(0)$ and $\dot{x}(0)$, the amplitude will increase or decrease, depending on whether x is small or large, and it will finally reach a stable state known as the *limit cycle*, graphically displayed by the phase plane plot of Fig. 13.4.3.

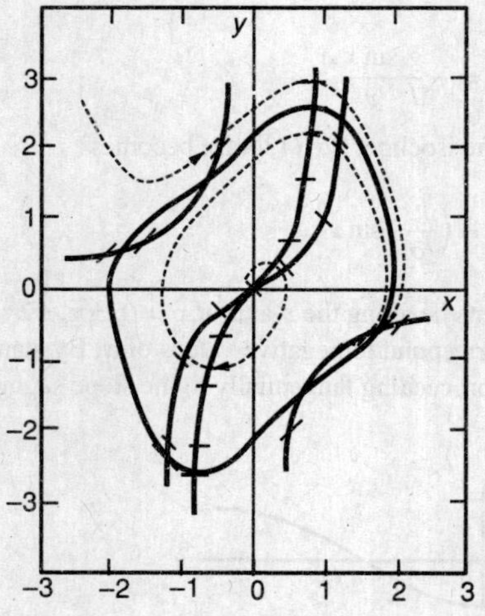

FIGURE 13.4.3. Isocline curves for van der Pol's equation with $\mu = 1.0$.

13.5 PERTURBATION METHOD

The *perturbation method* is applicable to problems in which a small parameter μ is associated with the nonlinear term of the differential equation. The solution is formed in terms of a series of the perturbation parameter μ, the result being a development in the neighborhood of the solution of the linearized problem. If the solution of the linearized problem is periodic, and if μ is small, we can expect the perturbed solution to be periodic also. We can reason from the phase plane that the periodic solution must represent a closed trajectory. The period, which depends on the initial conditions, is then a function of the amplitude of vibration.

Consider the free oscillation of a mass on a nonlinear spring, which is defined by the equation

$$\ddot{x} + \omega_n^2 x + \mu x^3 = 0 \tag{13.5.1}$$

with initial conditions $x(0) = A$ and $\dot{x}(0) = 0$. When $\mu = 0$, the frequency of oscillation is that of the linear system, $\omega_n = \sqrt{k/m}$.

We seek a solution in the form of an infinite series of the perturbation parameter μ as follows:

$$x = x_0(t) + \mu x_1(t) + \mu^2 x_2(t) + \cdots \tag{13.5.2}$$

Furthermore, we know that the frequency of the nonlinear oscillation will depend on the amplitude of oscillation as well as on μ. We express this fact also in terms of a series in μ:

$$\omega^2 = \omega_n^2 + \mu\alpha_1 + \mu^2\alpha_2 + \cdots \tag{13.5.3}$$

where the α_i are as yet undefined functions of the amplitude, and ω is the frequency of the nonlinear oscillations.

We consider only the first two terms of Eqs. (13.5.2) and (13.5.3), which will adequately illustrate the procedure. Substituting these into Eq. (13.5.1), we obtain

$$\ddot{x}_0 + \mu\ddot{x}_1 + (\omega^2 - \mu\alpha_1)(x_0 + \mu x_1) + \mu(x_0^3 + 3\mu x_0^2 x_1 + \cdots) = 0 \tag{13.5.4}$$

Because the perturbation parameter μ could have been chosen arbitrarily, the coefficients of the various powers of μ must be equated to zero. This leads to a system of equations that can be solved successively:

$$\begin{aligned} \ddot{x}_0 + \omega^2 x_0 &= 0 \\ \ddot{x}_1 + \omega^2 x_1 &= \alpha_1 x_0 - x_0^3 \end{aligned} \tag{13.5.5}$$

The solution to the first equation, subject to the initial conditions $x(0) = A$, and $\dot{x}(0) = 0$ is

$$x_0 = A\cos\omega t \tag{13.5.6}$$

which is called the *generating solution*. Substituting this into the right side of the second equation in Eq. (13.5.5), we obtain

$$\begin{aligned} \ddot{x}_1 + \omega^2 x_1 &= \alpha_1 A\cos\omega t - A^3\cos^3\omega t \\ &= \left(\alpha_1 - \frac{3}{4}A^3\right)A\cos\omega t - \frac{A^3}{4}\cos 3\omega t \end{aligned} \tag{13.5.7}$$

where $\cos^3\omega t = \frac{3}{4}\cos\omega t + \frac{1}{4}\cos 3\omega t$ has been used. We note here that the forcing term $\cos\omega t$ would lead to a secular term $t\cos\omega t$ in the solution for x_1 (i.e., we have a condition of resonance). Such terms violate the initial stipulation that the motion is to be periodic; hence, we impose the condition

$$\alpha_1 - \frac{3}{4}A^2 = 0$$

Thus, α_1, which we stated earlier to be some function of the amplitude A, is evaluated to be

$$\alpha_1 = \frac{3}{4}A^2 \tag{13.5.8}$$

With the forcing term cos ωt eliminated from the right side of the equation, the general solution for x_1 is

$$x_1 = C_1 \sin \omega t + C_2 \cos \omega t + \frac{A^3}{32\omega^2} \cos 3\omega t$$
$$\omega^2 = \omega_n^2 + \frac{3}{4}\mu A^2 \tag{13.5.9}$$

By imposing the initial conditions $x_1(0) = \dot{x}_1(0)$, constants C_1 and C_2 are

$$C_1 = 0 \quad C_2 = -\frac{A^3}{32\omega^2}$$

Thus,

$$x_1 = \frac{A^3}{32\omega^2}(\cos 3\omega t - \cos \omega t) \tag{13.5.10}$$

and the solution at this point from Eq. (13.5.2) becomes

$$x = A \cos \omega t + \mu \frac{A^3}{32\omega^2}(\cos 3\omega t - \cos \omega t)$$
$$\omega = \omega_n \sqrt{1 + \frac{3}{4}\frac{\mu A^2}{\omega_0^2}} \tag{13.5.11}$$

The solution is thus found to be periodic, and the fundamental frequency ω is found to increase with the amplitude, as expected for a hardening spring.

Mathieu equation. Consider the nonlinear equation

$$\ddot{x} + \omega_n^2 x + \mu x^3 = F \cos \omega t \tag{13.5.12}$$

and assume a perturbation solution

$$x = x_1(t) + \xi(t) \tag{13.5.13*}$$

Substituting Eq. (13.5.13) into (13.5.12), we obtain the following two equations:

$$\ddot{x}_1 + \omega_n^2 x_1 + \mu x_1^3 = F \cos \omega t \tag{13.5.14}$$
$$\ddot{\xi} + (\omega_n^2 + \mu 3 x_1^2)\xi = 0 \tag{13.5.15}$$

If μ is assumed to be small, we can let

$$x_1 \cong A \sin \omega t \tag{13.5.16}$$

and substitute it into Eq. (13.5.15), which becomes

$$\ddot{\xi} + \left[\left(\omega_n^2 + \frac{3\mu}{2}A^2\right) - \frac{3\mu}{2}A^2 \cos 2\omega t\right]\xi = 0 \tag{13.5.17}$$

This equation is of the form

$$\frac{d^2y}{dz^2} + (a - 2b \cos 2z)y = 0 \tag{13.5.18}$$

which is known as the *Mathieu equation*. The stable and unstable regions of the Mathieu equation depend on the parameters a and b, and are shown in Fig. 13.5.1.

*See Ref. [1], pp. 259–273.

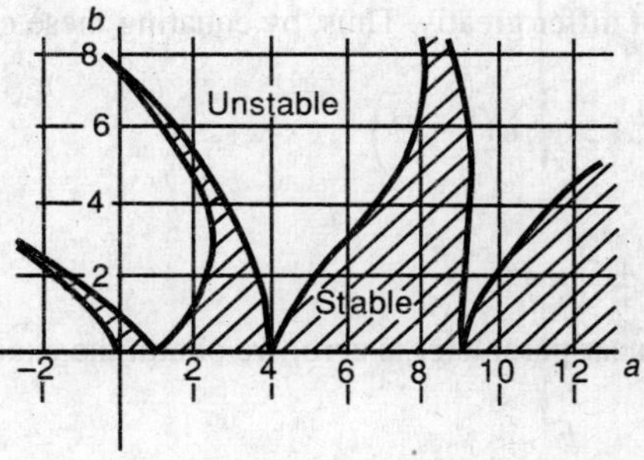

FIGURE 13.5.1. Stable region of Mathieu equation indicated by the shaded area, which is symmetric about the horizontal axis.

13.6 METHOD OF ITERATION

Duffing[2] made an exhaustive study of the equation

$$m\ddot{x} + c\dot{x} + kx \pm \mu x^3 = F \cos \omega t$$

which represents a mass on a cubic spring, excited harmonically. The $\pm$ sign signifies a hardening or softening spring. The equation is nonautonomous in that the time t appears explicitly in the forcing term.

In this section, we wish to examine a simpler equation where damping is zero, written in the form

$$\ddot{x} + \omega_n^2 x \pm \mu x^3 = F \cos \omega t \tag{13.6.1}$$

We seek only the steady-state harmonic solution by the *method of iteration*, which is essentially a process of *successive approximation*. An assumed solution is substituted into the differential equation, which is integrated to obtain a solution of improved accuracy. The procedure can be repeated any number of times to achieve the desired accuracy.

For the first assumed solution, let

$$x_0 = A \cos \omega t \tag{13.6.2}$$

and substitute into the differential equation

$$\begin{aligned}\ddot{x} &= -\omega_n^2 A \cos \omega t \mp \mu A^3 \left(\frac{3}{4} \cos \omega t + \frac{1}{4} \cos 3\omega t\right) + F \cos \omega t \\ &= \left(-\omega_n^2 A \mp \frac{3}{4}\mu A^3 + F\right) \cos \omega t \mp \frac{1}{4}\mu A^3 \cos 3\omega t\end{aligned}$$

In integrating this equation, it is necessary to set the constants of integration to zero if the solution is to be harmonic with period $\tau = 2\pi/\omega$. Thus, we obtain for the improved solution

$$x_1 = \frac{1}{\omega^2}\left(\omega_n^2 \pm \frac{3}{4}\mu A^3 - F\right) \cos \omega t \mp \cdots \tag{13.6.3}$$

where the higher harmonic term is ignored.

The procedure can be repeated, but we will not go any further. Duffing reasoned at this point that if the first and second approximations are reasonable solutions to the problem, then the coefficients of cos ωt in Eqs. (13.6.2) and (13.6.3) must not differ greatly. Thus, by equating these coefficients, we obtain

$$A = \frac{1}{\omega^2}\left(\omega_n^2 A \pm \frac{3}{4}\mu A^3 - F\right) \tag{13.6.4}$$

which can be solved for ω^2:

$$\omega^2 = \omega_n^2 \pm \frac{3}{4}\mu A^2 - \frac{F}{A} \tag{13.6.5}$$

It is evident from this equation that if the nonlinear parameter is zero, we obtain the exact result for the linear system

$$A = \frac{F}{\omega_n^2 - \omega^2}$$

For $\mu \neq 0$, the frequency ω is a function of μ, F, and A. It is evident that when $F = 0$, we obtain the frequency equation for free vibration

$$\frac{\omega^2}{\omega_n^2} = 1 \pm \frac{3}{4}\mu\frac{A^2}{\omega_n^2}$$

discussed in the previous section. Here we see that the frequency increases with amplitude for the hardening spring (+) and decreases for the softening spring (−).

For $\mu \neq 0$ and $F \neq 0$, it is convenient to hold both μ and F constant and plot $|A|$ against ω/ω_n. In the construction of these curves, it is helpful to rearrange Eq. (13.6.5) to

$$\frac{3}{4}\mu\frac{A^3}{\omega_n^2} = \left(1 - \frac{\omega^2}{\omega_n^2}\right)A - \frac{F}{\omega_n^2} \tag{13.6.6}$$

each side of which can be plotted against A, as shown in Fig. 13.6.1. The left side of this equation is a cubic, whereas the right side is a straight line of slope $(1 - \omega^2/\omega_n^2)$ and intercept $-F/\omega_n^2$. For $\omega/\omega_n < 1$, the two curves intersect at three points, 1, 2, and 3, which are also shown in the amplitude–frequency plot. As ω/ω_n increases toward unity, points 2 and 3 approach each other, after which only one value of the amplitude satisfies Eq. (13.6.6). When $\omega/\omega_n = 1$, or when $\omega/\omega_n > 1$, these points are 4 or 5.

The jump phenomenon. In problems of this type, it is found that amplitude A undergoes a sudden discontinuous jump near resonance. The *jump phenomenon* can be described as follows. For the softening spring, with increasing frequency of excitation, the amplitude gradually increases until

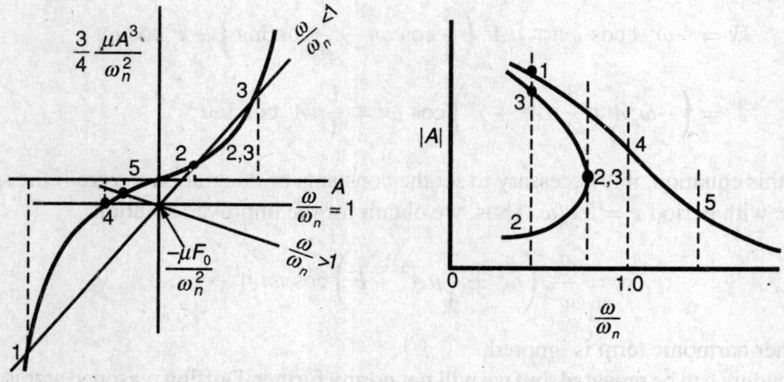

FIGURE 13.6.1. Solution of Eq. (13.6.6).

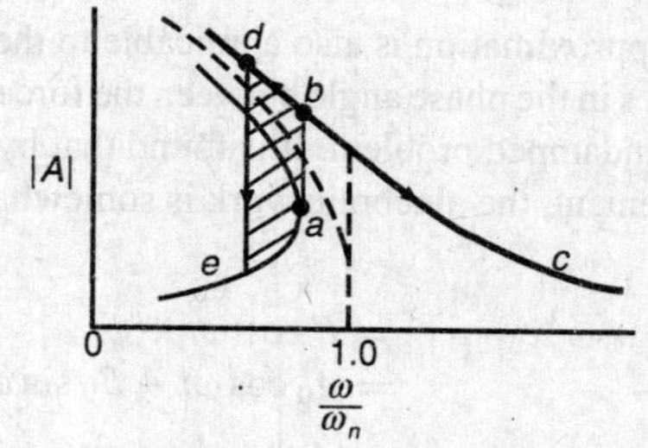

FIGURE 13.6.2. The jump phenomenon for the softening spring.

point a in Fig. 13.6.2 is reached. It then suddenly jumps to a larger value indicated by point b, and diminishes along the curve to its right. In decreasing the frequency from some point c, the amplitude continues to increase beyond b to point d, and suddenly drops to a smaller value at e. The shaded region in the amplitude–frequency plot is unstable; the extent of unstableness depends on a number of factors such as the amount of damping present and the rate of change of the exciting frequency. If a hardening spring had been chosen instead of a softening spring, the same type of analysis would be applicable and the result would be a curve of the type shown in Fig. 13.6.3.

Effect of damping. In the undamped case, the amplitude–frequency curves approach the backbone curve (shown dashed) asymptotically. This is also the case for the linear system, where the backbone curve is the vertical line at $\omega/\omega_n = 1.0$.

With a small amount of damping present, the behavior of the system cannot differ appreciably from that of the undamped system. The upper end of the curve, instead of approaching the backbone curve asymptotically, crosses in a continuous curve, as shown in Fig. 13.6.4. The jump phenomenon is also present here, but damping generally tends to reduce the size of the unstable region.

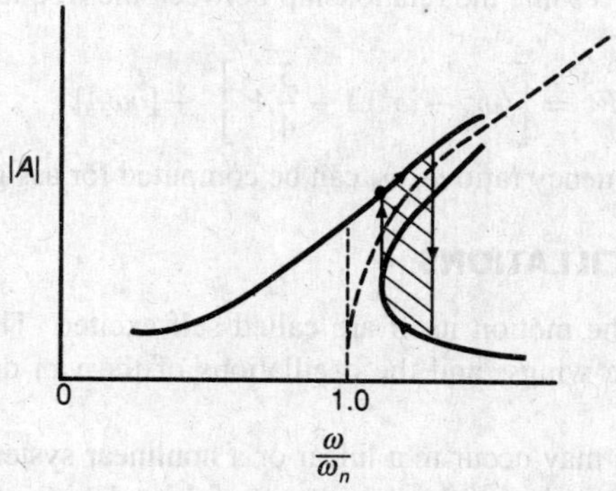

FIGURE 13.6.3. The jump phenomenon for the hardening spring.

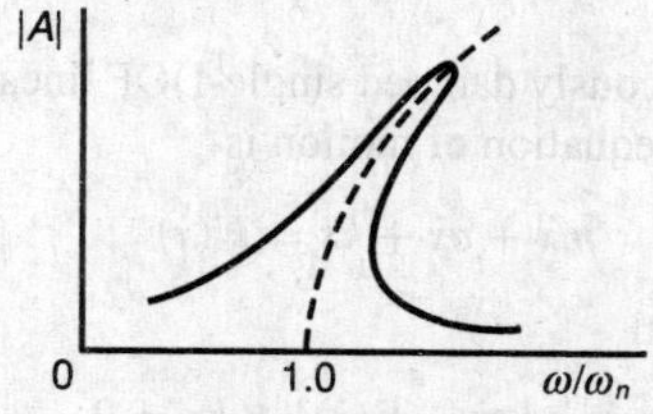

FIGURE 13.6.4.

The method of successive approximation is also applicable to the damped vibration case. The major difference in its treatment lies in the phase angle between the force and the displacement, which is no longer 0° or 180° as in the undamped problem. It is found that by introducing the phase in the force term rather than the displacement, the algebraic work is somewhat simplified. The differential equation can then be written as

$$\begin{aligned} \ddot{x} + c\dot{x} + \omega_n^2 x + \mu x^3 &= F\cos(\omega t + \phi) \\ &= A_0 \cos\omega t - B_0 \sin\omega t \end{aligned} \tag{13.6.7}$$

where the magnitude of the force is

$$F = \sqrt{A_0^2 + B_0^2} \tag{13.6.8}$$

and the phase can be determined from

$$\tan\phi = \frac{B_0}{A_0}$$

By assuming the first approximation to be

$$x_0 = A\cos\omega t$$

its substitution into the differential equation results in

$$\begin{aligned} \left[(\omega_n^2 - \omega^2)A + \frac{3}{4}\mu A^3\right]\cos\omega t - c\omega A\sin\omega t + \frac{1}{4}\mu A^3\cos 3\omega t \\ = A_0\cos\omega t - B_0\sin\omega t \end{aligned} \tag{13.6.9}$$

We again ignore the $\cos 3\omega t$ term and equate coefficients of $\cos\omega t$ and $\sin\omega t$ to obtain

$$\begin{aligned} (\omega_n^2 - \omega^2)A + \frac{3}{4}\mu A^3 &= A_0 \\ c\omega A &= B_0 \end{aligned} \tag{13.6.10}$$

By squaring and adding these results, the relationship between the frequency, amplitude, and force becomes

$$F^2 = \left[(\omega_n^2 - \omega^2)A + \frac{3}{4}A^3\right]^2 + [c\omega A]^2 \tag{13.6.11}$$

By fixing μ, c, and F, the frequency ratio ω/ω_n can be computed for assigned values of A.

13.7 SELF-EXCITED OSCILLATIONS

Oscillations that depend on the motion itself are called self-excited. The shimmy of automobile wheels, the flutter of airplane wings, and the oscillations of the van der Pol equation are some examples.

Self-excited oscillations may occur in a linear or a nonlinear system. The motion is induced by an excitation that is some function of the velocity or of the velocity and the displacement. If the motion of the system tends to increase the energy of the system, the amplitude will increase, and the system may become unstable.

As an example, consider a viscously damped single-DOF linear system excited by a force that is some function of the velocity. Its equation of motion is

$$m\ddot{x} + c\dot{x} + kx = F(\dot{x}) \tag{13.7.1}$$

Rearranging the equation to the form

$$m\ddot{x} + [c\dot{x} - F(\dot{x})] + kx = 0 \tag{13.7.2}$$

we can recognize the possibility of negative damping if $F(\dot{x})$ becomes greater than cx.

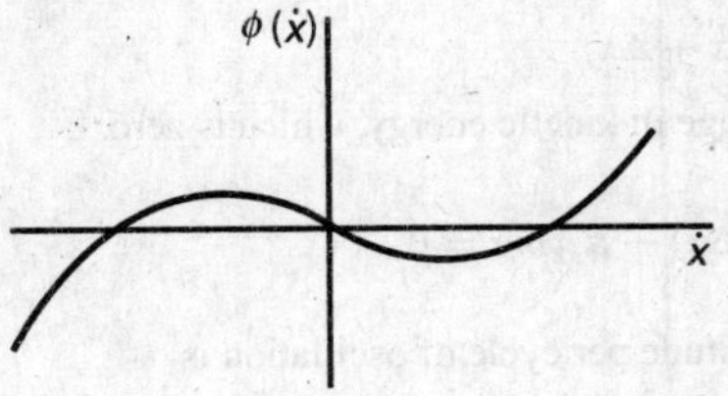

FIGURE 13.7.1. System with apparent damping $\phi(\dot{x}) = c(\dot{x}) - F(\dot{x})$.

Suppose that $\phi(\dot{x}) = c\dot{x} - F(\dot{x})$ in the preceding equations varies as in Fig. 13.7.1. For small velocities, the apparent damping $\phi(\dot{x})$ is negative, and the amplitude of oscillation increases. For large velocities, the opposite is true, and hence the oscillations tend to a limit cycle.

Example 13.7.1

The coefficient of kinetic friction μ_k is generally less than the coefficient of static friction μ_s, this difference increasing somewhat with the velocity. Thus, if the belt of Fig. 13.7.2 is started, the mass will move with the belt until the spring force is balanced by the static friction.

$$kx_0 = \mu_s mg \tag{a}$$

At this point, the mass starts to move back to the left, and the forces are again balanced on the basis of kinetic friction when

$$k(x_0 - x) = \mu_{kl} mg$$

From these two equations, the amplitude of oscillation is

$$x = x_0 - \mu_{kl}\frac{mg}{k} = \frac{(\mu_s - \mu_{kl})g}{\omega_n^2} \tag{b}$$

While the mass is moving to the left, the relative velocity between it and the belt is greater than when it is moving to the right; thus, μ_{kl} is less than μ_{kr}, where subscripts l and r refer to left and right, respectively. It is evident then that the work done by the friction force while moving to the right is greater than that while moving to the left; so more energy is put into the spring-mass system than taken out. This then represents one type of self-excited oscillation and the amplitude continues to increase.

The work done by the spring from 2 to 3 is

$$-\frac{1}{2}k[(x_0 + \Delta x) + (x_0 - 2x)](2x + \Delta x)$$

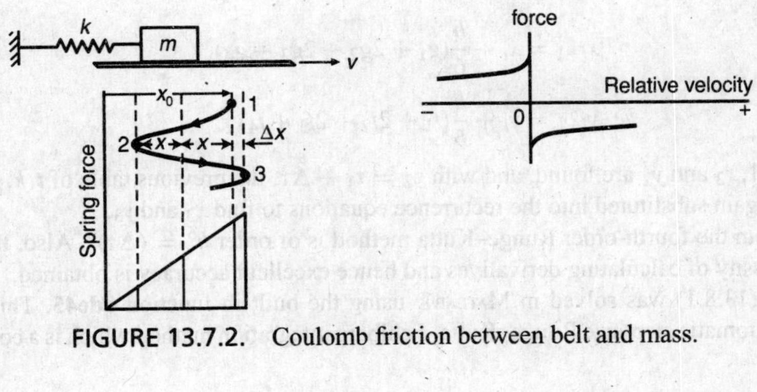

FIGURE 13.7.2. Coulomb friction between belt and mass.

The work done by friction from 2 to 3 is

$$\mu_{kr} mg(2x + \Delta x)$$

Equating the net work done between 2 and 3 to the change in kinetic energy, which is zero,

$$-\frac{1}{2}k(2x_0 - 2x + \Delta x) + \mu_{kr} mg = 0 \tag{c}$$

By substituting (a) and (b) into (c), the increase in amplitude per cycle of oscillation is

$$\Delta x = \frac{2g(\mu_{kr} - \mu_{kl})}{\omega_n^2} \tag{d}$$

■

13.8 RUNGE–KUTTA METHOD

The Runge–Kutta method discussed in Chapter 4 can be used to solve nonlinear differential equations. We consider the nonlinear equation

$$\frac{d^2x}{d\tau^2} + 0.4\frac{dx}{d\tau} + x + 0.5x^3 = 0.5\cos 0.5\tau \tag{13.8.1}$$

and rewrite it in first-order form by letting

$$y = \frac{dx}{d\tau} \tag{13.8.2}$$

as follows:

$$\frac{dy}{d\tau} = 0.5\cos 0.5\tau - x - 0.5x^3 - 0.4y = F(\tau, x, y) \tag{13.8.3}$$

The computational equations to be used are programmed for the digital computer in the following order:

τ	x	y	F
$t_1 = \tau_1$	$k_1 = x_1$	$g_1 = y_1$	$f_1 = F(t_1, k_1, g_1)$
$t_2 = \tau_1 + h/2$	$k_2 = x_1 + g_1 h/2$	$g_2 = y_1 + f_1 h/2$	$f_2 = F(t_2, k_2, g_2)$
$t_3 = \tau_1 + h/2$	$k_3 = x_1 + g_2 h/2$	$g_3 = y_1 + f_2 h/2$	$f_3 = F(t_3, k_3, g_3)$
$t_4 = \tau_1 + h$	$k_4 = x_1 + g_3 h$	$g_4 = y_1 + f_3 h$	$f_4 = F(t_4, k_4, g_4)$

From these results, the values of x and y are determined from the following recurrence equations, where $h = \Delta t$:

$$x_{i+1} = x_i + \frac{h}{6}(g_1 + 2g_2 + 2g_3 + g_4) \tag{13.8.4}$$

$$y_{i+1} = y_i + \frac{h}{6}(f_1 + 2f_2 + 2f_3 + f_4) \tag{13.8.5}$$

Thus, with $i = 1, x_2$ and y_2 are found, and with $\tau_2 = \tau_1 + \Delta\tau$, the previous table of $t, k, g,$ and f is computed and again substituted into the recurrence equations to find x_3 and y_3.

The error in the fourth-order Runge–Kutta method is of order $h^5 = (\Delta\tau)^5$. Also, the method avoids the necessity of calculating derivatives and hence excellent accuracy is obtained.

Equation (13.8.1) was solved in MATLAB® using the built in function **ode45**. This function consists of an automatic step-size Runge–Kutta–Fehlberg integration method which is a combination of a fourth- and fifth-order method. In order to use this function to solve a differential equation, the equation must first be written as a system of first order equations. Equations (13.8.2) and (13.8.3) are the system of equations which comes from Eq. (13.8.1). These equations need to be put in a function file, which **ode45** can access. For this example, the function file is called **nonlin.m** and it contains the following commands:

```
function xdot = nonlin(t,x)
        xdot = [0.5 * cos(0.5. * t) - x(2) - 0.5 * x(2)^3 - 0.4 * x(1); x(1)];
```

The function **ode45** also needs to be given an initial time t_0, a final time t_f, and a column vector of initial conditions x_0. Figure 13.8.1 is the result of the following commands in MATLAB®:

```
t0 = 0;
tf = 40;
x0 = [0, 0.05]';
[t,x] = ode45 ('nonlin', t0, tf,x0)
x1 = x(:, 1);
x2 = x(:, 2);
plot    (x2,x1)
```

It is evident that the limit cycle was reached in less than two cycles.

Figure 13.8.2 is obtained from the van der Pol equation:

$$\ddot{x} - \mu\dot{x}(1 - x^2) + x = 0$$

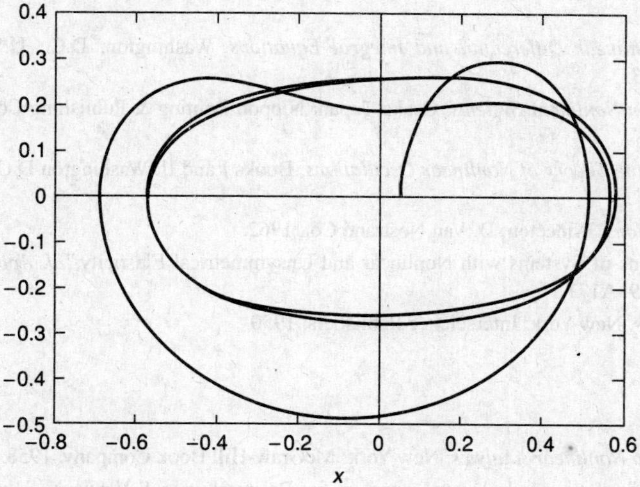

FIGURE 13.8.1.

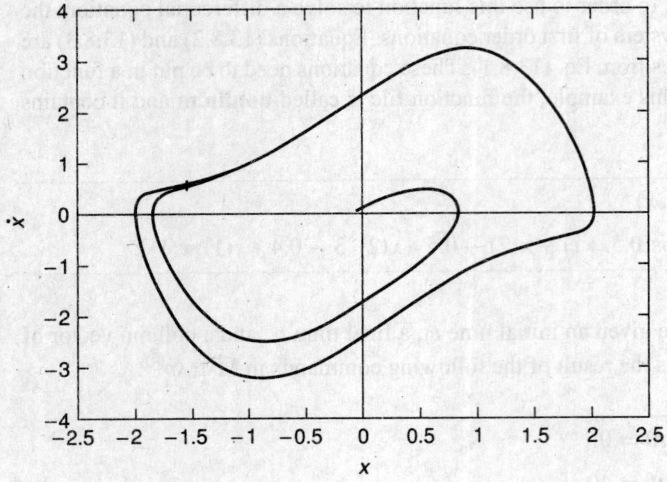

FIGURE 13.8.2.

This equation can be rewritten as the following system of first-order equations:

$$\dot{x}_1 = \mu x_1(1 - x_2^2) - x_2$$

$$\dot{x}_2 = x_1$$

Figure 13.8.2 is the result of using **ode45** with $\mu = 1.5$ and the initial conditions $x_1 = 0$ and $x_2 = 0.05$. The effect of the nonlinearity is quite evident in this figure.

SUGGESTED READING

[1] Bellman, R. *Peturbation Techniques in Mathematics, Physics and Engineering.* New York: Holt, Rinehart & Winston, 1964.

[2] Brock, J. E. "An Iterative Numerical Method for Nonlinear Vibrations," *J. Appl. Mech.* (March 1951), pp. 1–11.

[3] Butenin, N. V. *Elements of the Theory of Nonlinear Oscillations.* New York: Blaisdell Publishing Co., 1965.

[4] Davis, H. T. *Introduction to Nonlinear Differential and Integral Equations.* Washington, D.C.: U.S. Government Printing Office, 1956.

[5] Hayashi, C. *Forced Oscillations in Nonlinear Systems.* Osaka, Japan: Nippon Printing & Publishing Co., 1953.

[6] Malkin, I. G. *Some Problems in the Theory of Nonlinear Oscillations*, Books I and II. Washington D.C.: Department of Commerce, 1959.

[7] Minorsky, N. *Nonlinear Oscillations.* Princeton: D. Van Nostrand Co., 1962.

[8] Rauscher, M. "Steady Oscillations of Systems with Nonlinear and Unsymmetrical Elasticity," *J. Appl. Mech.* (December 1938), pp. A169–A177.

[9] Stoker, J. J. *Nonlinear Vibrations.* New York: Interscience Publishers, 1950.

REFERENCES

[1] Cunningham, W. J. *Introduction to Nonlinear Analysis.* New York: McGraw-Hill Book Company, 1958.

[2] Duffing, G. *Erwugene Schwingungen bei veranderlicher Eigenfrequenz.* Braunschweig: F. Vieweg u. Sohn, 1918.

PROBLEMS

13.1. A mass is attached to the midpoint of a string of length $2l$, as shown in Fig. P13.1. Determine the differential equation of motion for large deflection. Assume string tension to be T.

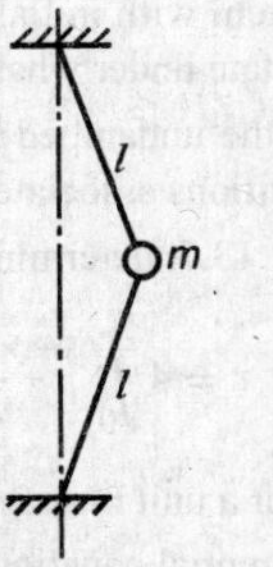

FIGURE P13.1.

13.2. A buoy is composed of two cones of diameter $2r$ and height h, as shown in Fig. P13.2. A weight attached to the bottom allows it to float in the equilibrium position x_0. Establish the differential equation of motion for vertical oscillation.

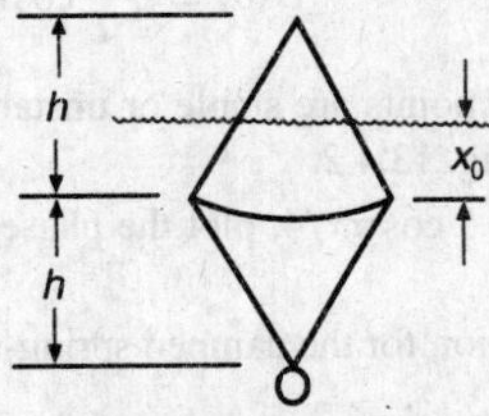

FIGURE P13.2.

13.3. Determine the differential equation of motion for the spring-mass system with the discontinuous stiffness resulting from the free gaps of Fig. P13.3.

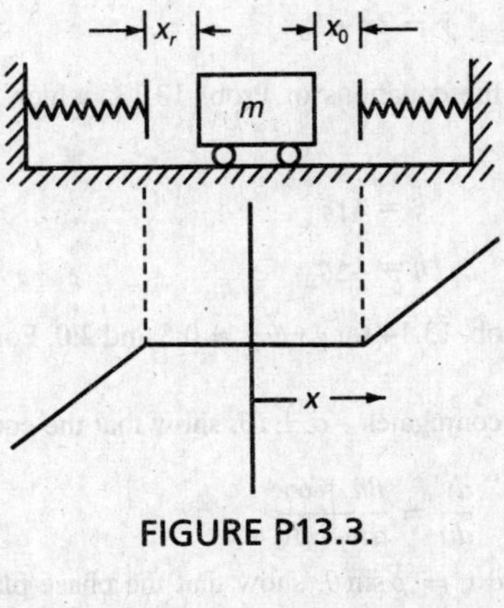

FIGURE P13.3.

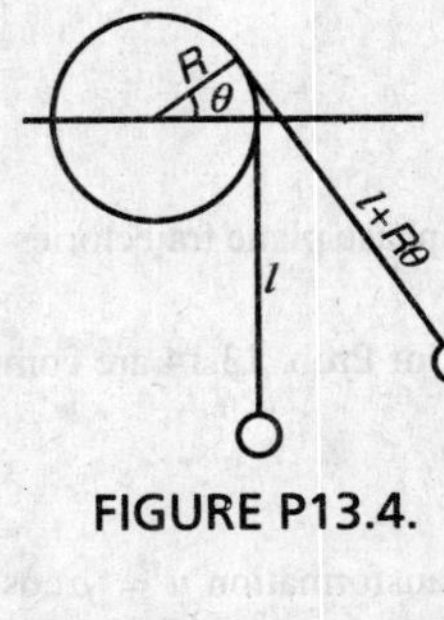

FIGURE P13.4.

13.4. The cord of a simple pendulum is wrapped around a fixed cylinder of radius R such that its length is l when in the vertical position, as shown in Fig. P13.4. Determine the differential equation of motion.

13.5. Using the nonlinear equation

$$\ddot{x} + x^3 = 0$$

show that if x_1 and x_2 are solutions satisfying the differential equation, their superposition $(x_1 + x_2)$ is not a solution.

13.6. For the undamped spring-mass system with initial conditions $x(0) = A$ and $\dot{x}(0) = 0$, determine the equation for the state speed V and state under what condition the system is in equilibrium.

13.7. Plot the phase plane trajectory for the undamped spring-mass system, including the potential energy curve $U(x)$. Discuss the initial conditions associated with the plot.

13.8. From the plot of $U(x)$ vs. x of Prob. 13.7, determine the period from the equation

$$\tau = 4\int_0^{x_{\max}} \frac{dx}{\sqrt{2[E - U(x)]}}$$

(Remember that E in the text was for a unit mass.)

M **13.9.** The solution to a certain linear differential equation is given as

$$x = \cos 2\pi t + \sin \pi t$$

Determine $y = \dot{x}$ and plot a phase plane diagram.

13.10. If the potential energy of a simple pendulum is given with the positive sign

$$U(\theta) = +\frac{g}{l}\cos\theta$$

determine which of the singular points are stable or unstable and explain their physical implications. Compare the phase plane with Fig. 13.4.2.

M **13.11.** Given the potential $U(x) = 8 - 2\cos \pi x/4$, plot the phase plane trajectories for $E = 6, 7, 8, 10$, and 12, and discuss the curves.

M **13.12.** Determine the phase plane equation for the damped spring-mass system

$$\ddot{x} + 2\zeta\omega_n\dot{x} + \omega_n^2 x = 0$$

and plot one of the trajectories with $v = y/\omega_n$ and x as coordinates.

13.13. Determine the eigenvalues and eigenvectors of the equations

$$\dot{x} = 5x - y$$

$$\dot{y} = 2x + 2y$$

13.14. Determine the modal transformation of the equations of Prob. 13.13, which will decouple them to the form

$$\dot{\xi} = \lambda_1\xi$$

$$\dot{\eta} = \lambda_2\eta$$

M **13.15.** Plot the ξ, η phase plane trajectories of Prob. 13.14 for $\lambda_1/\lambda_2 = 0.5$ and 2.0. For $\lambda_1/\lambda_2 = 2.0$, plot the trajectory y vs. x.

13.16. If λ_1 and λ_2 of Prob. 13.14 are complex conjugates $-\alpha \pm i\beta$, show that the equation in the u, v plane becomes

$$\frac{dv}{du} = \frac{\beta u + \alpha v}{\alpha u - \beta v}$$

13.17. Using the transformation $u = \rho\cos\theta$ and $v = \rho\sin\theta$, show that the phase plane equation for Prob. 13.16 becomes

$$\frac{d\rho}{\rho} = \frac{\alpha}{\beta}d\theta$$

with the trajectories identified as logarithmic spirals

$$\rho = e^{(\alpha/\beta)\theta}$$

13.18. Near a singular point in the xy-plane, the trajectories appear as shown in Fig. P13.18. Determine the form of the phase plane equation and the corresponding trajectories in the $\xi\eta$-plane.

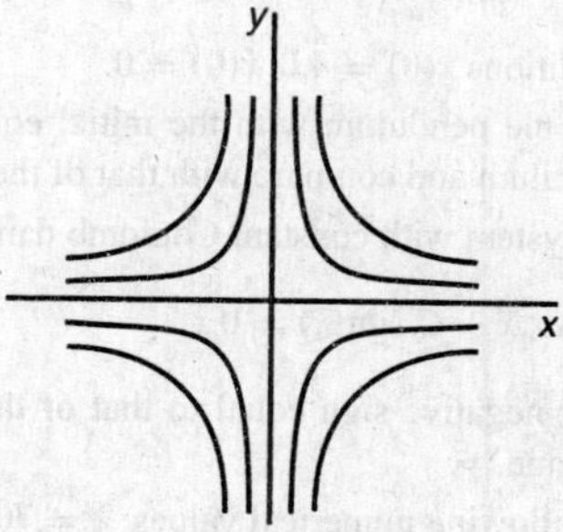

FIGURE P13.18.

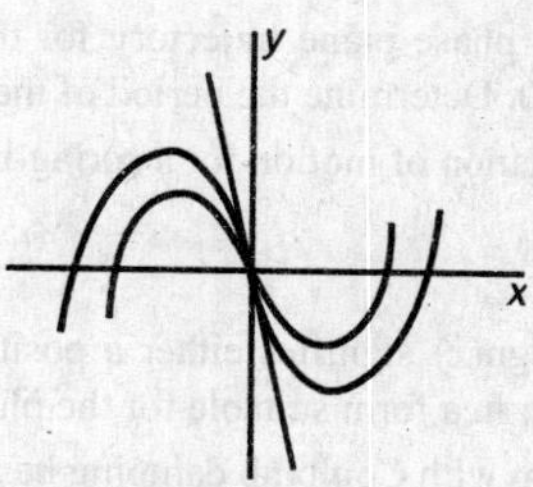

FIGURE P13.19.

13.19. The phase plane trajectories in the vicinity of a singularity of an overdamped system ($\zeta > 1$) are shown in Fig. P13.19. Identify the phase plane equation and plot the corresponding trajectories in the $\xi\eta$-plane.

13.20. Show that the solution of the equation

$$\frac{dy}{dx} = \frac{-x - y}{x + 3y}$$

is $x^2 + 2xy + 3y^2 = C$, which is a family of ellipses with axes rotated from the x, y coordinates. Determine the rotation of the semimajor axis and plot one of the ellipses.

13.21. Show that the isoclines of the linear differential equation of second order are straight lines.

M **13.22.** Draw the isoclines for the equation

$$\frac{dy}{dx} = xy(y - 2)$$

13.23. Consider the nonlinear equation

$$\ddot{x} + \omega_n^2 x + \mu x^3 = 0$$

Replacing $\ddot{x}$ by $y(dy/dx)$, where $y = \dot{x}$, gives the integral

$$y^2 + \omega_n^2 x^2 + \frac{1}{2}\mu x^4 = 2E$$

With $y = 0$ when $x = A$, show that the period is available from

$$\tau = 4\int_0^A \frac{dx}{\sqrt{2[E - U(x)]}}$$

What do the isoclines look like?

M **13.24.** Plot the isoclines of the van der Pol's equation

$$\ddot{x} - \mu\dot{x}(1 - x^2) + x = 0$$

for $\mu = 4.0$ and $dy/dx = 0, -1$ and $+1$.

13.25. The equation for the free oscillation of a damped system with a hardening spring is

$$m\ddot{x} + c\dot{x} + kx + \mu x^3 = 0$$

Express this equation in the phase plane form.

M **13.26.** The following numerical values are given for the equation in Prob. 13.25:

$$\omega_n^2 = \frac{k}{m} = 25 \qquad \frac{c}{m} = 2\zeta\omega_n = 2.0 \qquad \frac{\mu}{m} = 5$$

Plot the phase trajectory for the initial conditions $x(0) = 4.0, \dot{x}(0) = 0$.

M **13.27.** Plot the phase plane trajectory for the simple pendulum with the initial conditions $\theta(0) = 60°$ and $\dot{\theta}(0) = 0$. Determine the period of the pendulum and compare with that of the linear system.

13.28. The equation of motion for a spring-mass system with constant Coulomb damping can be written as

$$\ddot{x} + \omega_n^2 x + C\ \mathrm{sgn}(\dot{x}) = 0$$

where $\mathrm{sgn}(\dot{x})$ signifies either a positive or negative sign equal to that of the sign of $\dot{x}$. Express this equation in a form suitable for the phase plane.

M **13.29.** A system with Coulomb damping has the following numerical values: $k = 700$ N/m, $m = 0.05$ kg, and $\mu = 0.20$. Using the phase plane, plot the trajectory for $x(0) = 0.5$ m, $\dot{x}(0) = 0$.

13.30. Consider the motion of the simple pendulum with viscous damping and determine the singular points. With the aid of Fig. 13.4.2, and the knowledge that the trajectories must spiral into the origin, draw some approximate trajectories.

13.31. Apply the perturbation method to the simple pendulum with sin θ replaced by $\theta - \frac{1}{6}\theta^3$. Use only the first two terms of the series for x and ω. From the perturbation method, what is the equation for the period of the simple pendulum as a function of amplitude?

M **13.32.** For a given system, the numerical values of Eq. (13.7.7) are

$$\ddot{x} + 0.15\dot{x} + 10x + x^3 = 5\cos(\omega t + \phi)$$

Plot A vs. ω from Eq. (13.7.11) by first assuming a value of A and solving for ω^2. Determine the phase angle ϕ vs. ω.

13.33. The supporting end of a simple pendulum is given a motion, as shown in Fig. P13.33. Show that the equation of motion is

$$\ddot{\theta} + \left(\frac{g}{l} - \frac{\omega^2 y_0}{l}\cos 2\omega t\right)\sin\theta = 0$$

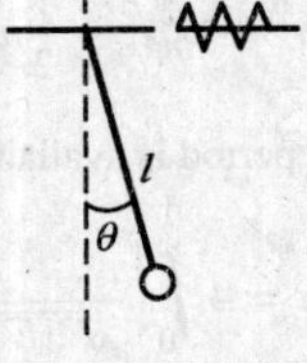

FIGURE P13.33.

13.34. For a given value of g/l, determine the frequencies of the excitation for which the simple pendulum of Prob. 13.33 with a stiff arm l will be stable in the inverted position.

13.35. Determine the perturbation solution for the system shown in Fig. P13.35 leading to a Mathieu equation. Use initial conditions $\dot{x}(0) = 0, x(0) = A$.

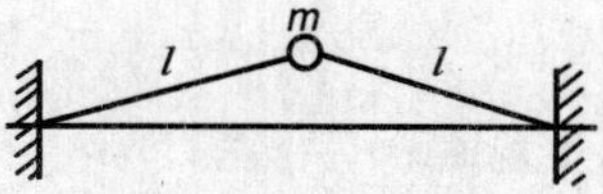

FIGURE P13.35.

M **13.36.** Using the Runge–Kutta routine and $g/l = 1.0$, calculate the angle θ for the simple pendulum of Prob. 13.27.

M **13.37.** With damping added to Prob. 13.36, the equation of motion is

$$\ddot{\theta} + 0.30\dot{\theta} + \sin\theta = 0$$

Using the Runge–Kutta method, solve for the initial conditions $\theta(0) = 60°, \dot{\theta}(0) = 0$.

M **13.38.** Obtain a numerical solution for the system of Prob. 13.35 by using (a) the central difference method and (b) the Runge–Kutta method.

M **13.39.** Consider the large-amplitude motion of the pendulum of mass m and length l, forced by sinusoidal forcing of frequency Ω and amplitude F_0. The Poincaré plot of the motion is obtained by plotting the initial position and velocity and then plotting the position and velocity of the pendulum after time $T, 2T, 3T, \ldots$ has elapsed. The angle θ must be presented on the fundamental interval $[0, 2\pi]$. Simulate the motion for various initial conditions in MATLAB®, for the amplitude of perturbation ranging from very small to 1 and for different frequencies of forcing. If the amplitude of the perturbation is non-zero, is the transition from the oscillatory to rotational motion possible?

M **13.40.** Consider the forced and damped Duffing oscillator described in Sec. 13.6. Simulate the equation of motion in MATLAB® for $c = 0.2, F = 0.3, k = 1, \mu = 1$, and $\omega = 1$. Make the Poincaré plot. What do you observe?

APPENDIX A

Specifications of Vibration Bounds

Specifications for vibrations are often based on harmonic motion.

$$x = x_0 \sin \omega t$$

The velocity and acceleration are then available from differentiation and the following relationships for the peak values can be written.

$$\dot{x} = 2\pi f x_0$$

$$\ddot{x}_0 = -4\pi^2 f^2 x_0 = -2\pi f \dot{x}_0$$

These equations can be represented on log–log paper by rewriting them in the form

$$\ln \dot{x}_0 = \ln x_0 + \ln 2\pi f$$

$$\ln \dot{x}_0 = -\ln \ddot{x}_0 - \ln 2\pi f$$

By letting x_0 = constant, the plot of $\ln \dot{x}_0$ against $\ln 2\pi f$ is a straight line slope equal to $+1$. By letting $\ddot{x}_0$ = constant, the plot of x_0 vs. $\ln 2\pi f$ is again a straight line of slope -1. These lines are shown graphically in Fig. A.1. The graph is often used to specify bounds for the vibration. Shown in heavy lines are bounds for a maximum acceleration of $10g$, minimum and maximum frequencies of 5 and 500 cps, and an upper limit for the displacement of 0.30 in.

100
10
1
.1
.01
.001
.1
1
10
100
1000
VELOCITY - INCHES / SEC
FREQUENCY - CPS
10 INCHES
1 INCH
.1 INCH
.01 INCH
.001 INCH
.0001 INCH
.00001 INCH
.000001 INCH
e/g = 100
e/g = 10
e/g = 1
e/g = .1
e/g = .01
e/g = .001
e/g = .0001
e/g = .00001

FIGURE A.1.

APPENDIX B

Introduction to Laplace Transformation

Definition

If $f(t)$ is a known function of t for values of $t > 0$, its Laplace transform (LT), $\bar{f}(s)$, is defined by the equation

$$\bar{f}(s) = \int_0^\infty e^{-st} f(t)\, dt = \mathcal{L}f(t) \tag{B.1}$$

where s is a complex variable. The integral exists for the real part of $s > 0$ provided $f(t)$ is an absolutely integrable function of t in the time interval 0 to ∞.

Example B.1

Let $f(t)$ be a constant c for $t > 0$. Its LT is

$$\mathcal{L}c = \int_0^\infty ce^{-st}\, dt = -\left.\frac{ce^{-st}}{s}\right|_0^\infty = \frac{c}{s}$$

which exists for $R(s) > 0$.

■

Example B.2

Let $f(t) = t$. Its LT is found by integration by parts, letting

$$u = t \qquad du = dt$$
$$dv = e^{-st}\, dt \qquad v = -\frac{e^{-st}}{s}$$

The result is

$$\mathcal{L}t = -\left.\frac{te^{-st}}{s}\right|_0^\infty + \frac{1}{s}\int_0^\infty e^{-st}\, dt = \frac{1}{s^2} \qquad R(s) > 0$$

■

LT of derivatives. If $\mathcal{L}f(t) = \bar{f}(s)$ exists, where $f(t)$ is continuous, then $f(t)$ tends to $f(0)$ as $t \to 0$ and the LT of its derivative $f'(t) = df(t)/dt$ is equal to

$$\mathcal{L}f'(t) = s\bar{f}(s) - f(0) \tag{B.2}$$

This relation is found by integration by parts

$$\int_0^\infty e^{-st} f'(t)\, dt = e^{-st} f(t)\Big|_0^\infty + s\int_0^\infty e^{-st} f(t)\, dt$$

Similarly, the LT of the second derivative can be shown to be

$$\mathcal{L}f''(t) = s^2\bar{f}(s) - sf(0) - f'(0) \tag{B.3}$$

Shifting Theorem

Consider the LT of the function $e^{at}x(t)$.

$$\mathcal{L}e^{at}x(t) = \int_0^\infty e^{-st}[e^{at}x(t)]\, dt = \int_0^\infty e^{-(s-a)t}x(t)\, dt$$

We conclude from this expression that

$$\mathcal{L}e^{at}x(t) = \bar{x}(s-a) \tag{B.4}$$

where $\mathcal{L}x(t) = \bar{x}(s)$. Thus, the multiplication of $x(t)$ by e^{at} shifts the transform by a, where a can be any number, real or complex.

Transformation of Ordinary Differential Equations

Consider the differential equation

$$m\ddot{x} + c\dot{x} + kx = F(t) \tag{B.5}$$

Its LT is

$$m[s^2\bar{x}(s) - sx(0) - \dot{x}(0)] + c[s\bar{x}(s) - x(0)] + k\bar{x}(s) = \bar{F}(s)$$

which can be rearranged to

$$\bar{x}(s) = \frac{\bar{F}(s)}{ms^2 + cs + k} + \frac{(ms + c)x(0) + m\dot{x}(0)}{ms^2 + cs + k} \tag{B.6}$$

The last equation is called the subsidiary equation of the differential equation. The response $x(t)$ is found from the inverse transformation, the first term representing the forced response and the second term the response due to the initial conditions.

For the more general case, the subsidiary equation can be written in the form

$$\bar{x}(s) = \frac{A(s)}{B(s)} \tag{B.7}$$

where $A(s)$ and $B(s)$ are polynomials. $B(s)$ is in general of higher order than $A(s)$.

Transforms Having Simple Poles

Considering the subsidiary equation

$$\bar{x}(s) = \frac{A(s)}{B(s)}$$

we examine the case where $B(s)$ is factorable in terms of n roots a_k, which are distinct (simple poles).

$$B(s) = (s - a_1)(s - a_2) \cdots (s - a_n)$$

The subsidiary equation can then be expanded in the following partial fractions:

$$\bar{x}(s) = \frac{A(s)}{B(s)} = \frac{C_1}{s - a_1} + \frac{C_2}{s - a_2} + \cdots + \frac{C_n}{s - a_n} \tag{B.8}$$

To determine the constants C_k, we multiply both sides of the preceding equation by $(s - a_k)$ and let $s = a_k$. Every term on the right will then be zero except C_k and we arrive at the result

$$C_k = \lim_{s \to a_k} (s - a_k) \frac{A(s)}{B(s)} \tag{B.9}$$

Because $\mathcal{L}^{-1} C_k/(s - a_k) = C_k e^{a_k t}$, the inverse transform of $\bar{x}(s)$ becomes

$$x(t) = \sum_{k=1}^{n} \lim_{s \to a_k} (s - a_k) \frac{A(s)}{B(s)} e^{a_k t} \tag{B.10}$$

Another expression for the last equation becomes apparent by noting that

$$\begin{aligned} B(s) &= (s - a_k) B_1(s) \\ B'(s) &= (s - a_k) B_1'(s) + B_1(s) \\ \lim_{s \to a_k} B'(s) &= B_1(a_k) \end{aligned}$$

Because $(s - a_k)A(s)/B(s) = A(s)/B_1(s)$, it is evident that

$$x(t) = \sum_{k=1}^{n} \frac{A(a_k)}{B'(a_k)} e^{a_k t} \tag{B.11}$$

Transforms Having Poles of Higher Order

If in the subsidary equation

$$\bar{x}(s) = \frac{A(s)}{B(s)}$$

a factor in $B(s)$ is repeated m times, we say that $\bar{x}(s)$ has an mth-order pole. Assuming that there is an m-th order pole at $a_1, B(s)$ will have the form

$$B(s) = (s - a_1)^m (s - a_2)(s - a_3) \cdots$$

The partial fraction expansion of $\bar{x}(s)$ then becomes

$$\bar{x}(s) = \frac{C_{11}}{(s - a_1)^m} + \frac{C_{12}}{(s - a_1)^{m-1}} + \cdots + \frac{C_{1m}}{(s - a_1)} + \frac{C_2}{(s - a_2)} + \frac{C_3}{(s - a_3)} + \cdots \quad \text{(B.12)}$$

The coefficient C_{11} is determined by multiplying both sides of the equation by $(s - a_1)^m$ and letting $s = a_1$,

$$(s - a_1)^m \bar{x}(s) = C_{11} + (s - a_1)C_{12} + \cdots + (s - a_1)^{m-1} C_{1m} + \frac{(s - a_1)^m}{s - a_2} C_2 + \cdots \quad \text{(B.13)}$$

$$\therefore C_{11} = [(s - a_1)^m \bar{x}(s)]_{s=a_1}$$

The coefficient C_{12} is determined by differentiating the equation for $(s - a_1)^m \bar{x}(s)$ with respect to s and then letting $s = a_1$,

$$C_1 = \left[\frac{d}{ds}(s - a_1)^m \bar{x}(s)\right]_{s=a_1} \quad \text{(B.14)}$$

It is evident then that

$$C_{1n} = \frac{1}{(n-1)!}\left[\frac{d^{n-1}}{ds^{n-1}}(s - a_1)^m \bar{x}(s)\right]_{s=a_1} \quad \text{(B.15)}$$

The remaining coefficients $C_2, C_3, \ldots$, are evaluated as in the previous section for simple poles.

Because by the shifting theorem,

$$\mathcal{L}^{-1}\frac{1}{(s - a_1)^n} = \frac{t^{n-1}}{(n-1)!}^{a_1 t}$$

the inverse transform of $\bar{x}(s)$ becomes

$$x(t) = \left[C_{11}\frac{t^{m-1}}{(m-1)!} + C_{12}\frac{t^{m-2}}{(m-2)!} + \cdots\right] e^{a_1 t} + C_2 e^{a_2 t} + C_3 e^{a_3 t} + \cdots \quad \text{(B.16)}$$

Most ordinary differential equations can be solved by the elementary theory of LT. Table B.1 gives the LT of simple functions. The table is also used to establish the inverse LT, because if

$$\mathcal{L}f(t) = \bar{f}(s)$$

then

$$f(t) = \mathcal{L}^{-1}\bar{f}(s)$$

TABLE B.1 Short Table of Laplace Transforms

	$f(s)$	$f(t)$
(1)	1	$\delta(t) =$ unit impulse at $t = 0$
(2)	$\frac{1}{s}$	$\mathcal{U}(t) =$ unit step function at $t = 0$
(3)	$\frac{1}{s^n}\ (n = 1, 2, \ldots)$	$\frac{t^{n-1}}{(n-1)!}$
(4)	$\frac{1}{s+a}$	e^{-at}
(5)	$\frac{1}{(s+a)^2}$	te^{-at}
(6)	$\frac{1}{(s+a)^n}\ (n = 1, 2, \ldots)$	$\frac{1}{(n-1)!} t^{n-1} e^{-at}$
(7)	$\frac{1}{s(s+a)}$	$\frac{1}{a}(1 - e^{-at})$
(8)	$\frac{1}{s^2(s+a)}$	$\frac{1}{a^2}(e^{-at} + at - 1)$
(9)	$\frac{s}{s^2 + a^2}$	$\cos at$
(10)	$\frac{s}{s^2 - a^2}$	$\cosh at$
(11)	$\frac{1}{s^2 + a^2}$	$\frac{1}{a} \sin at$
(12)	$\frac{1}{s^2 - a^2}$	$\frac{1}{a} \sinh at$
(13)	$\frac{1}{s(s^2 + a^2)}$	$\frac{1}{a^2}(1 - \cos at)$
(14)	$\frac{1}{s^2(s^2 + a^2)}$	$\frac{1}{a^3}(at - \sin at)$
(15)	$\frac{1}{(s^2 + a^2)^2}$	$\frac{1}{2a^3}(\sin at - at \cos at)$
(16)	$\frac{s}{(s^2 + a^2)^2}$	$\frac{t}{2a} \sin at$
(17)	$\frac{s^2 - a^2}{(s^2 + a^2)^2}$	$t \cos at$
(18)	$\frac{1}{s^2 + 2\zeta\omega_0 s + \omega_0^2}$	$\frac{1}{\omega_0\sqrt{1-\zeta^2}} e^{-\zeta\omega_0\tau} \sin \omega_0\sqrt{1-\zeta^2}\,t$

SUGGESTED READING

[1] THOMSON, W. T. *Laplace Transformation*, 2nd Ed. Englewood Cliffs, NJ: Prentice-Hall 1960.

APPENDIX C

Determinants and Matrices

C.1 DETERMINANT

A determinant of the second order and its numerical evaluation are defined by the following notation and operation

$$D = \begin{vmatrix} a & b \\ c & d \end{vmatrix} = ad - bc$$

An nth-order determinant has n rows and n columns, and in order to identify the position of its elements, the following notation is adopted:

$$\begin{vmatrix} a_{11} & a_{12} & a_{13} & \cdots & a_{1n} \\ a_{21} & a_{22} & a_{23} & \cdots & a_{2n} \\ \vdots & \vdots & \vdots & & \vdots \\ a_{n1} & a_{n2} & a_{n3} & \cdots & a_{nn} \end{vmatrix}$$

Minors

A minor M_{ij} of the element a_{ij} is a determinant formed by deleting the ith row and the jth column from the original determinant.

Cofactor

The cofactor C_{ij} of the element a_{ij} is defined by the equation

$$C_{ij} = (-1)^{i+j} M_{ij}$$

Example C.1.1

Given the third-order determinant

$$\begin{vmatrix} 2 & 1 & 5 \\ 4 & 2 & 1 \\ 2 & 0 & 3 \end{vmatrix}$$

The minor of the term $a_{21} = 4$ is

$$M_{21} \text{ of } \begin{vmatrix} 2 & 1 & 5 \\ 4 & 2 & 1 \\ 2 & 0 & 3 \end{vmatrix} = \begin{vmatrix} 1 & 5 \\ 0 & 3 \end{vmatrix} = 3$$

and its cofactor is

$$C_{21} = (-1)^{2+1}3 = -3$$

■

Expansion of a Determinant

The order of a determinant can be reduced by 1 by expanding any row or column in terms of its cofactors.

Example C.1.2

The determinant of the previous example is expanded in terms of the second column as

$$D = \begin{vmatrix} 2 & 1 & 5 \\ 4 & 2 & 1 \\ 2 & 0 & 3 \end{vmatrix} = 1(-1)^{1+2}\begin{vmatrix} 4 & 1 \\ 2 & 3 \end{vmatrix} + 2(-1)^{2+2}\begin{vmatrix} 2 & 5 \\ 2 & 3 \end{vmatrix}$$
$$+ 0(-1)^{3+2}\begin{vmatrix} 2 & 5 \\ 4 & 1 \end{vmatrix}$$
$$= -10 - 8 = -18$$

■

Properties of Determinants

The following properties of determinants are stated without proof:

1. Interchange of any two columns or rows changes the sign of the determinant.
2. If two rows or two columns are identical, the determinant is zero.
3. Any row or column may be multiplied by a constant and added to another row or column without changing the value of the determinant.

C.2 MATRICES

Matrix. A rectangular array of terms arranged in m rows and n columns is called a matrix. For example,

$$A = \begin{bmatrix} a_{11} & a_{12} & a_{13} & a_{14} \\ a_{21} & a_{22} & a_{23} & a_{24} \\ a_{31} & a_{32} & a_{33} & a_{34} \end{bmatrix}$$

is a 3×4 matrix.

Square matrix. A square matrix is one in which the number of rows is equal to the number of columns. It is referred to as an $n \times n$ matrix or a matrix of order n.

Symmetric matrix. A square matrix is said to be symmetric if the elements on the upper right half can be obtained by flipping the matrix about the diagonal.

$$A = \begin{bmatrix} 2 & 1 & 3 \\ 1 & 5 & 0 \\ 3 & 0 & 1 \end{bmatrix} = \text{symmetric matrix}$$

Trace. The sum of the diagonal elements of a square matrix is called the trace. For the previous matrix,

$$\text{Trace } A = 2 + 5 + 1 = 8$$

Singular matrix. If the determinant of a matrix is zero, the matrix is said to be singular.

Row matrix. A row matrix has $m = 1$.

$$B = [\ b_1 \quad b_2 \quad b_3\ ]$$

Column matrix. A column matrix has $n = 1$.

$$C = \begin{Bmatrix} C_1 \\ C_2 \\ C_3 \end{Bmatrix}$$

Zero matrix. The zero matrix is defined as one in which all elements are zero.

$$0 = \begin{bmatrix} 0 & 0 & 0 \\ 0 & 0 & 0 \end{bmatrix}$$

Unit matrix. The unit matrix

$$I = \begin{bmatrix} 1 & 0 & 0 \\ 0 & 1 & 0 \\ 0 & 0 & 1 \end{bmatrix}$$

is a square matrix in which the diagonal elements from the top left to the bottom right are unity with all other elements equal to zero.

Diagonal matrix. A square matrix having elements a_{ii} along the diagonal with all other elements equal to zero is a diagonal matrix.

$$[a_{ii}] = \begin{bmatrix} a_{11} & 0 & 0 \\ 0 & a_{22} & 0 \\ 0 & 0 & a_{33} \end{bmatrix}$$

Transpose. The transpose A^T of a matrix A is one in which the rows and columns are interchanged. For example,

$$A = \begin{bmatrix} a_{11} & a_{12} & a_{13} \\ a_{21} & a_{22} & a_{23} \end{bmatrix} \qquad A^T = \begin{bmatrix} a_{11} & a_{21} \\ a_{12} & a_{22} \\ a_{13} & a_{23} \end{bmatrix}$$

The transpose of a column matrix is a row matrix.

Minor. A minor M_{ij} of a matrix A is formed by deleting the ith row and the jth column from the determinant of the original matrix.

$$\text{Let } A = \begin{bmatrix} a_{11} & a_{12} & a_{13} \\ a_{21} & a_{22} & a_{23} \\ a_{31} & a_{32} & a_{33} \end{bmatrix}$$

$$M_{12} \begin{vmatrix} a_{11} & a_{12} & a_{13} \\ a_{21} & a_{22} & a_{23} \\ a_{31} & a_{32} & a_{33} \end{vmatrix} = \begin{vmatrix} a_{21} & a_{23} \\ a_{31} & a_{33} \end{vmatrix}$$

Cofactor. The cofactor C_{ij} is equal to the signed minor $(-1)^{i+j}M_{ij}$. From the previous example,

$$C_{12} = (-1)^{1+2}M_{12} = -M_{12}$$

Adjoint matrix. An adjoint matrix of a square matrix A is a transpose of the matrix of cofactors of A.

Let cofactor matrix of A be

$$[C_{ij}] = \begin{bmatrix} C_{11} & C_{12} & C_{13} \\ C_{21} & C_{22} & C_{23} \\ C_{31} & C_{32} & C_{33} \end{bmatrix}$$

$$\text{adj } A = [C_{ij}]^T = [C_{ji}] = \begin{bmatrix} C_{11} & C_{21} & C_{31} \\ C_{12} & C_{22} & C_{32} \\ C_{13} & C_{23} & C_{33} \end{bmatrix}$$

Inverse matrix. The inverse A^{-1} of a matrix A satisfies the relationship

$$A^{-1}A = AA^{-1} = I$$

Orthogonal matrix. An orthogonal matrix A satisfies the relationship

$$A^TA = AA^T = I$$

From the definition of an inverse matrix, it is evident that for an orthogonal matrix $A^T = A^{-1}$.

C.3 RULES OF MATRIX OPERATIONS

Addition. Two matrices having the same n mber of rows and columns can be added by summing the corresponding elements.

Example C.3.1

$$\begin{bmatrix} 1 & 3 & 2 \\ 4 & 1 & 1 \end{bmatrix} + \begin{bmatrix} 2 & 0 & 4 \\ 1 & -2 & -3 \end{bmatrix} = \begin{bmatrix} 3 & 3 & 6 \\ 5 & -1 & -2 \end{bmatrix}$$

■

Multiplication. The product of two matrices A and B is another matrix C.

$$AB = C$$

The element C_{ij} of C is determined by multiplying the elements of the ith row in A by the elements of the jth column in B according to the rule

$$c_{ij} = \sum_k a_{ik} b_{kj}$$

Example C.3.2

$$\text{Let } A = \begin{bmatrix} 1 & 1 & 1 \\ 1 & 2 & 2 \\ 1 & 2 & 3 \end{bmatrix} \quad B = \begin{bmatrix} 2 & 0 \\ 0 & 1 \\ 3 & -1 \end{bmatrix}$$

$$AB = \begin{bmatrix} 1 & 1 & 1 \\ 1 & 2 & 2 \\ 1 & 2 & 3 \end{bmatrix} \begin{bmatrix} 2 & 0 \\ 0 & 1 \\ 3 & -1 \end{bmatrix} = \begin{bmatrix} 5 & 0 \\ 8 & 0 \\ 11 & -1 \end{bmatrix} = C$$

i.e.,

$$c_{21} = 1 \times 2 + 2 \times 0 + 2 \times 3 = 8$$

It is evident that the number of columns in A must equal the number of rows in B, or that the matrices must be conformable. We also note that $AB \neq BA$.

The postmultiplication of a matrix by a column matrix results in a column matrix.

■

Example C.3.3

$$\begin{bmatrix} 1 & 1 & 1 \\ 1 & 5 & 2 \\ 2 & 1 & 3 \end{bmatrix} \begin{Bmatrix} 1 \\ 3 \\ 2 \end{Bmatrix} = \begin{Bmatrix} 6 \\ 20 \\ 11 \end{Bmatrix}$$

Premultiplication of a matrix by a row matrix (or transpose of a column matrix) results in a row matrix.

■

Example C.3.4

$$[1 \quad 3 \quad 2]\begin{bmatrix} 1 & 1 & 1 \\ 1 & 5 & 2 \\ 2 & 1 & 3 \end{bmatrix} = [8 \quad 18 \quad 13]$$

The transpose of a product $AB = C$ is $C^T = B^T A^T$.

■

Example C.3.5

$$\text{Let } A = \begin{bmatrix} 1 & 1 \\ 2 & 3 \end{bmatrix} \quad B = \begin{bmatrix} 2 & 1 \\ 1 & 1 \end{bmatrix}$$

$$C = AB = \begin{bmatrix} 3 & 2 \\ 7 & 5 \end{bmatrix} \quad C^T = B^T A^T = \begin{bmatrix} 2 & 1 \\ 1 & 1 \end{bmatrix}\begin{bmatrix} 1 & 2 \\ 1 & 3 \end{bmatrix} = \begin{bmatrix} 3 & 7 \\ 2 & 5 \end{bmatrix}$$

■

Inversion of a matrix. Consider a set of equations

$$\begin{aligned} a_{11}x_1 + a_{12}x_2 + a_{13}x_3 &= y_1 \\ a_{21}x_1 + a_{22}x_2 + a_{23}x_3 &= y_2 \\ a_{31}x_1 + a_{32}x_2 + a_{33}x_3 &= y_3 \end{aligned} \tag{C.3.1}$$

which can be expressed in the matrix form

$$AX = Y \tag{C.3.2}$$

Premultiplying by the inverse A^{-1}, we obtain the solution

$$X = A^{-1}Y \tag{C.3.3}$$

We can identify the term A^{-1} by the Cramer's rule as follows. The solution for x_1 is

$$\begin{aligned} x_1 &= \frac{1}{|A|}\begin{vmatrix} y_1 & a_{12} & a_{13} \\ y_2 & a_{22} & a_{23} \\ y_3 & a_{32} & a_{33} \end{vmatrix} \\ &= \frac{1}{|A|}\left\{ y_1 \begin{vmatrix} a_{22} & a_{23} \\ a_{32} & a_{33} \end{vmatrix} - y_2 \begin{vmatrix} a_{12} & a_{13} \\ a_{32} & a_{33} \end{vmatrix} + y_3 \begin{vmatrix} a_{12} & a_{13} \\ a_{22} & a_{23} \end{vmatrix} \right\} \\ &= \frac{1}{|A|}\{y_1 C_{11} + y_2 C_{21} + y_3 C_{31}\} \end{aligned}$$

where A is the determinant of the coefficient matrix A, and C_{11}, C_{21}, and C_{31} are the cofactors of A corresponding to elements 11, 21, and 31. We can also write similar expressions for x_2 and x_3 by replacing the second and third columns by the y column, respectively. Thus, the complete solution can be written in matrix form as

$$\begin{Bmatrix} x_1 \\ x_2 \\ x_3 \end{Bmatrix} = \frac{1}{|A|} \begin{bmatrix} C_{11} & C_{21} & C_{31} \\ C_{12} & C_{22} & C_{32} \\ C_{13} & C_{23} & C_{33} \end{bmatrix} \begin{Bmatrix} y_1 \\ y_2 \\ y_3 \end{Bmatrix} \tag{C.3.4}$$

or

$$\{x\} = \frac{1}{|A|}[C_{ji}]\{y\} = \frac{1}{|A|}[\text{adj } A]\{y\}$$

Thus, by comparison with Eq. (C.3.3), we arrive at the result

$$A^{-1} = \frac{1}{|A|}\text{adj } A \tag{C.3.5}$$

Example C.3.6

Find the inverse of the matrix

$$A = \begin{bmatrix} 1 & 1 & 1 \\ 1 & 2 & 2 \\ 1 & 0 & 3 \end{bmatrix}$$

(a) The determinant of A is $|A| = 3$.
(b) The minors of A are

$$M_{11} = \begin{vmatrix} 2 & 2 \\ 0 & 3 \end{vmatrix} = 6, \quad M_{12} = \begin{vmatrix} 1 & 2 \\ 1 & 3 \end{vmatrix} = 1, \ldots$$

(c) Supply the signs $(-1)^{i+j}$ to the minors to form the cofactors

$$[C_{ij}] = \begin{vmatrix} 6 & -1 & -2 \\ -3 & 2 & 1 \\ 0 & -1 & 1 \end{vmatrix}$$

(d) The adjoint matrix is the transpose of the cofactor matrix, or $[C_{ij}]^T = [C_{ji}]$. Thus, the inverse A^{-1} is

$$A^{-1} = \frac{1}{|A|}\text{adj } A = \frac{1}{3}\begin{bmatrix} 6 & -3 & 0 \\ -1 & 2 & -1 \\ -2 & 1 & 1 \end{bmatrix}$$

(e) The result can be checked as follows:

$$A^{-1}A = \frac{1}{3}\begin{bmatrix} 6 & -2 & 0 \\ -1 & 2 & -1 \\ -2 & 1 & 1 \end{bmatrix}\begin{bmatrix} 1 & 1 & 1 \\ 1 & 2 & 2 \\ 1 & 0 & 3 \end{bmatrix}$$

$$= \frac{1}{3}\begin{bmatrix} 3 & 0 & 0 \\ 0 & 3 & 0 \\ 0 & 0 & 3 \end{bmatrix} = \begin{bmatrix} 1 & 0 & 0 \\ 0 & 1 & 0 \\ 0 & 0 & 1 \end{bmatrix}$$

It should be noted that for an inverse to exist, the determinant $|A|$ must not be zero.

Equation (C.3.5) for the inverse offers another means of evaluating a determinant. Premultiply Eq. (C.3.5) by A:

$$AA^{-1} = \frac{A}{|A|}\text{adj } A = I$$

Thus, we obtain the expression

$$|A|I = A \text{ adj } A \tag{C.3.6}$$

■

Transpose of a Product

The following operations are given without proof:

$$\begin{aligned} (AB)^T &= B^T A^T \\ (A+B)^T &= A^T + B^T \end{aligned} \tag{C.3.7}$$

Orthogonal transformation. A matrix P is orthogonal if

$$P^{-1} = P^T$$

The determinant of an orthogonal matrix is equal to ± 1. If A = symmetric matrix, then

$$P^{-1}AP = D = P^T AP \quad \text{a diagonal matrix} \tag{C.3.8}$$

If A is a symmetric matrix, then

$$\begin{aligned} P^T A &= AP \\ \{x\}^T A &= A\{x\} \end{aligned} \tag{C.3.9}$$

Partitioned Matrices

A matrix can be partitioned into submatrices by horizontal and vertical lines, as shown by the following example:

$$\left[\begin{array}{cc:c} 2 & 4 & -1 \\ 0 & -3 & 4 \\ 1 & 2 & 2 \\ \hdashline 3 & -1 & -5 \end{array}\right] = \left[\begin{array}{c:c} [A] & [B] \\ \hdashline [C] & [D] \end{array}\right]$$

where the submatrices are

$$A = \begin{bmatrix} 2 & 4 \\ 0 & -3 \\ 1 & 2 \end{bmatrix} \qquad B = \begin{Bmatrix} -1 \\ 4 \\ 2 \end{Bmatrix}$$

$$C = [\,3 \quad -1\,] \qquad D = [-5]$$

Partitioned matrices obey the normal rules of matrix algebra and can be added, subtracted, and multiplied as though the submatrices were ordinary matrix elements. Thus,

$$\left[\begin{array}{c|c} A & B \\ \hline C & D \end{array}\right]\left\{\begin{array}{c} x \\ \hline y \end{array}\right\} = \left[\begin{array}{c} A\{x\} + B\{y\} \\ C\{x\} + D\{y\} \end{array}\right]$$

$$\left[\begin{array}{c|c} A & B \\ \hline C & D \end{array}\right]\left[\begin{array}{c|c} E & F \\ \hline G & H \end{array}\right] = \left[\begin{array}{c|c} AE + BG & AF + BH \\ \hline CE + DG & CE + DH \end{array}\right]$$

C.4 DETERMINATION OF EIGENVECTORS

The eigenvector X_i corresponding to the eigenvalue λ_i can be found from the cofactors of any row of the characteristic equation.

Let $[A - \lambda_i I]X_i = 0$ be written out for a third-order system as

$$\begin{bmatrix} (a_{11} - \lambda_1) & a_{12} & a_{13} \\ a_{21} & (a_{22} - \lambda_i) & a_{23} \\ a_{31} & a_{32} & (a_{33} - \lambda_i) \end{bmatrix} \begin{Bmatrix} x_1 \\ x_2 \\ x_3 \end{Bmatrix}_i = 0 \tag{C.4.1}$$

Its characteristic equation $|A - \lambda_i I| = 0$ written out in determinant form is

$$\begin{vmatrix} (a_{11} - \lambda_i) & a_{12} & a_{13} \\ a_{21} & (a_{22} - \lambda_i) & a_{23} \\ a_{31} & a_{32} & (a_{33} - \lambda_i) \end{vmatrix} = 0 \tag{C.4.2}$$

The determinant expanded in terms of the cofactors of the first row is

$$(a_{11} - \lambda_1)C_{11} + a_{12}C_{12} + a_{13}C_{13} = 0 \tag{C.4.3}$$

Next replace the first row of the determinant by the second row, leaving the other two rows unchanged. The value of the determinant is still zero because of two identical rows:

$$\begin{vmatrix} a_{21} & (a_{22} - \lambda_i) & a_{23} \\ a_{21} & (a_{22} - \lambda_i) & a_{23} \\ a_{31} & a_{32} & (a_{33} - \lambda_i) \end{vmatrix} = 0 \tag{C.4.4}$$

Again expand in terms of the cofactors of the first row, which are identical to the cofactors of the previous determinant:

$$a_{21}C_{11} + (a_{22} - \lambda_i)C_{12} + a_{23}C_{13} = 0 \tag{C.4.5}$$

Finally, replace the first row by the third row and expand in terms of the first row of the new determinant.

$$\begin{vmatrix} a_{31} & a_{32} & (a_{33} - \lambda_i) \\ a_{21} & (a_{22} - \lambda_i) & a_{23} \\ a_{31} & a_{32} & (a_{33} - \lambda_i) \end{vmatrix} = 0 \tag{C.4.6}$$

$$a_{31}C_{11} + a_{32}C_{12} + (a_{33} - \lambda_i)C_{13} = 0 \tag{C.4.7}$$

Equations (C.4.3), (C.4.5), and (C.4.7) can now be assembled in a single matrix equation:

$$\begin{bmatrix} (a_{11} - \lambda_i) & a_{12} & a_{13} \\ a_{21} & (a_{22} - \lambda_i) & a_{23} \\ a_{31} & a_{32} & (a_{33} - \lambda_i) \end{bmatrix} \begin{Bmatrix} C_{11} \\ C_{12} \\ C_{13} \end{Bmatrix} = 0 \tag{C.4.8}$$

Comparison of Eqs. (C.4.1) and (C.4.8) indicates that the eigenvector X_i can be determined from the cofactors of the characteristic equation with $\lambda = \lambda_i$. Because the eigenvectors are relative to a normalized coordinate, the column of cofactors can differ by a multiplying factor.

$$\begin{Bmatrix} x_1 \\ x_2 \\ x_3 \end{Bmatrix} = \alpha \begin{Bmatrix} C_{11} \\ C_{12} \\ C_{13} \end{Bmatrix}$$

Instead of the first row, any other row may have been used for the determination of the cofactors.

APPENDIX D

Normal Modes of Uniform Beams

We assume the free vibrations of a uniform beam to be governed by Euler's differential equation.

$$EI\frac{\partial^4 y}{\partial x^4} + m\frac{\partial^2 y}{\partial t^2} = 0 \tag{D.1}$$

To determine the normal modes of vibration, the solution in the form

$$y(x,t) = \phi_n(x)e^{i\omega_n t} \tag{D.2}$$

is substituted into Eq. (D.1) to obtain the equation

$$\frac{d^4\phi_n(x)}{dx^4} - \beta_n^4\phi_n(x) = 0 \tag{D.3}$$

where

$\phi_n(x)$ = characteristic function describing the deflection of the nth mode

m = mass density per unit length

$\beta_n^4 = m\,\omega_n^2/EI$

$\omega_n = (\beta_n l)^2\sqrt{EI/ml^4}$ = natural frequency of the nth mode

The characteristic functions $\phi_n(x)$ and the normal mode frequencies ω_n depend on the boundary conditions and have been tabulated by Young and Felgar. An abbreviated summary taken from this work* is presented here.

---

*D. Young, and R. P. Felgar, Jr., *Tables of Characteristic Functions Representing Normal Modes of Vibration of a Uniform Beam*. The University of Texas Publication No. 4913, July 1, 1949.

D.1 CLAMPED–CLAMPED BEAM

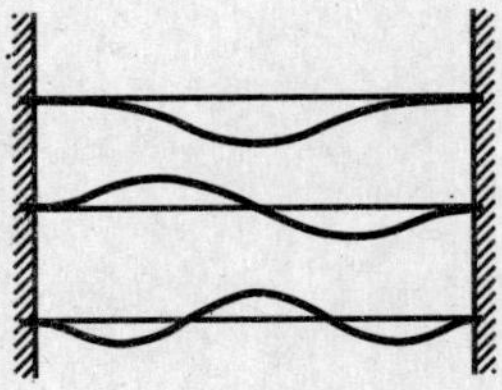

n	$\beta_n l$	$(\beta_n l)^2$	ω_n/ω_1
1	4.7300	22.3733	1.0000
2	7.8532	61.6728	2.7565
3	10.9956	120.9034	5.4039

D.2 FREE–FREE BEAM

The natural frequencies of the free–free beam are equal to those of the clamped–clamped beam. The characteristic functions of the free–free beam are related to those of the clamped–clamped beam as follows:

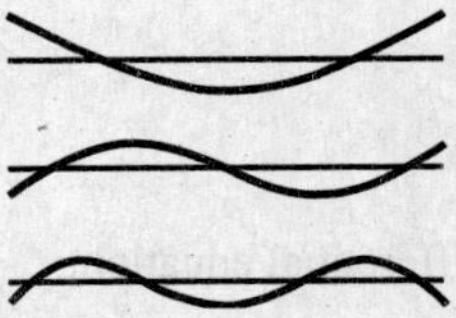

free–free		clamped–clamped
ϕ_n	=	ϕ''_n
ϕ'_n	=	ϕ'''_n
ϕ''_n	=	ϕ_n
ϕ'''_n	=	ϕ'_n

The characteristic functions of the first and second mode ($n = 1$ and 2) of a *clamped–clamped* beam are given in Tables D.1 and D.2 respectively.

D.3 CLAMPED–FREE BEAM

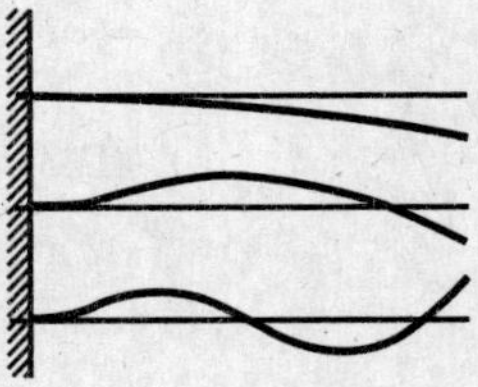

n	$\beta_n l$	$(\beta_n l)^2$	ω_n/ω_1
1	1.8751	3.5160	1.0000
2	4.6941	22.0345	6.2669
3	7.8548	61.6972	17.5475

The characteristic functions of the first and second mode ($n = 1$ and 2) of a *clamped–free* beam are given in Tables D.3 and D.4 respectively.

D.4 CLAMPED–PINNED BEAM

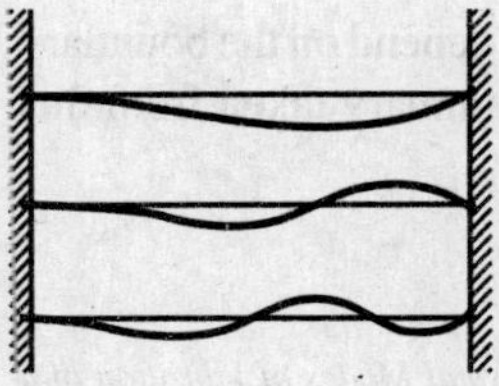

n	$\beta_n l$	$(\beta_n l)^2$	ω_n/ω_1
1	3.9266	15.4182	1.0000
2	7.0686	49.9645	3.2406
3	10.2101	104.2477	6.7613

D.5 FREE–PINNED BEAM

The natural frequencies of the free–pinned beam are equal to those of the clamped–pinned beam. The characteristic functions of the free–pinned beam are related to those of the clamped–pinned beam as follows:

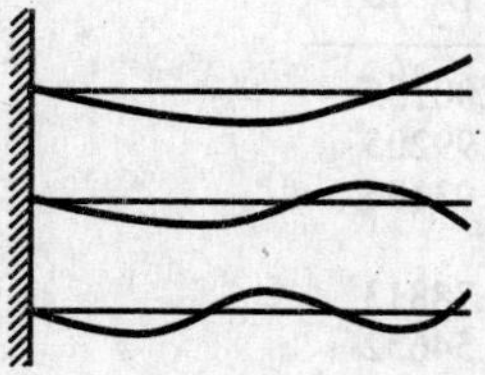

free–pinned		clamped–pinned
ϕ_n	=	ϕ_n''
ϕ_n'	=	ϕ_n'''
ϕ_n''	=	ϕ_n
ϕ_n'''	=	ϕ_n'

The characteristic functions of the first and second mode ($n = 1$ and 2) of a *clamped–pinned* beam are given in Tables D.5 and D.6 respectively.

TABLE D.1 Characteristic Functions and Derivatives
Clamped–Clamped Beam
First Mode

$\frac{x}{l}$	ϕ_1	$\phi_1' = \frac{1}{\beta_1}\frac{d\phi_1}{dx}$	$\phi_1'' = \frac{1}{\beta_1^2}\frac{d^2\phi_1}{dx^2}$	$\phi_1''' = \frac{1}{\beta_1^3}\frac{d^3\phi_1}{dx^3}$
0.00	0.00000	0.00000	2.00000	−1.96500
0.04	0.03358	0.34324	1.62832	−1.96285
0.08	0.12545	0.61624	1.25802	−1.94862
0.12	0.26237	0.81956	0.89234	−1.91254
0.16	0.43126	0.95451	0.53615	−1.84732
0.20	0.61939	1.02342	0.19545	−1.74814
0.24	0.81459	1.02986	−0.12305	−1.61250
0.28	1.00546	0.97870	−0.41240	−1.44017
0.32	1.18168	0.87608	−0.66581	−1.23296
0.36	1.33419	0.72992	−0.87699	−0.99452
0.40	1.45545	0.54723	−1.04050	−0.73007
0.44	1.53962	0.33897	−1.15202	−0.44611
0.48	1.58271	0.11478	−1.20854	−0.15007
0.52	1.58271	−0.11478	−1.20854	0.15007
0.56	1.53962	−0.33897	−1.15202	0.44611
0.60	1.45545	−0.54723	−1.04050	0.73007
0.64	1.33419	−0.72992	−0.87699	0.99452
0.68	1.18168	−0.87608	−0.66581	1.23296
0.72	1.00546	−0.97870	−0.41240	1.44017
0.76	0.81459	−1.02986	−0.12305	1.61250
0.80	0.61939	−1.02342	0.19545	1.74814
0.84	0.43126	−0.95451	0.53615	1.84732
0.88	0.26237	−0.81956	0.89234	1.91254
0.92	0.12545	−0.61624	1.25802	1.94862
0.96	0.03358	−0.34324	1.62832	1.96285
1.00	0.00000	0.00000	2.00000	1.96500

TABLE D.2 Characteristic Functions and Derivatives
Clamped–Clamped Beam
Second Mode

$\frac{x}{l}$	ϕ_2	$\phi_2' = \frac{1}{\beta_2}\frac{d\phi_2}{dx}$	$\phi_2'' = \frac{1}{\beta_2^2}\frac{d^2\phi_2}{dx^2}$	$\phi_2''' = \frac{1}{\beta_2^3}\frac{d^3\phi_2}{dx^3}$
0.00	0.00000	0.00000	2.00000	−2.00155
0.04	0.08834	0.52955	1.37202	−1.99205
0.08	0.31214	0.86296	0.75386	−1.93186
0.12	0.61058	1.00644	0.16713	−1.78813
0.16	0.92602	0.97427	−0.35923	−1.54652
0.20	1.20674	0.79030	−0.79450	−1.21002
0.24	1.41005	0.48755	−1.11133	−0.79651
0.28	1.50485	0.10660	−1.28991	−0.33555
0.32	1.47357	−0.30736	−1.32106	0.13566
0.36	1.31314	−0.70819	−1.20786	0.57665
0.40	1.03457	−1.05271	−0.96605	0.94823
0.44	0.66150	−1.30448	−0.62296	1.21670
0.48	0.22751	−1.43728	−0.21508	1.35744
0.52	−0.22751	−1.43728	0.21508	1.35744
0.56	−0.66150	−1.30448	0.62296	1.21670
0.60	−1.03457	−1.05271	0.96605	0.94823
0.64	−1.31314	−0.70819	1.20786	0.57665
0.68	−1.47357	−0.30736	1.32106	0.13566
0.72	−1.50485	0.10660	1.28991	−0.33555
0.76	−1.41005	0.48755	1.11133	−0.79651
0.80	−1.20674	0.70930	0.79450	−1.21002
0.84	−0.92602	0.97427	0.35923	−1.54652
0.88	−0.61058	1.00644	−0.16713	−1.78813
0.92	−0.31214	0.86296	−0.75386	−1.93186
0.96	−0.08834	0.52955	−1.37202	−1.99205
1.00	0.00000	0.00000	−2.00000	−2.00155

TABLE D.3 Characteristic Functions and Derivatives
Clamped–Free Beam
First Mode

$\frac{x}{l}$	ϕ_1	$\phi_1' = \frac{1}{\beta_1}\frac{d\phi_1}{dx}$	$\phi_1'' = \frac{1}{\beta_1^2}\frac{d^2\phi_1}{dx^2}$	$\phi_1''' = \frac{1}{\beta_1^3}\frac{d^3\phi_1}{dx^3}$
0.00	0.00000	0.00000	2.00000	−1.45819
0.04	0.00552	0.14588	1.88988	−1.46805
0.08	0.02168	0.28350	1.77980	−1.46710
0.12	0.04784	0.41286	1.66985	−1.46455
0.16	0.08340	0.53400	1.56016	−1.45968
0.20	0.12774	0.64692	1.45096	−1.45182
0.24	0.18024	0.75167	1.34247	−1.44032
0.28	0.24030	0.84832	1.23500	−1.42459
0.32	0.30730	0.93696	1.23889	−1.40410
0.36	0.38065	1.01771	1.02451	−1.37834
0.40	0.45977	1.09070	0.92227	−1.34685
0.44	0.54408	1.15612	0.82262	−1.30924
0.48	0.63301	1.21418	0.72603	−1.26512
0.52	0.72603	1.26512	0.63301	−1.21418
0.56	0.82262	1.30924	0.54408	−1.15612
0.60	0.92227	1.34685	0.45977	−1.09070
0.64	1.02451	1.37834	0.38065	−1.01771
0.68	1.12889	1.40410	0.30730	−0.93696
0.72	1.23500	1.42459	0.24030	−0.84832
0.76	1.34247	1.44032	0.18024	−0.75167
0.80	1.45096	1.45182	0.12774	−0.64692
0.84	1.56016	1.45968	0.08340	−0.53400
0.88	1.66985	1.46455	0.04784	−0.41286
0.92	1.77980	1.46710	0.02168	−0.28350
0.96	1.88988	1.46805	0.00552	−0.14588
1.00	2.00000	1.46819	0.00000	0.00000

TABLE D.4 Characteristic Functions and Derivatives
Clamped–Free Beam
Second Mode

$\frac{x}{l}$	ϕ_2	$\phi_2' = \frac{1}{\beta_2}\frac{d\phi_2}{dx}$	$\phi_2'' = \frac{1}{\beta_2^2}\frac{d^2\phi_2}{dx^2}$	$\phi_2''' = \frac{1}{\beta_2^3}\frac{d^3\phi_2}{dx^3}$
0.00	0.00000	0.00000	2.00000	−2.03693
0.04	0.03301	0.33962	1.61764	−2.03483
0.08	0.12305	0.60754	1.23660	−2.02097
0.12	0.25670	0.80728	0.86004	−1.98590
0.16	0.42070	0.93108	0.49261	−1.92267
0.20	0.60211	0.99020	0.14007	−1.82682
0.24	0.78852	0.98502	−0.19123	−1.69625
0.28	0.96827	0.92013	−0.49475	−1.53113
0.32	1.13068	0.80136	−0.76419	−1.33373
0.36	1.26626	0.63565	−0.99384	−1.10821
0.40	1.36694	0.43094	−1.17895	−0.86040
0.44	1.42619	0.19593	−1.31600	−0.59748
0.48	1.43920	−0.06012	−1.40289	−0.32772
0.52	1.40289	−0.32772	−1.43920	−0.06012
0.56	1.31600	−0.59748	−1.42619	0.19593
0.60	1.17895	−0.86040	−1.36693	0.43094
0.64	0.99384	−1.10821	−1.26626	0.63565
0.68	0.76419	−1.33373	−1.13068	0.80136
0.72	0.49475	−1.53113	−0.96827	0.92013
0.76	0.19123	−1.69625	−0.78852	0.98502
0.80	−0.14007	−1.82682	−0.60211	0.99020
0.84	−0.49261	−1.92267	−0.42070	0.93108
0.88	−0.86004	−1.98590	−0.25670	0.80428
0.92	−1.23660	−2.02097	−0.12305	0.60754
0.96	−1.61764	−2.03483	−0.03301	0.33962
1.00	−2.00000	−2.03693	0.00000	0.00000

TABLE D.5 Characteristic Functions and Derivatives
Clamped–Pinned Beam
First Mode

$\frac{x}{l}$	ϕ_1	$\phi_1' = \frac{1}{\beta_1}\frac{d\phi_1}{dx}$	$\phi_1'' = \frac{1}{\beta_1^2}\frac{d^2\phi_1}{dx^2}$	$\phi_1''' = \frac{1}{\beta_1^3}\frac{d^3\phi_1}{dx^3}$
0.00	0.00000	0.00000	2.00000	−2.00155
0.04	0.02338	0.29844	1.68568	−2.00031
0.08	0.08834	0.52955	1.37202	−1.99203
0.12	0.18715	0.72055	1.06060	−1.97079
0.16	0.31214	0.86296	0.75386	−1.93187
0.20	0.45574	0.95776	0.45486	−1.87177
0.24	0.61058	1.00643	0.16712	−1.78812
0.28	0.76958	1.01105	−0.10554	−1.67975
0.32	0.92601	0.97427	−0.35923	−1.54652
0.36	1.07363	0.89940	−0.59009	−1.38932
0.40	1.20675	0.79029	−0.79450	−1.21002
0.44	1.32032	0.65138	−0.96918	−1.01128
0.48	1.41006	0.48755	−1.11133	−0.79652
0.52	1.47245	0.30410	−1.21875	−0.56977
0.56	1.50485	0.10661	−1.28992	−0.33555
0.60	1.50550	−0.09916	−1.32402	−0.09872
0.64	1.47357	−0.30736	−1.32106	0.13566
0.68	1.40913	−0.51224	−1.28180	0.36247
0.72	1.31313	−0.70820	−1.20786	0.57666
0.76	1.18741	−0.88996	−1.10157	0.77340
0.80	1.03457	−1.05270	−0.96606	0.94823
0.84	0.85795	−1.19210	−0.80507	1.09714
0.88	0.66151	−1.30448	−0.62295	1.21670
0.92	0.44974	−1.38692	−0.42455	1.30414
0.96	0.22752	−0.22752	−0.21507	1.35743
1.00	0.00000	−1.45420	0.00000	1.37533

TABLE D.6 Characteristic Functions and Derivatives
Clamped–Pinned Beam
Second Mode

$\frac{x}{l}$	ϕ_2	$\phi_2' = \frac{1}{\beta_2}\frac{d\phi_2}{dx}$	$\phi_2'' = \frac{1}{\beta_2^2}\frac{d^2\phi_2}{dx^2}$	$\phi_2''' = \frac{1}{\beta_2^3}\frac{d^3\phi_2}{dx^3}$
0.00	0.00000	0.00000	2.00000	−2.00000
0.04	0.07241	0.48557	1.43502	−1.99300
0.08	0.25958	0.81207	0.87658	−1.94824
0.12	0.51697	0.98325	0.33937	−1.83960
0.16	0.80176	1.00789	−0.15633	−1.65333
0.20	1.07449	0.90888	−0.58802	−1.38736
0.24	1.30078	0.68345	−0.93412	−1.05012
0.28	1.45308	0.38242	−1.17673	−0.65879
0.32	1.51208	0.02894	−1.30380	−0.23724
0.36	1.46765	−0.34350	−1.31068	0.18649
0.40	1.31923	−0.70122	−1.20092	0.58286
0.44	1.07550	−1.01270	−0.98634	0.92349
0.48	0.75348	−1.25090	−0.68631	1.18364
0.52	0.37700	−1.39515	−0.32640	1.34442
0.56	−0.02536	−1.43265	0.06348	1.39438
0.60	−0.42268	−1.35944	0.45136	1.33056
0.64	−0.78413	−1.18058	0.80569	1.15876
0.68	−1.08158	−0.90972	1.09776	0.89319
0.72	−1.29186	−0.56793	1.30395	0.55537
0.76	−1.39848	−0.18205	1.40755	0.17245
0.80	−1.39351	0.21752	1.40010	−0.22494
0.84	−1.27727	0.59923	1.28198	−0.60506
0.88	−1.05919	0.93288	1.06244	−0.93759
0.92	−0.75676	1.19208	0.75879	−1.19604
0.96	−0.39406	1.35629	0.39504	−1.35983
1.00	0.00000	1.41251	0.00000	−1.41592

A P P E N D I X   E

Introduction to MATLAB®

MATLAB® is a commercially available interactive software package that can be used along with the programs included with this text to solve many problems in vibrations. The programs for this text work with *The Student Edition of MATLAB®*. The individual programs will be discussed as they are needed. The following can be considered as a general introduction to MATLAB®. For the purposes of this introduction we will concentrate on the commands that one will need throughout the rest of the book. For a complete description of MATLAB®, the reader should consult *The Student Edition of MATLAB®*.

Upon entering MATLAB®, one should see the prompt ≫. This prompt distinguishes a MATLAB® command line. Inside MATLAB®, one can get information about a command by typing "help" followed by the command name. It is important to note that MATLAB® is case sensitive, so all commands and variables need to be in the appropriate case.

MATLAB® works with either arrays of numbers or matrices. In order to create an array of numbers you can use the command

```
x : y : z
```

that gives an array of numbers starting at x and incremented by y until z or the closest number that is less than or equal to z. For example, the command

```
0 : 1 : 3
```

generates the array

```
0 1 2 3
```

and the command

```
0: −.1: −1
```

generates the array

```
0   −.1   −.2   −.3   −.4   −.5   −.6   −.7   −.8   −.9   −1.
```

Functions can be applied to an entire array, for example, the following two commands

$$x = 0 : .5 : \pi$$

$$y = \cos(x)$$

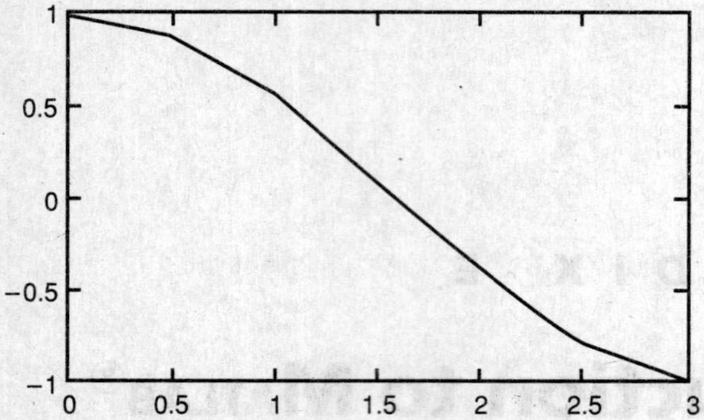

FIGURE E.1. Plot of cos(x).

generate the arrays

x = 0.0000 0.5000 1.000 1.500 2.000 2.5000 3.0000

and

y = 1.0000 0.8776 0.5403 0.0707 −0.4161 −0.8011 −0.9900.

One can plot these two arrays in MATLAB® by using the command **plot (x,y)**. The result of this command is shown in Figure E.1.

A few of the functions which are available in MATLAB® are given in the following table. MATLAB® assumes that the argument of a trigonometric function is in radians.

Function	Effect
sin ()	Gives the sine of each element in an array or matrix.
cos ()	Gives the cosine of each element in an array or matirx.
exp ()	Gives the exponential function of each element in an array or matrix.

A matrix can be input easily into MATLAB®. For example, consider the matrix

$$A = \begin{bmatrix} 0.5 & 0.5 & 0.5 \\ 0.5 & 1.5 & 1.5 \\ 0.5 & 1.5 & 2.5 \end{bmatrix}$$

This matrix can be input into MATLAB® by typing the following on a MATLAB® command line:

$$A = [0.5\ 0.5\ 0.5; 0.5\ 1.5\ 1.5; 0.5\ 1.5\ 2.5]$$

where there is a space between each element and a semi-colon at the end of each row. Alternatively, you can separate matrix elements by commas instead of spaces and you can indicate the end of each row by a carriage return. MATLAB® can efficiently implement many functions of matrices. A few functions are:

Function	Effect
eig ()	Gives the eigenvalues and eigenvectors of a matrix.
inv ()	Gives the inverse of a matrix.
det ()	Gives the determinant of a matrix.

For example, consider the computation of the eigenvalues for the following matrix

$$A = \begin{bmatrix} -2 & 1 \\ .5 & -1 \end{bmatrix}$$

The eigenvalues are the values of λ which satisfy

$$\begin{vmatrix} (-2-\lambda) & 1 \\ .5 & (-1-\lambda) \end{vmatrix} = 0$$

This calculation results in the following characteristic polynomial:

$$\lambda^2 + 3\lambda + 1.5 = 0$$

In MATLAB®, the roots of this equation can be computed by typing the command **roots(c)** where c is the vector containing the coefficients of the polynomial in descending order. For this example,

$$c = [1,\ 3,\ 1.5]$$

and the command $\lambda =$ **roots(c)** results in the following:

$$\lambda = \begin{bmatrix} -2.3660 \\ -0.6340 \end{bmatrix}$$

You can compute the eigenvalues in MATLAB®, directly from the matrix A using the command

y = eig(A)

which produces

$$y = \begin{bmatrix} -2.3660 \\ -0.6340 \end{bmatrix}$$

In order to compute both the eigenvalues and eigenvectors we use the command

[U, D] = eig(A)

This command produces two matrices. D is a diagonal matrix with the eigenvalues along the diagonal and U contains the corresponding eigenvectors as column vectors. For the above matrix we get

$$U = \begin{bmatrix} -0.9392 & -0.5907 \\ 0.3437 & -0.8069 \end{bmatrix}$$

and

$$D = \begin{bmatrix} -2.3660 & 0 \\ 0 & -0.6340 \end{bmatrix}$$

The inverse of this matrix can be computed using the command

I = inv(A)

The result for the example matrix is

$$I = \begin{bmatrix} -0.6667 & -0.6667 \\ -0.3333 & -1.3333 \end{bmatrix}$$

It is possible to have operations on pairs of matrices or arrays. Array operations act componentwise. The following table illustrates such operations:

Matrix Operations	Array Operations
+ addition	+ addition
− subtraction	− subtraction
* multiplication	.* multiplication
/ division	./ division
^ power	.^ power
' conjugate transpose	.' conjugate transpose

Consider the arrays $x = [1, 1, 2, 4]$ and the matrix

$$A = \begin{bmatrix} 1 & 1 & 1 \\ 1 & 3 & 3 \\ 1 & 3 & 5 \end{bmatrix}$$

The command that generates an array y whose components are the squares of the components of x is

$$\mathbf{y = x.\hat{}2}$$

For the above example, this command produces

$$y = [1,\ 1,\ 4,\ 16]$$

If this operation is used with a matrix instead of a vector, the result is each element of the matrix is squared. For the matrix A above, the following command

$$\mathbf{A2 = A.\hat{}2}$$

produces the matrix

$$A2 = \begin{bmatrix} 1 & 1 & 1 \\ 1 & 9 & 9 \\ 1 & 9 & 25 \end{bmatrix}$$

Contrast this with the matrix operation that is obtained from the vector operation by deleting the period. The matrix command is $B = A\hat{}2$ and it will generate a matrix that is the matrix product of A times A. It is given by:

$$B = \begin{bmatrix} 3 & 7 & 9 \\ 7 & 19 & 25 \\ 9 & 25 & 35 \end{bmatrix}$$

These basic commands along with the programs provided will allow you to solve many vibrations problems. As you become more familiar with MATLAB®, its versatility and power will become evident.

PROBLEMS

E.1. Generate an array containing 10 elements between θ and π. Generate a second array that contains the cosine of these elements.

E.2. Produce a plot for the sine function.

E.3. Given the matrices

$$A = \begin{bmatrix} 1 & 2 & 2 \\ 2 & 4 & 3 \\ 2 & 3 & 5 \end{bmatrix}$$

$$B = \begin{bmatrix} 1 & 1 & 1 \\ 0 & 3 & 3 \\ 0 & 0 & 5 \end{bmatrix}$$

produce the matrix $C = A + B$. What are the eigenvalues of C?

E.4. Construct the characteristic polynomial for the matrix C and compute the roots of this polynomial.

APPENDIX F

Computer Programs

This appendix describes how to run the programs which accompany this text. A brief discussion about the program can be found at the beginning of each program.

RUNGA

Program RUNGA solves the differential equation

$$m\ddot{x} + c\dot{x} + kx = f(t)$$

using the fourth-order Runge–Kutta method, which is described in detail in Sec. 4.8 of Chapter 4. For a complete discussion of this method, see this section of the main text.

The program RUNGA.m is a MATLAB® script file. Script files are the MATLAB® equivalent of a main program. This program can be run from the command window by typing RUNGA at the prompt. The program will ask the user to input the values of m, c, and k, h, the timestep and the initial values $x(0)$ and $\dot{x}(0)$. See Fig. F.1 for the flow chart for this program. It requires a function file that contains the function $f(t)$. For example, if we want to solve the equation

$$m\ddot{x} + c\dot{x} + kx = \sin(t),$$

we would need to create a function file containing the following commands.

```
function [force] = f(t)
force =sin(t)
end
```

This function file must be named **f.m.** There are several function files available. Since the program RUNGA.m requires the function file to be named **f.m**, the user must copy whichever function file

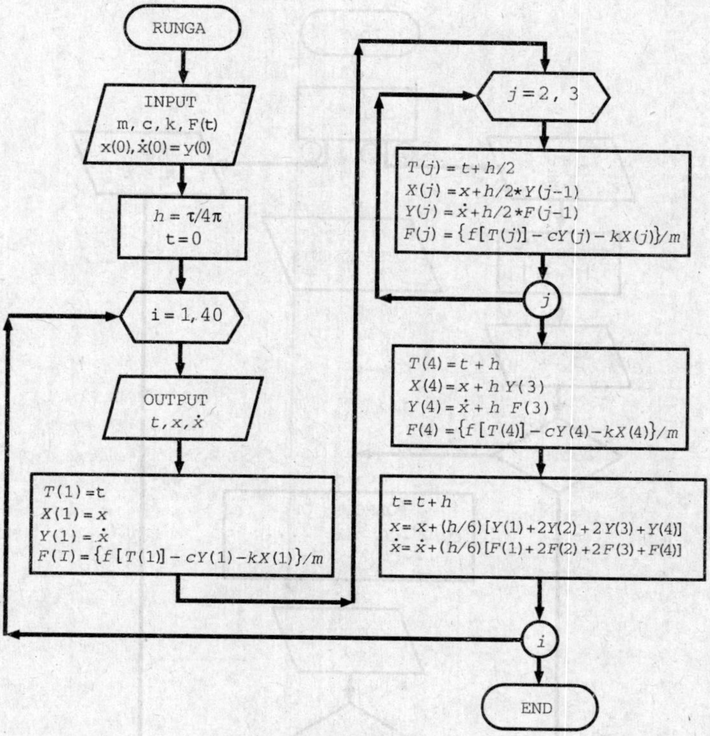

FIGURE F.1.

he wants to use to a file named **f.m.** Any function files that the user creates to use with RUNGA.m must also be named **f.m.** The program RUNGA.m outputs both numerical data and a plot.

POLY

The three options available for the program POLY are shown by the block labeled choice. See Fig. F.2. In option ①, mass M and stiffness K are inputted, and the characteristic determinant $|M - \lambda K| = 0$ is reduced to the polynomial form $c_1\lambda^n + c_2\lambda^{n-1} + \cdots + c_n = 0$ in the block *Polcof.* The coefficients c_i of the polynomial are then outputted.

If no further information is sought, option ① is now complete. If, however, the roots of the polynomial equation are desired, the decision block sends the coefficients to option ②, where the search for the roots is carried out in the block *Polroot* and outputted as the eigenvalues λ.

If the eigenvectors are also desired, the eigenvalues are sent to option ③, where the eigenvectors ϕ are found.

When the coefficients c_i are initially available, option ② can be used directly for the eigenvalues λ.

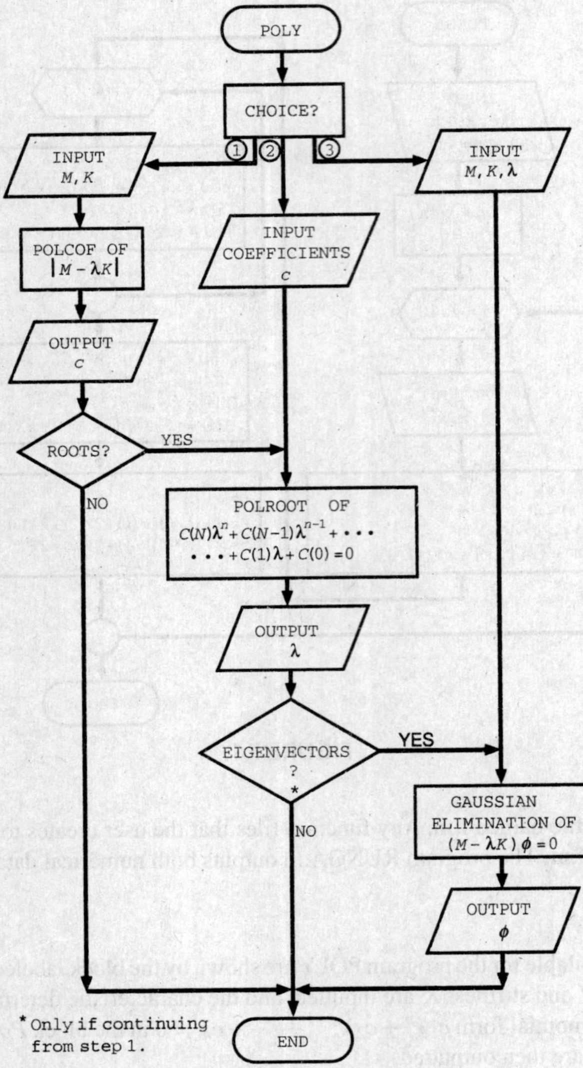

FIGURE F.2.

When M, K, and λ are initially available, option ③ can be used directly to determine the eigenvectors ϕ.

Iteration

In the flow diagram for the iteration method (see Fig. F.3), the method input block shows matrix order N, mass matrix M, and stiffness matrix K. The equation of motion is expressed in the form

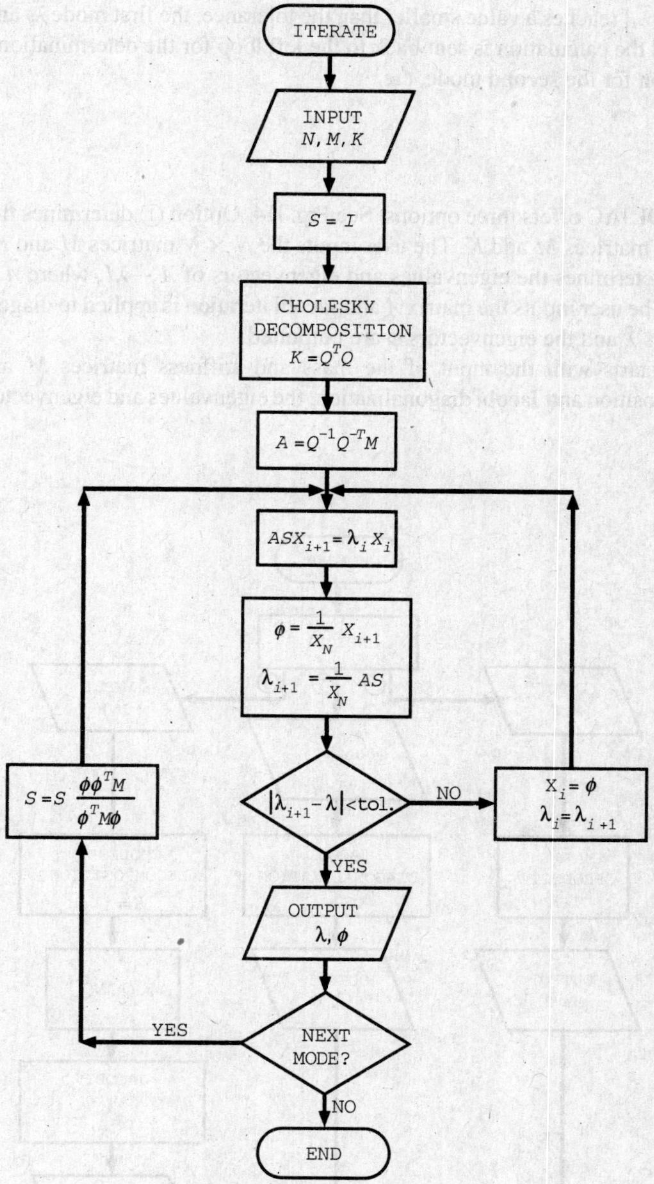

FIGURE F.3.

$K^{-1}MX = \bar{\lambda}X$, and the stiffness matrix $K = Q^TQ$ is first decomposed by the Cholesky method for the determination of Q, Q^{-1}, and Q^{-T} and the dynamic matrix $A = K^{-1}M = Q^{-1}Q^{-T}M$, which in this case is generally unsymmetric. The sweeping matrix S is introduced as a unit matrix I for the first mode.

The iteration procedure follows in the block $ASX_{i+1} = \bar{\lambda}_i X_i$, which is normalized in the next block and tested for convergence in the decision block and looped back for further iteration. When the difference $|\bar{\lambda}_{i+1} - \bar{\lambda}_i|$ reaches a value smaller than the tolerance, the first mode $\bar{\lambda}_i$ and its eigenvector ϕ is complete, and the calculation is sent back to the left loop for the determination of the sweeping matrix and iteration for the second mode, etc.

CHOLJAC

The program CHOLJAC offers three options. See Fig. F.4. Option ① determines the product $M * K$ of any two square matrices M and K. The user inputs the $N \times N$ matrices M and K.

Option ② determines the eigenvalues and eigenvectors of $\tilde{A} - \lambda I$, where $\tilde{A}$ is the symmetric dynamic matrix. The user inputs the matrix $\tilde{A}$ and Jacobi iteration is applied to diagonalize the matrix $\tilde{A}$. The eigenvalues $\bar{\lambda}$ and the eigenvectors ϕ are outputted.

Option ③ starts with the input of the mass and stiffness matrices M and K. By using Cholesky decomposition and Jacobi diagonalization, the eigenvalues and eigenvectors of $(M - \lambda K)\phi$

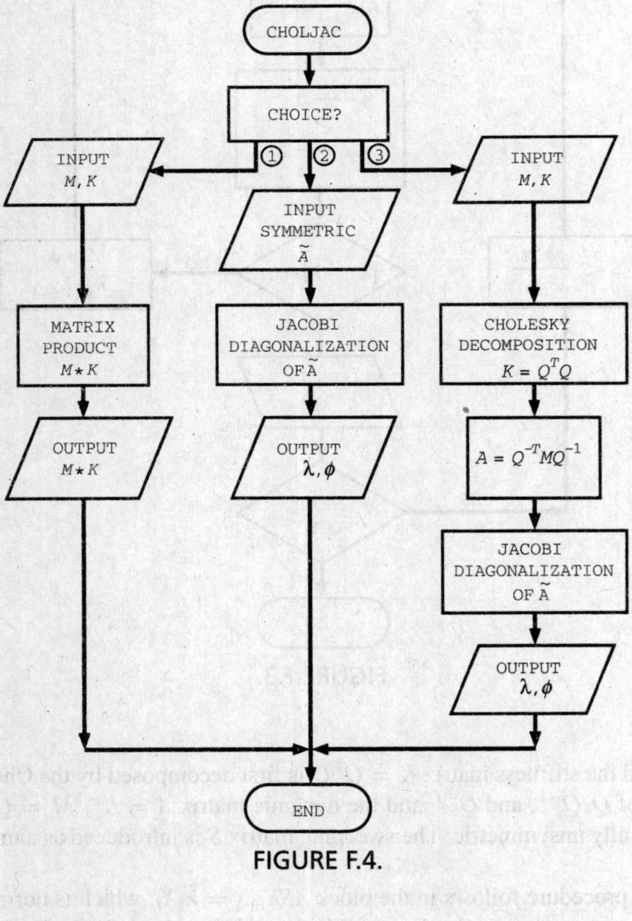

FIGURE F.4.

are determined. The program decomposes the first matrix inputted, which for the flow diagram shown is the stiffness matrix. The eigenvalues are then proportional to the reciprocal of the natural frequencies ω^2.

BAR AND BEAM

These two programs use the finite element approach presented in Chapter 11 to produce the natural frequencies for the cantilever bar and the uniform beam. See Sec. 11.6 for a complete discussion of the finite element method for the BAR and Sec. 11.10 for a discussion of this method for the BEAM. For the flow charts for these two programs see Figs. F.5 and F.6, respectively. Both programs construct the mass and the stiffness matrix for the finite element configuration. From this the dynamic matrix,

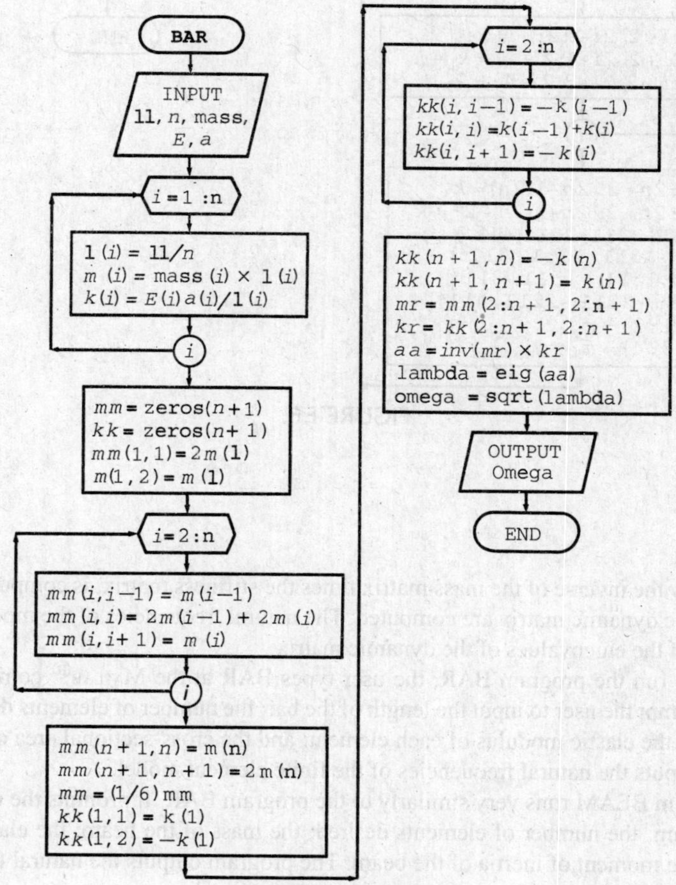

FIGURE F.5.

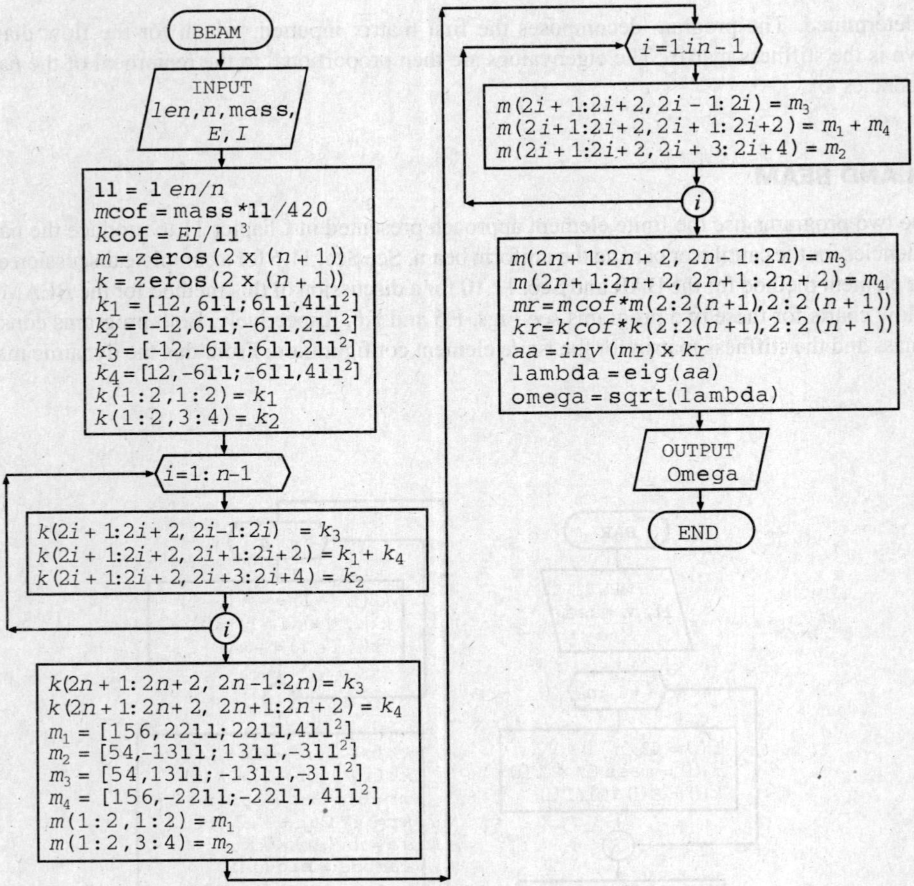

FIGURE F.6.

which is given by the inverse of the mass matrix times the stiffness matrix, is computed. Finally, the eigenvalues of the dynamic matrix are computed. The natural frequencies of the model are given by the square root of the eigenvalues of the dynamic matrix.

In order to run the program BAR, the user types BAR at the MATLAB® command line. The program will prompt the user to input the length of the bar; the number of elements desired; the mass of each element; the elastic modulus of each element; and the cross-sectional area of each element. The program outputs the natural frequencies of the finite element model.

The program BEAM runs very similarly to the program BAR. It prompts the user to input the length of the beam; the number of elements desired; the mass of the beam; the elastic modulus of the beam; and the moment of inertia of the beam. The program outputs the natural frequency of the finite element model.

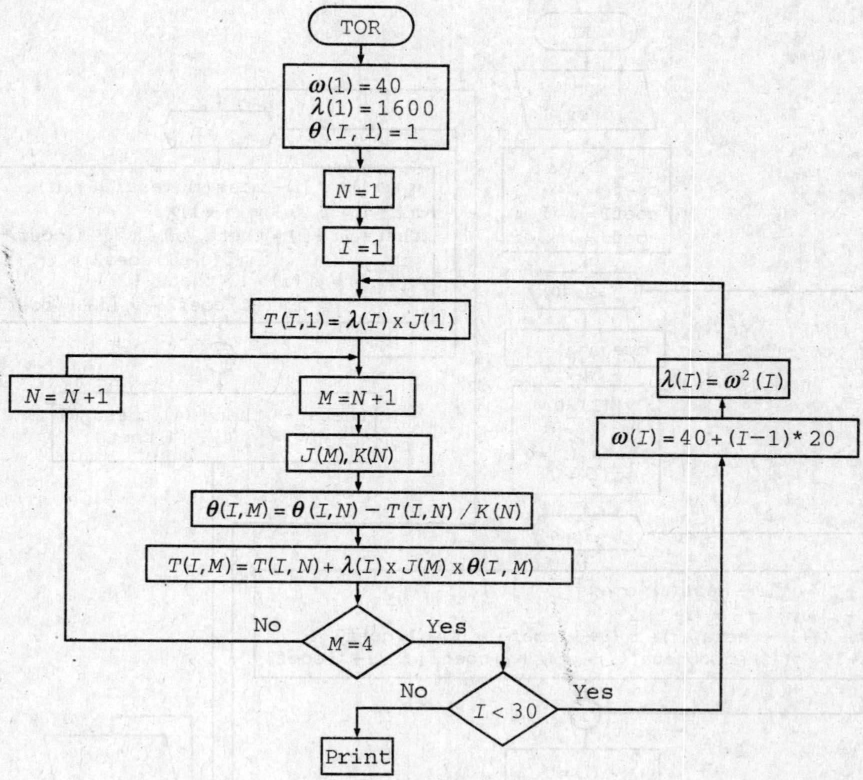

FIGURE F.7.

TOR

This program uses Holzer's method to compute the natural frequencies of a torsional system (see Fig. F.7). This method is discussed in Secs. 10.4 and 10.5. This program computes the torsional displacement of each disk, θ, and the torque carried by each shaft, T, for a range of frequencies. The quantities are determined by the equations

$$\theta(I,N+1) = \theta(I,N) - T(I,N)/K(N)$$
$$T(I,N+1) = T(I,N) + \lambda(I) * J(N+1) * \theta(I,N+1)$$

The natural frequency has been found if $\theta = 0$ at the fixed end or $T = 0$ at the free end.

MYKL

This program uses the lumped mass approach to determine the natural frequencies of the cantilever beam. This method is known as Myklestad's method and it is discussed in detail in Sec. 10.6.

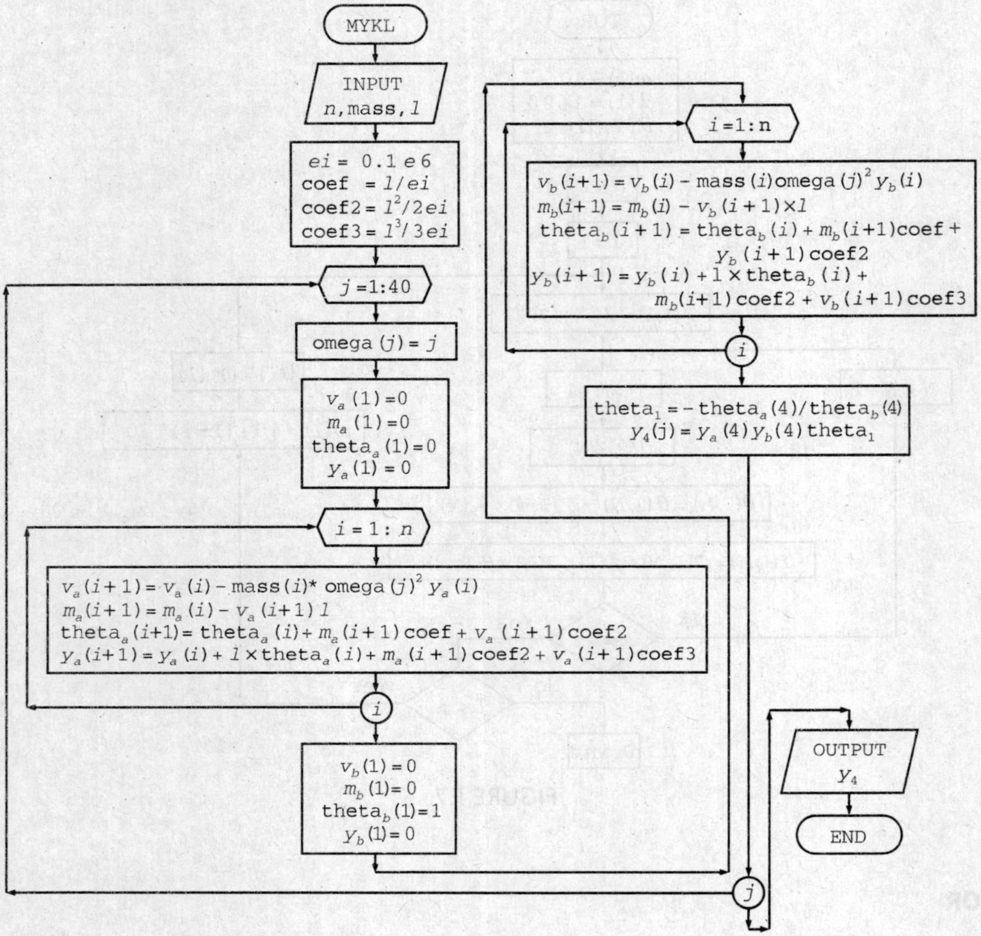

FIGURE F.8.

Figure F.8 gives the flow chart for the program. The natural frequencies for this system are given by the values of omega for which the deflection y_4 is zero. The method proceeds by systematically calculating the values of y_4 for a series of values of omega.

This program prompts the user to input the number of masses; the value of each mass; the spacing between the masses; the initial value of omega; the final value of omega; and the spacing of the omegas. The program outputs a table of omega versus y_4 and a plot.

SUGGESTED READING

[1] Ralson, A. and Wilf, H. S. *Mathematical Methods for Digital Computers*, Vol. 1. New York: John Wiley & Sons, 1960.

[2] *The Student Edition of Matlab® Version 4 User's Guide*, Englewood Cliffs, NJ: Prentice Hall, 1995.

APPENDIX G

Convergence to Higher Modes

In Sec. 7.4, we have shown that when the equation of motion is formulated in terms of flexibility, the iteration procedure converges to the lowest mode. It is evident that if the lowest mode is absent in the assumed deflection, the iteration will converge to the next lowest, or the second, mode. However, because round-off errors will always reintroduce a small component of ϕ_1 during each iteration, it will be necessary to remove this component from each iterated vector in order for the iteration to converge to ϕ_2.

To accomplish this removal procedure, we again start with the expansion theorem:

$$X = c_1\phi_1 + c_2\phi_2 + c_3\phi_3 + \cdots \tag{G.1}$$

Next, premultiply this equation by $\phi_1^T M$, where ϕ_1 is the first normal mode, which was already found:

$$\phi_1^T MX = c_1\phi_1^T M\phi_1 + c_2\phi_1^T M\phi_2 + c_3\phi_1^T M\phi_3 + \cdots \tag{G.2}$$

Due to orthogonality, all the terms on the right side of this equation except the first are zero and we have

$$\phi_1^T MX = c_1\phi_1^T M\phi_1 \tag{G.3}$$

We note from Eq. (G.1) that if $c_1 = 0$, we have a displacement free from ϕ_1. Also because $\phi_1^T M\phi_1$ cannot be zero, with $c_1 = 0$, Eq. (G.3) is reduced to

$$\phi_1^T MX = 0 \tag{G.4}$$

which is the *constraint equation.*

Writing out this equation for a 3 × 3 problem, we have

$$\begin{aligned}\phi_1^T MX &= \left(x_1^{(1)} x_2^{(1)} x_3^{(3)}\right)\begin{bmatrix} m_1 & & \\ & m_2 & \\ & & m_3\end{bmatrix}\begin{Bmatrix} x_1 \\ x_2 \\ x_3\end{Bmatrix} \\ &= m_1x_1^{(1)}x_1 + m_2x_2^{(1)}x_2 + m_3x_3^{(1)}x_3 = 0\end{aligned}$$

where $x_1^{(1)}, x_2^{(1)}$, and $x_3^{(1)}$ are known, and the x_i without the superscript belong to the ith iterated vector X. From the preceding equation, we obtain

$$\begin{aligned} x_1 &= -\left(\frac{m_2}{m_1}\right)\left(\frac{x_2}{x_1}\right)^{(1)} x_2 - \left(\frac{m_3}{m_1}\right)\left(\frac{x_3}{x_1}\right)^{(1)} x_3 \\ x_2 &= x_2 \\ x_3 &= x_3 \end{aligned}$$

where the last two equations have been introduced as identities. Expressed in matrix form, this equation is

$$\begin{Bmatrix} x_1 \\ x_2 \\ x_3 \end{Bmatrix} = \begin{bmatrix} 0 & -\left(\frac{m_2}{m_1}\right)\left(\frac{x_2}{x_1}\right)^{(1)} & -\left(\frac{m_3}{m_1}\right)\left(\frac{x_3}{x_1}\right)^{(1)} \\ 0 & 1 & 0 \\ 0 & 0 & 1 \end{bmatrix} \begin{Bmatrix} x_1 \\ x_2 \\ x_3 \end{Bmatrix} \tag{G.5}$$

$$= [S][X]$$

This is the constraint equation for removing the first mode, and $[S]$ is the *sweeping matrix*. By replacing X on the left side of Eq. (7.3.1) by this constraint equation, it becomes

$$\overline{A}SX = \overline{\lambda}X \tag{G.6}$$

Iteration of this equation now sweeps out the undesired ϕ_1 component in each iteration step and converges to the second mode ϕ_2.

For the third and higher modes, the sweeping procedure is repeated with the normal modes already found. This reduces the order of the matrix equation by 1 each time. Thus, the matrix $[\overline{A}S]$ is referred to as the *deflated matrix*.

It is well to mention that the convergence for higher modes becomes more critical if impurities are introduced through the sweeping matrix, i.e., the lower modes used for the sweeping matrix must be accurately found. The highest mode can be checked by the inversion of the original equation, which is the equation formulated in terms of the stiffness matrix.

COMPUTER NOTES

To program the iteration procedure for the digital computer, it is convenient to develop another form of the sweeping matrix S based on the Gram-Schmidt orthogonalization.* Rewriting Eq. (7.4.2) as

$$X_2 = X_1 - \alpha_1\phi_2 = c_2\phi_2 + c_3\phi_3 + \cdots \tag{G.7}$$

where $\alpha_1\phi_1$ is the unwanted ϕ_1 component, we again premultiply this equation by $\phi_1^T M$ to obtain

$$\phi_1^T M(X_1 - \alpha\phi_1) = 0$$

The constant α_1 then becomes

$$\alpha_1 = \frac{\phi_1^T M X_1}{\phi_1^T M \phi_1} \tag{G.8}$$

*Wilson E. Klus-Jurgen Bathe, *Numerical Methods in Finite Element Analysis* (Englewood Cliffs, NJ: Prentice-Hall, 1976), p. 440.

which substituted into Eq. (G.7) gives

$$
\begin{aligned}
X_2 &= X_1 - \alpha\phi_1 = X_1 - \phi_1\alpha \\
&= X_1 - \phi_1 \frac{\phi_1^T M X_1}{\phi_1^T M \phi_1} \\
&= X_1 - \frac{\phi_1\phi_1^T M}{\phi_1^T M \phi_1} X_1 = \left[I - \frac{\phi_1\phi_1^T M}{\phi_1^T M \phi_1} \right] X_1
\end{aligned}
$$

Thus,

$$S = \left[I - \frac{\phi_1\phi_1^T M}{\phi_1^T M \phi_1} \right]$$

is another expression for the sweeping matrix, which can be more easily programmed.

Example G.1

Consider the same system of Example 6.5.1, in which the eigenvalue and eigenvector for the first mode were found as

$$\overline{\lambda_1} = 14.32 \qquad \phi_1 = \begin{Bmatrix} x_1 \\ x_2 \\ x_3 \end{Bmatrix}^{(1)} = \begin{Bmatrix} 0.250 \\ 0.790 \\ 1.000 \end{Bmatrix}$$

To determine the second mode, we form the sweeping matrix given by Eq. (G.3):

$$S = \begin{bmatrix} 0 & -\frac{1}{2}\left(\frac{0.79}{0.25}\right) & -\frac{1}{4}\left(\frac{1.00}{0.25}\right) \\ 0 & 1 & 0 \\ 0 & 0 & 1 \end{bmatrix} = \begin{bmatrix} 0 & -1.58 & -1 \\ 0 & 1 & 0 \\ 0 & 0 & 1 \end{bmatrix}$$

The new equation for the second mode iteration is found from Eq. (G.6):

$$[\overline{AS}]X = \overline{\lambda}X$$

$$\begin{bmatrix} 4 & 2 & 1 \\ 4 & 8 & 4 \\ 4 & 8 & 7 \end{bmatrix} \begin{bmatrix} 0 & -1.58 & -1 \\ 0 & 1 & 0 \\ 0 & 0 & 1 \end{bmatrix} \begin{Bmatrix} x_1 \\ x_2 \\ x_3 \end{Bmatrix} = \overline{\lambda} \begin{Bmatrix} x_1 \\ x_2 \\ x_3 \end{Bmatrix}$$

or

$$\begin{bmatrix} 0 & -4.32 & -3.0 \\ 0 & 1.67 & 0 \\ 0 & 1.67 & 3.0 \end{bmatrix} \begin{Bmatrix} x_1 \\ x_2 \\ x_3 \end{Bmatrix} = \overline{\lambda} \begin{Bmatrix} x_1 \\ x_2 \\ x_3 \end{Bmatrix}$$

Knowing that the second mode would have a node, we might start the iteration with an arbitrary test column:

$$X = \begin{Bmatrix} 0.5 \\ -0.2 \\ 1.0 \end{Bmatrix}$$

The first iteration then becomes

$$\begin{bmatrix} 0 & -4.32 & -3.0 \\ 0 & 1.67 & 0 \\ 0 & 1.67 & 3.0 \end{bmatrix} \begin{Bmatrix} 0.5 \\ -0.2 \\ 1.0 \end{Bmatrix} = \begin{Bmatrix} -2.136 \\ -0.334 \\ 2.666 \end{Bmatrix} = 2.666 \begin{Bmatrix} -0.801 \\ -0.125 \\ 1.00 \end{Bmatrix}$$

With this normalized column, the second iteration becomes

$$\begin{bmatrix} 0 & -4.32 & -3.0 \\ 0 & 1.67 & 0 \\ 0 & 1.67 & 3.0 \end{bmatrix} \begin{Bmatrix} -0.801 \\ 0.125 \\ 1.00 \end{Bmatrix} = \begin{Bmatrix} -2.46 \\ -0.21 \\ 2.79 \end{Bmatrix} = 2.79 \begin{Bmatrix} -0.881 \\ -0.075 \\ 1.00 \end{Bmatrix}$$

The third iteration gives

$$\begin{bmatrix} 0 & -4.32 & -3.0 \\ 0 & 1.67 & 0 \\ 0 & 1.67 & 3.0 \end{bmatrix} \begin{Bmatrix} -0.881 \\ -0.075 \\ 1.00 \end{Bmatrix} = \begin{Bmatrix} -2.68 \\ -0.125 \\ 2.87 \end{Bmatrix} = 2.87 \begin{Bmatrix} -0.933 \\ -0.044 \\ 1.00 \end{Bmatrix}$$

After a few more iterations, the convergence is to

$$3.0 \begin{Bmatrix} -1.0 \\ 0 \\ 1.0 \end{Bmatrix}$$

Thus, the eigenvalue and eigenvector for the second mode are

$$\overline{\lambda_2} = \frac{3k}{\omega^2 m} = 3.0 \qquad \omega_2 = \sqrt{\frac{k}{m}}$$

$$\phi_2 = \begin{Bmatrix} -1.0 \\ 0 \\ 1.0 \end{Bmatrix}^{(2)}$$

For the determination of the third mode, we impose the condition $c_1 = c_2 = 0$ from the orthogonality equation:

$$c_1 = \sum_{i=1}^{3} m_i (x_i)^{(1)} x_i = 4(0.25)x_1 + 2(0.79)x_2 + 1(1.0)x_3 = 0$$

$$c_2 = \sum_{i=1}^{3} m_i (x_i)^{(2)} x_i = 4(-1.0)x_1 + 2(0)x_2 + 1(1.0)x_3 = 0$$

From these two equations, we obtain

$$x_1 = 0.25x_3 \qquad x_2 = -0.79x_3$$

which can be expressed by the matrix equation

$$\begin{Bmatrix} x_1 \\ x_2 \\ x_3 \end{Bmatrix} = \begin{bmatrix} 0 & 0 & 0.25 \\ 0 & 0 & -0.79 \\ 0 & 0 & 1.00 \end{bmatrix} \begin{Bmatrix} x_1 \\ x_2 \\ x_3 \end{Bmatrix}$$

This matrix is devoid of the first two modes and can be used as a sweeping matrix for the third mode. Applying this to the original equation, we obtain

$$\begin{bmatrix} 4 & 2 & 1 \\ 4 & 8 & 4 \\ 4 & 8 & 7 \end{bmatrix} \begin{bmatrix} 0 & 0 & 0.25 \\ 0 & 0 & -0.79 \\ 0 & 0 & 1.00 \end{bmatrix} \begin{Bmatrix} x_1 \\ x_2 \\ x_3 \end{Bmatrix} = \left(\frac{3k}{\omega^2 m}\right) \begin{Bmatrix} x_1 \\ x_2 \\ x_3 \end{Bmatrix}$$

This equation results immediately in the third mode, which is

$$1.68 \begin{Bmatrix} 0.25 \\ -0.79 \\ 1.00 \end{Bmatrix} = \left(\frac{3k}{\omega^2 m}\right) \begin{Bmatrix} x_1 \\ x_2 \\ x_3 \end{Bmatrix}$$

The natural frequency of the third mode is then found to be

$$\omega_3 = \sqrt{\frac{3k}{1.68m}} = 1.34\sqrt{\frac{k}{m}}$$

These natural frequencies were checked by solving the stiffness equation, which is

$$m\begin{bmatrix} 4 & 0 & 0 \\ 0 & 2 & 0 \\ 0 & 0 & 1 \end{bmatrix}\begin{Bmatrix} \ddot{x}_1 \\ \ddot{x}_2 \\ \ddot{x}_3 \end{Bmatrix} + k\begin{bmatrix} 4 & -1 & 0 \\ -1 & 2 & -1 \\ 0 & -1 & 1 \end{bmatrix}\begin{Bmatrix} x_1 \\ x_2 \\ x_3 \end{Bmatrix} = 0$$

With $\lambda = m\omega^2/k$, the determinant of this equation set equal to zero gives

$$8(1-\lambda)^3 - 5(1-\lambda) = (1-\lambda)[8(1-\lambda)^2 - 5] = 0$$

Its solutions are

$$\lambda_1 = 0.2094 \quad \omega_1 = 0.4576\sqrt{\frac{k}{m}} \quad \phi_1 = \begin{Bmatrix} 0.250 \\ 0.791 \\ 1.000 \end{Bmatrix}$$

$$\lambda_2 = 1.0000 \quad \omega_2 = 1.0000\sqrt{\frac{k}{m}} \quad \phi_2 = \begin{Bmatrix} -1 \\ 0 \\ 1 \end{Bmatrix}$$

$$\lambda_3 = 1.7906 \quad \omega_3 = 1.3381\sqrt{\frac{k}{m}} \quad \phi_3 = \begin{Bmatrix} 0.250 \\ -0.791 \\ 1.000 \end{Bmatrix}$$

■

Answers to Selected Problems

Chapter 1

1.1 $x_{max} = 6.37\, cm, \qquad \tau = 66.67\, ms, \qquad \ddot{x}_{max} = 57.65g$

1.2 $\dot{x}_{max} = 5.03\, cm/s, \qquad \ddot{x}_{max} = 126.33\, cm/s^2$

1.6 $A = 10, \qquad \theta = 36.9^0$

1.9 $x(t) = \frac{1}{2} - \frac{4}{\pi^2}\left(cos\omega_1 t + \frac{1}{9}cos3\omega_1 t + \ldots\right)$

1.11 $x(t) = \frac{8}{\pi}\left(sin\omega_1 t + \frac{1}{3}sin3\omega_1 t + \ldots\right)$

1.13 $\sqrt{\overline{x^2}} = A/2$

1.14 $\overline{x^2} = 1/3$

1.16 $a_0 = 1/3, \qquad a_n = \frac{1}{n\pi}sin\frac{n\pi}{3}, \qquad b_n = \frac{1}{n\pi}\left(1 - cos\frac{n\pi}{3}\right)$

1.19 rms = 0.447A

1.21 error $= 10^{\pm\frac{1}{40}}$

1.22 $\frac{x_{res}}{x_{low}} = 10^{0.8}$

Chapter 2

2.1 $k_2 = k_1/15$

2.3 70.461 N/m

2.5 $J_0 = 0.46309Nms^2$

2.7 $\kappa = 0.2032m$

2.9 $\omega_n = \sqrt{\dfrac{k}{m_0 + J_0/r^2}}$

2.11 Amplitude = 0.0416 m, Accleration = $0.3744 m/s^2$

2.13 $\tau = 1.969s$

2.17 $\omega_{locked} = 0.936\omega_{unlocked}$

2.19 $\omega_n = \sqrt{\dfrac{kb^2 + k_2a^2}{J + mb^2}}$

2.21 m = 0.0300 kg

2.23 $\zeta = 0.548$

2.27 $\zeta = 4.934e - 2, \quad \delta = 0.3104, \quad \dfrac{x_1}{x_2} = 1.3364$

2.29 $c_c = \dfrac{2l}{a}\sqrt{km}, \quad \omega_d = \dfrac{a}{l}\sqrt{\dfrac{k}{m} - \left(\dfrac{c}{2m}\right)^2\left(\dfrac{a}{l}\right)^2}$

2.31 $\zeta = 8.164e - 3$

2.33 $\tau = 0.15s, \quad \dot{x} = 28.24 m/s, \quad C_c = 12601.7\, Ns/m$

2.35 $\zeta_1 = 0.5911, \quad 37.83\%$

2.37 $K_{eff} = \dfrac{k_3\,(k_1 + k_2)}{k_1 + k_2 + k_3}$

2.39 $K_{eff} = \dfrac{k_2 a + k_1 b}{b}$

2.47 $\omega_n = \sqrt{\dfrac{k_1 k_2}{(k_1 + k_2)\, m}}$

2.49 $m\ddot{x} + c\dot{x} + \dfrac{k_1 k_2}{k_1 + k_2}x = 0.$

Chapter 3

3.2 $\zeta = 0.169$

3.3 c = 39.81 Ns/m

3.5 $X = 7.91\, mm, \quad \phi = 72.11^0$

3.9 Add 41.51 gms at 30.59^0 ccw to the reference plane

3.12 $\omega_n = 104.72\, Hz, \quad \zeta = 0.028, \quad X = 3.6\, mm, \quad \phi = 171.32^0$

3.16 $\omega = 15.9\, rad/s$

3.17 $F_{2.5} = 403.32\, N, \quad F_{2.0} = 130.76\, N$

3.21 $V = \dfrac{L}{2\pi}\sqrt{\dfrac{k}{m}}$

3.26 $k = 3.354\ N/mm$ each spring

3.27 $X = 0.1267\ mm, \quad F_{TR} = 42.758\ N$

3.28 $\omega^2 X = 6\ cm/s^2$

3.38 $frequency_1 = 16.82\ cps, \quad frequency_2 = 7.79\ cps$

3.39 correct amplitude = −0.048 cm

3.41 $voltage_{20} = 273.23\ mV, \quad voltage_{1500} = 3.643\ mV$

3.44 $E_{withoutcable} = 40\ mV/g, \quad E_{withcable} = 27\ mV/g$

Chapter 4

4.3 $x = \dfrac{F_0}{k}\left(cos\omega_n\left(t - t_1\right) - cos\omega_n t\right)$

4.10 x = 1.345 m

4.13 x = 0.307m $t = 0.392$ s

4.14 $tan\omega_n t = \dfrac{\sqrt{mgs/k}}{s - mg/4k}$

4.21 1.57

4.29 1.653g

4.32 $x(t) = \dfrac{F_0}{c\omega_n}\left\{\dfrac{e^{-\zeta\omega_n t}}{\sqrt{1-\zeta^2}} sin\left(\sqrt{1-\zeta^2}\omega_n t + sin^{-1}\sqrt{1-\zeta^2}\right) - cos\omega_n t\right\}$

4.43 $y(t) = y(0)cos\omega t + \dfrac{\dot{y}(0)}{\omega} sin\omega t + \dfrac{V}{\omega}(\omega t - sin\omega t) - \dfrac{g}{\omega^2}(1 - cos\omega t)$

Chapter 5

5.4 $\lambda = (1 + n) \pm n$

5.8 $\omega_1 = 0, \quad \omega_2 = 2697.4\ rad/sec, \quad \phi_1 = \begin{Bmatrix} 1 \\ 1 \end{Bmatrix}, \quad \phi_2 = \begin{Bmatrix} -0.6 \\ 1 \end{Bmatrix}$

5.12 $\ddot{\theta}_1 + \dfrac{2g}{l}\theta_1 - \dfrac{g}{l}\theta_2 = 0 \quad \& \ \ddot{\theta}_1 + \ddot{\theta}_2 + \dfrac{g}{l}\theta_2 = 0$

5.14 $\omega = \sqrt{\dfrac{g}{l} + \dfrac{k}{ml^2}(1 \pm 1)}, \quad \tau = 0.162s$

5.21 $\begin{bmatrix} m & 0 \\ 0 & J \end{bmatrix}\begin{Bmatrix} \ddot{x} \\ \ddot{\theta} \end{Bmatrix} + \begin{bmatrix} 2k & \frac{kl}{4} \\ \frac{kl}{4} & \frac{5kl^2}{16} \end{bmatrix}\begin{Bmatrix} x \\ \theta \end{Bmatrix} = \begin{Bmatrix} 0 \\ 0 \end{Bmatrix}$

5.22 5.11 – Static coupling, 5.12 – Dynamic coupling

5.23 $\omega_1 = 6.1\ rad/s, \ \omega_2 = 8.38\ rad/s, \quad \phi_1 = \begin{Bmatrix} -3.29 \\ 1 \end{Bmatrix}, \phi_2 = \begin{Bmatrix} 0.452 \\ 1 \end{Bmatrix}$

5.28 $\omega_1 = 34.16\ rad/s, \ \omega_2 = 68.31\ rad/s, \quad \phi_1 = \begin{Bmatrix} 0.5 \\ 1 \end{Bmatrix}, \phi_2 = \begin{Bmatrix} -1 \\ 1 \end{Bmatrix}$

5.30 $x_1 = \frac{8}{9}cos\omega_1 t + \frac{1}{9}cos\omega_2 t \,\&\, x_2 = \frac{4}{9}cos\omega_1 t - \frac{1}{9}cos\omega_2 t$

5.36 $\begin{bmatrix} J & 0 \\ 0 & 2J \end{bmatrix}\begin{Bmatrix} \ddot{\theta}_1 \\ \ddot{\theta}_2 \end{Bmatrix} + \begin{bmatrix} 2K & -K \\ -K & K \end{bmatrix}\begin{Bmatrix} \theta_1 \\ \theta_2 \end{Bmatrix} = \begin{Bmatrix} 0 \\ 0 \end{Bmatrix}, \quad \begin{Bmatrix} \theta_1 \\ \theta_2 \end{Bmatrix}_1 = \begin{Bmatrix} 1.00 \\ 1.78 \end{Bmatrix},$
$\begin{Bmatrix} \theta_1 \\ \theta_2 \end{Bmatrix}_2 = \begin{Bmatrix} 1.00 \\ -0.28 \end{Bmatrix}$

5.40 $\tilde{P} = \begin{bmatrix} 0.207 & -1.208 \\ 0.293 & 1.707 \end{bmatrix}$

5.41 $P = \begin{bmatrix} 1.44/l & -8.40/l \\ 1.00 & 1.00 \end{bmatrix}$

5.45 $F = \dfrac{k + (k+k_1)\left(\frac{\omega c}{k_1}\right)^2}{1 + \left(\frac{\omega c}{k_1}\right)^2}\left\{1 + i\dfrac{\omega c}{k + (k+k_1)\left(\frac{\omega c}{k_1}\right)^2}\right\}x = k^*(1+i\gamma)x$

5.46 $[K] = k\begin{bmatrix} 2 & -1 \\ -1 & 2 \end{bmatrix}, \quad [C] = c\begin{bmatrix} 2 & -1 \\ -1 & 1 \end{bmatrix}, \quad \therefore$ *Not proportional*

5.51 $\ddot{q}_2 + 0.8902\zeta_2\sqrt{\frac{k}{m}}\dot{q}_2 + 0.1981\frac{k}{m}q_2 = 0.4068\ddot{u}_0(t)$

$\ddot{q}_3 + 1.4614\zeta_3\sqrt{\frac{k}{m}}\dot{q}_3 + 0.5339\frac{k}{m}q_3 = -0.3268\ddot{u}_0(t)$

5.52 $\left|\dfrac{kx(10)}{ma_0}\right| = 1.90 + \sqrt{0.610^2 + 0.369^2} = 2.61$

5.57 $\alpha = \dfrac{2\omega_1\omega_2(\zeta_1\omega_2 - \zeta_2\omega_1)}{\omega_2^2 - \omega_1^2}, \quad \beta = \dfrac{2(\zeta_2\omega_2 - \zeta_1\omega_1)}{\omega_2^2 - \omega_1^2}, \quad \zeta_i = \dfrac{\alpha + \beta\omega_i^2}{2\omega_i}, \quad \zeta_3 = 0.1867$

5.58 $C_1 = 0.89865, \quad C_2 = -0.1477, \quad C_3 = 0.3886$

5.60 $\overline{a}_{11} = \dfrac{l^3}{3EI} + \dfrac{1}{k} + \dfrac{l^2}{K}$

$\overline{a}_{12} = \overline{a}_{21} = \dfrac{l^2}{2EI} + \dfrac{1}{K}$

$\overline{a}_{22} = \dfrac{l}{EI} + \dfrac{1}{K}$

5.69 $d_2 = 12.75mm$

5.71 $weight = 2.8kg, \quad k = 1652.69N/m$

5.73 $\zeta_0 = 0.105, \quad \omega/\omega_n = 0.943$

5.80 $\begin{bmatrix} J_1 & 0 \\ 0 & J_2 \end{bmatrix}\begin{Bmatrix} \ddot{\theta}_1 \\ \ddot{\theta}_2 \end{Bmatrix} + l^2\begin{bmatrix} \frac{9}{16}k_1 & -\frac{9}{16}k_1 \\ -\frac{9}{16}k_1 & (-\frac{9}{16}k_1 + -\frac{1}{4}k_2) \end{bmatrix}\begin{Bmatrix} \theta_1 \\ \theta_2 \end{Bmatrix} = \begin{Bmatrix} 0 \\ 0 \end{Bmatrix}$
$J_1 = m_1 l^2/3, \quad J_2 = (7/48)m_2 l^2$

5.87 $$\begin{bmatrix} m_1 & & \\ & m_2 & \\ & & m_3 \end{bmatrix} \begin{Bmatrix} \ddot{x}_1 \\ \ddot{x}_2 \\ \ddot{x}_3 \end{Bmatrix} + \begin{bmatrix} (k_1+k_2+k_5) & -k_2 & -k_5 \\ -k_2 & (k_2+k_3+k_4) & -k_3 \\ -k_5 & -k_3 & (k_3+k_5) \end{bmatrix} \begin{Bmatrix} x_1 \\ x_2 \\ x_3 \end{Bmatrix} = \begin{Bmatrix} 0 \\ 0 \\ 0 \end{Bmatrix}$$

Chapter 6

6.1 $\tau = 2\pi\sqrt{\dfrac{R(\pi-2)}{g}}$

6.2 $\tau = 2\pi\dfrac{L}{a}\sqrt{\dfrac{h}{3g}}$

6.5 $m_{eff} = \frac{3}{8}ml$

6.7 $m_A = \dfrac{J + m_v b^2 + \frac{1}{3}m_s b^2}{a^2}$

6.10 $K_{eff} = \dfrac{K_1K_2}{K_1+K_2} + K_2, \quad \tau = 2\pi\sqrt{\dfrac{J}{K}}$

6.12 $J_{eff} = J_1 + J_2\left(\dfrac{r_1}{r_2}\right)^2$

6.13 *Constraints*, $u_2 = u_5 = 0, \quad u_1 = u_3, \quad u_4 = u_6,$ System has 2 DOF

6.14 Let $u_3 = q_1,\ u_6 = q_2,\quad \begin{Bmatrix} u_3 \\ u_6 \end{Bmatrix} = \begin{bmatrix} 1 & 0 \\ 0 & 1 \end{bmatrix}\begin{Bmatrix} q_1 \\ q_2 \end{Bmatrix}$

6.15 $tan\theta = \left(\dfrac{l_1}{l_2}\right)^2$

6.17 $tan\theta = \left(\dfrac{m_2 - m_1}{m_1 + m_2}\right)\dfrac{l}{\sqrt{(2R)^2 + l^2}}$

6.19 $tan\theta = \dfrac{1}{\mu}$

6.21 $sin\theta = \dfrac{3h}{4l} - \dfrac{mg}{2kl}$

6.23 $\omega_d = \dfrac{a}{l}\sqrt{\dfrac{3k}{m}}\sqrt{1 - \dfrac{3}{4km}\left(\dfrac{cl}{a}\right)^2}, \quad C_c = \dfrac{2}{3}\dfrac{a}{l}\sqrt{3km}$

6.24 $\ddot{\theta}_\sim + \dfrac{3}{2}g\left(\dfrac{l_2^2 cos\theta_0 + l_1^2 sin\theta_0}{l_1^3 + l_2^3}\right)\theta_\sim = 0,$ *where* $tan\theta_0 = (l_1/l_2)^2$

6.25 $(m_1+m_2)R^2\ddot{\theta}_\sim + g\left[(m_1+m_2)\sqrt{R^2 + (l/2)^2}cos\theta_0 + (m_2 - m_1)\dfrac{l}{2}sin\theta_0\right]\theta_\sim = 0$

6.28 $m_0\left(\ddot{r} - r\dot{\theta}^2\right) + k\,(r - r_0) = m_0 g cos\theta$

$; m_0 r(r\ddot{\theta} + 2\dot{r}\dot{\theta}) + m_{rod}\frac{l^2}{3}\ddot{\theta} + m_0 g\,(r - r_0)\,sin\theta + m_{rod} g\frac{l}{2} sin\theta = 0$

6.31 $\left[J_1 + (m_1 + m_2)\,4l^2\right]\ddot{q}_1 + \left[K + l^2\,(k_1 + 4k_2)\right]q_1 + 4l^2 k_2 q_2 = 0$
$J_2\ddot{q}_2 + 4l^2 k_2\,(q_1 + q_2) = 0$

6.33 $[k] = \frac{EI}{l^3}\begin{bmatrix} 20.43 & -5.25l \\ -5.25l & 7.0l^2 \end{bmatrix}$

6.35 $R = \dfrac{P\left(l_1^3/3 + l_1^2 l_2/2\right) + M(l_1^2/2 + l_1 l_2)}{(l_1^3/3 + 2l_2^3/3 + l_1^2 l_2 + l_1 l_2^2)}, \quad M = R(l_1 + l_2) = Pl_1 - M$

Chapter 7

7.1 $\left|\begin{bmatrix} 0.5 & 0.5 & 0.5 \\ 0.5 & 1.5 & 1.5 \\ 0.5 & 1.5 & 2.5 \end{bmatrix}\begin{bmatrix} 2 & & \\ & 2 & \\ & & 2 \end{bmatrix} - \overline{\lambda} I\right| = 0, \quad \overline{\lambda} = \frac{k}{m\omega^2}$

$\overline{\lambda}_1 = 7.4641, \quad \overline{\lambda}_2 = 1.00, \quad \overline{\lambda}_3 = 0.5359$

$\omega_1 = 0.3660\sqrt{\frac{k}{m}}, \quad \omega_2 = \sqrt{\frac{k}{m}}, \quad \omega_3 = 1.3660\sqrt{\frac{k}{m}}$

7.4 $\omega_1 = 0.445\sqrt{\frac{k}{m}}, \quad \omega_2 = 1.247\sqrt{\frac{k}{m}}, \quad \omega_3 = 1.802\sqrt{\frac{k}{m}}$

7.5 $\left|-\lambda\begin{bmatrix} m_1 & & & 0 \\ & m_2 & & \\ & & m_3 & \\ 0 & & & m_4 \end{bmatrix} + \begin{bmatrix} (k_1 + k_2 + k_3) & -k_2 & -k_5 & 0 \\ -k_2 & (k_2 + k_3) & -k_3 & 0 \\ -k_5 & -k_3 & (k_3 + k_4 + k_5) & -k_4 \\ 0 & 0 & -k_4 & k_4 \end{bmatrix}\right| =$

7.8 $\left|-\lambda\begin{bmatrix} 1478 & & & \\ & 2200 & & \\ & & 61.2 & \\ & & & 61.2 \end{bmatrix} + \begin{bmatrix} 73000 & 15600 & -35000 & -38000 \\ 15600 & 178420 & 49000 & -64600 \\ -35000 & 49000 & 435000 & 0 \\ -38000 & -64600 & 0 & 438000 \end{bmatrix}\right| = 0$

Solution by CHOLJAC with $\lambda = \omega^2$

$\lambda_1 = 43.3 \quad \lambda_2 = 76.1 \quad \lambda_3 = 7112.3 \quad \lambda_4 = 7163.5$
$\omega_1 = 6.5083 \quad \omega_2 = 8.7235 \quad \omega_3 = 84.3345 \quad \omega_4 = 84.6375$
$f_1 = 1.0478cps \quad f_2 = 1.3891cps \quad f_3 = 13.4291cps \quad f_4 = 13.4773cps$

7.9 $\omega_1 = 0.223\sqrt{\frac{EI}{l^3}}, \quad \phi_1 = \begin{Bmatrix} -1.00 \\ 2.588 \end{Bmatrix}, \quad \omega_2 = 0.4774\sqrt{\frac{EI}{l^3}}, \quad \phi_2 = \begin{Bmatrix} 1.00 \\ 1.932 \end{Bmatrix}$

7.10 $\omega_1 = 0.584\sqrt{\frac{k}{m}}, \quad \omega_1 = 1.2\sqrt{\frac{k}{m}}, \quad \omega_1 = 1.642\sqrt{\frac{k}{m}}$

7.11 $\omega_1 = 0.2925\sqrt{\dfrac{EI}{ml^3}}, \quad \phi_1 = \begin{Bmatrix} 1.00 \\ 0.5318 \\ 0.1565 \end{Bmatrix}, \quad \omega_2 = 1.916\sqrt{\dfrac{EI}{ml^3}},$

$\phi_1 = \begin{Bmatrix} 1.00 \\ -1.507 \\ -1.2687 \end{Bmatrix}, \quad \omega_3 = 5.146\sqrt{\dfrac{EI}{ml^3}}, \quad \phi_3 = \begin{Bmatrix} 1.00 \\ -3.2481 \\ 4.6471 \end{Bmatrix}$

7.14 $U^T U = K, \quad U = \begin{bmatrix} 1.414 & -0.707 \\ 0 & 1.875 \end{bmatrix}$

7.16 $\left| \begin{bmatrix} 1.667 & -0.5774 \\ -0.5774 & 2.0 \end{bmatrix} - \lambda I \right| = 0, \quad \lambda = \dfrac{m\omega^2}{k}$

7.18 $\lambda = \dfrac{m\omega^2}{k}, \quad \omega_1 = 0.769\sqrt{\dfrac{k}{m}}, \quad \omega_2 = 1.187\sqrt{\dfrac{k}{m}}, \quad \phi_1 = \begin{Bmatrix} 0.816 \\ 1.0 \end{Bmatrix},$

$\phi_2 = \begin{Bmatrix} -0.816 \\ 1.0 \end{Bmatrix}$

7.20 $\left[\begin{bmatrix} 0.5 & -0.3873 & 0.1519 \\ -0.3873 & 0.7000 & -0.6667 \\ 0.1519 & -0.6667 & 0.9923 \end{bmatrix} - \lambda I \right] \begin{Bmatrix} x_1 \\ x_2 \\ x_3 \end{Bmatrix} = \begin{Bmatrix} 0 \\ 0 \\ 0 \end{Bmatrix}, \quad \lambda = \dfrac{m\omega^2}{k}$

7.22 $\omega_1 = 0.613\sqrt{\dfrac{k}{m}}, \quad \phi_1 = \begin{Bmatrix} 0.3717 \\ 0.6015 \\ 0.3717 \\ 0.6015 \end{Bmatrix}, \quad \omega_2 = 1.543\sqrt{\dfrac{k}{m}}, \quad \phi_2 = \begin{Bmatrix} -0.3717 \\ -0.6015 \\ 0.3717 \\ 0.6015 \end{Bmatrix},$

$\omega_3 = 1.618\sqrt{\dfrac{k}{m}}, \quad \phi_3 = \begin{Bmatrix} -0.6015 \\ 0.3717 \\ -0.6015 \\ 0.3717 \end{Bmatrix}, \quad \omega_4 = 2.149\sqrt{\dfrac{k}{m}}, \quad \phi_4 = \begin{Bmatrix} 0.6015 \\ -0.3717 \\ -0.6015 \\ 0.3717 \end{Bmatrix}$

Chapter 8

8.1 $f = \dfrac{n}{2l}\sqrt{\dfrac{T}{l}}, \quad n = 1, 2, 3, \ldots$

8.2 $tan\dfrac{\omega l}{c} = -\left(\dfrac{T}{kl}\right)\dfrac{\frac{\omega l}{c}}{1 - \left(\frac{\omega}{\omega_n}\right)^2}, \quad \omega_n = \sqrt{\dfrac{k}{m}}$

8.8 4.792e3 m/s

8.14 $\omega_n = (2n-1)\dfrac{\pi}{l}\sqrt{\dfrac{G}{\rho}}, \quad n = 1, 2, 3, \ldots$

8.17 $tan\dfrac{\omega l}{c} = \dfrac{2\left(\frac{J_0}{J_s}\frac{\omega l}{c}\right)}{\left(\frac{J_0}{J_s}\frac{\omega l}{c}\right)^2 - 1}$

8.18 4.2677e11 Nm/rad

8.20 T = 11.88e7 N, K = 4.752e10 Nm/rad $f_1 = 0.05742 Hz, \quad f_2 = 0.1148 Hz$
Torsional freq = 0.32813 Hz

8.25 $E = 2.145e10 N/m^2$

8.26 $\omega = \beta^2\sqrt{EI/\rho}$, where β is determined from $(1 + cosh\beta l.cos\beta l)$
$= \beta l\dfrac{W_0}{W_b}(sinh\beta l.cos\beta l - cosh\beta l.sin\beta l)$

8.27 $\omega_1 = \sqrt{\dfrac{3EI_g}{w_0 + 0.237W_b}}$

8.33 $w_n = 2\sqrt{\dfrac{k}{m}}sin\dfrac{n\pi}{2(N+1)}$

8.34 $w_k = 2\sqrt{\dfrac{K}{J}}sin\dfrac{(2k-1)\pi}{2(2N+1)}$

8.37 $-2cos\beta\left(N + \dfrac{1}{2}\right)\cdot sin\dfrac{\beta}{2} = \dfrac{K_N}{k}sin\beta N$

Chapter 9

9.1 $\Gamma_i = \dfrac{p_o}{l}\displaystyle\int_0^l \phi_i(x)dx$

9.6 $y(x,t) = \dfrac{4p_0 l}{\pi M\omega_2^2}sin\dfrac{2x\pi}{l}(1 - cos\omega_2 t)$

9.11 Modes absent are $2^{nd}, 5^{th}, 8^{th}$, etc.

9.12 $\Gamma = \sqrt{2}cos\dfrac{(2n-1)\pi}{6}, \quad D_n = (1 - cos\omega_n t)$

$$u = \frac{2F_0 l}{AE}\left\{\frac{cos(\pi/6)cos(\pi/2)(x/l)}{(\pi/2)^2}D_1 + \frac{cos(5\pi/6)cos(5\pi/2)(x/l)}{(5\pi/2)^2}D_2 + \ldots\ldots\right\}$$

9.13 $\Gamma_1 = \dfrac{1}{l}\displaystyle\int_0^l \phi_1(x)dx = 0.784$

$\Gamma_2 = \dfrac{1}{l}\displaystyle\int_0^l \phi_2(x)dx = 0.434$

$\Gamma_3 = \dfrac{1}{l}\displaystyle\int_0^l \phi_3(x)dx = 0.254$

9.17 $\left(\dfrac{\omega}{\omega_1}\right)^2 = 1 + \dfrac{k}{M\omega_1^2}\phi_1^2(a), \left\{1 + \dfrac{K\varphi_2'^2(0)}{M\omega_1^2[1-(\omega/\omega_1)^2]}\right\}\left\{1 + \dfrac{K\varphi_2'^2(0)}{M\omega_2^2[1-(\omega/\omega_2)^2]}\right\}$

$$= \left\{1 + \frac{K\varphi_1'(0)\varphi_2'(0)}{M\omega_1^2[1-(\omega/\omega_1)^2]}\right\}\left\{1 + \frac{K\varphi_1'(0)\varphi_2'(0)}{M\omega_2^2[1-(\omega/\omega_2)^2]}\right\}$$

$\varphi_1 = \sqrt{2}sin\dfrac{\pi x}{l}, \quad \varphi_1' = \dfrac{\pi}{l}\sqrt{2}cos\dfrac{\pi x}{l}$, etc. Once mode approximation gives

$$\left(\frac{\omega}{\omega_1}\right)^2 = 1 + \frac{2K}{M\omega_1^2}\left(\frac{\pi}{l}\right)^2, \quad \omega_1 = \pi^2\sqrt{\frac{EI}{Ml^3}}$$

9.19 One mode approximation

$$\left(\frac{\omega}{\omega_1}\right)^2 = 1 + \frac{4K}{M\omega_1^2}\left(\frac{\pi}{l}\right)^2$$

$$\left(\frac{\omega}{\omega_1}\right)^2 = \frac{M_1}{M_1 + M_0\varphi_1^2(0) - [M_0^2\varphi_1^2(0)/(M_0 + 2ml)]}$$

where $M_1 = \int \varphi_1^2(x) m dx = 2ml, \quad \omega_1 = 22.4\sqrt{\frac{EI}{m(2l)^4}}$

Chapter 10

10.1 $\omega_1 = 4.63\sqrt{\frac{EI}{Ml^3}}$

10.2 $\omega_1 = 1.62\sqrt{\frac{EI}{Ml^3}}$

10.8 $\omega_1 = \sqrt{\frac{3EI/l^3 + 2k}{\frac{33}{140}ml + \frac{2}{3}m_0}}$

10.10 $\omega_1 = 9.96\sqrt{\frac{EI}{(0.2188m_0l)\,l^3}}$, where $0.2188m_0l$ = total mass

10.13 $\omega_1^2 = \frac{3EI}{l^3}\frac{1}{27m_1 + 8m_2 + m_3}$

10.14 $f_{11} = 495.2cps$

10.16 $\left(\frac{ml}{2}\omega^2\right)^2 - \left[5EAl\left(\frac{\pi}{2l}\right)^2 + 2k_0\right]\left(\frac{ml}{2}\omega^2\right) + \left[\frac{EAl}{2}\left(\frac{\pi}{2l}\right)^2 + k_0\right]\left[\frac{EAl}{2}\left(\frac{3\pi}{2l}\right)^2 + k_0\right] - k_0^2 = 0$

10.17 $\left(\frac{1}{6} - \frac{1}{\pi^2}\right)\left(ml^2\omega^2\right)^2 - \left(\frac{\pi^4}{6}\frac{EI}{l^3} + \frac{k}{2}\right)\left(ml^2\omega^2\right) + \frac{\pi^4}{2}\frac{EI}{l^3}k = 0$

10.22 $\omega_1 = 0.629\sqrt{K/J}, \quad \begin{Bmatrix}\theta_1\\ \theta_2\\ \theta_3\end{Bmatrix}_1 = \begin{Bmatrix}1.000\\ 0.604\\ 0.287\end{Bmatrix}$

10.24 $\omega_1 = 0.445\sqrt{k/m}, \quad \begin{Bmatrix}x_1\\ x_2\\ x_3\end{Bmatrix}_1 = \begin{Bmatrix}1.000\\ 0.802\\ 0.445\end{Bmatrix}$

$\omega_2 = 1.247\sqrt{k/m}, \quad \begin{Bmatrix}x_1\\ x_2\\ x_3\end{Bmatrix}_2 = \begin{Bmatrix}-1.000\\ 0.555\\ 1.247\end{Bmatrix}$

$\omega_3 = 1.802\sqrt{k/m}, \quad \begin{Bmatrix}x_1\\ x_2\\ x_3\end{Bmatrix}_3 = \begin{Bmatrix}1.000\\ -2.247\\ 1.802\end{Bmatrix}$

10.30 $\omega_1 = 1.651\sqrt{\frac{EI}{ml^3}}, \begin{Bmatrix}y_1\\ y_2\end{Bmatrix}_1 = \begin{Bmatrix}0.320\\ 1.000\end{Bmatrix}$

10.31 $\omega_1 = \sqrt{\frac{6EI}{Ml^3}\left(1 + \frac{n}{2}\right)}, \quad \frac{y_1}{y_2} = -n/2$

10.32 $u_{43} - \dfrac{u_{41}u_{23}}{u_{21}} = 0$

10.36 $\omega_1 = 22.5, \quad \omega_2 = 52.3$

10.39 $\omega = 22.7$

10.41 $\omega_1 = 0, \quad \omega_2 = 0.5375\sqrt{\dfrac{K}{J}}, \begin{Bmatrix} 1.00 \\ 0.714 \\ 0.239 \\ -0.326 \end{Bmatrix}, \quad \omega_3 = 1.272\sqrt{\dfrac{K}{J}}, \begin{Bmatrix} 1.00 \\ -0.614 \\ -1.237 \\ 0.1416 \end{Bmatrix},$

$$\omega_4 = 1.805\sqrt{\frac{K}{J}}, \begin{Bmatrix} 1.00 \\ -2.27 \\ 1.87 \\ -0.1005 \end{Bmatrix}$$

10.44 $\omega_1 = 0.5375\sqrt{K/J}, \quad \begin{Bmatrix} \theta_1 \\ \theta_2 \\ \theta_3 \\ \theta_4 \end{Bmatrix}_1 = \begin{Bmatrix} 1.000 \\ 0.714 \\ 0.239 \\ -0.326 \end{Bmatrix}$

$$\omega_3 = 1.805\sqrt{K/J}, \quad \begin{Bmatrix} \theta_1 \\ \theta_2 \\ \theta_3 \\ \theta_4 \end{Bmatrix}_3 = \begin{Bmatrix} 1.000 \\ -2.270 \\ 1.870 \\ -0.141 \end{Bmatrix}$$

Chapter 11

11.2 $a_{11} = \dfrac{k_2 + k_3}{\sum k_i k_j}, \quad a_{12} = a_{21} = \dfrac{k_2}{\sum k_i k_j}, \quad a_{22} = \dfrac{k_1 + k_2}{\sum k_i k_j}$

11.3 $a_{11} = 0.0147l^3/EI, \quad a_{21} = a_{12} = 0.0123l^3/EI, \quad a_{22} = 0.0147^3/EI$

11.6 $[a] = \dfrac{l^3}{EI}\begin{bmatrix} 7/96 & 1/8 \\ 1/8 & 5/6 \end{bmatrix}$

11.7 $[K] = \begin{bmatrix} (K_1 + K_2) & -K_2 & 0 \\ -K_2 & (K_2 + K_3) & -K_3 \\ 0 & -K_3 & K_3 \end{bmatrix}$

$$[a] = \begin{bmatrix} 1/K_1 & 1/K_1 & 1/K_1 \\ 1/K_1 & (1/K_1 + 1/K_2) & (1/K_1 + 1/K_2) \\ 1/K_1 & (1/K_1 + 1/K_2) & (1/K_1 + 1/K_2 + 1/K_3) \end{bmatrix}$$

11.9 $[a] = \dfrac{l^3}{12EI}\begin{bmatrix} 1 & 1 & 1 & 1 \\ 1 & 2 & 2 & 2 \\ 1 & 2 & 3 & 3 \\ 1 & 2 & 3 & 4 \end{bmatrix}$

11.10 $\begin{Bmatrix} F_1 \\ M_2 \\ M_3 \end{Bmatrix} = \begin{bmatrix} 24EI_1/l_1^3 & -6EI_1/l^2 & -6EI_1/l_1^2 \\ -6EI_1/l_1^2 & (4EI_1/l_1 + 4EI_2/l_2) & 2EI_2/l_2 \\ -6EI_1/l_1^2 & 2EI_2/l_2 & (4EI_1/l_1 + 4EI_2/l_2) \end{bmatrix} \begin{Bmatrix} u_1 \\ \theta_1 \\ \theta_2 \end{Bmatrix}$

11.16 $\omega_1 = 1.403\sqrt{\dfrac{EA_2}{M_2 l}}, \quad \begin{Bmatrix} u_1 \\ u_2 \end{Bmatrix}_1 = \begin{Bmatrix} 0.577 \\ 1.00 \end{Bmatrix}$

$\omega_2 = 3.648\sqrt{\dfrac{EA_2}{M_2 l}}, \quad \begin{Bmatrix} u_1 \\ u_2 \end{Bmatrix}_2 = \begin{Bmatrix} -0.526 \\ 1.00 \end{Bmatrix}$

11.17 $\dfrac{M}{18}\begin{bmatrix} 4 & 1 & 0 \\ 1 & 4 & 1 \\ 0 & 1 & 2 \end{bmatrix}\begin{Bmatrix} \ddot{u}_1 \\ \ddot{u}_2 \\ \ddot{u}_3 \end{Bmatrix} + \dfrac{3EA}{l}\begin{bmatrix} 2 & -1 & 0 \\ -1 & 2 & -1 \\ 0 & -1 & 1 \end{bmatrix}\begin{Bmatrix} u_1 \\ u_2 \\ u_3 \end{Bmatrix} = \begin{Bmatrix} 0 \\ 0 \\ 0 \end{Bmatrix}$

11.19 $\omega_1 = 1.611\sqrt{\dfrac{GA}{Ml}}, \quad \omega_2 = 5.629\sqrt{\dfrac{GA}{Ml}}$

11.22 $\omega_1 = 2.368\sqrt{\dfrac{E}{\rho l^2}}, \quad \omega_2 = 8.664\sqrt{\dfrac{E}{\rho l^2}}, \quad \rho = \textit{mass density}$

11.25 $v_1 = 0.1333\dfrac{Pl}{AE}, \quad u_2 = 0.563\dfrac{Pl}{AE}$

11.26 $\dfrac{EA}{l}\begin{bmatrix} \left(1+\frac{0.5}{\sqrt{2}}\right) & \frac{0.5}{\sqrt{2}} & -1 & 0 \\ \frac{0.5}{\sqrt{2}} & \left(1+\frac{0.5}{\sqrt{2}}\right) & 0 & 0 \\ -1 & 0 & 1 & 0 \\ 0 & 0 & 0 & 1 \end{bmatrix}\begin{Bmatrix} \bar{u}_3 \\ \bar{v}_3 \\ \bar{u}_4 \\ \bar{v}_4 \end{Bmatrix} = \begin{Bmatrix} F_{3x} = 0 \\ F_{3y} = 0 \\ F_{4x} = P \\ F_{4y} = 0 \end{Bmatrix}$

11.28 $\bar{v}_2 = -\dfrac{Pl^3}{192EI}, \quad \theta_2 = -\dfrac{Ml}{16EI}$

11.29 $\omega_1 = 22.74\sqrt{\dfrac{EI}{ml^4}}, \quad \omega_2 = 81.67\sqrt{\dfrac{EI}{ml^4}}$

11.31 $\omega_1 = 0, \quad \omega_2 = 17.54\sqrt{\dfrac{EI}{ml^4}}, \quad \omega_3 = \sqrt{\dfrac{EI}{ml^4}}$

Exact values $\omega_1 = 0, \quad \omega_2 = 15.4\sqrt{\dfrac{EI}{ml^4}}, \quad \omega_3 = 50.0\sqrt{\dfrac{EI}{ml^4}}$

11.33 $\dfrac{EI}{8l^3}\begin{bmatrix} (2.5R+6) & 0.5(R-12) & 8.484l & \\ 0.5(R-12) & (0.5R+30) & 15.52l & \\ -1 & 0 & 1 & 0 \\ 8.484l & 15.52l & 40.0l^2 & \end{bmatrix}\begin{Bmatrix} \bar{u}_2 \\ \bar{v}_2 \\ \theta_2 \\ \bar{v}_4 \end{Bmatrix} = \begin{Bmatrix} -P \\ 0 \\ M \end{Bmatrix}, \quad R = \left(\dfrac{44Al^2}{I}\right)$

11.34 $\dfrac{EI}{l^3}\begin{bmatrix} 12 & -6l & 0 & 0 \\ -6l & 8l^2 & 6l & 2l^2 \\ 0 & 6l & \left(12+\frac{kl^3}{EI}\right) & 6l \\ 0 & 2l^2 & 6l & 4l^2 \end{bmatrix}\begin{Bmatrix} \bar{v}_2 \\ \theta_2 \\ \bar{u}_3 \\ \theta_3 \end{Bmatrix} = \begin{Bmatrix} 0 \\ -M \\ 0 \\ 0 \end{Bmatrix}$

11.40(a) $\begin{Bmatrix} \overline{F}_2 \\ \overline{M}_2 \\ \overline{F}_3 \\ \overline{M}_3 \end{Bmatrix} = -p_0 l\begin{Bmatrix} 0.2875 \\ -0.2271l \\ 0.0375 \\ 0.0146l \end{Bmatrix}$

11.40(b) $\bar{v}_2 = -\dfrac{0.2031}{192}\dfrac{pl^4}{EI}, \quad \theta_2 = -\dfrac{0.0286}{16}\dfrac{pl^3}{EI}$

Chapter 12

12.5 $\bar{x} = A_0, \quad \overline{x^2} = A_0^2 + \frac{1}{2}A_1^2$

12.7 $\bar{x} = 0.50, \quad \overline{x^2} = 0.333$

12.12 A triangle of twice the base, symmetric about t = 0.

12.16 $R(\tau) = 5 \quad at \quad \tau = 0$ and linearly decreases to $R(1) = 1$.

12.19 $rms = 53.85g = 528.3/s^2$

12.20 $rms = 50.54mm, \quad \sigma = 24.86$

12.22 $f(t) = \frac{2}{\pi}(sin\omega_1 t - \frac{1}{2}sin2\omega_1 t + \frac{1}{3}sin3\omega_1 t - \ldots)$

$S(\omega) = \Sigma_n \frac{1}{2}C_n^2 = \frac{2}{\pi^2}\Sigma_n \frac{1}{n^2}$

12.25 $x(t) = \frac{2A}{\pi}\Sigma_{n=-\infty}^{\infty}\frac{1}{in}e^{in\omega_1 t}$, for n = odd

$x(t) = \frac{4A}{\pi}(sin\omega_1 t + \frac{1}{3}sin3\omega_1 t + \ldots),\ S(\omega_n) = C_n C_n^*/2 = \frac{4A^2}{n^2\pi^2}$

12.28 $f_{1,2} = f_n\left(1 \mp \frac{1}{2Q}\right)$

12.30 $53.2g = 2\sigma, \quad \begin{matrix} P[x > 2\sigma] = 4.6\% \\ P[X > 2\sigma] = 13.5\% \end{matrix}$

12.33 $F(t) = 10^6\left(\frac{1}{4} + \sum_{n=1}^{\infty}\frac{2}{n\pi}sin\frac{n\pi}{4}.cos\, n\frac{2\pi}{T}t\right)$

$S_F(\omega_n) = \frac{1}{2} \times 10^{12}[(\frac{1}{16})_{n=0} + \sum_{n=1}^{\infty}(\frac{2}{n\pi})^2 sin^2(\frac{n\pi}{4})]$

$\overline{y^2} = \sum \frac{1}{k^2}\frac{S_F(\omega_n)}{[1-(\frac{n\omega_1}{2\pi}T)^2]^2}, \quad k = (\frac{2\pi}{T})^2 m$

12.35 $\sigma = 0.0039m,\ P[|y| > 0.012] = .3\%$

12.37 $\overline{y^2} = \sigma^2 \cong \frac{S_0}{k^2}\frac{f_n\pi}{4\zeta} = 0.000438, \quad \sigma = 0.0662m, \quad P[|y| > 0.132] = 2\sigma = 4.6\%$

Chapter 13

13.1 $m\ddot{x} + \frac{2T_0}{l_0}x\left[1 + \frac{1}{2}\left(\frac{EA}{T_0} - 1\right)\left(\frac{x}{l}\right)^2\right] = 0$

13.2 $m\ddot{x} + \frac{\pi r_0^2\rho}{3(h-x_0)}[(h-x)^3 - (h-x_0)^3] = 0,$

r_0 = radius of circle at water line, $\rho = wt/vol$ of water

13.6 $V = \sqrt{y^2 + \omega_n^4 x^2}$, x = y = 0 for equilibrium

13.10 Shift origin of phase to π in Fig. 13.4.2

13.13 $\lambda_{1,2} = 3, 4, \quad \begin{Bmatrix} x \\ y \end{Bmatrix}_1 = \begin{Bmatrix} 0.50 \\ 1.00 \end{Bmatrix}, \quad \begin{Bmatrix} x \\ y \end{Bmatrix}_2 = \begin{Bmatrix} 1.00 \\ 1.00 \end{Bmatrix}$

13.14 $\begin{Bmatrix} x \\ y \end{Bmatrix} = \begin{bmatrix} 0.5 & 1 \\ 1 & 1 \end{bmatrix} \begin{Bmatrix} \zeta \\ \eta \end{Bmatrix}$

13.23 $y = \dfrac{-x\left(\omega_n^2 + \mu x^2\right)}{c}, \quad \dfrac{dy}{dx} = c$

13.25 $\dfrac{dy}{dx} = \dfrac{-(x+\delta)}{y}$, where $\delta = \left(\frac{c}{m}y + \frac{\mu}{\omega_n^2 m}x^3\right), \quad \omega_n^2 = k/m, \quad \tau = \omega_n t, \quad y = \frac{dx}{d\tau}$

13.27 $\tau = 4\sqrt{\dfrac{l}{g}}\displaystyle\int_0^{60^\circ} \dfrac{d\theta}{\sqrt{2(\,cos\theta - \;cos\theta_0)}} = 4\sqrt{\dfrac{l}{g}}\int_0^{\pi/2} \dfrac{d\theta}{\sqrt{(1-k^2 sin^2\phi)}},$

where $k = sin\dfrac{\theta_0}{2}, \quad sin\dfrac{\theta}{2} = ksin\phi$

13.31 $\omega \cong \sqrt{\dfrac{g}{l}}\left(1 + \dfrac{1}{16}\theta_0^2\right)$

13.35 $m\ddot{x}_1 + \left(\dfrac{2T_0}{l_0}\right)x_2 + \left(\dfrac{2k}{l_0^2}\right)x_1^3 = 0, \quad T = T_0 + K\dfrac{x^2}{l_0}$ Second approximation

$m\ddot{x}_2 + \left(\frac{2T_0}{l_0}\right)x_2 + 3\alpha x_1^2 x_2 = 0, \quad \alpha = \frac{2K}{l_0^2}$

$m\ddot{x}_2 + \left[\left(\frac{2T_0}{l_0} + \frac{3}{2}\alpha A^2\right) + \frac{3}{2}\alpha A^2 cos2\omega_n t\right]x_2 = 0$

Index